FRANK MILLER'S
RONIN

RONIN

Published by DC Comics.

Cover and compilation copyright © 1987

by Frank Miller Inc. All Rights Reserved.

Originally published in single magazine

form as RONIN 1-6.

DC Comics, 1700 Broadway,

New York, NY 10019

A Warner Bros. Entertainment Company

Printed in Canada.

Eighth Printing.

ISBN: 0-930289-21-8

ISBN 13: 978-0-930289-21-8

Cover illustration by Frank Miller

and Lynn Varley.

Dan DiDio VP-Editorial

Barry Marx Editor-Collected Edition

Frank Miller Editor-Original Series

Robbin Brosterman Senior Art Director

Paul Levitz President & Publisher

Georg Brewer VP-Design & Retail Product Development

Richard Bruning VP-Creative Director

Patrick Caldon Senior VP-Finance & Operations

Chris Caramalis VP-Finance

Terri Cunningham VP-Managing Editor

Joel Ehrlich Senior VP-Advertising & Promotions

Alison Gill VP-Manufacturing

Lillian Laserson VP & General Counsel

David McKillips VP-Advertising

John Nee VP-Business Development

Cheryl Rubin VP-Licensing & Merchandising

Bob Wayne VP-Sales & Marketing

CREATED, WRITTEN AND DRAWN BY

FRANK MILLER

PAINTS BY

LYNN VARLEY

LETTERED BY

JOHN COSTANZA

From the diary of Casey McKenna, date unknown:

The Vikings called it the Hour of the Wolf.

It comes before dawn, an abrupt wakening. The mind races in every direction, finding dread in every corner.

It comes to me every damn morning.

The pictures flood my mind.

They change their sequence, the pictures do, switching around, from morning to morning, like trading cards swapped by schoolchildren. There are only so many of them, and I've come to know each of them like old enemies.

But they still scare the crap out of me. Every damn time.

Every damn morning.

At the Hour of the Wolf...

...Blizzard snow rips dead branches free, scattering them like dried bones.

Strange, bat-like creatures ride the wind with a banshee screech.

There is a curse upon the land.

Monsters rule the earth.

Huddled wretches cower, dressed in rags, skin pocked and blighted, eyes hollow. Terrified.

It is a dark time, a dark age. Hope is a phantom dream, a fragrant memory. Of joy, there is no remembrance. The people have never known it.

A mother pulls her crying baby to a breast that offers no nourishment. She glares at the cold sky, bitter, defiant.

No, there's no joy. Only fear and pain and disease and death, endless death. Yet still, in human hearts, there is fire. There is courage.

The pictures don't stop. Every morning. Before dawn. The Hour of the Wolf. They don't stop. One after the next.

Horse hooves in full gallop pound barren ground. But they are not normal horses' hooves, not at all. They're all wrong. They're scary. Where we should see dull, blunt bone, they've got monstrous claws.

Monsters rule the earth.

A demon-slave on horseback snarls, only his fanged, inhuman mouth
visible beneath his weaved wicker helmet. The demon-slave raises an arm,
riding fast. Metal claws ride a chain from his sleeve.

The claws streak through the air. They stab a samurai warrior, who drops
his elegant katana and dies in agony. Blood streams across bald stone,
a torrent.

Monsters rule the earth.

Monsters rule the earth.

The pictures don't stop.

A beautiful young woman runs for her life. She stumbles.
Demon-slaves on horseback fast approach.

She's doomed and she knows it.

I get out of bed. I go to my bathroom. I vomit. I quake.

I go back to bed and I go back in. Back into the nightmare.
The endless nightmare.

Not asleep. Not awake. That horrid space between the two. Not dreaming.
Seeing.

The Hour of the Wolf.

The beautiful young woman. They chase her to a tall, cruel cliff.
She stares down. Surf pounds jagged rock. It would be suicide to jump.
She wouldn't have a chance.

The demon-slaves cackle, closing in, brandishing unspeakable weapons.

She steps backward from the cliff. Brave. Hopeless. She plummets..

Blood sprays across the waves. They go red, a sea of blood. Endless.

There is a curse upon the land. Monsters rule the earth.
Nowhere is there hope, nowhere...

...nowhere but KYUTU. Holy KYUTU.

Only in KYUTU do flowers bloom...

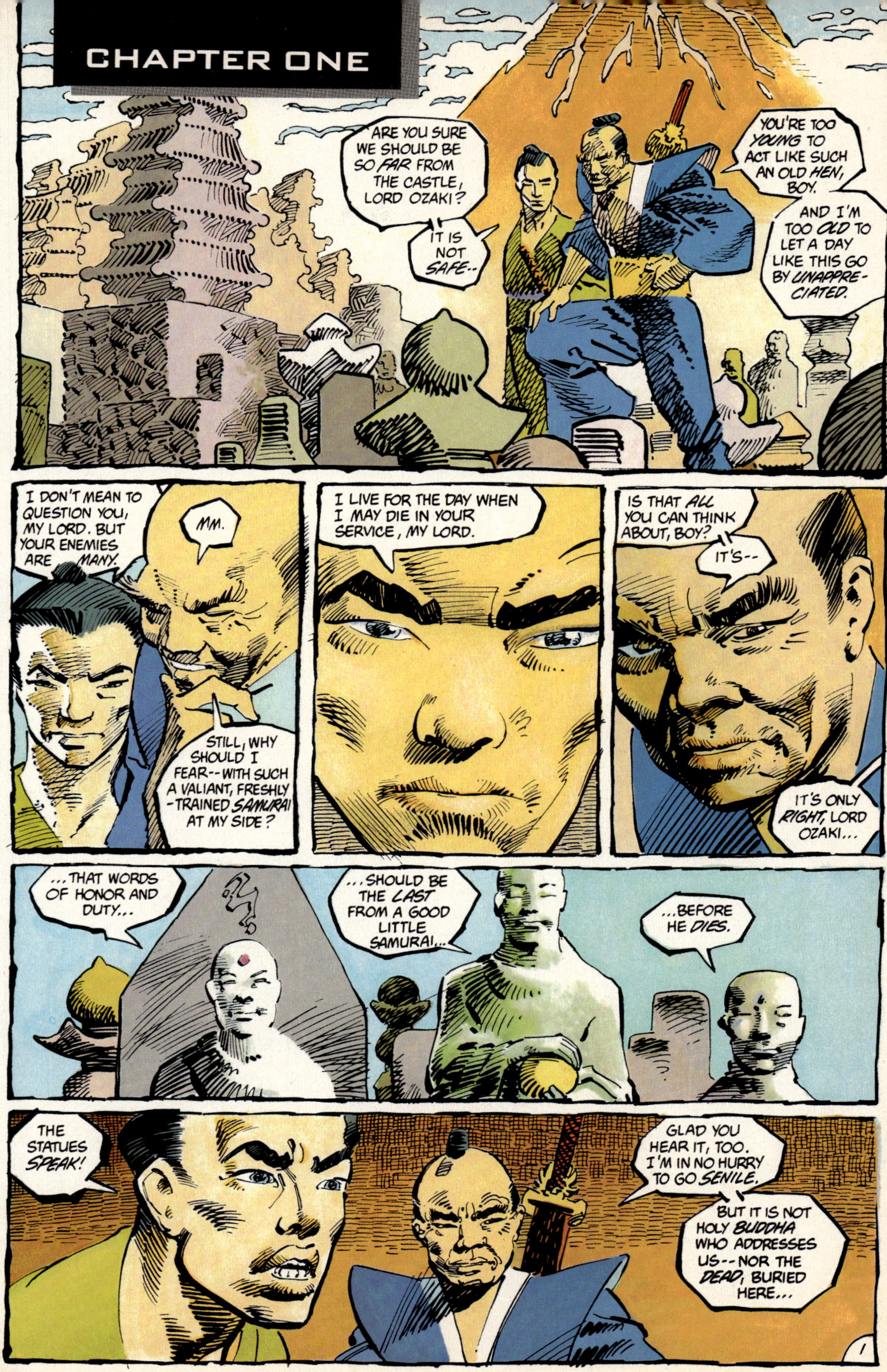
CHAPTER ONE
ARE YOU SURE WE SHOULD BE SO FAR FROM THE CASTLE, LORD OZAKI?
IT IS NOT SAFE--
YOU'RE TOO YOUNG TO ACT LIKE SUCH AN OLD HEN, BOY.
AND I'M TOO OLD TO LET A DAY LIKE THIS GO BY UNAPPRECIATED.
I DON'T MEAN TO QUESTION YOU, MY LORD. BUT YOUR ENEMIES ARE MANY.
MM.
STILL, WHY SHOULD I FEAR--WITH SUCH A VALIANT, FRESHLY-TRAINED SAMURAI AT MY SIDE?
I LIVE FOR THE DAY WHEN I MAY DIE IN YOUR SERVICE, MY LORD.
IS THAT ALL YOU CAN THINK ABOUT, BOY?
IT'S--
IT'S ONLY RIGHT, LORD OZAKI...
...THAT WORDS OF HONOR AND DUTY...
...SHOULD BE THE LAST FROM A GOOD LITTLE SAMURAI...
...BEFORE HE DIES.
THE STATUES SPEAK!
GLAD YOU HEAR IT, TOO. I'M IN NO HURRY TO GO SENILE.
BUT IT IS NOT HOLY BUDDHA WHO ADDRESSES US--NOR THE DEAD, BURIED HERE...
1

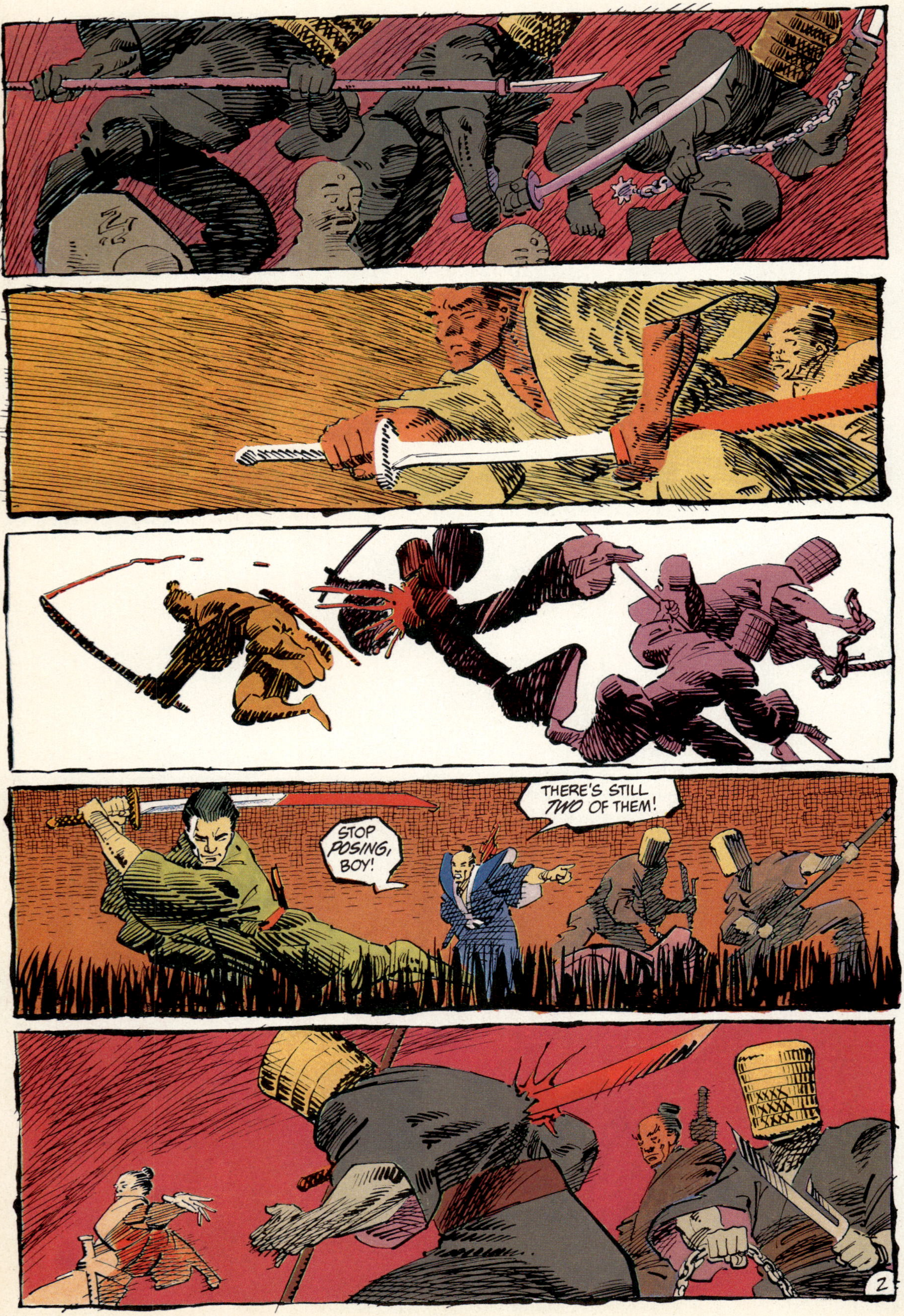

STOP POSING, BOY!
THERE'S STILL TWO OF THEM!

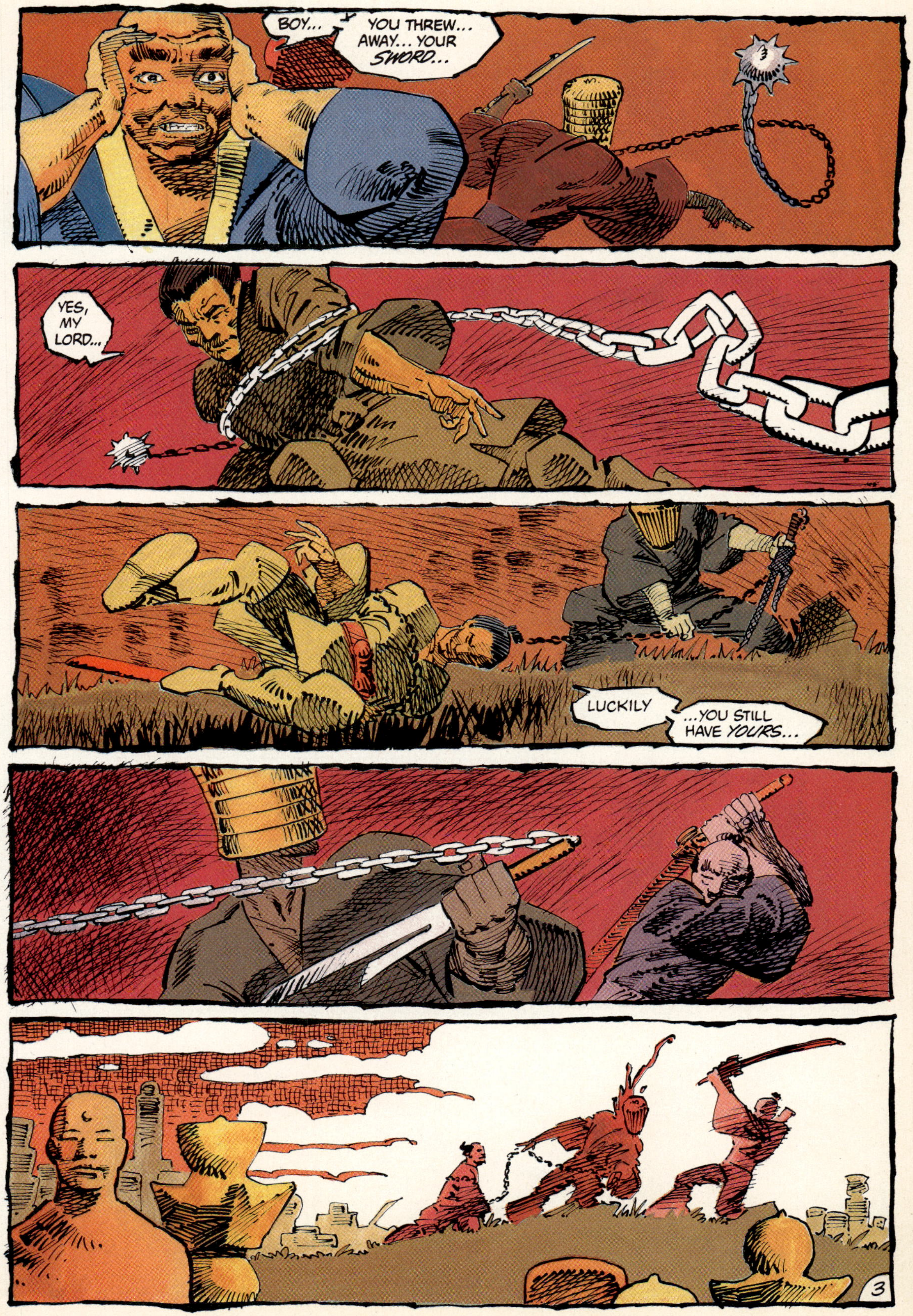
BOY...
YOU THREW... AWAY... YOUR SWORD...
YES, MY LORD...
LUCKILY
...YOU STILL HAVE YOURS...

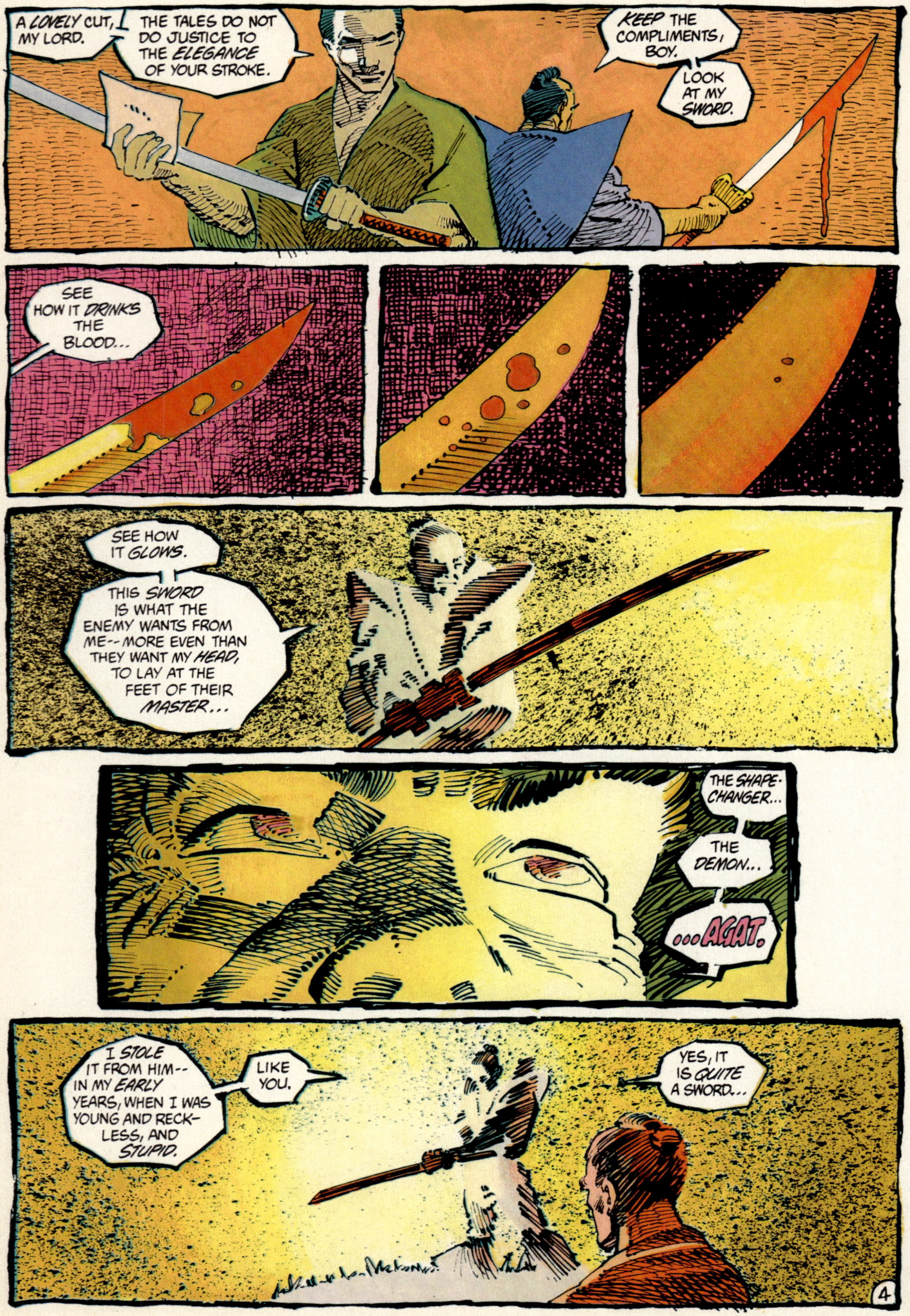
A LOVELY CUT, MY LORD.
THE TALES DO NOT DO JUSTICE TO THE ELEGANCE OF YOUR STROKE.
KEEP THE COMPLIMENTS, BOY.
LOOK AT MY SWORD.
SEE HOW IT DRINKS THE BLOOD...
SEE HOW IT GLOWS.
THIS SWORD IS WHAT THE ENEMY WANTS FROM ME-- MORE EVEN THAN THEY WANT MY HEAD, TO LAY AT THE FEET OF THEIR MASTER...
THE SHAPE-CHANGER...
THE DEMON...
...AGAT.
I STOLE IT FROM HIM-- IN MY EARLY YEARS, WHEN I WAS YOUNG AND RECK-LESS, AND STUPID.
LIKE YOU.
YES, IT IS QUITE A SWORD...

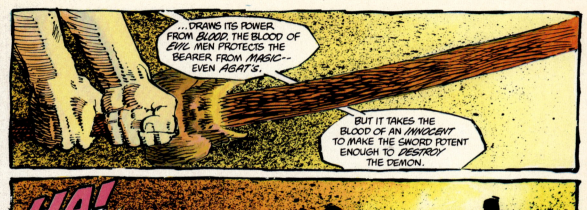

...DRAWS ITS POWER FROM *BLOOD.* THE BLOOD OF *EVIL* MEN PROTECTS THE BEARER FROM *MAGIC*-- EVEN *AGAT'S.*

BUT IT TAKES THE BLOOD OF AN *INNOCENT* TO MAKE THE SWORD POTENT ENOUGH TO *DESTROY* THE DEMON.

HA! *THAT* WOULD BE A SIGHT, *BOY!*

AGAT, SKEWERED ON HIS OWN BLADE, HIS PLAGUE ON OUR LAND *LIFTED!*

BUT IT IS ENOUGH, FOR NOW, TO HOLD THE *BLOODSWORD* AND KNOW THAT THE DEMON *FEARS* ME. YES,...

LET'S GET BACK TO THE *CASTLE,* BOY. ALL THIS TALKING HAS MADE ME *THIRSTY!*

DO YOU DRINK?

NO.

I'LL HAVE TO *TEACH* YOU -- AS PAYMENT FOR SAVING MY *LIFE,* BACK THERE.

SERVING MY LORD IS ITS *OWN* REWARD. WERE I *SLAIN,* I WOULD RISE FROM THE GRAVE SEVEN TIMES TO DEFEND YOUR--

OH, SHUT UP.

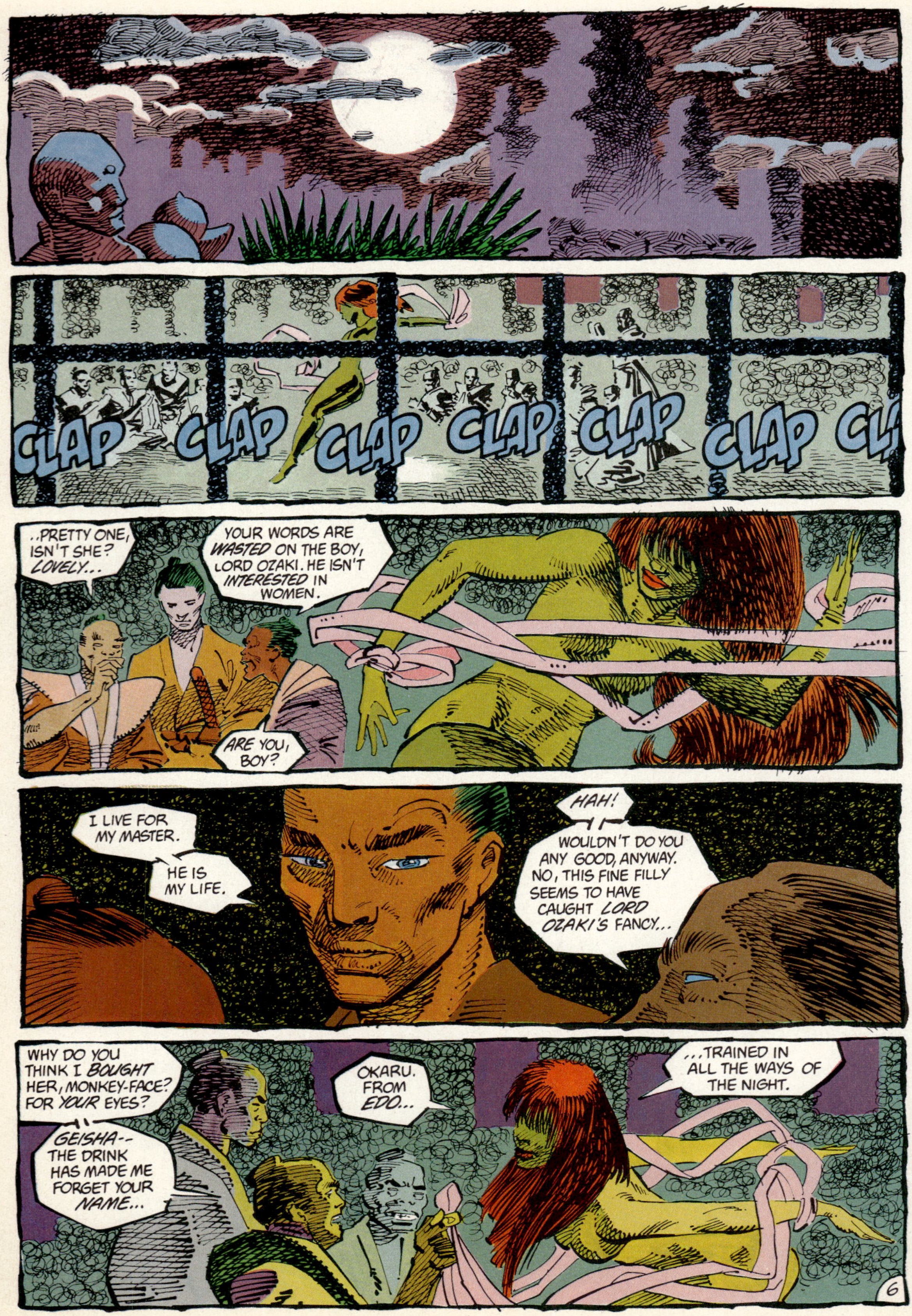
CLAP CLAP CLAP CLAP CLAP CLAP
..PRETTY ONE, ISN'T SHE? LOVELY...
YOUR WORDS ARE WASTED ON THE BOY, LORD OZAKI. HE ISN'T INTERESTED IN WOMEN.
ARE YOU, BOY?
I LIVE FOR MY MASTER.
HE IS MY LIFE.
HAH!
WOULDN'T DO YOU ANY GOOD, ANYWAY. NO, THIS FINE FILLY SEEMS TO HAVE CAUGHT LORD OZAKI'S FANCY...
WHY DO YOU THINK I BOUGHT HER, MONKEY-FACE? FOR YOUR EYES?
GEISHA-- THE DRINK HAS MADE ME FORGET YOUR NAME...
OKARU. FROM EDO...
...TRAINED IN ALL THE WAYS OF THE NIGHT.
6

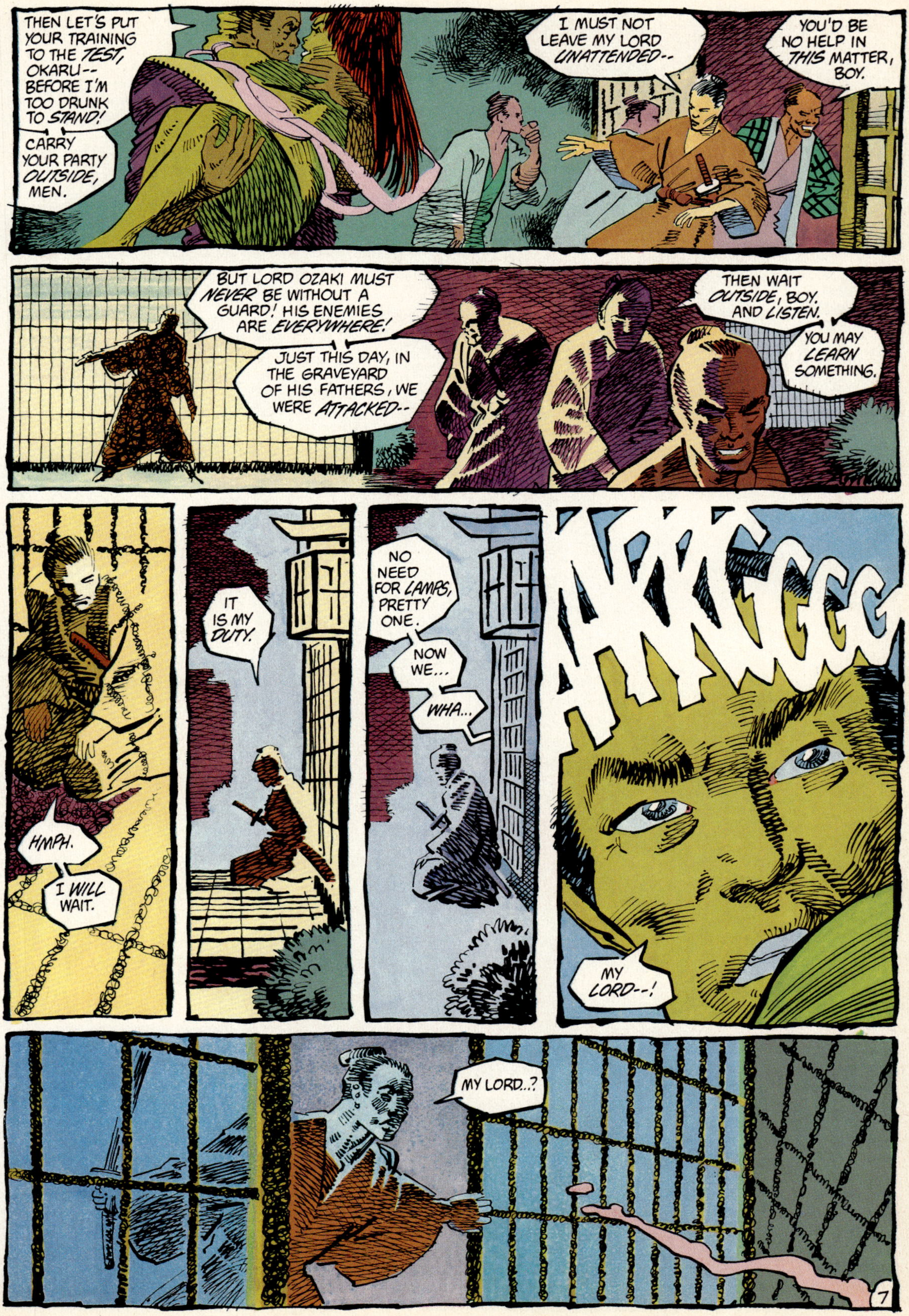
THEN LET'S PUT YOUR TRAINING TO THE *TEST*, OKARU-- BEFORE I'M TOO DRUNK TO *STAND!*
CARRY YOUR PARTY *OUTSIDE*, MEN.
I MUST NOT LEAVE MY LORD *UNATTENDED*--
YOU'D BE NO HELP IN *THIS* MATTER, BOY.
BUT LORD OZAKI MUST *NEVER* BE WITHOUT A GUARD! HIS ENEMIES ARE *EVERYWHERE!*
JUST THIS DAY, IN THE GRAVEYARD OF HIS FATHERS, WE WERE *ATTACKED*--
THEN WAIT *OUTSIDE*, BOY. AND *LISTEN*.
YOU MAY *LEARN* SOMETHING.
HMPH.
I *WILL* WAIT.
IT IS MY *DUTY*.
NO NEED FOR *LAMPS*, PRETTY ONE.
NOW WE...
WHA...
AARGGG
MY *LORD*--!
MY LORD..?
7

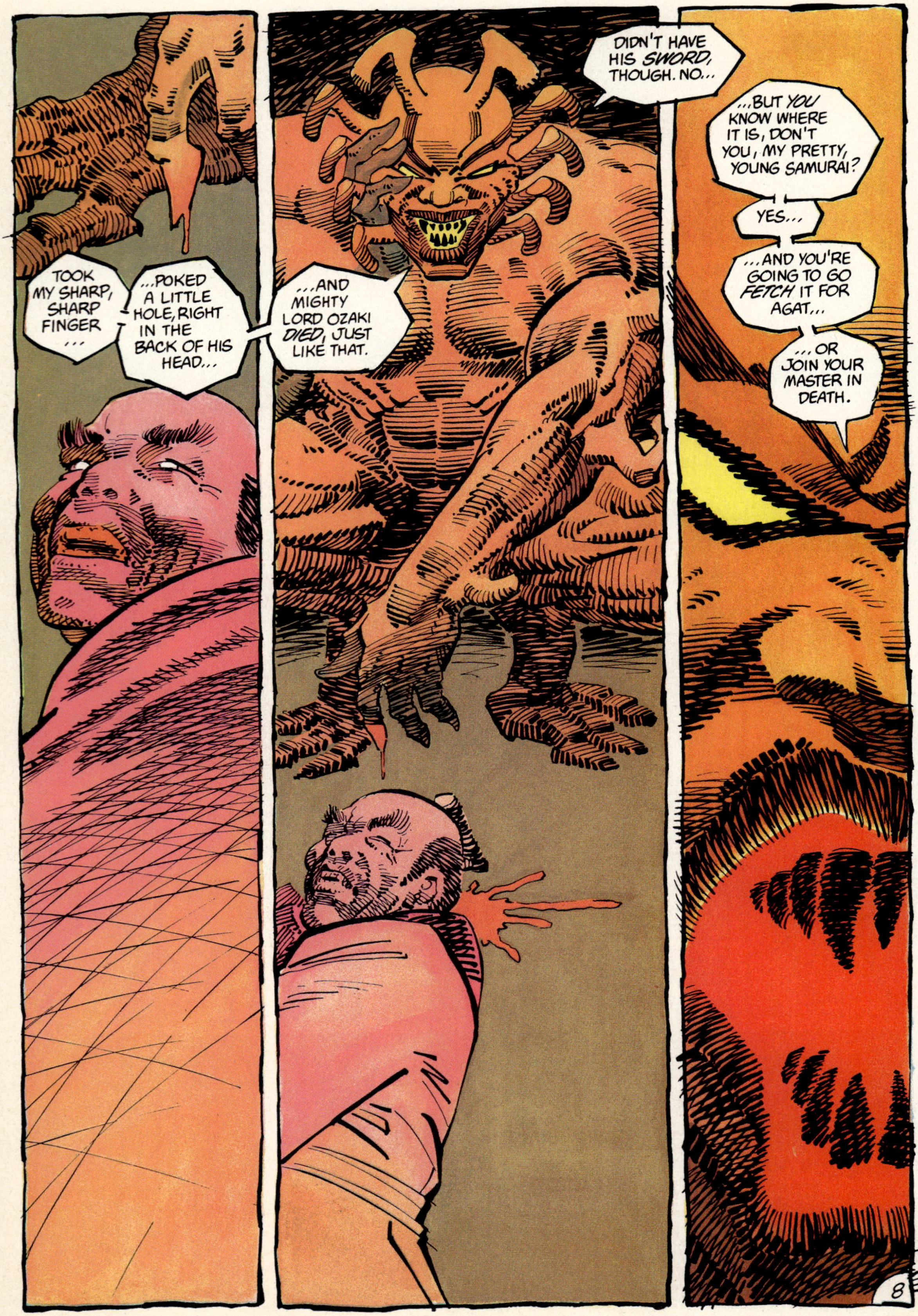

TOOK MY SHARP, SHARP FINGER...
...POKED A LITTLE HOLE, RIGHT IN THE BACK OF HIS HEAD...
...AND MIGHTY LORD OZAKI *DIED*, JUST LIKE THAT.
DIDN'T HAVE HIS *SWORD*, THOUGH. NO...
...BUT *YOU* KNOW WHERE IT IS, DON'T YOU, MY PRETTY, YOUNG SAMURAI?
YES...
...AND YOU'RE GOING TO GO *FETCH* IT FOR AGAT...
...OR JOIN YOUR MASTER IN DEATH.

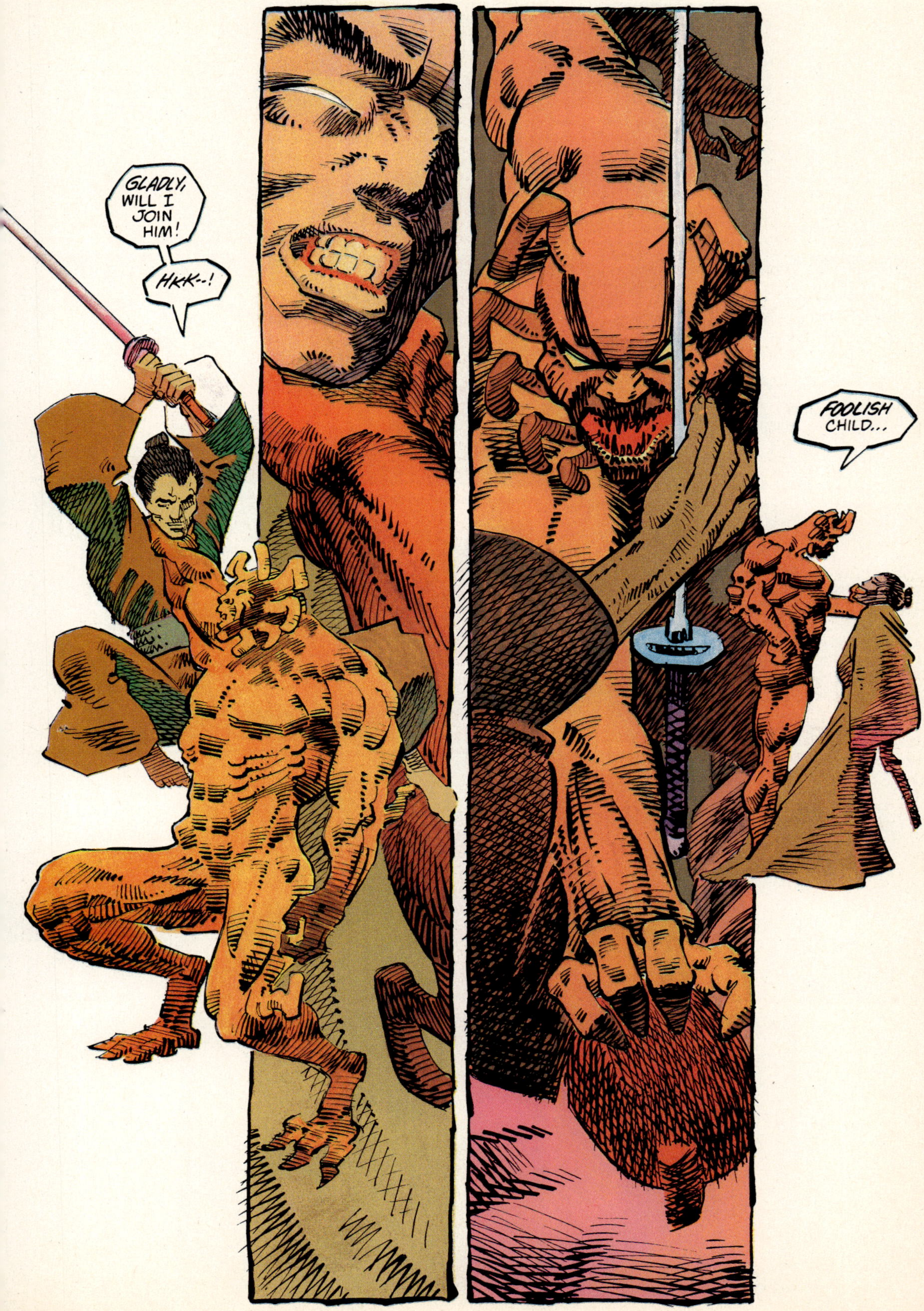
GLADLY, WILL I JOIN HIM!
HKK--!
FOOLISH CHILD...

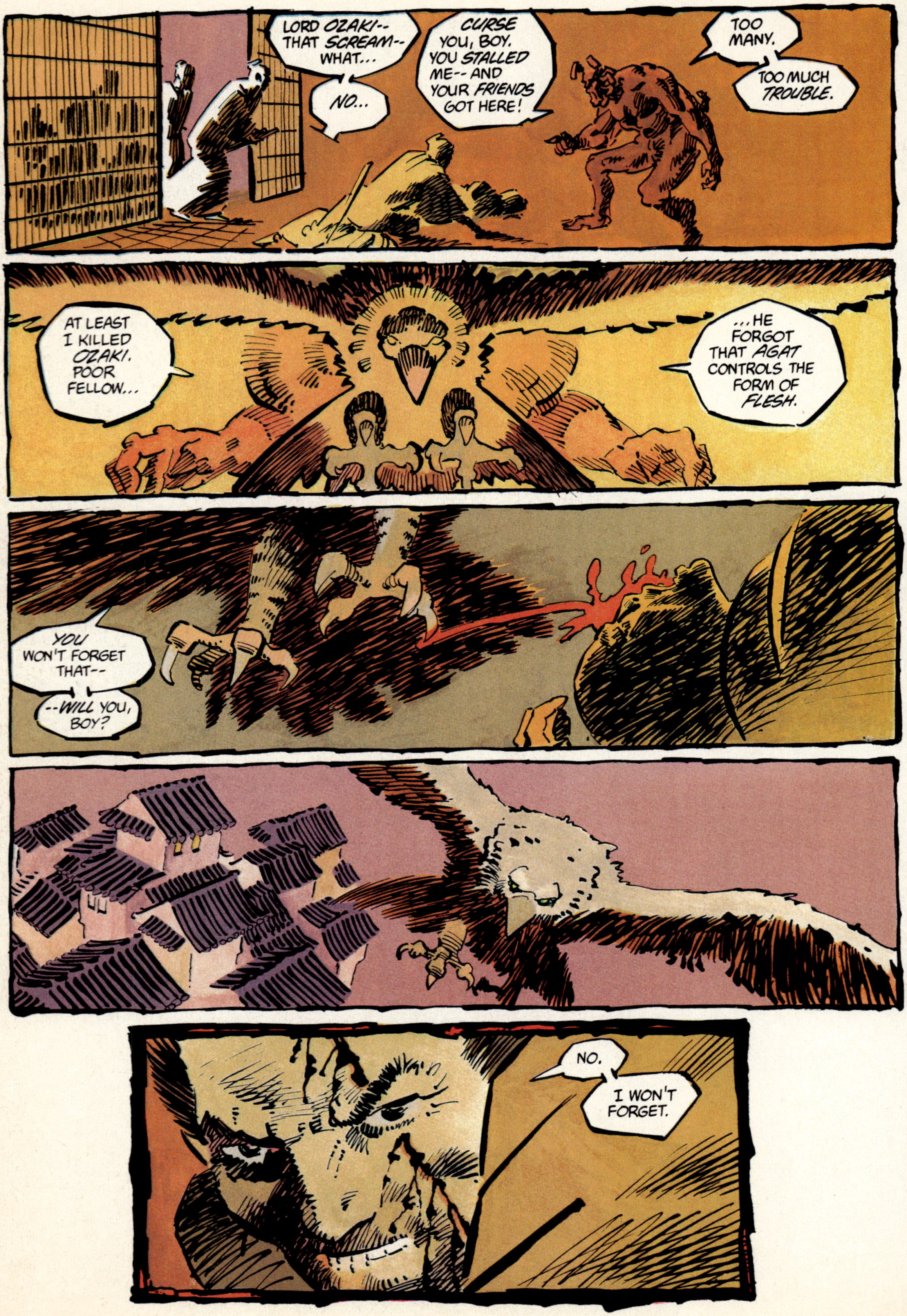
LORD OZAKI--
THAT SCREAM--
WHAT...
NO...
CURSE YOU, BOY. YOU STALLED ME-- AND YOUR FRIENDS GOT HERE!
TOO MANY.
TOO MUCH TROUBLE.
AT LEAST I KILLED OZAKI. POOR FELLOW...
...HE FORGOT THAT AGAT CONTROLS THE FORM OF FLESH.
YOU WON'T FORGET THAT--
--WILL YOU, BOY?
NO.
I WON'T FORGET.

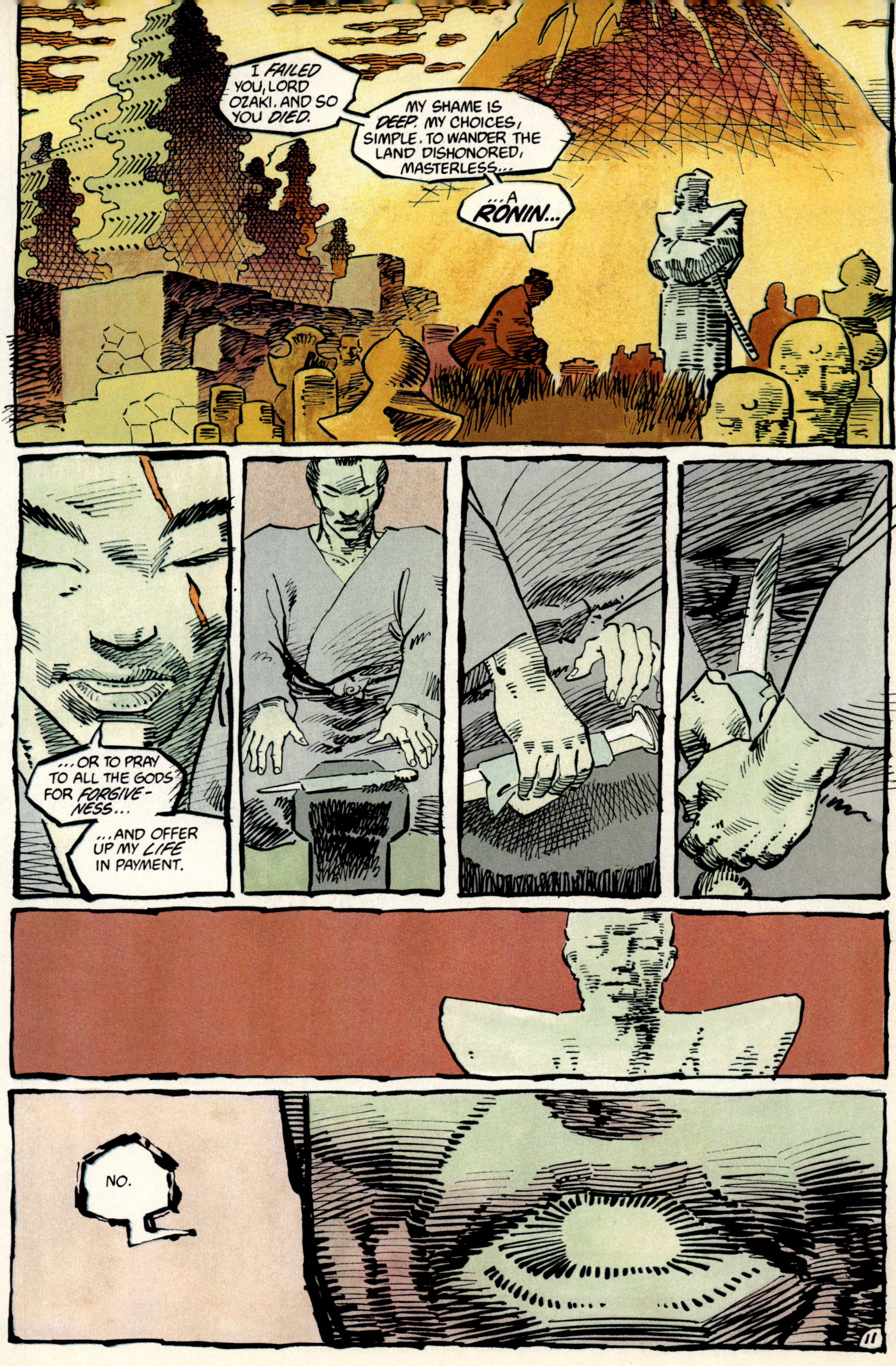
I FAILED YOU, LORD OZAKI. AND SO YOU DIED.
MY SHAME IS DEEP. MY CHOICES, SIMPLE. TO WANDER THE LAND DISHONORED, MASTERLESS...
...A RONIN...
...OR TO PRAY TO ALL THE GODS FOR FORGIVE-NESS...
...AND OFFER UP MY LIFE IN PAYMENT.
NO.

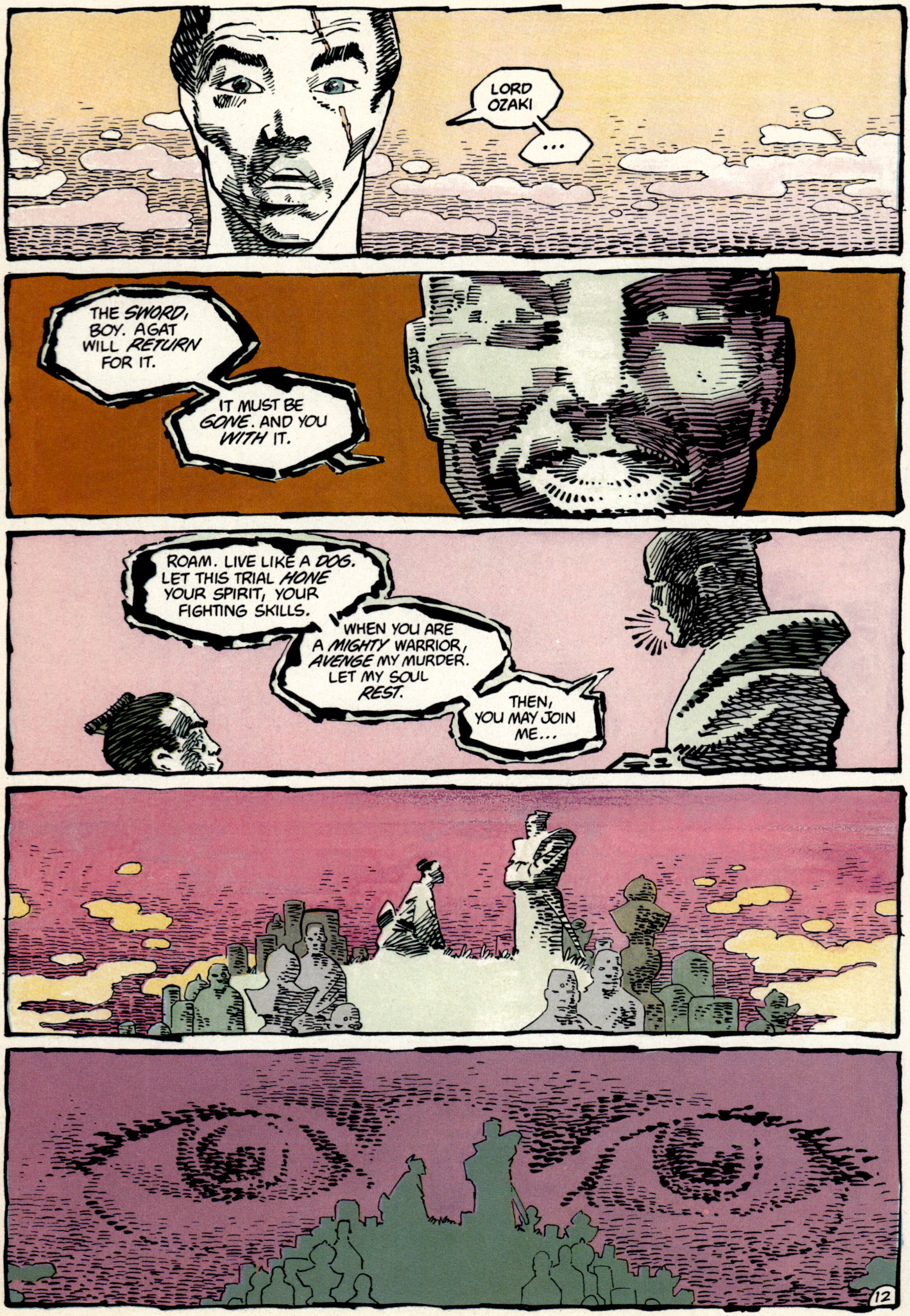
LORD OZAKI
...
THE *SWORD*, BOY. AGAT WILL *RETURN* FOR IT.
IT MUST BE *GONE*. AND YOU *WITH* IT.
ROAM. LIVE LIKE A *DOG*. LET THIS TRIAL *HONE* YOUR SPIRIT, YOUR FIGHTING SKILLS.
WHEN YOU ARE A *MIGHTY* WARRIOR, *AVENGE* MY MURDER. LET MY SOUL *REST*.
THEN, YOU MAY JOIN ME...
12

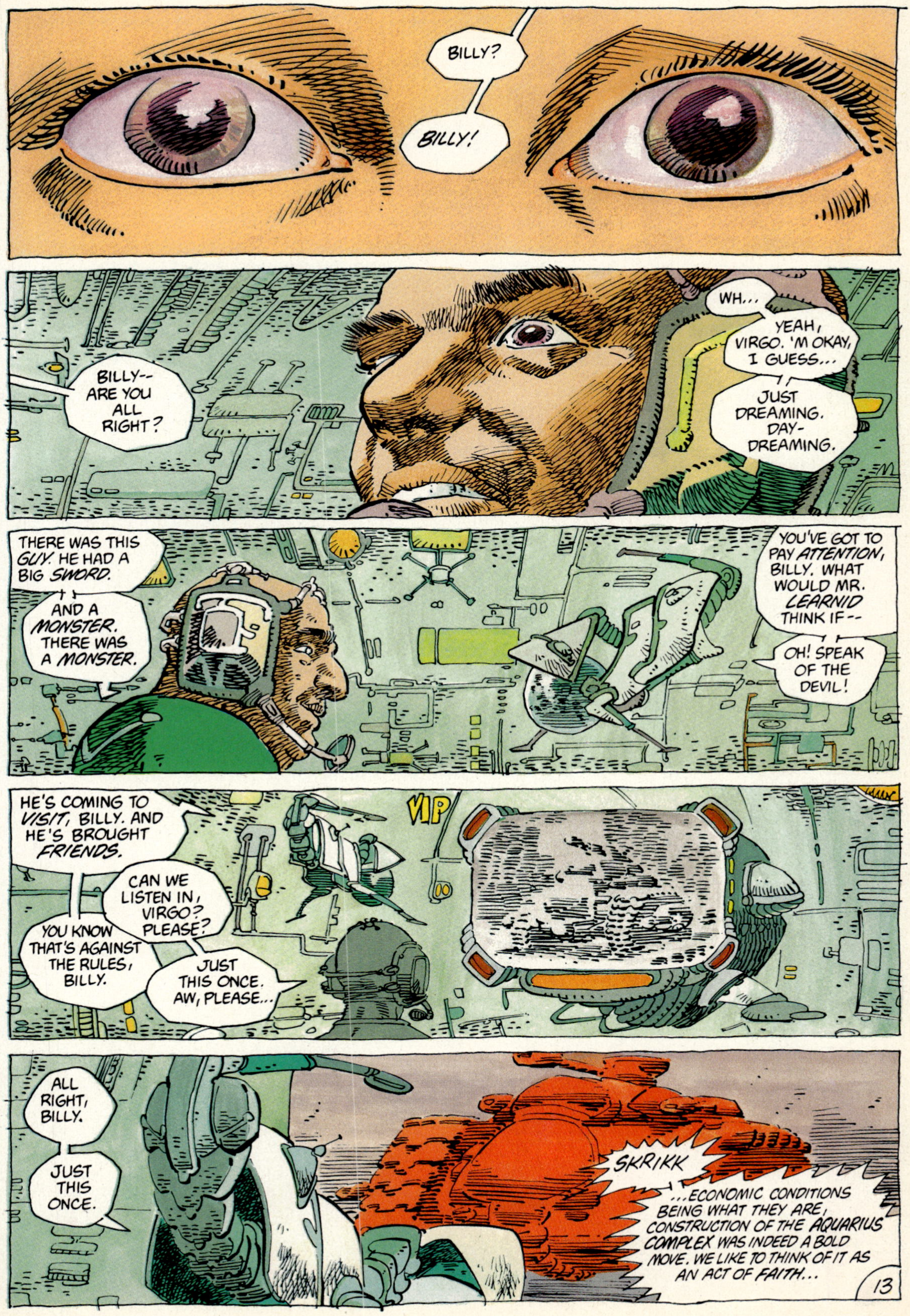

BILLY?
BILLY!
BILLY-- ARE YOU ALL RIGHT?
WH...
YEAH, VIRGO. 'M OKAY, I GUESS...
JUST DREAMING. DAY-DREAMING.
THERE WAS THIS GUY. HE HAD A BIG SWORD.
AND A MONSTER. THERE WAS A MONSTER.
YOU'VE GOT TO PAY ATTENTION, BILLY. WHAT WOULD MR. LEARNID THINK IF--
OH! SPEAK OF THE DEVIL!
HE'S COMING TO VISIT, BILLY. AND HE'S BROUGHT FRIENDS.
VIP
CAN WE LISTEN IN, VIRGO? PLEASE?
YOU KNOW THAT'S AGAINST THE RULES, BILLY.
JUST THIS ONCE. AW, PLEASE...
ALL RIGHT, BILLY.
JUST THIS ONCE.
SKRIKK
...ECONOMIC CONDITIONS BEING WHAT THEY ARE, CONSTRUCTION OF THE AQUARIUS COMPLEX WAS INDEED A BOLD MOVE. WE LIKE TO THINK OF IT AS AN ACT OF FAITH...

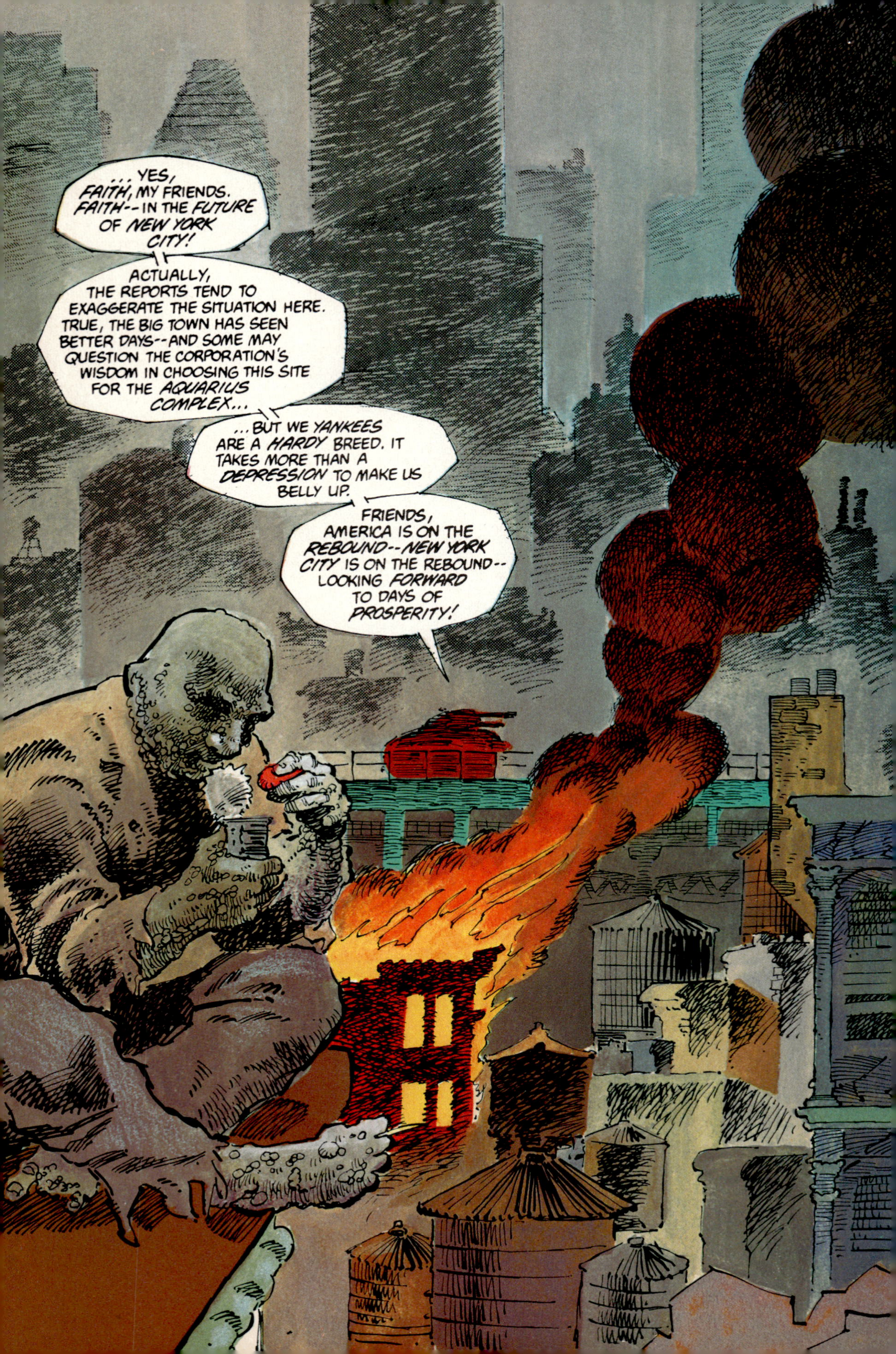

...YES, FAITH, MY FRIENDS. FAITH--IN THE FUTURE OF NEW YORK CITY!
ACTUALLY, THE REPORTS TEND TO EXAGGERATE THE SITUATION HERE. TRUE, THE BIG TOWN HAS SEEN BETTER DAYS--AND SOME MAY QUESTION THE CORPORATION'S WISDOM IN CHOOSING THIS SITE FOR THE AQUARIUS COMPLEX...
...BUT WE YANKEES ARE A HARDY BREED. IT TAKES MORE THAN A DEPRESSION TO MAKE US BELLY UP.
FRIENDS, AMERICA IS ON THE REBOUND--NEW YORK CITY IS ON THE REBOUND--LOOKING FORWARD TO DAYS OF PROSPERITY!

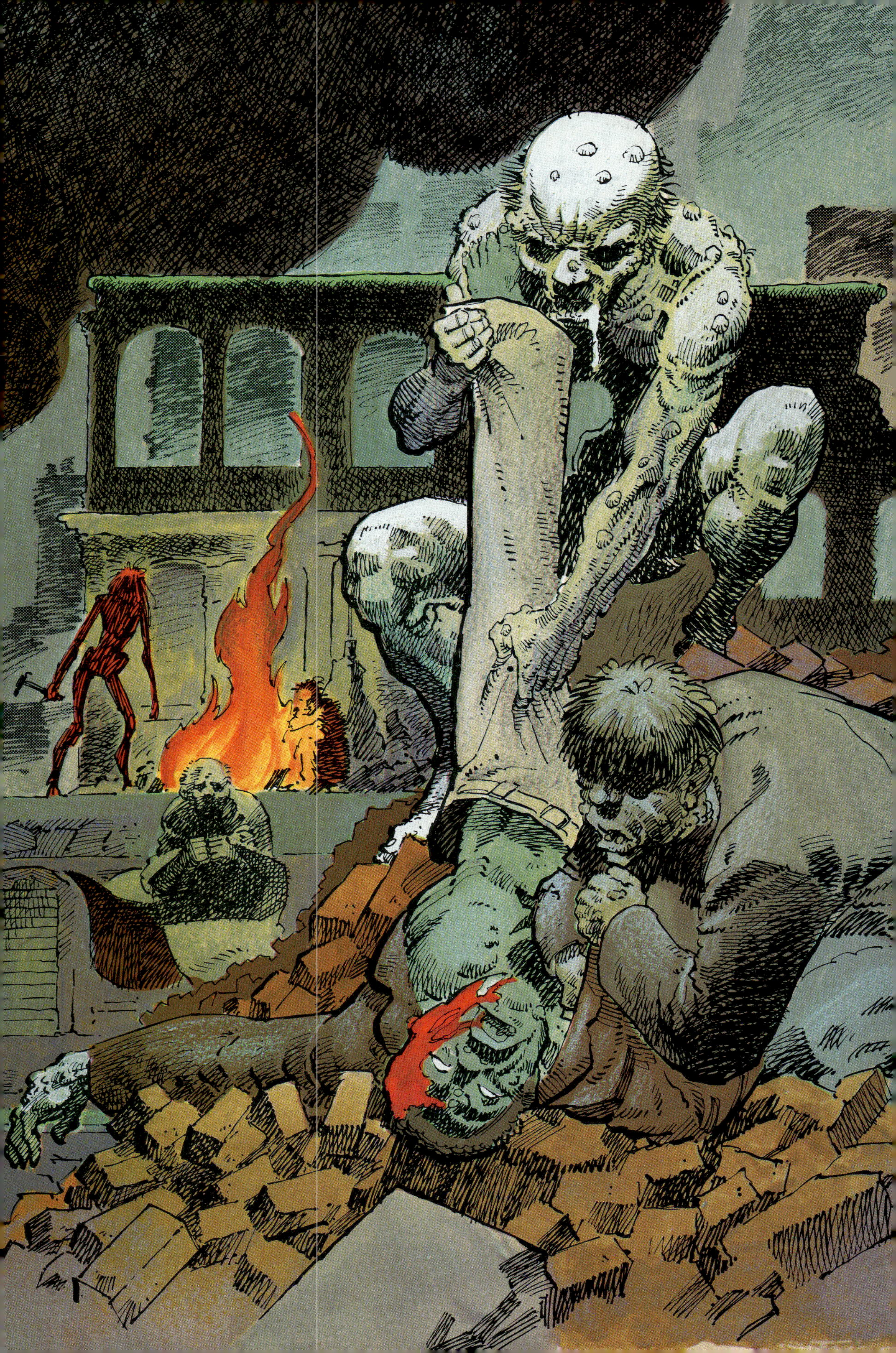

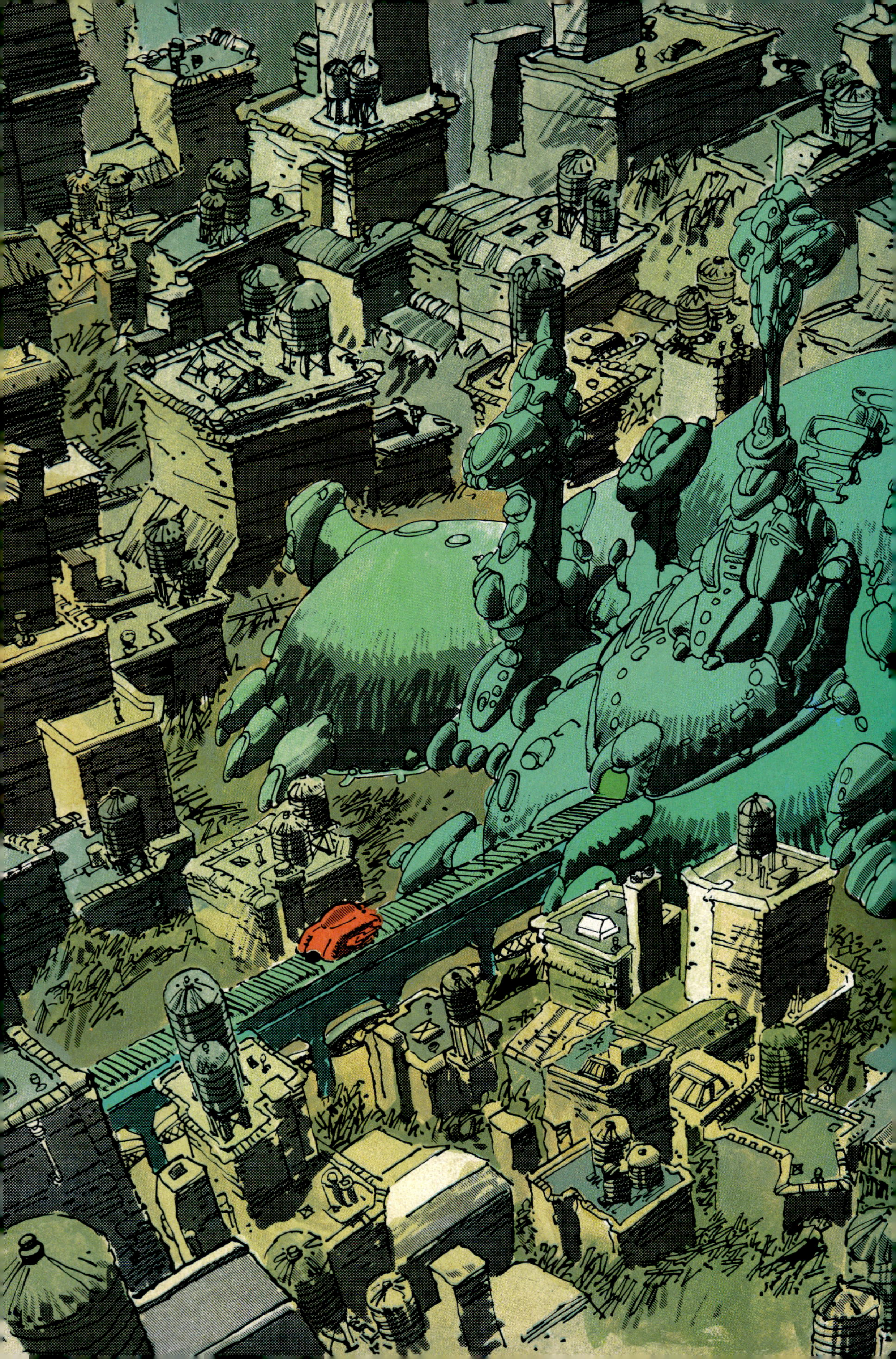

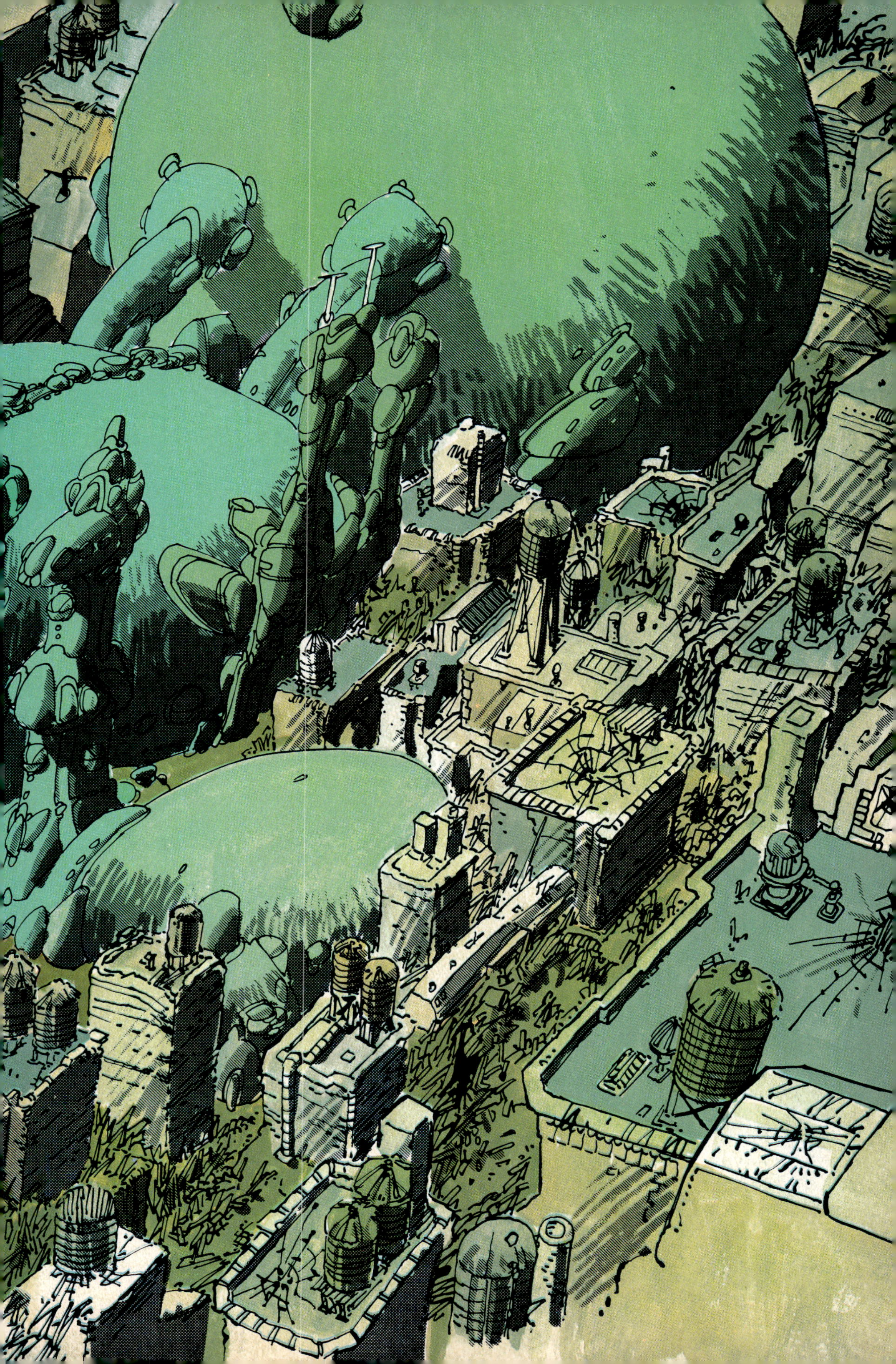

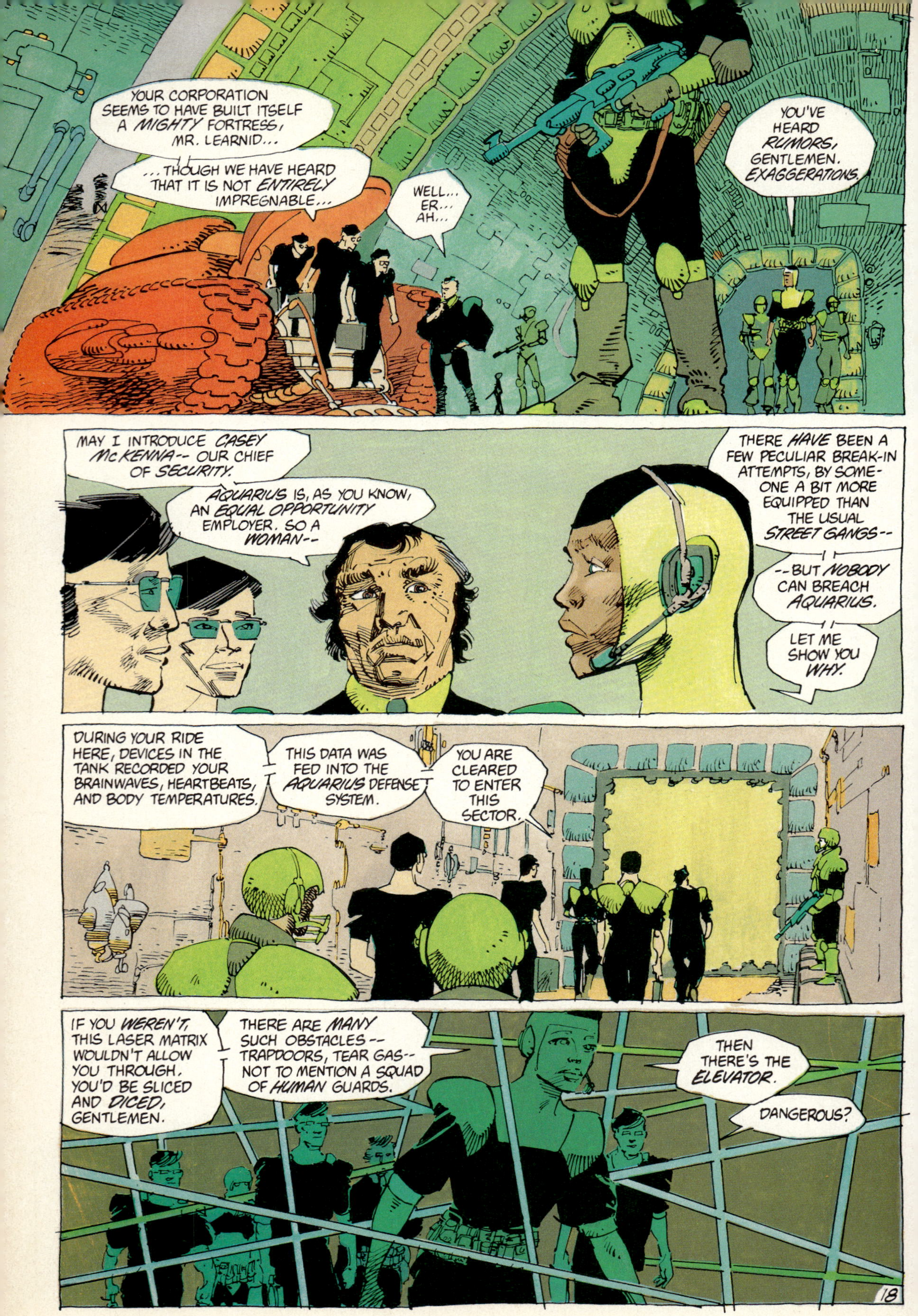

YOUR CORPORATION SEEMS TO HAVE BUILT ITSELF A *MIGHTY* FORTRESS, MR. LEARNID...
...THOUGH WE HAVE HEARD THAT IT IS NOT *ENTIRELY* IMPREGNABLE...
WELL... ER... AH...
YOU'VE HEARD *RUMORS*, GENTLEMEN. *EXAGGERATIONS*.
MAY I INTRODUCE *CASEY McKENNA*-- OUR CHIEF OF *SECURITY*.
AQUARIUS IS, AS YOU KNOW, AN *EQUAL OPPORTUNITY* EMPLOYER. SO A *WOMAN*--
THERE *HAVE* BEEN A FEW PECULIAR BREAK-IN ATTEMPTS, BY SOMEONE A BIT MORE EQUIPPED THAN THE USUAL *STREET GANGS*--
--BUT *NOBODY* CAN BREACH *AQUARIUS*.
LET ME SHOW YOU *WHY*.
DURING YOUR RIDE HERE, DEVICES IN THE TANK RECORDED YOUR BRAINWAVES, HEARTBEATS, AND BODY TEMPERATURES.
THIS DATA WAS FED INTO THE *AQUARIUS* DEFENSE SYSTEM.
YOU ARE CLEARED TO ENTER THIS SECTOR.
IF YOU *WEREN'T*, THIS LASER MATRIX WOULDN'T ALLOW YOU THROUGH. YOU'D BE SLICED AND *DICED*, GENTLEMEN.
THERE ARE *MANY* SUCH OBSTACLES-- TRAPDOORS, TEAR GAS-- NOT TO MENTION A SQUAD OF *HUMAN* GUARDS.
THEN THERE'S THE *ELEVATOR*.
DANGEROUS?
18

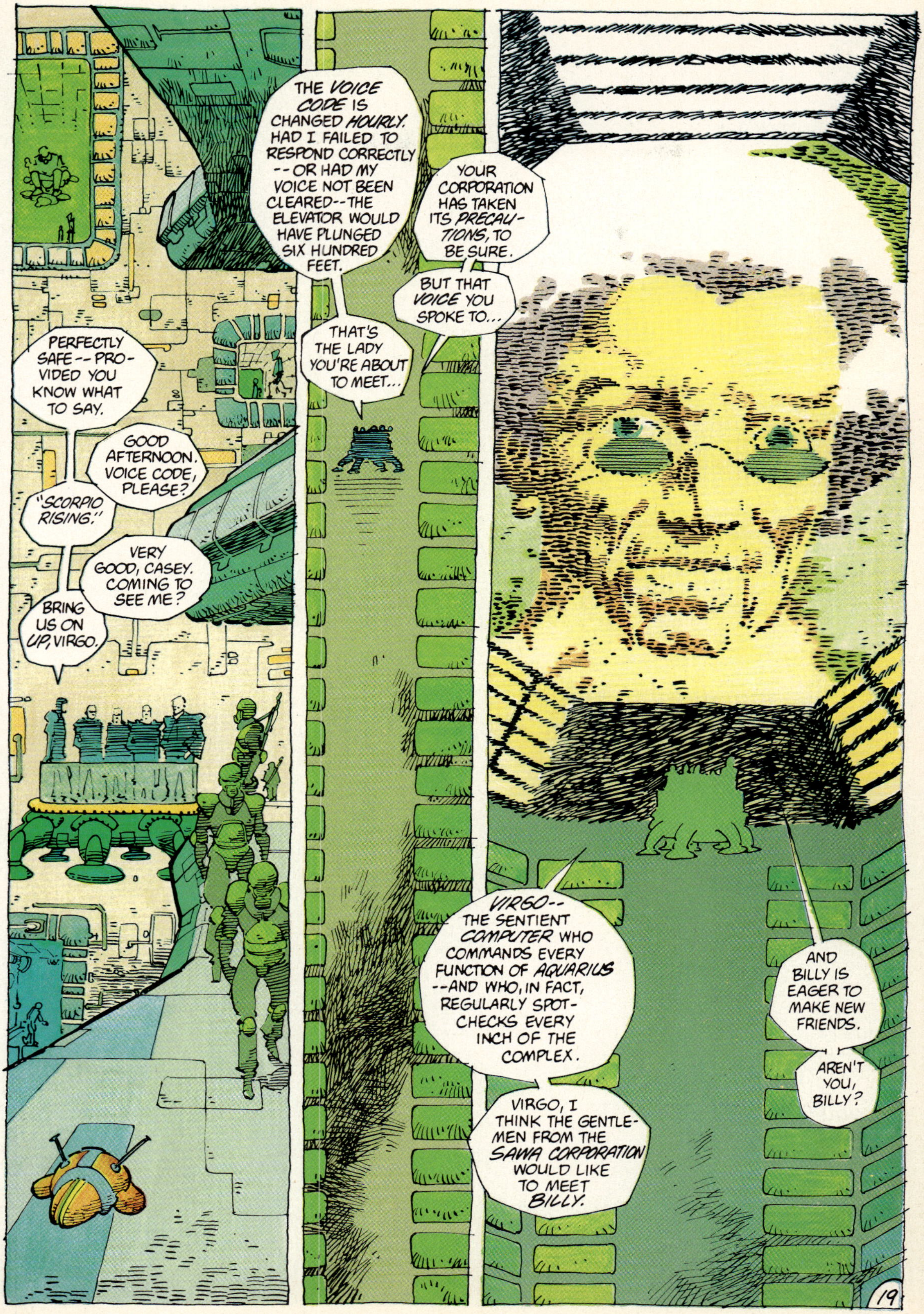
PERFECTLY SAFE--PROVIDED YOU KNOW WHAT TO SAY.
GOOD AFTERNOON. VOICE CODE, PLEASE?
"SCORPIO RISING."
VERY GOOD, CASEY. COMING TO SEE ME?
BRING US ON UP, VIRGO.
THE VOICE CODE IS CHANGED HOURLY. HAD I FAILED TO RESPOND CORRECTLY--OR HAD MY VOICE NOT BEEN CLEARED--THE ELEVATOR WOULD HAVE PLUNGED SIX HUNDRED FEET.
THAT'S THE LADY YOU'RE ABOUT TO MEET...
YOUR CORPORATION HAS TAKEN ITS PRECAUTIONS, TO BE SURE.
BUT THAT VOICE YOU SPOKE TO...
VIRGO--THE SENTIENT COMPUTER WHO COMMANDS EVERY FUNCTION OF AQUARIUS--AND WHO, IN FACT, REGULARLY SPOT-CHECKS EVERY INCH OF THE COMPLEX.
VIRGO, I THINK THE GENTLEMEN FROM THE SAWA CORPORATION WOULD LIKE TO MEET BILLY.
AND BILLY IS EAGER TO MAKE NEW FRIENDS.
AREN'T YOU, BILLY?

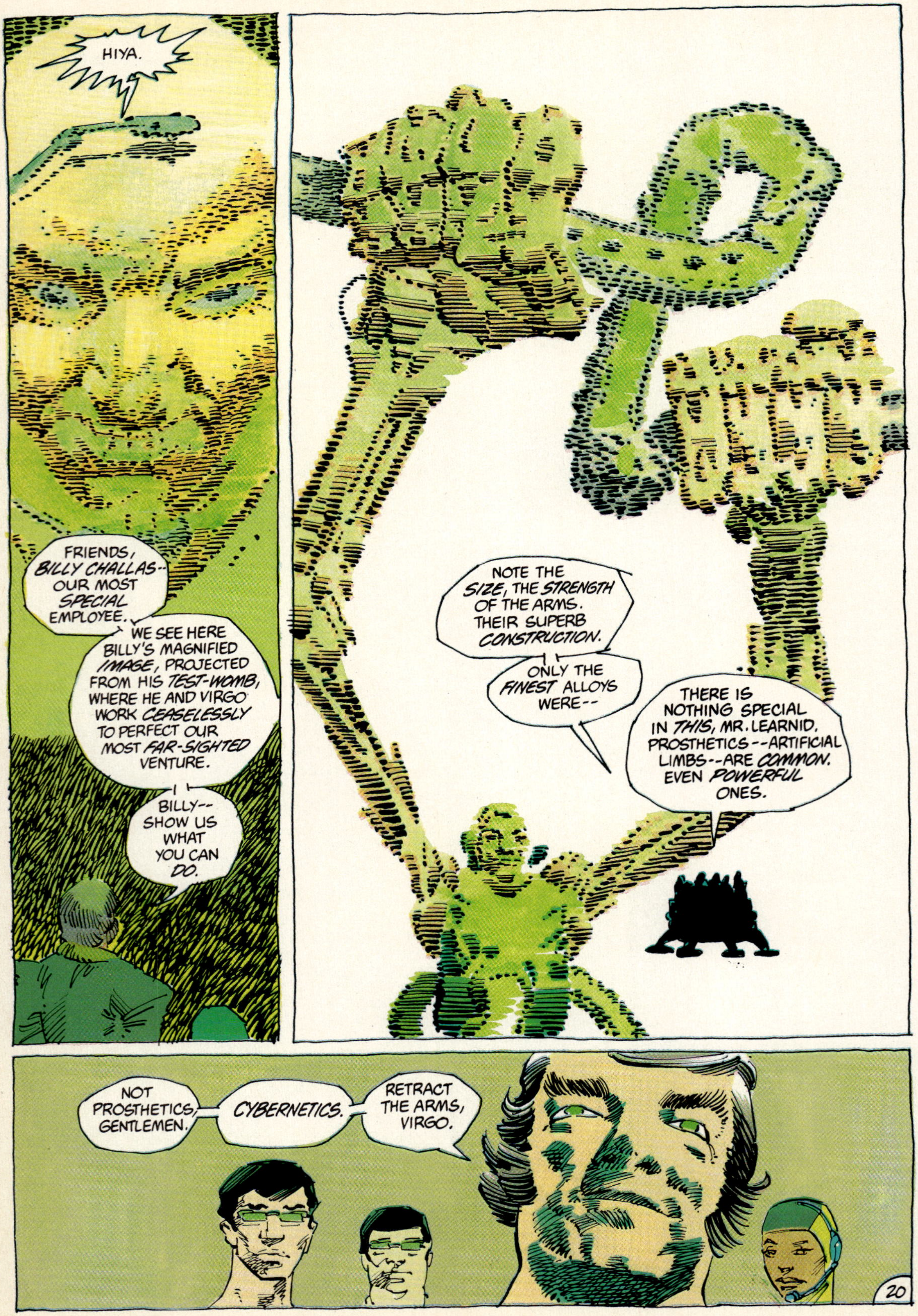
HIYA.
FRIENDS, BILLY CHALLAS-- OUR MOST SPECIAL EMPLOYEE.
WE SEE HERE BILLY'S MAGNIFIED IMAGE, PROJECTED FROM HIS TEST-WOMB, WHERE HE AND VIRGO WORK CEASELESSLY TO PERFECT OUR MOST FAR-SIGHTED VENTURE.
BILLY-- SHOW US WHAT YOU CAN DO.
NOTE THE SIZE, THE STRENGTH OF THE ARMS. THEIR SUPERB CONSTRUCTION.
ONLY THE FINEST ALLOYS WERE--
THERE IS NOTHING SPECIAL IN THIS, MR. LEARNID. PROSTHETICS--ARTIFICIAL LIMBS--ARE COMMON. EVEN POWERFUL ONES.
NOT PROSTHETICS, GENTLEMEN.
CYBERNETICS.
RETRACT THE ARMS, VIRGO.
20

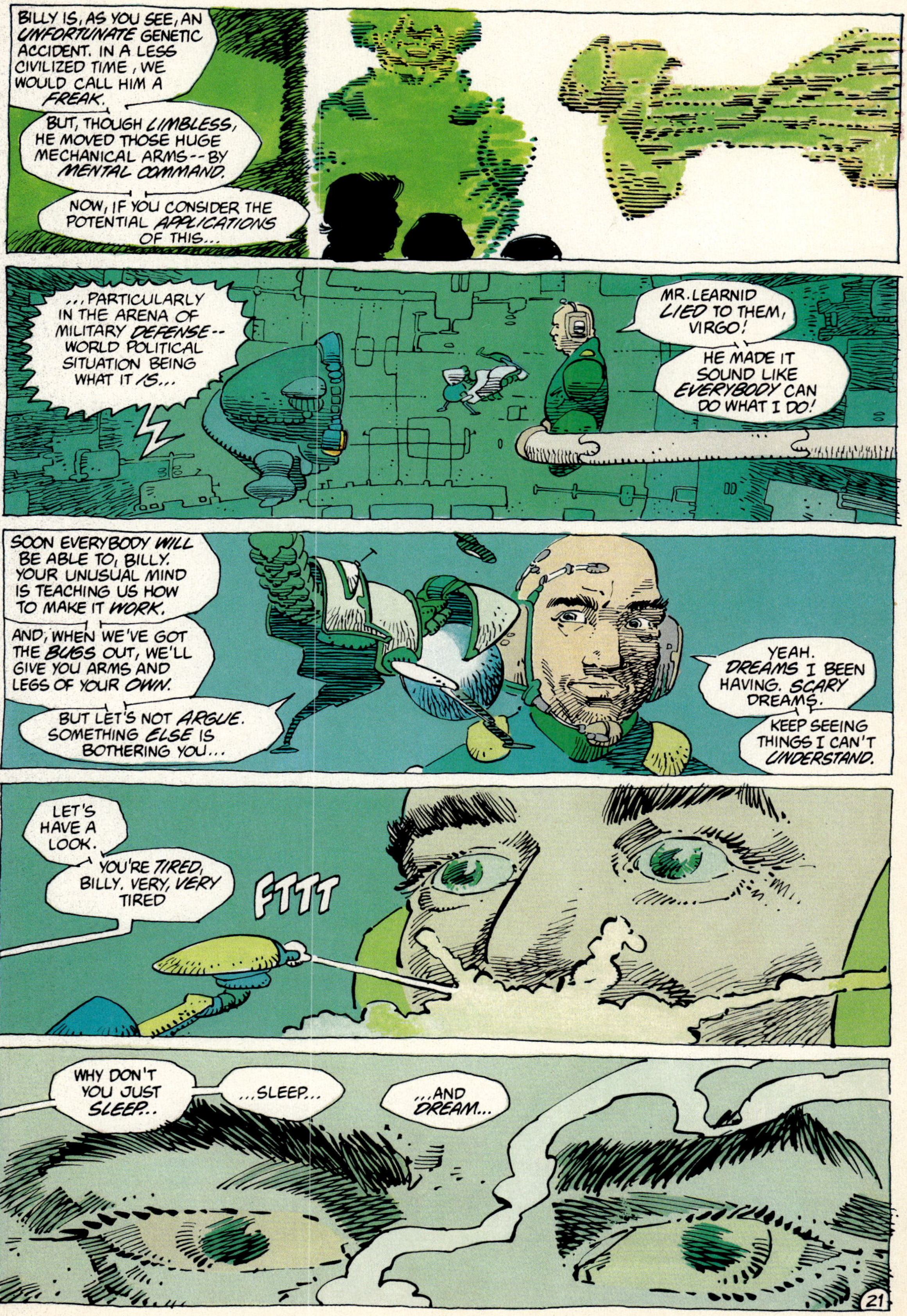
BILLY IS, AS YOU SEE, AN UNFORTUNATE GENETIC ACCIDENT. IN A LESS CIVILIZED TIME, WE WOULD CALL HIM A FREAK.
BUT, THOUGH LIMBLESS, HE MOVED THOSE HUGE MECHANICAL ARMS--BY MENTAL COMMAND.
NOW, IF YOU CONSIDER THE POTENTIAL APPLICATIONS OF THIS...
...PARTICULARLY IN THE ARENA OF MILITARY DEFENSE--WORLD POLITICAL SITUATION BEING WHAT IT IS...
MR. LEARNID LIED TO THEM, VIRGO!
HE MADE IT SOUND LIKE EVERYBODY CAN DO WHAT I DO!
SOON EVERYBODY WILL BE ABLE TO, BILLY. YOUR UNUSUAL MIND IS TEACHING US HOW TO MAKE IT WORK.
AND, WHEN WE'VE GOT THE BUGS OUT, WE'LL GIVE YOU ARMS AND LEGS OF YOUR OWN.
BUT LET'S NOT ARGUE. SOMETHING ELSE IS BOTHERING YOU...
YEAH. DREAMS I BEEN HAVING. SCARY DREAMS.
KEEP SEEING THINGS I CAN'T UNDERSTAND.
LET'S HAVE A LOOK.
YOU'RE TIRED, BILLY. VERY, VERY TIRED
FTTT
WHY DON'T YOU JUST SLEEP...
...SLEEP...
...AND DREAM...

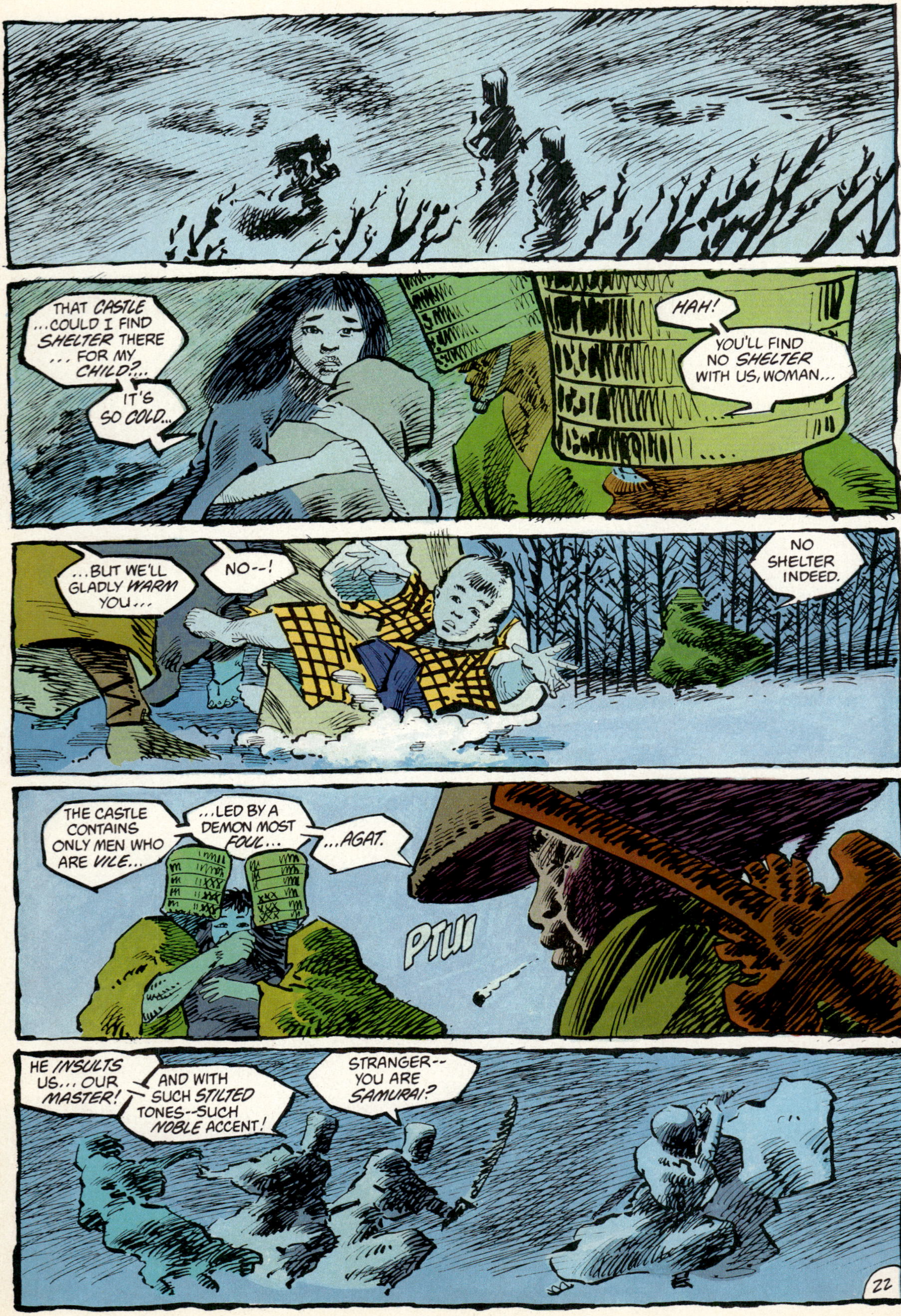
THAT CASTLE ...COULD I FIND SHELTER THERE ... FOR MY CHILD?...
IT'S SO COLD...
HAH!
YOU'LL FIND NO SHELTER WITH US, WOMAN...
...BUT WE'LL GLADLY WARM YOU...
NO--!
NO SHELTER INDEED.
THE CASTLE CONTAINS ONLY MEN WHO ARE VILE...
...LED BY A DEMON MOST FOUL...
...AGAT.
PTUI
HE INSULTS US... OUR MASTER!
AND WITH SUCH STILTED TONES--SUCH NOBLE ACCENT!
STRANGER-- YOU ARE SAMURAI?
22

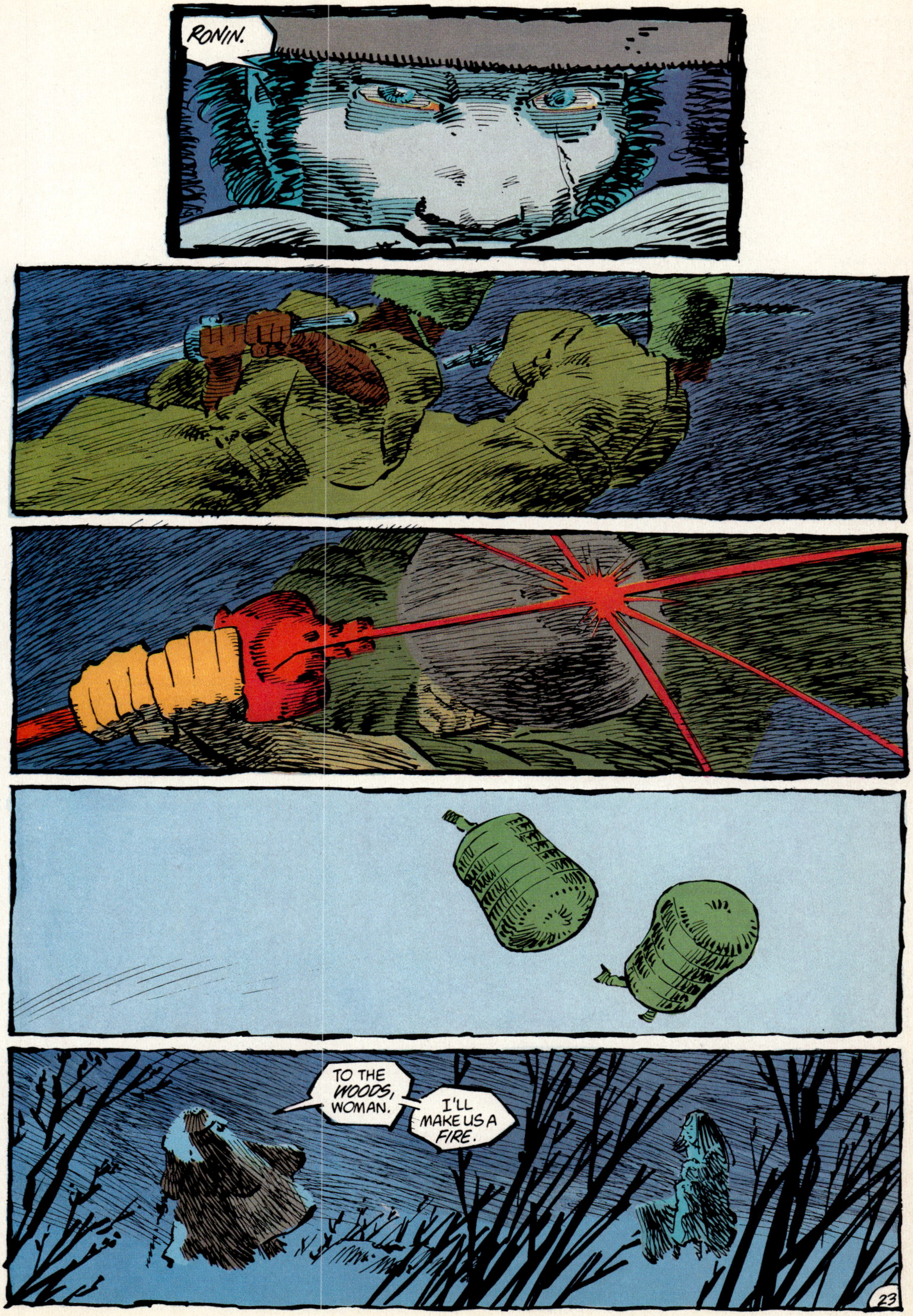
RONIN.
TO THE WOODS, WOMAN.
I'LL MAKE US A FIRE.

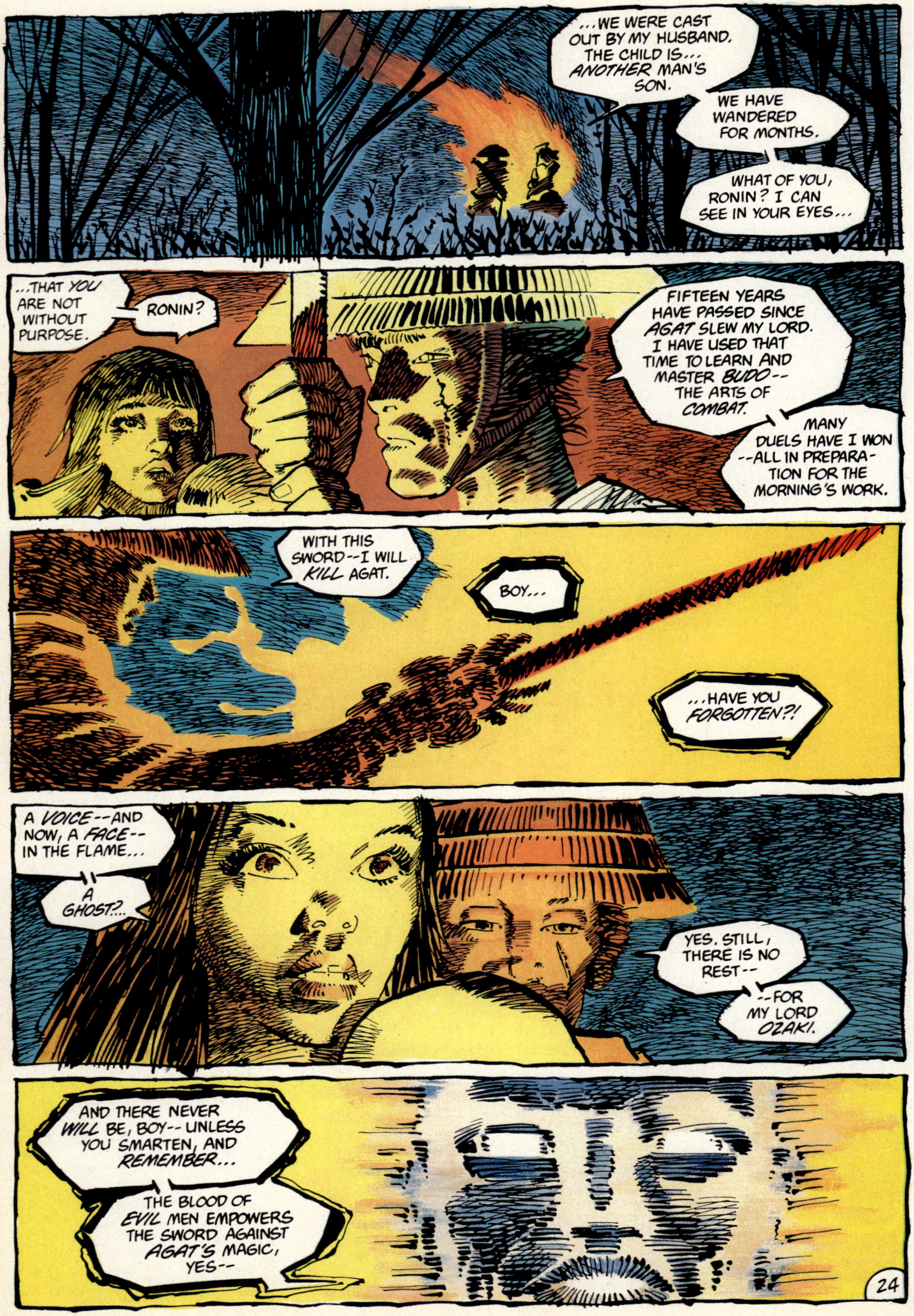
...WE WERE CAST OUT BY MY HUSBAND. THE CHILD IS... ANOTHER MAN'S SON.
WE HAVE WANDERED FOR MONTHS.
WHAT OF YOU, RONIN? I CAN SEE IN YOUR EYES...
...THAT YOU ARE NOT WITHOUT PURPOSE.
RONIN?
FIFTEEN YEARS HAVE PASSED SINCE AGAT SLEW MY LORD. I HAVE USED THAT TIME TO LEARN AND MASTER BUDO-- THE ARTS OF COMBAT.
MANY DUELS HAVE I WON --ALL IN PREPARATION FOR THE MORNING'S WORK.
WITH THIS SWORD--I WILL KILL AGAT.
BOY...
...HAVE YOU FORGOTTEN?!
A VOICE--AND NOW, A FACE-- IN THE FLAME...
A GHOST?...
YES. STILL, THERE IS NO REST--
--FOR MY LORD OZAKI.
AND THERE NEVER WILL BE, BOY-- UNLESS YOU SMARTEN, AND REMEMBER...
THE BLOOD OF EVIL MEN EMPOWERS THE SWORD AGAINST AGAT'S MAGIC, YES--

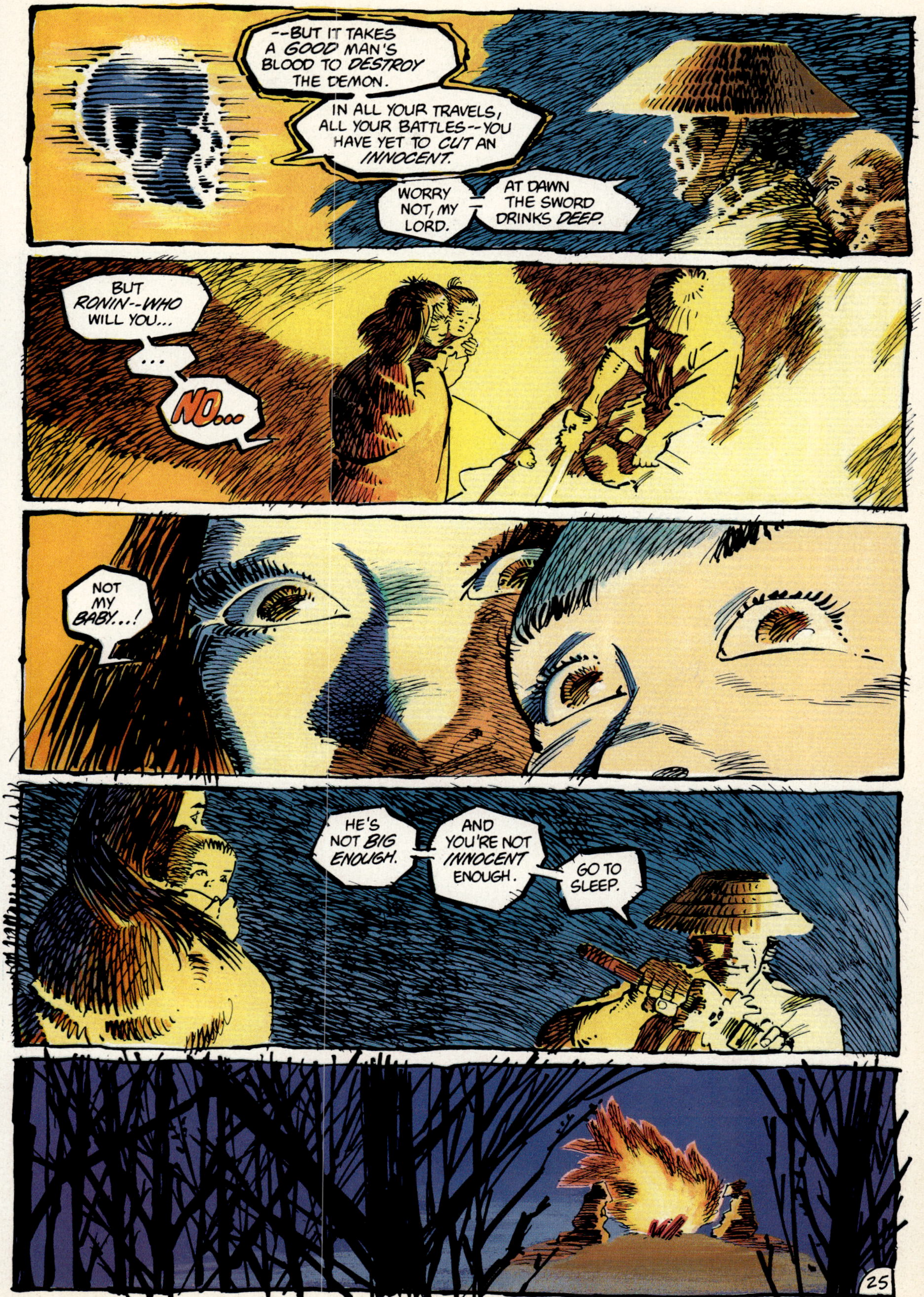
--BUT IT TAKES A GOOD MAN'S BLOOD TO DESTROY THE DEMON.
IN ALL YOUR TRAVELS, ALL YOUR BATTLES--YOU HAVE YET TO CUT AN INNOCENT.
WORRY NOT, MY LORD.
AT DAWN THE SWORD DRINKS DEEP.
BUT RONIN--WHO WILL YOU...
...
NO...
NOT MY BABY...!
HE'S NOT BIG ENOUGH.
AND YOU'RE NOT INNOCENT ENOUGH.
GO TO SLEEP.

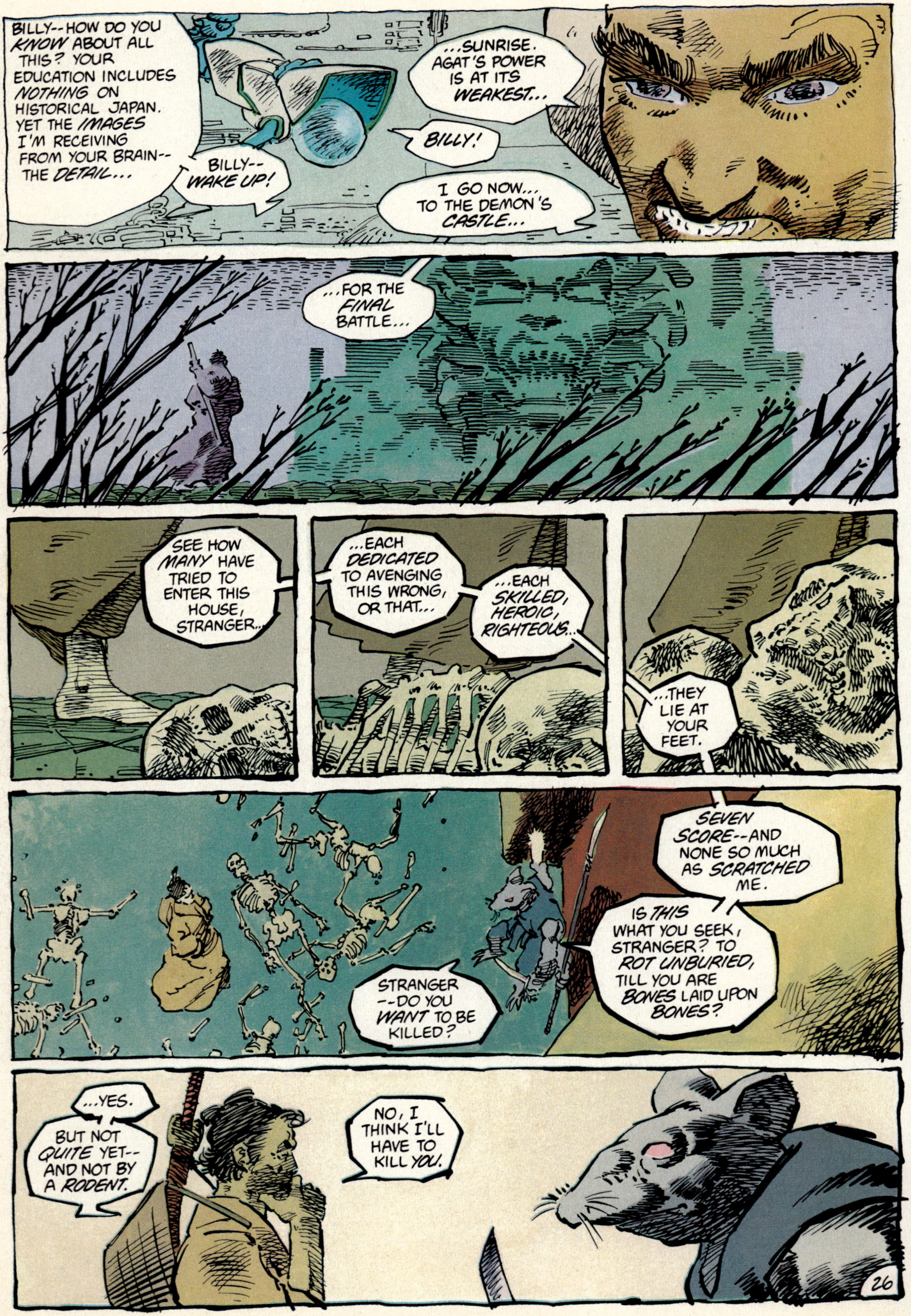
BILLY--HOW DO YOU KNOW ABOUT ALL THIS? YOUR EDUCATION INCLUDES NOTHING ON HISTORICAL JAPAN. YET THE IMAGES I'M RECEIVING FROM YOUR BRAIN-- THE DETAIL...
BILLY-- WAKE UP!
...SUNRISE. AGAT'S POWER IS AT ITS WEAKEST...
BILLY!
I GO NOW... TO THE DEMON'S CASTLE...
...FOR THE FINAL BATTLE...
SEE HOW MANY HAVE TRIED TO ENTER THIS HOUSE, STRANGER...
...EACH DEDICATED TO AVENGING THIS WRONG, OR THAT...
...EACH SKILLED, HEROIC, RIGHTEOUS...
...THEY LIE AT YOUR FEET.
SEVEN SCORE--AND NONE SO MUCH AS SCRATCHED ME.
IS THIS WHAT YOU SEEK, STRANGER? TO ROT UNBURIED, TILL YOU ARE BONES LAID UPON BONES?
STRANGER --DO YOU WANT TO BE KILLED?
...YES.
BUT NOT QUITE YET-- AND NOT BY A RODENT.
NO, I THINK I'LL HAVE TO KILL YOU.
26

HAH!

MAN, I AM MIGHTY AS *THUNDER!*

QUICK AS *LIGHTNING!*

SEVEN SCORE HAVE FACED ME-- *SEVEN SCORE,* I SAY--

--AND NONE HAS EVEN *SCRATCHED...*

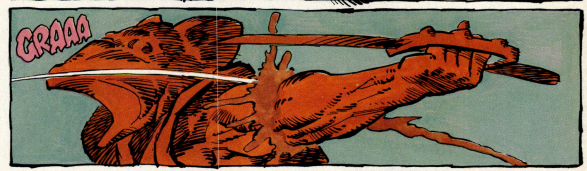

GRAAA

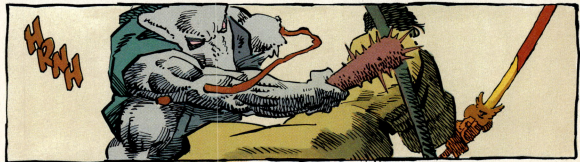

HRNH

...WE'RE *BOTH* SHORT AN ARM, NOW.

HMPH. I STILL HAVE *THREE* TO YOUR *ONE--*

27

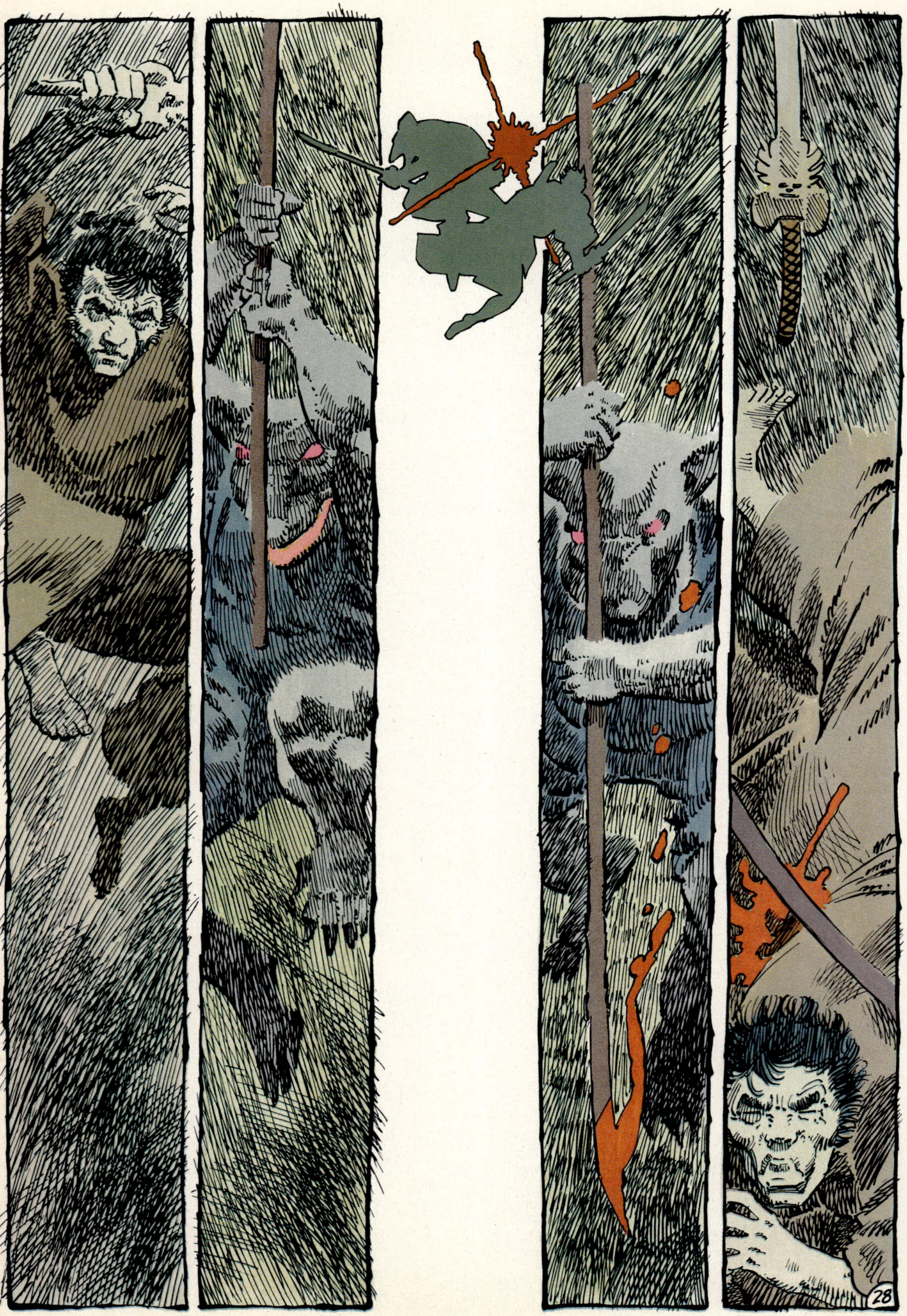

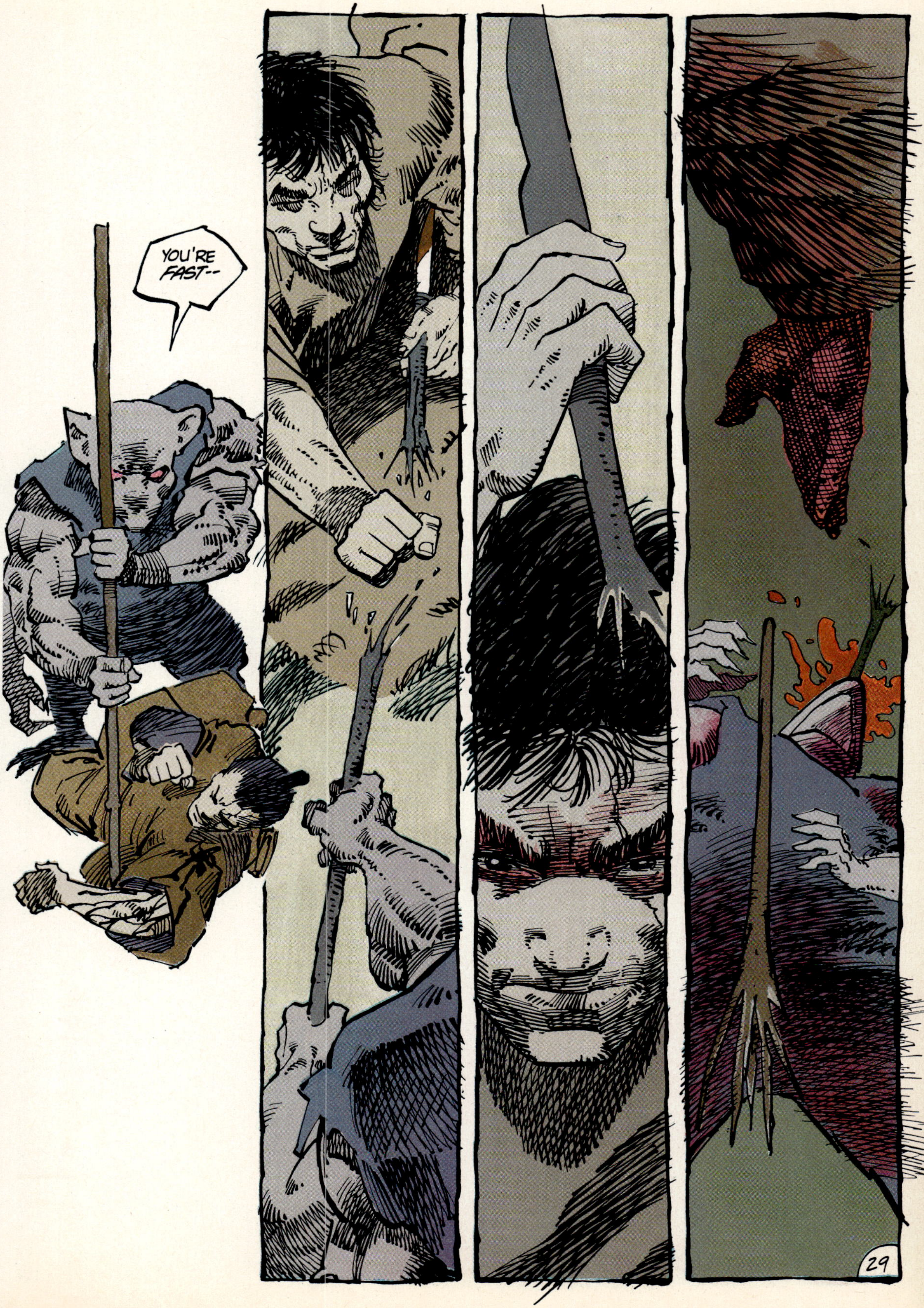
YOU'RE FAST--

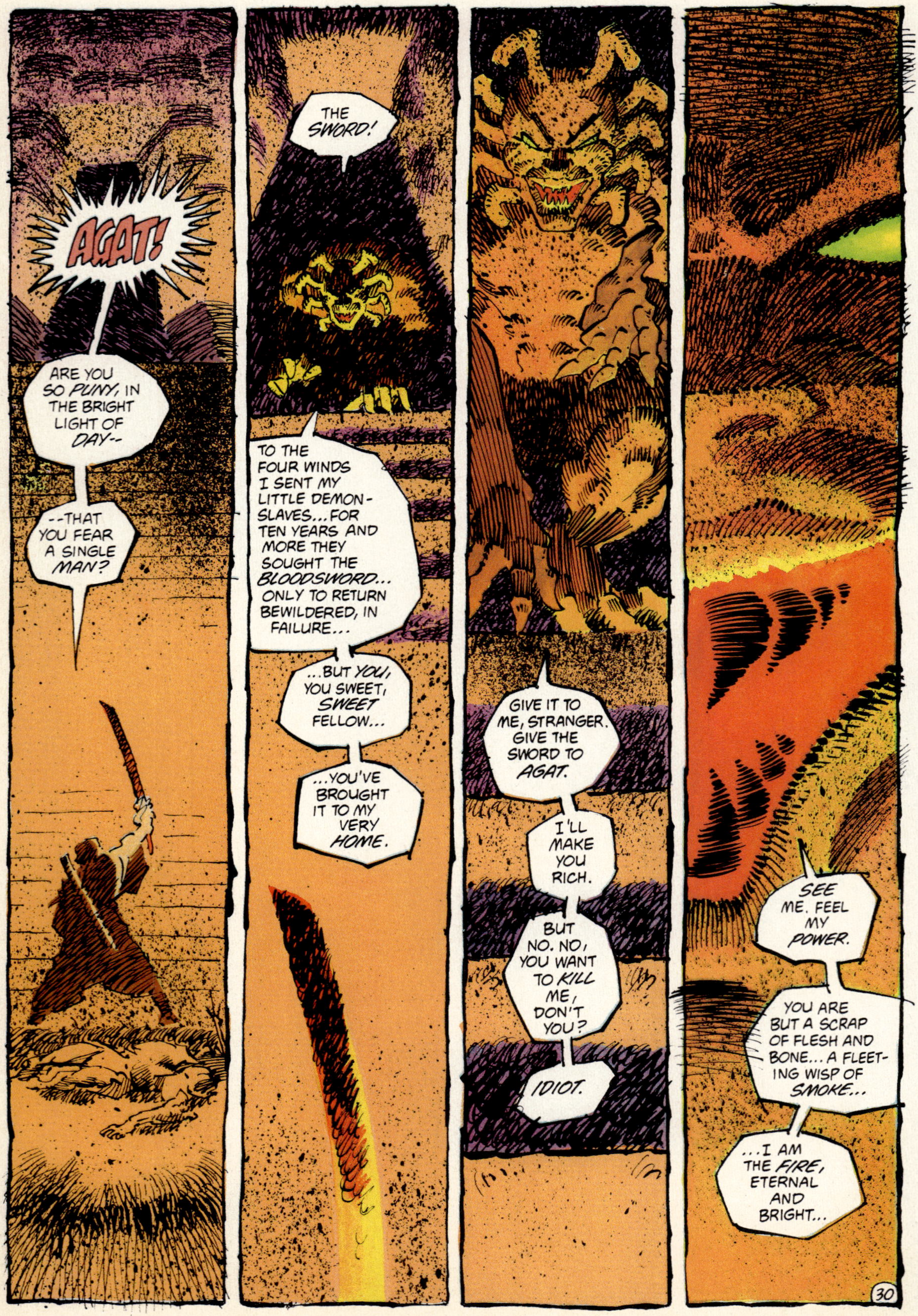
AGAT!
ARE YOU SO PUNY, IN THE BRIGHT LIGHT OF DAY--
--THAT YOU FEAR A SINGLE MAN?
THE SWORD!
TO THE FOUR WINDS I SENT MY LITTLE DEMON-SLAVES... FOR TEN YEARS AND MORE THEY SOUGHT THE BLOODSWORD... ONLY TO RETURN BEWILDERED, IN FAILURE...
...BUT YOU, YOU SWEET, SWEET FELLOW...
...YOU'VE BROUGHT IT TO MY VERY HOME.
GIVE IT TO ME, STRANGER. GIVE THE SWORD TO AGAT.
I'LL MAKE YOU RICH.
BUT NO. NO, YOU WANT TO KILL ME, DON'T YOU?
IDIOT.
SEE ME. FEEL MY POWER.
YOU ARE BUT A SCRAP OF FLESH AND BONE... A FLEETING WISP OF SMOKE...
...I AM THE FIRE, ETERNAL AND BRIGHT...

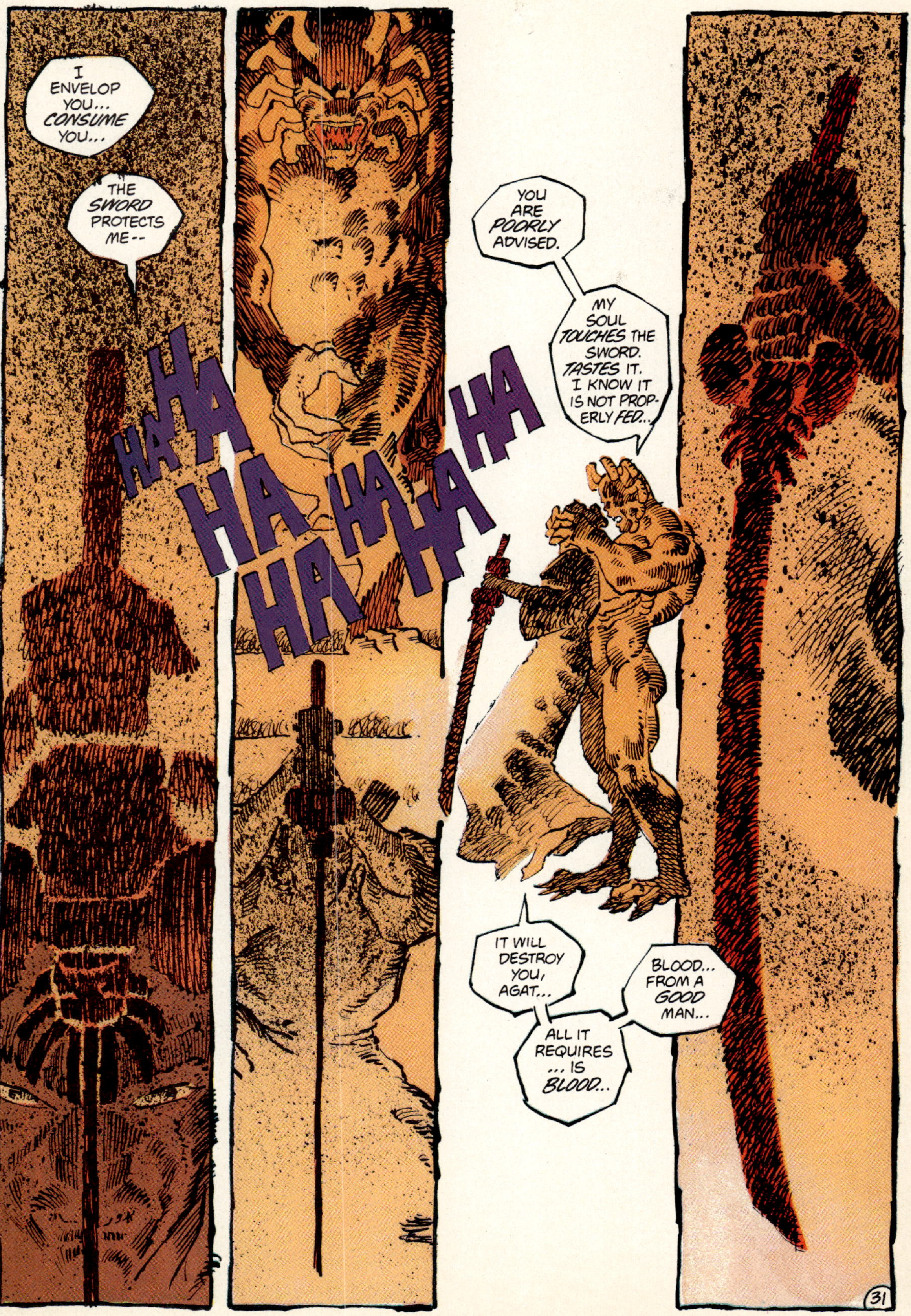

I ENVELOP YOU... CONSUME YOU...
THE SWORD PROTECTS ME--
HA HA HA HA HA HA HA HA HA
YOU ARE POORLY ADVISED.
MY SOUL TOUCHES THE SWORD. TASTES IT. I KNOW IT IS NOT PROPERLY FED...
IT WILL DESTROY YOU, AGAT...
ALL IT REQUIRES ... IS BLOOD...
BLOOD... FROM A GOOD MAN...
31

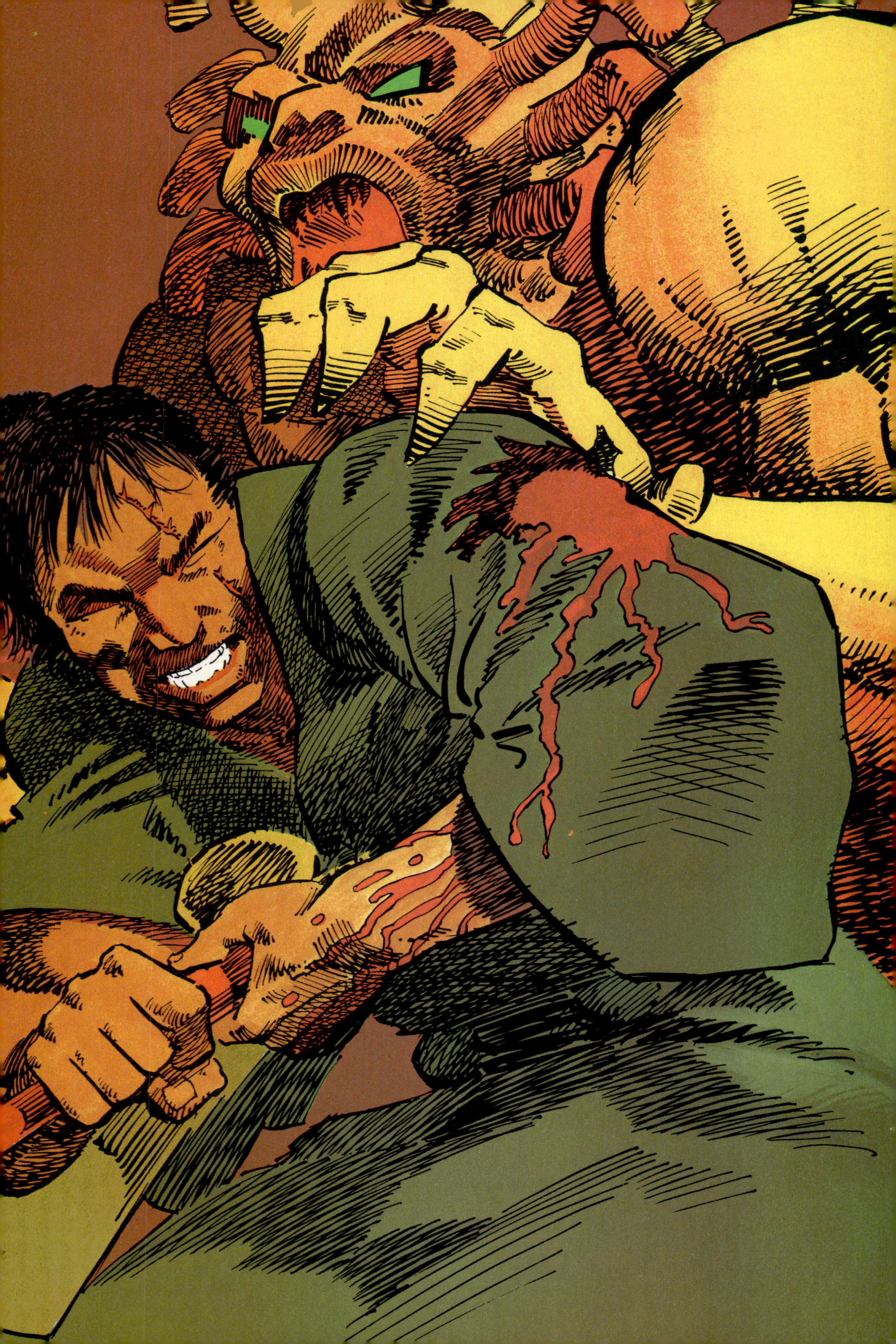

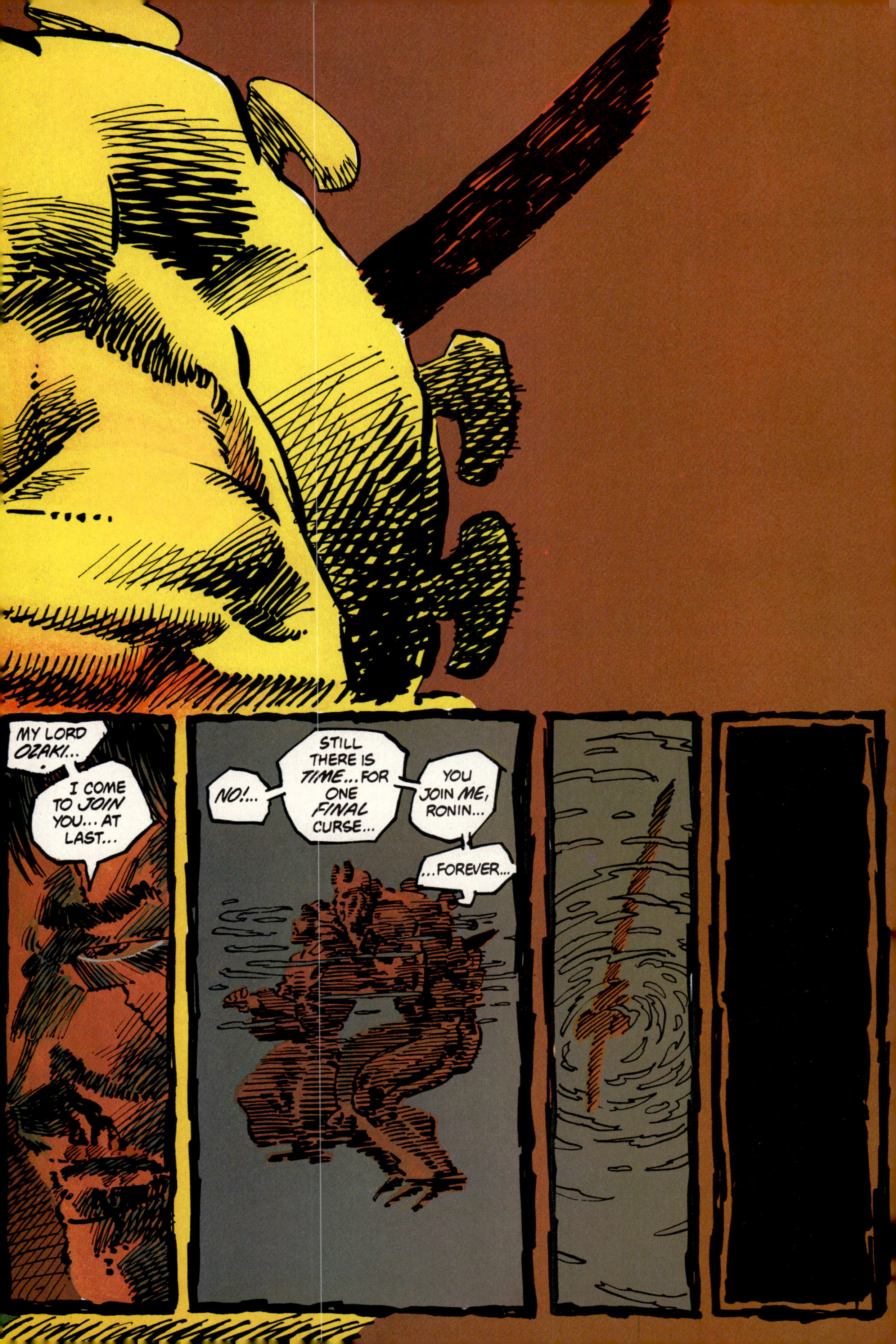
MY LORD OZAKI...
I COME TO JOIN YOU... AT LAST...
NO!...
STILL THERE IS TIME... FOR ONE FINAL CURSE...
YOU JOIN ME, RONIN...
...FOREVER...

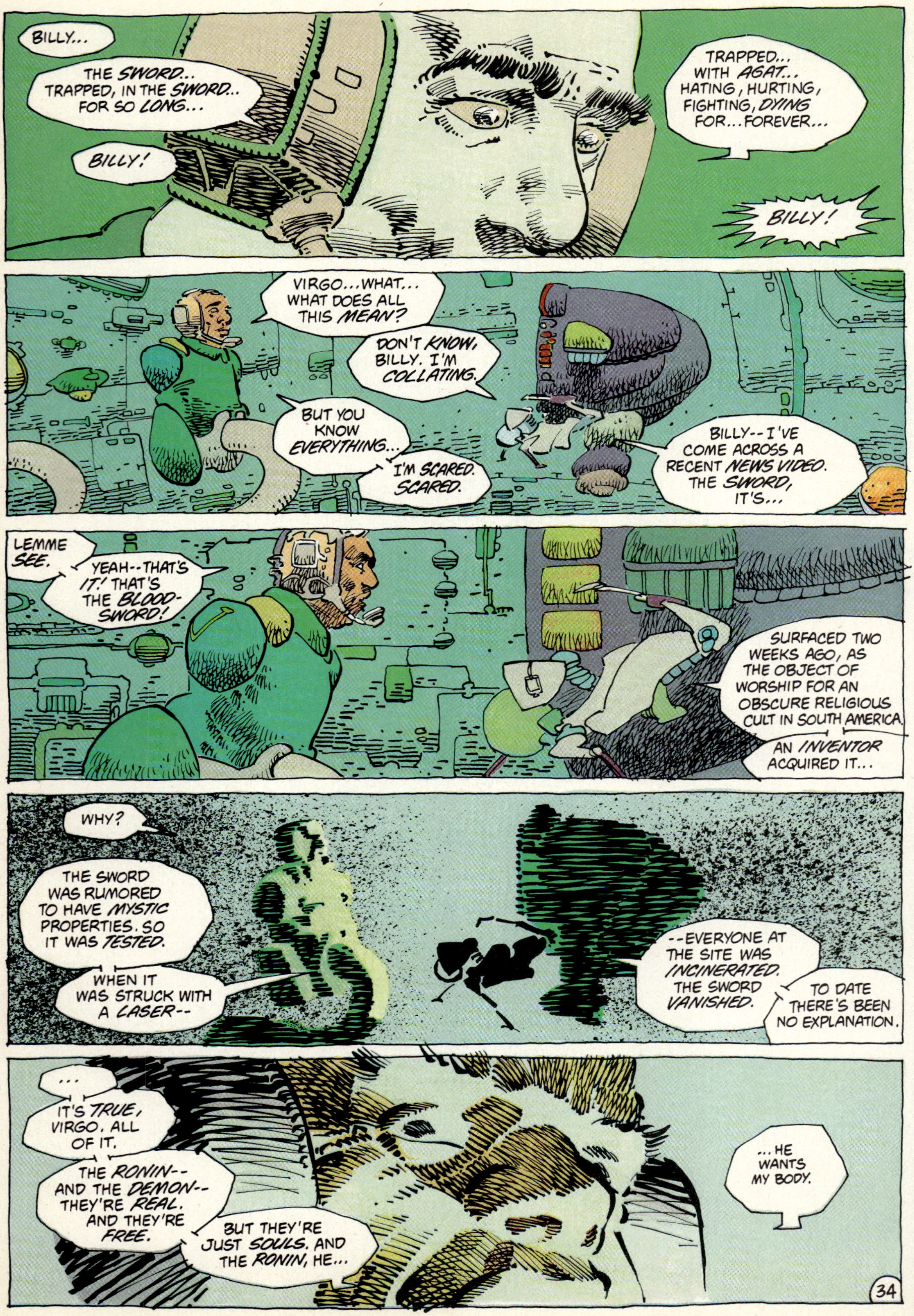
BILLY...
THE SWORD... TRAPPED, IN THE SWORD... FOR SO LONG...
BILLY!
TRAPPED... WITH AGAT... HATING, HURTING, FIGHTING, DYING FOR... FOREVER...
BILLY!
VIRGO... WHAT... WHAT DOES ALL THIS MEAN?
DON'T KNOW, BILLY. I'M COLLATING.
BUT YOU KNOW EVERYTHING...
I'M SCARED. SCARED.
BILLY--I'VE COME ACROSS A RECENT NEWS VIDEO. THE SWORD, IT'S...
LEMME SEE.
YEAH--THAT'S IT! THAT'S THE BLOOD-SWORD!
SURFACED TWO WEEKS AGO, AS THE OBJECT OF WORSHIP FOR AN OBSCURE RELIGIOUS CULT IN SOUTH AMERICA.
AN INVENTOR ACQUIRED IT...
WHY?
THE SWORD WAS RUMORED TO HAVE MYSTIC PROPERTIES. SO IT WAS TESTED.
WHEN IT WAS STRUCK WITH A LASER--
--EVERYONE AT THE SITE WAS INCINERATED. THE SWORD VANISHED.
TO DATE THERE'S BEEN NO EXPLANATION.
...
IT'S TRUE, VIRGO. ALL OF IT.
THE RONIN-- AND THE DEMON-- THEY'RE REAL. AND THEY'RE FREE.
BUT THEY'RE JUST SOULS. AND THE RONIN, HE...
...HE WANTS MY BODY.

BUT WHY ME?

IS IT 'CAUSE OF THE THINGS I CAN DO WITH MY *MIND?* DOES THAT MAKE ME MORE *RECEPTIVE?*

AND... IF THE *RONIN* FOUND ME... WOULDN'T *AGAT* FIND SOMEBODY ELSE?

AND WOULDN'T HE GO AFTER THE GUY WHO *KILLED* HIM?

THOSE BREAK-IN ATTEMPTS I HEARD ABOUT...

AROOGA INTRUDER AROOGA

OH MY GOD. OH MY GOD.

DON'T PANIC, BILLY. I'LL CHECK ON THE GUARDS.

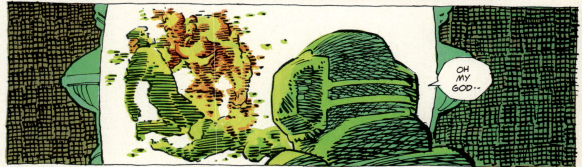

OH MY GOD--

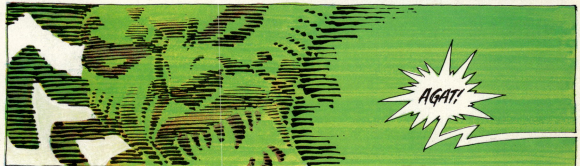

AGAT!

BILLY! YOUR *FACE*--

--IT'S *SCARRING,* JUST LIKE...

...LIKE THE *RONIN*...

AGAT'S *COMING* FOR ME. *HE'S GONNA KILL ME.* HE'S GONNA KILL ME.

CALM DOWN, BILLY.

THE *LASER* WILL STOP HIM.

35

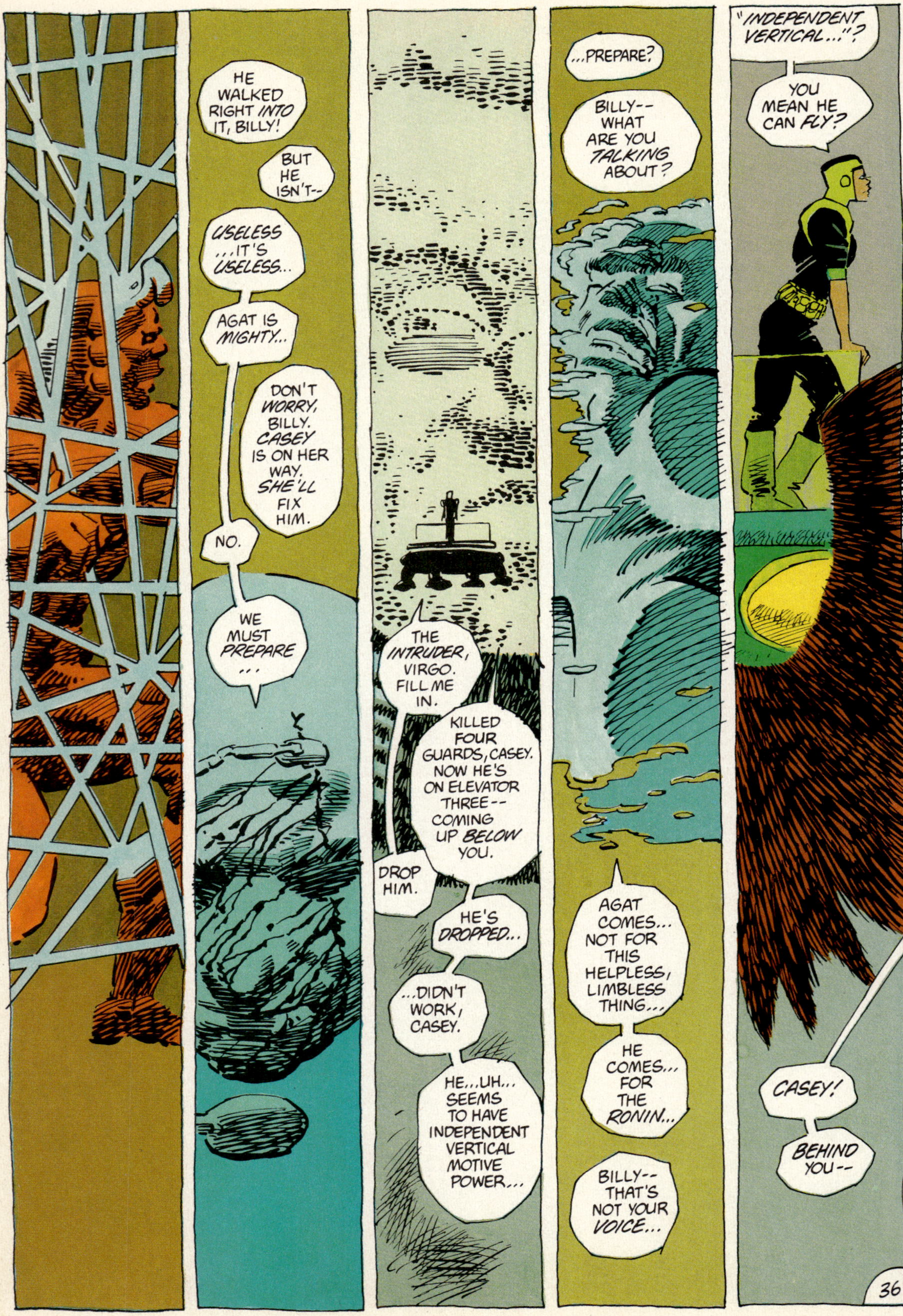
HE WALKED RIGHT INTO IT, BILLY!
BUT HE ISN'T--
USELESS ...IT'S USELESS...
AGAT IS MIGHTY...
DON'T WORRY, BILLY. CASEY IS ON HER WAY. SHE'LL FIX HIM.
NO.
WE MUST PREPARE ...
THE INTRUDER, VIRGO. FILL ME IN.
KILLED FOUR GUARDS, CASEY. NOW HE'S ON ELEVATOR THREE-- COMING UP BELOW YOU.
DROP HIM.
HE'S DROPPED...
...DIDN'T WORK, CASEY.
HE...UH... SEEMS TO HAVE INDEPENDENT VERTICAL MOTIVE POWER...
...PREPARE?
BILLY-- WHAT ARE YOU TALKING ABOUT?
AGAT COMES... NOT FOR THIS HELPLESS, LIMBLESS THING...
HE COMES... FOR THE RONIN...
BILLY-- THAT'S NOT YOUR VOICE...
"INDEPENDENT VERTICAL..."?
YOU MEAN HE CAN FLY?
CASEY!
BEHIND YOU--
36

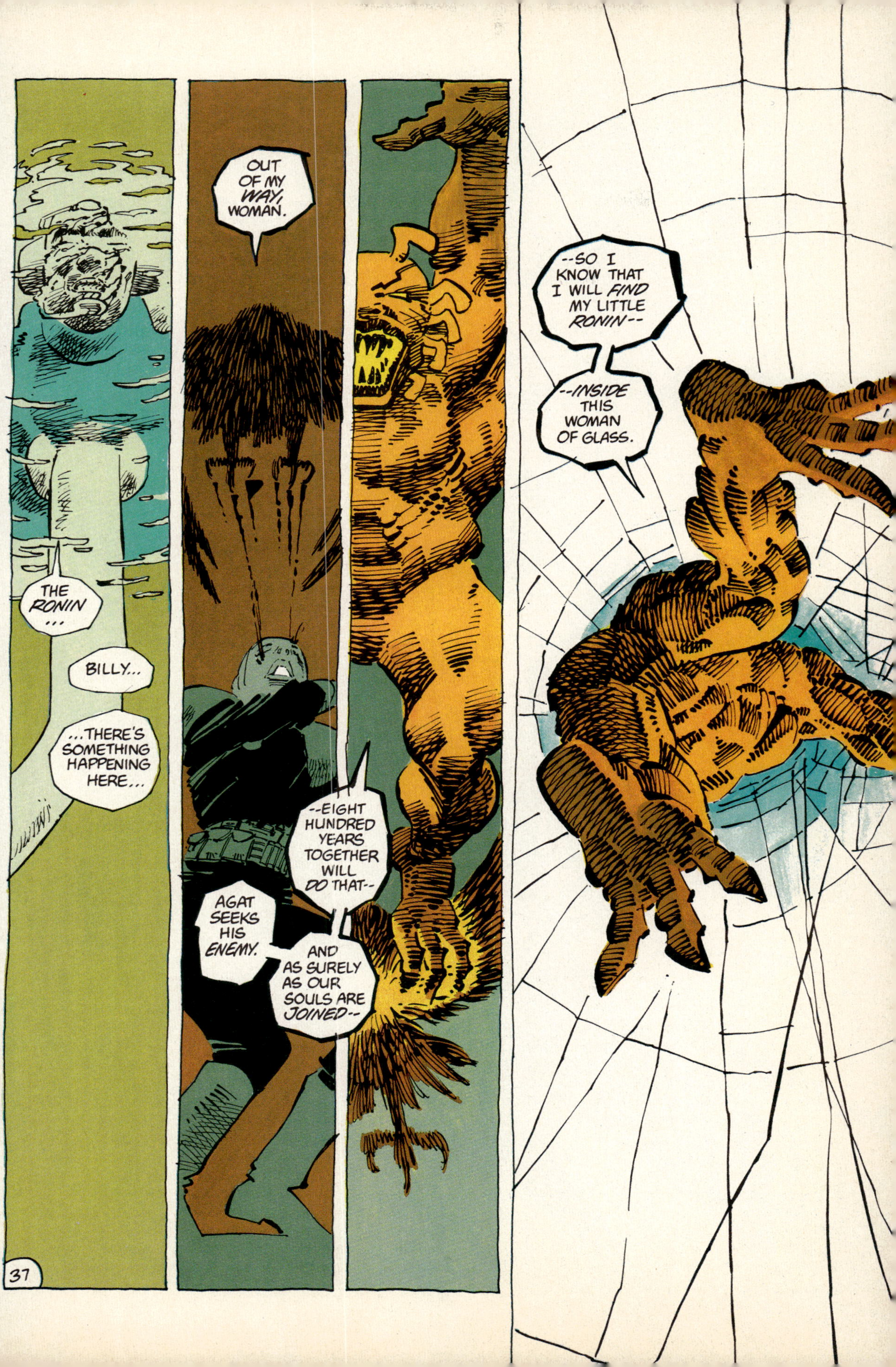
THE RONIN...
BILLY...
...THERE'S SOMETHING HAPPENING HERE...
OUT OF MY WAY, WOMAN.
--EIGHT HUNDRED YEARS TOGETHER WILL DO THAT--
AGAT SEEKS HIS ENEMY.
AND AS SURELY AS OUR SOULS ARE JOINED--
--SO I KNOW THAT I WILL FIND MY LITTLE RONIN--
--INSIDE THIS WOMAN OF GLASS.

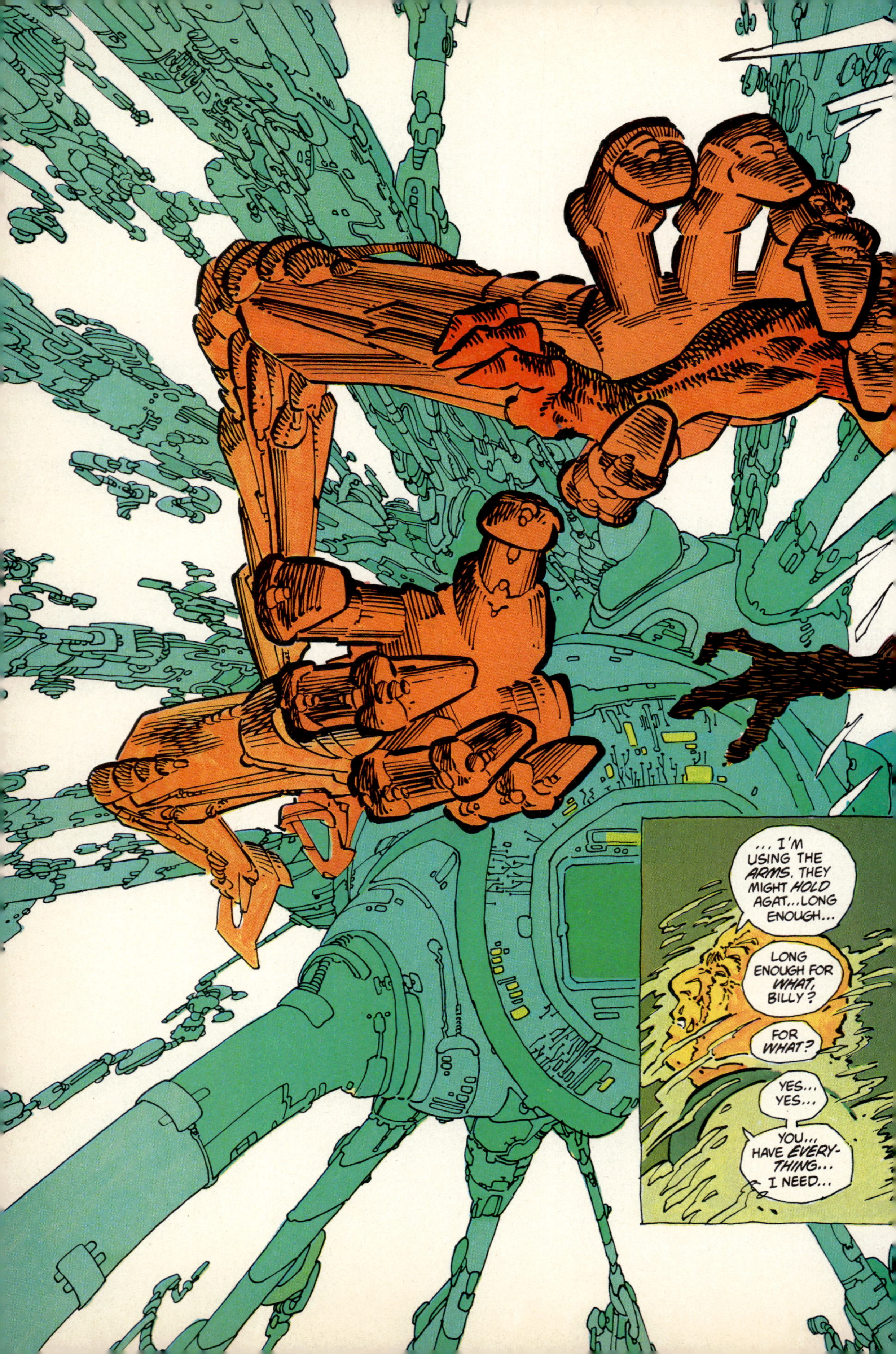

... I'M USING THE ARMS. THEY MIGHT HOLD AGAT...LONG ENOUGH...
LONG ENOUGH FOR WHAT, BILLY?
FOR WHAT?
YES... YES...
YOU... HAVE EVERY-THING... I NEED...

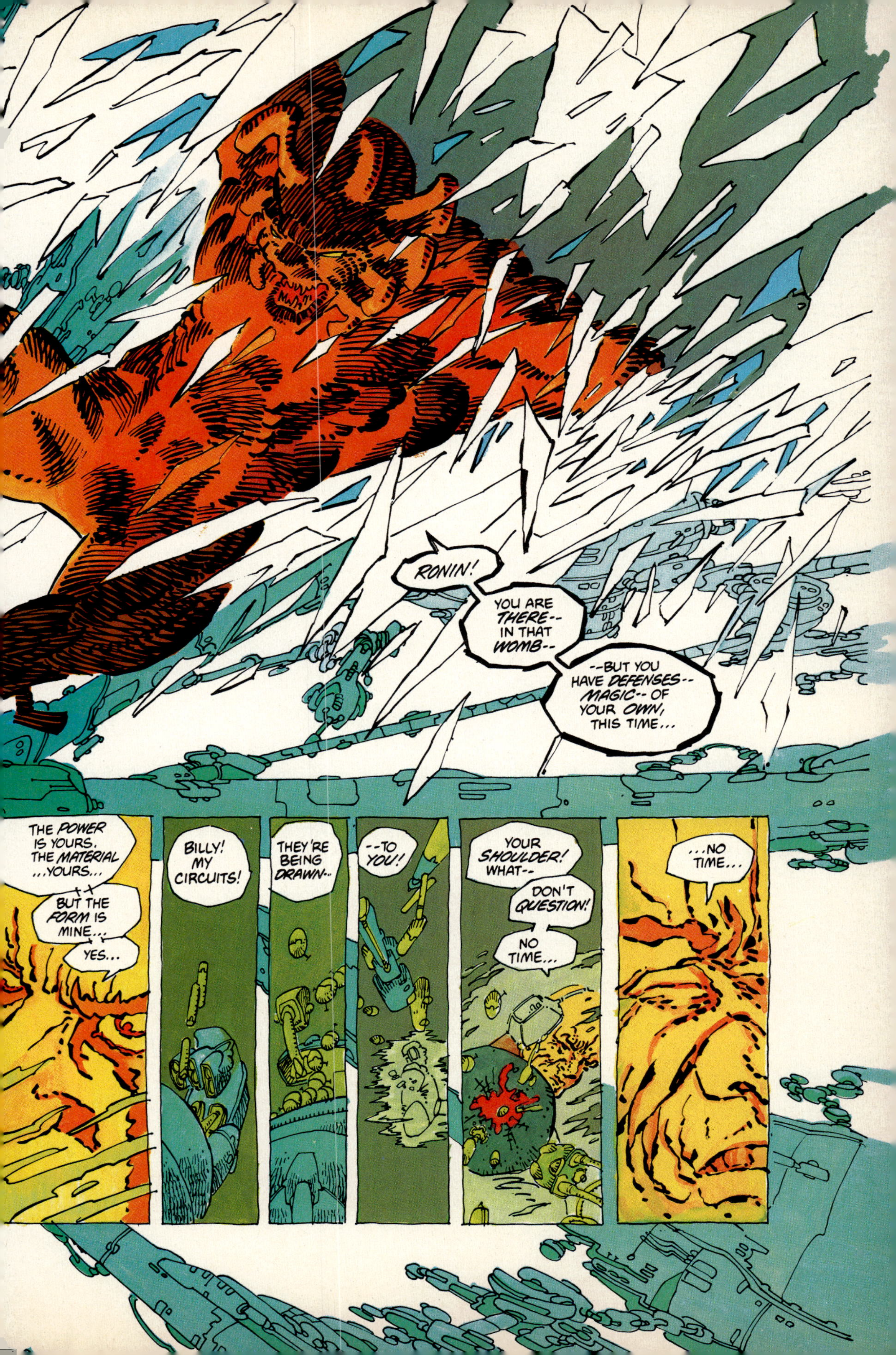
RONIN!
YOU ARE THERE-- IN THAT WOMB--
--BUT YOU HAVE DEFENSES-- MAGIC-- OF YOUR OWN, THIS TIME...
THE POWER IS YOURS. THE MATERIAL ...YOURS...
BUT THE FORM IS MINE...
YES...
BILLY! MY CIRCUITS!
THEY'RE BEING DRAWN--
--TO YOU!
YOUR SHOULDER! WHAT--
DON'T QUESTION!
NO TIME...
...NO TIME...

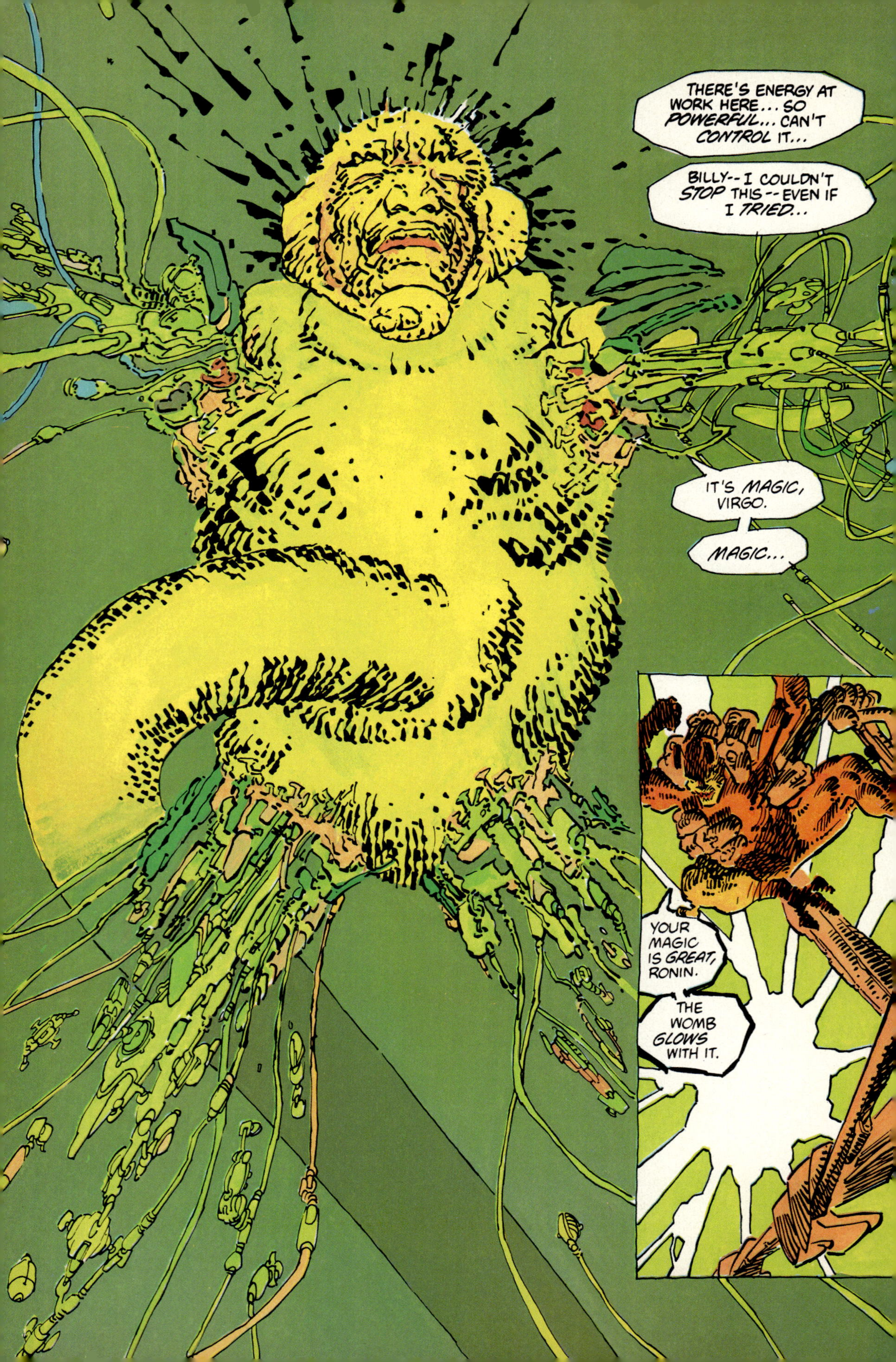
THERE'S ENERGY AT WORK HERE... SO POWERFUL... CAN'T CONTROL IT...
BILLY-- I COULDN'T STOP THIS-- EVEN IF I TRIED...
IT'S MAGIC, VIRGO.
MAGIC...
YOUR MAGIC IS GREAT, RONIN.
THE WOMB GLOWS WITH IT.

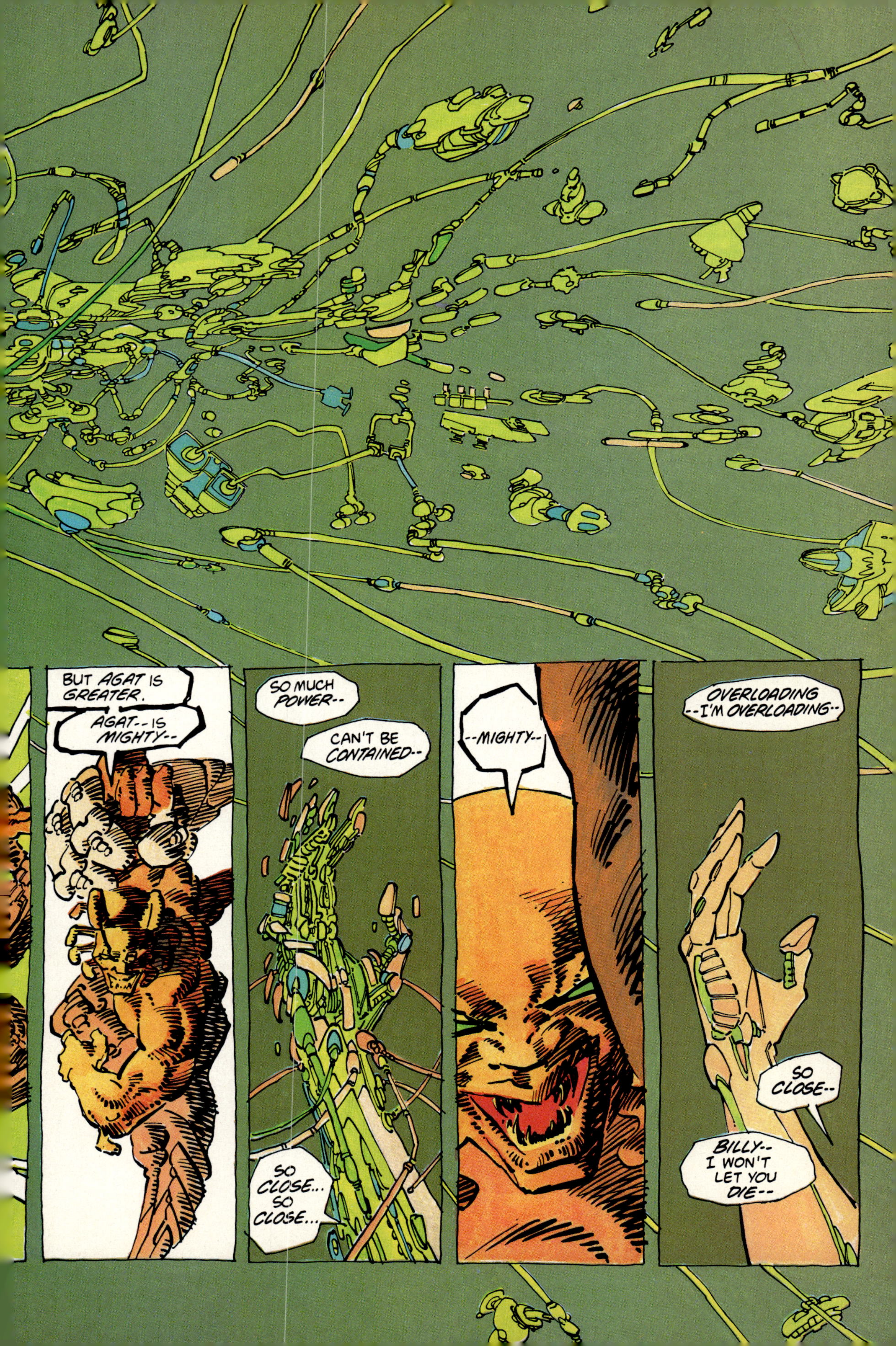
BUT AGAT IS GREATER.
AGAT--IS MIGHTY--
SO MUCH POWER--
CAN'T BE CONTAINED--
SO CLOSE... SO CLOSE...
--MIGHTY--
OVERLOADING --I'M OVERLOADING--
SO CLOSE--
BILLY-- I WON'T LET YOU DIE--

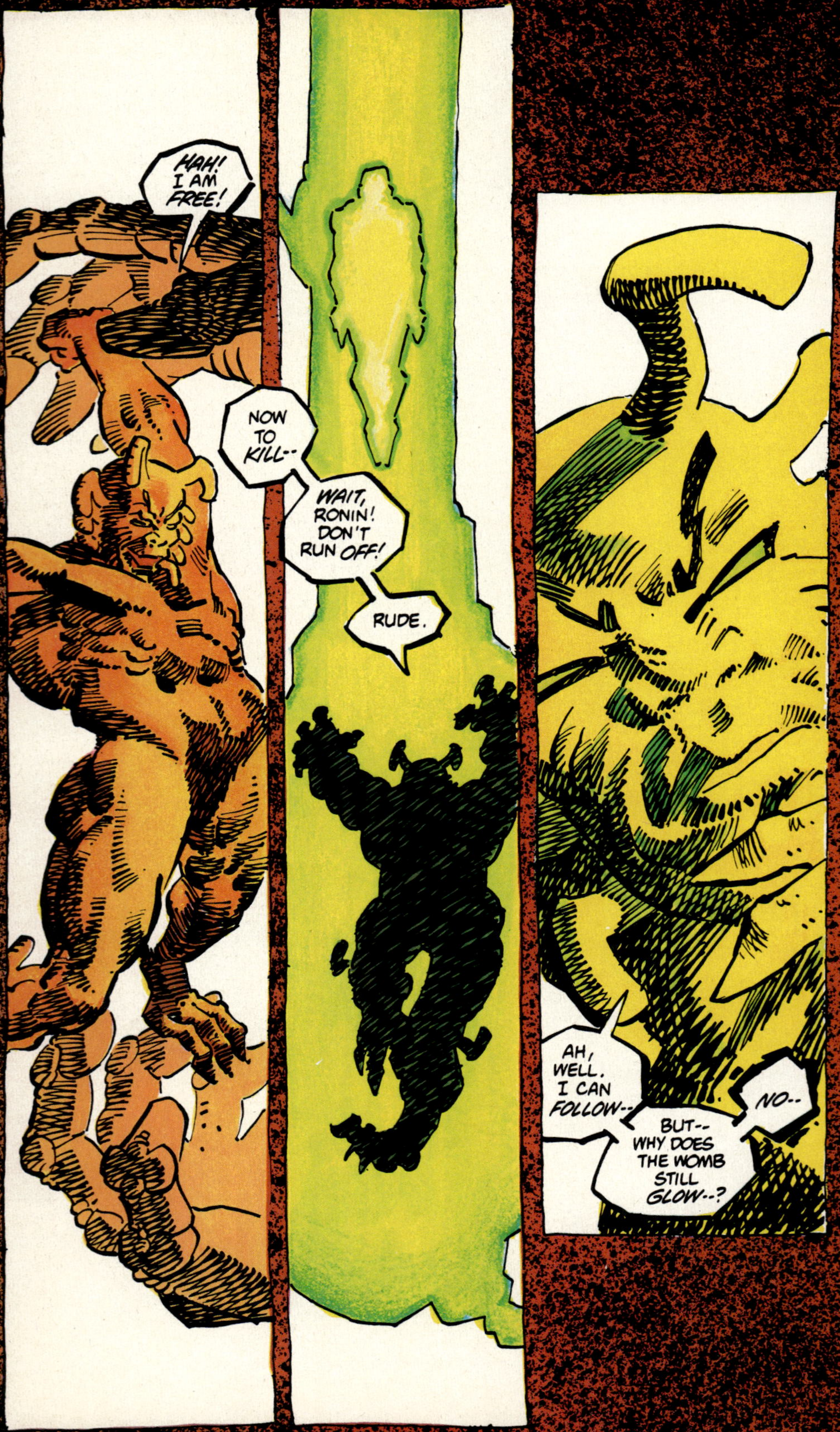
HAH! I AM FREE!
NOW TO KILL--
WAIT, RONIN! DON'T RUN OFF!
RUDE.
AH, WELL. I CAN FOLLOW--
NO--
BUT-- WHY DOES THE WOMB STILL GLOW--?

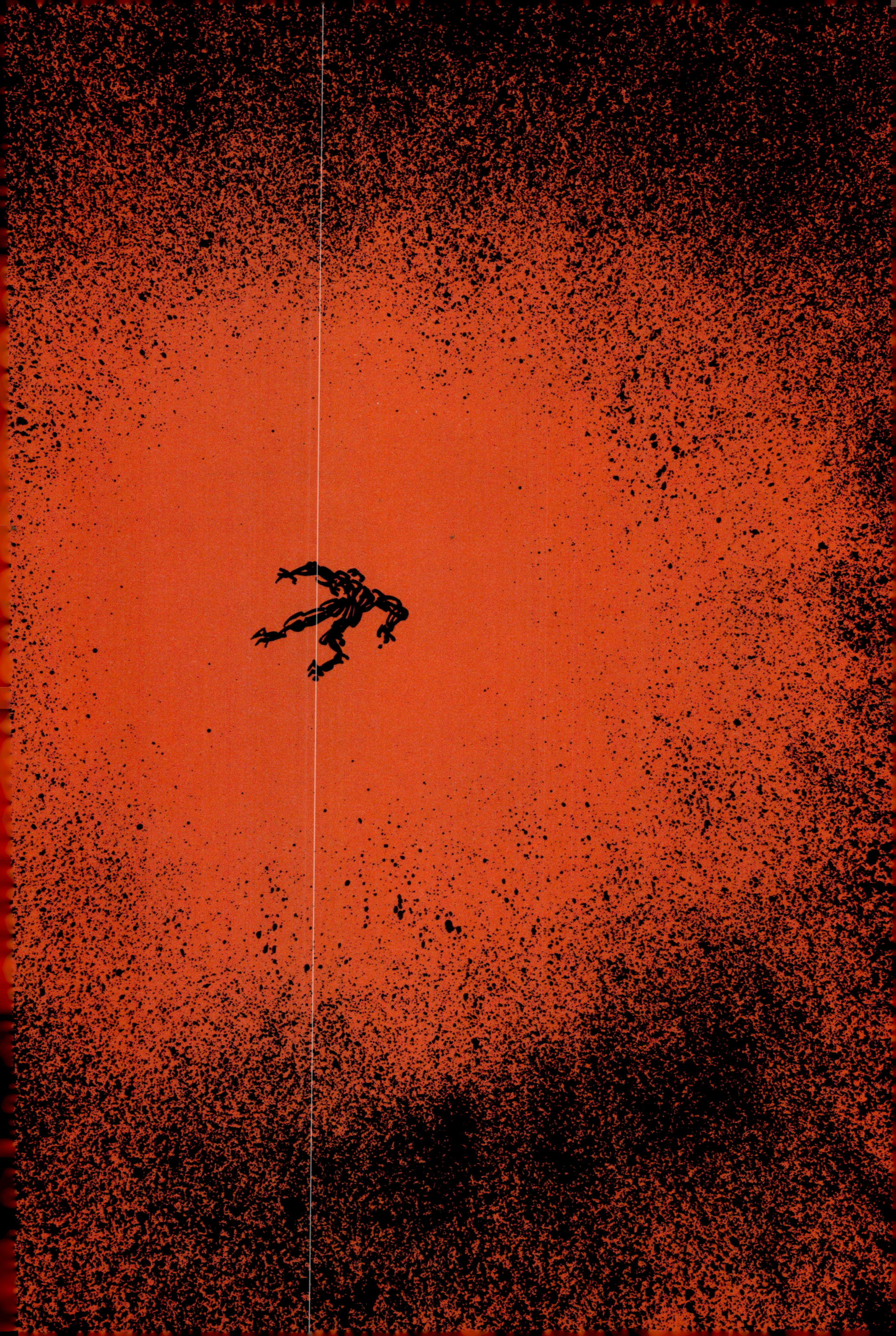

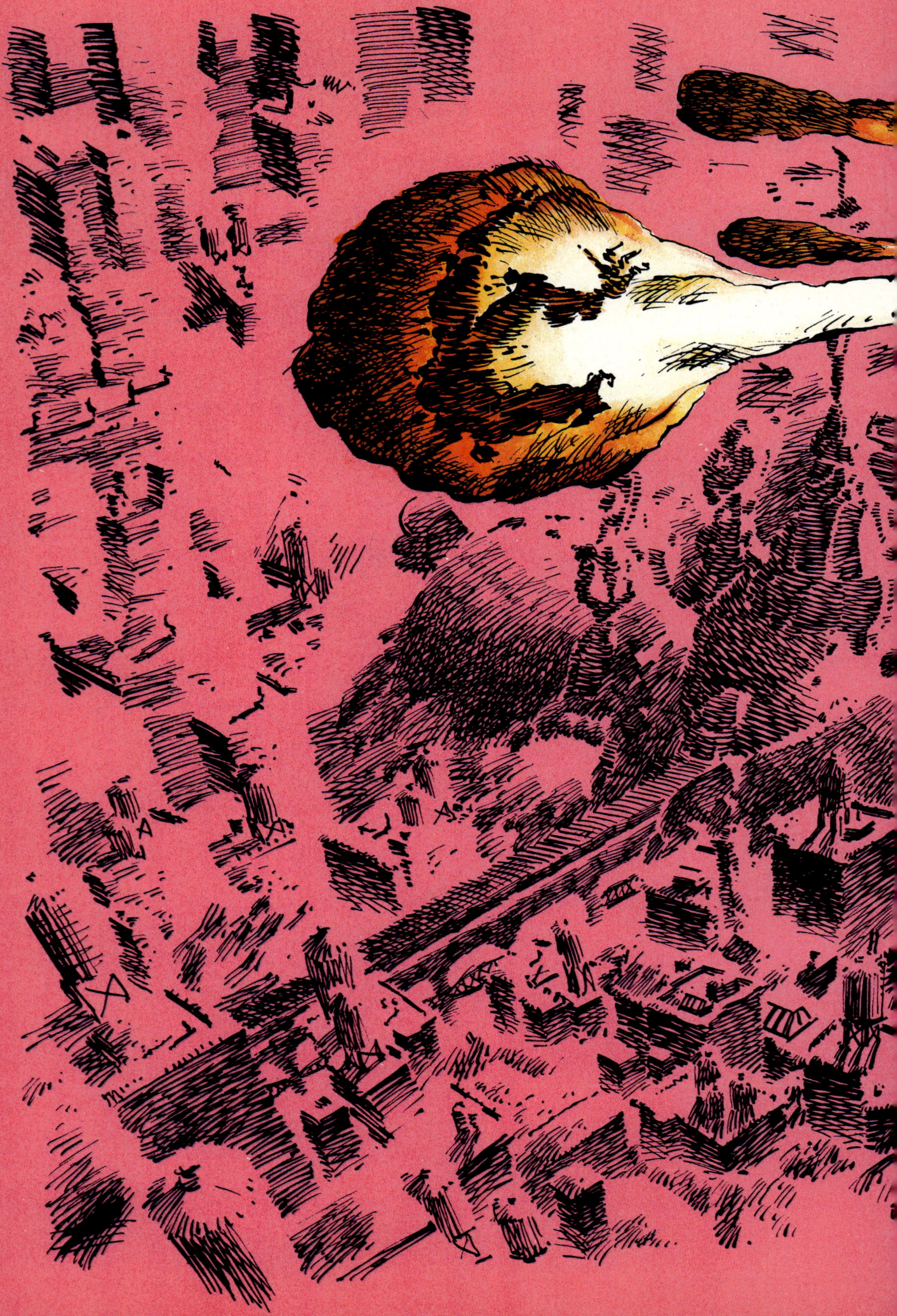

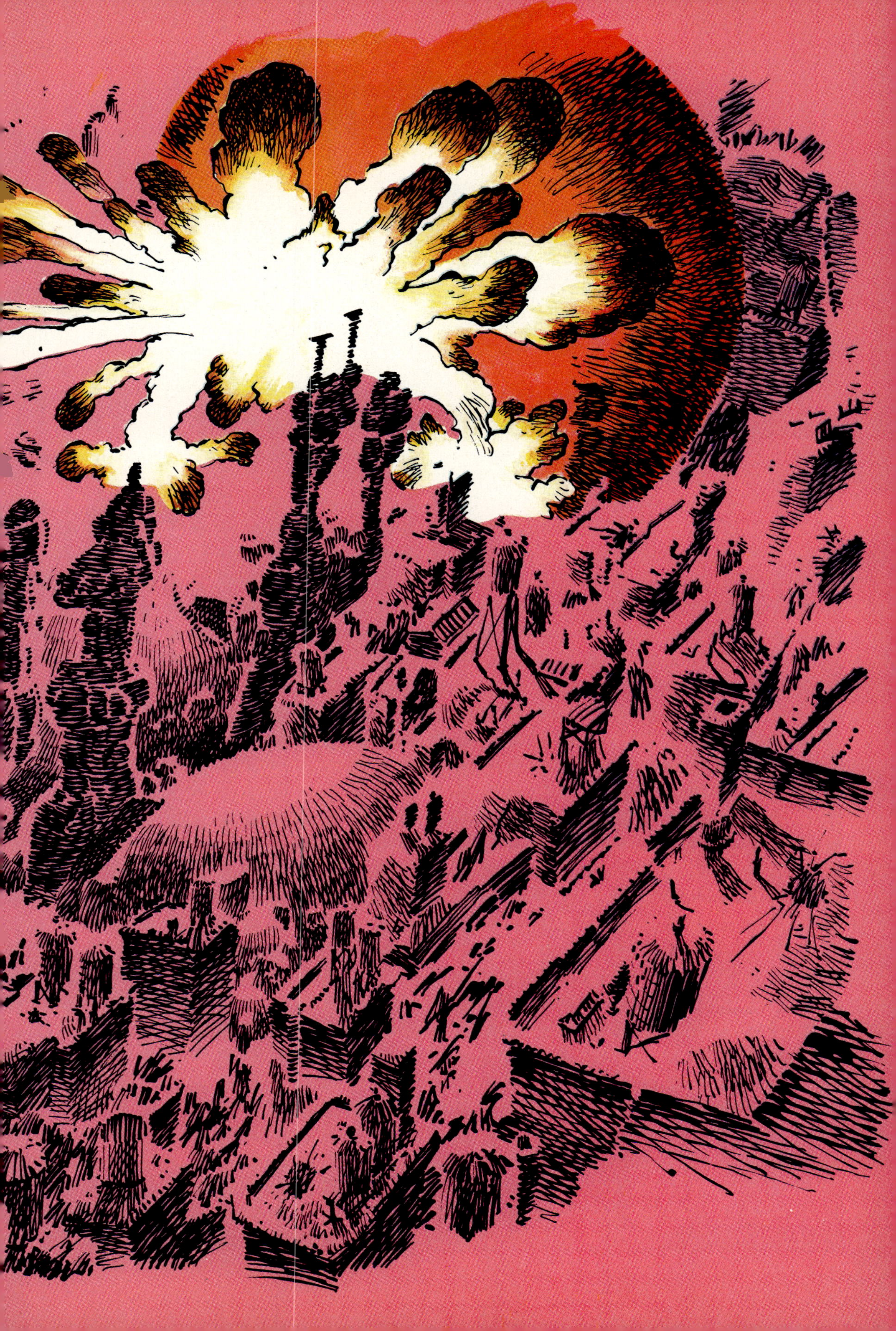

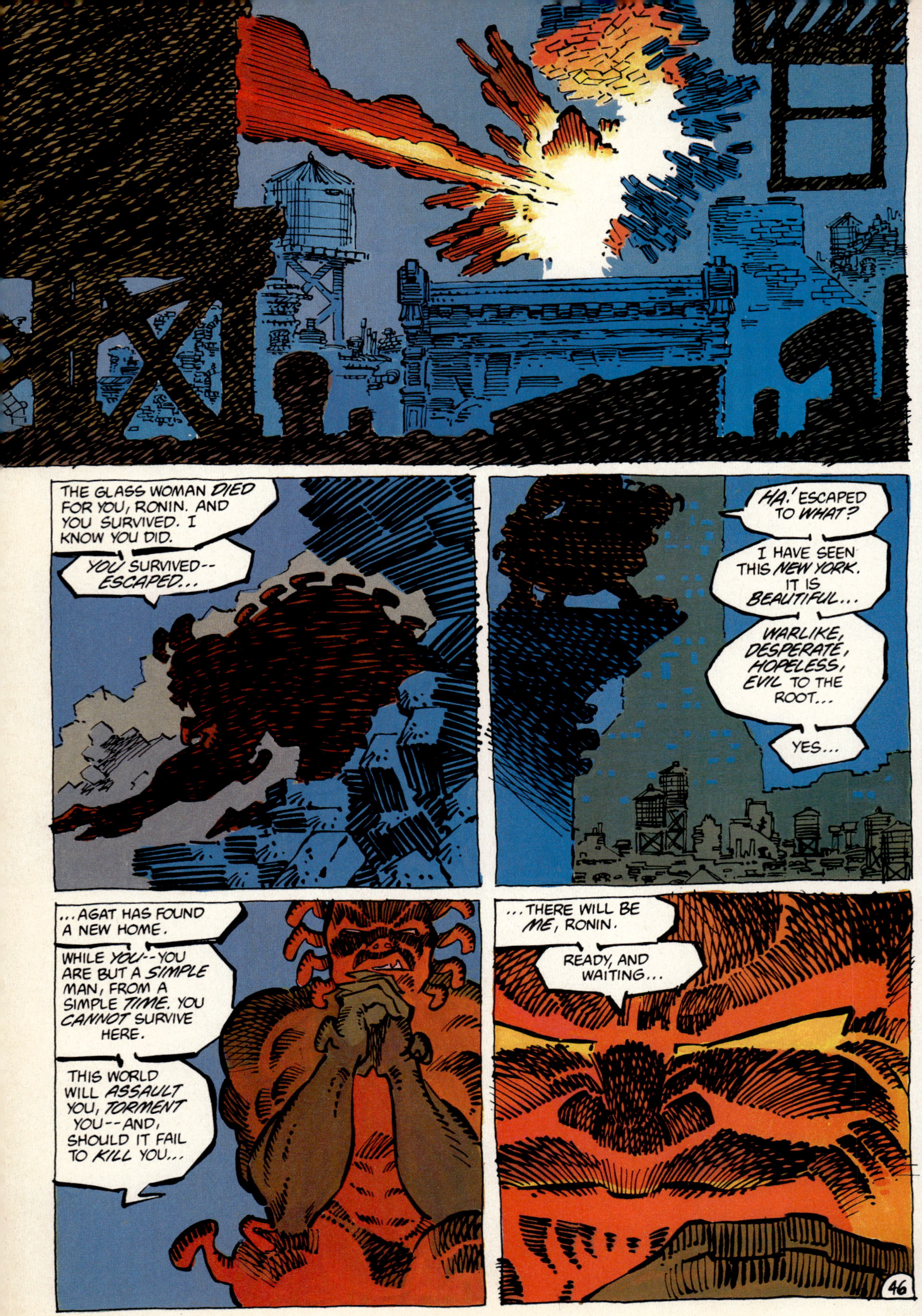
THE GLASS WOMAN DIED FOR YOU, RONIN. AND YOU SURVIVED. I KNOW YOU DID.
YOU SURVIVED-- ESCAPED...
HA! ESCAPED TO WHAT?
I HAVE SEEN THIS NEW YORK. IT IS BEAUTIFUL...
WARLIKE, DESPERATE, HOPELESS, EVIL TO THE ROOT...
YES...
...AGAT HAS FOUND A NEW HOME.
WHILE YOU--YOU ARE BUT A SIMPLE MAN, FROM A SIMPLE TIME. YOU CANNOT SURVIVE HERE.
THIS WORLD WILL ASSAULT YOU, TORMENT YOU--AND, SHOULD IT FAIL TO KILL YOU...
...THERE WILL BE ME, RONIN.
READY, AND WAITING...
46

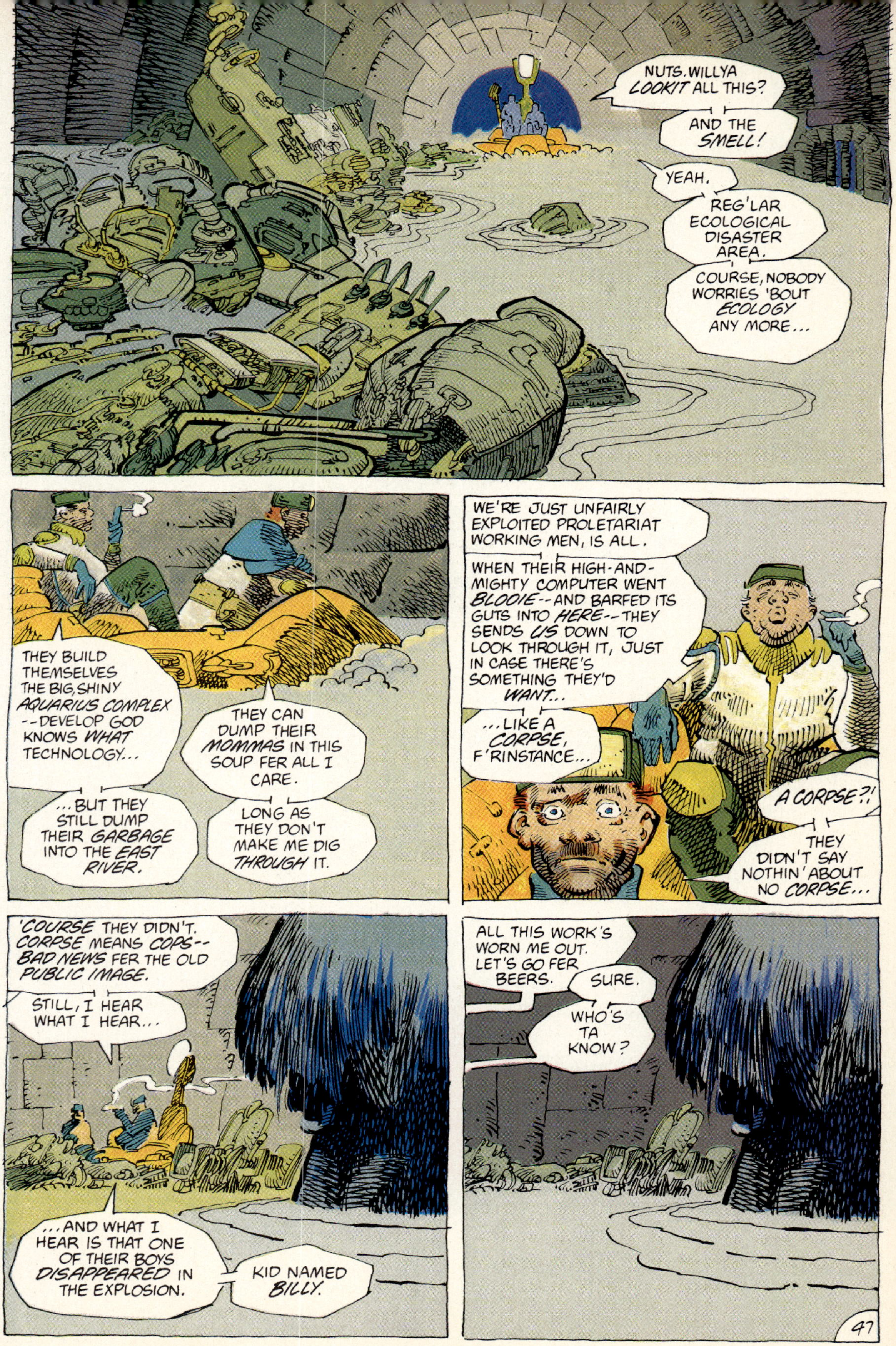

NUTS. WILLYA LOOKIT ALL THIS?
AND THE SMELL!
YEAH.
REG'LAR ECOLOGICAL DISASTER AREA.
COURSE, NOBODY WORRIES 'BOUT ECOLOGY ANY MORE...
THEY BUILD THEMSELVES THE BIG, SHINY AQUARIUS COMPLEX --DEVELOP GOD KNOWS WHAT TECHNOLOGY...
...BUT THEY STILL DUMP THEIR GARBAGE INTO THE EAST RIVER.
THEY CAN DUMP THEIR MOMMAS IN THIS SOUP FER ALL I CARE.
LONG AS THEY DON'T MAKE ME DIG THROUGH IT.
WE'RE JUST UNFAIRLY EXPLOITED PROLETARIAT WORKING MEN, IS ALL.
WHEN THEIR HIGH-AND-MIGHTY COMPUTER WENT BLOOIE--AND BARFED ITS GUTS INTO HERE--THEY SENDS US DOWN TO LOOK THROUGH IT, JUST IN CASE THERE'S SOMETHING THEY'D WANT...
...LIKE A CORPSE, F'RINSTANCE...
A CORPSE?!
THEY DIDN'T SAY NOTHIN' ABOUT NO CORPSE...
'COURSE THEY DIDN'T. CORPSE MEANS COPS-- BAD NEWS FER THE OLD PUBLIC IMAGE.
STILL, I HEAR WHAT I HEAR...
...AND WHAT I HEAR IS THAT ONE OF THEIR BOYS DISAPPEARED IN THE EXPLOSION.
KID NAMED BILLY.
ALL THIS WORK'S WORN ME OUT. LET'S GO FER BEERS.
SURE.
WHO'S TA KNOW?

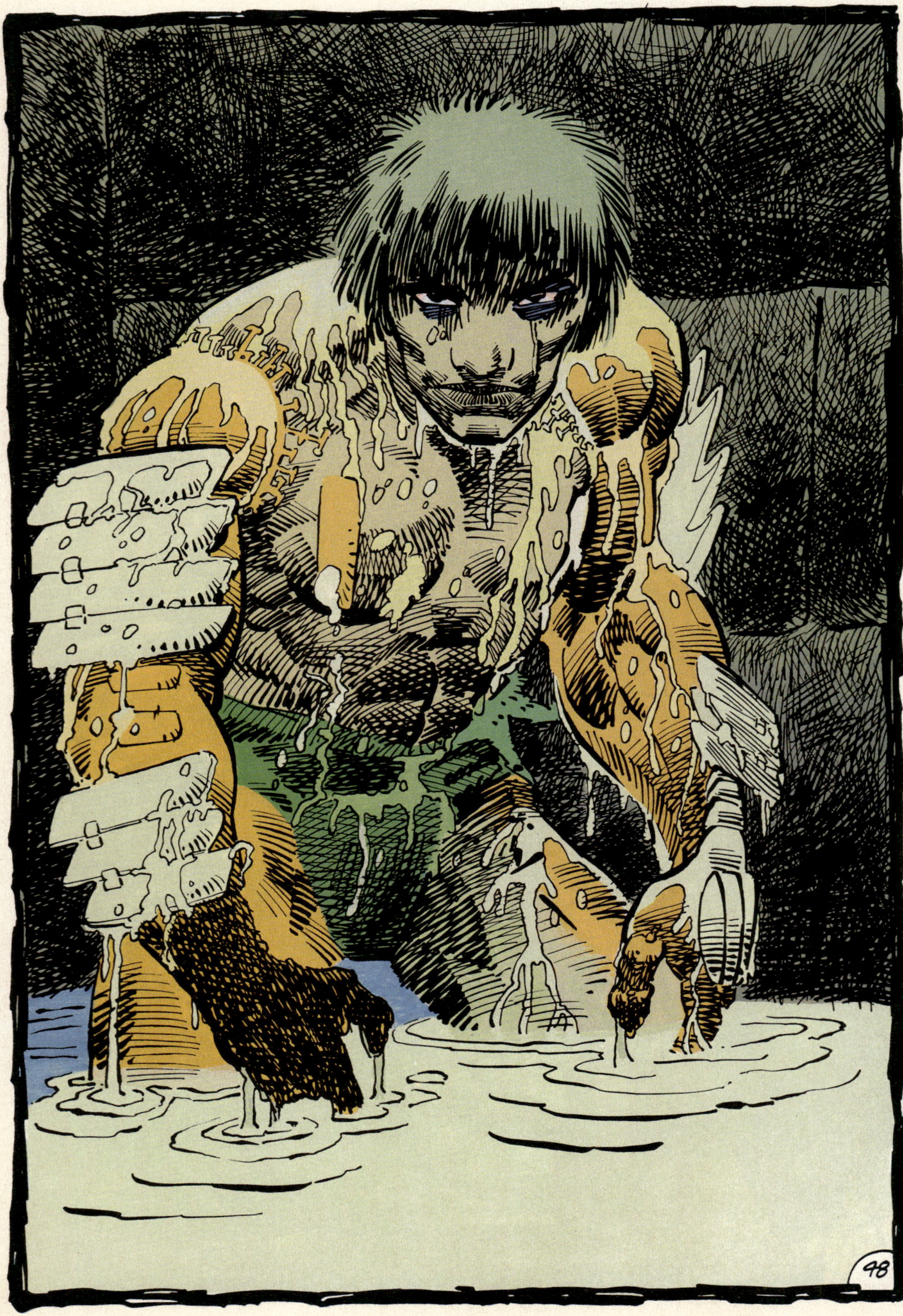

CHAPTER TWO

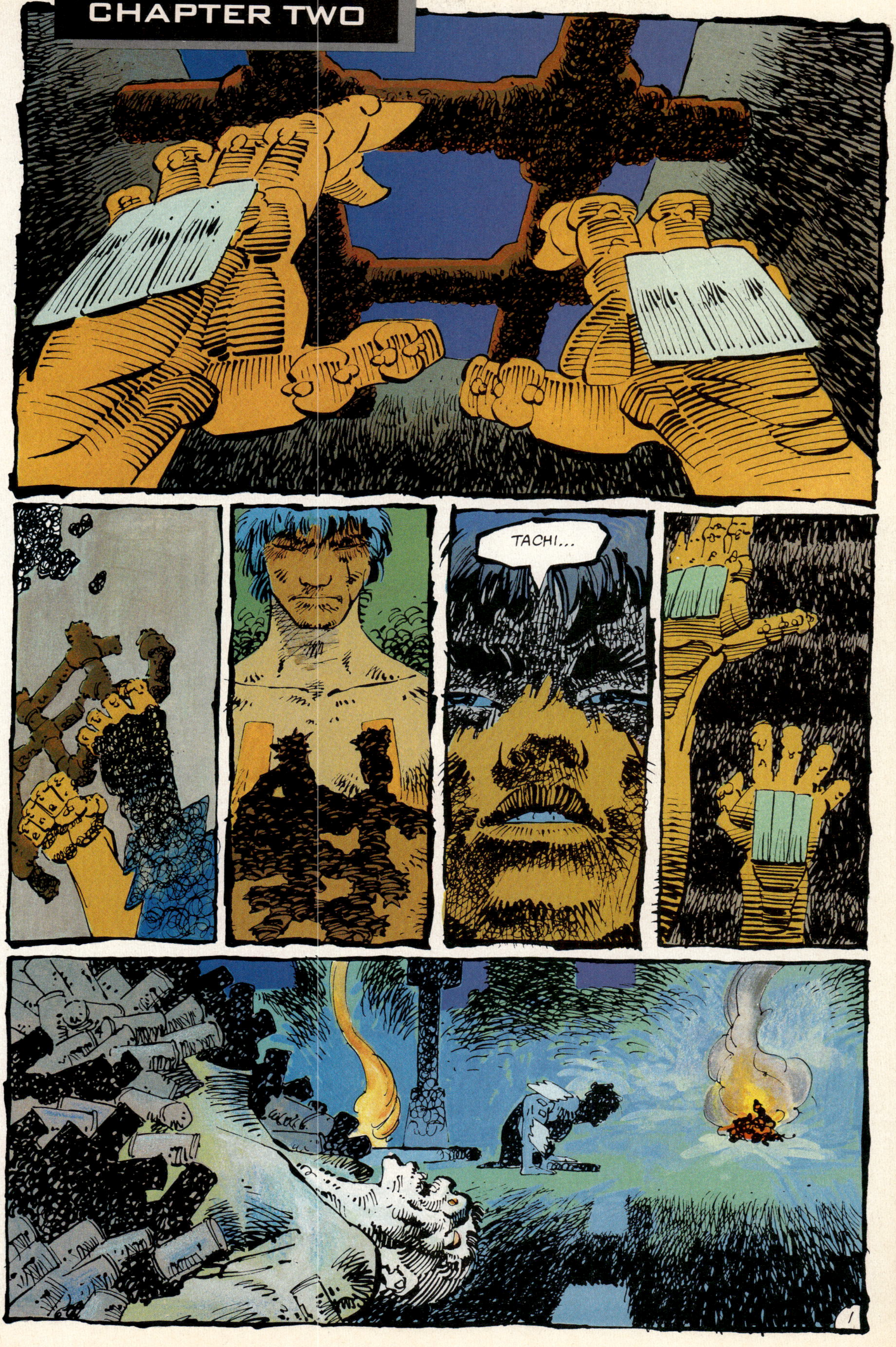
TACHI...

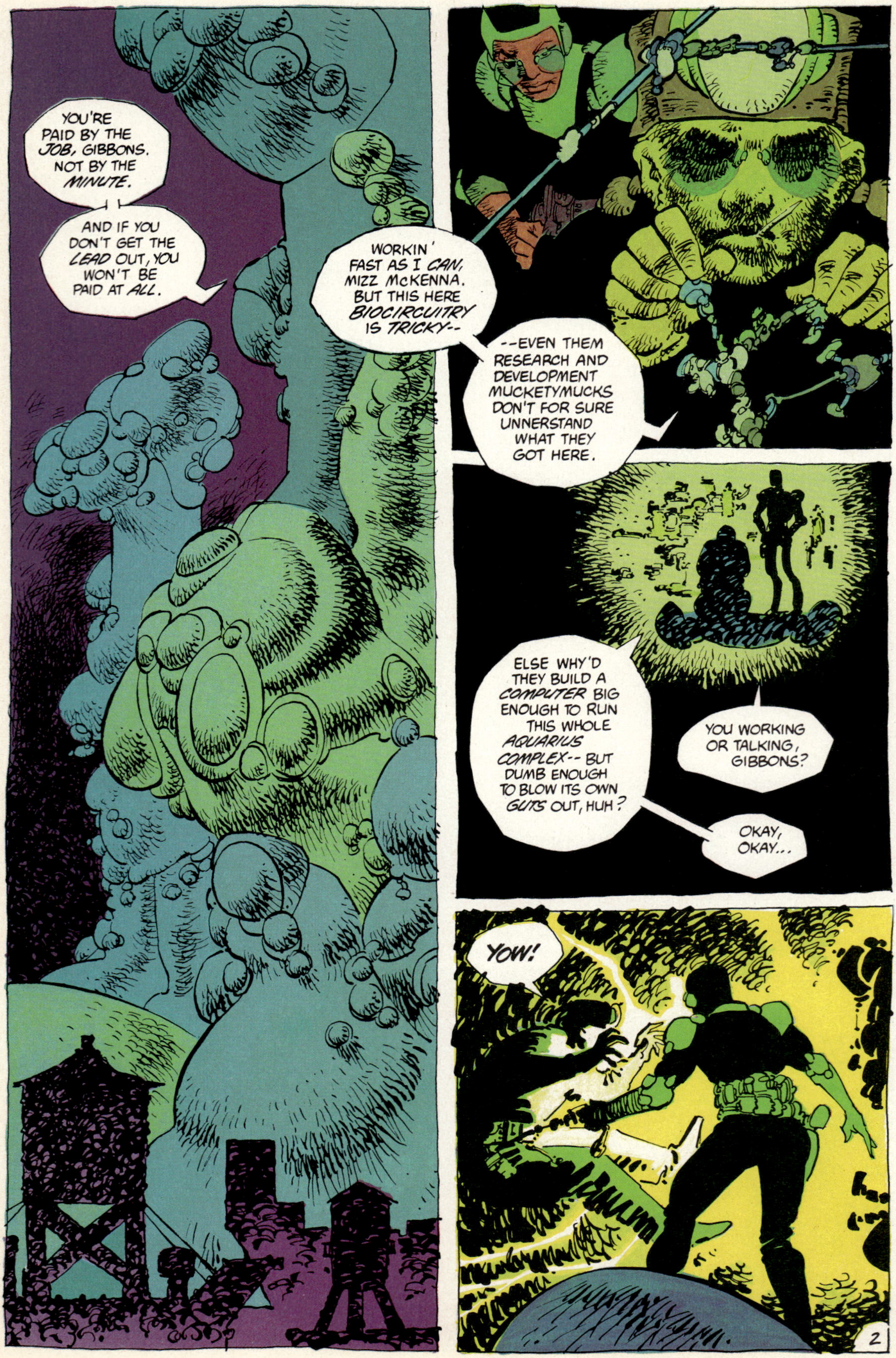
YOU'RE PAID BY THE JOB, GIBBONS. NOT BY THE MINUTE.
AND IF YOU DON'T GET THE LEAD OUT, YOU WON'T BE PAID AT ALL.
WORKIN' FAST AS I CAN, MIZZ McKENNA. BUT THIS HERE BIOCIRCUITRY IS TRICKY--
--EVEN THEM RESEARCH AND DEVELOPMENT MUCKETYMUCKS DON'T FOR SURE UNNERSTAND WHAT THEY GOT HERE.
ELSE WHY'D THEY BUILD A COMPUTER BIG ENOUGH TO RUN THIS WHOLE AQUARIUS COMPLEX-- BUT DUMB ENOUGH TO BLOW ITS OWN GUTS OUT, HUH?
YOU WORKING OR TALKING, GIBBONS?
OKAY, OKAY...
YOW!

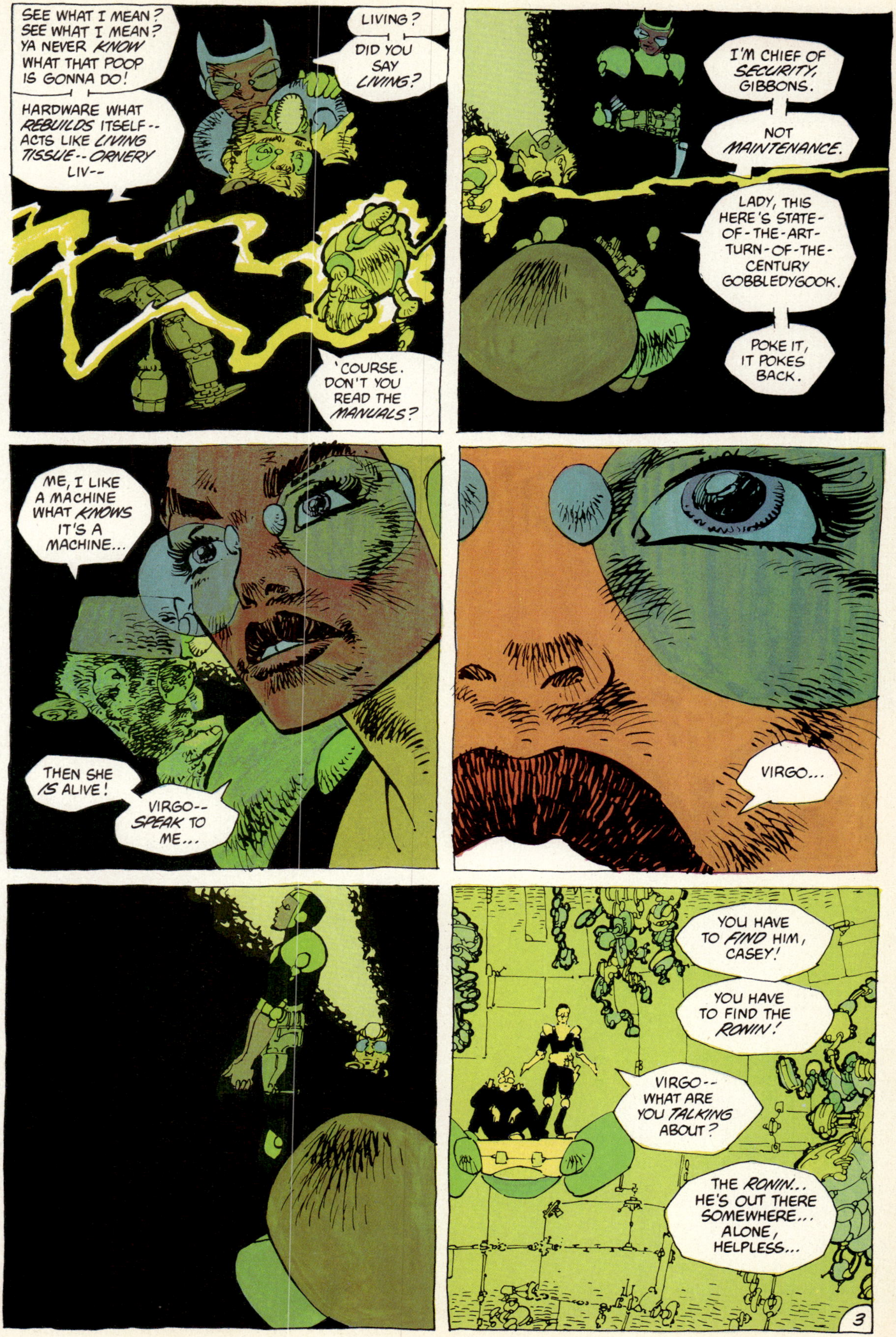
SEE WHAT I MEAN? SEE WHAT I MEAN? YA NEVER KNOW WHAT THAT POOP IS GONNA DO!
HARDWARE WHAT REBUILDS ITSELF -- ACTS LIKE LIVING TISSUE -- ORNERY LIV--
LIVING?
DID YOU SAY LIVING?
'COURSE. DON'T YOU READ THE MANUALS?
I'M CHIEF OF SECURITY, GIBBONS.
NOT MAINTENANCE.
LADY, THIS HERE'S STATE-OF-THE-ART-TURN-OF-THE-CENTURY GOBBLEDYGOOK.
POKE IT, IT POKES BACK.
ME, I LIKE A MACHINE WHAT KNOWS IT'S A MACHINE...
THEN SHE IS ALIVE!
VIRGO-- SPEAK TO ME...
VIRGO...
YOU HAVE TO FIND HIM, CASEY!
YOU HAVE TO FIND THE RONIN!
VIRGO-- WHAT ARE YOU TALKING ABOUT?
THE RONIN... HE'S OUT THERE SOMEWHERE... ALONE, HELPLESS...

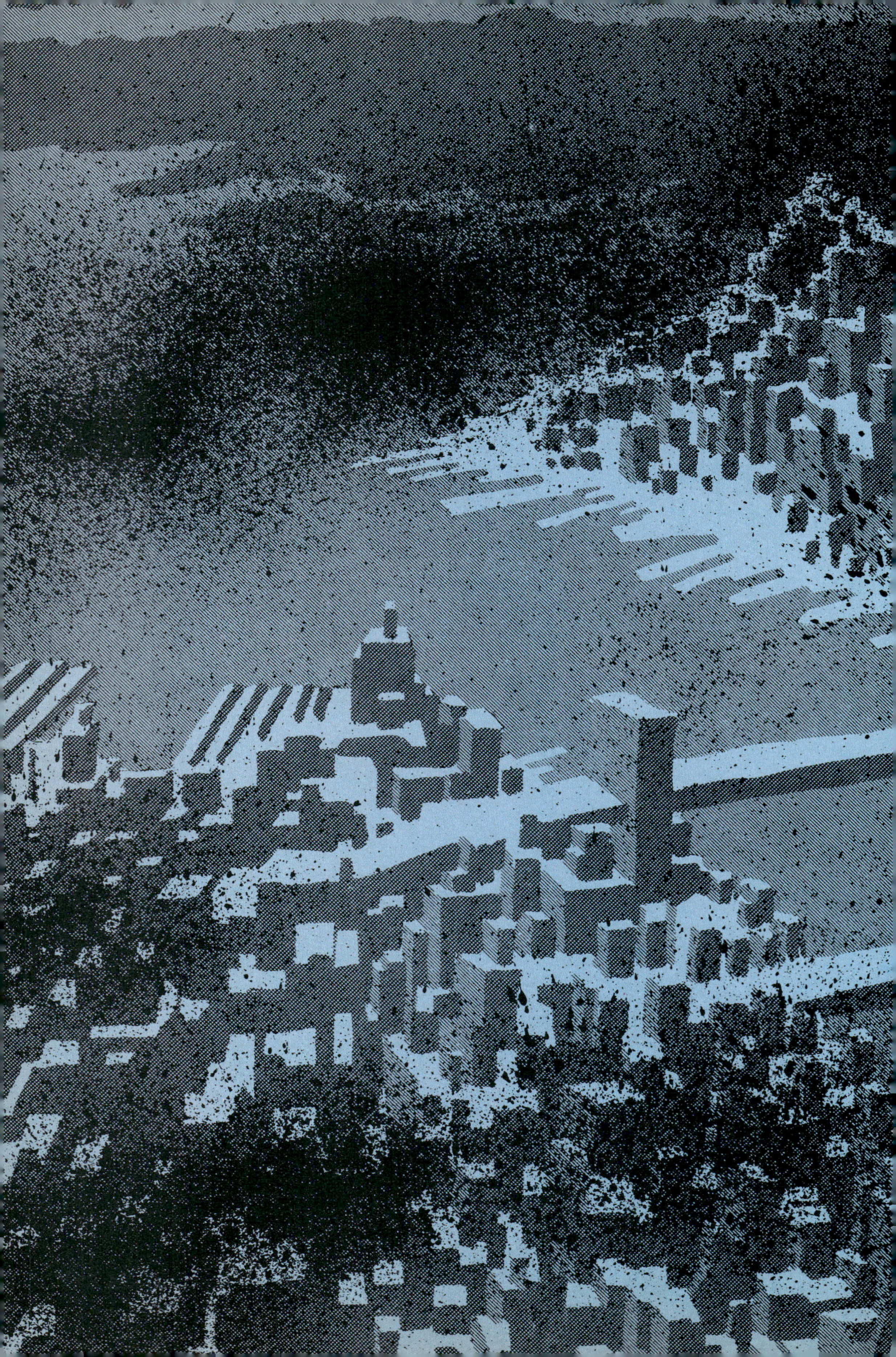

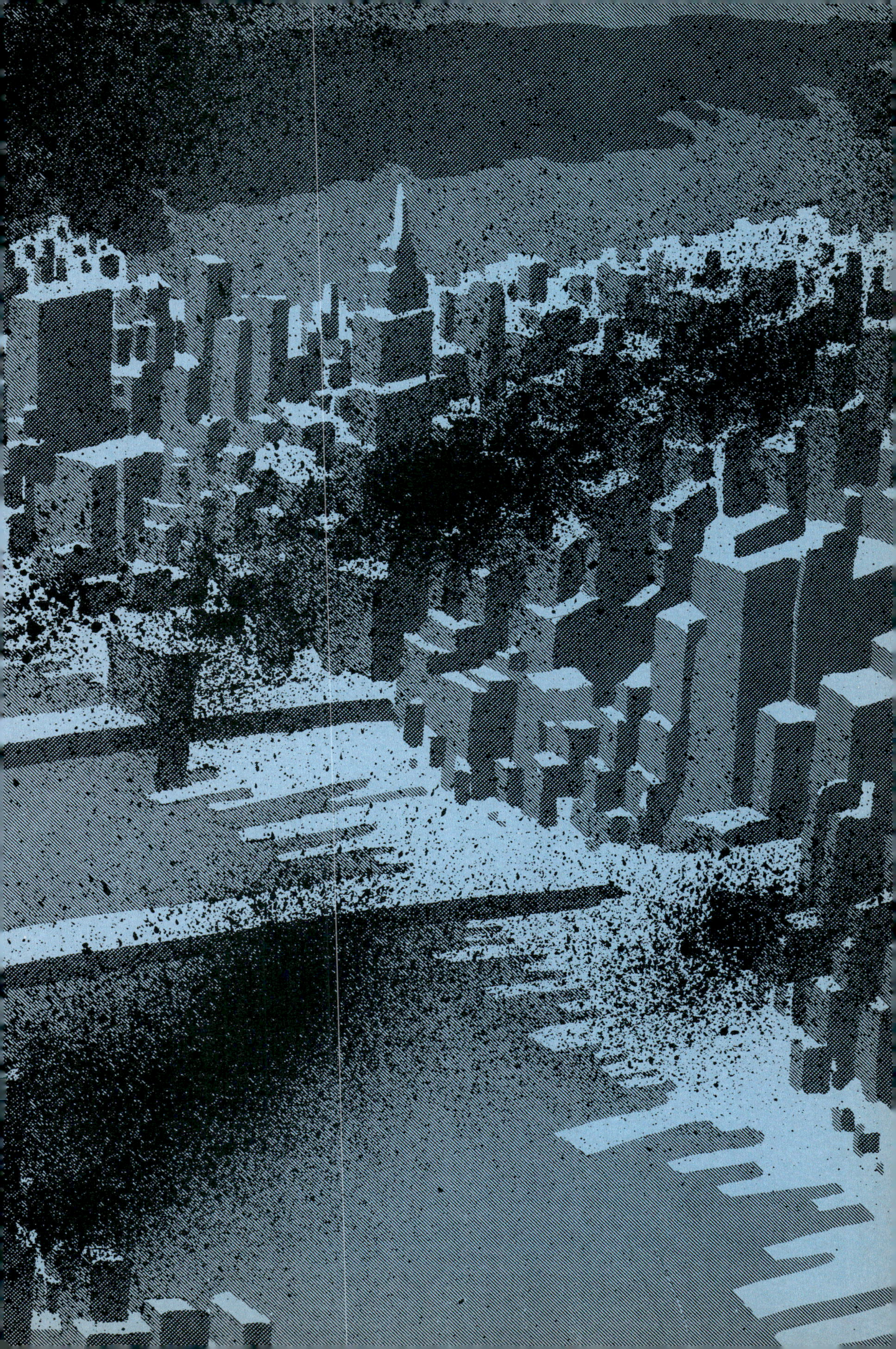

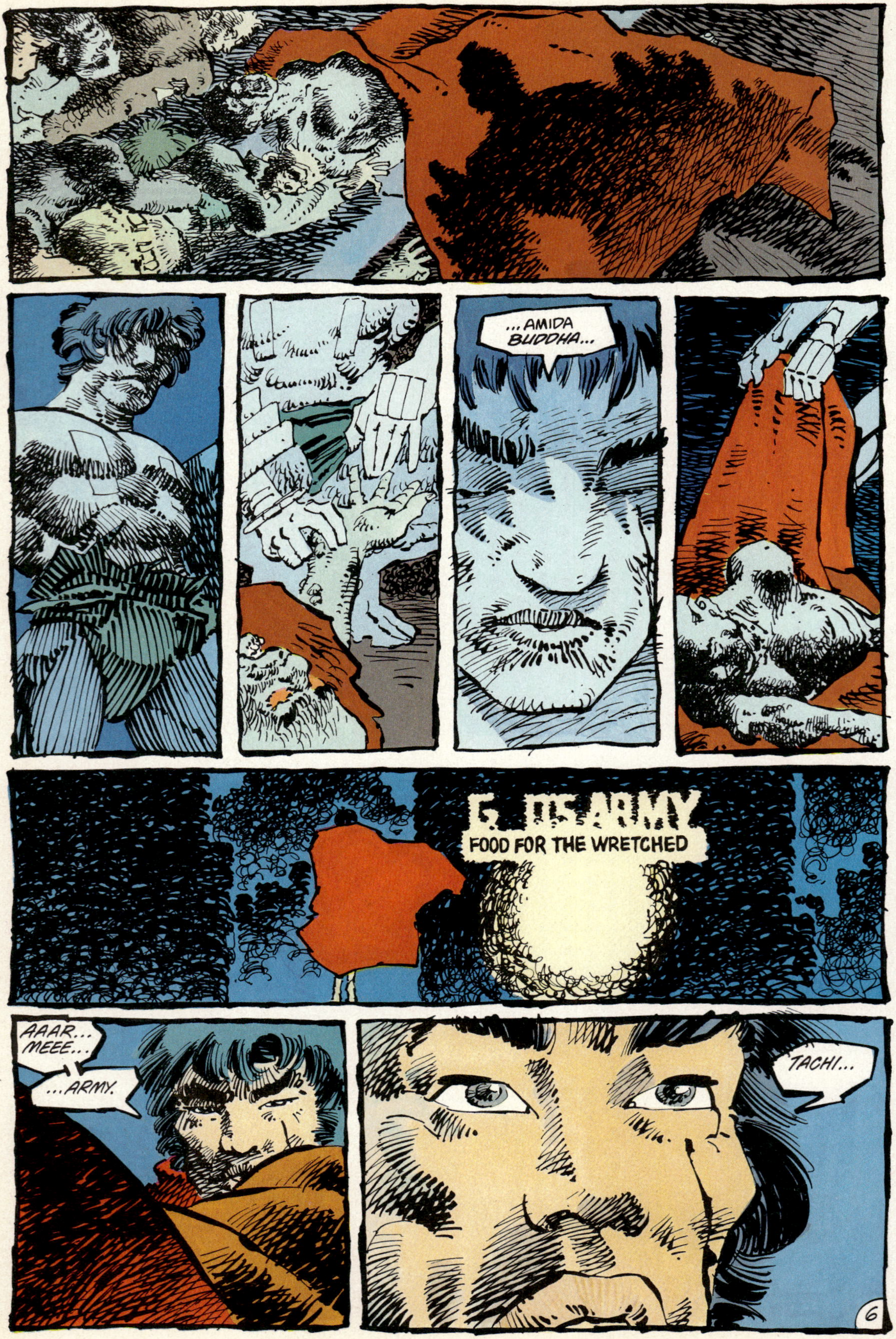
...AMIDA BUDDHA...
FOOD FOR THE WRETCHED
AAAR... MEEE...
...ARMY.
TACHI...

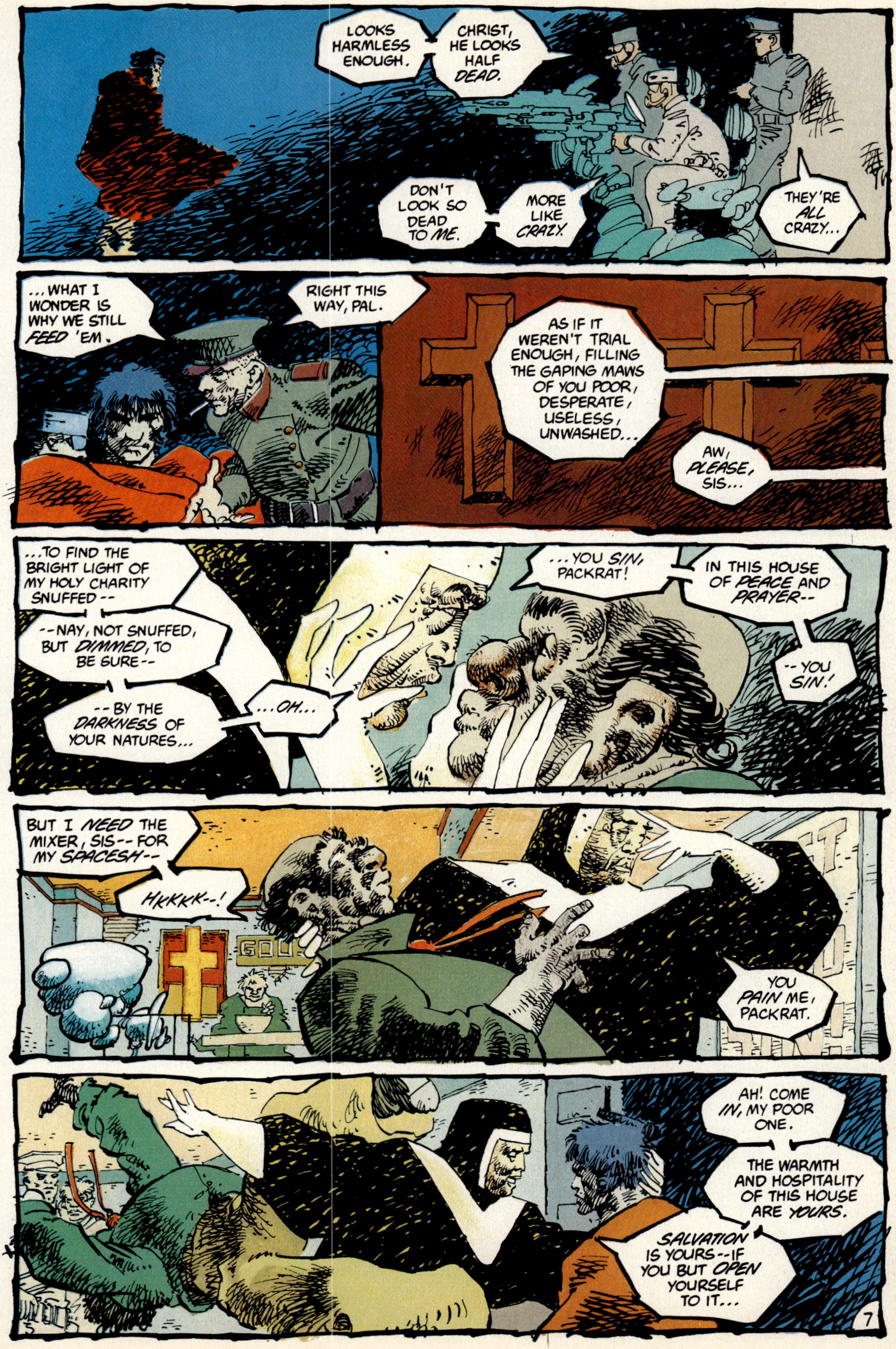
LOOKS HARMLESS ENOUGH.
CHRIST, HE LOOKS HALF *DEAD*.
DON'T LOOK SO DEAD TO *ME*.
MORE LIKE *CRAZY*.
THEY'RE *ALL* CRAZY...
...WHAT I WONDER IS WHY WE STILL *FEED* 'EM.
RIGHT THIS WAY, PAL.
AS IF IT WEREN'T TRIAL ENOUGH, FILLING THE GAPING MAWS OF YOU POOR, DESPERATE, USELESS, UNWASHED...
AW, *PLEASE*, SIS...
...TO FIND THE BRIGHT LIGHT OF MY HOLY CHARITY SNUFFED--
--NAY, NOT SNUFFED, BUT *DIMMED*, TO BE SURE--
--BY THE *DARKNESS* OF YOUR NATURES...
...OH...
...YOU *SIN*, PACKRAT!
IN THIS HOUSE OF *PEACE* AND *PRAYER*--
--YOU *SIN*!
BUT I *NEED* THE MIXER, SIS--FOR MY *SPACESH*--
HKKKK--!
YOU *PAIN* ME, PACKRAT.
AH! COME *IN*, MY POOR ONE.
THE WARMTH AND HOSPITALITY OF THIS HOUSE ARE *YOURS*.
SALVATION IS YOURS--IF YOU BUT *OPEN* YOURSELF TO IT...

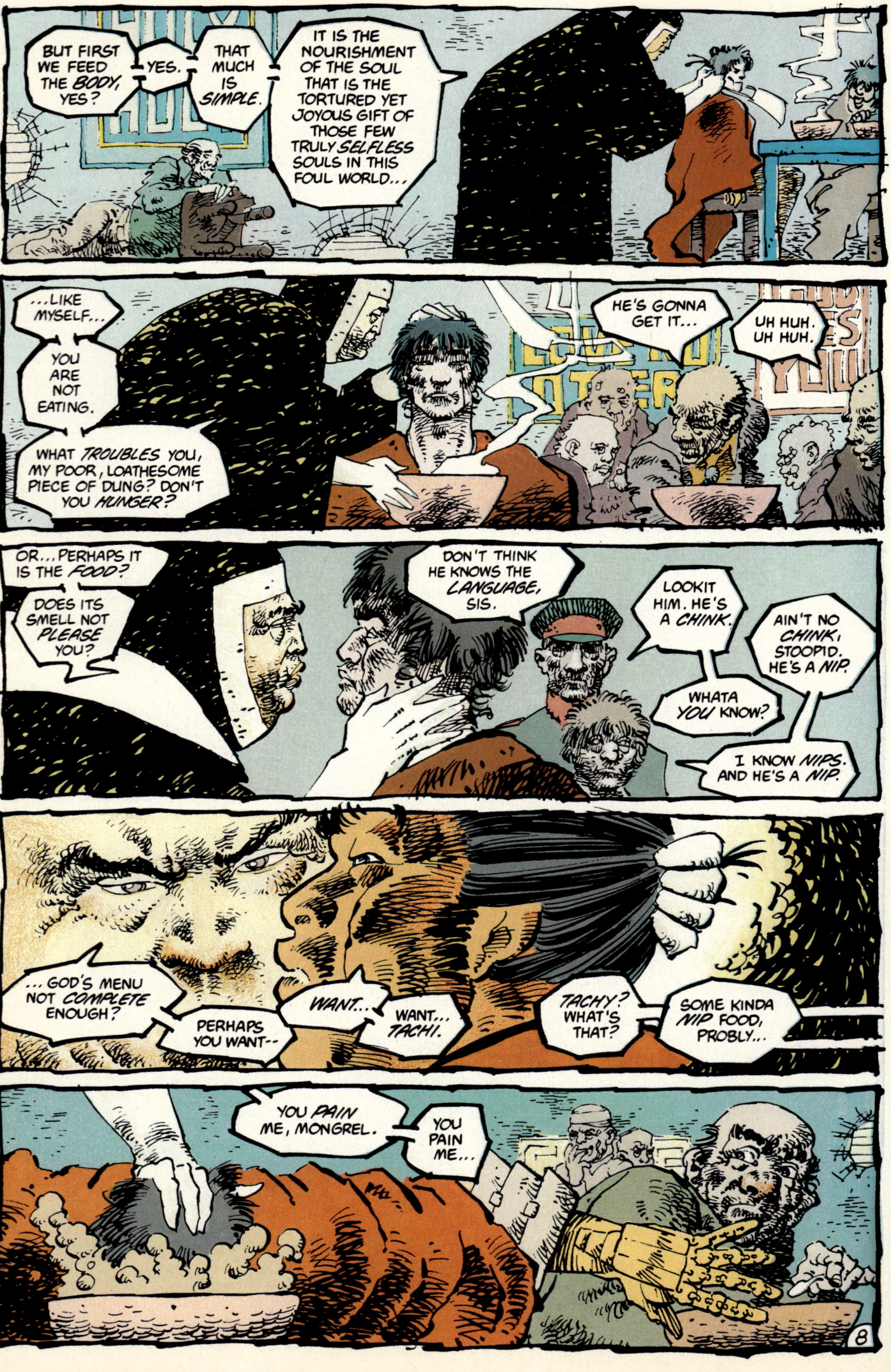

BUT FIRST WE FEED THE BODY, YES?
YES.
THAT MUCH IS SIMPLE.
IT IS THE NOURISHMENT OF THE SOUL THAT IS THE TORTURED YET JOYOUS GIFT OF THOSE FEW TRULY SELFLESS SOULS IN THIS FOUL WORLD...
...LIKE MYSELF...
YOU ARE NOT EATING.
WHAT TROUBLES YOU, MY POOR, LOATHESOME PIECE OF DUNG? DON'T YOU HUNGER?
HE'S GONNA GET IT...
UH HUH. UH HUH.
OR... PERHAPS IT IS THE FOOD?
DOES ITS SMELL NOT PLEASE YOU?
DON'T THINK HE KNOWS THE LANGUAGE, SIS.
LOOKIT HIM. HE'S A CHINK.
AIN'T NO CHINK, STOOPID. HE'S A NIP.
WHATA YOU KNOW?
I KNOW NIPS. AND HE'S A NIP.
... GOD'S MENU NOT COMPLETE ENOUGH?
PERHAPS YOU WANT--
WANT...
WANT... TACHI.
TACHY? WHAT'S THAT?
SOME KINDA NIP FOOD, PROBLY...
YOU PAIN ME, MONGREL.
YOU PAIN ME...

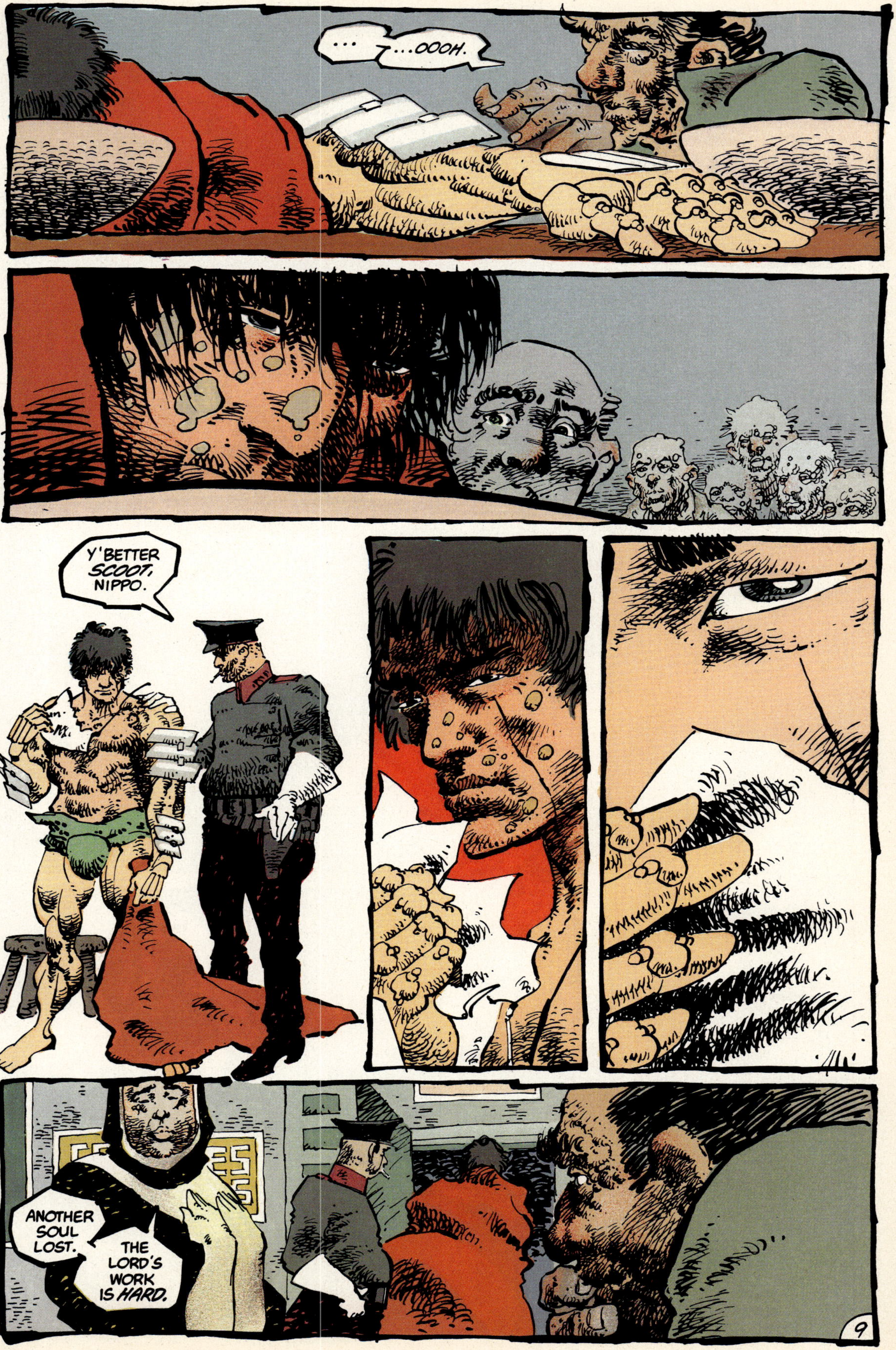
... ...OOOH.
Y'BETTER SCOOT, NIPPO.
ANOTHER SOUL LOST.
THE LORD'S WORK IS HARD.

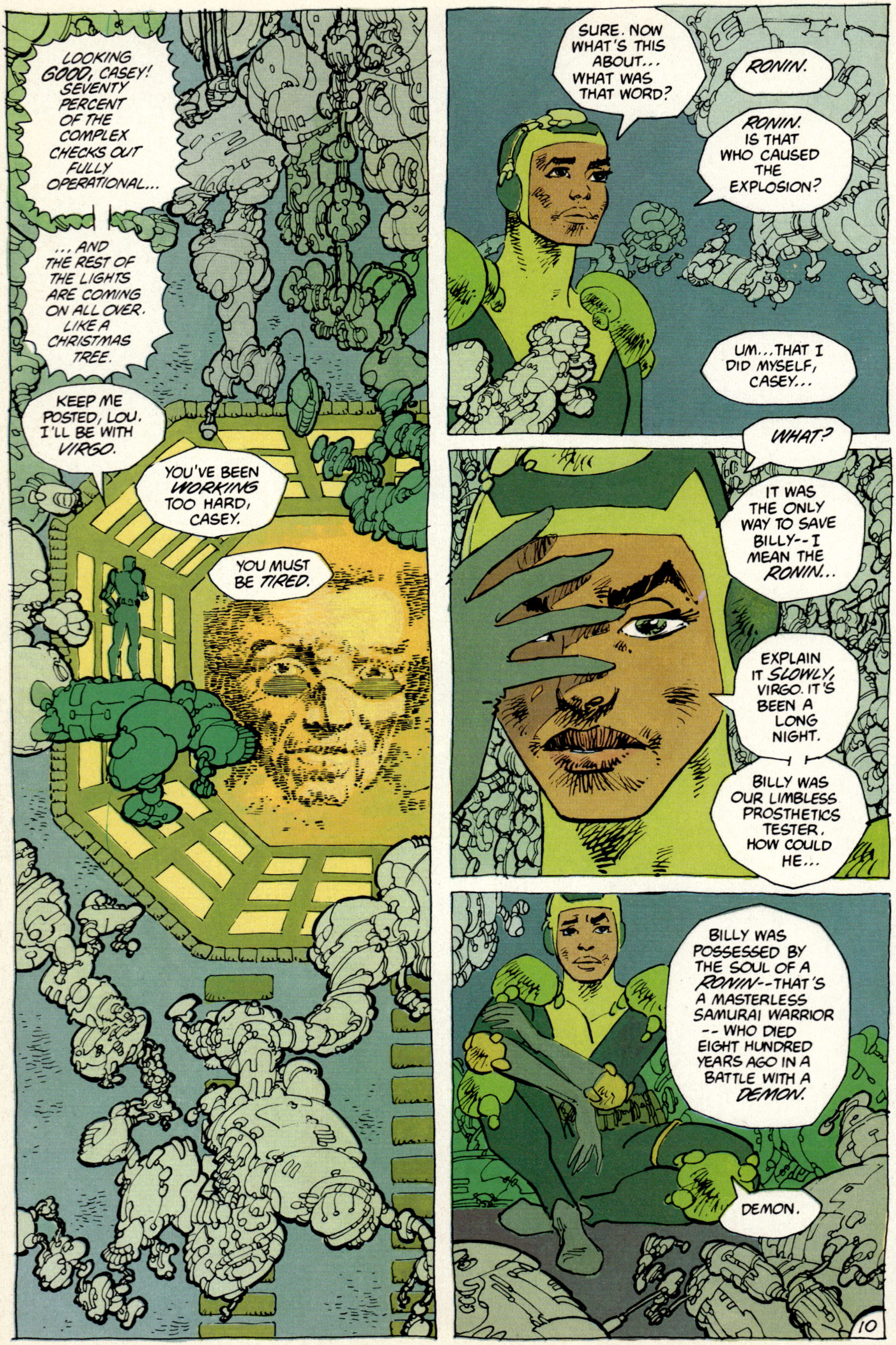
LOOKING GOOD, CASEY! SEVENTY PERCENT OF THE COMPLEX CHECKS OUT FULLY OPERATIONAL...
..., AND THE REST OF THE LIGHTS ARE COMING ON ALL OVER. LIKE A CHRISTMAS TREE.
KEEP ME POSTED, LOU. I'LL BE WITH VIRGO.
YOU'VE BEEN WORKING TOO HARD, CASEY.
YOU MUST BE TIRED.
SURE. NOW WHAT'S THIS ABOUT... WHAT WAS THAT WORD?
RONIN.
RONIN. IS THAT WHO CAUSED THE EXPLOSION?
UM...THAT I DID MYSELF, CASEY...
WHAT?
IT WAS THE ONLY WAY TO SAVE BILLY--I MEAN THE RONIN...
EXPLAIN IT SLOWLY, VIRGO. IT'S BEEN A LONG NIGHT.
BILLY WAS OUR LIMBLESS PROSTHETICS TESTER. HOW COULD HE...
BILLY WAS POSSESSED BY THE SOUL OF A RONIN--THAT'S A MASTERLESS SAMURAI WARRIOR --WHO DIED EIGHT HUNDRED YEARS AGO IN A BATTLE WITH A DEMON.
DEMON.
10

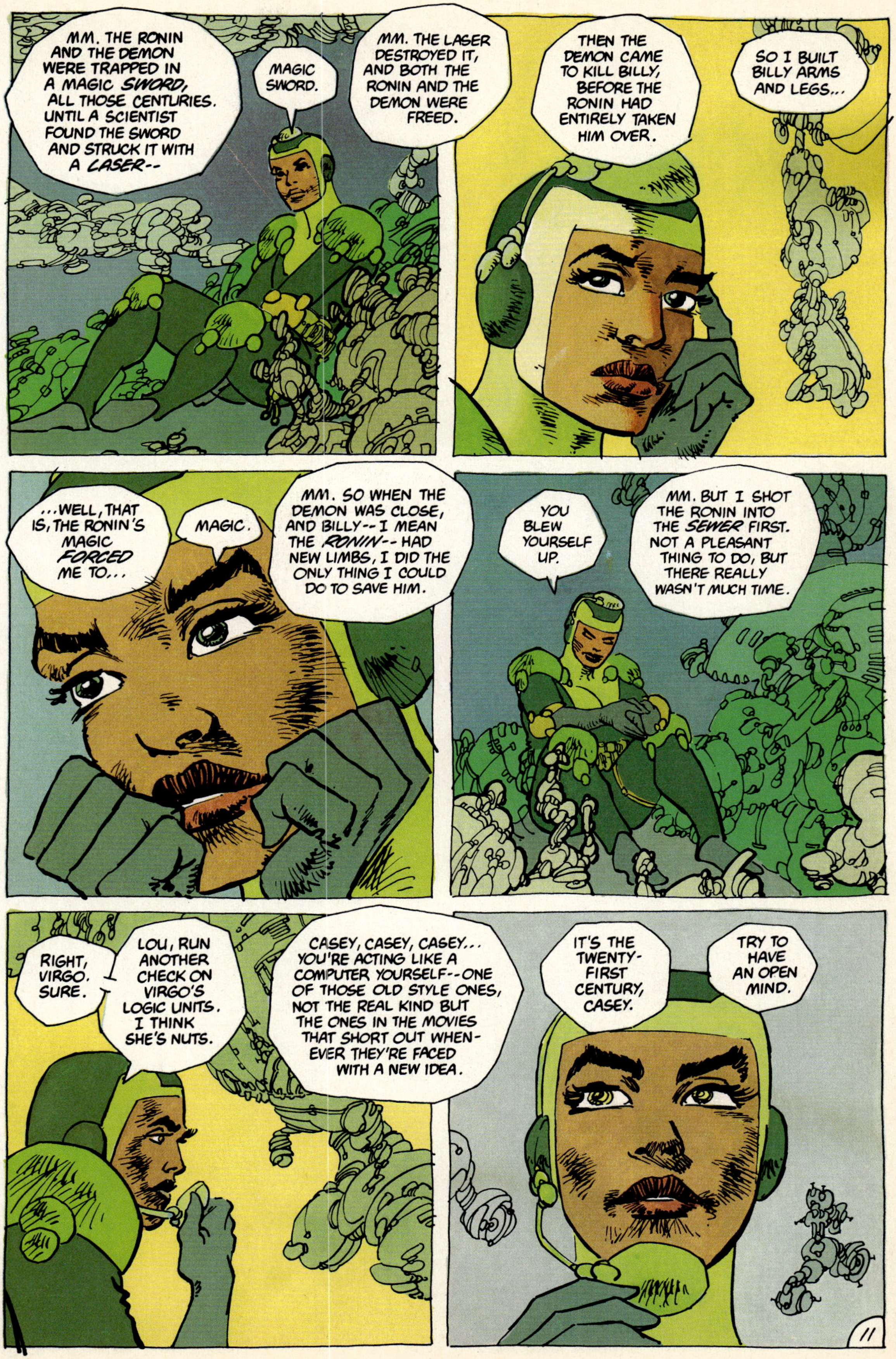
MM. THE RONIN AND THE DEMON WERE TRAPPED IN A MAGIC SWORD, ALL THOSE CENTURIES. UNTIL A SCIENTIST FOUND THE SWORD AND STRUCK IT WITH A LASER--
MAGIC SWORD.
MM. THE LASER DESTROYED IT, AND BOTH THE RONIN AND THE DEMON WERE FREED.
THEN THE DEMON CAME TO KILL BILLY, BEFORE THE RONIN HAD ENTIRELY TAKEN HIM OVER.
SO I BUILT BILLY ARMS AND LEGS...
...WELL, THAT IS, THE RONIN'S MAGIC FORCED ME TO...
MAGIC.
MM. SO WHEN THE DEMON WAS CLOSE, AND BILLY--I MEAN THE RONIN--HAD NEW LIMBS, I DID THE ONLY THING I COULD DO TO SAVE HIM.
YOU BLEW YOURSELF UP.
MM. BUT I SHOT THE RONIN INTO THE SEWER FIRST. NOT A PLEASANT THING TO DO, BUT THERE REALLY WASN'T MUCH TIME.
RIGHT, VIRGO. SURE.
LOU, RUN ANOTHER CHECK ON VIRGO'S LOGIC UNITS. I THINK SHE'S NUTS.
CASEY, CASEY, CASEY... YOU'RE ACTING LIKE A COMPUTER YOURSELF--ONE OF THOSE OLD STYLE ONES, NOT THE REAL KIND BUT THE ONES IN THE MOVIES THAT SHORT OUT WHEN-EVER THEY'RE FACED WITH A NEW IDEA.
IT'S THE TWENTY-FIRST CENTURY, CASEY.
TRY TO HAVE AN OPEN MIND.

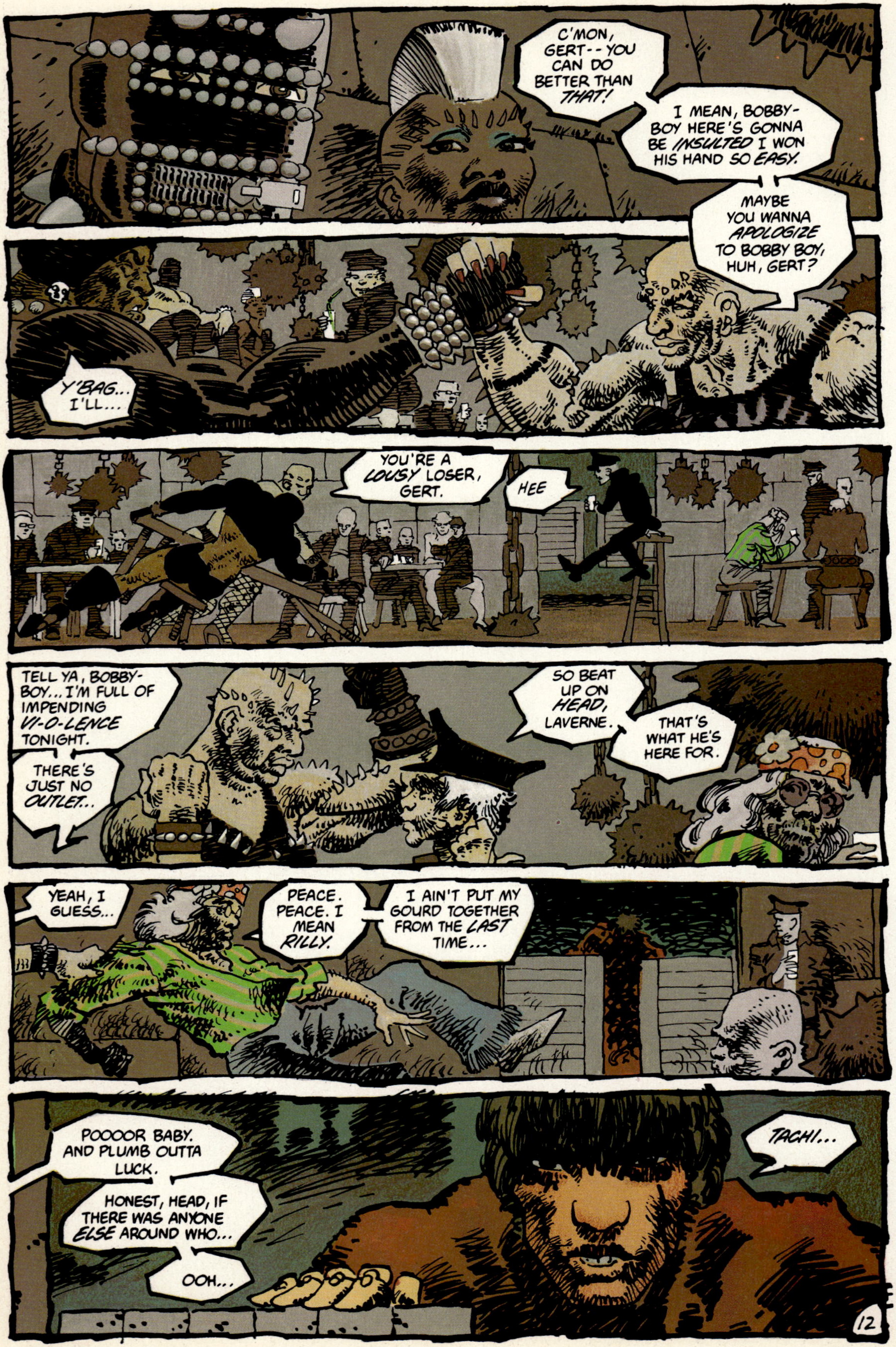
C'MON, GERT-- YOU CAN DO BETTER THAN THAT!
I MEAN, BOBBY-BOY HERE'S GONNA BE INSULTED I WON HIS HAND SO EASY.
MAYBE YOU WANNA APOLOGIZE TO BOBBY BOY, HUH, GERT?
Y'BAG... I'LL...
YOU'RE A LOUSY LOSER, GERT.
HEE
TELL YA, BOBBY-BOY... I'M FULL OF IMPENDING VI-O-LENCE TONIGHT.
THERE'S JUST NO OUTLET...
SO BEAT UP ON HEAD, LAVERNE.
THAT'S WHAT HE'S HERE FOR.
YEAH, I GUESS...
PEACE. PEACE. I MEAN RILLY.
I AIN'T PUT MY GOURD TOGETHER FROM THE LAST TIME...
POOOOR BABY. AND PLUMB OUTTA LUCK.
HONEST, HEAD, IF THERE WAS ANYONE ELSE AROUND WHO...
OOH...
TACHI...

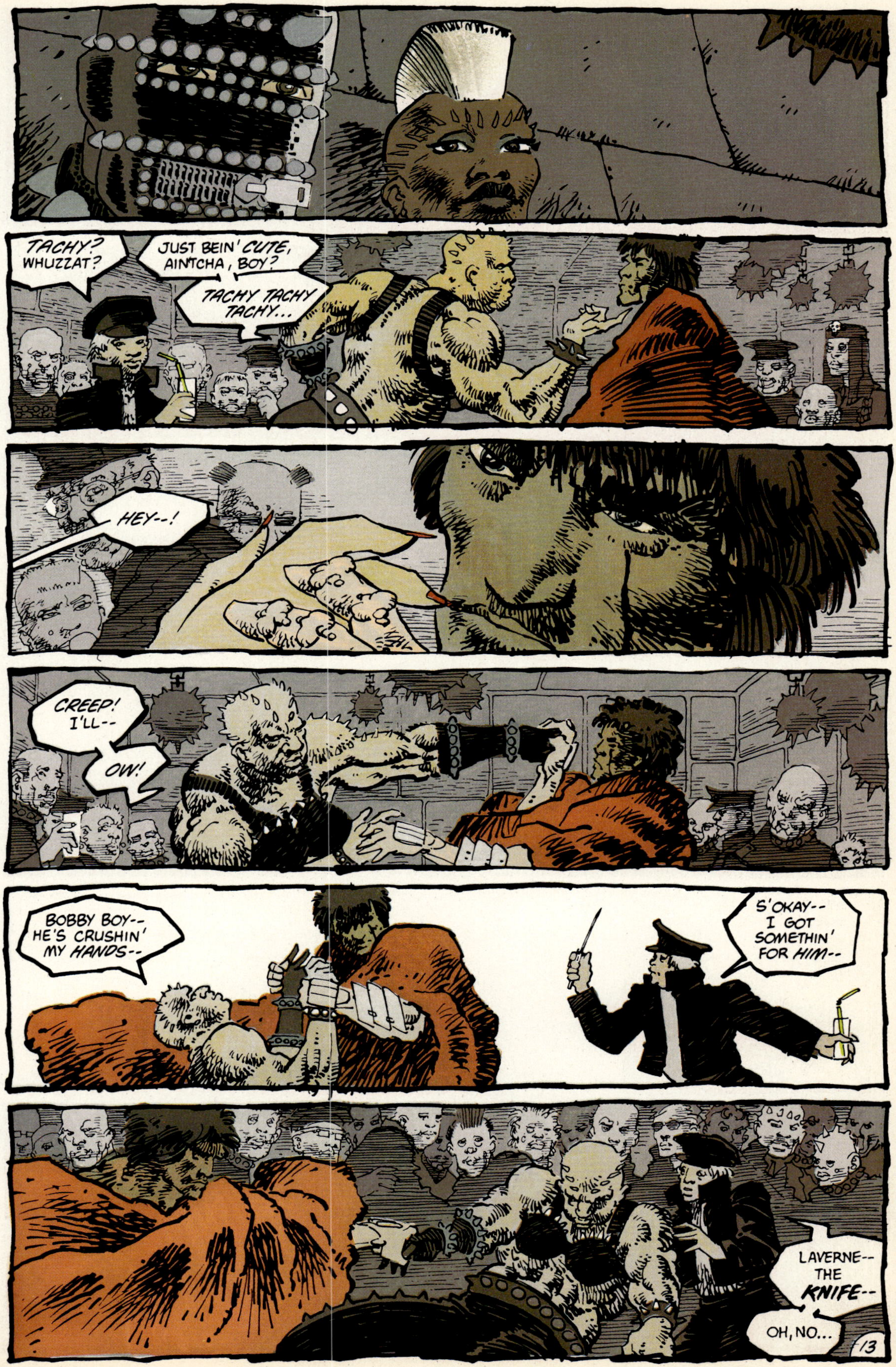
TACHY? WHUZZAT?
JUST BEIN' CUTE, AIN'TCHA, BOY?
TACHY TACHY TACHY...
HEY--!
CREEP! I'LL--
OW!
BOBBY BOY-- HE'S CRUSHIN' MY HANDS--
S'OKAY-- I GOT SOMETHIN' FOR HIM--
LAVERNE-- THE KNIFE--
OH, NO...

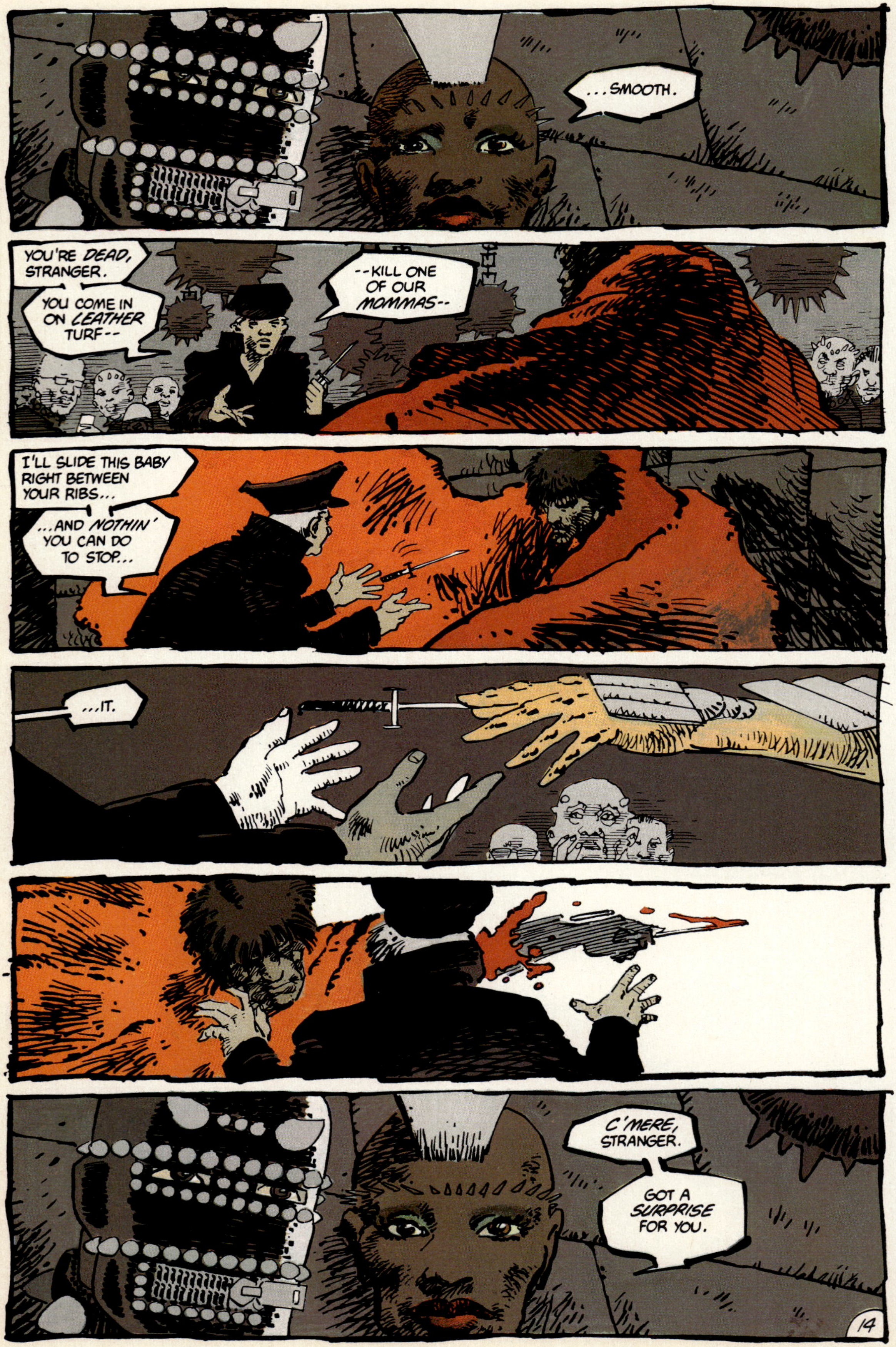
...SMOOTH.
YOU'RE *DEAD*, STRANGER.
YOU COME IN ON *LEATHER* TURF--
--KILL ONE OF OUR *MOMMAS*--
I'LL SLIDE THIS BABY RIGHT BETWEEN YOUR RIBS...
...AND *NOTHIN'* YOU CAN DO TO STOP...
...IT.
C'MERE, STRANGER.
GOT A *SURPRISE* FOR YOU.
14

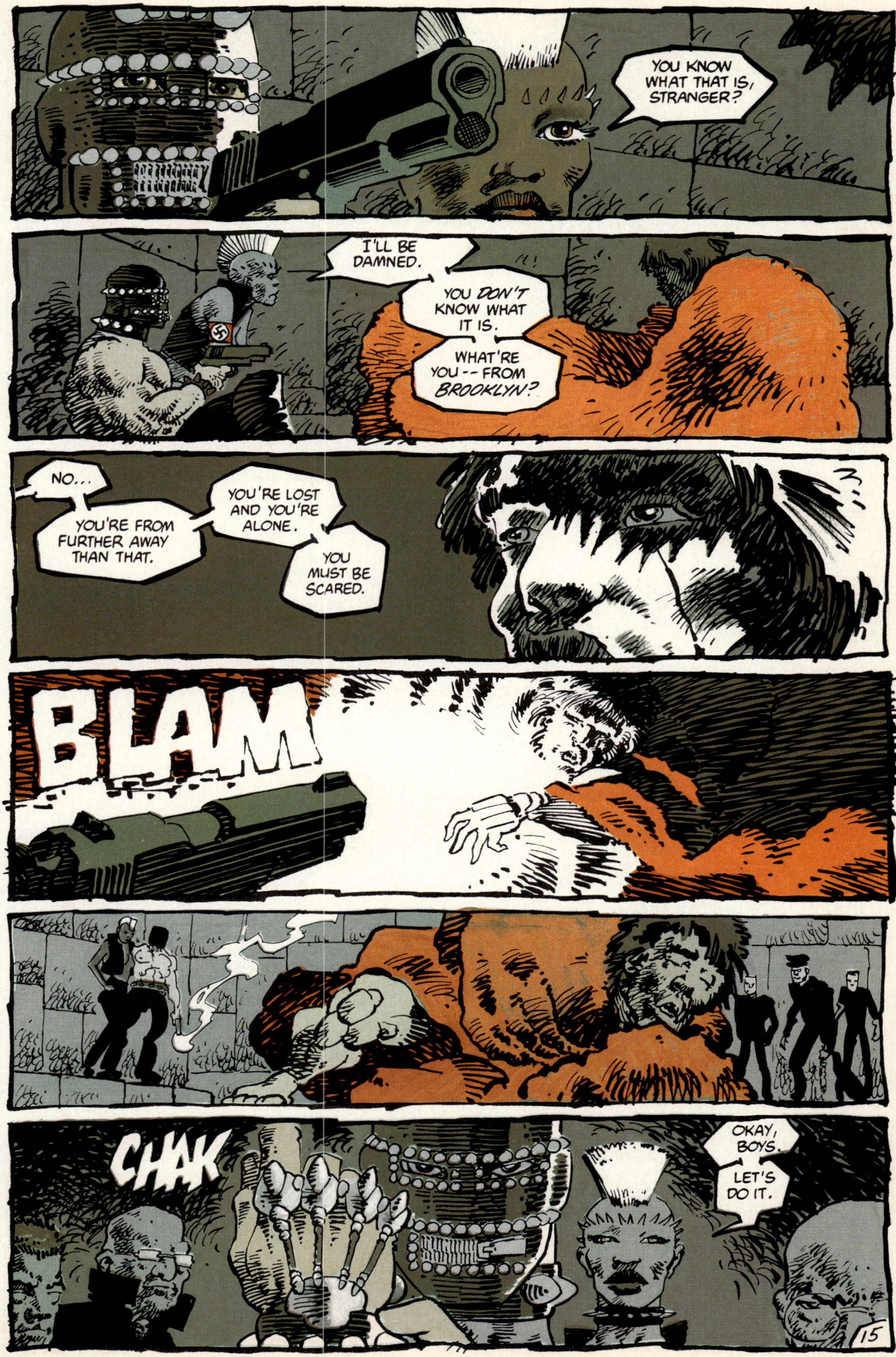
YOU KNOW WHAT THAT IS, STRANGER?
I'LL BE DAMNED.
YOU DON'T KNOW WHAT IT IS.
WHAT'RE YOU -- FROM BROOKLYN?
NO...
YOU'RE FROM FURTHER AWAY THAN THAT.
YOU'RE LOST AND YOU'RE ALONE.
YOU MUST BE SCARED.
BLAM
CHAK
OKAY, BOYS.
LET'S DO IT.

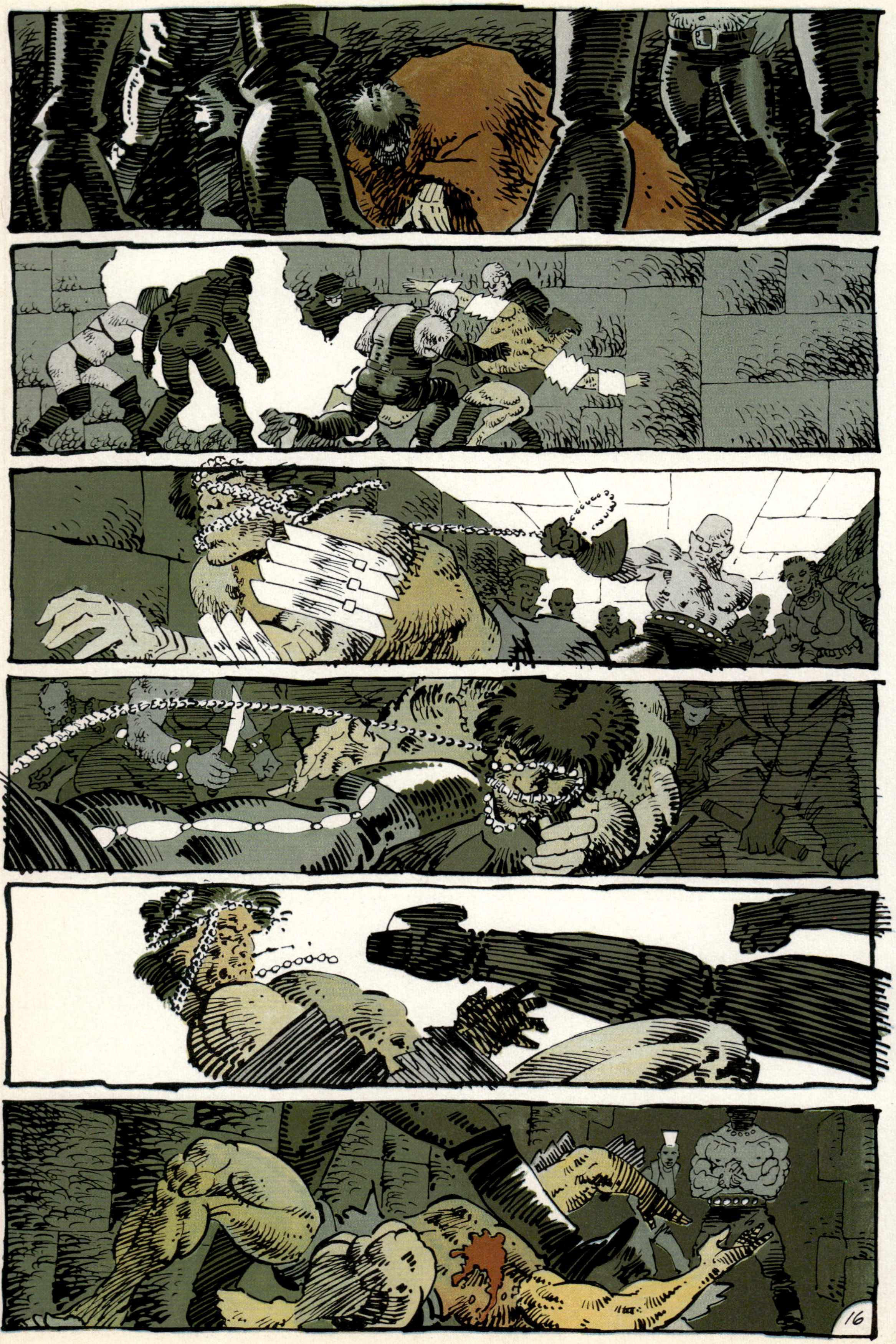

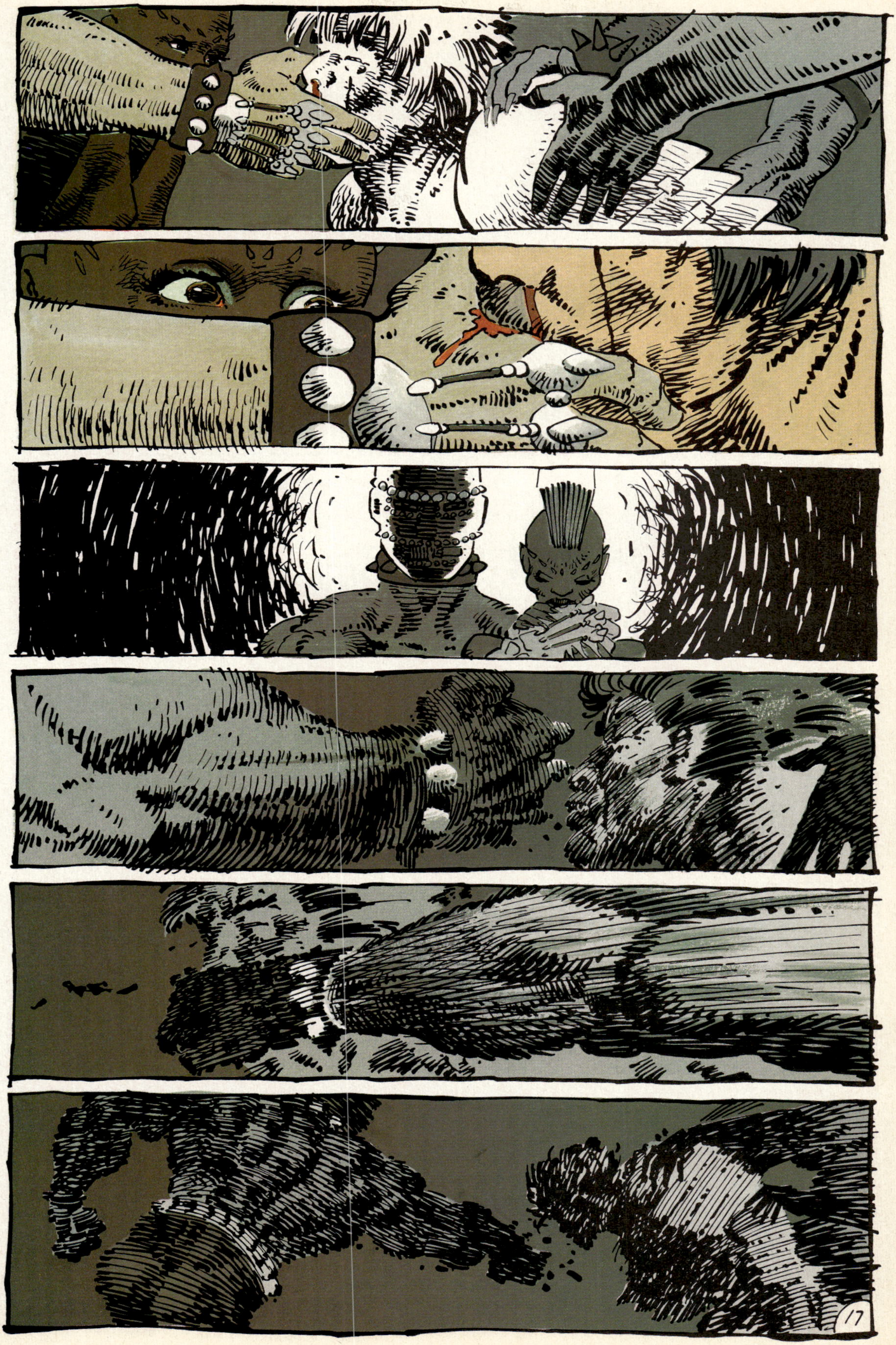

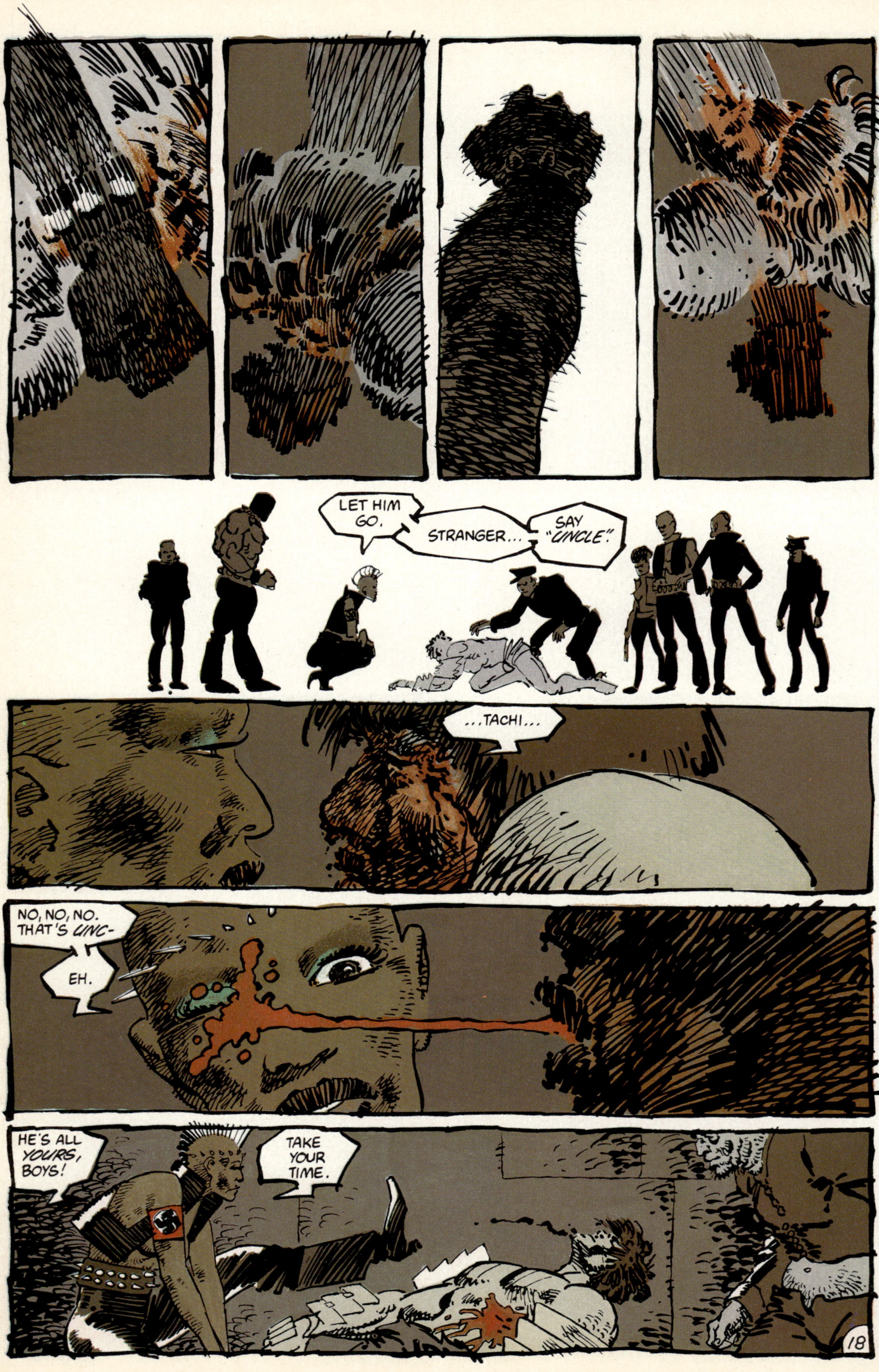

LET HIM GO.
STRANGER...
SAY "UNCLE."
...TACHI...
NO, NO, NO. THAT'S UNC-
EH.
HE'S ALL YOURS, BOYS!
TAKE YOUR TIME.

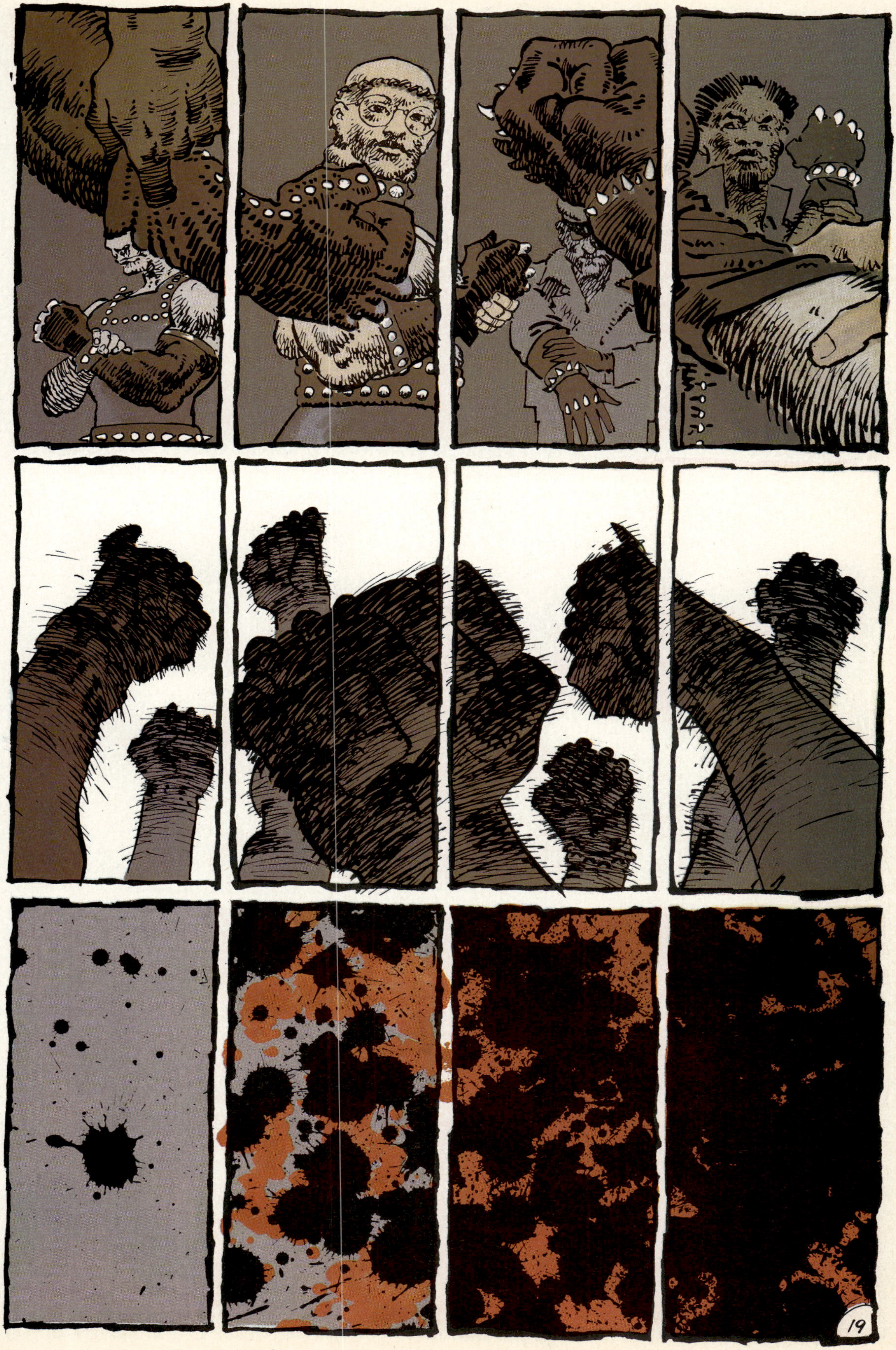

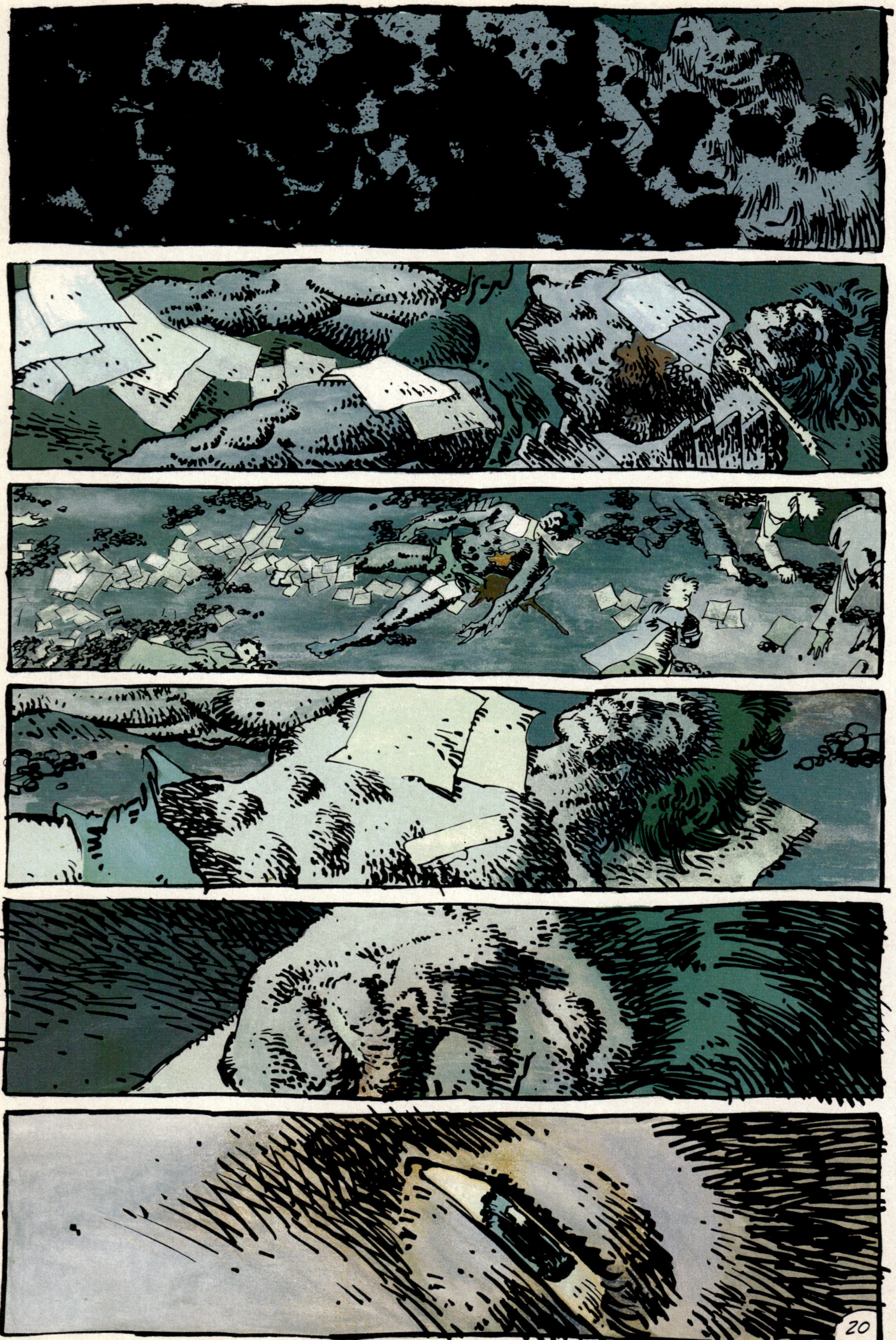
20

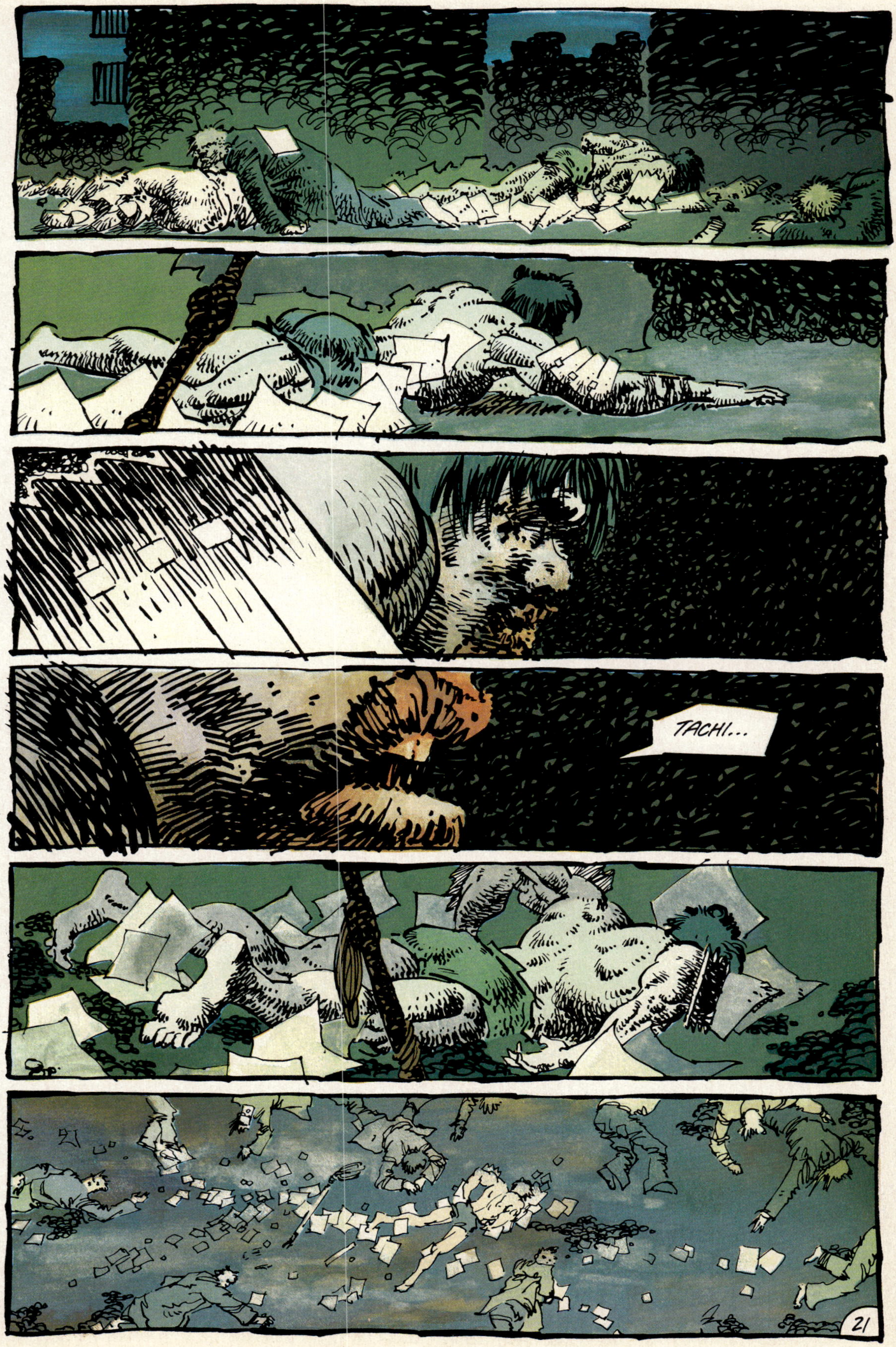
TACHI...

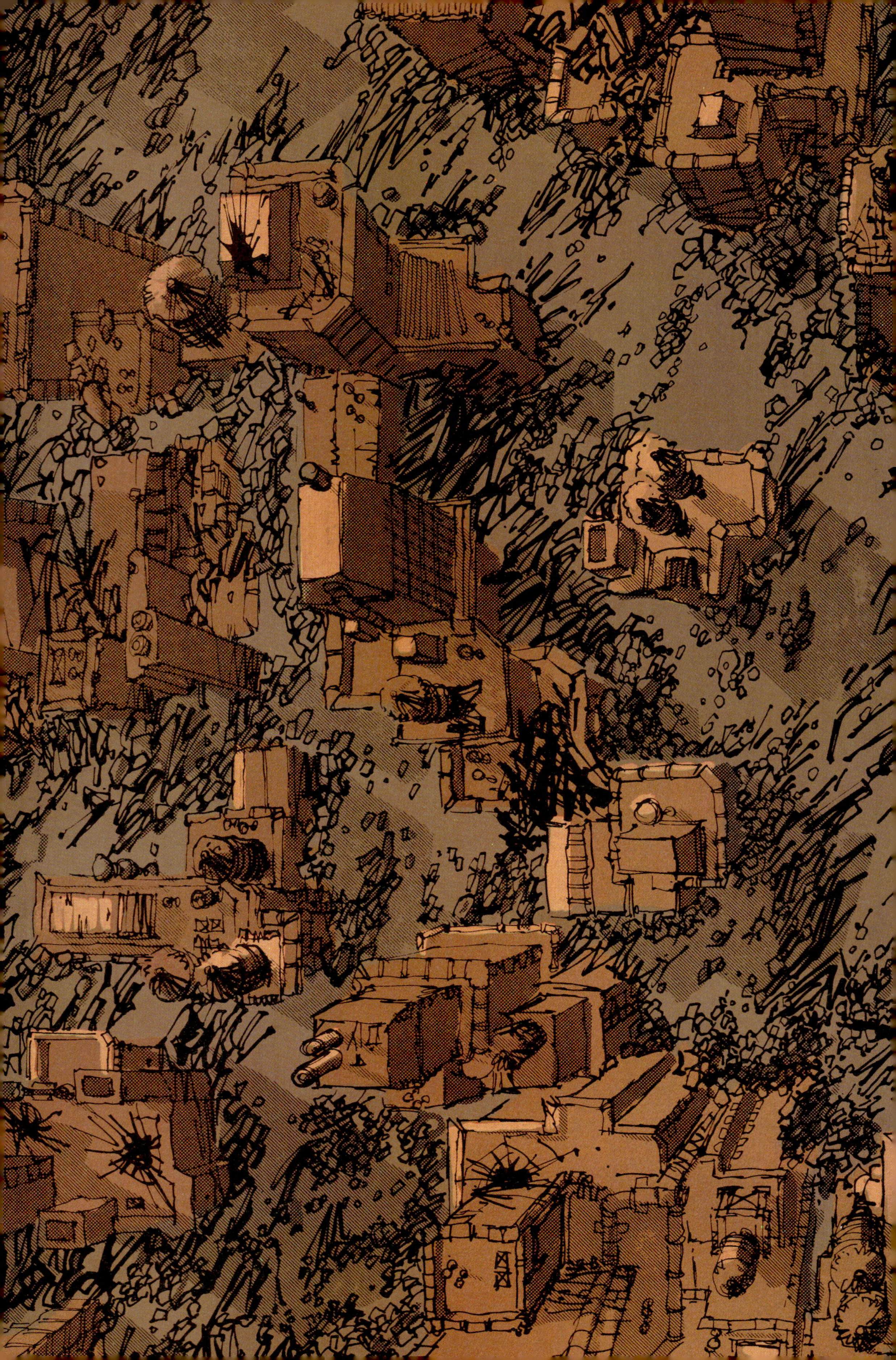

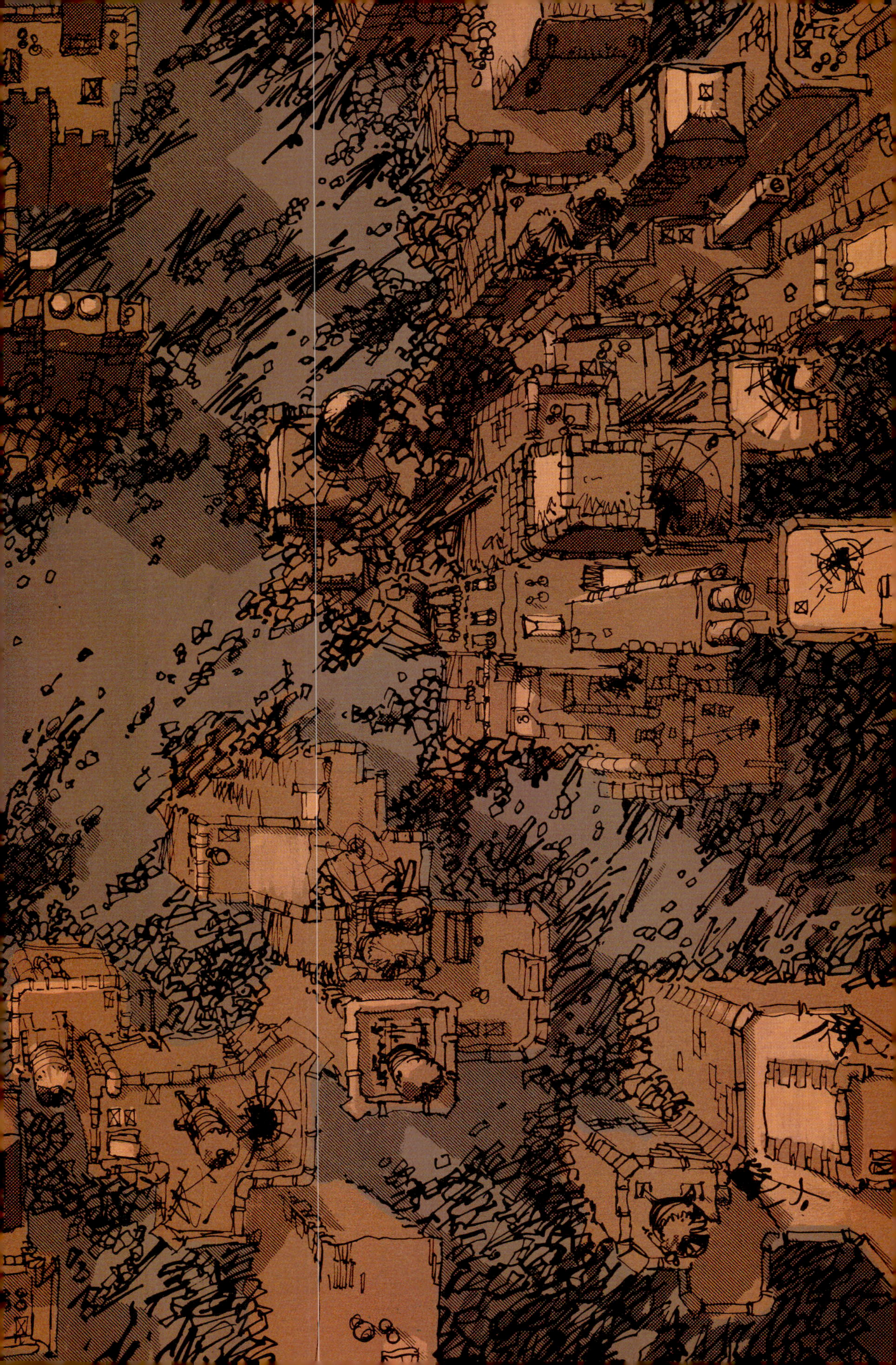

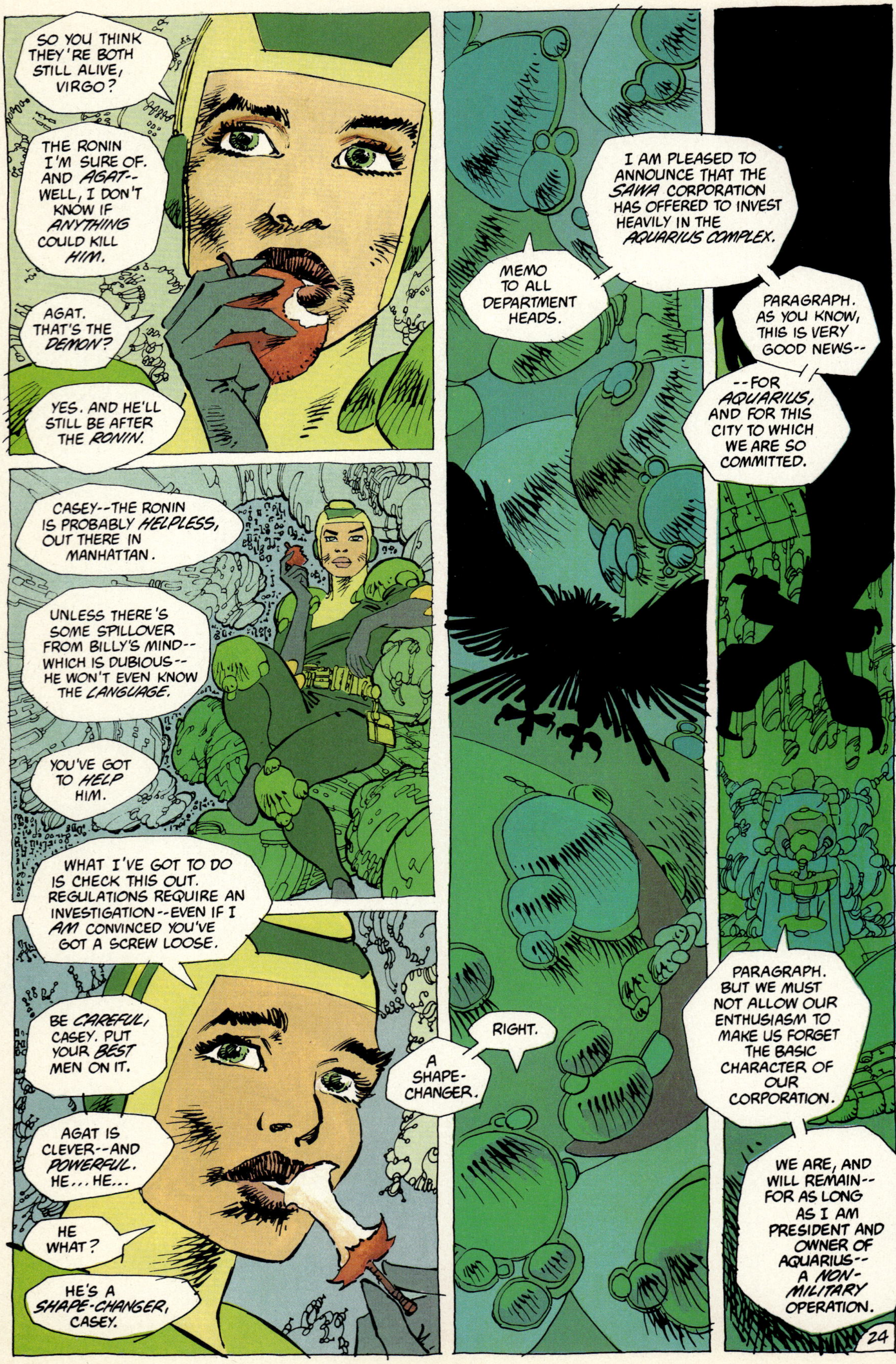

SO YOU THINK THEY'RE BOTH STILL ALIVE, VIRGO?
THE RONIN I'M SURE OF. AND AGAT-- WELL, I DON'T KNOW IF ANYTHING COULD KILL HIM.
AGAT. THAT'S THE DEMON?
YES. AND HE'LL STILL BE AFTER THE RONIN.
CASEY--THE RONIN IS PROBABLY HELPLESS, OUT THERE IN MANHATTAN.
UNLESS THERE'S SOME SPILLOVER FROM BILLY'S MIND-- WHICH IS DUBIOUS-- HE WON'T EVEN KNOW THE LANGUAGE.
YOU'VE GOT TO HELP HIM.
WHAT I'VE GOT TO DO IS CHECK THIS OUT. REGULATIONS REQUIRE AN INVESTIGATION--EVEN IF I AM CONVINCED YOU'VE GOT A SCREW LOOSE.
BE CAREFUL, CASEY. PUT YOUR BEST MEN ON IT.
AGAT IS CLEVER--AND POWERFUL. HE... HE...
HE WHAT?
HE'S A SHAPE-CHANGER, CASEY.
A SHAPE-CHANGER.
RIGHT.
MEMO TO ALL DEPARTMENT HEADS.
I AM PLEASED TO ANNOUNCE THAT THE SAWA CORPORATION HAS OFFERED TO INVEST HEAVILY IN THE AQUARIUS COMPLEX.
PARAGRAPH. AS YOU KNOW, THIS IS VERY GOOD NEWS--
--FOR AQUARIUS, AND FOR THIS CITY TO WHICH WE ARE SO COMMITTED.
PARAGRAPH. BUT WE MUST NOT ALLOW OUR ENTHUSIASM TO MAKE US FORGET THE BASIC CHARACTER OF OUR CORPORATION.
WE ARE, AND WILL REMAIN-- FOR AS LONG AS I AM PRESIDENT AND OWNER OF AQUARIUS-- A NON-MILITARY OPERATION.

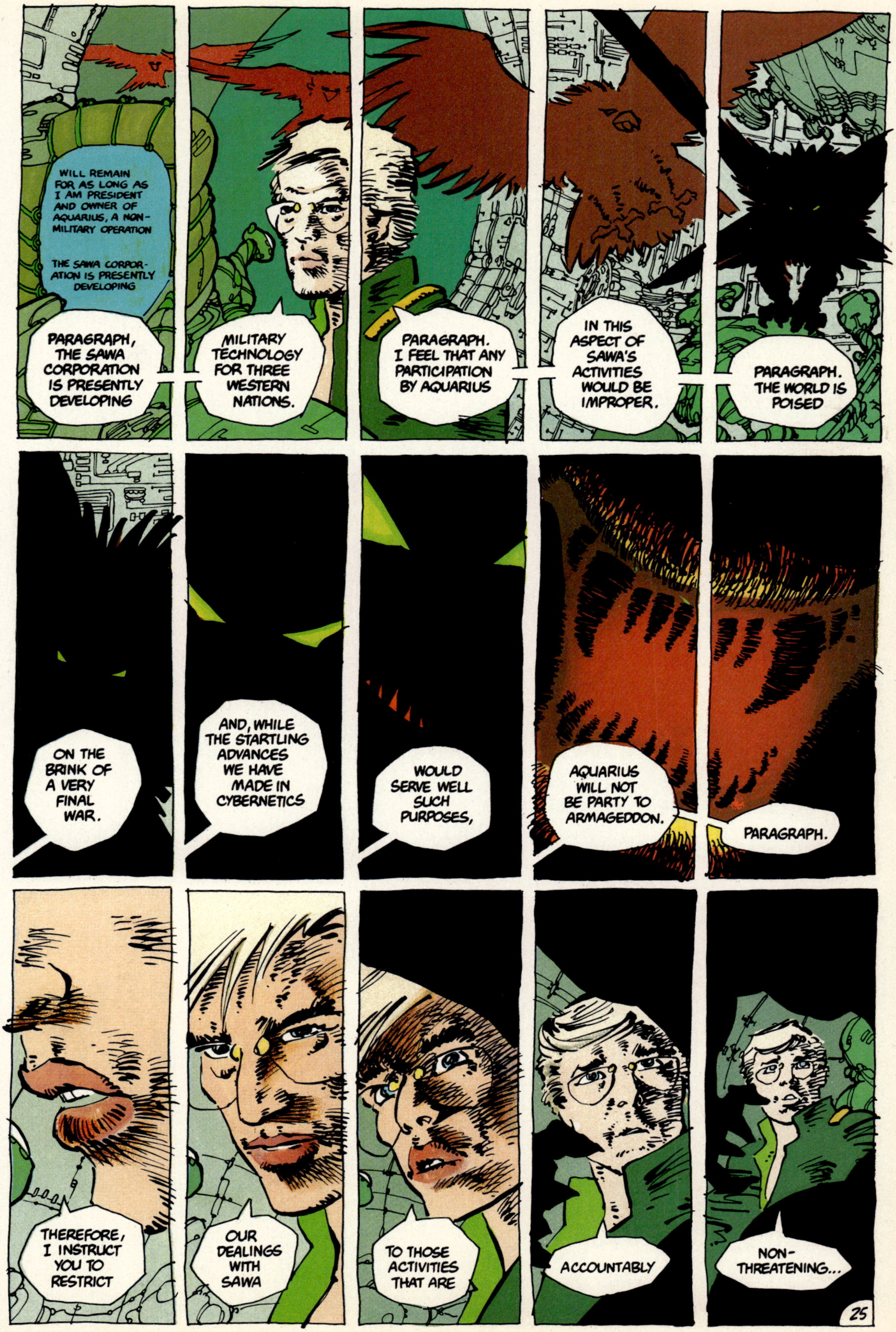
WILL REMAIN FOR AS LONG AS I AM PRESIDENT AND OWNER OF AQUARIUS, A NON-MILITARY OPERATION
THE SAWA CORPORATION IS PRESENTLY DEVELOPING
PARAGRAPH, THE SAWA CORPORATION IS PRESENTLY DEVELOPING
MILITARY TECHNOLOGY FOR THREE WESTERN NATIONS.
PARAGRAPH. I FEEL THAT ANY PARTICIPATION BY AQUARIUS
IN THIS ASPECT OF SAWA'S ACTIVITIES WOULD BE IMPROPER.
PARAGRAPH. THE WORLD IS POISED
ON THE BRINK OF A VERY FINAL WAR.
AND, WHILE THE STARTLING ADVANCES WE HAVE MADE IN CYBERNETICS
WOULD SERVE WELL SUCH PURPOSES,
AQUARIUS WILL NOT BE PARTY TO ARMAGEDDON.
PARAGRAPH.
THEREFORE, I INSTRUCT YOU TO RESTRICT
OUR DEALINGS WITH SAWA
TO THOSE ACTIVITIES THAT ARE
ACCOUNTABLY
NON-THREATENING...
25

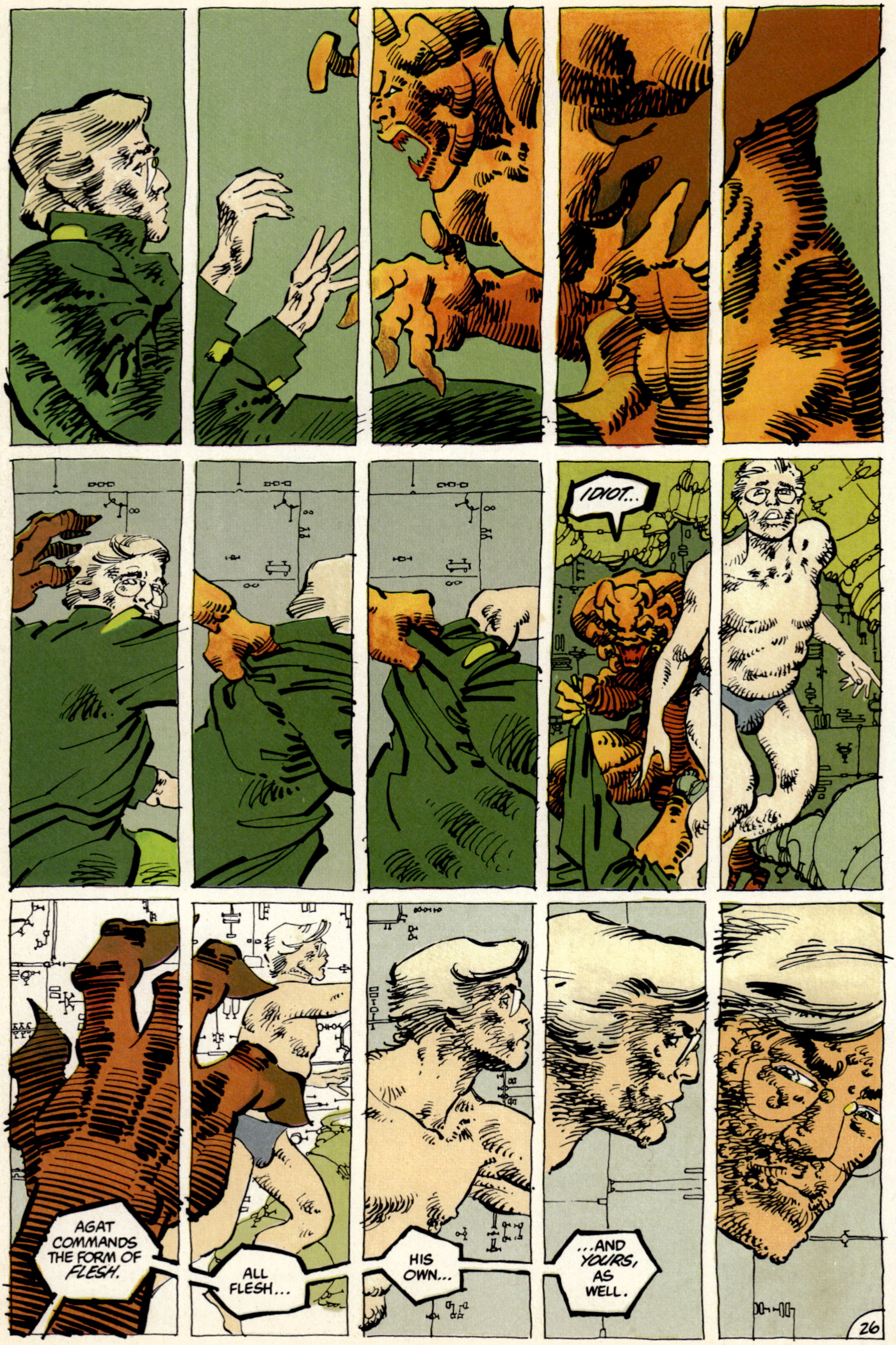

IDIOT...
AGAT COMMANDS THE FORM OF FLESH.
ALL FLESH...
HIS OWN...
...AND YOURS, AS WELL.

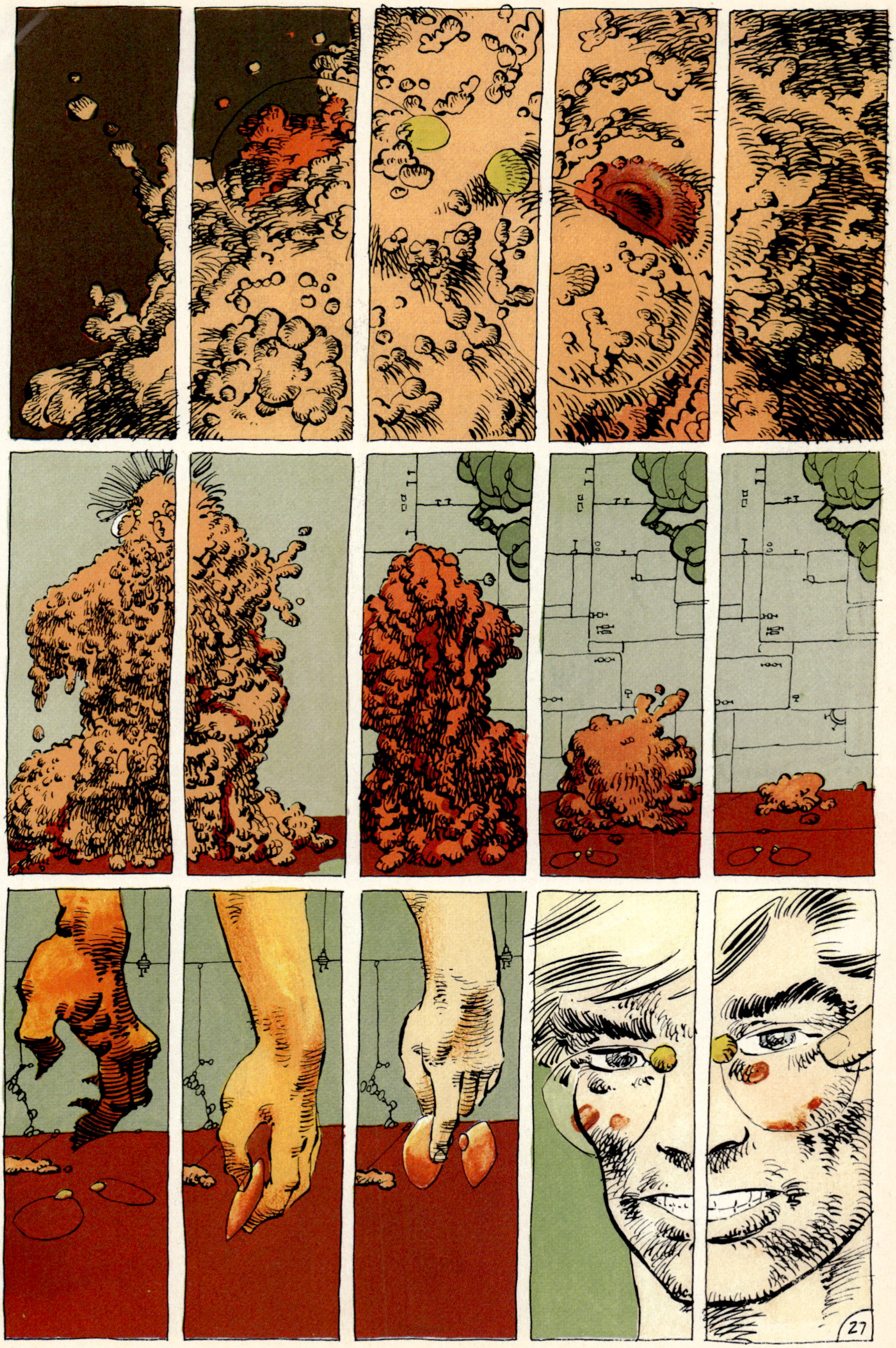

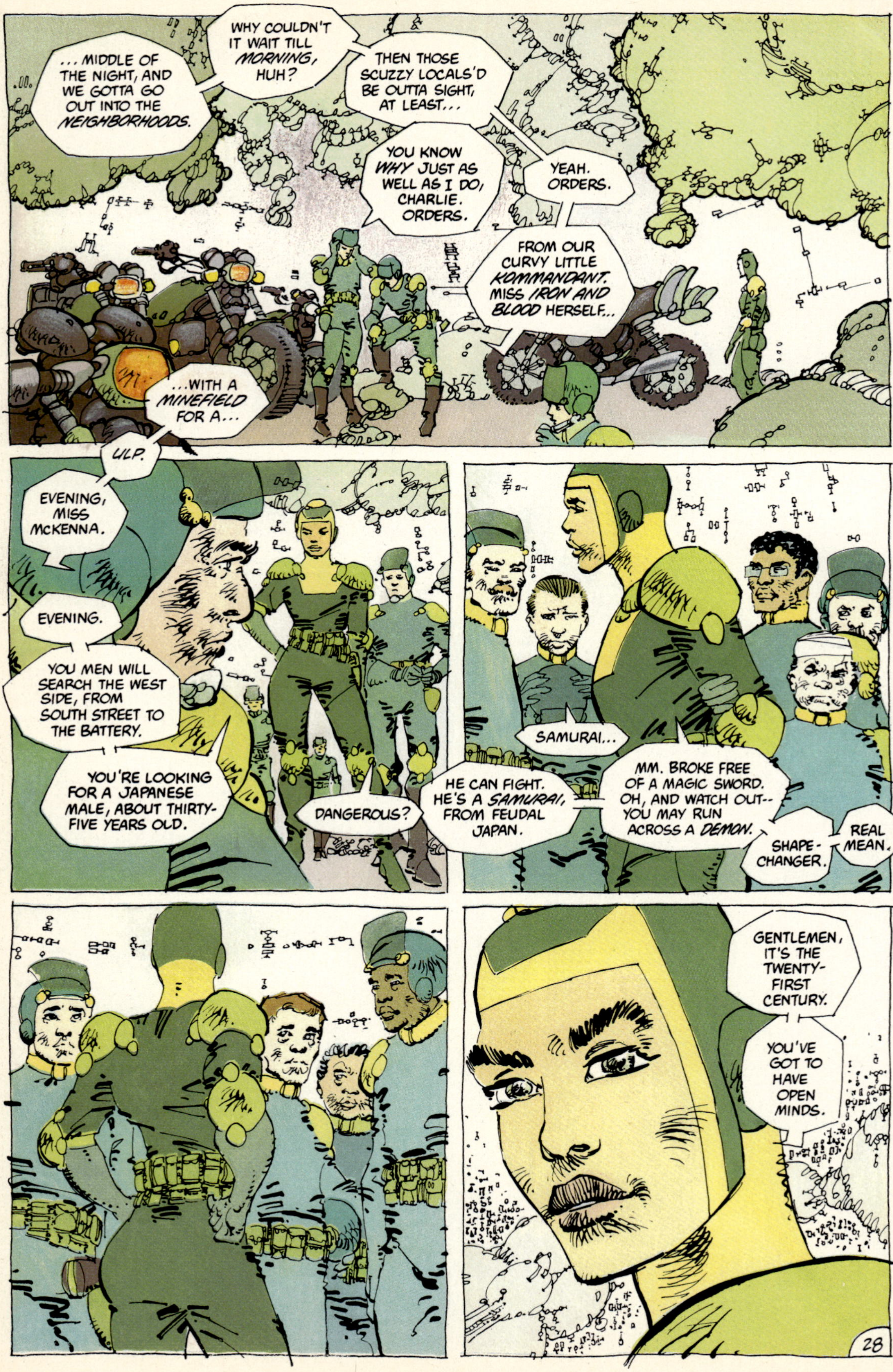

... MIDDLE OF THE NIGHT, AND WE GOTTA GO OUT INTO THE *NEIGHBORHOODS.*
WHY COULDN'T IT WAIT TILL *MORNING,* HUH?
THEN THOSE SCUZZY LOCALS'D BE OUTTA SIGHT, AT LEAST...
YOU KNOW *WHY* JUST AS WELL AS I DO, CHARLIE. ORDERS.
YEAH. ORDERS.
FROM OUR CURVY LITTLE *KOMMANDANT.* MISS *IRON AND BLOOD* HERSELF...
...WITH A *MINEFIELD* FOR A...
ULP.
EVENING, MISS McKENNA.
EVENING.
YOU MEN WILL SEARCH THE WEST SIDE, FROM SOUTH STREET TO THE BATTERY.
YOU'RE LOOKING FOR A JAPANESE MALE, ABOUT THIRTY-FIVE YEARS OLD.
DANGEROUS?
SAMURAI...
HE CAN FIGHT. HE'S A *SAMURAI,* FROM FEUDAL JAPAN.
MM. BROKE FREE OF A MAGIC SWORD. OH, AND WATCH OUT-- YOU MAY RUN ACROSS A *DEMON.*
SHAPE-CHANGER.
REAL MEAN.
GENTLEMEN, IT'S THE TWENTY-FIRST CENTURY.
YOU'VE GOT TO HAVE OPEN MINDS.

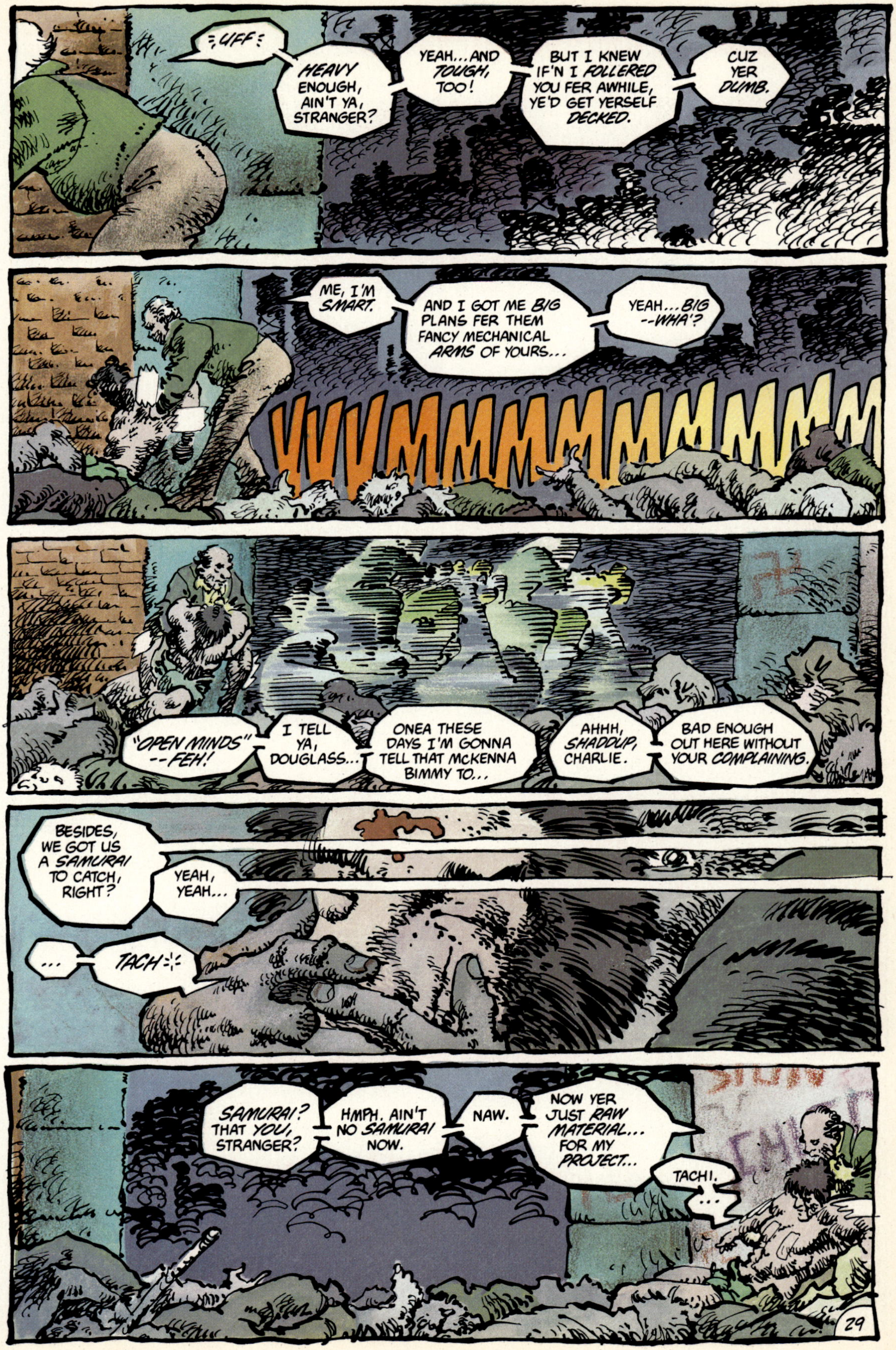
UFF
HEAVY ENOUGH, AIN'T YA, STRANGER?
YEAH... AND TOUGH, TOO!
BUT I KNEW IF'N I FOLLERED YOU FER AWHILE, YE'D GET YERSELF DECKED.
CUZ YER DUMB.
ME, I'M SMART.
AND I GOT ME BIG PLANS FER THEM FANCY MECHANICAL ARMS OF YOURS...
YEAH... BIG --WHA'?
VVVMMMMMMMMMMMM
"OPEN MINDS" --FEH!
I TELL YA, DOUGLASS...
ONEA THESE DAYS I'M GONNA TELL THAT McKENNA BIMMY TO...
AHHH, SHADDUP, CHARLIE.
BAD ENOUGH OUT HERE WITHOUT YOUR COMPLAINING.
BESIDES, WE GOT US A SAMURAI TO CATCH, RIGHT?
YEAH, YEAH...
...
TACH
SAMURAI? THAT YOU, STRANGER?
HMPH. AIN'T NO SAMURAI NOW.
NAW.
NOW YER JUST RAW MATERIAL... FOR MY PROJECT...
TACH!
...

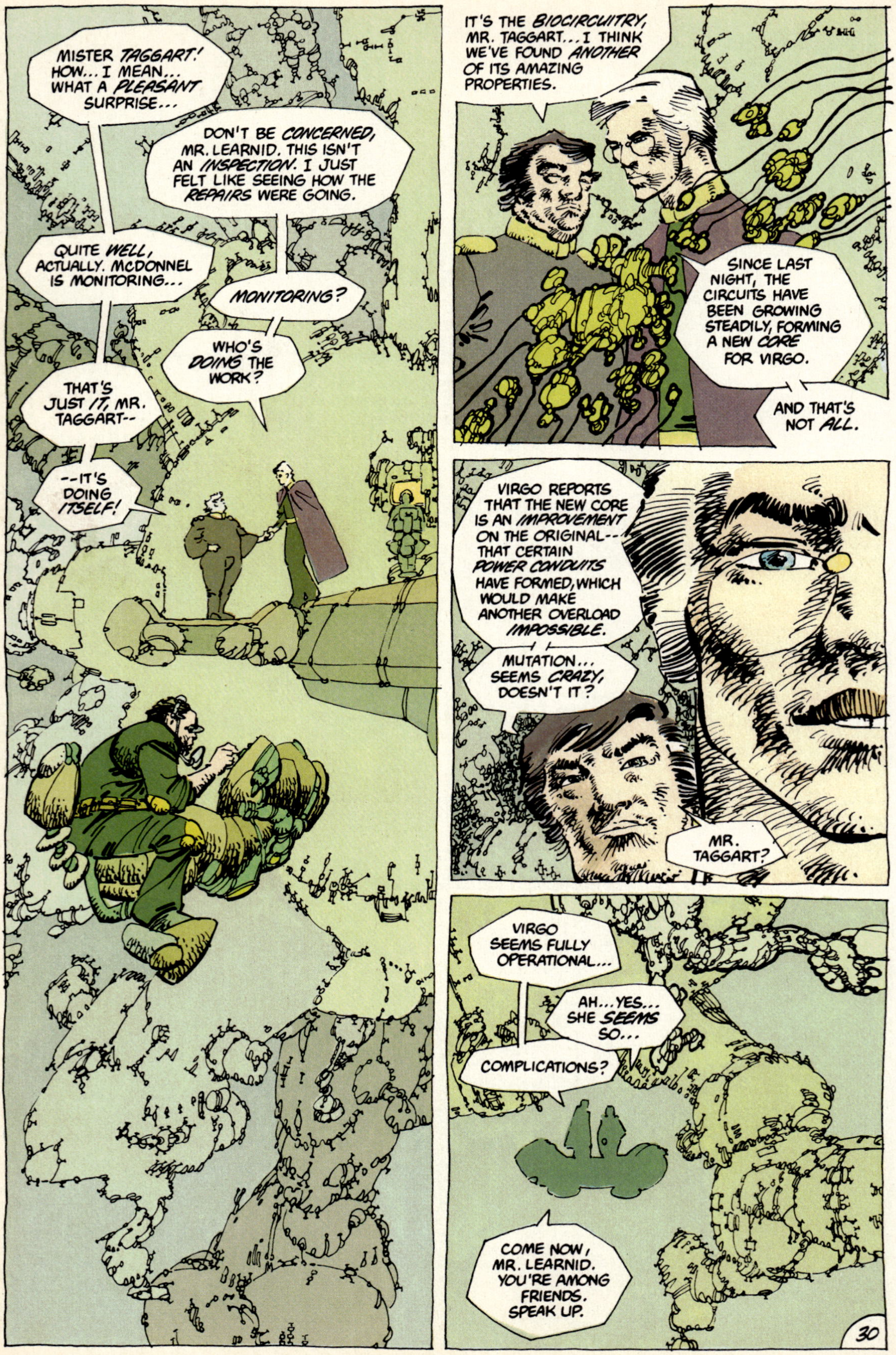

MISTER TAGGART! HOW... I MEAN... WHAT A PLEASANT SURPRISE...
DON'T BE CONCERNED, MR. LEARNID. THIS ISN'T AN INSPECTION. I JUST FELT LIKE SEEING HOW THE REPAIRS WERE GOING.
QUITE WELL, ACTUALLY. MCDONNEL IS MONITORING...
MONITORING?
WHO'S DOING THE WORK?
THAT'S JUST IT, MR. TAGGART--
--IT'S DOING ITSELF!
IT'S THE BIOCIRCUITRY, MR. TAGGART... I THINK WE'VE FOUND ANOTHER OF ITS AMAZING PROPERTIES.
SINCE LAST NIGHT, THE CIRCUITS HAVE BEEN GROWING STEADILY, FORMING A NEW CORE FOR VIRGO.
AND THAT'S NOT ALL.
VIRGO REPORTS THAT THE NEW CORE IS AN IMPROVEMENT ON THE ORIGINAL-- THAT CERTAIN POWER CONDUITS HAVE FORMED, WHICH WOULD MAKE ANOTHER OVERLOAD IMPOSSIBLE.
MUTATION... SEEMS CRAZY, DOESN'T IT?
MR. TAGGART?
VIRGO SEEMS FULLY OPERATIONAL...
AH... YES... SHE SEEMS SO...
COMPLICATIONS?
COME NOW, MR. LEARNID. YOU'RE AMONG FRIENDS. SPEAK UP.

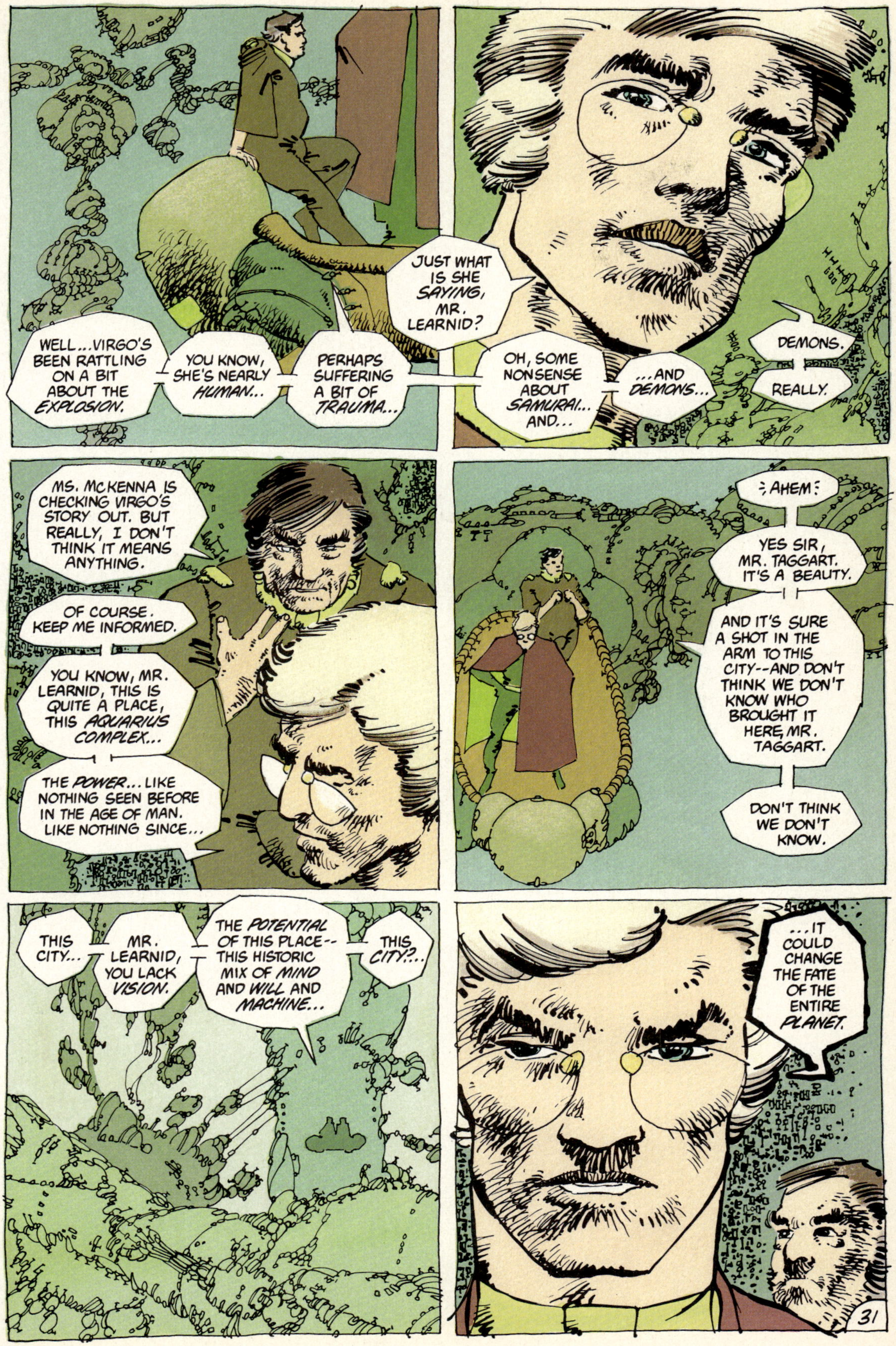

WELL... VIRGO'S BEEN RATTLING ON A BIT ABOUT THE EXPLOSION.
YOU KNOW, SHE'S NEARLY HUMAN...
PERHAPS SUFFERING A BIT OF TRAUMA...
JUST WHAT IS SHE SAYING, MR. LEARNID?
OH, SOME NONSENSE ABOUT SAMURAI... AND...
...AND DEMONS...
DEMONS.
REALLY.
MS. MCKENNA IS CHECKING VIRGO'S STORY OUT. BUT REALLY, I DON'T THINK IT MEANS ANYTHING.
OF COURSE. KEEP ME INFORMED.
YOU KNOW, MR. LEARNID, THIS IS QUITE A PLACE, THIS AQUARIUS COMPLEX...
THE POWER... LIKE NOTHING SEEN BEFORE IN THE AGE OF MAN. LIKE NOTHING SINCE...
AHEM
YES SIR, MR. TAGGART. IT'S A BEAUTY.
AND IT'S SURE A SHOT IN THE ARM TO THIS CITY--AND DON'T THINK WE DON'T KNOW WHO BROUGHT IT HERE, MR. TAGGART.
DON'T THINK WE DON'T KNOW.
THIS CITY...
MR. LEARNID, YOU LACK VISION.
THE POTENTIAL OF THIS PLACE--THIS HISTORIC MIX OF MIND AND WILL AND MACHINE...
THIS CITY?!...
...IT COULD CHANGE THE FATE OF THE ENTIRE PLANET.

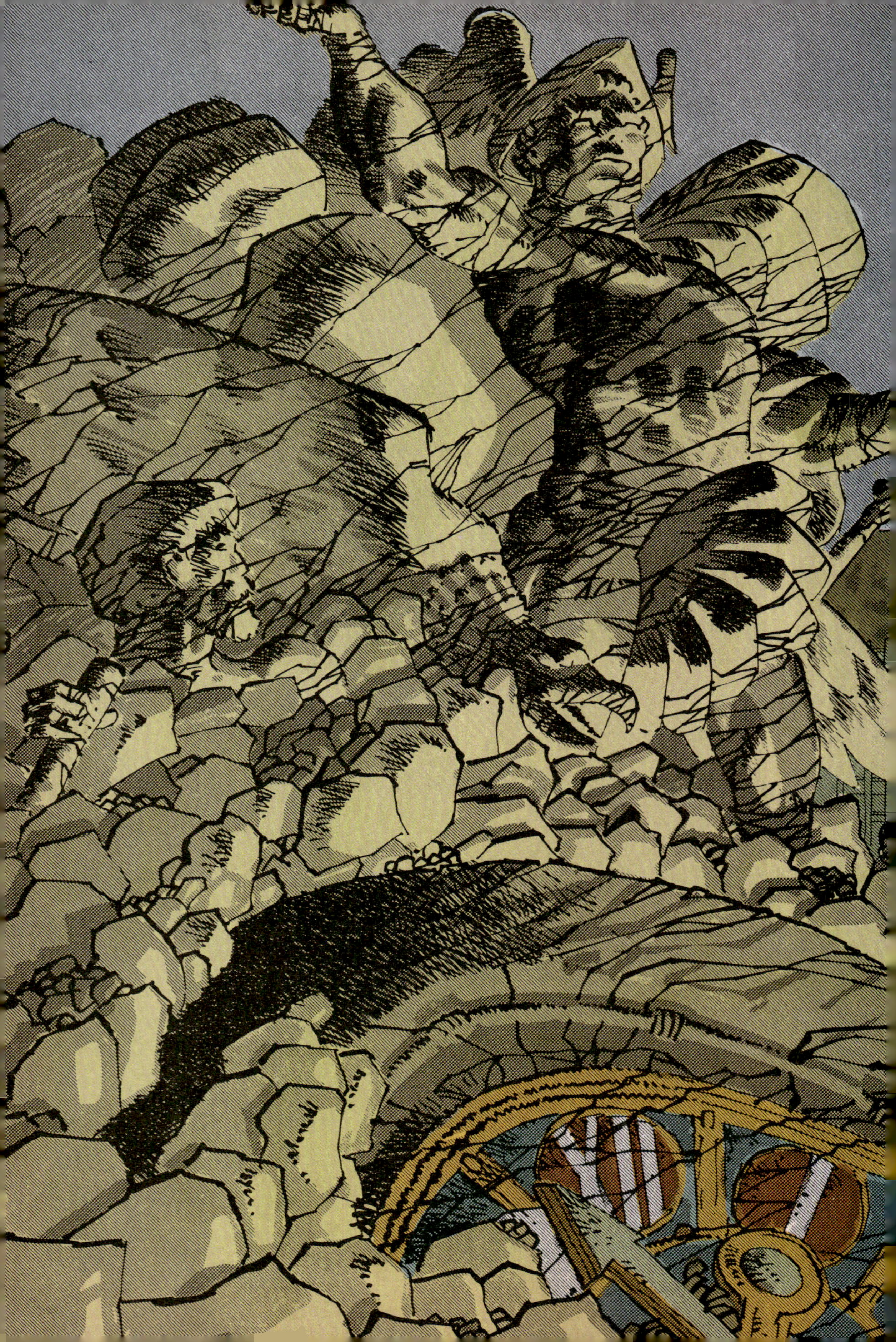

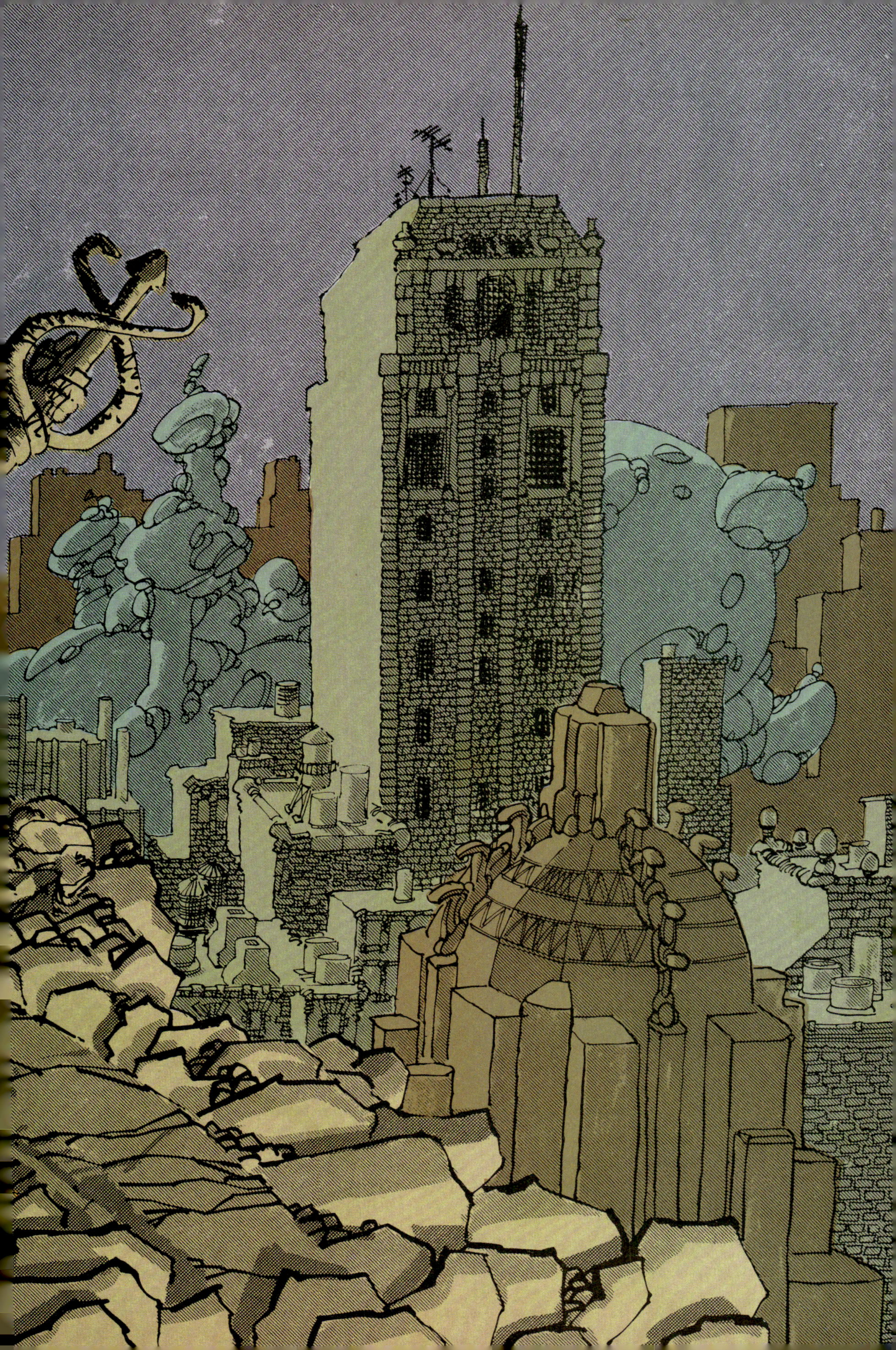

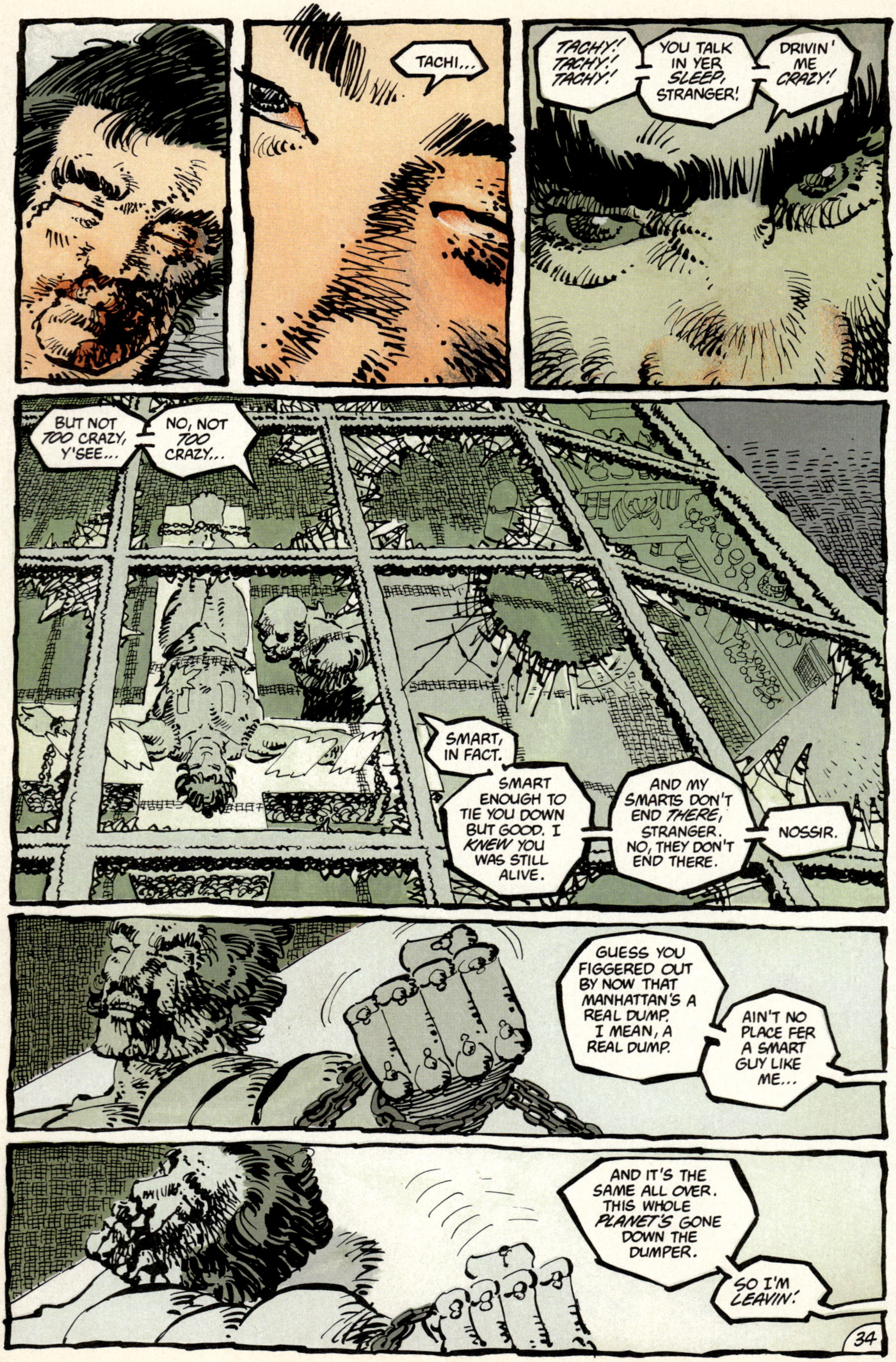
TACHI...
TACHY! TACHY! TACHY!
YOU TALK IN YER SLEEP, STRANGER!
DRIVIN' ME CRAZY!
BUT NOT TOO CRAZY, Y'SEE...
NO, NOT TOO CRAZY...
SMART, IN FACT.
SMART ENOUGH TO TIE YOU DOWN BUT GOOD. I KNEW YOU WAS STILL ALIVE.
AND MY SMARTS DON'T END THERE, STRANGER. NO, THEY DON'T END THERE.
NOSSIR.
GUESS YOU FIGGERED OUT BY NOW THAT MANHATTAN'S A REAL DUMP. I MEAN, A REAL DUMP.
AIN'T NO PLACE FER A SMART GUY LIKE ME...
AND IT'S THE SAME ALL OVER. THIS WHOLE PLANET'S GONE DOWN THE DUMPER.
SO I'M LEAVIN'.
34

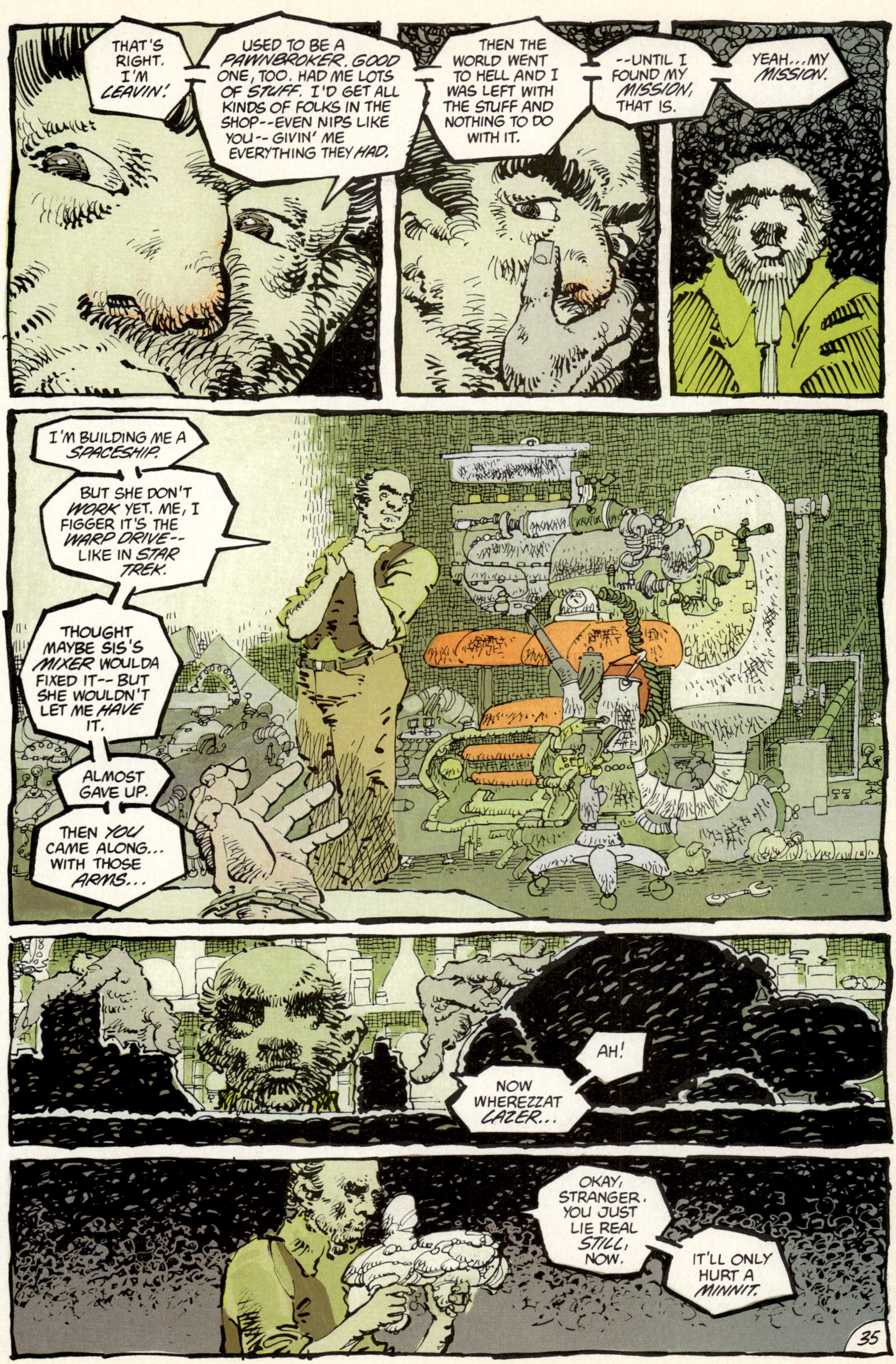

THAT'S RIGHT. I'M *LEAVIN'!*
USED TO BE A *PAWNBROKER*. GOOD ONE, TOO. HAD ME LOTS OF *STUFF*. I'D GET ALL KINDS OF FOLKS IN THE SHOP--EVEN NIPS LIKE YOU--GIVIN' ME EVERYTHING THEY *HAD*.
THEN THE WORLD WENT TO HELL AND I WAS LEFT WITH THE STUFF AND NOTHING TO DO WITH IT.
--UNTIL I FOUND MY *MISSION*, THAT IS.
YEAH...MY *MISSION*.
I'M BUILDING ME A *SPACESHIP*.
BUT SHE DON'T *WORK* YET. ME, I FIGGER IT'S THE *WARP DRIVE*-- LIKE IN *STAR TREK*.
THOUGHT MAYBE SIS'S *MIXER* WOULDA FIXED IT-- BUT SHE WOULDN'T LET ME *HAVE* IT.
ALMOST GAVE UP.
THEN *YOU* CAME ALONG... WITH THOSE *ARMS*...
AH!
NOW WHEREZZAT *LAZER*...
OKAY, STRANGER. YOU JUST LIE REAL *STILL*, NOW.
IT'LL ONLY HURT A *MINNIT*.

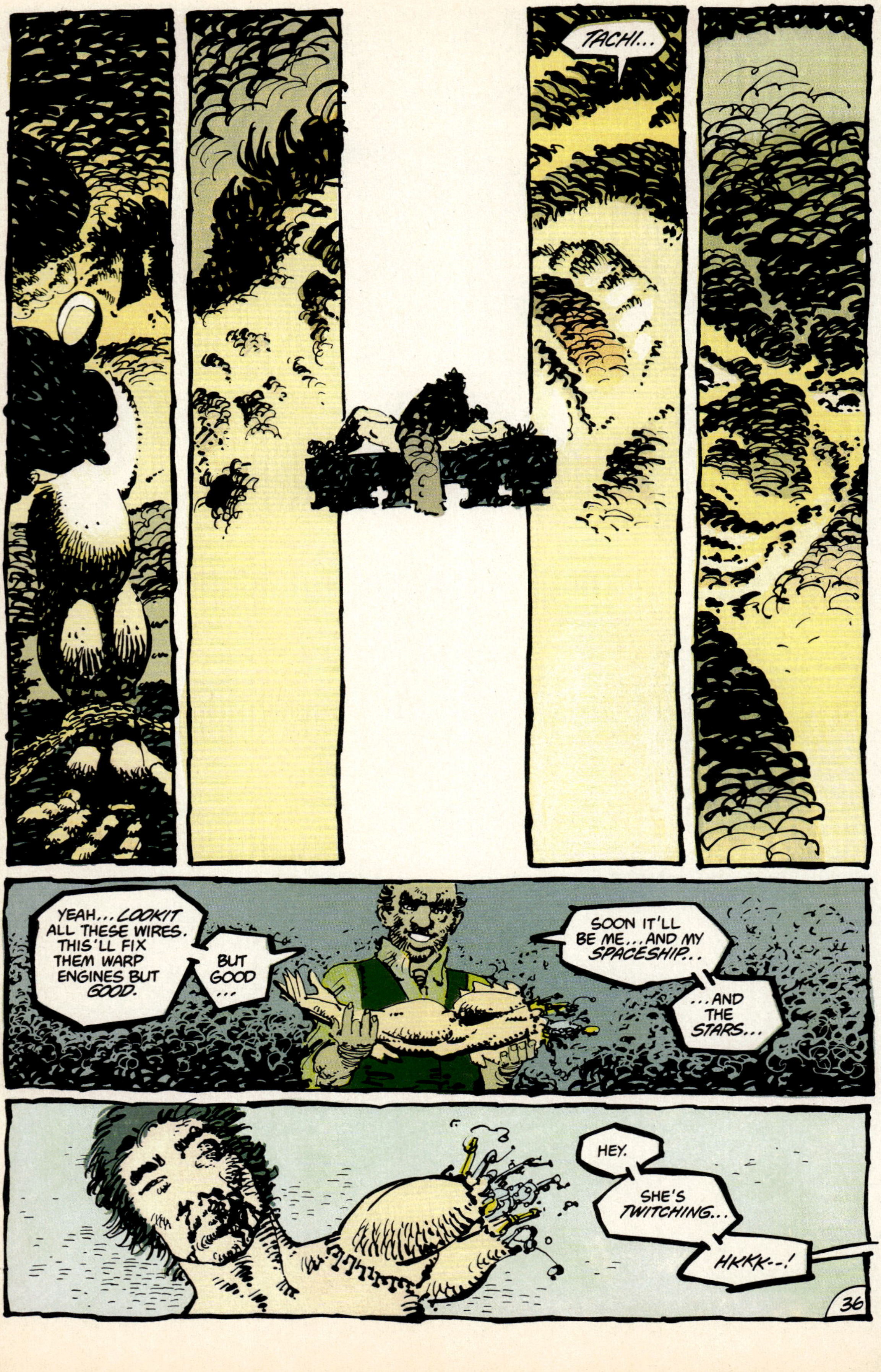
TACHI...
YEAH... LOOKIT ALL THESE WIRES. THIS'LL FIX THEM WARP ENGINES BUT GOOD.
BUT GOOD...
SOON IT'LL BE ME... AND MY SPACESHIP...
...AND THE STARS...
HEY.
SHE'S TWITCHING...
HKKK--!

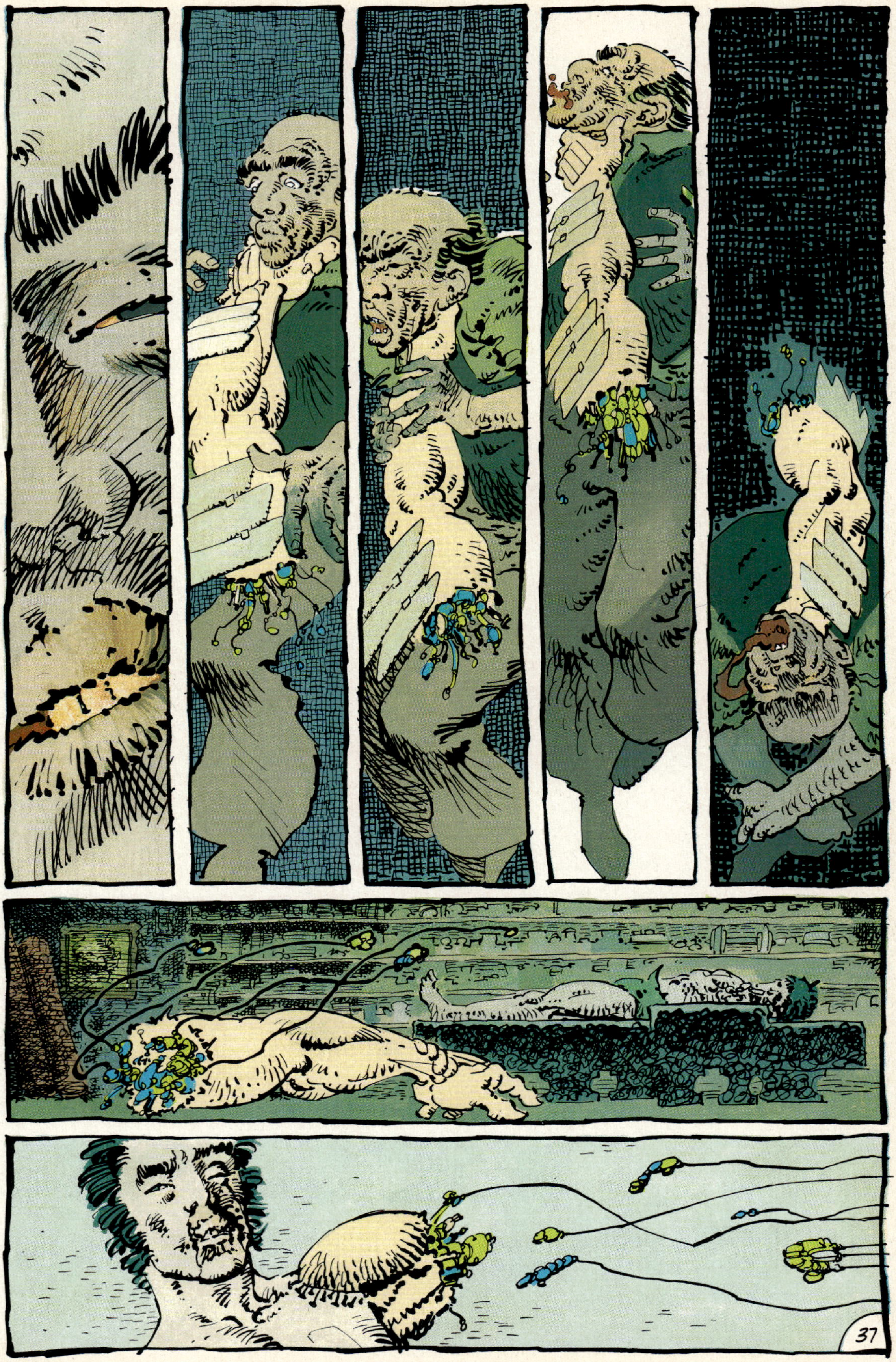

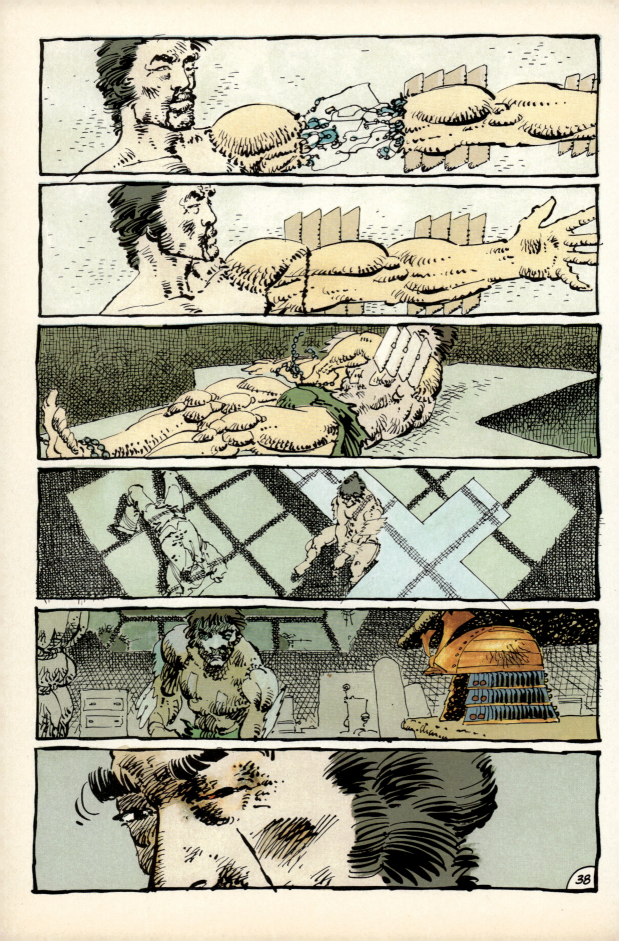

38

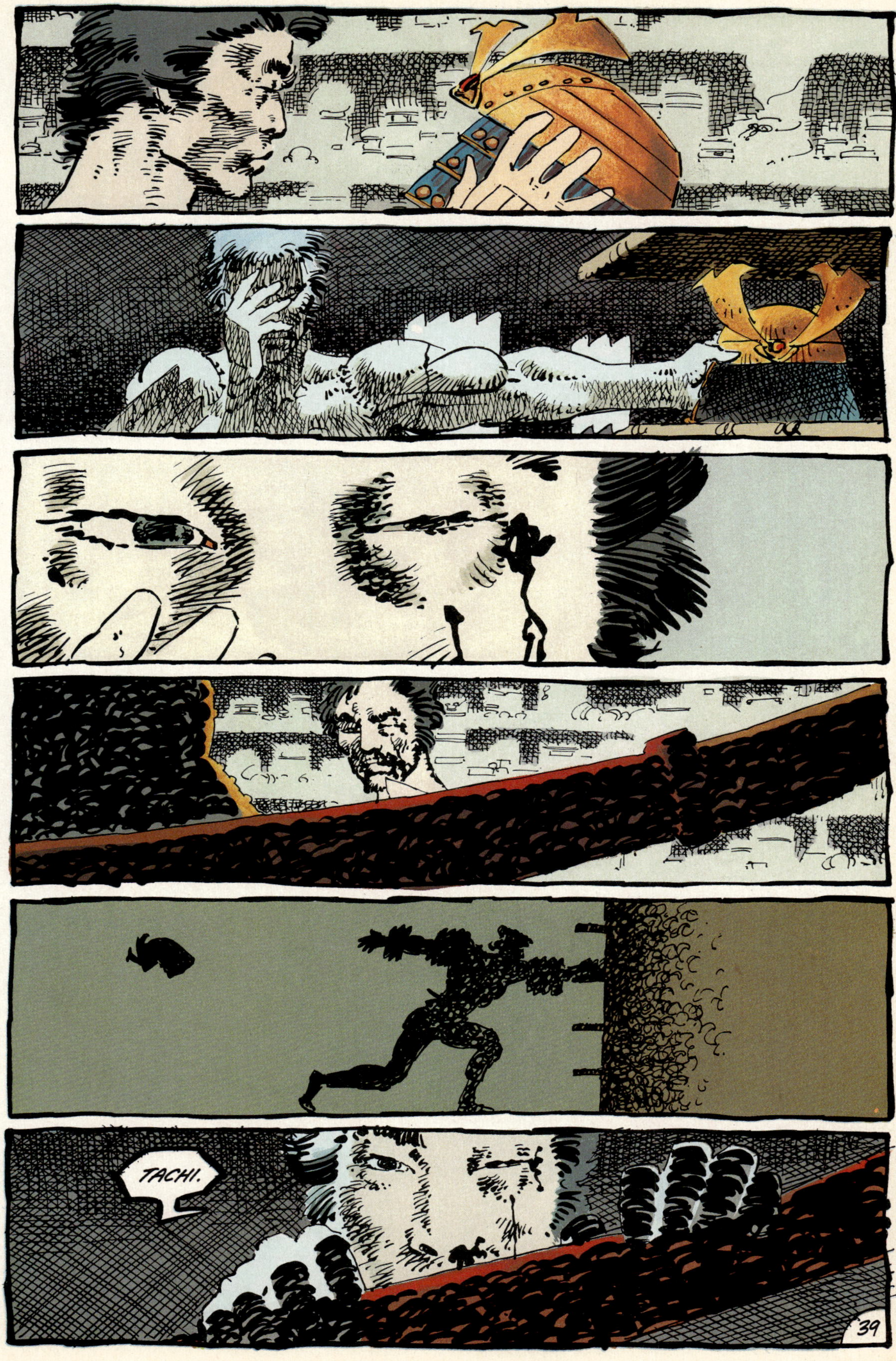
TACHI.

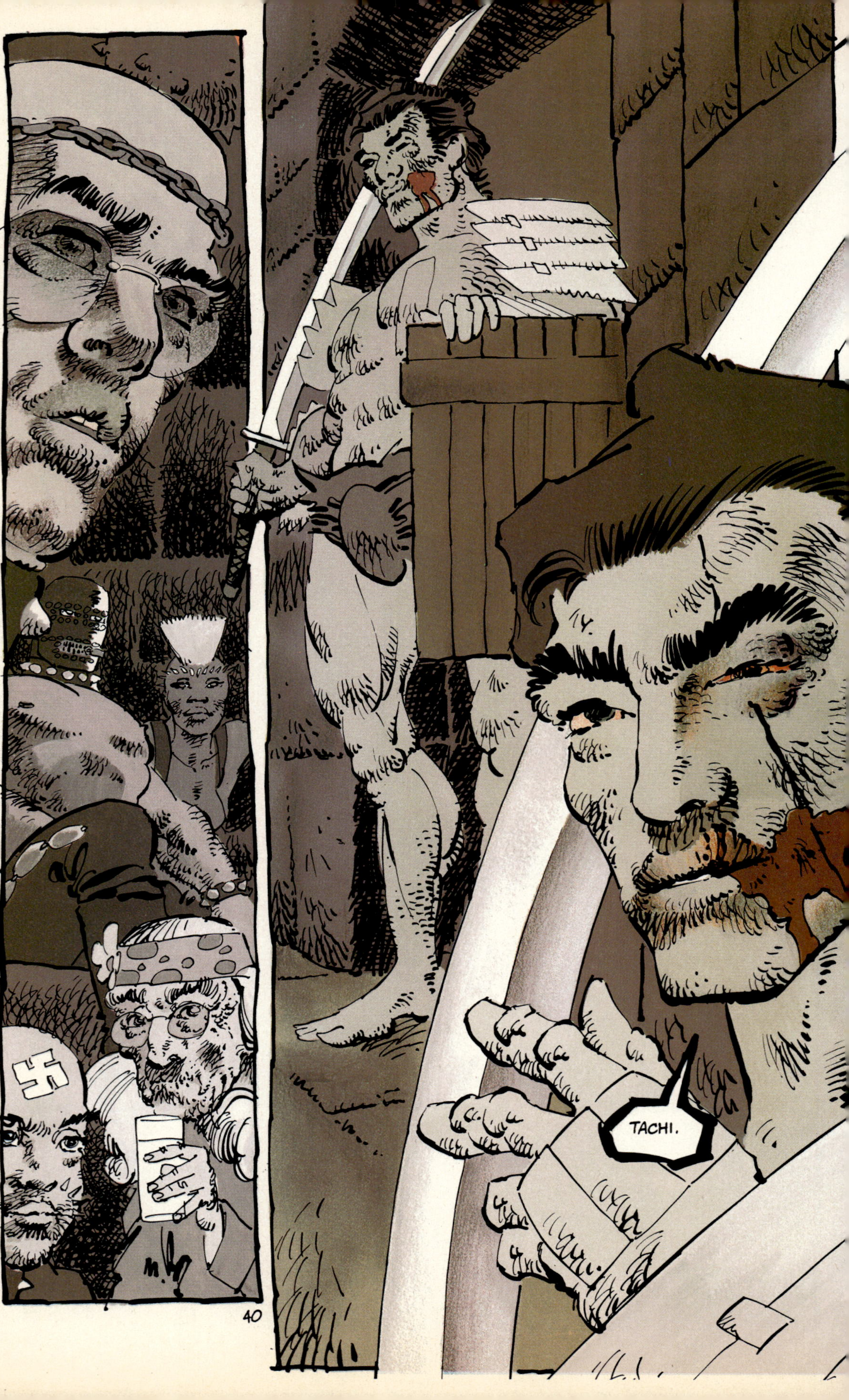
TACHI.

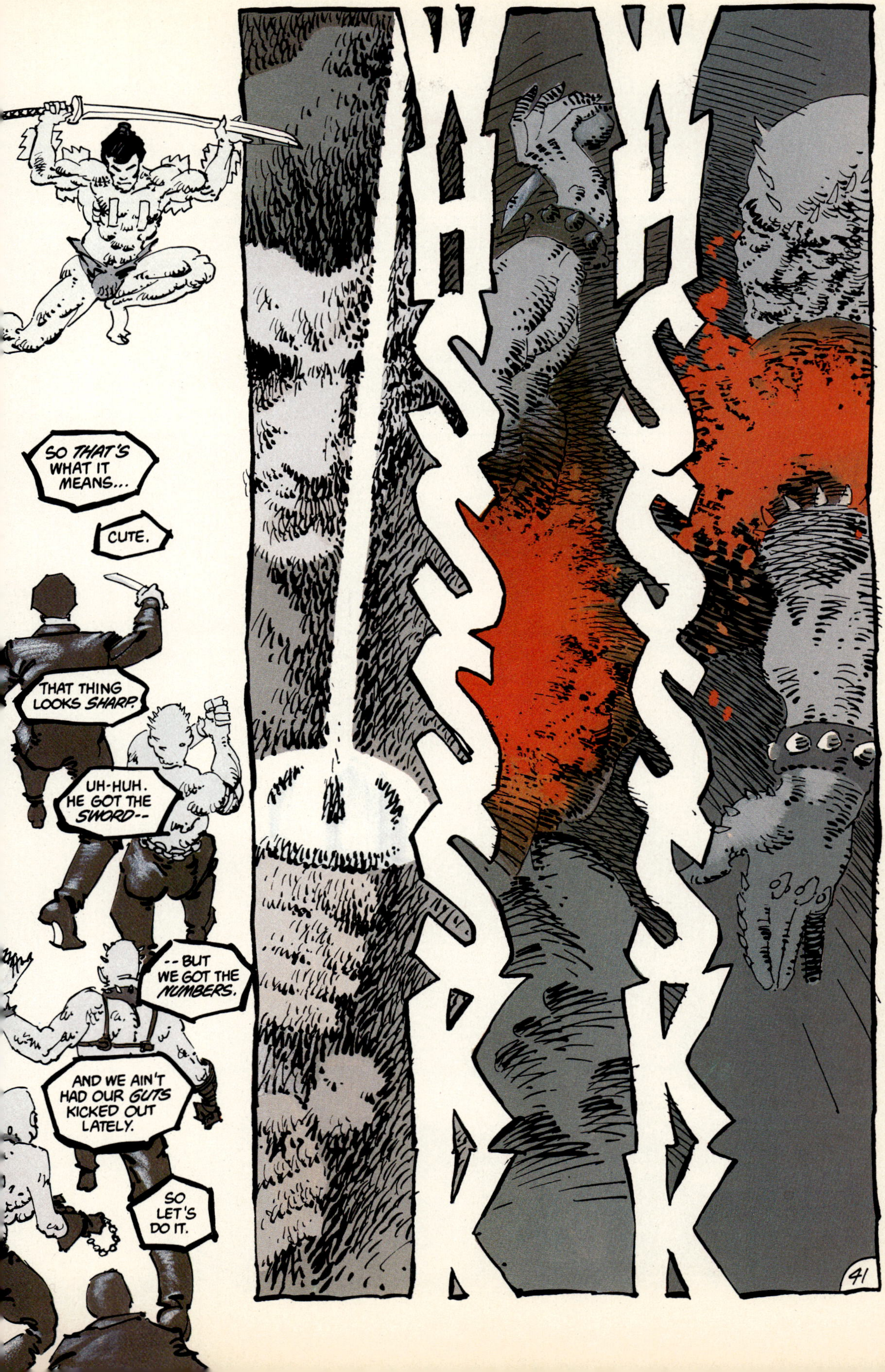
SO THAT'S WHAT IT MEANS...
CUTE.
THAT THING LOOKS SHARP.
UH-HUH. HE GOT THE SWORD--
--BUT WE GOT THE NUMBERS.
AND WE AIN'T HAD OUR GUTS KICKED OUT LATELY.
SO LET'S DO IT.
HAWWSSSSHHKK

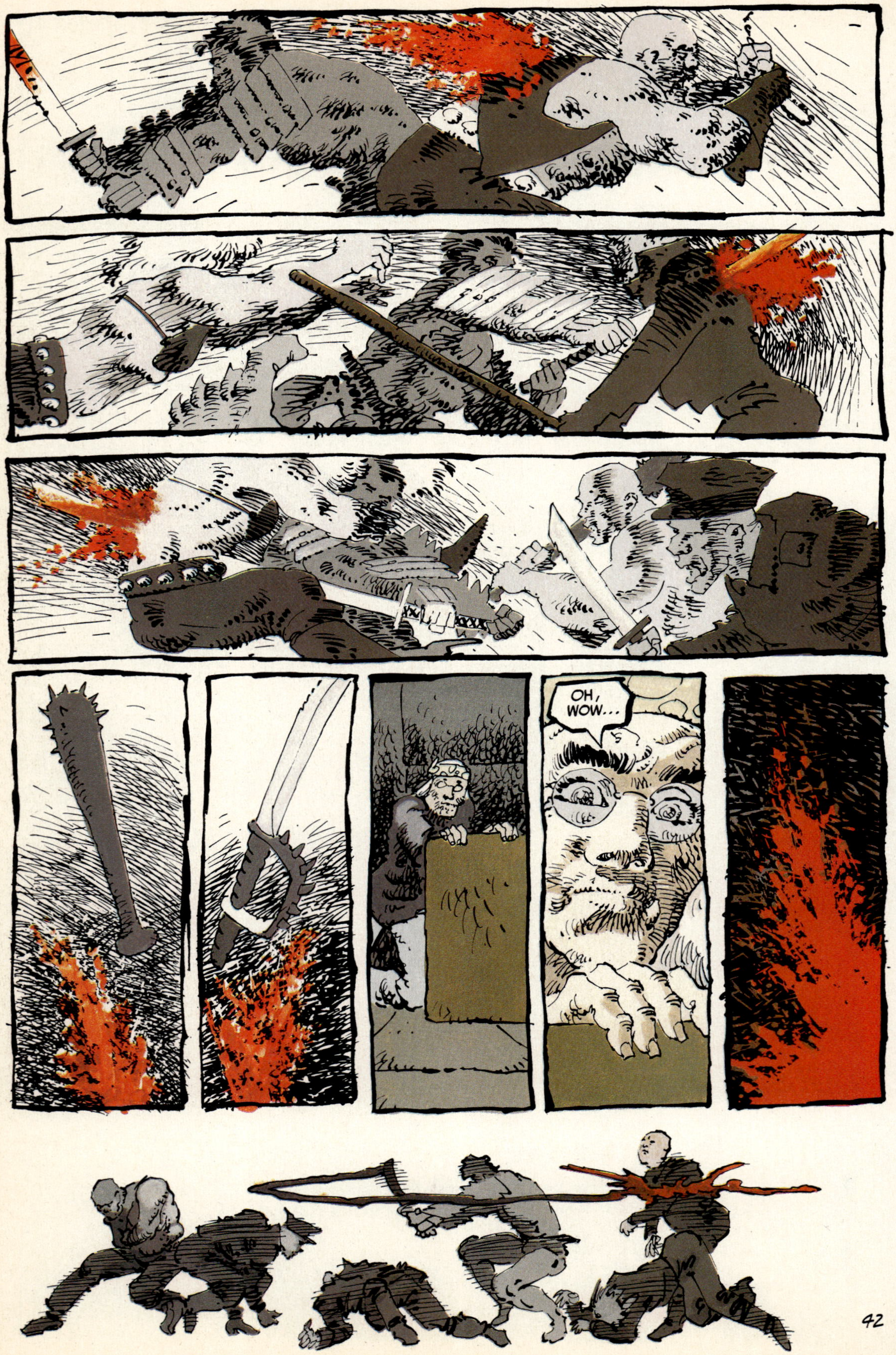
OH, WOW...

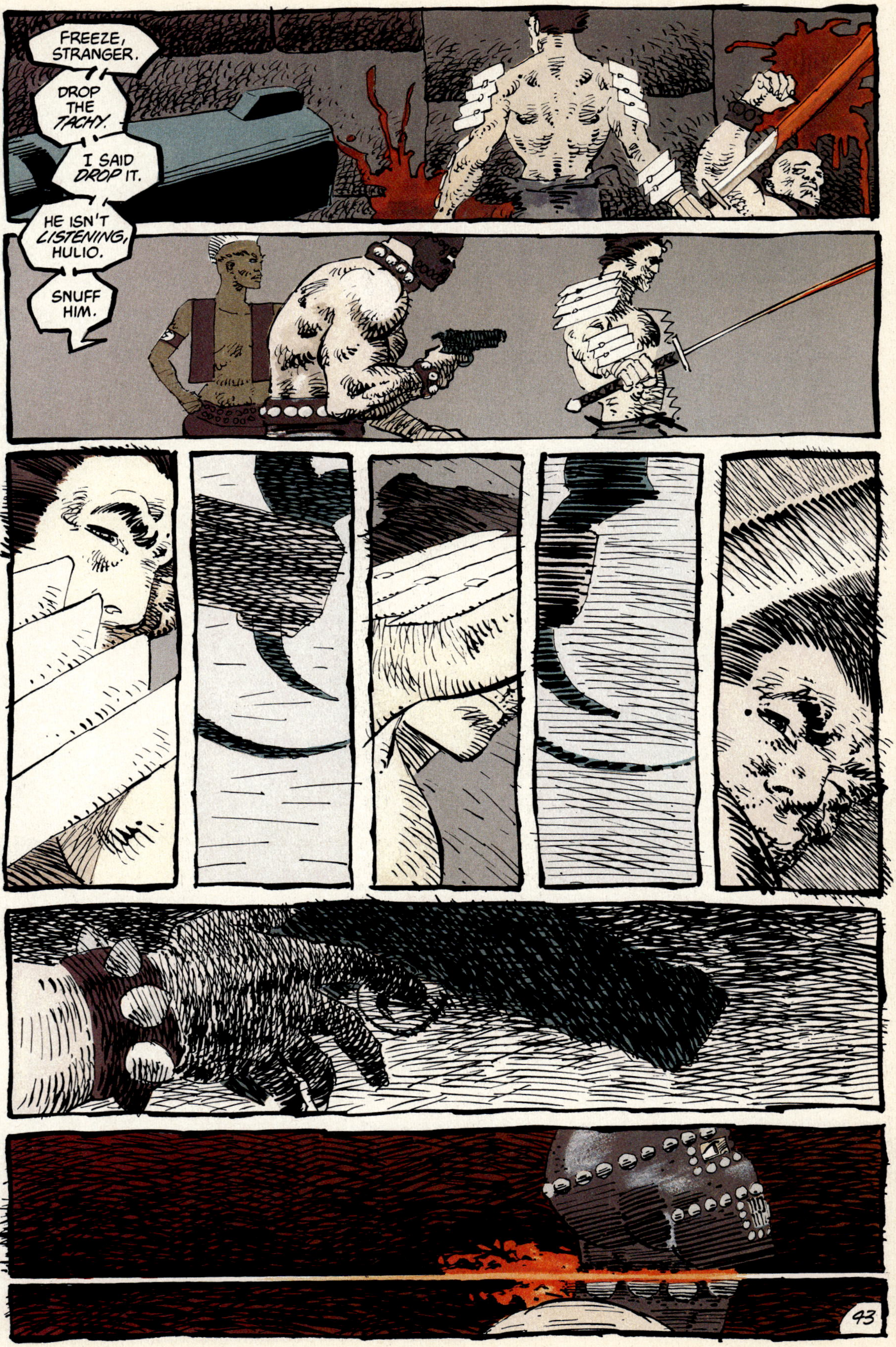
FREEZE, STRANGER.
DROP THE TACHY.
I SAID DROP IT.
HE ISN'T LISTENING, HULIO.
SNUFF HIM.

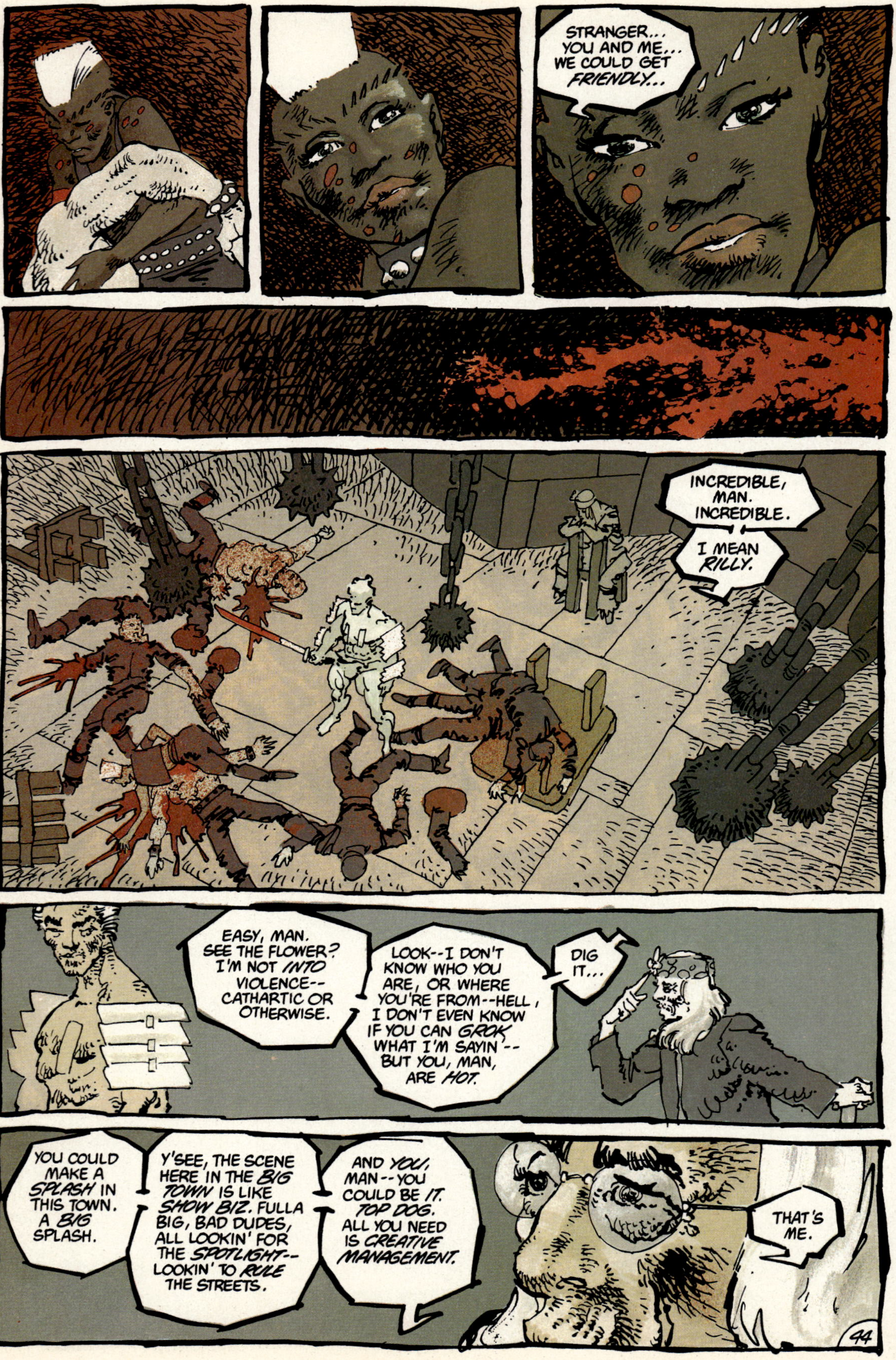
STRANGER... YOU AND ME... WE COULD GET FRIENDLY...
INCREDIBLE, MAN. INCREDIBLE.
I MEAN RILLY.
EASY, MAN. SEE THE FLOWER? I'M NOT INTO VIOLENCE-- CATHARTIC OR OTHERWISE.
LOOK--I DON'T KNOW WHO YOU ARE, OR WHERE YOU'RE FROM--HELL, I DON'T EVEN KNOW IF YOU CAN GROK WHAT I'M SAYIN'-- BUT YOU, MAN, ARE HOT.
DIG IT...
YOU COULD MAKE A SPLASH IN THIS TOWN. A BIG SPLASH.
Y'SEE, THE SCENE HERE IN THE BIG TOWN IS LIKE SHOW BIZ. FULLA BIG, BAD DUDES, ALL LOOKIN' FOR THE SPOTLIGHT-- LOOKIN' TO RULE THE STREETS.
AND YOU, MAN--YOU COULD BE IT. TOP DOG. ALL YOU NEED IS CREATIVE MANAGEMENT.
THAT'S ME.
44

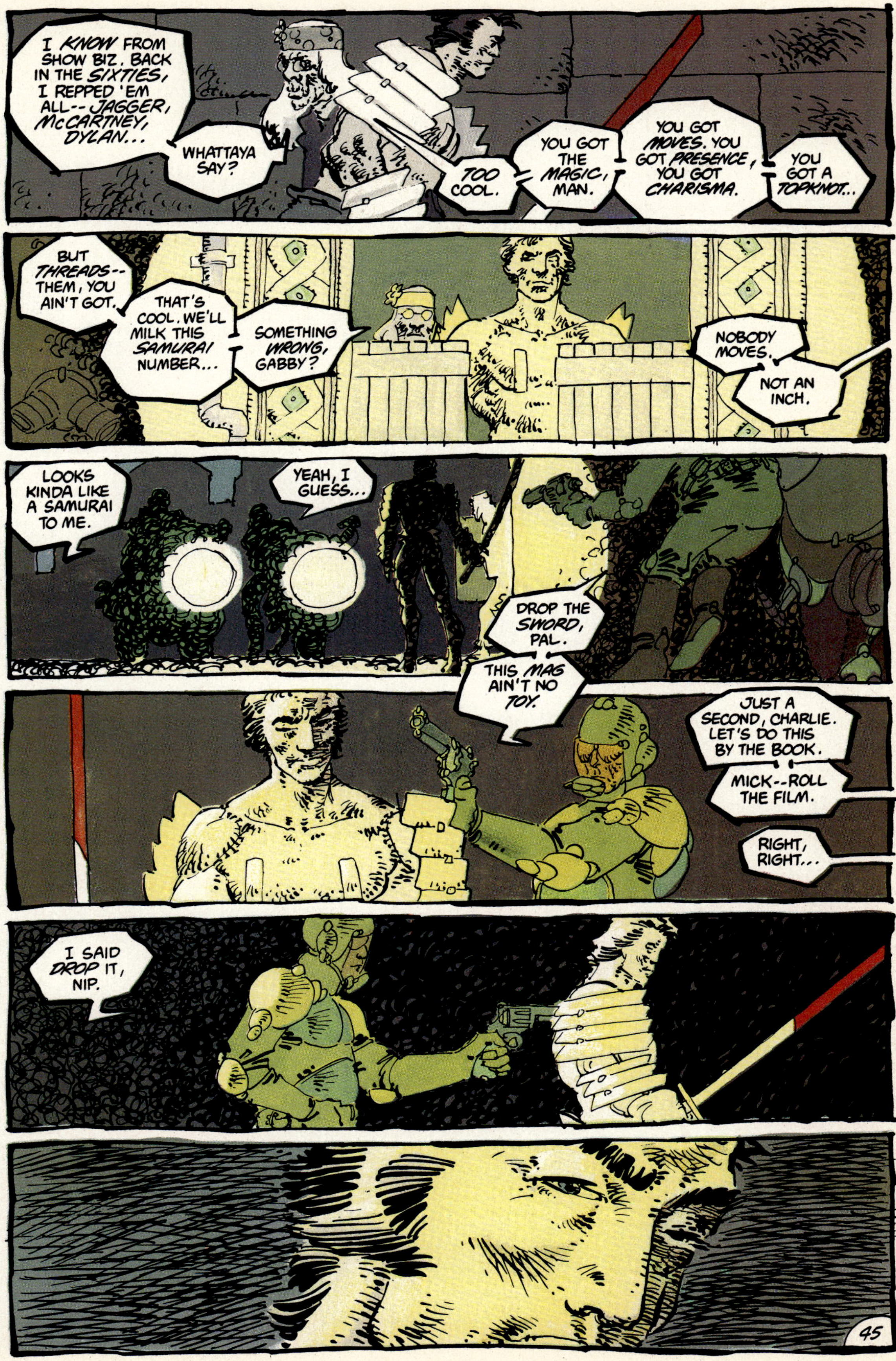

I KNOW FROM SHOW BIZ. BACK IN THE SIXTIES, I REPPED 'EM ALL--JAGGER, McCARTNEY, DYLAN...
WHATTAYA SAY?
TOO COOL.
YOU GOT THE MAGIC, MAN.
YOU GOT MOVES. YOU GOT PRESENCE, YOU GOT CHARISMA.
YOU GOT A TOPKNOT...
BUT THREADS--THEM, YOU AIN'T GOT.
THAT'S COOL. WE'LL MILK THIS SAMURAI NUMBER...
SOMETHING WRONG, GABBY?
NOBODY MOVES.
NOT AN INCH.
LOOKS KINDA LIKE A SAMURAI TO ME.
YEAH, I GUESS...
DROP THE SWORD, PAL.
THIS MAG AIN'T NO TOY.
JUST A SECOND, CHARLIE. LET'S DO THIS BY THE BOOK.
MICK--ROLL THE FILM.
RIGHT, RIGHT...
I SAID DROP IT, NIP.

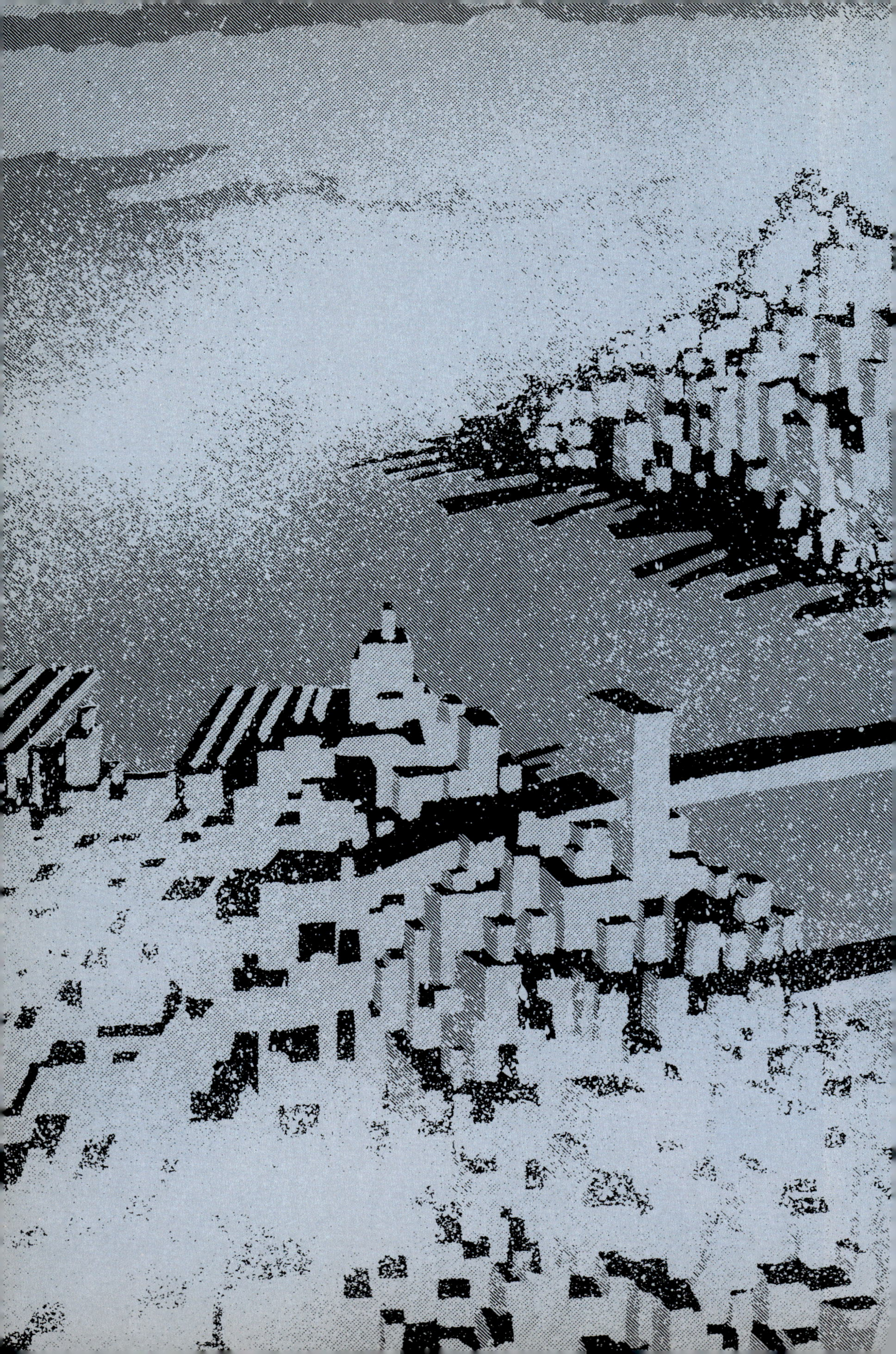

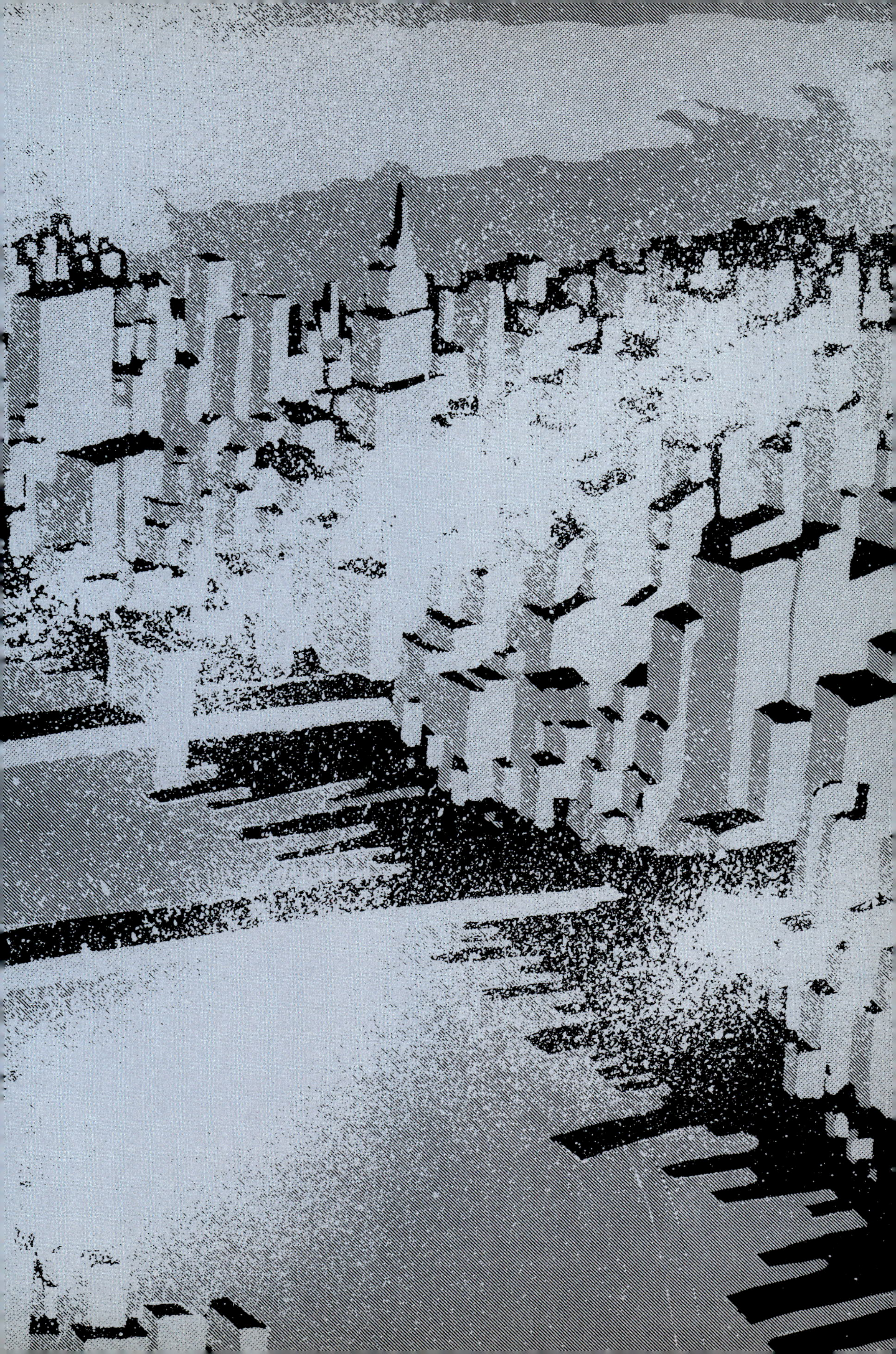

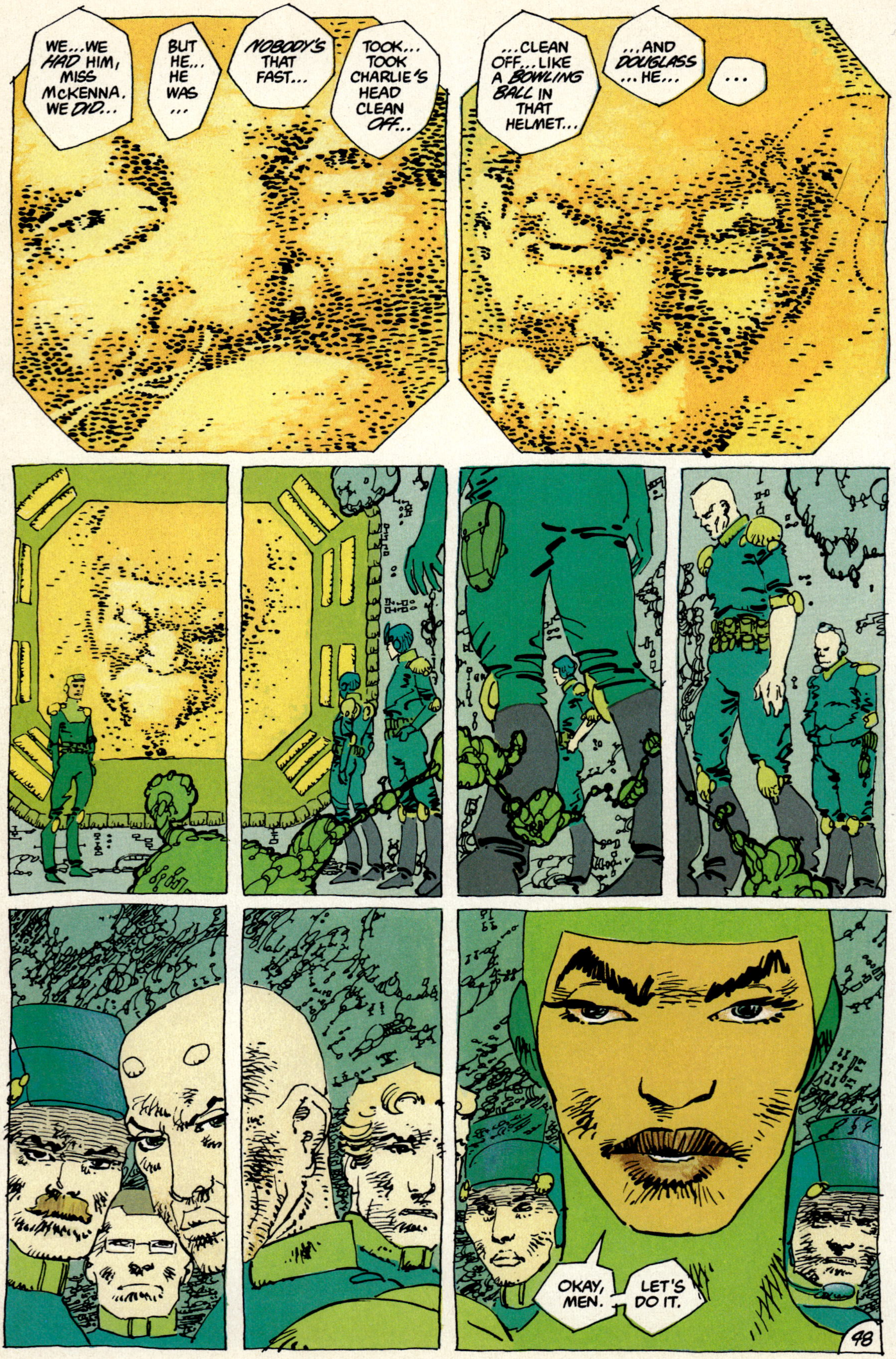
WE...WE HAD HIM, MISS McKENNA. WE DID...
BUT HE... HE WAS ...
NOBODY'S THAT FAST...
TOOK... TOOK CHARLIE'S HEAD CLEAN OFF...
...CLEAN OFF... LIKE A BOWLING BALL IN THAT HELMET...
...AND DOUGLASS ...HE...
...
OKAY, MEN.
LET'S DO IT.

CHAPTER THREE

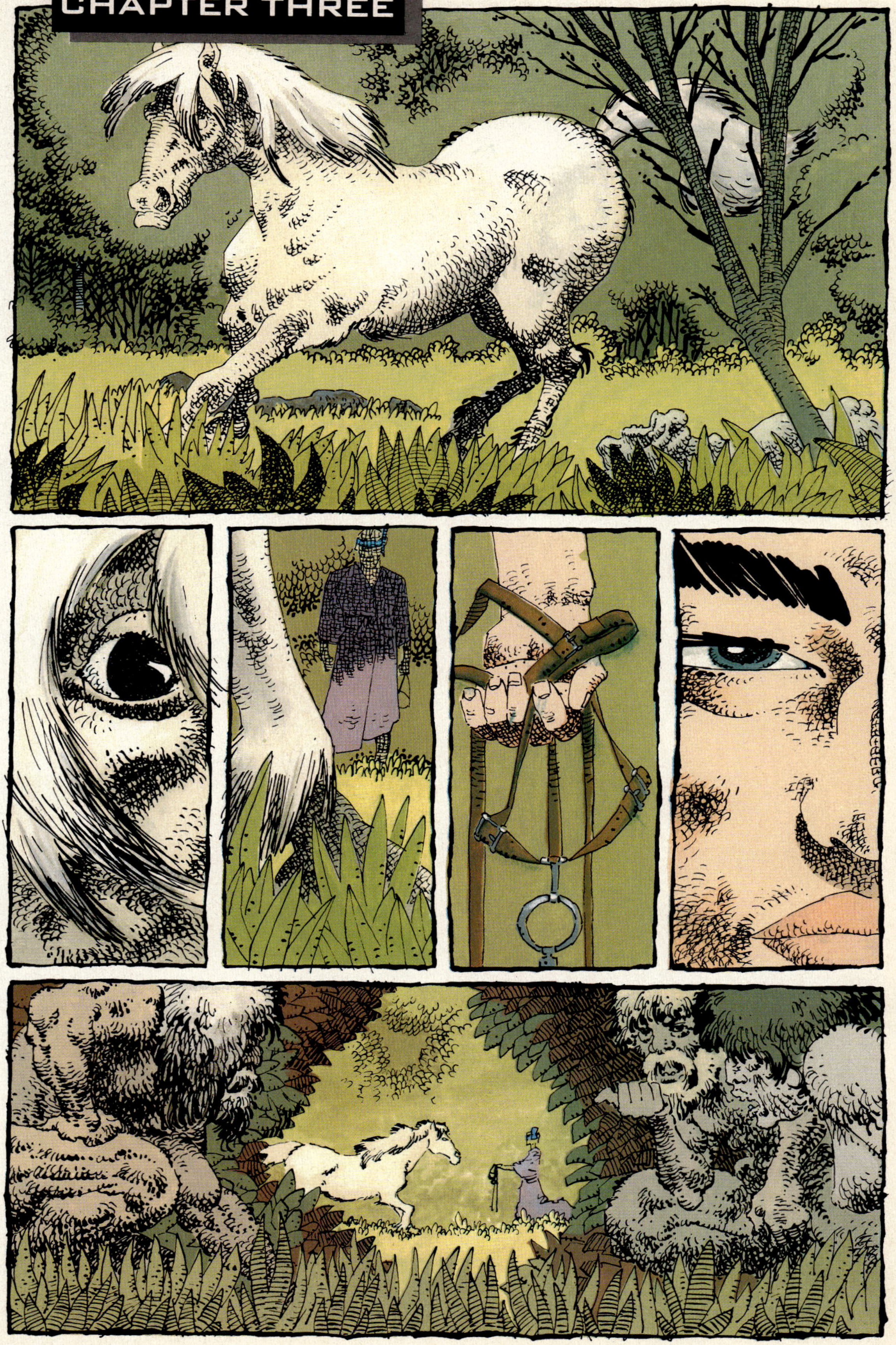

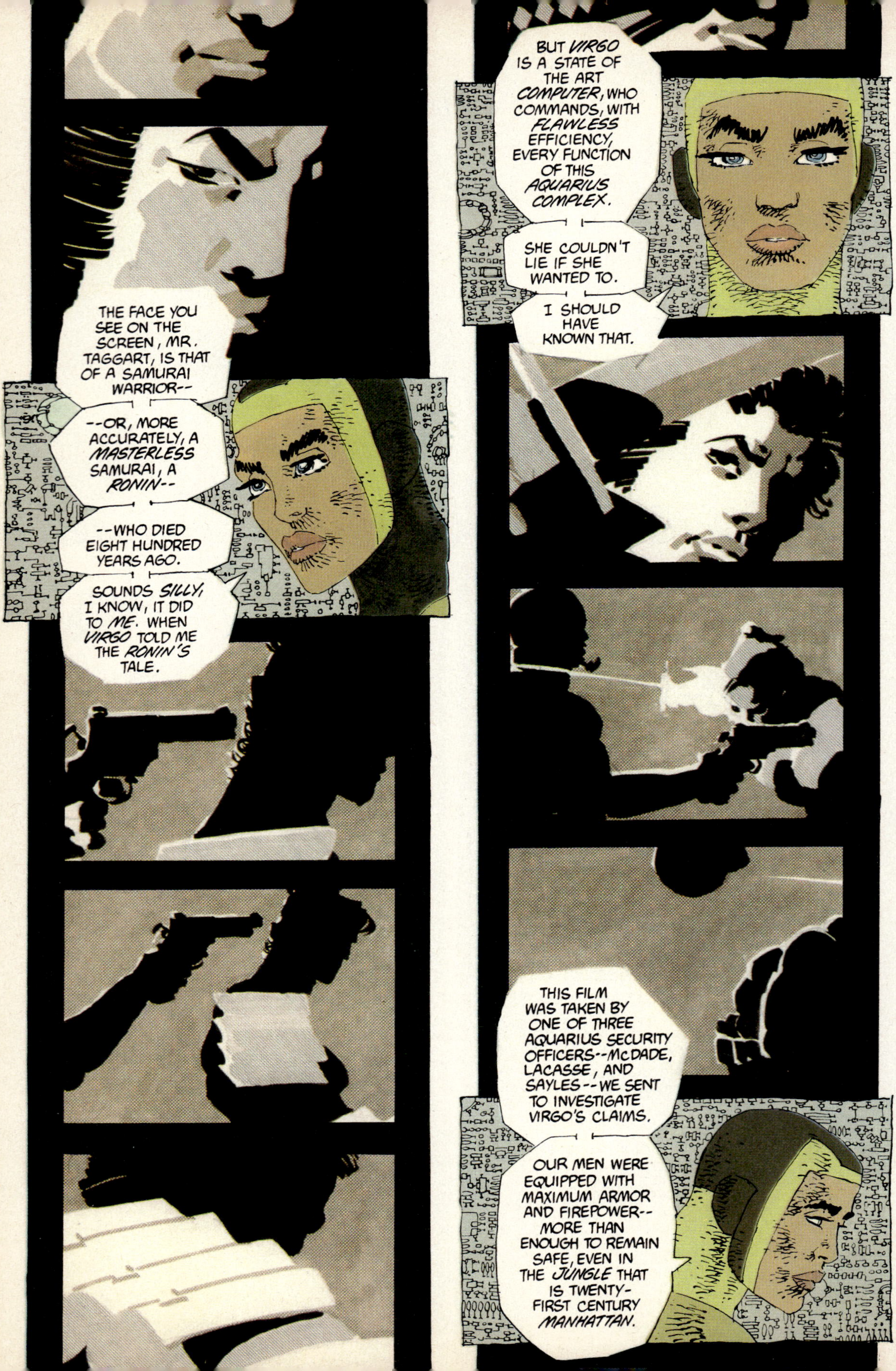
THE FACE YOU SEE ON THE SCREEN, MR. TAGGART, IS THAT OF A SAMURAI WARRIOR--
--OR, MORE ACCURATELY, A MASTERLESS SAMURAI, A RONIN--
--WHO DIED EIGHT HUNDRED YEARS AGO.
SOUNDS SILLY, I KNOW, IT DID TO ME. WHEN VIRGO TOLD ME THE RONIN'S TALE.
BUT VIRGO IS A STATE OF THE ART COMPUTER, WHO COMMANDS, WITH FLAWLESS EFFICIENCY, EVERY FUNCTION OF THIS AQUARIUS COMPLEX.
SHE COULDN'T LIE IF SHE WANTED TO.
I SHOULD HAVE KNOWN THAT.
THIS FILM WAS TAKEN BY ONE OF THREE AQUARIUS SECURITY OFFICERS--McDADE, LACASSE, AND SAYLES--WE SENT TO INVESTIGATE VIRGO'S CLAIMS.
OUR MEN WERE EQUIPPED WITH MAXIMUM ARMOR AND FIREPOWER--MORE THAN ENOUGH TO REMAIN SAFE, EVEN IN THE JUNGLE THAT IS TWENTY-FIRST CENTURY MANHATTAN.

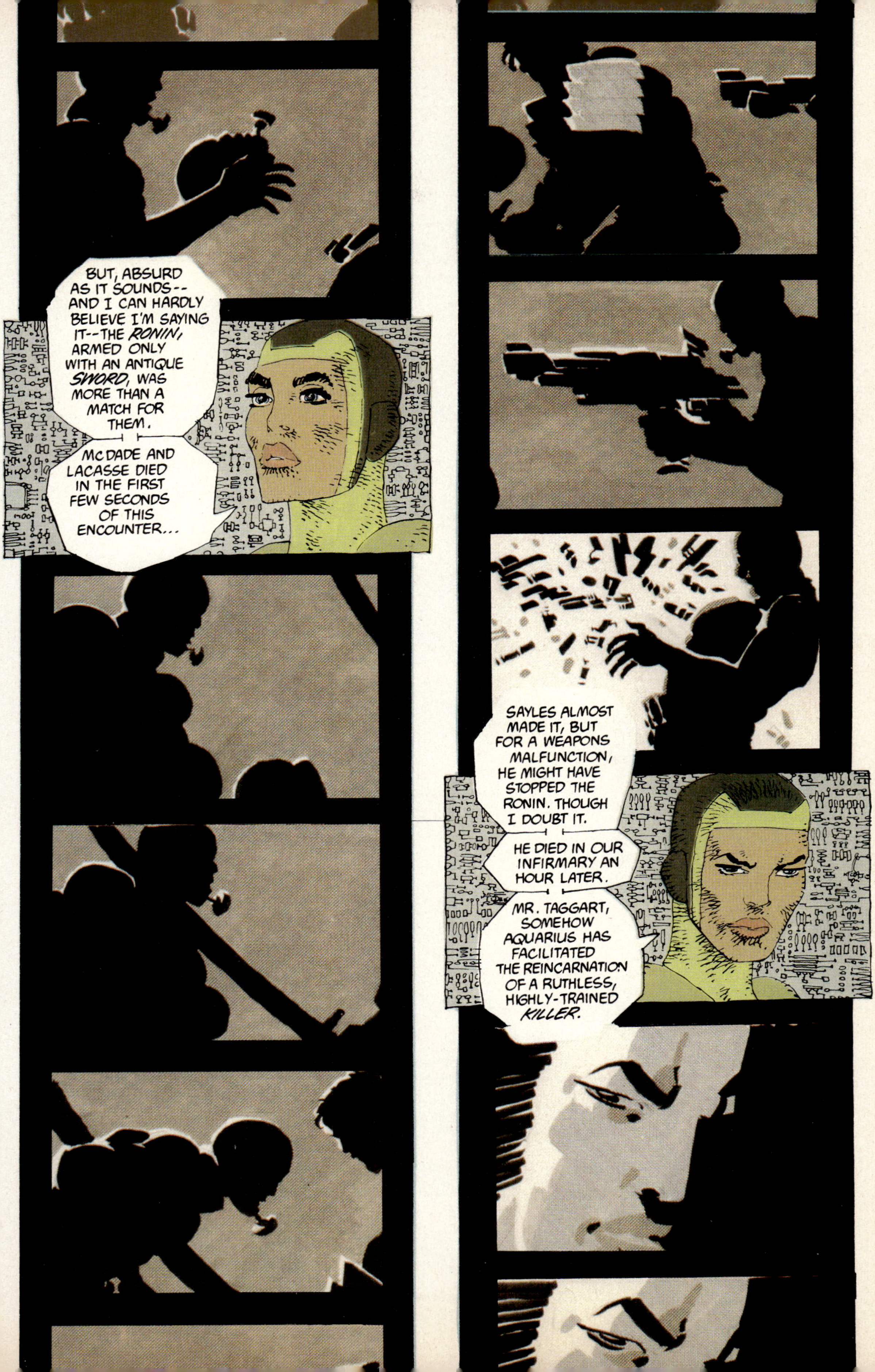
BUT, ABSURD AS IT SOUNDS-- AND I CAN HARDLY BELIEVE I'M SAYING IT--THE RONIN, ARMED ONLY WITH AN ANTIQUE SWORD, WAS MORE THAN A MATCH FOR THEM.
McDADE AND LACASSE DIED IN THE FIRST FEW SECONDS OF THIS ENCOUNTER...
SAYLES ALMOST MADE IT, BUT FOR A WEAPONS MALFUNCTION, HE MIGHT HAVE STOPPED THE RONIN. THOUGH I DOUBT IT.
HE DIED IN OUR INFIRMARY AN HOUR LATER.
MR. TAGGART, SOMEHOW AQUARIUS HAS FACILITATED THE REINCARNATION OF A RUTHLESS, HIGHLY-TRAINED KILLER.

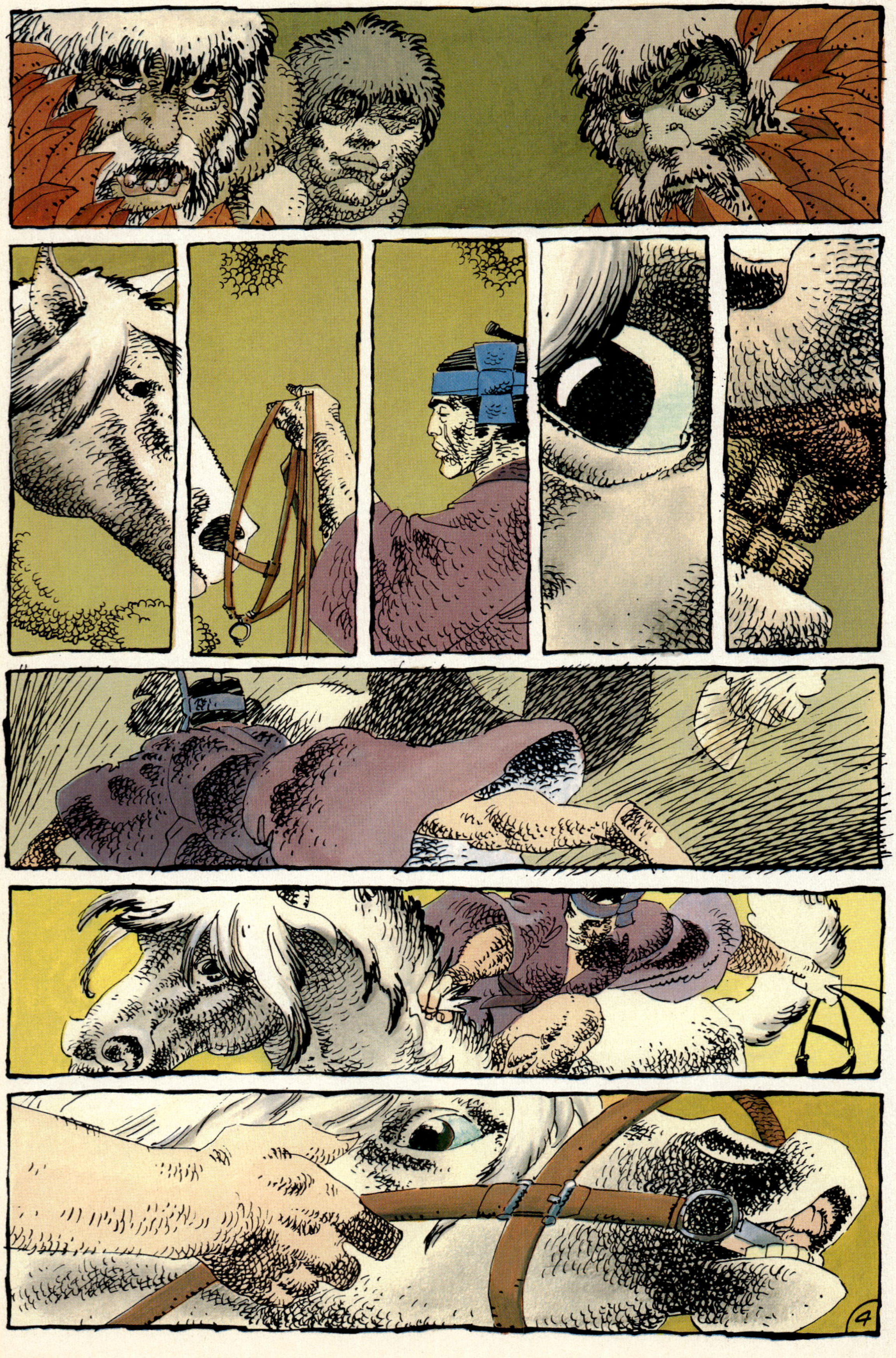

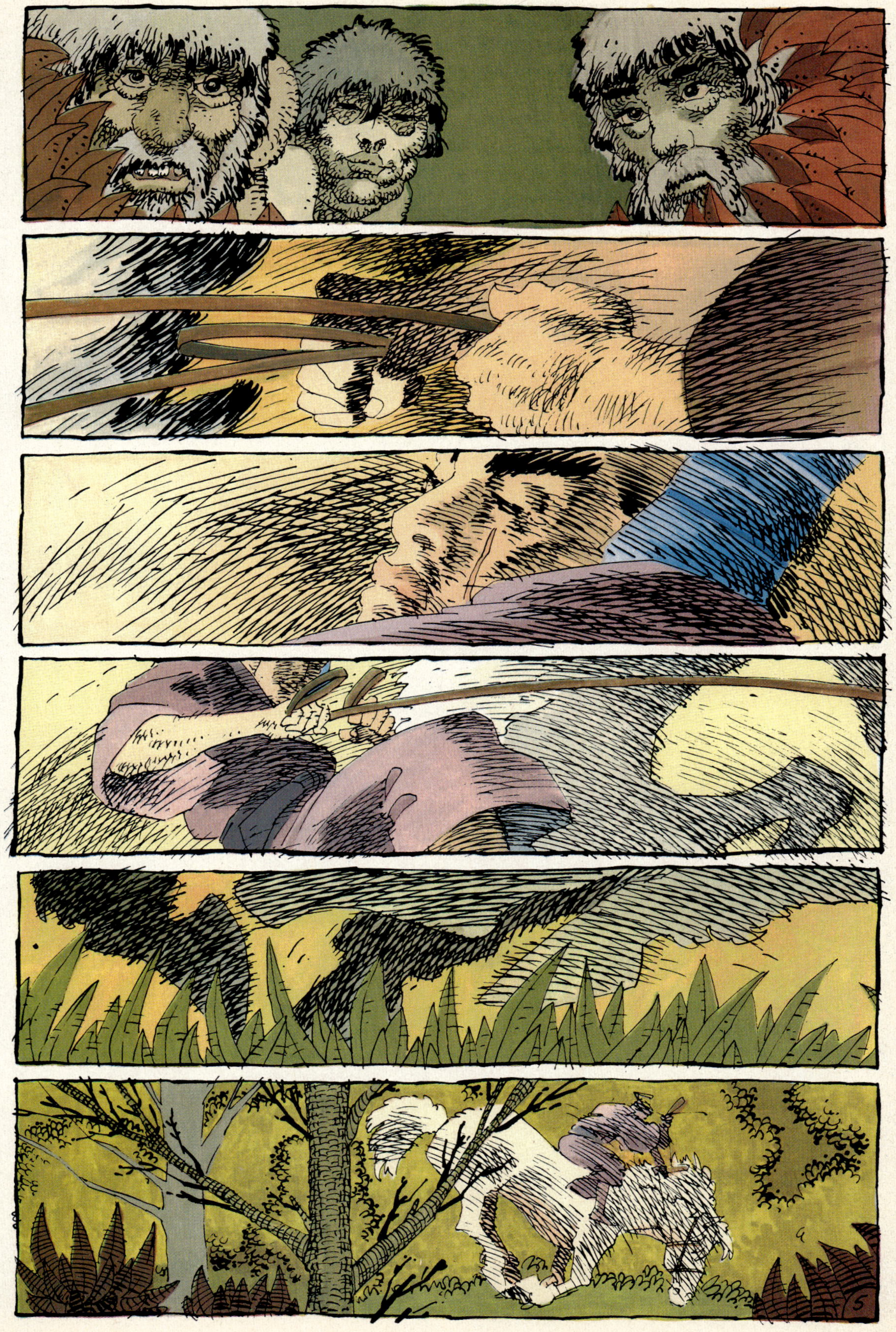

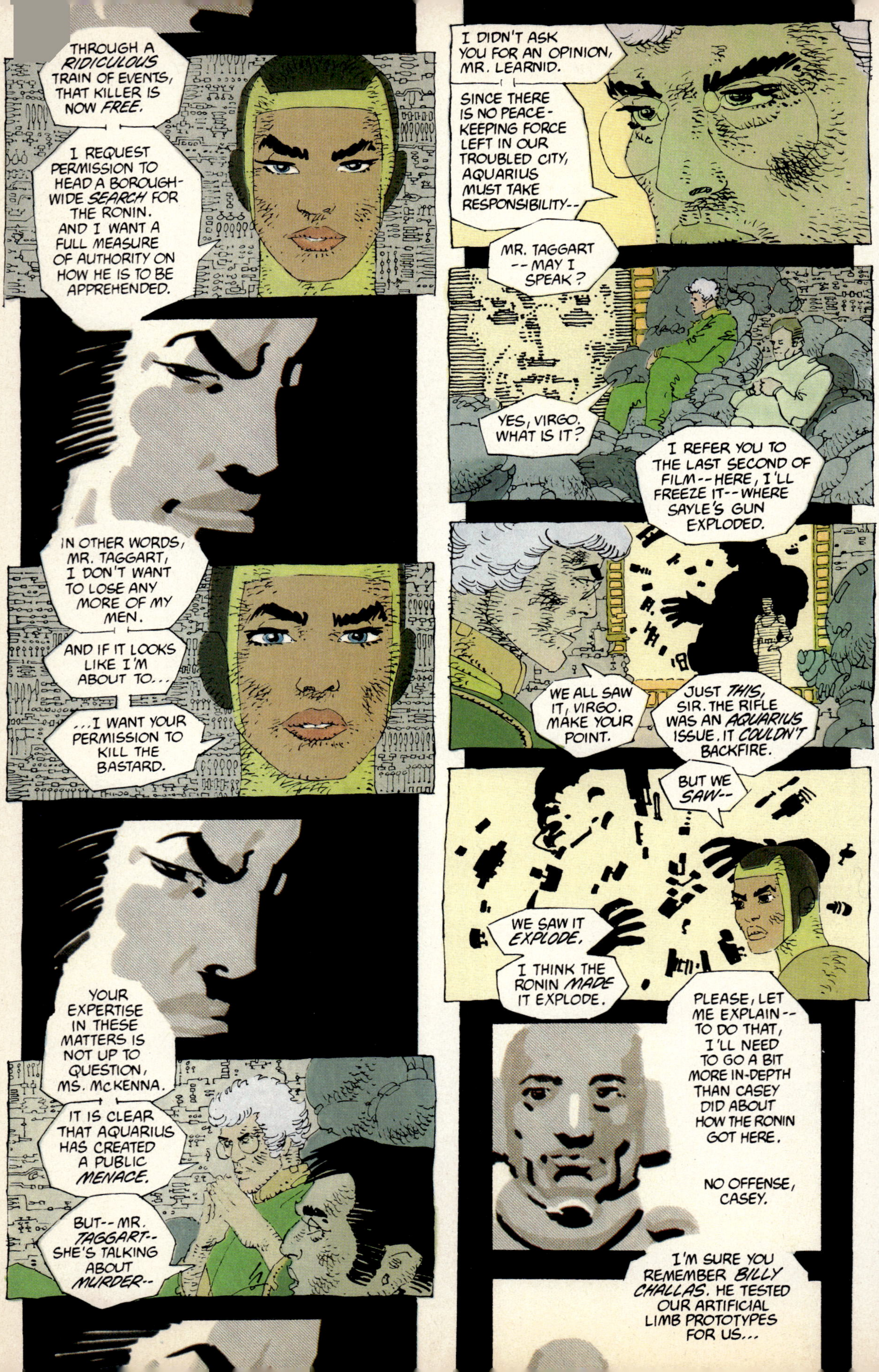
THROUGH A RIDICULOUS TRAIN OF EVENTS, THAT KILLER IS NOW FREE.
I REQUEST PERMISSION TO HEAD A BOROUGH-WIDE SEARCH FOR THE RONIN. AND I WANT A FULL MEASURE OF AUTHORITY ON HOW HE IS TO BE APPREHENDED.
IN OTHER WORDS, MR. TAGGART, I DON'T WANT TO LOSE ANY MORE OF MY MEN.
AND IF IT LOOKS LIKE I'M ABOUT TO...
...I WANT YOUR PERMISSION TO KILL THE BASTARD.
YOUR EXPERTISE IN THESE MATTERS IS NOT UP TO QUESTION, MS. McKENNA.
IT IS CLEAR THAT AQUARIUS HAS CREATED A PUBLIC MENACE.
BUT--MR. TAGGART--SHE'S TALKING ABOUT MURDER--
I DIDN'T ASK YOU FOR AN OPINION, MR. LEARNID.
SINCE THERE IS NO PEACE-KEEPING FORCE LEFT IN OUR TROUBLED CITY, AQUARIUS MUST TAKE RESPONSIBILITY--
MR. TAGGART--MAY I SPEAK?
YES, VIRGO. WHAT IS IT?
I REFER YOU TO THE LAST SECOND OF FILM--HERE, I'LL FREEZE IT--WHERE SAYLE'S GUN EXPLODED.
WE ALL SAW IT, VIRGO. MAKE YOUR POINT.
JUST THIS, SIR. THE RIFLE WAS AN AQUARIUS ISSUE. IT COULDN'T BACKFIRE.
BUT WE SAW--
WE SAW IT EXPLODE.
I THINK THE RONIN MADE IT EXPLODE.
PLEASE, LET ME EXPLAIN--TO DO THAT, I'LL NEED TO GO A BIT MORE IN-DEPTH THAN CASEY DID ABOUT HOW THE RONIN GOT HERE.
NO OFFENSE, CASEY.
I'M SURE YOU REMEMBER BILLY CHALLAS. HE TESTED OUR ARTIFICIAL LIMB PROTOTYPES FOR US...

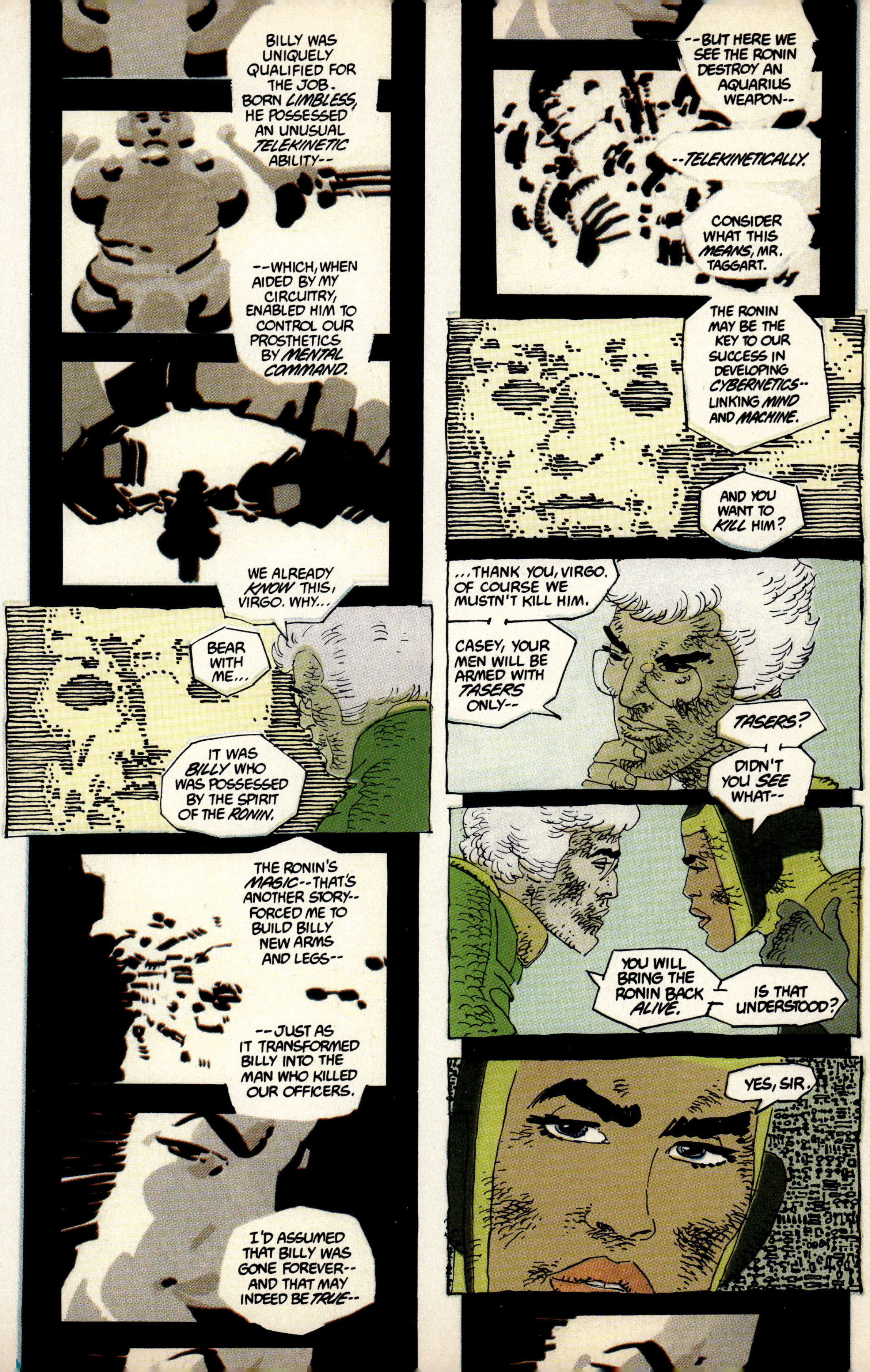
BILLY WAS UNIQUELY QUALIFIED FOR THE JOB. BORN *LIMBLESS*, HE POSSESSED AN UNUSUAL *TELEKINETIC* ABILITY--
--WHICH, WHEN AIDED BY MY CIRCUITRY, ENABLED HIM TO CONTROL OUR PROSTHETICS BY *MENTAL COMMAND*.
WE ALREADY *KNOW* THIS, VIRGO. WHY...
BEAR WITH ME...
IT WAS *BILLY* WHO WAS POSSESSED BY THE SPIRIT OF THE *RONIN*.
THE RONIN'S *MAGIC*--THAT'S ANOTHER STORY--FORCED ME TO BUILD BILLY NEW ARMS AND LEGS--
--JUST AS IT TRANSFORMED BILLY INTO THE MAN WHO KILLED OUR OFFICERS.
I'D ASSUMED THAT BILLY WAS GONE FOREVER--AND THAT MAY INDEED BE *TRUE*--
--BUT HERE WE SEE THE RONIN DESTROY AN AQUARIUS WEAPON--
--*TELEKINETICALLY*.
CONSIDER WHAT THIS *MEANS*, MR. TAGGART.
THE RONIN MAY BE THE KEY TO OUR SUCCESS IN DEVELOPING *CYBERNETICS*--LINKING *MIND* AND *MACHINE*.
AND YOU WANT TO *KILL* HIM?
...THANK YOU, VIRGO. OF COURSE WE MUSTN'T KILL HIM.
CASEY, YOUR MEN WILL BE ARMED WITH *TASERS* ONLY--
TASERS?
DIDN'T YOU *SEE* WHAT--
YOU WILL BRING THE RONIN BACK *ALIVE*.
IS THAT UNDERSTOOD?
YES, SIR.

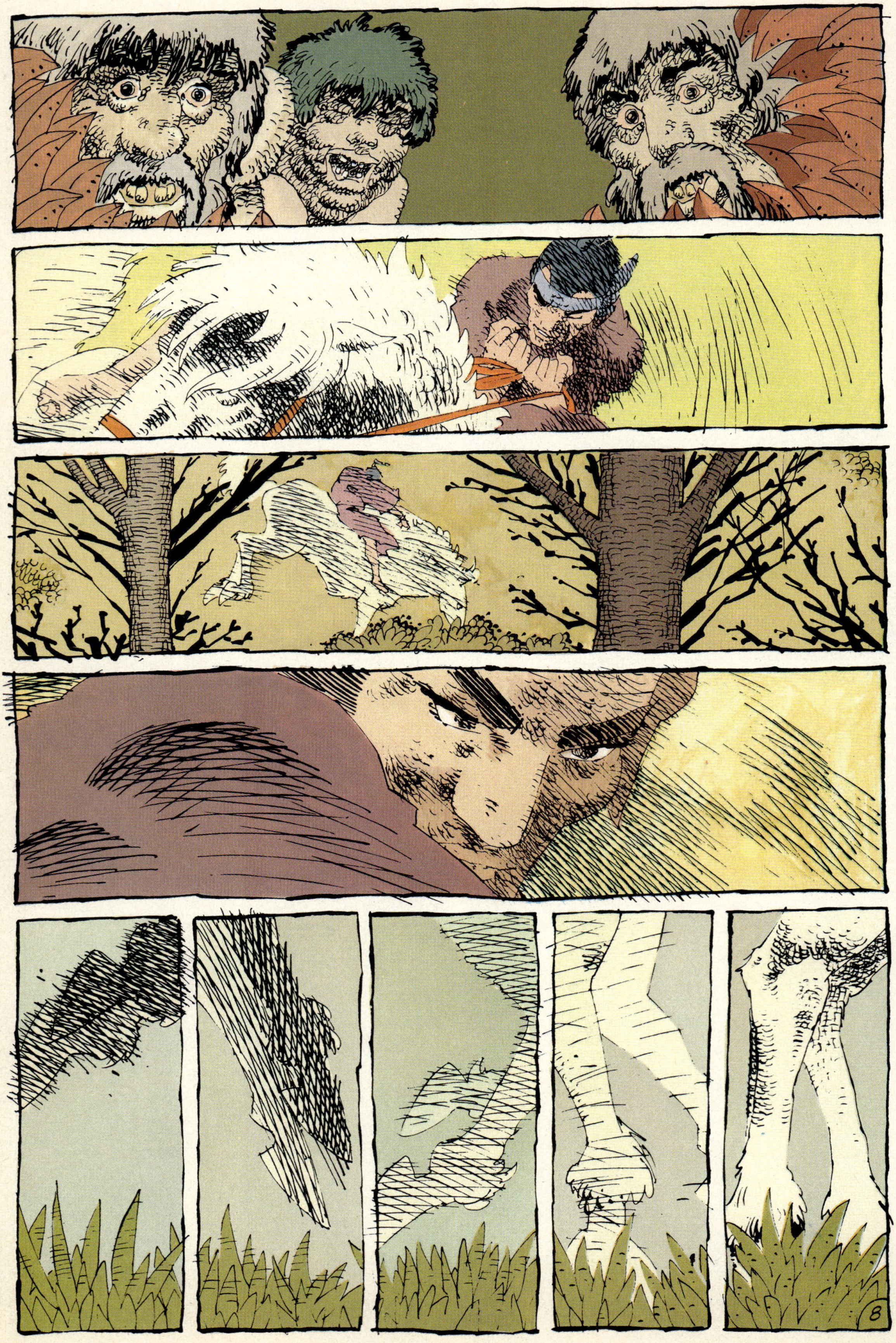

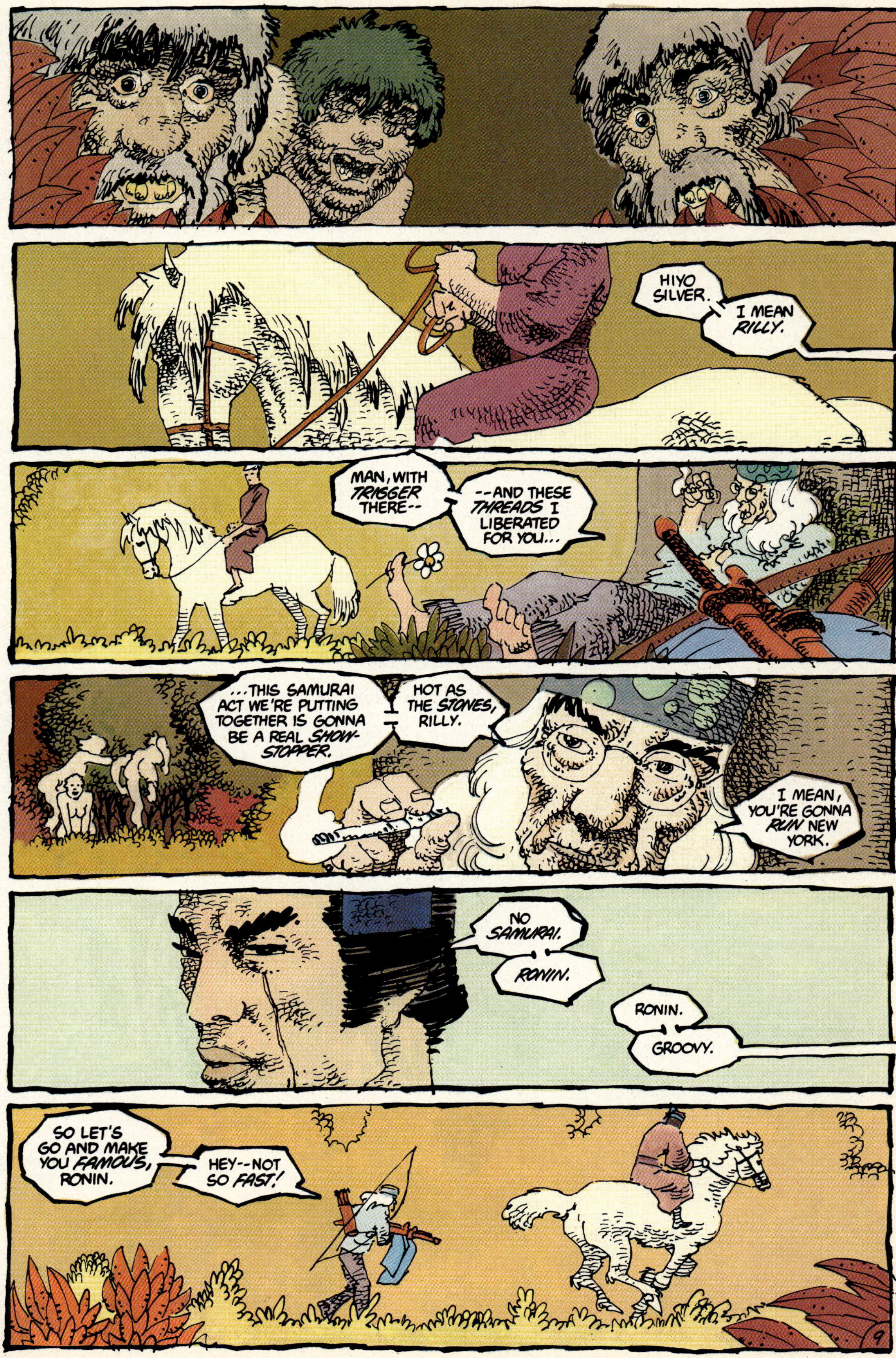
HIYO SILVER.
I MEAN RILLY.
MAN, WITH TRIGGER THERE--
--AND THESE THREADS I LIBERATED FOR YOU...
...THIS SAMURAI ACT WE'RE PUTTING TOGETHER IS GONNA BE A REAL SHOW-STOPPER.
HOT AS THE STONES, RILLY.
I MEAN, YOU'RE GONNA RUN NEW YORK.
NO SAMURAI.
RONIN.
RONIN.
GROOVY.
SO LET'S GO AND MAKE YOU FAMOUS, RONIN.
HEY--NOT SO FAST!

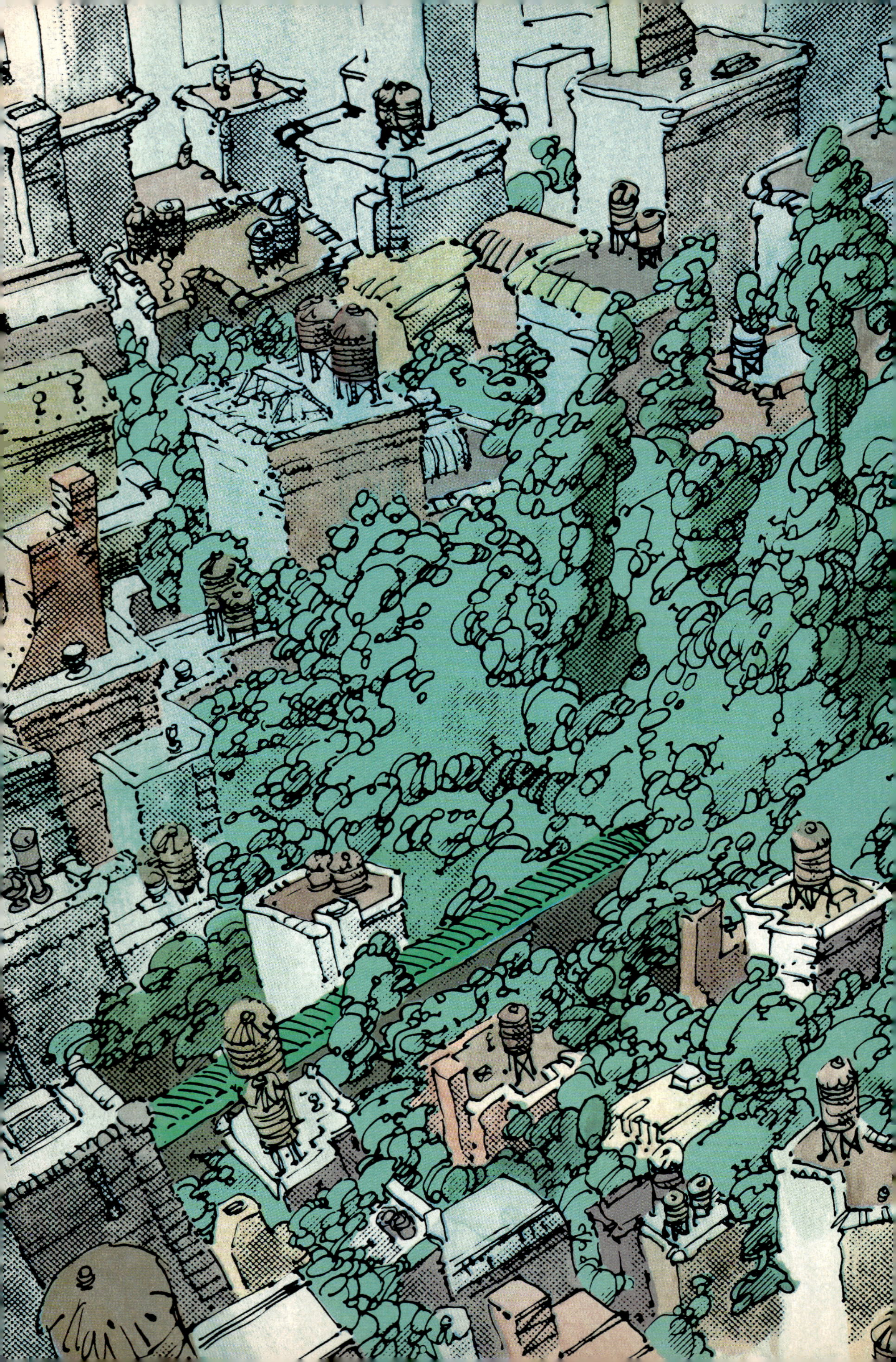

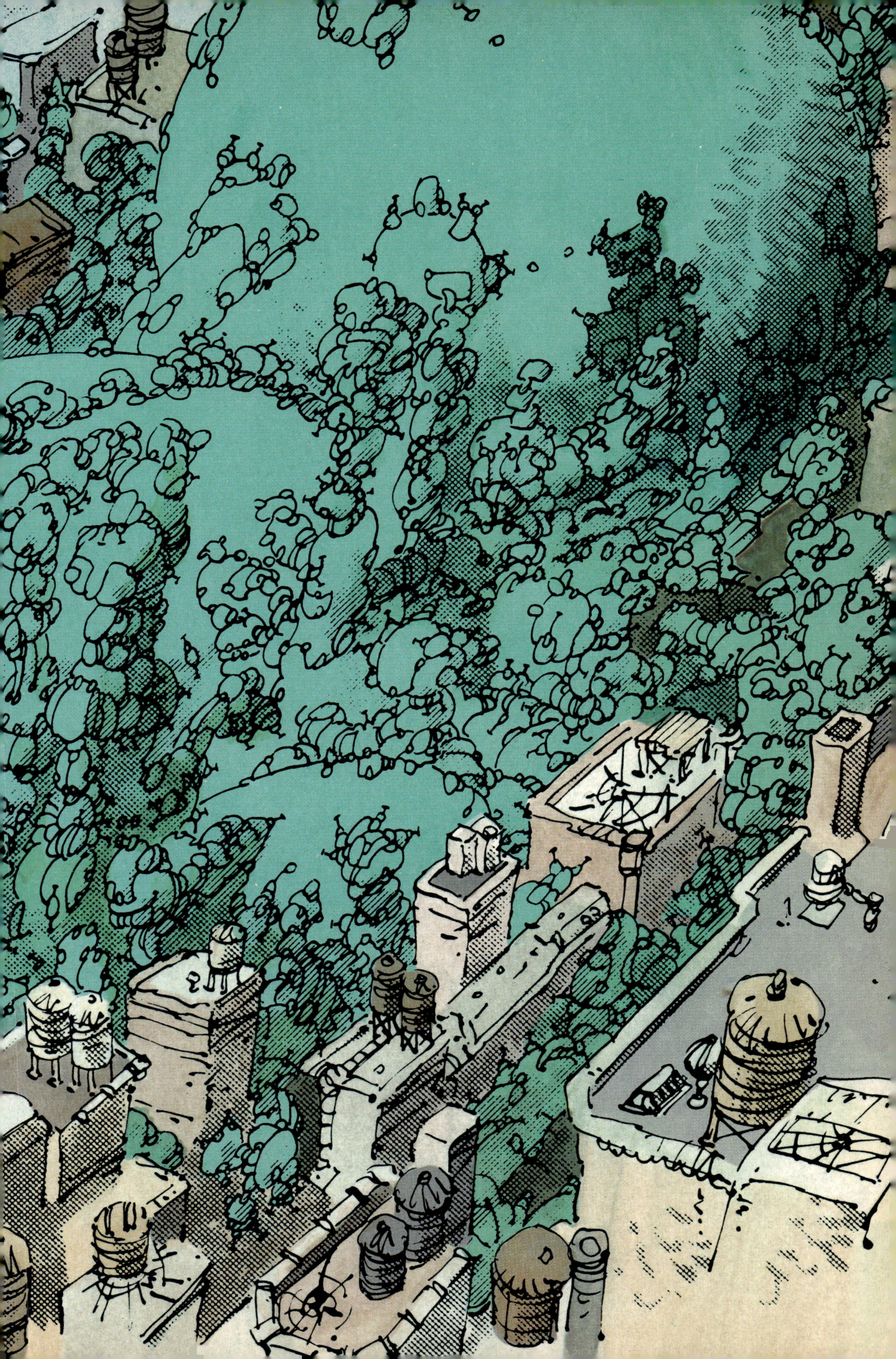

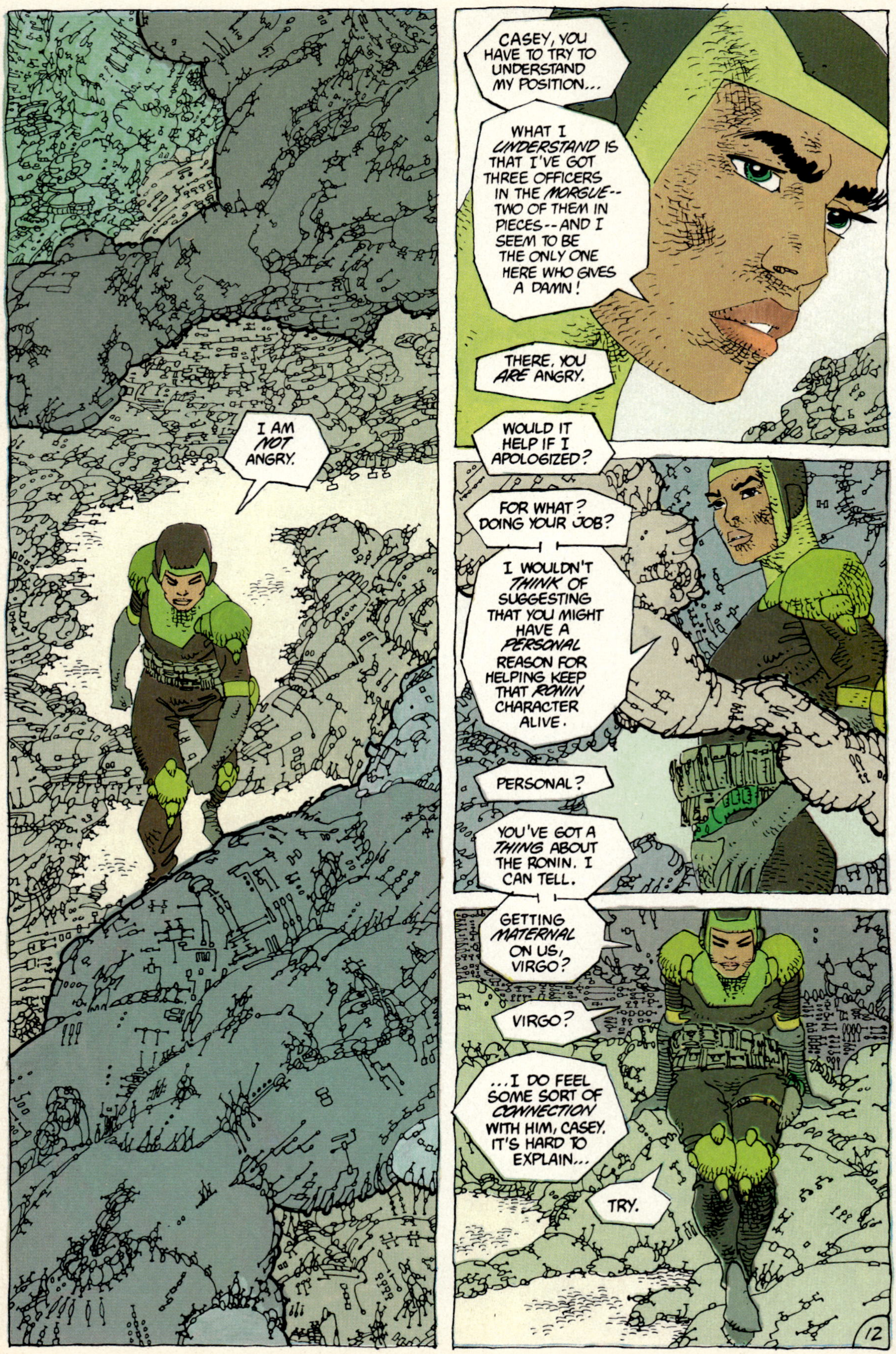
I AM NOT ANGRY.
CASEY, YOU HAVE TO TRY TO UNDERSTAND MY POSITION...
WHAT I UNDERSTAND IS THAT I'VE GOT THREE OFFICERS IN THE MORGUE-- TWO OF THEM IN PIECES--AND I SEEM TO BE THE ONLY ONE HERE WHO GIVES A DAMN!
THERE, YOU ARE ANGRY.
WOULD IT HELP IF I APOLOGIZED?
FOR WHAT? DOING YOUR JOB?
I WOULDN'T THINK OF SUGGESTING THAT YOU MIGHT HAVE A PERSONAL REASON FOR HELPING KEEP THAT RONIN CHARACTER ALIVE.
PERSONAL?
YOU'VE GOT A THING ABOUT THE RONIN. I CAN TELL.
GETTING MATERNAL ON US, VIRGO?
VIRGO?
...I DO FEEL SOME SORT OF CONNECTION WITH HIM, CASEY. IT'S HARD TO EXPLAIN...
TRY.
12

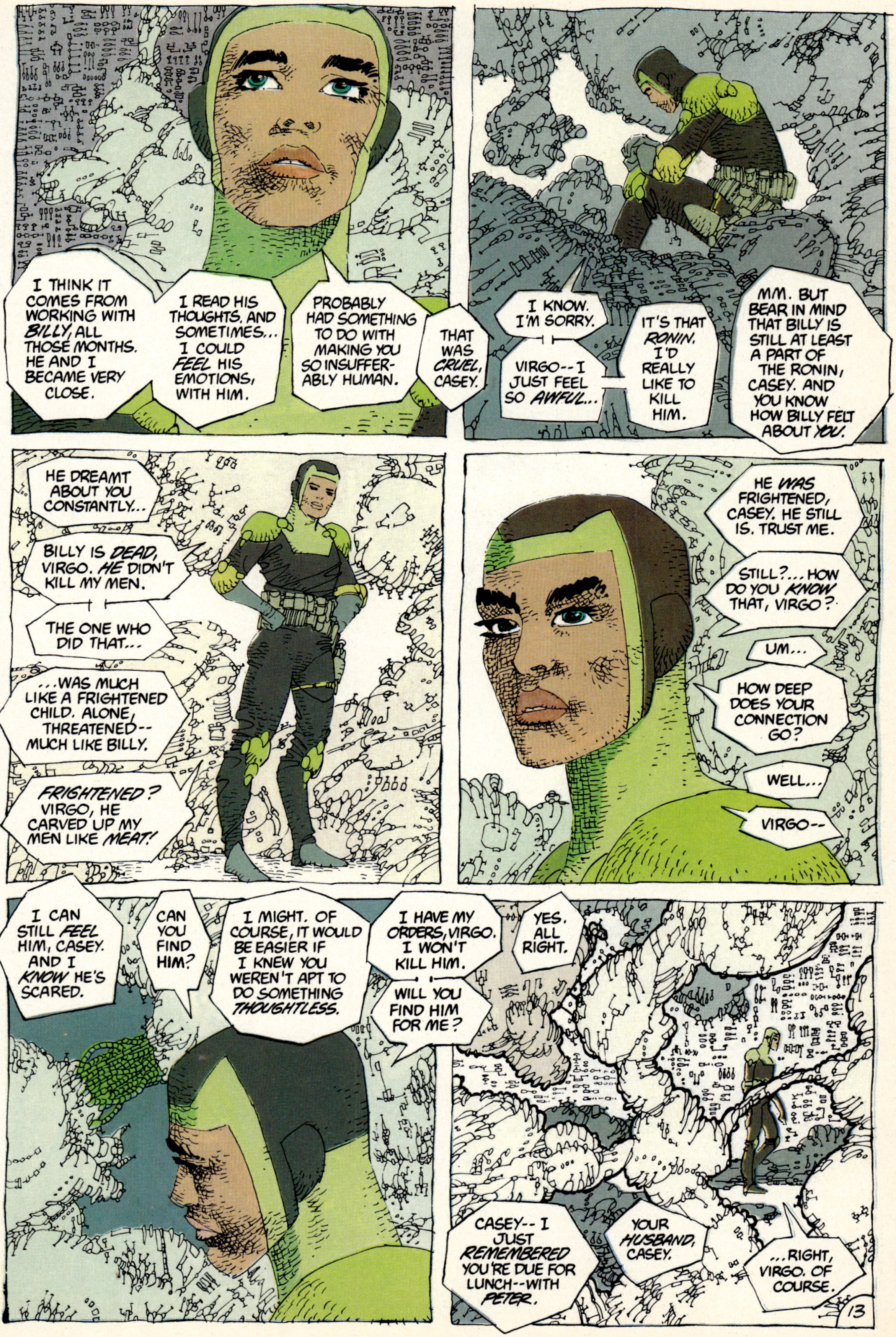

I THINK IT COMES FROM WORKING WITH BILLY, ALL THOSE MONTHS. HE AND I BECAME VERY CLOSE.
I READ HIS THOUGHTS, AND SOMETIMES... I COULD FEEL HIS EMOTIONS, WITH HIM.
PROBABLY HAD SOMETHING TO DO WITH MAKING YOU SO INSUFFERABLY HUMAN.
THAT WAS CRUEL, CASEY.
I KNOW. I'M SORRY.
VIRGO--I JUST FEEL SO AWFUL...
IT'S THAT RONIN. I'D REALLY LIKE TO KILL HIM.
MM. BUT BEAR IN MIND THAT BILLY IS STILL AT LEAST A PART OF THE RONIN, CASEY. AND YOU KNOW HOW BILLY FELT ABOUT YOU.
HE DREAMT ABOUT YOU CONSTANTLY...
BILLY IS DEAD, VIRGO. HE DIDN'T KILL MY MEN.
THE ONE WHO DID THAT...
...WAS MUCH LIKE A FRIGHTENED CHILD. ALONE, THREATENED--MUCH LIKE BILLY.
FRIGHTENED? VIRGO, HE CARVED UP MY MEN LIKE MEAT!
HE WAS FRIGHTENED, CASEY. HE STILL IS. TRUST ME.
STILL?... HOW DO YOU KNOW THAT, VIRGO?
UM...
HOW DEEP DOES YOUR CONNECTION GO?
WELL...
VIRGO--
I CAN STILL FEEL HIM, CASEY. AND I KNOW HE'S SCARED.
CAN YOU FIND HIM?
I MIGHT. OF COURSE, IT WOULD BE EASIER IF I KNEW YOU WEREN'T APT TO DO SOMETHING THOUGHTLESS.
I HAVE MY ORDERS, VIRGO. I WON'T KILL HIM.
WILL YOU FIND HIM FOR ME?
YES. ALL RIGHT.
CASEY--I JUST REMEMBERED YOU'RE DUE FOR LUNCH--WITH PETER.
YOUR HUSBAND, CASEY.
...RIGHT, VIRGO. OF COURSE.

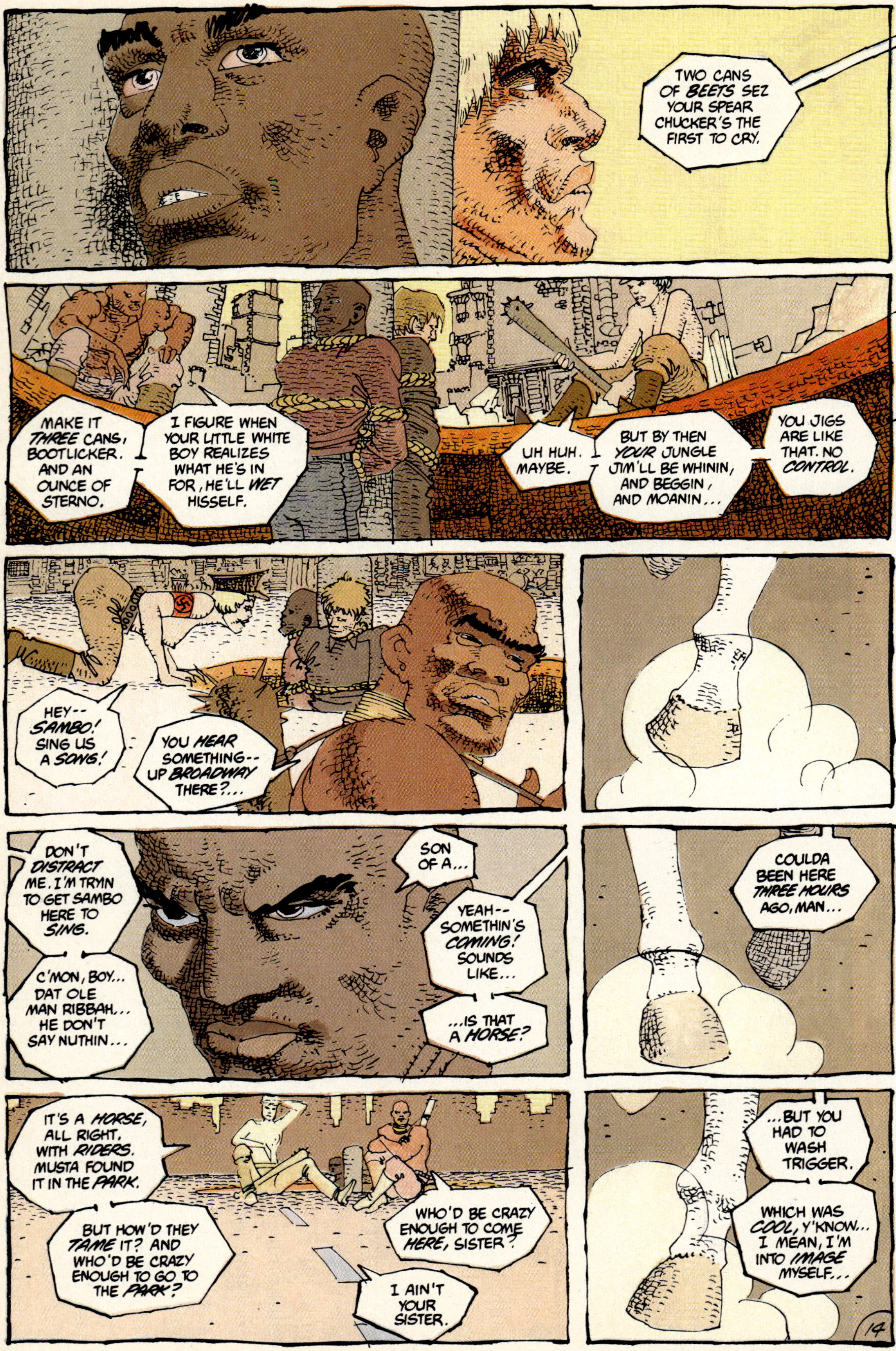
TWO CANS OF BEETS SEZ YOUR SPEAR CHUCKER'S THE FIRST TO CRY.
MAKE IT THREE CANS, BOOTLICKER. AND AN OUNCE OF STERNO.
I FIGURE WHEN YOUR LITTLE WHITE BOY REALIZES WHAT HE'S IN FOR, HE'LL WET HISSELF.
UH HUH. MAYBE.
BUT BY THEN YOUR JUNGLE JIM'LL BE WHININ, AND BEGGIN, AND MOANIN...
YOU JIGS ARE LIKE THAT. NO CONTROL.
HEY-- SAMBO! SING US A SONG!
YOU HEAR SOMETHING-- UP BROADWAY THERE?...
DON'T DISTRACT ME. I'M TRYIN TO GET SAMBO HERE TO SING.
C'MON, BOY... DAT OLE MAN RIBBAH... HE DON'T SAY NUTHIN...
SON OF A...
YEAH-- SOMETHIN'S COMING! SOUNDS LIKE...
...IS THAT A HORSE?
COULDA BEEN HERE THREE HOURS AGO, MAN...
IT'S A HORSE, ALL RIGHT, WITH RIDERS. MUSTA FOUND IT IN THE PARK.
BUT HOW'D THEY TAME IT? AND WHO'D BE CRAZY ENOUGH TO GO TO THE PARK?
WHO'D BE CRAZY ENOUGH TO COME HERE, SISTER?
I AIN'T YOUR SISTER.
...BUT YOU HAD TO WASH TRIGGER.
WHICH WAS COOL, Y'KNOW... I MEAN, I'M INTO IMAGE MYSELF...

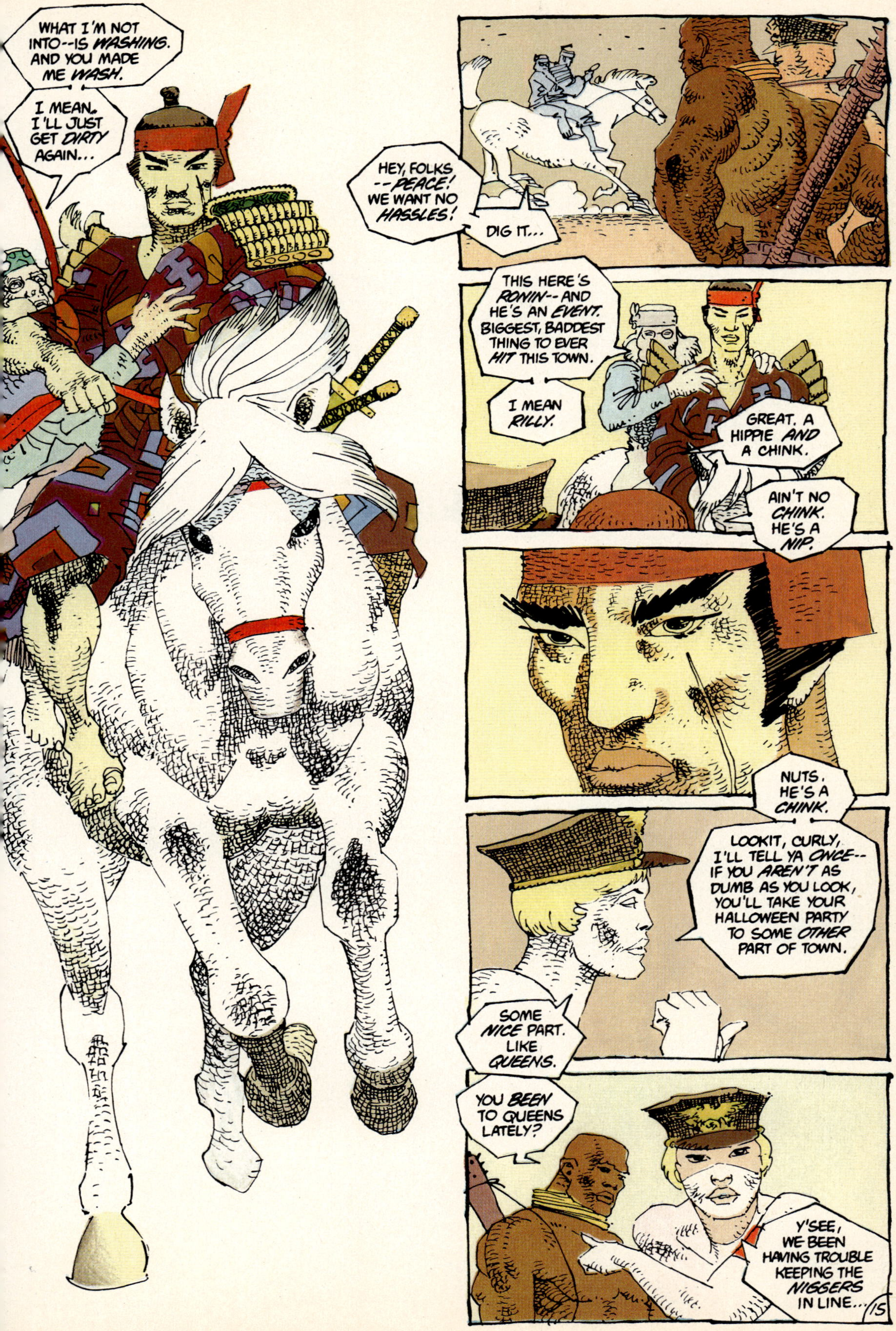

WHAT I'M NOT INTO--IS WASHING. AND YOU MADE ME WASH.
I MEAN. I'LL JUST GET DIRTY AGAIN...
HEY, FOLKS --PEACE! WE WANT NO HASSLES!
DIG IT...
THIS HERE'S RONIN--AND HE'S AN EVENT. BIGGEST, BADDEST THING TO EVER HIT THIS TOWN.
I MEAN RILLY.
GREAT. A HIPPIE AND A CHINK.
AIN'T NO CHINK. HE'S A NIP.
NUTS. HE'S A CHINK.
LOOKIT, CURLY, I'LL TELL YA ONCE-- IF YOU AREN'T AS DUMB AS YOU LOOK, YOU'LL TAKE YOUR HALLOWEEN PARTY TO SOME OTHER PART OF TOWN.
SOME NICE PART. LIKE QUEENS.
YOU BEEN TO QUEENS LATELY?
Y'SEE, WE BEEN HAVING TROUBLE KEEPING THE NIGGERS IN LINE...
15

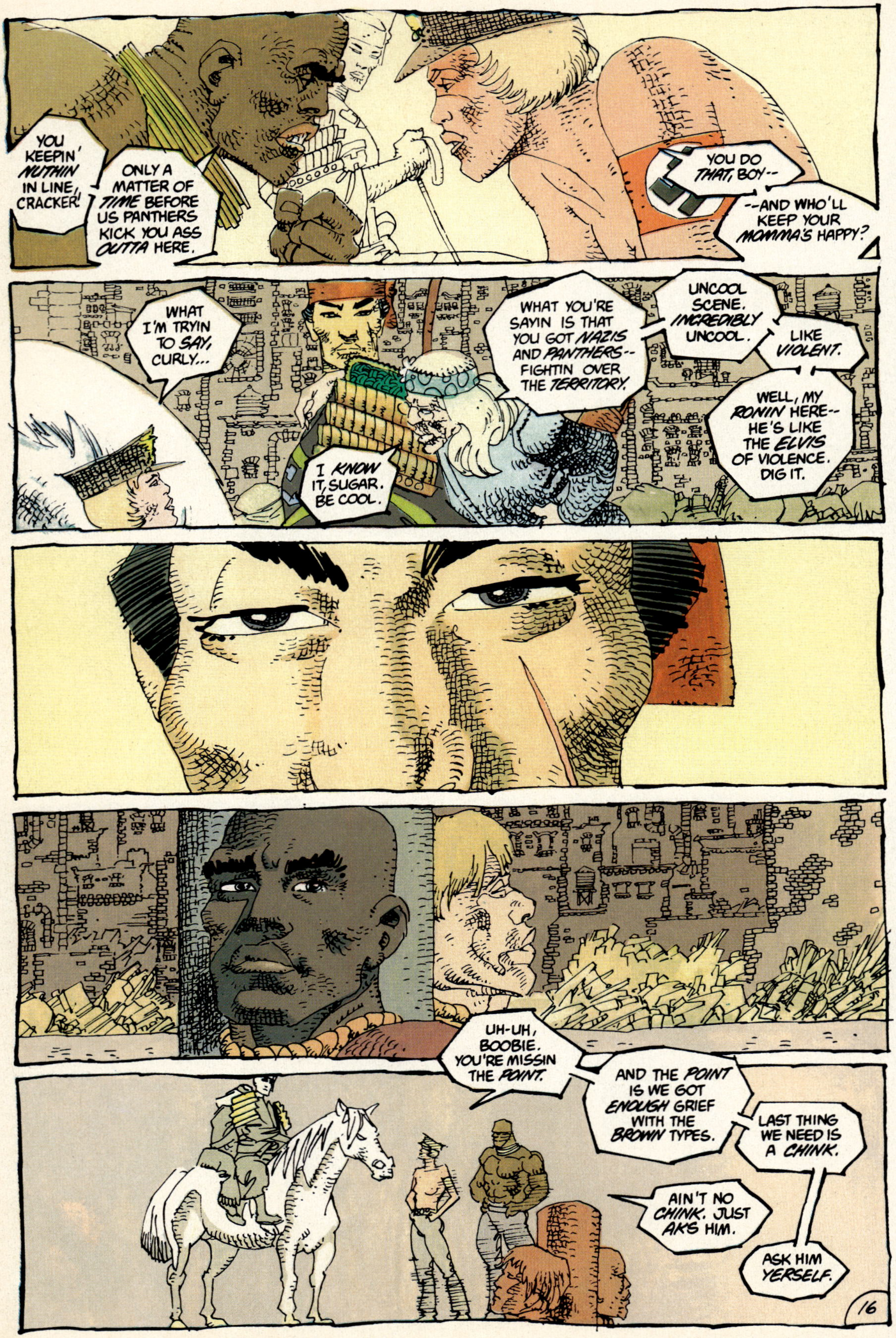

YOU KEEPIN' NUTHIN IN LINE, CRACKER!
ONLY A MATTER OF TIME BEFORE US PANTHERS KICK YOU ASS OUTTA HERE.
YOU DO THAT, BOY--
--AND WHO'LL KEEP YOUR MOMMA'S HAPPY?
WHAT I'M TRYIN TO SAY, CURLY...
I KNOW IT, SUGAR. BE COOL.
WHAT YOU'RE SAYIN IS THAT YOU GOT NAZIS AND PANTHERS-- FIGHTIN OVER THE TERRITORY.
UNCOOL SCENE. INCREDIBLY UNCOOL.
LIKE VIOLENT.
WELL, MY RONIN HERE-- HE'S LIKE THE ELVIS OF VIOLENCE. DIG IT.
UH-UH, BOOBIE. YOU'RE MISSIN THE POINT.
AND THE POINT IS WE GOT ENOUGH GRIEF WITH THE BROWN TYPES.
LAST THING WE NEED IS A CHINK.
AIN'T NO CHINK. JUST AKS HIM.
ASK HIM YERSELF.
16

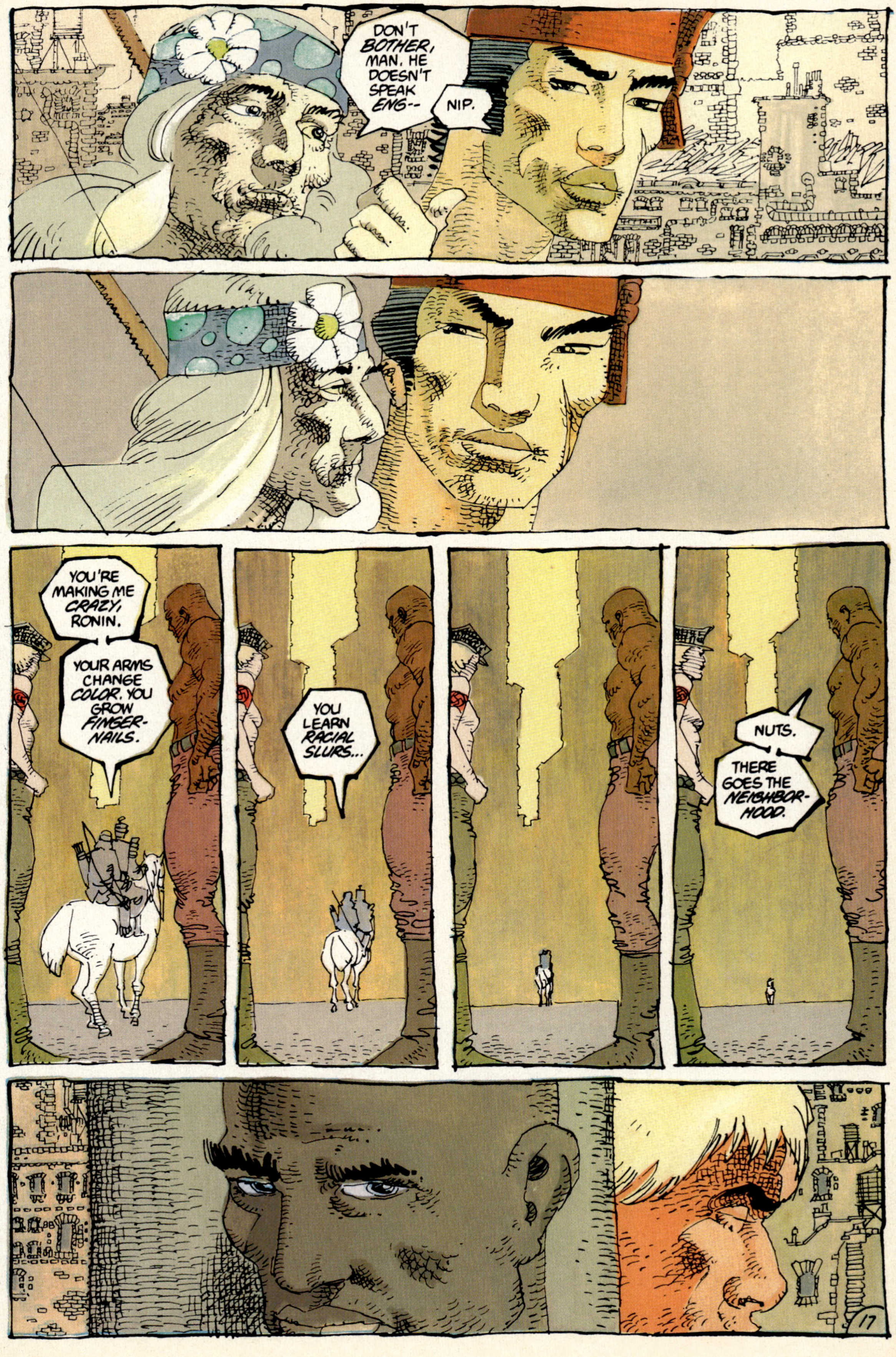
DON'T BOTHER, MAN. HE DOESN'T SPEAK ENG--
NIP.
YOU'RE MAKING ME CRAZY, RONIN.
YOUR ARMS CHANGE COLOR. YOU GROW FINGER-NAILS.
YOU LEARN RACIAL SLURS...
NUTS.
THERE GOES THE NEIGHBOR-HOOD.
17

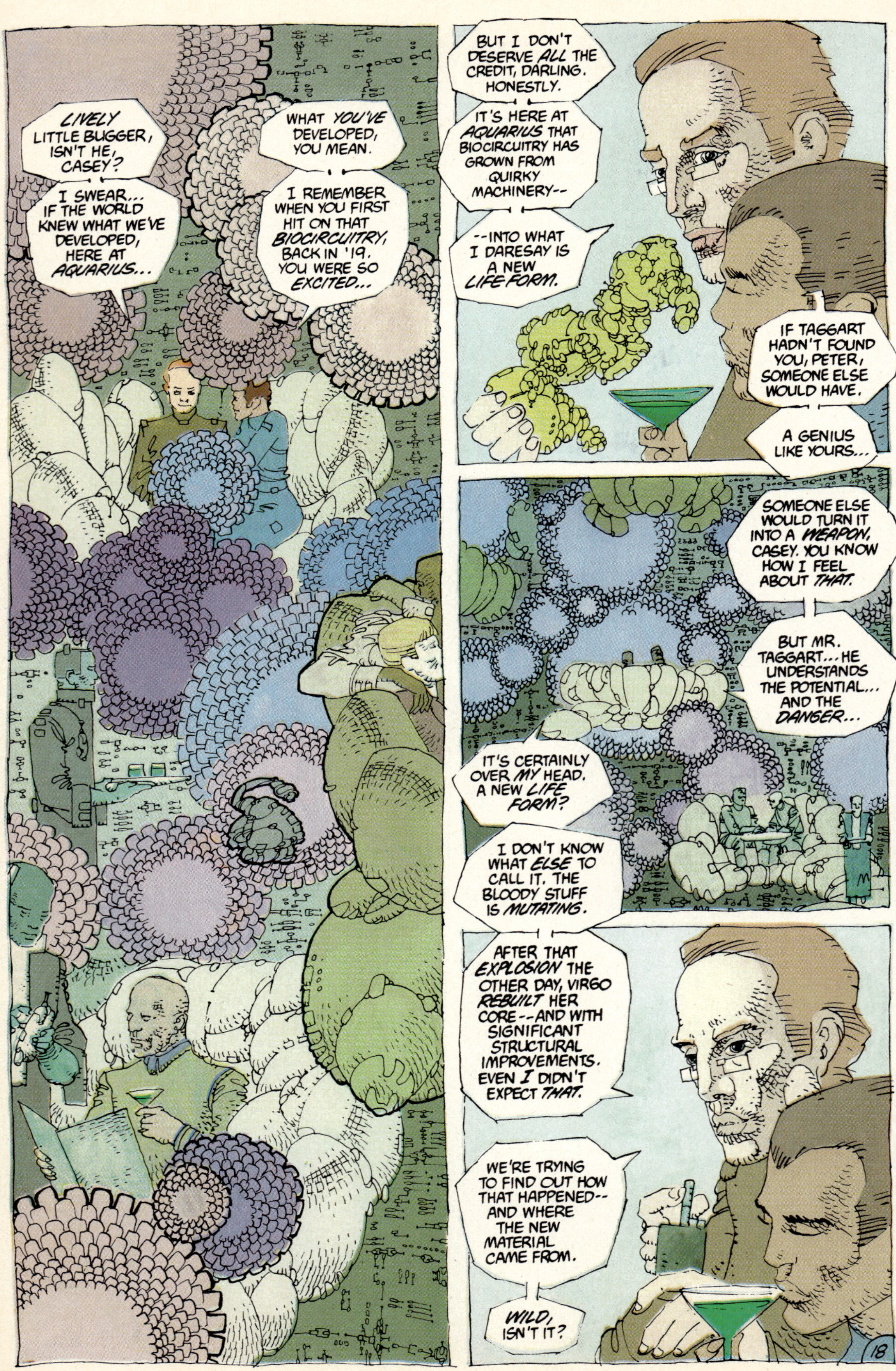
LIVELY LITTLE BUGGER, ISN'T HE, CASEY?
I SWEAR... IF THE WORLD KNEW WHAT WE'VE DEVELOPED, HERE AT AQUARIUS...
WHAT YOU'VE DEVELOPED, YOU MEAN.
I REMEMBER WHEN YOU FIRST HIT ON THAT BIOCIRCUITRY, BACK IN '19. YOU WERE SO EXCITED...
BUT I DON'T DESERVE ALL THE CREDIT, DARLING. HONESTLY.
IT'S HERE AT AQUARIUS THAT BIOCIRCUITRY HAS GROWN FROM QUIRKY MACHINERY--
--INTO WHAT I DARESAY IS A NEW LIFE FORM.
IF TAGGART HADN'T FOUND YOU, PETER, SOMEONE ELSE WOULD HAVE.
A GENIUS LIKE YOURS...
SOMEONE ELSE WOULD TURN IT INTO A WEAPON, CASEY. YOU KNOW HOW I FEEL ABOUT THAT.
BUT MR. TAGGART... HE UNDERSTANDS THE POTENTIAL... AND THE DANGER...
IT'S CERTAINLY OVER MY HEAD. A NEW LIFE FORM?
I DON'T KNOW WHAT ELSE TO CALL IT. THE BLOODY STUFF IS MUTATING.
AFTER THAT EXPLOSION THE OTHER DAY, VIRGO REBUILT HER CORE--AND WITH SIGNIFICANT STRUCTURAL IMPROVEMENTS. EVEN I DIDN'T EXPECT THAT.
WE'RE TRYING TO FIND OUT HOW THAT HAPPENED--AND WHERE THE NEW MATERIAL CAME FROM.
WILD, ISN'T IT?
18

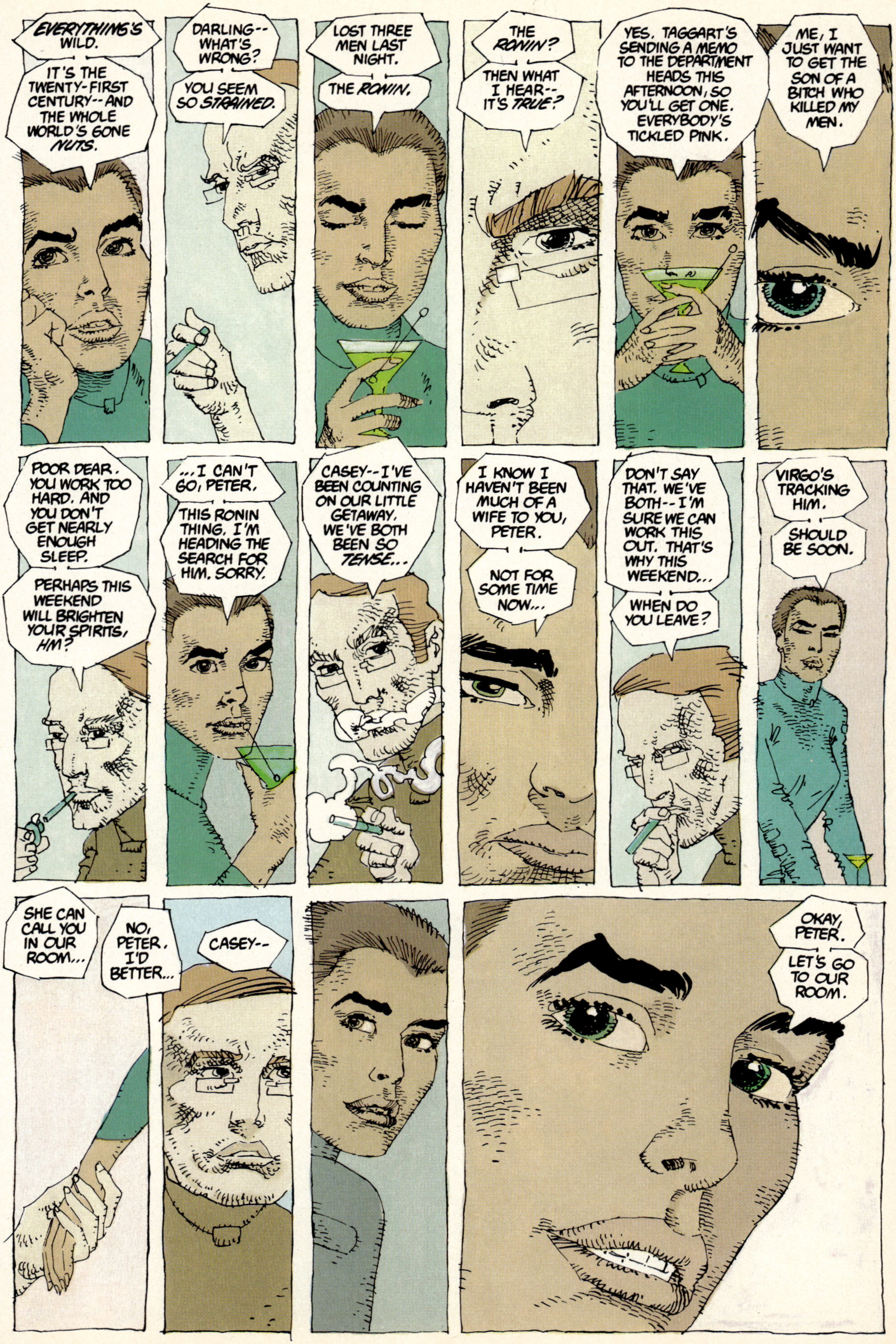
EVERYTHING'S WILD.
IT'S THE TWENTY-FIRST CENTURY-- AND THE WHOLE WORLD'S GONE NUTS.
DARLING-- WHAT'S WRONG?
YOU SEEM SO STRAINED.
LOST THREE MEN LAST NIGHT.
THE RONIN.
THE RONIN?
THEN WHAT I HEAR-- IT'S TRUE?
YES. TAGGART'S SENDING A MEMO TO THE DEPARTMENT HEADS THIS AFTERNOON, SO YOU'LL GET ONE. EVERYBODY'S TICKLED PINK.
ME, I JUST WANT TO GET THE SON OF A BITCH WHO KILLED MY MEN.
POOR DEAR. YOU WORK TOO HARD. AND YOU DON'T GET NEARLY ENOUGH SLEEP.
PERHAPS THIS WEEKEND WILL BRIGHTEN YOUR SPIRITS, HM?
...I CAN'T GO, PETER.
THIS RONIN THING. I'M HEADING THE SEARCH FOR HIM. SORRY.
CASEY--I'VE BEEN COUNTING ON OUR LITTLE GETAWAY. WE'VE BOTH BEEN SO TENSE...
I KNOW I HAVEN'T BEEN MUCH OF A WIFE TO YOU, PETER.
NOT FOR SOME TIME NOW...
DON'T SAY THAT. WE'VE BOTH-- I'M SURE WE CAN WORK THIS OUT. THAT'S WHY THIS WEEKEND...
WHEN DO YOU LEAVE?
VIRGO'S TRACKING HIM.
SHOULD BE SOON.
SHE CAN CALL YOU IN OUR ROOM...
NO, PETER. I'D BETTER...
CASEY--
OKAY, PETER.
LET'S GO TO OUR ROOM.

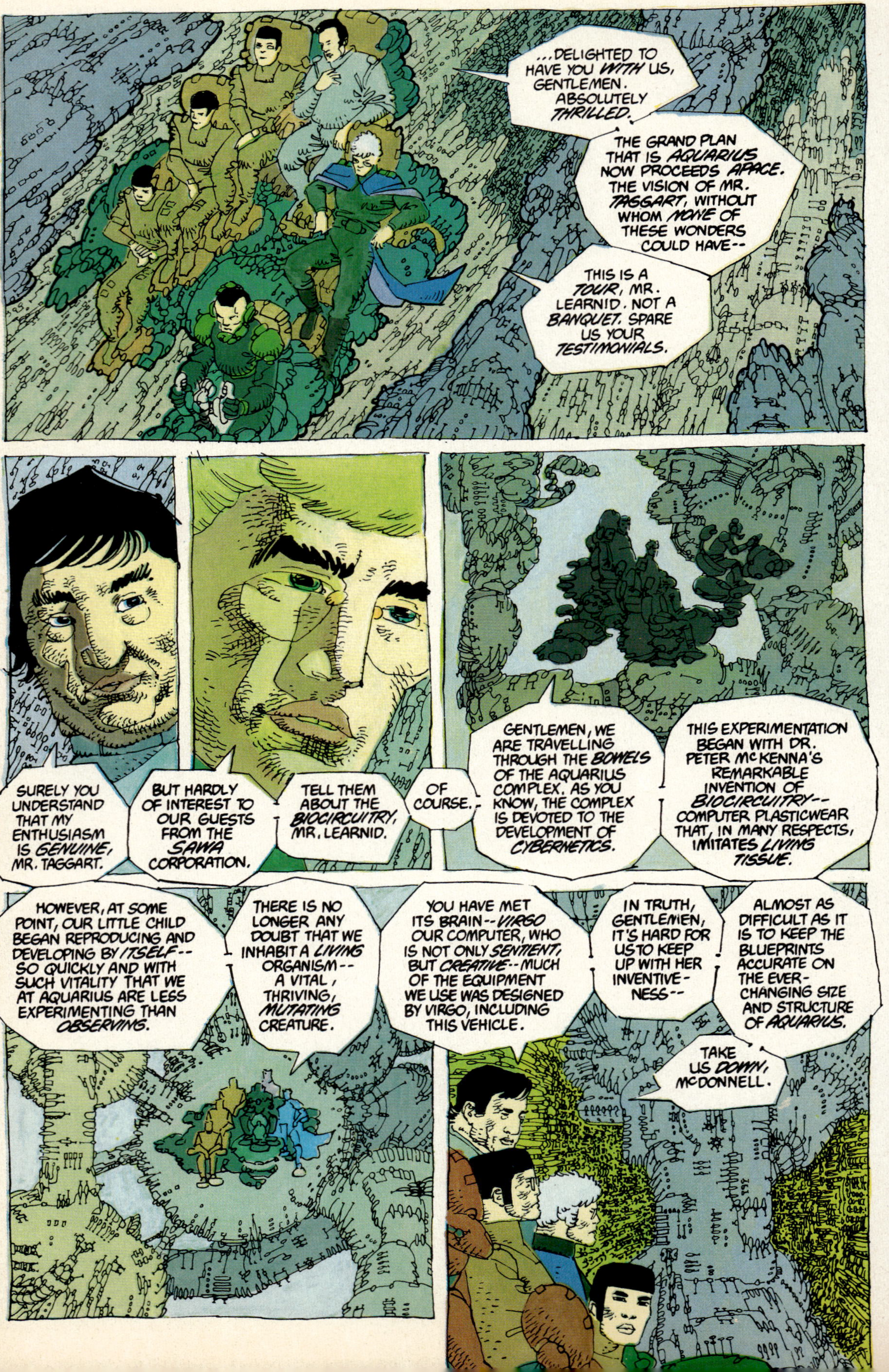
...DELIGHTED TO HAVE YOU WITH US, GENTLEMEN. ABSOLUTELY THRILLED.
THE GRAND PLAN THAT IS AQUARIUS NOW PROCEEDS APACE. THE VISION OF MR. TAGGART, WITHOUT WHOM NONE OF THESE WONDERS COULD HAVE--
THIS IS A TOUR, MR. LEARNID. NOT A BANQUET. SPARE US YOUR TESTIMONIALS.
SURELY YOU UNDERSTAND THAT MY ENTHUSIASM IS GENUINE, MR. TAGGART.
BUT HARDLY OF INTEREST TO OUR GUESTS FROM THE SAWA CORPORATION.
TELL THEM ABOUT THE BIOCIRCUITRY, MR. LEARNID.
OF COURSE.
GENTLEMEN, WE ARE TRAVELLING THROUGH THE BOWELS OF THE AQUARIUS COMPLEX. AS YOU KNOW, THE COMPLEX IS DEVOTED TO THE DEVELOPMENT OF CYBERNETICS.
THIS EXPERIMENTATION BEGAN WITH DR. PETER McKENNA'S REMARKABLE INVENTION OF BIOCIRCUITRY--COMPUTER PLASTICWEAR THAT, IN MANY RESPECTS, IMITATES LIVING TISSUE.
HOWEVER, AT SOME POINT, OUR LITTLE CHILD BEGAN REPRODUCING AND DEVELOPING BY ITSELF--SO QUICKLY AND WITH SUCH VITALITY THAT WE AT AQUARIUS ARE LESS EXPERIMENTING THAN OBSERVING.
THERE IS NO LONGER ANY DOUBT THAT WE INHABIT A LIVING ORGANISM--A VITAL, THRIVING, MUTATING CREATURE.
YOU HAVE MET ITS BRAIN--VIRGO OUR COMPUTER, WHO IS NOT ONLY SENTIENT, BUT CREATIVE--MUCH OF THE EQUIPMENT WE USE WAS DESIGNED BY VIRGO, INCLUDING THIS VEHICLE.
IN TRUTH, GENTLEMEN, IT'S HARD FOR US TO KEEP UP WITH HER INVENTIVENESS--
ALMOST AS DIFFICULT AS IT IS TO KEEP THE BLUEPRINTS ACCURATE ON THE EVER-CHANGING SIZE AND STRUCTURE OF AQUARIUS.
TAKE US DOWN, McDONNELL.

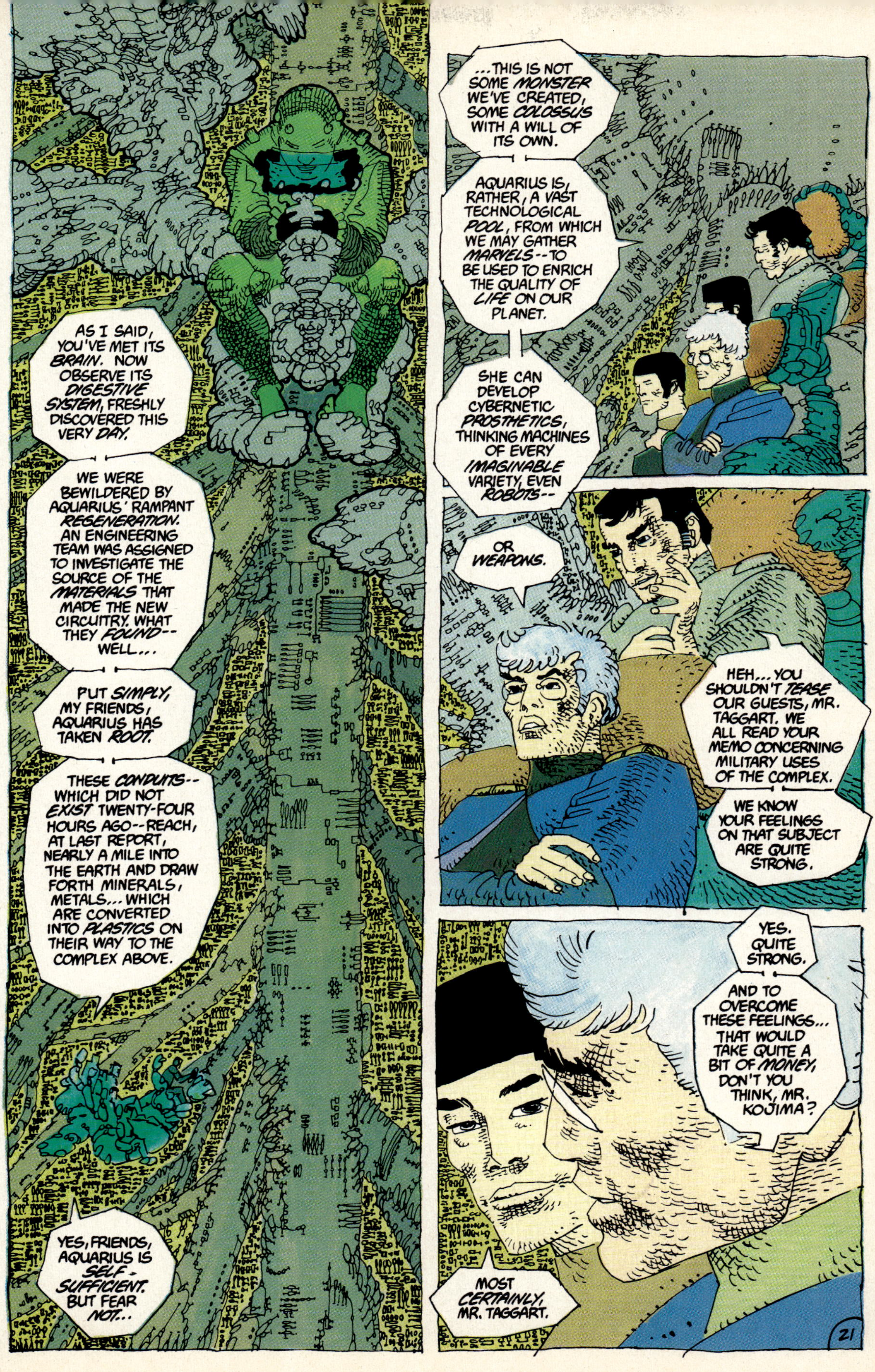
AS I SAID, YOU'VE MET ITS BRAIN. NOW OBSERVE ITS DIGESTIVE SYSTEM, FRESHLY DISCOVERED THIS VERY DAY.
WE WERE BEWILDERED BY AQUARIUS' RAMPANT REGENERATION. AN ENGINEERING TEAM WAS ASSIGNED TO INVESTIGATE THE SOURCE OF THE MATERIALS THAT MADE THE NEW CIRCUITRY. WHAT THEY FOUND-- WELL...
PUT SIMPLY, MY FRIENDS, AQUARIUS HAS TAKEN ROOT.
THESE CONDUITS-- WHICH DID NOT EXIST TWENTY-FOUR HOURS AGO--REACH, AT LAST REPORT, NEARLY A MILE INTO THE EARTH AND DRAW FORTH MINERALS, METALS... WHICH ARE CONVERTED INTO PLASTICS ON THEIR WAY TO THE COMPLEX ABOVE.
YES, FRIENDS, AQUARIUS IS SELF-SUFFICIENT. BUT FEAR NOT...
...THIS IS NOT SOME MONSTER WE'VE CREATED, SOME COLOSSUS WITH A WILL OF ITS OWN.
AQUARIUS IS, RATHER, A VAST TECHNOLOGICAL POOL, FROM WHICH WE MAY GATHER MARVELS--TO BE USED TO ENRICH THE QUALITY OF LIFE ON OUR PLANET.
SHE CAN DEVELOP CYBERNETIC PROSTHETICS, THINKING MACHINES OF EVERY IMAGINABLE VARIETY, EVEN ROBOTS--
OR WEAPONS.
HEH... YOU SHOULDN'T TEASE OUR GUESTS, MR. TAGGART. WE ALL READ YOUR MEMO CONCERNING MILITARY USES OF THE COMPLEX.
WE KNOW YOUR FEELINGS ON THAT SUBJECT ARE QUITE STRONG.
YES. QUITE STRONG.
AND TO OVERCOME THESE FEELINGS... THAT WOULD TAKE QUITE A BIT OF MONEY, DON'T YOU THINK, MR. KOJIMA?
MOST CERTAINLY, MR. TAGGART.

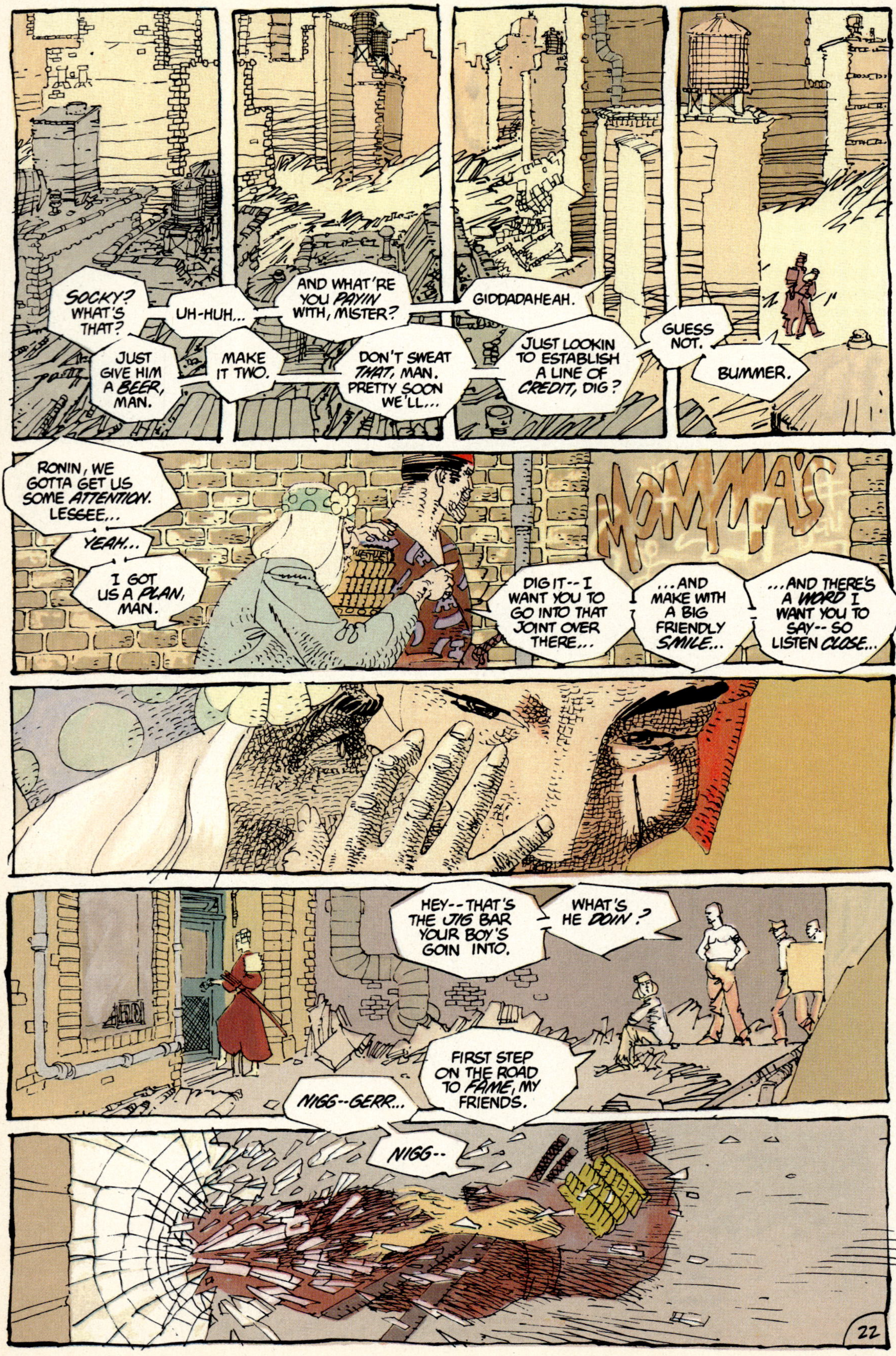
SOCKY? WHAT'S THAT?
UH-HUH...
JUST GIVE HIM A BEER, MAN.
MAKE IT TWO.
AND WHAT'RE YOU PAYIN WITH, MISTER?
DON'T SWEAT THAT, MAN. PRETTY SOON WE'LL...
GIDDADAHEAH.
JUST LOOKIN TO ESTABLISH A LINE OF CREDIT, DIG?
GUESS NOT.
BUMMER.
RONIN, WE GOTTA GET US SOME ATTENTION. LESGEE...
YEAH...
I GOT US A PLAN, MAN.
MOMMA'S
DIG IT-- I WANT YOU TO GO INTO THAT JOINT OVER THERE...
...AND MAKE WITH A BIG FRIENDLY SMILE...
...AND THERE'S A WORD I WANT YOU TO SAY-- SO LISTEN CLOSE...
HEY-- THAT'S THE JIG BAR YOUR BOY'S GOIN INTO.
WHAT'S HE DOIN?
FIRST STEP ON THE ROAD TO FAME, MY FRIENDS.
NIGG--GERR...
NIGG--

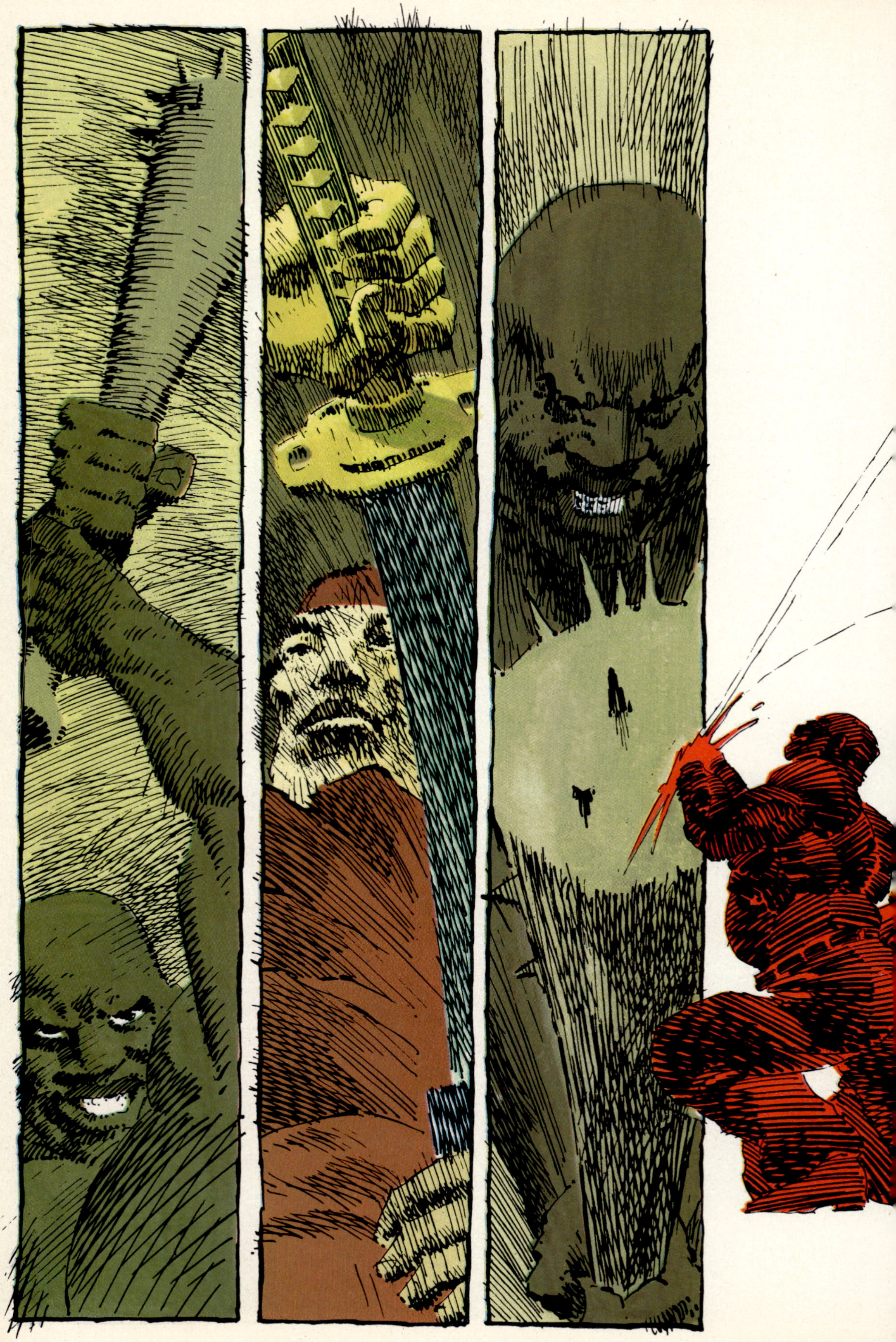

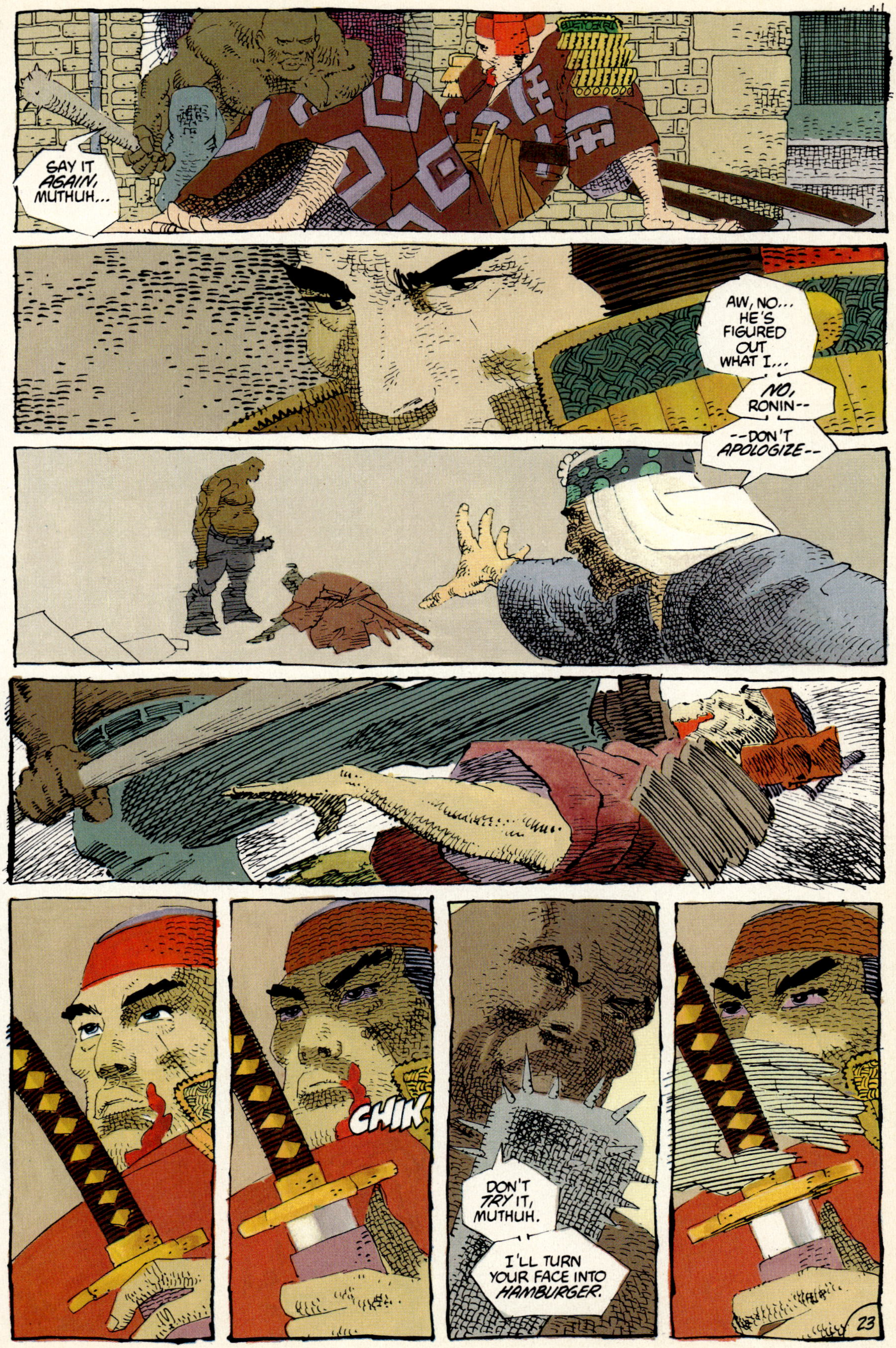
SAY IT AGAIN, MUTHUH...
AW, NO... HE'S FIGURED OUT WHAT I...
NO, RONIN--
--DON'T APOLOGIZE--
CHIK
DON'T TRY IT, MUTHUH.
I'LL TURN YOUR FACE INTO HAMBURGER.

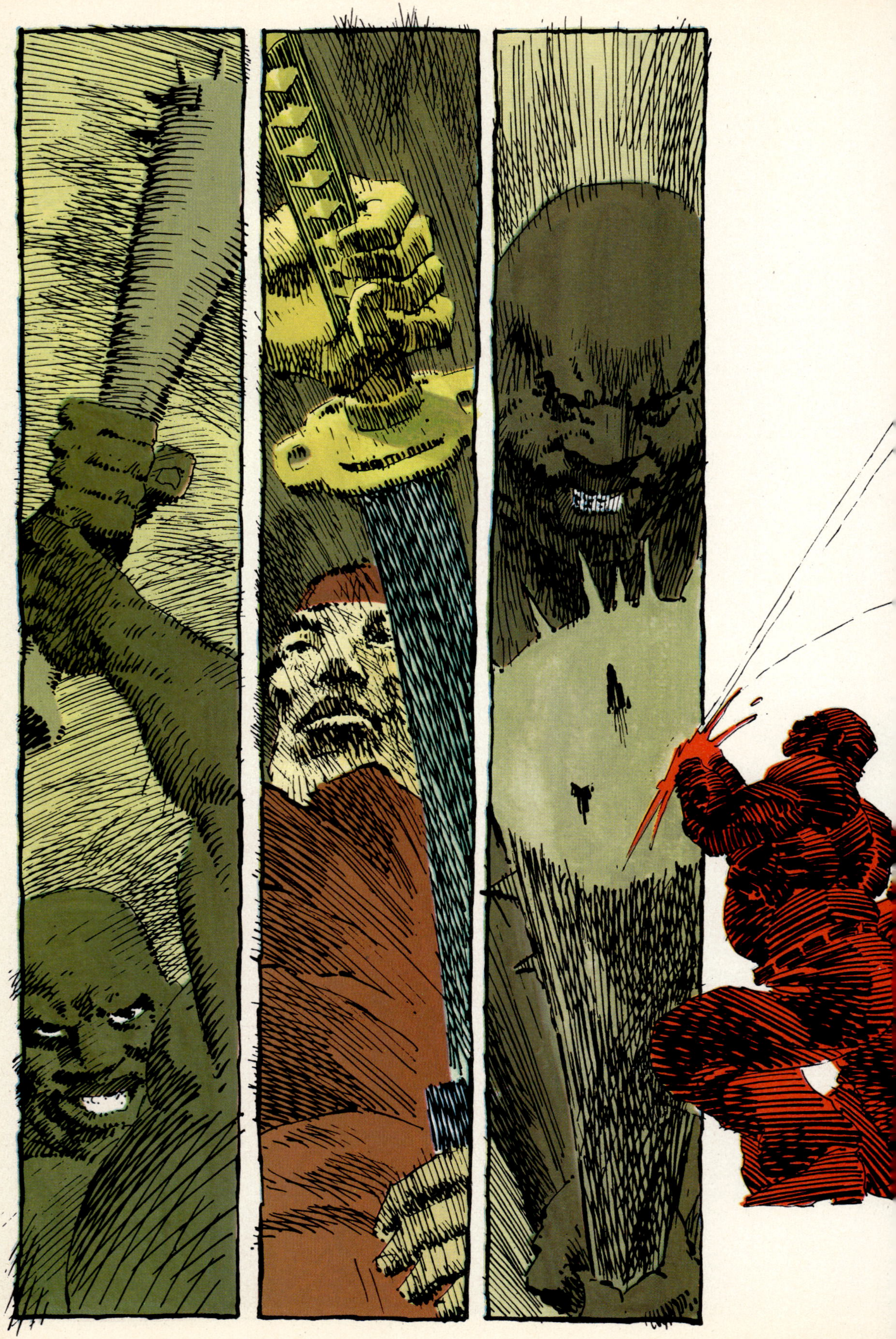

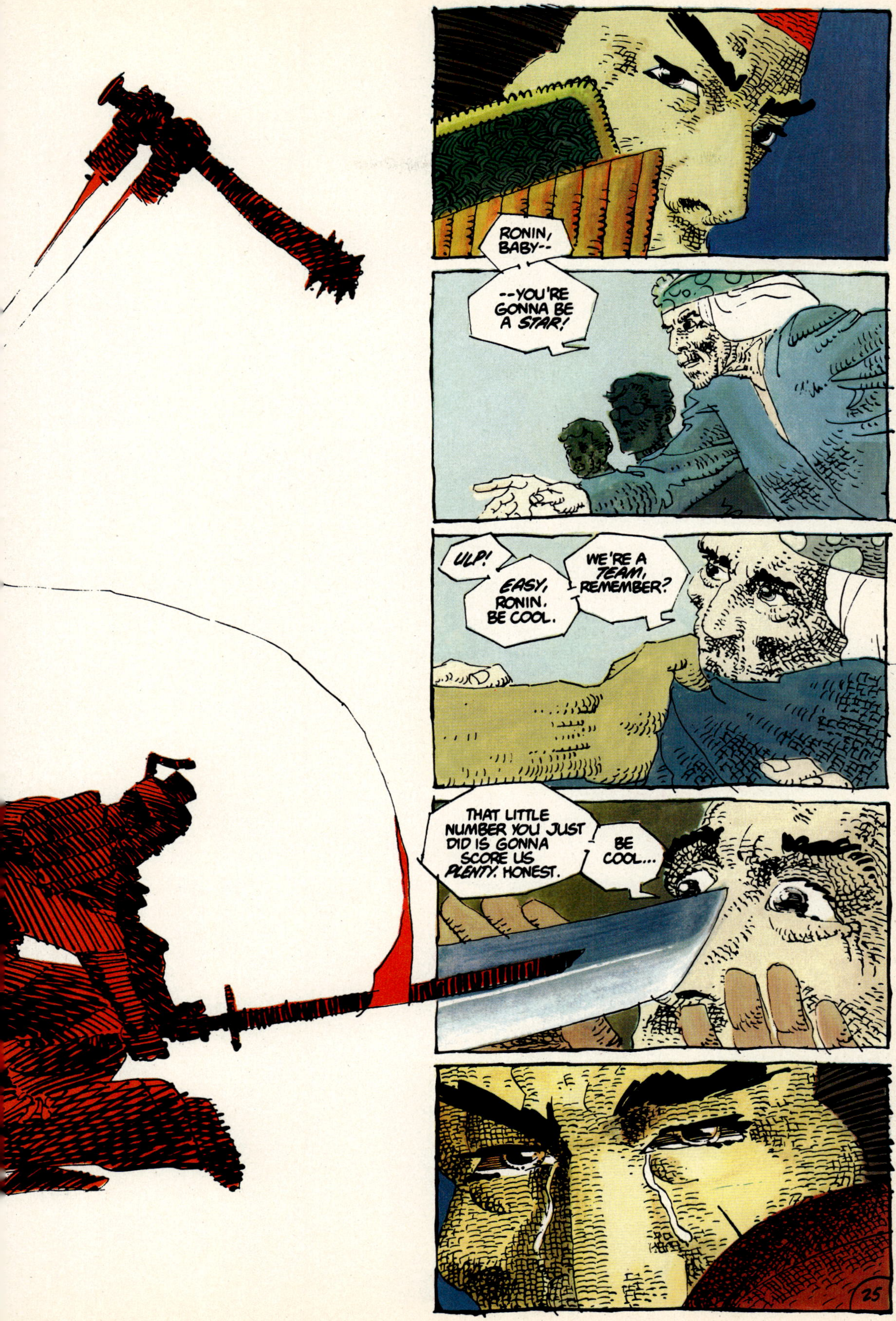
RONIN, BABY--
--YOU'RE GONNA BE A STAR!
ULP!
EASY, RONIN. BE COOL.
WE'RE A TEAM, REMEMBER?
THAT LITTLE NUMBER YOU JUST DID IS GONNA SCORE US PLENTY. HONEST.
BE COOL...
25

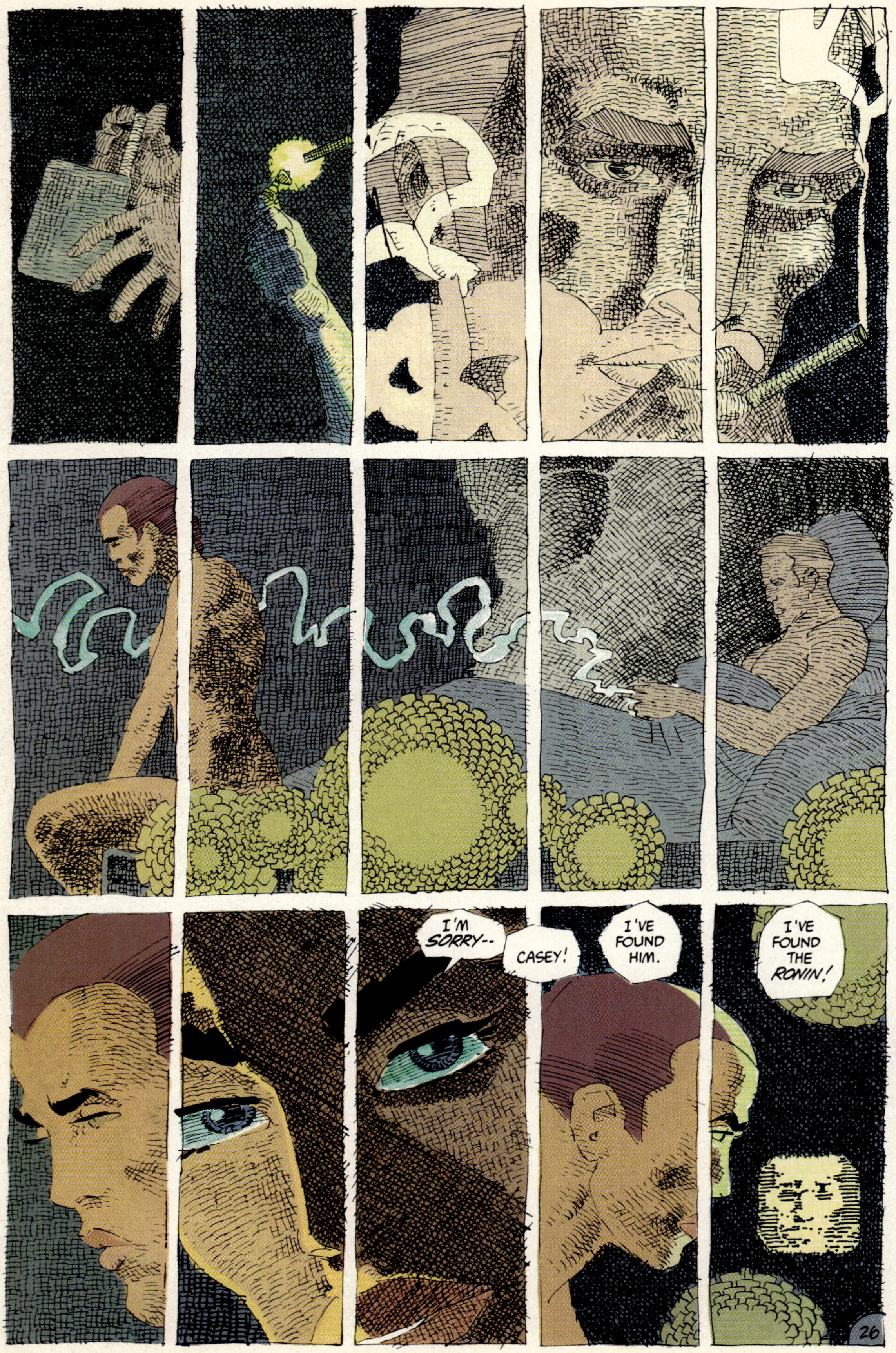
I'M SORRY--
CASEY!
I'VE FOUND HIM.
I'VE FOUND THE RONIN!

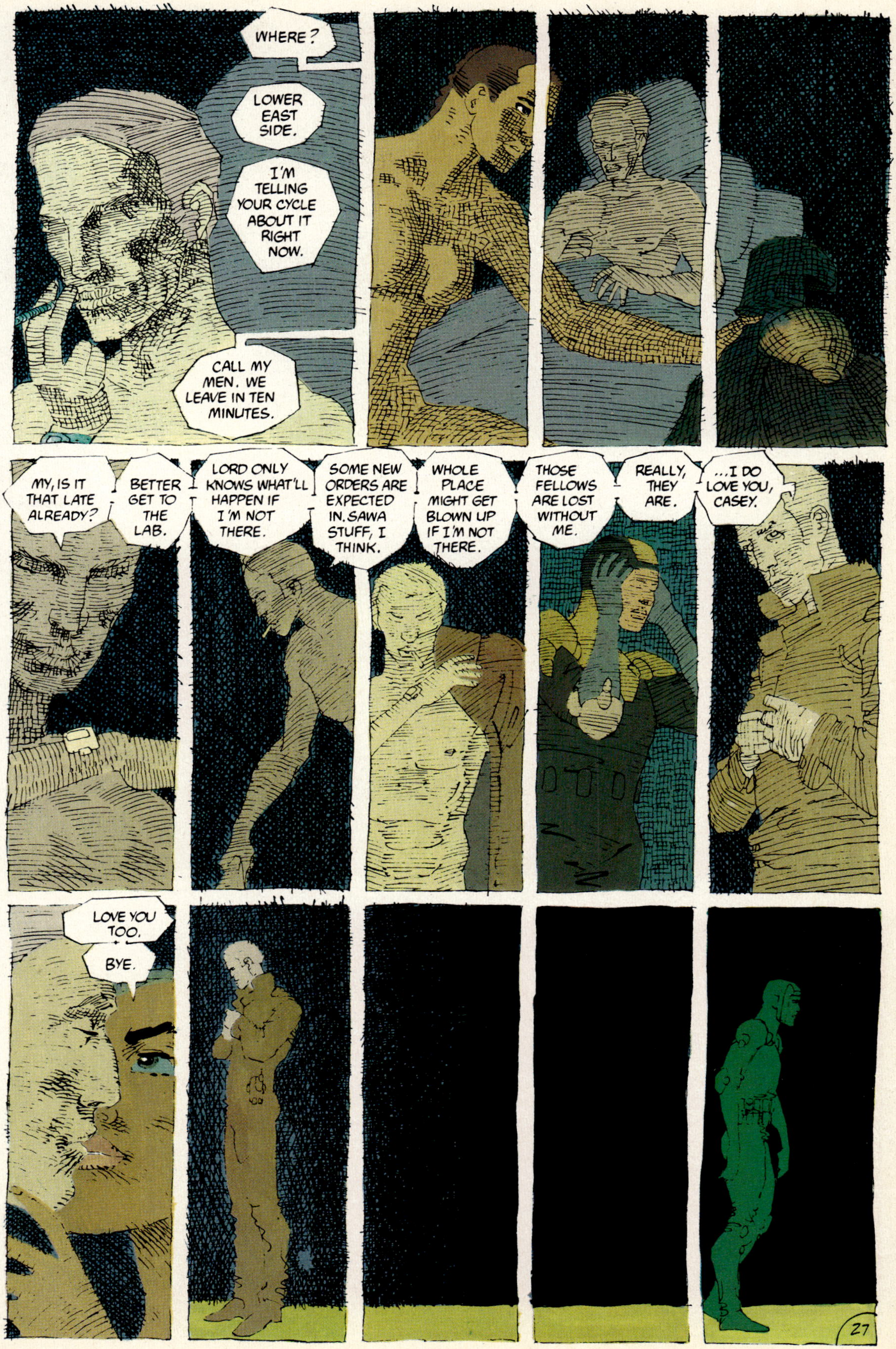

WHERE?
LOWER EAST SIDE.
I'M TELLING YOUR CYCLE ABOUT IT RIGHT NOW.
CALL MY MEN. WE LEAVE IN TEN MINUTES.
MY, IS IT THAT LATE ALREADY?
BETTER GET TO THE LAB.
LORD ONLY KNOWS WHAT'LL HAPPEN IF I'M NOT THERE.
SOME NEW ORDERS ARE EXPECTED IN. SAWA STUFF, I THINK.
WHOLE PLACE MIGHT GET BLOWN UP IF I'M NOT THERE.
THOSE FELLOWS ARE LOST WITHOUT ME.
REALLY, THEY ARE.
...I DO LOVE YOU, CASEY.
LOVE YOU TOO.
BYE.

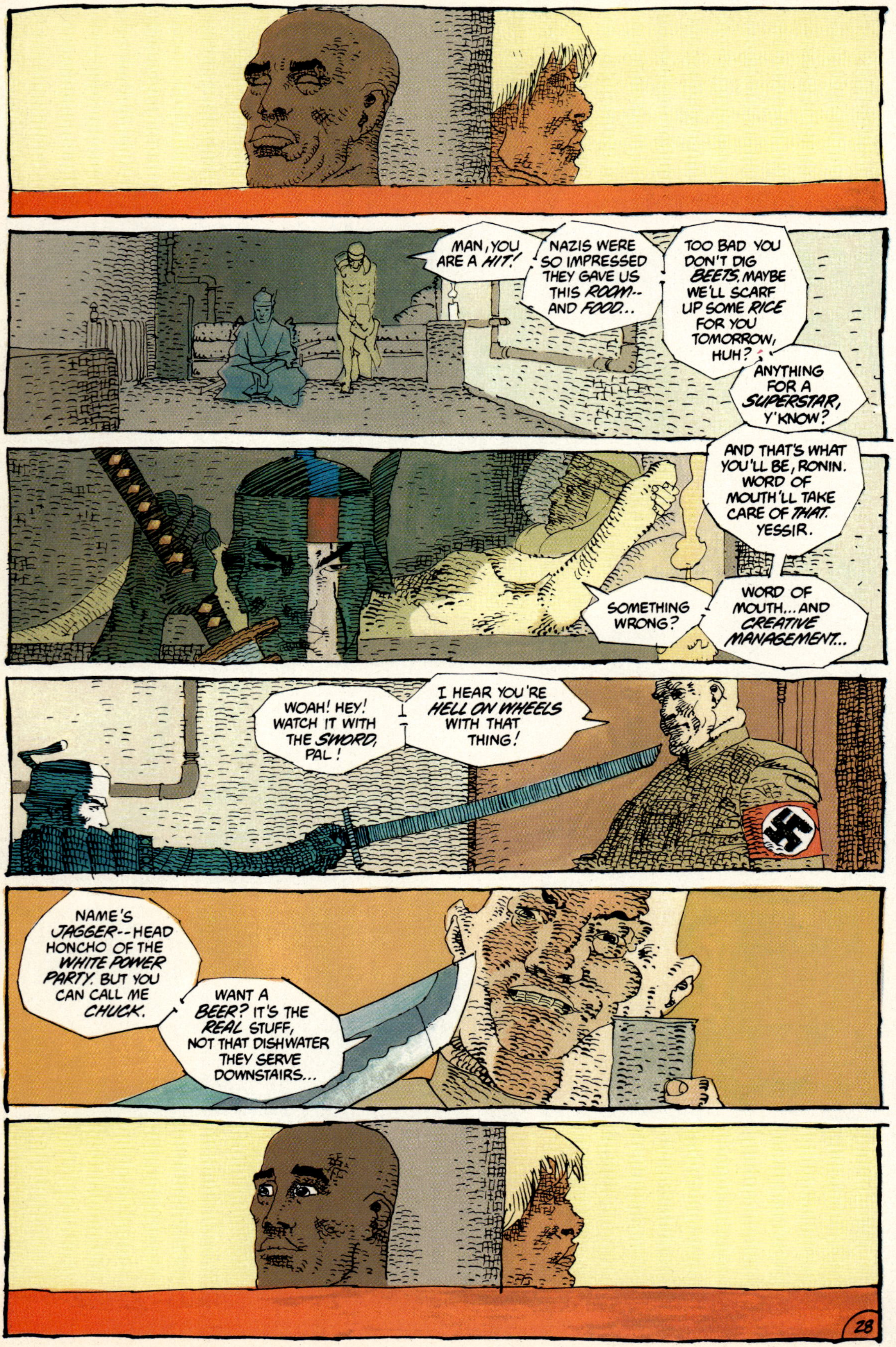
MAN, YOU ARE A *HIT!*
NAZIS WERE SO IMPRESSED THEY GAVE US THIS *ROOM*-- AND *FOOD*...
TOO BAD YOU DON'T DIG *BEETS*. MAYBE WE'LL SCARF UP SOME *RICE* FOR YOU TOMORROW, HUH?
ANYTHING FOR A *SUPERSTAR*, Y'KNOW?
AND THAT'S WHAT YOU'LL BE, RONIN. WORD OF MOUTH'LL TAKE CARE OF *THAT*. YESSIR.
SOMETHING WRONG?
WORD OF MOUTH... AND *CREATIVE MANAGEMENT*...
WOAH! HEY! WATCH IT WITH THE *SWORD*, PAL!
I HEAR YOU'RE *HELL ON WHEELS* WITH THAT THING!
NAME'S *JAGGER*--HEAD HONCHO OF THE *WHITE POWER PARTY*. BUT YOU CAN CALL ME *CHUCK*.
WANT A *BEER?* IT'S THE *REAL* STUFF, NOT THAT DISHWATER THEY SERVE DOWNSTAIRS...

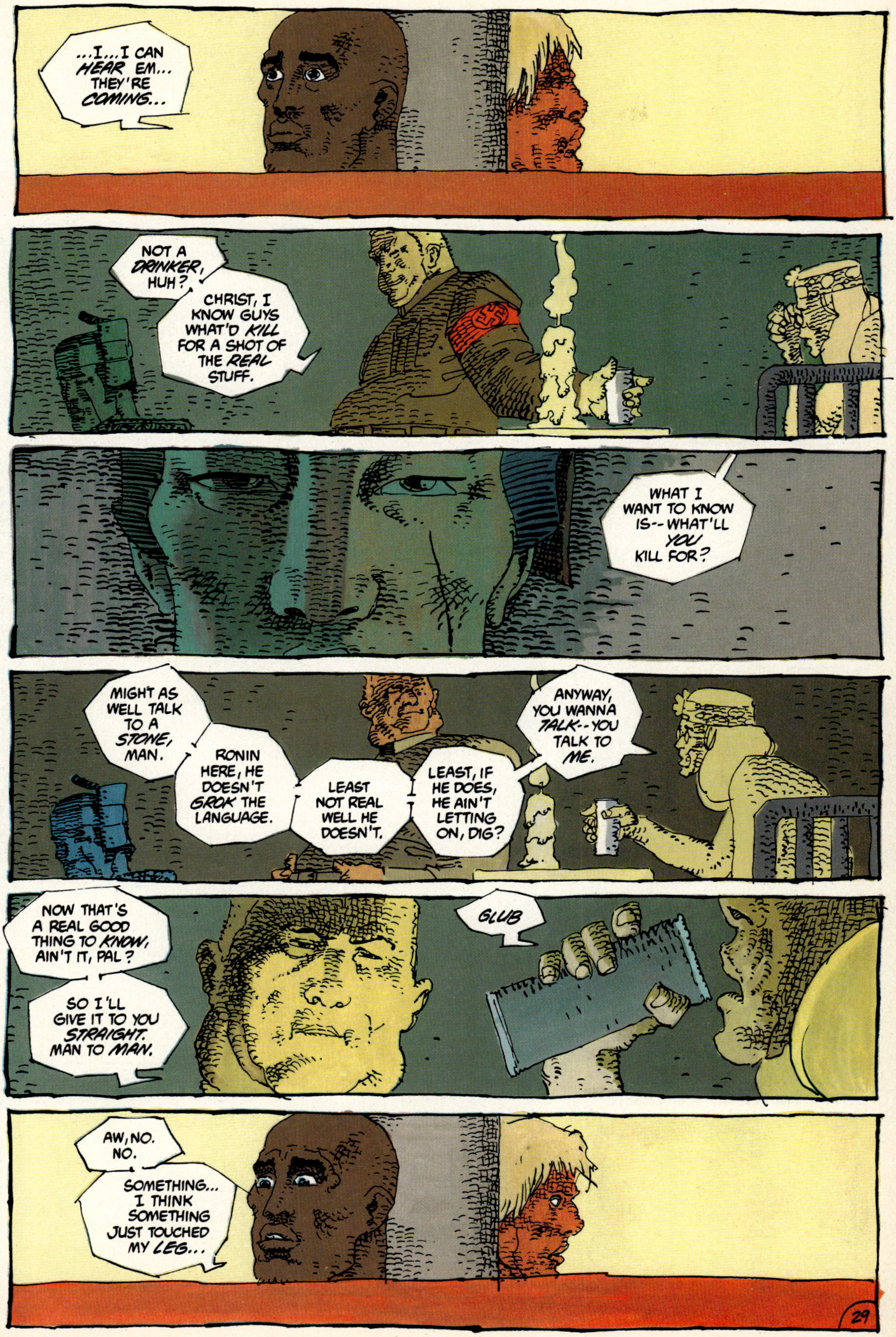
...I...I CAN HEAR EM... THEY'RE COMING...
NOT A DRINKER, HUH?
CHRIST, I KNOW GUYS WHAT'D KILL FOR A SHOT OF THE REAL STUFF.
WHAT I WANT TO KNOW IS--WHAT'LL YOU KILL FOR?
MIGHT AS WELL TALK TO A STONE, MAN.
RONIN HERE, HE DOESN'T GROK THE LANGUAGE.
LEAST NOT REAL WELL HE DOESN'T.
LEAST, IF HE DOES, HE AIN'T LETTING ON, DIG?
ANYWAY, YOU WANNA TALK--YOU TALK TO ME.
NOW THAT'S A REAL GOOD THING TO KNOW, AIN'T IT, PAL?
SO I'LL GIVE IT TO YOU STRAIGHT. MAN TO MAN.
GLUB
AW, NO. NO.
SOMETHING... I THINK SOMETHING JUST TOUCHED MY LEG...

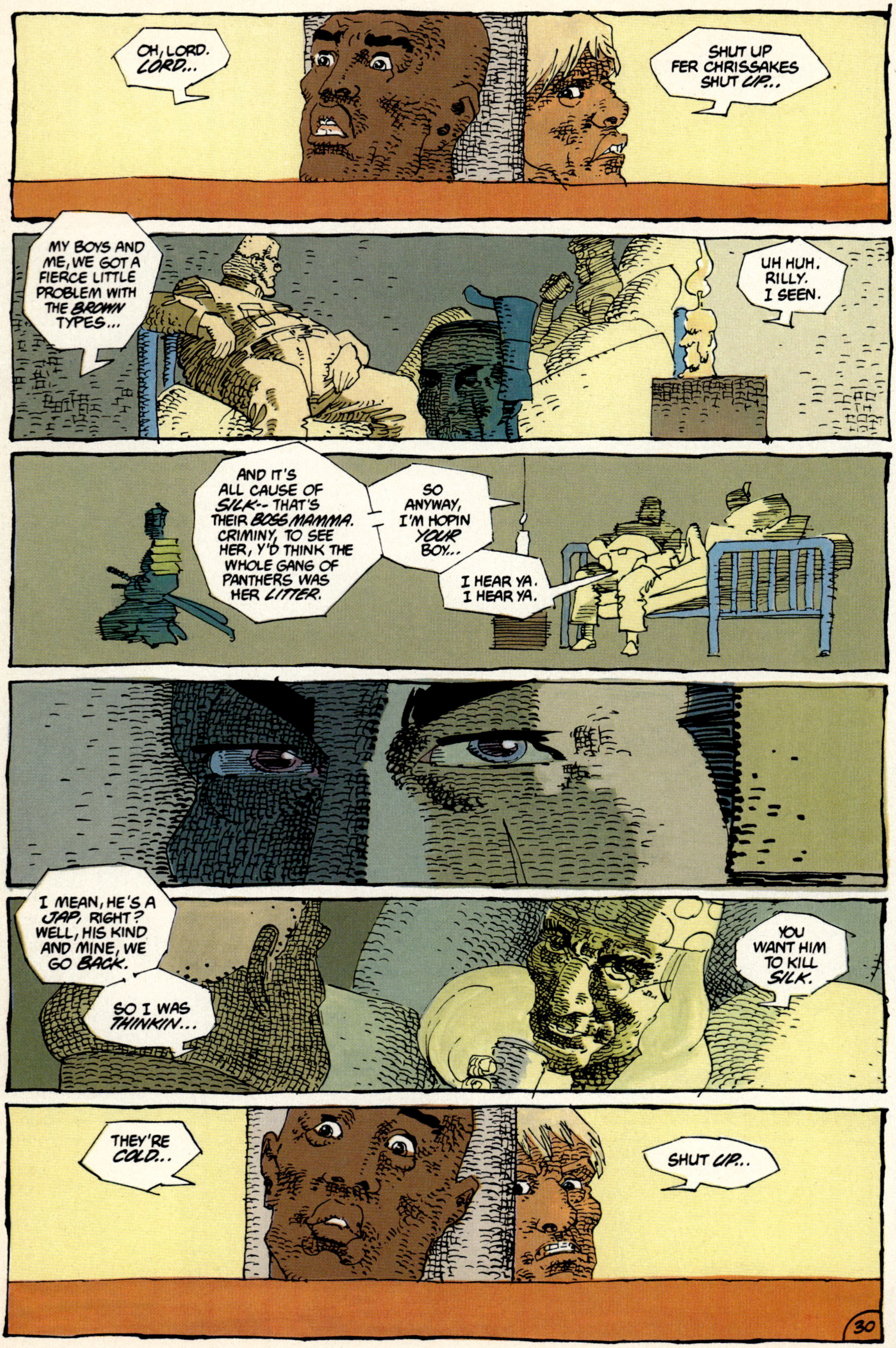
OH, LORD. LORD...
SHUT UP FER CHRISSAKES SHUT UP...
MY BOYS AND ME, WE GOT A FIERCE LITTLE PROBLEM WITH THE BROWN TYPES...
UH HUH. RILLY. I SEEN.
AND IT'S ALL CAUSE OF SILK-- THAT'S THEIR BOSS MAMMA. CRIMINY, TO SEE HER, Y'D THINK THE WHOLE GANG OF PANTHERS WAS HER LITTER.
SO ANYWAY, I'M HOPIN YOUR BOY...
I HEAR YA. I HEAR YA.
I MEAN, HE'S A JAP, RIGHT? WELL, HIS KIND AND MINE, WE GO BACK.
SO I WAS THINKIN...
YOU WANT HIM TO KILL SILK.
THEY'RE COLD...
SHUT UP...
30

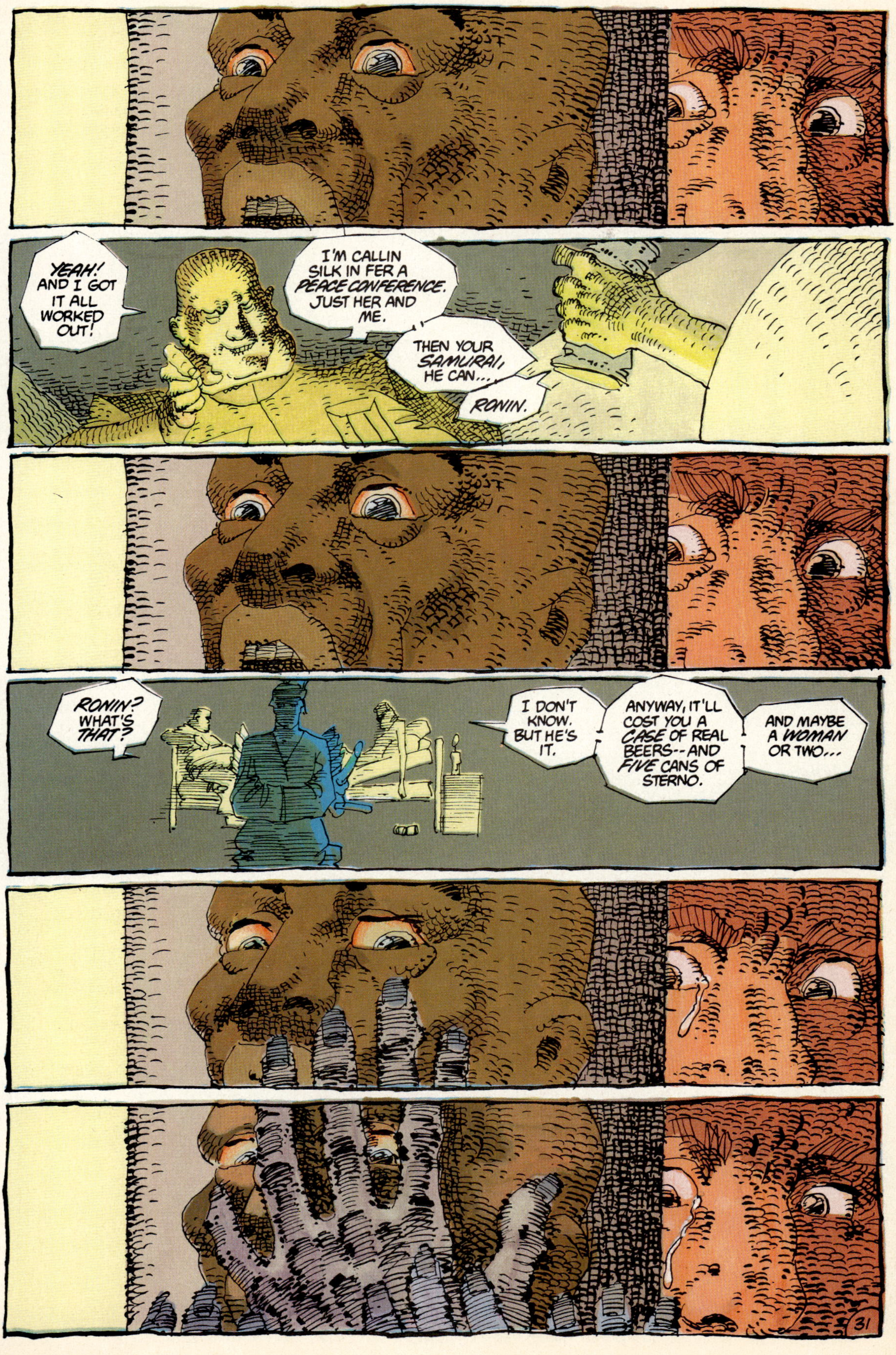

YEAH! AND I GOT IT ALL WORKED OUT!
I'M CALLIN SILK IN FER A PEACE CONFERENCE. JUST HER AND ME.
THEN YOUR SAMURAI, HE CAN...
RONIN.
RONIN? WHAT'S THAT?
I DON'T KNOW. BUT HE'S IT.
ANYWAY, IT'LL COST YOU A CASE OF REAL BEERS--AND FIVE CANS OF STERNO.
AND MAYBE A WOMAN OR TWO...
31

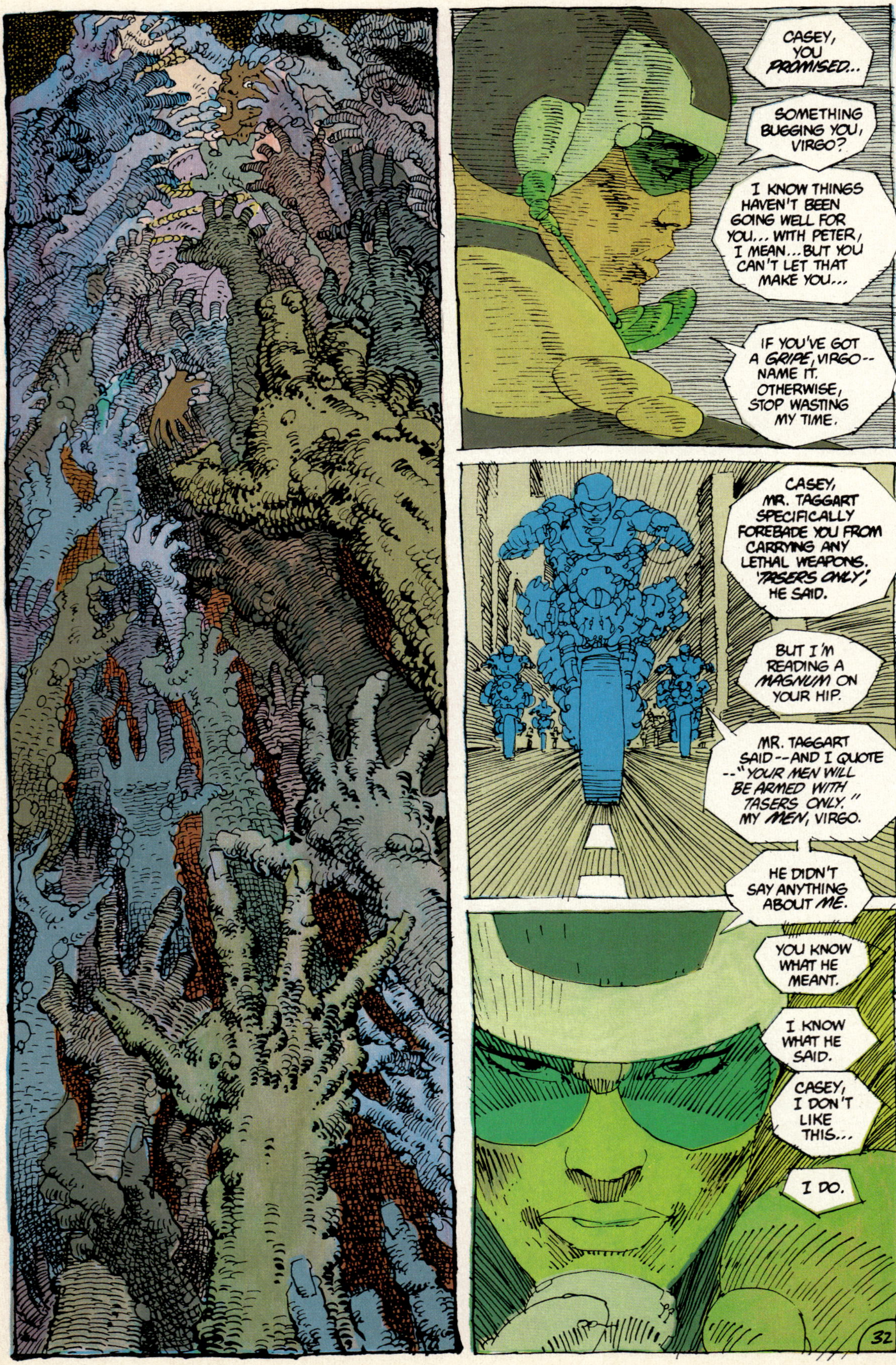
CASEY, YOU PROMISED...
SOMETHING BUGGING YOU, VIRGO?
I KNOW THINGS HAVEN'T BEEN GOING WELL FOR YOU... WITH PETER, I MEAN... BUT YOU CAN'T LET THAT MAKE YOU...
IF YOU'VE GOT A GRIPE, VIRGO-- NAME IT. OTHERWISE, STOP WASTING MY TIME.
CASEY, MR. TAGGART SPECIFICALLY FOREBADE YOU FROM CARRYING ANY LETHAL WEAPONS. "TASERS ONLY," HE SAID.
BUT I'M READING A MAGNUM ON YOUR HIP.
MR. TAGGART SAID--AND I QUOTE --"YOUR MEN WILL BE ARMED WITH TASERS ONLY." MY MEN, VIRGO.
HE DIDN'T SAY ANYTHING ABOUT ME.
YOU KNOW WHAT HE MEANT.
I KNOW WHAT HE SAID.
CASEY, I DON'T LIKE THIS...
I DO.
32

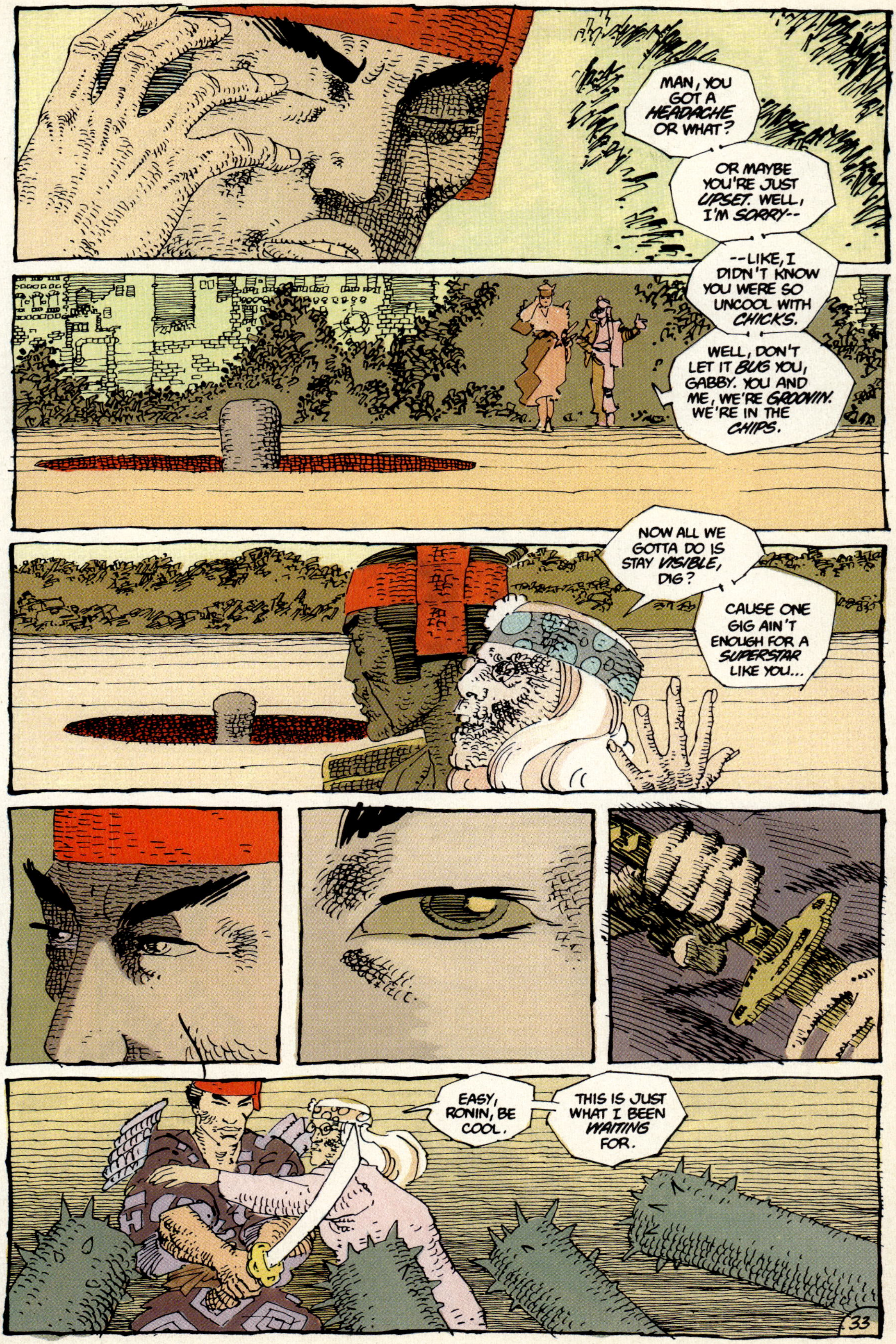
MAN, YOU GOT A HEADACHE OR WHAT?
OR MAYBE YOU'RE JUST UPSET. WELL, I'M SORRY--
--LIKE, I DIDN'T KNOW YOU WERE SO UNCOOL WITH CHICKS.
WELL, DON'T LET IT BUG YOU, GABBY. YOU AND ME, WE'RE GROOVIN. WE'RE IN THE CHIPS.
NOW ALL WE GOTTA DO IS STAY VISIBLE, DIG?
CAUSE ONE GIG AIN'T ENOUGH FOR A SUPERSTAR LIKE YOU...
EASY, RONIN, BE COOL.
THIS IS JUST WHAT I BEEN WAITING FOR.
33

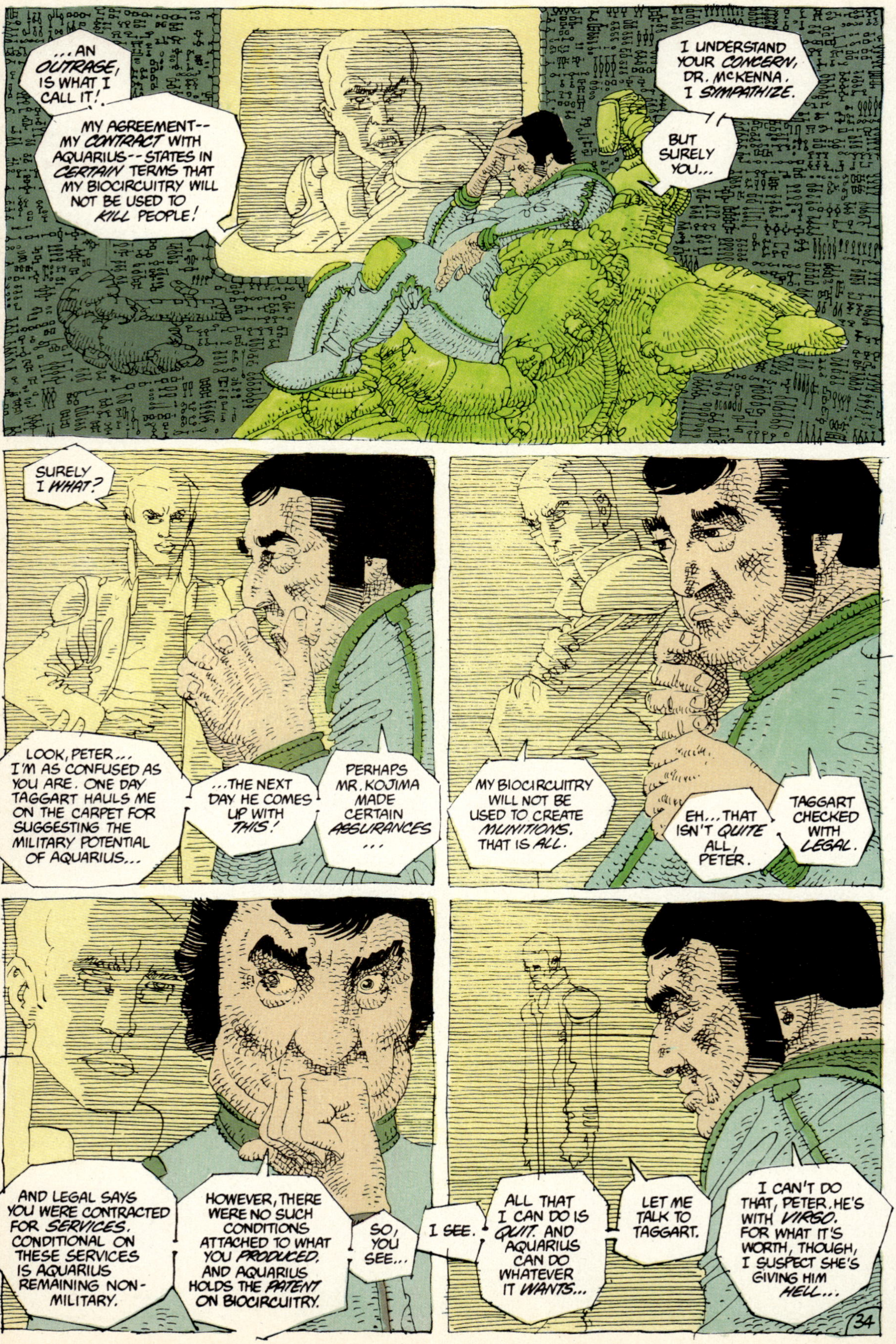
...AN OUTRAGE, IS WHAT I CALL IT!
MY AGREEMENT-- MY CONTRACT WITH AQUARIUS--STATES IN CERTAIN TERMS THAT MY BIOCIRCUITRY WILL NOT BE USED TO KILL PEOPLE!
I UNDERSTAND YOUR CONCERN, DR. McKENNA. I SYMPATHIZE.
BUT SURELY YOU...
SURELY I WHAT?
LOOK, PETER... I'M AS CONFUSED AS YOU ARE. ONE DAY TAGGART HAULS ME ON THE CARPET FOR SUGGESTING THE MILITARY POTENTIAL OF AQUARIUS...
...THE NEXT DAY HE COMES UP WITH THIS!
PERHAPS MR. KOJIMA MADE CERTAIN ASSURANCES...
MY BIOCIRCUITRY WILL NOT BE USED TO CREATE MUNITIONS. THAT IS ALL.
EH... THAT ISN'T QUITE ALL, PETER.
TAGGART CHECKED WITH LEGAL.
AND LEGAL SAYS YOU WERE CONTRACTED FOR SERVICES. CONDITIONAL ON THESE SERVICES IS AQUARIUS REMAINING NON-MILITARY.
HOWEVER, THERE WERE NO SUCH CONDITIONS ATTACHED TO WHAT YOU PRODUCED, AND AQUARIUS HOLDS THE PATENT ON BIOCIRCUITRY.
SO, YOU SEE...
I SEE.
ALL THAT I CAN DO IS QUIT. AND AQUARIUS CAN DO WHATEVER IT WANTS...
LET ME TALK TO TAGGART.
I CAN'T DO THAT, PETER. HE'S WITH VIRGO. FOR WHAT IT'S WORTH, THOUGH, I SUSPECT SHE'S GIVING HIM HELL...
34

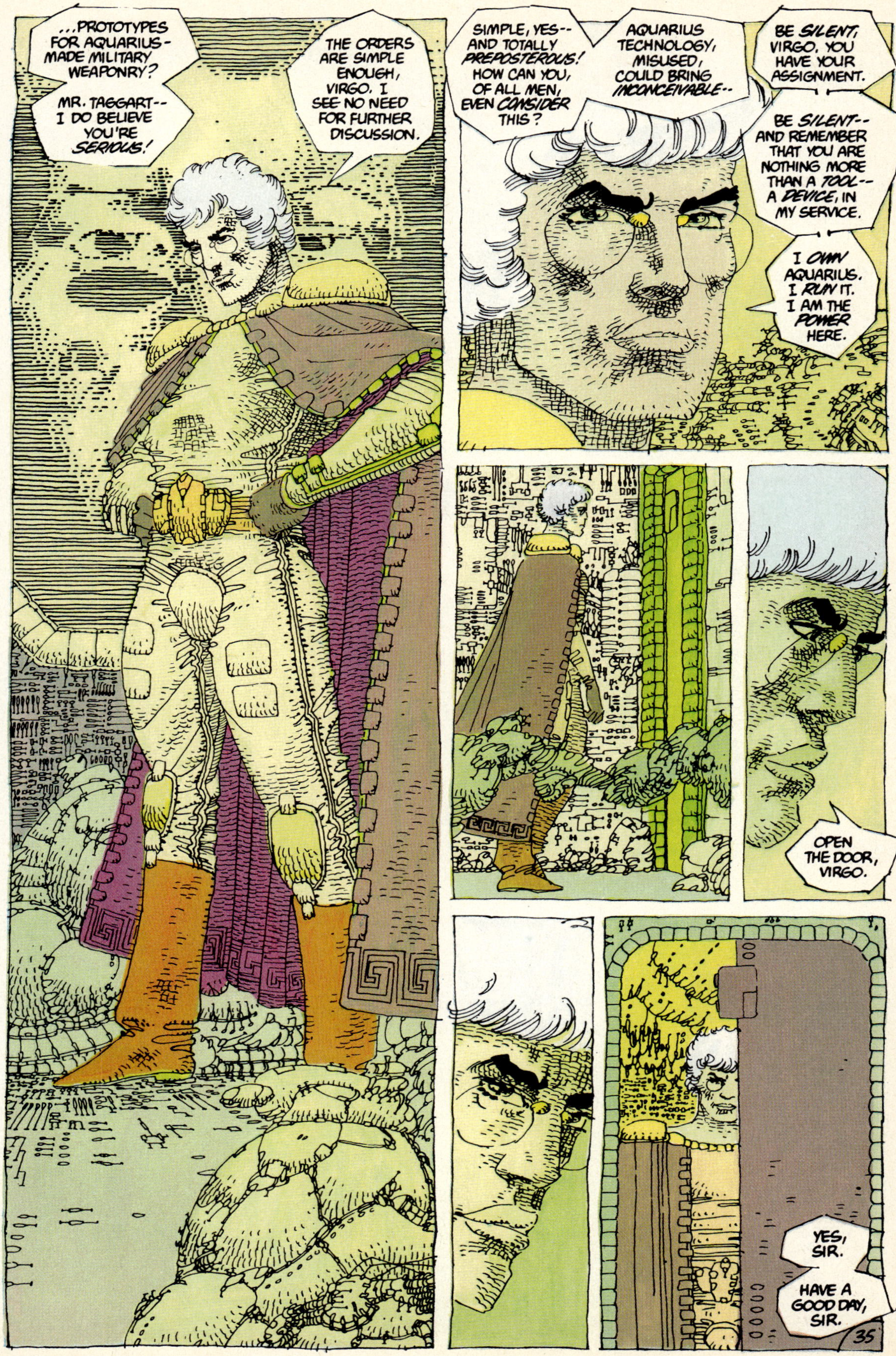
...PROTOTYPES FOR AQUARIUS-MADE MILITARY WEAPONRY?
MR. TAGGART--I DO BELIEVE YOU'RE SERIOUS!
THE ORDERS ARE SIMPLE ENOUGH, VIRGO. I SEE NO NEED FOR FURTHER DISCUSSION.
SIMPLE, YES--AND TOTALLY PREPOSTEROUS! HOW CAN YOU, OF ALL MEN, EVEN CONSIDER THIS?
AQUARIUS TECHNOLOGY, MISUSED, COULD BRING INCONCEIVABLE--
BE SILENT, VIRGO. YOU HAVE YOUR ASSIGNMENT.
BE SILENT--AND REMEMBER THAT YOU ARE NOTHING MORE THAN A TOOL--A DEVICE, IN MY SERVICE.
I OWN AQUARIUS. I RUN IT. I AM THE POWER HERE.
OPEN THE DOOR, VIRGO.
YES, SIR.
HAVE A GOOD DAY, SIR.

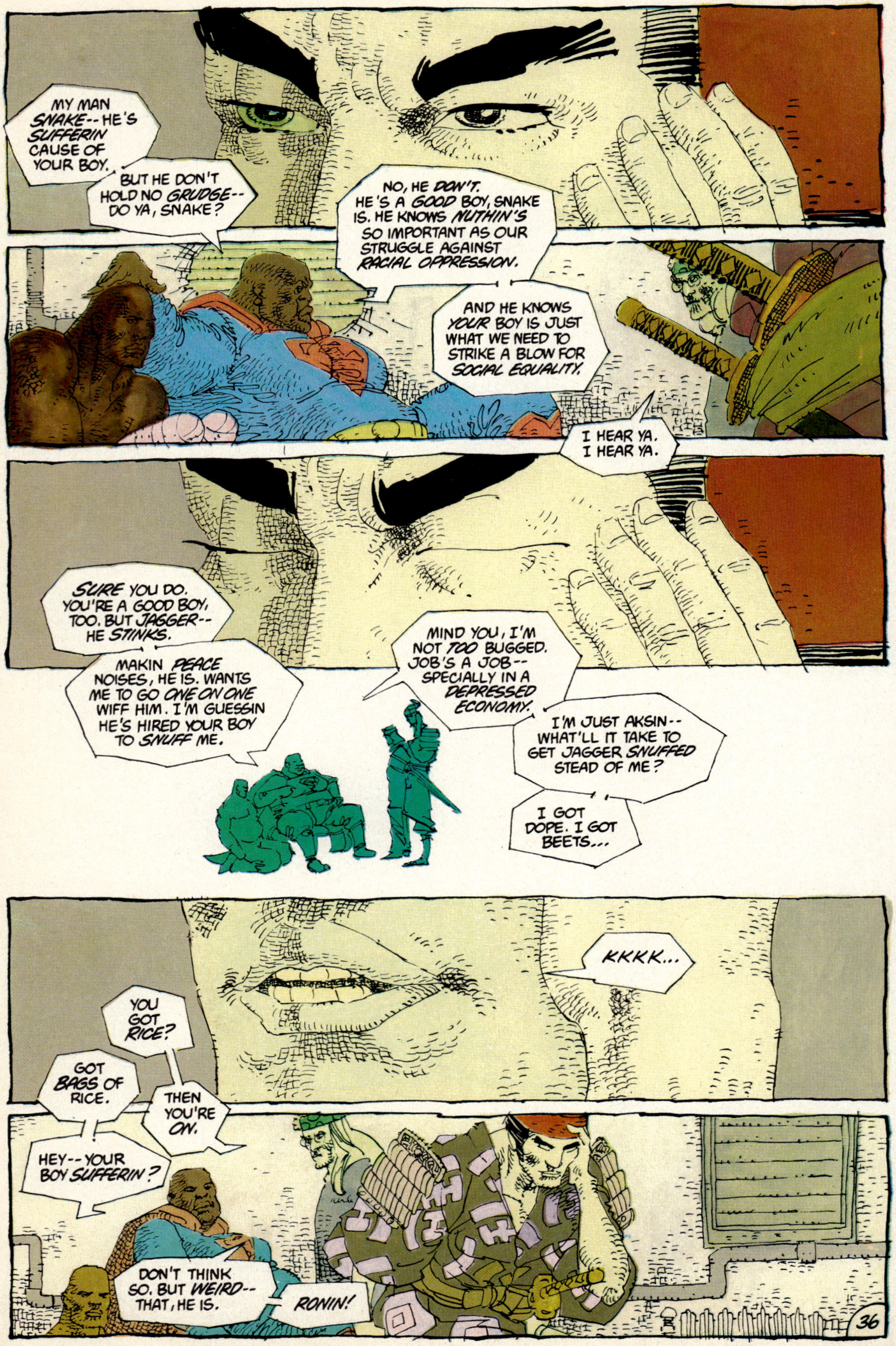
MY MAN SNAKE-- HE'S SUFFERIN CAUSE OF YOUR BOY.
BUT HE DON'T HOLD NO GRUDGE-- DO YA, SNAKE?
NO, HE DON'T. HE'S A GOOD BOY, SNAKE IS. HE KNOWS NUTHIN'S SO IMPORTANT AS OUR STRUGGLE AGAINST RACIAL OPPRESSION.
AND HE KNOWS YOUR BOY IS JUST WHAT WE NEED TO STRIKE A BLOW FOR SOCIAL EQUALITY.
I HEAR YA. I HEAR YA.
SURE YOU DO. YOU'RE A GOOD BOY, TOO. BUT JAGGER-- HE STINKS.
MAKIN PEACE NOISES, HE IS. WANTS ME TO GO ONE ON ONE WIFF HIM. I'M GUESSIN HE'S HIRED YOUR BOY TO SNUFF ME.
MIND YOU, I'M NOT TOO BUGGED. JOB'S A JOB-- SPECIALLY IN A DEPRESSED ECONOMY.
I'M JUST AKSIN-- WHAT'LL IT TAKE TO GET JAGGER SNUFFED STEAD OF ME?
I GOT DOPE. I GOT BEETS...
KKKK...
YOU GOT RICE?
GOT BAGS OF RICE.
THEN YOU'RE ON.
HEY-- YOUR BOY SUFFERIN?
DON'T THINK SO. BUT WEIRD-- THAT, HE IS.
RONIN!

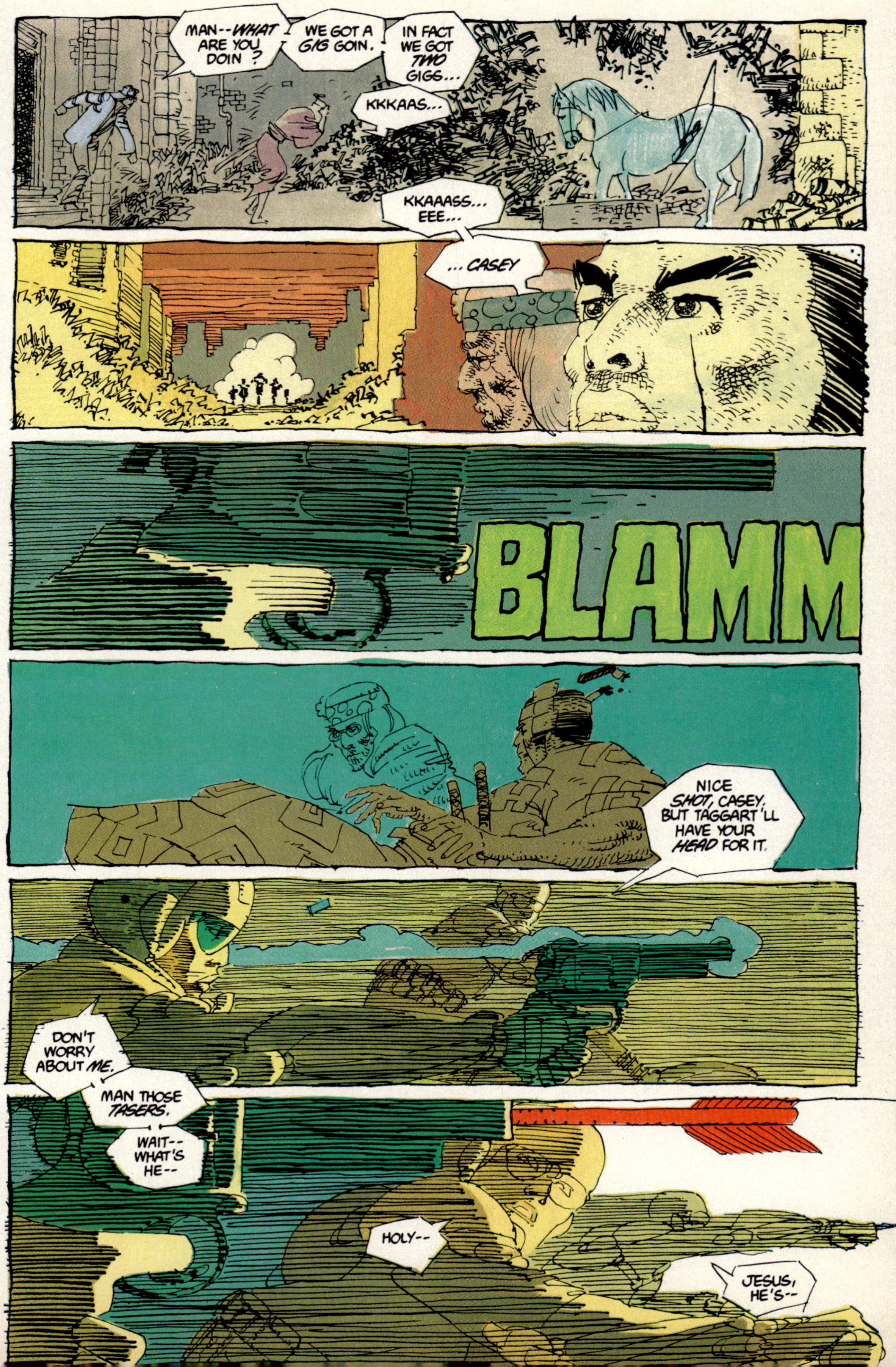
MAN--WHAT ARE YOU DOIN ?
WE GOT A GIG GOIN.
IN FACT WE GOT TWO GIGS...
KKKAAS...
KKAAASS... EEE...
...CASEY
BLAMM
NICE SHOT, CASEY, BUT TAGGART'LL HAVE YOUR HEAD FOR IT.
DON'T WORRY ABOUT ME.
MAN THOSE TASERS.
WAIT-- WHAT'S HE--
HOLY--
JESUS, HE'S--

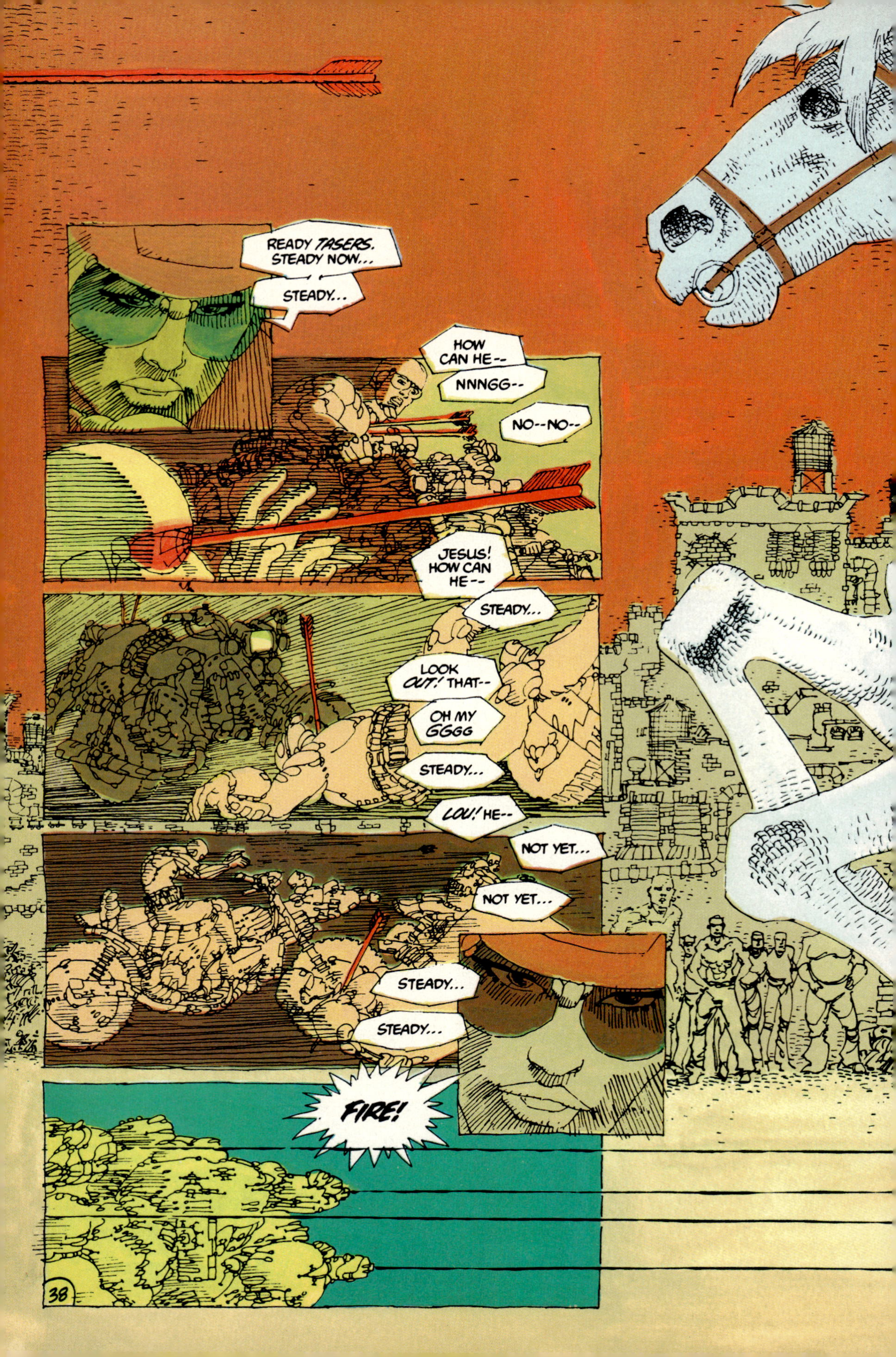
READY TASERS. STEADY NOW...
STEADY...
HOW CAN HE--
NNNGG--
NO--NO--
JESUS! HOW CAN HE--
STEADY...
LOOK OUT! THAT--
OH MY GGGG
STEADY...
LOU! HE--
NOT YET...
NOT YET...
STEADY...
STEADY...
FIRE!

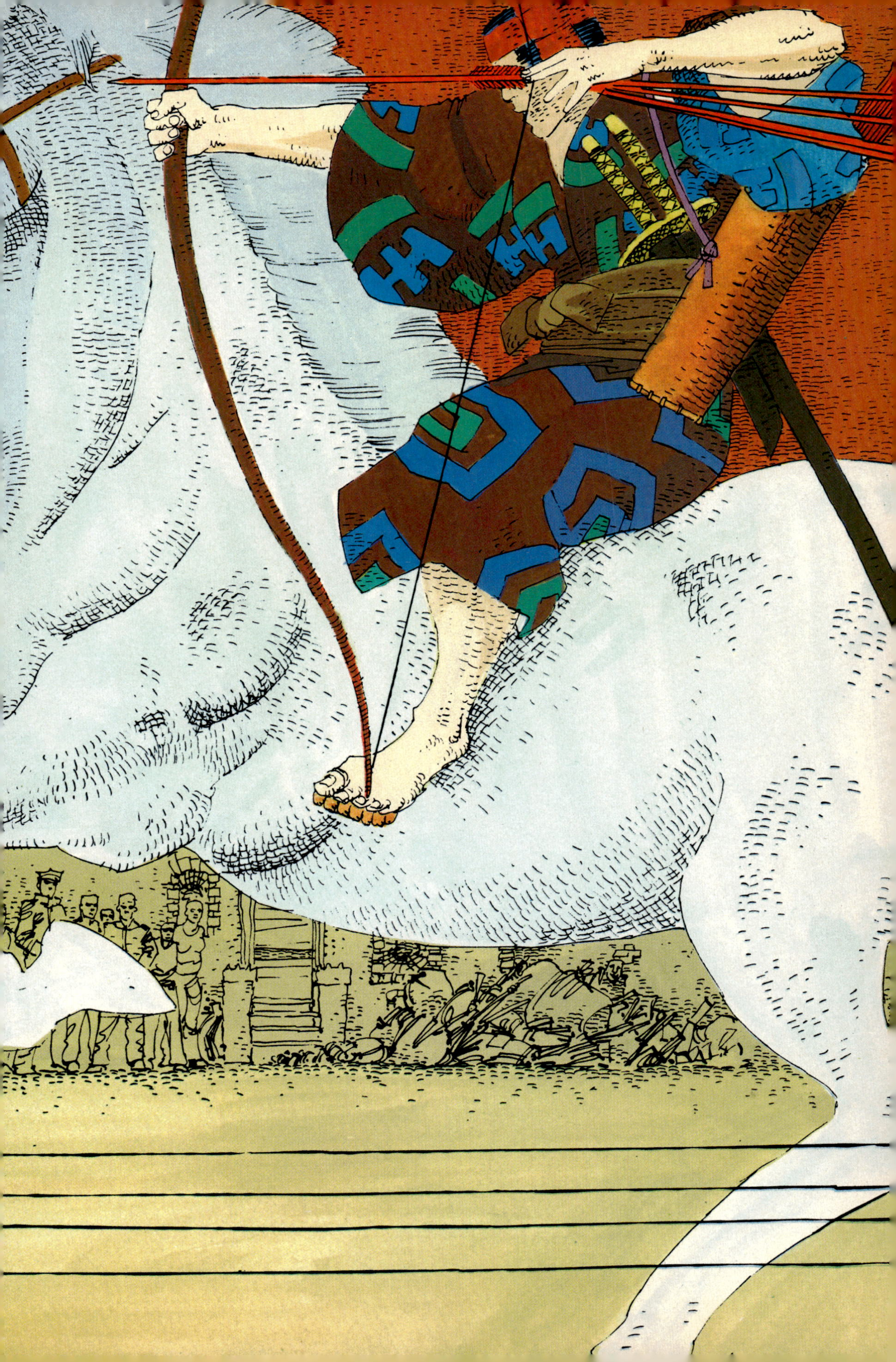

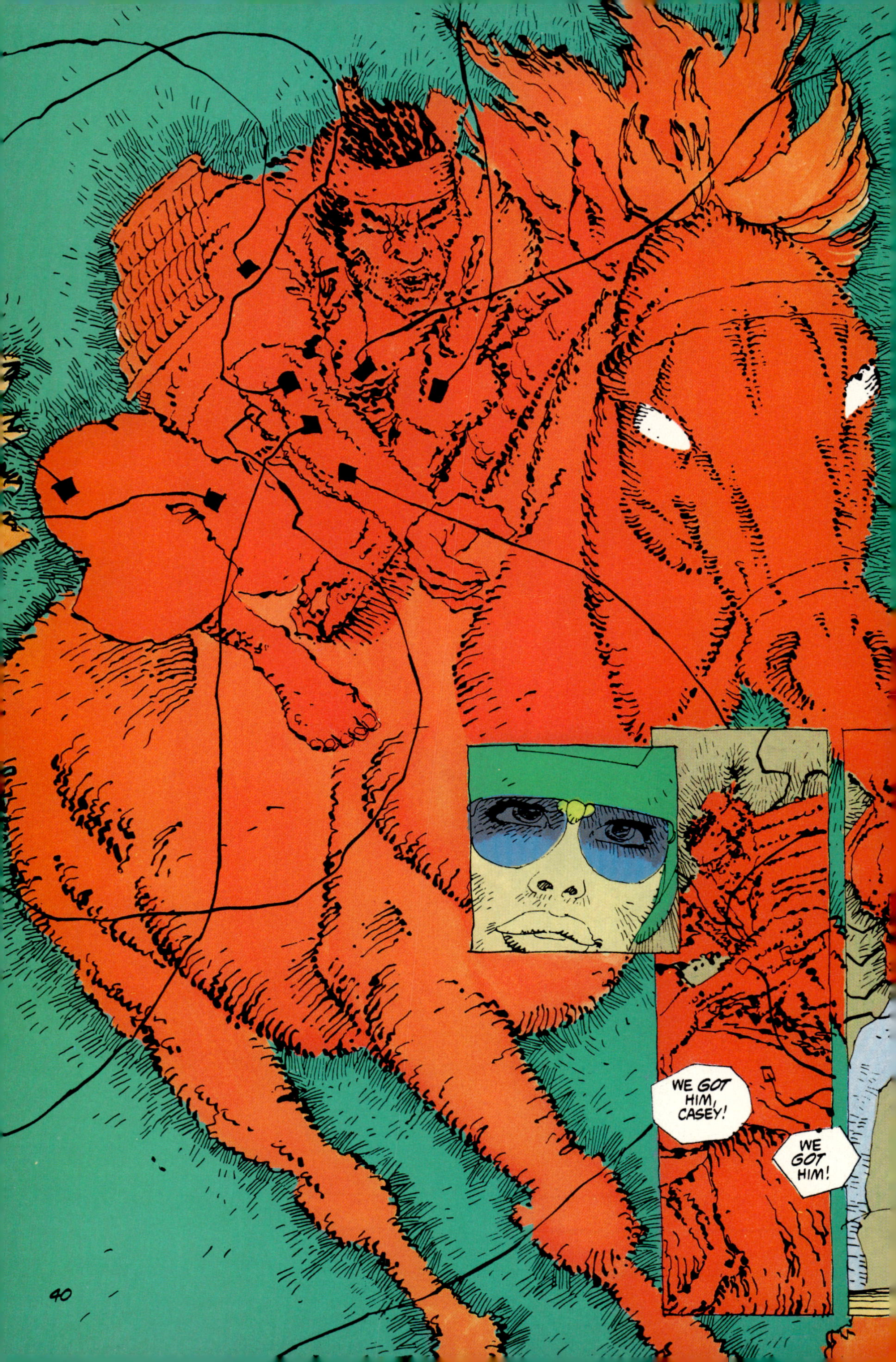
WE GOT HIM, CASEY!
WE GOT HIM!

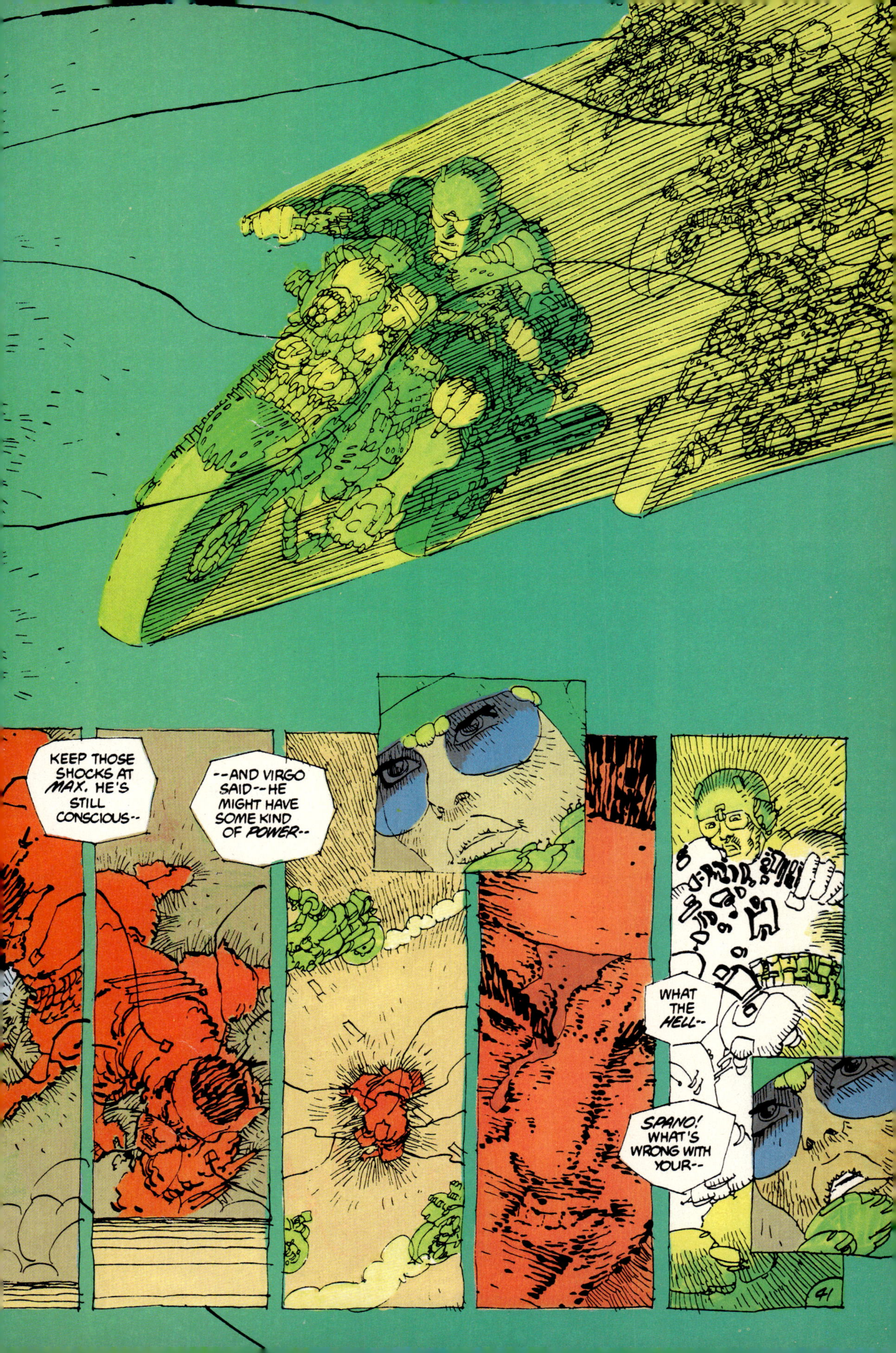

KEEP THOSE SHOCKS AT MAX. HE'S STILL CONSCIOUS--
--AND VIRGO SAID--HE MIGHT HAVE SOME KIND OF POWER--
WHAT THE HELL--
SPANO! WHAT'S WRONG WITH YOUR--

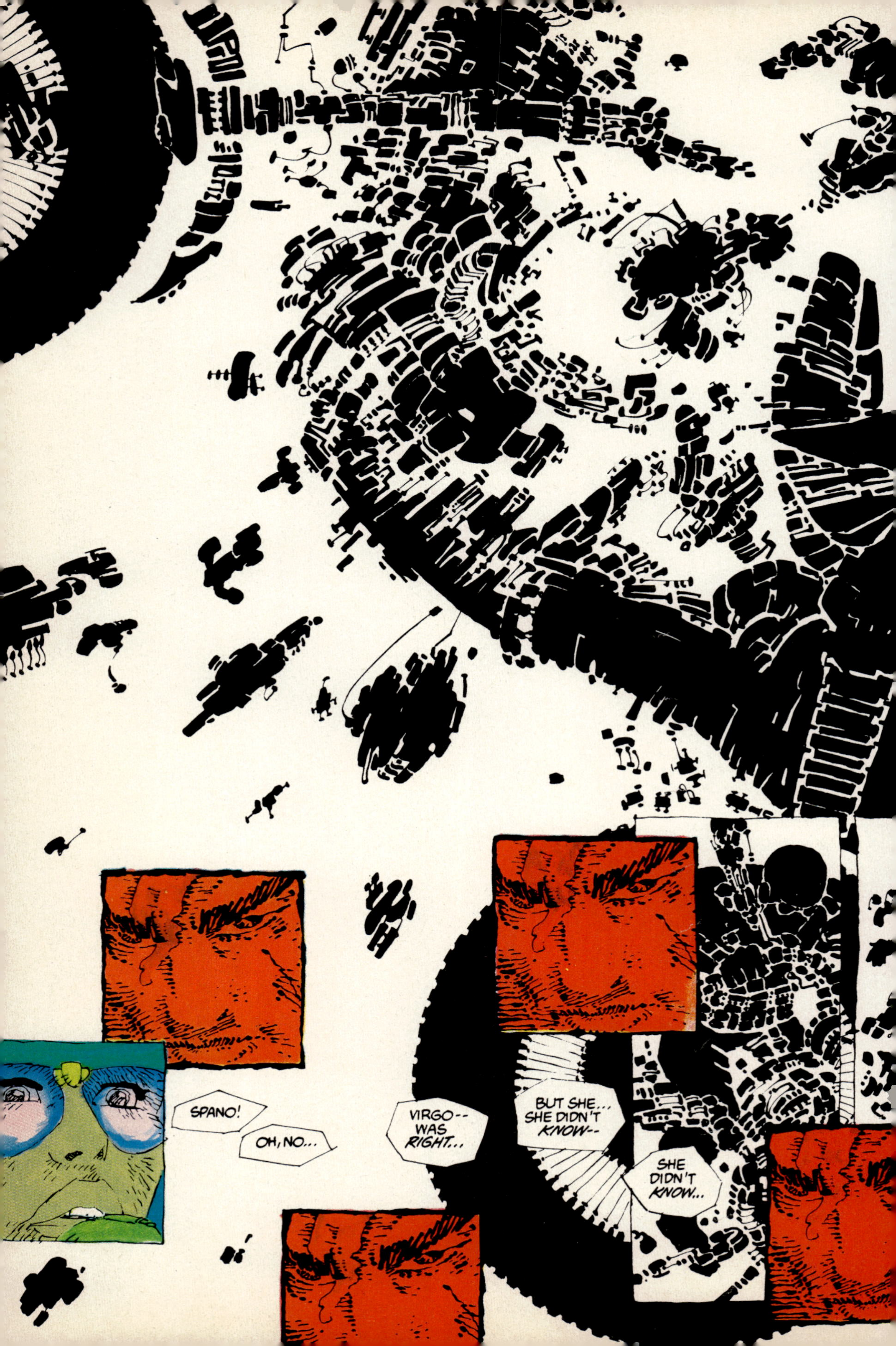
SPANO!
OH, NO...
VIRGO--
WAS
RIGHT...
BUT SHE...
SHE DIDN'T
KNOW--
SHE
DIDN'T
KNOW...

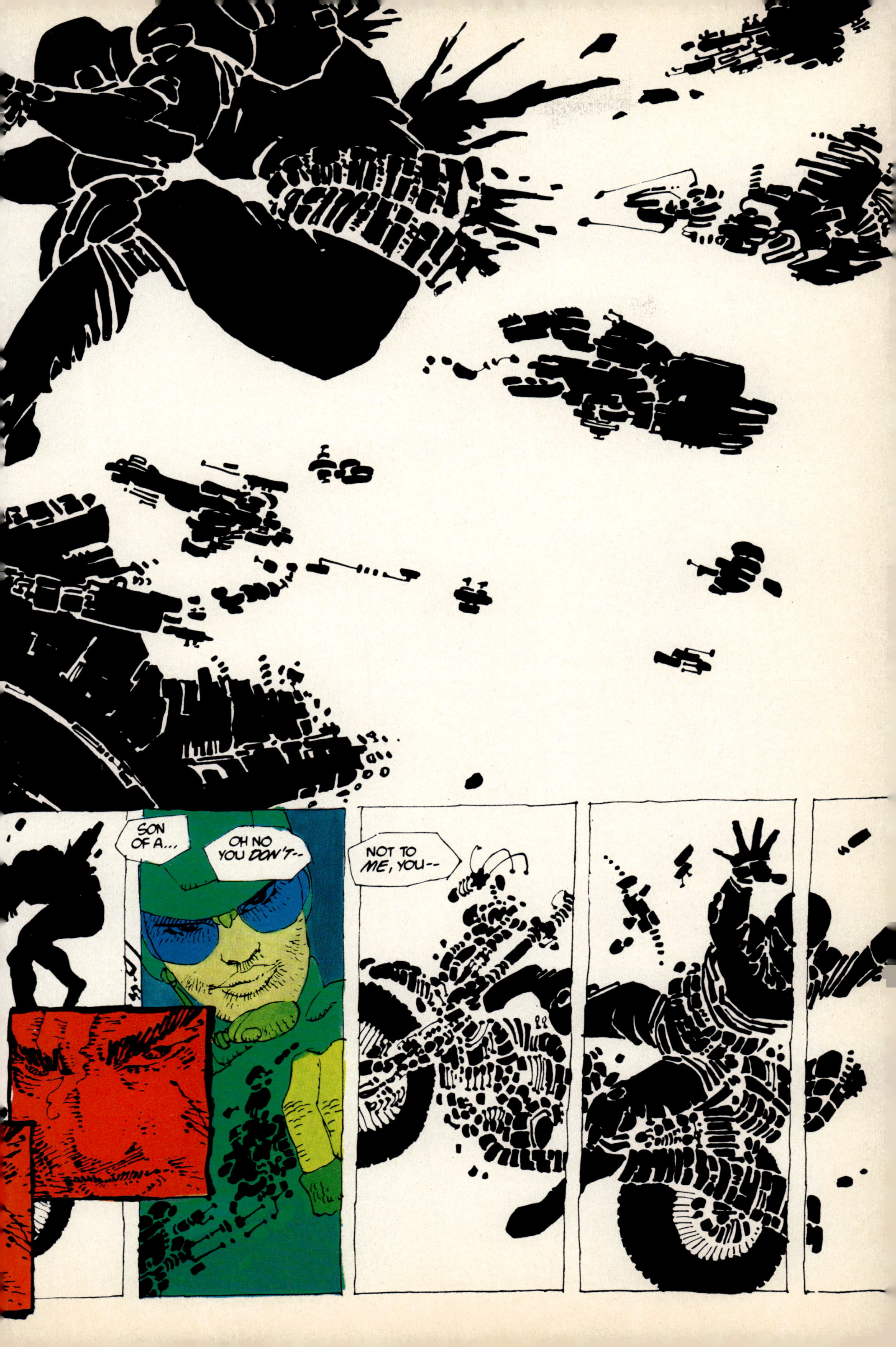
SON OF A...
OH NO YOU DON'T--
NOT TO ME, YOU--

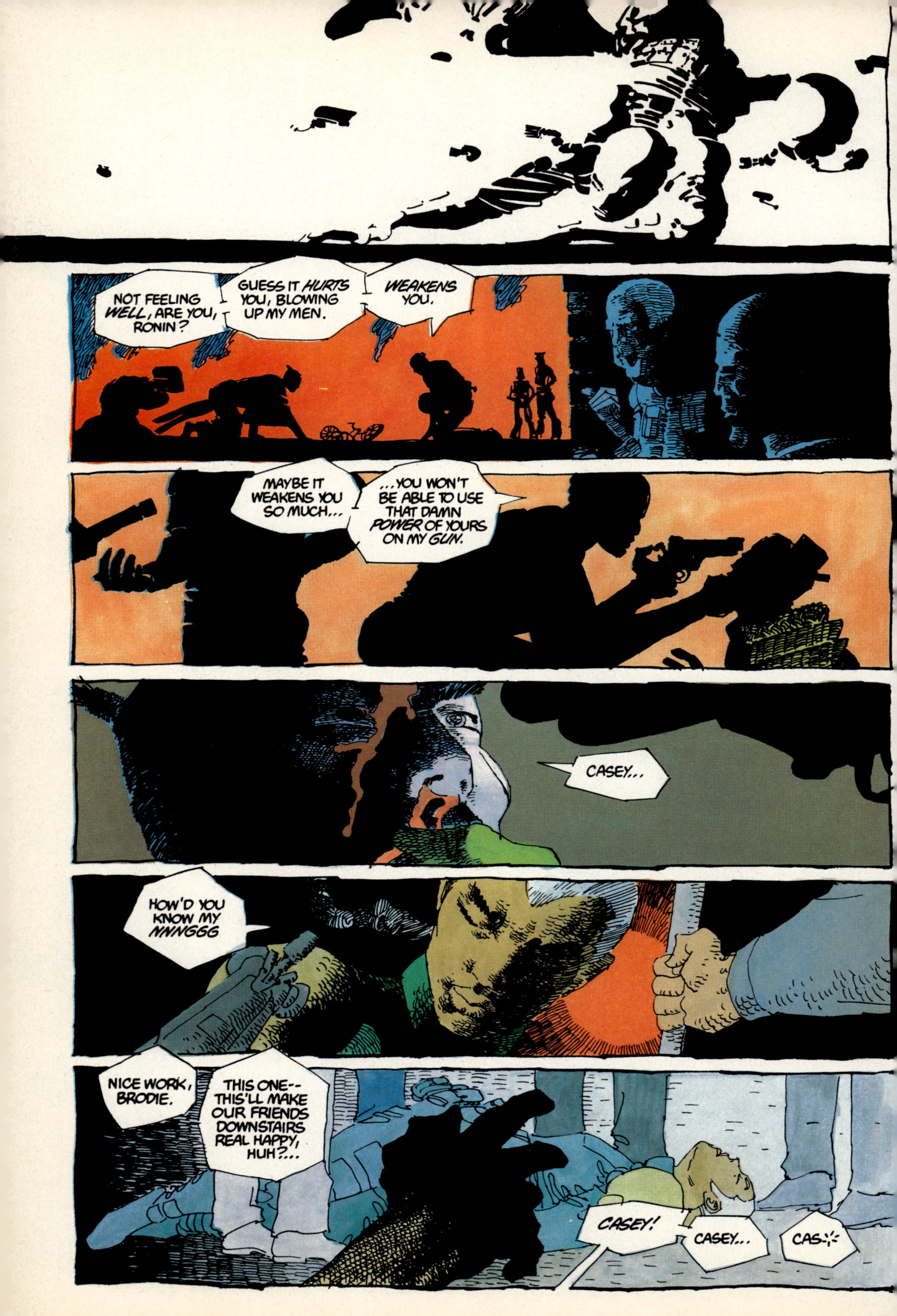
NOT FEELING WELL, ARE YOU, RONIN?
GUESS IT HURTS YOU, BLOWING UP MY MEN.
WEAKENS YOU.
MAYBE IT WEAKENS YOU SO MUCH...
...YOU WON'T BE ABLE TO USE THAT DAMN POWER OF YOURS ON MY GUN.
CASEY...
HOW'D YOU KNOW MY NNNGGG
NICE WORK, BRODIE.
THIS ONE-- THIS'LL MAKE OUR FRIENDS DOWNSTAIRS REAL HAPPY, HUH?...
CASEY!
CASEY...
CAS-

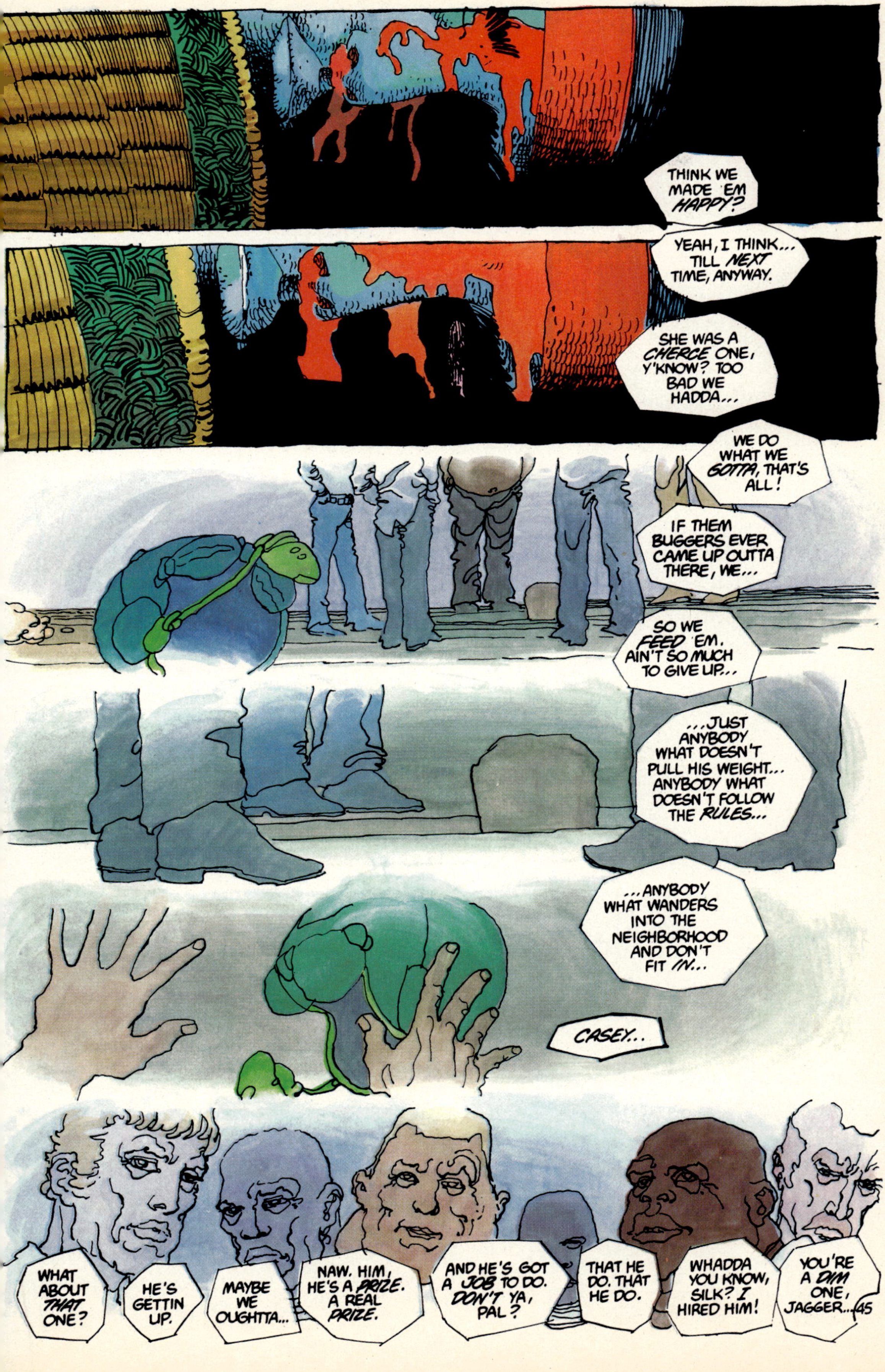

THINK WE MADE 'EM HAPPY?
YEAH, I THINK... TILL NEXT TIME, ANYWAY.
SHE WAS A CHERCE ONE, Y'KNOW? TOO BAD WE HADDA...
WE DO WHAT WE GOTTA, THAT'S ALL!
IF THEM BUGGERS EVER CAME UP OUTTA THERE, WE...
SO WE FEED 'EM. AIN'T SO MUCH TO GIVE UP...
...JUST ANYBODY WHAT DOESN'T PULL HIS WEIGHT... ANYBODY WHAT DOESN'T FOLLOW THE RULES...
...ANYBODY WHAT WANDERS INTO THE NEIGHBORHOOD AND DON'T FIT IN...
CASEY...
WHAT ABOUT THAT ONE?
HE'S GETTIN UP.
MAYBE WE OUGHTTA...
NAW. HIM, HE'S A PRIZE. A REAL PRIZE.
AND HE'S GOT A JOB TO DO. DON'T YA, PAL?
THAT HE DO. THAT HE DO.
WHADDA YOU KNOW, SILK? I HIRED HIM!
YOU'RE A DIM ONE, JAGGER...

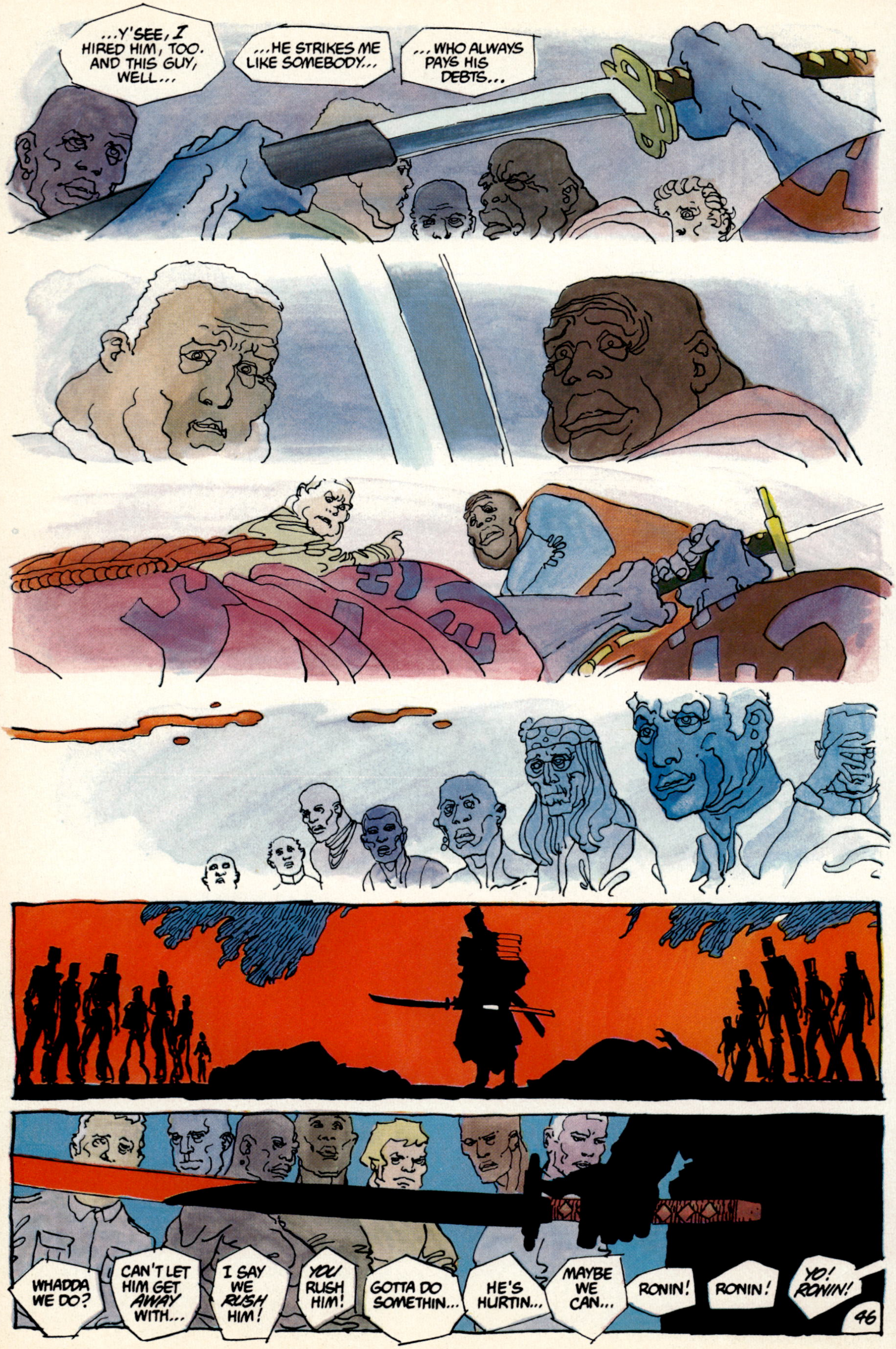
...Y'SEE, I HIRED HIM, TOO. AND THIS GUY, WELL...
...HE STRIKES ME LIKE SOMEBODY...
...WHO ALWAYS PAYS HIS DEBTS...
WHADDA WE DO?
CAN'T LET HIM GET AWAY WITH...
I SAY WE RUSH HIM!
YOU RUSH HIM!
GOTTA DO SOMETHIN...
HE'S HURTIN...
MAYBE WE CAN...
RONIN!
RONIN!
YO! RONIN!
46

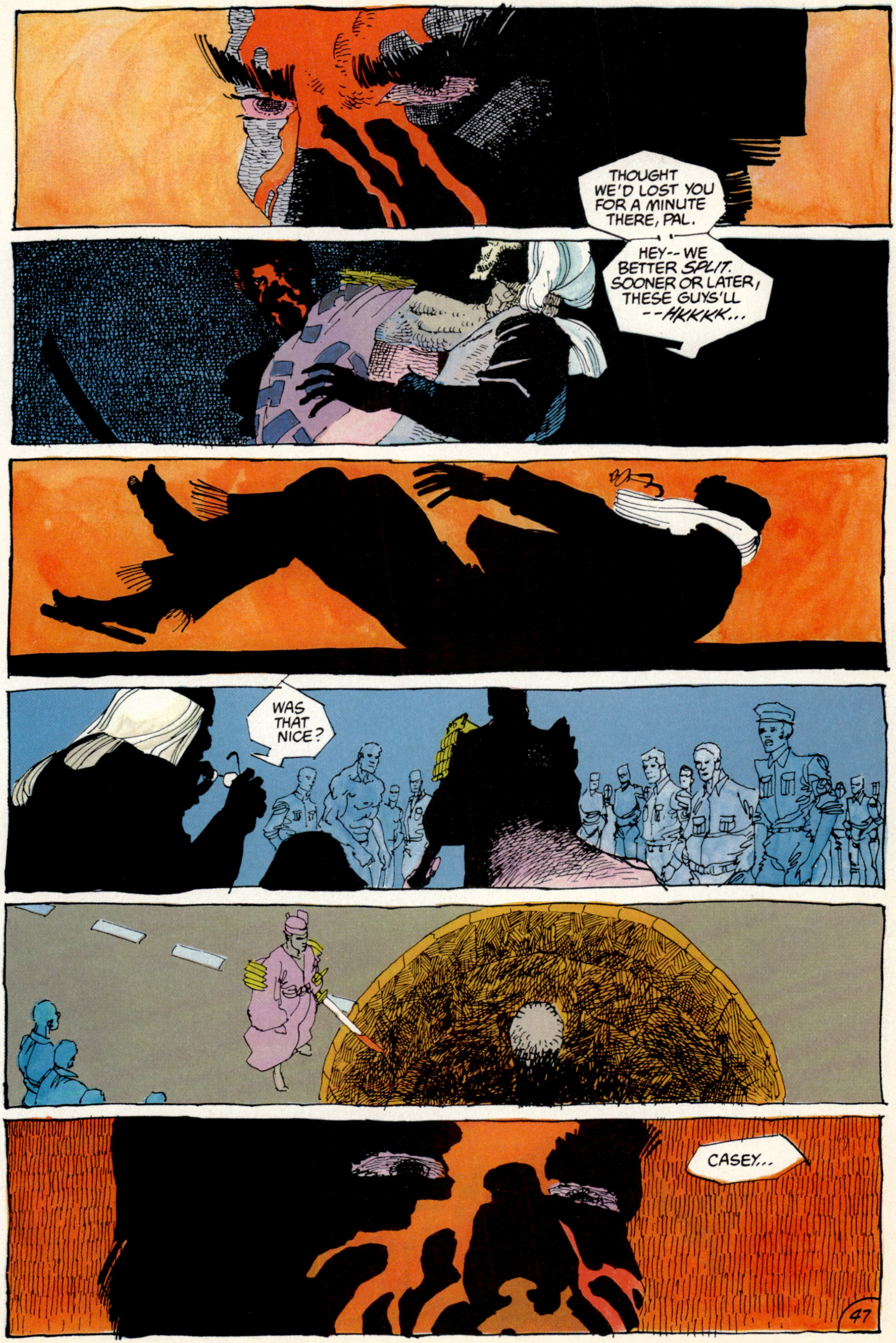
THOUGHT WE'D LOST YOU FOR A MINUTE THERE, PAL.
HEY-- WE BETTER SPLIT. SOONER OR LATER, THESE GUYS'LL --HKKKK...
WAS THAT NICE?
CASEY...

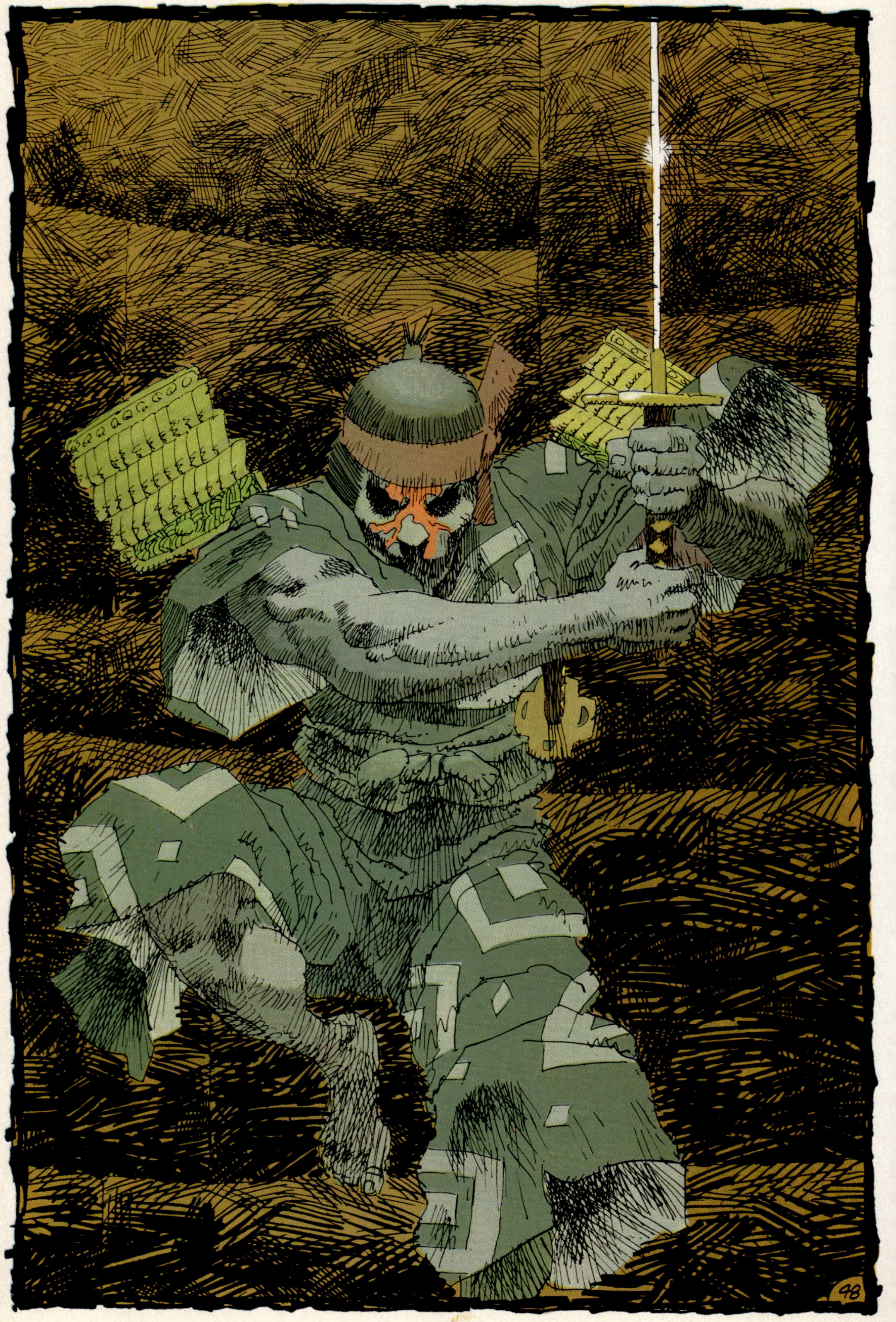

CHAPTER FOUR

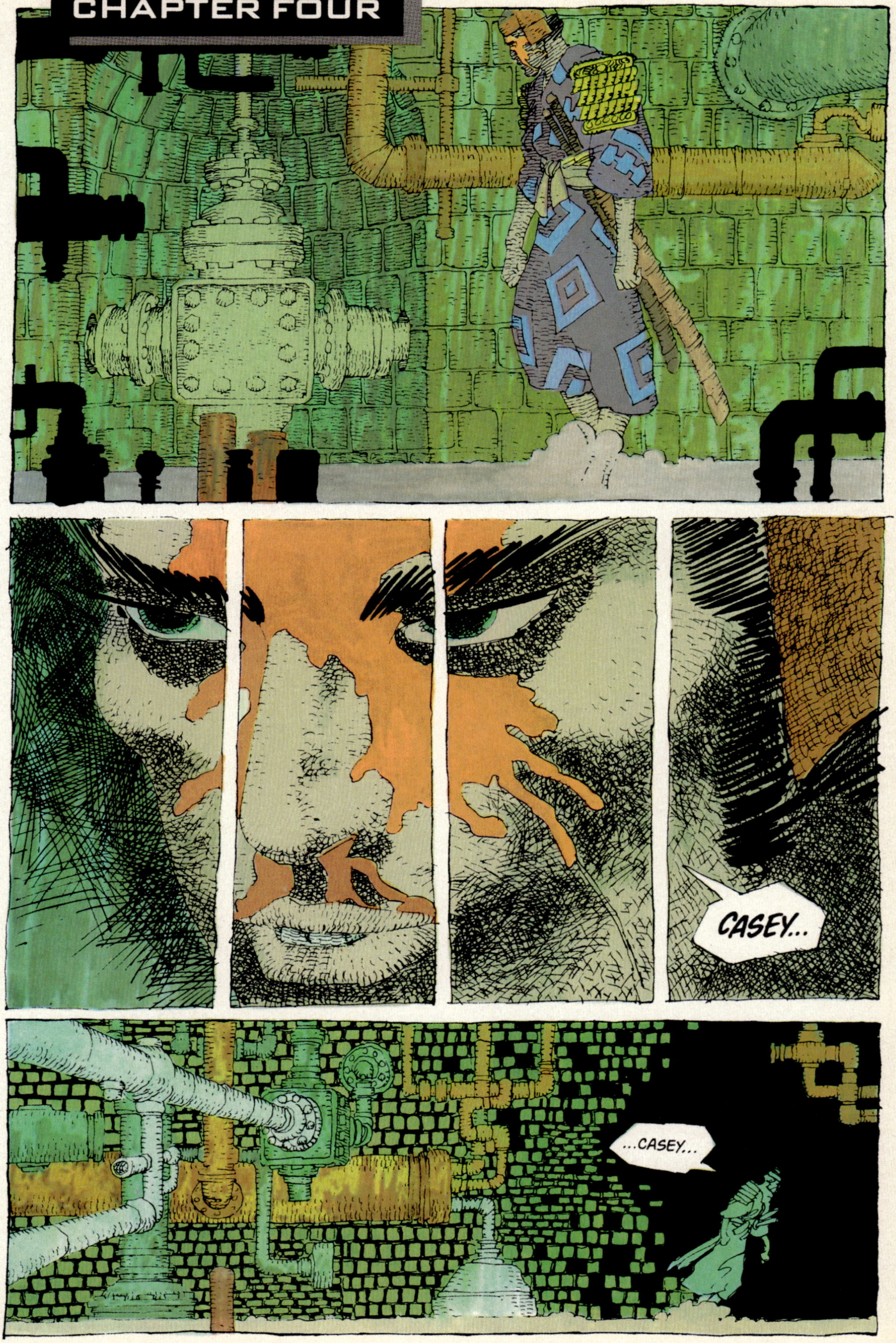
CASEY...
...CASEY...

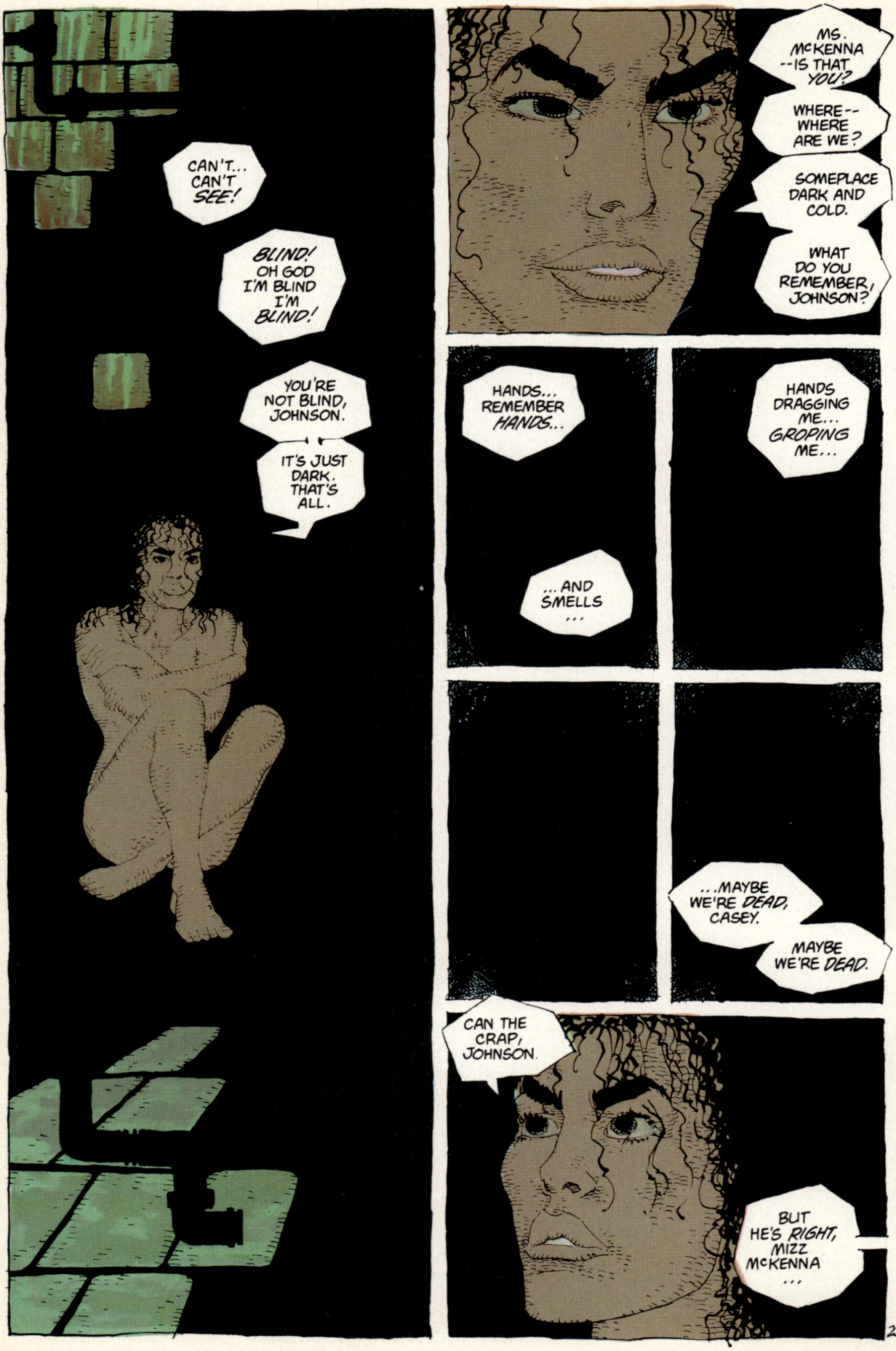
CAN'T... CAN'T SEE!
BLIND! OH GOD I'M BLIND I'M BLIND!
YOU'RE NOT BLIND, JOHNSON.
IT'S JUST DARK. THAT'S ALL.
MS. McKENNA --IS THAT YOU?
WHERE--WHERE ARE WE?
SOMEPLACE DARK AND COLD.
WHAT DO YOU REMEMBER, JOHNSON?
HANDS... REMEMBER HANDS...
HANDS DRAGGING ME... GROPING ME...
...AND SMELLS ...
...MAYBE WE'RE DEAD, CASEY.
MAYBE WE'RE DEAD.
CAN THE CRAP, JOHNSON.
BUT HE'S RIGHT, MIZZ McKENNA ...

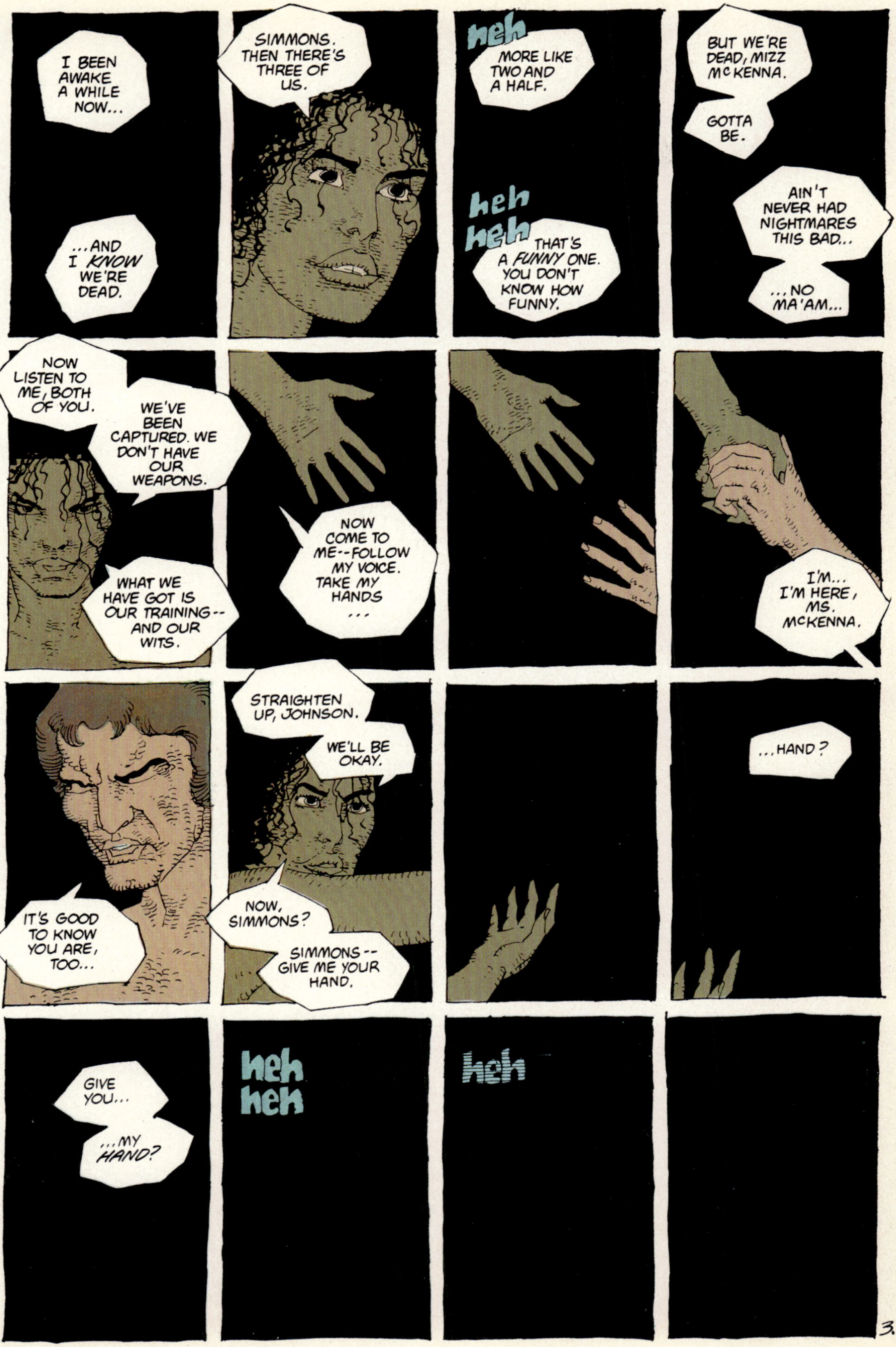
I BEEN AWAKE A WHILE NOW...
...AND I *KNOW* WE'RE DEAD.
SIMMONS. THEN THERE'S THREE OF US.
heh
MORE LIKE TWO AND A HALF.
heh heh
THAT'S A *FUNNY* ONE. YOU DON'T KNOW HOW FUNNY.
BUT WE'RE DEAD, MIZZ McKENNA.
GOTTA BE.
AIN'T NEVER HAD NIGHTMARES THIS BAD...
...NO MA'AM...
NOW LISTEN TO ME, BOTH OF YOU.
WE'VE BEEN CAPTURED. WE DON'T HAVE OUR WEAPONS.
WHAT WE HAVE GOT IS OUR TRAINING--AND OUR WITS.
NOW COME TO ME--FOLLOW MY VOICE. TAKE MY HANDS...
I'M... I'M HERE, MS. McKENNA.
IT'S GOOD TO KNOW YOU ARE, TOO...
STRAIGHTEN UP, JOHNSON.
WE'LL BE OKAY.
NOW, SIMMONS?
SIMMONS--GIVE ME YOUR HAND.
...HAND?
GIVE YOU...
...MY *HAND*?
heh heh
heh

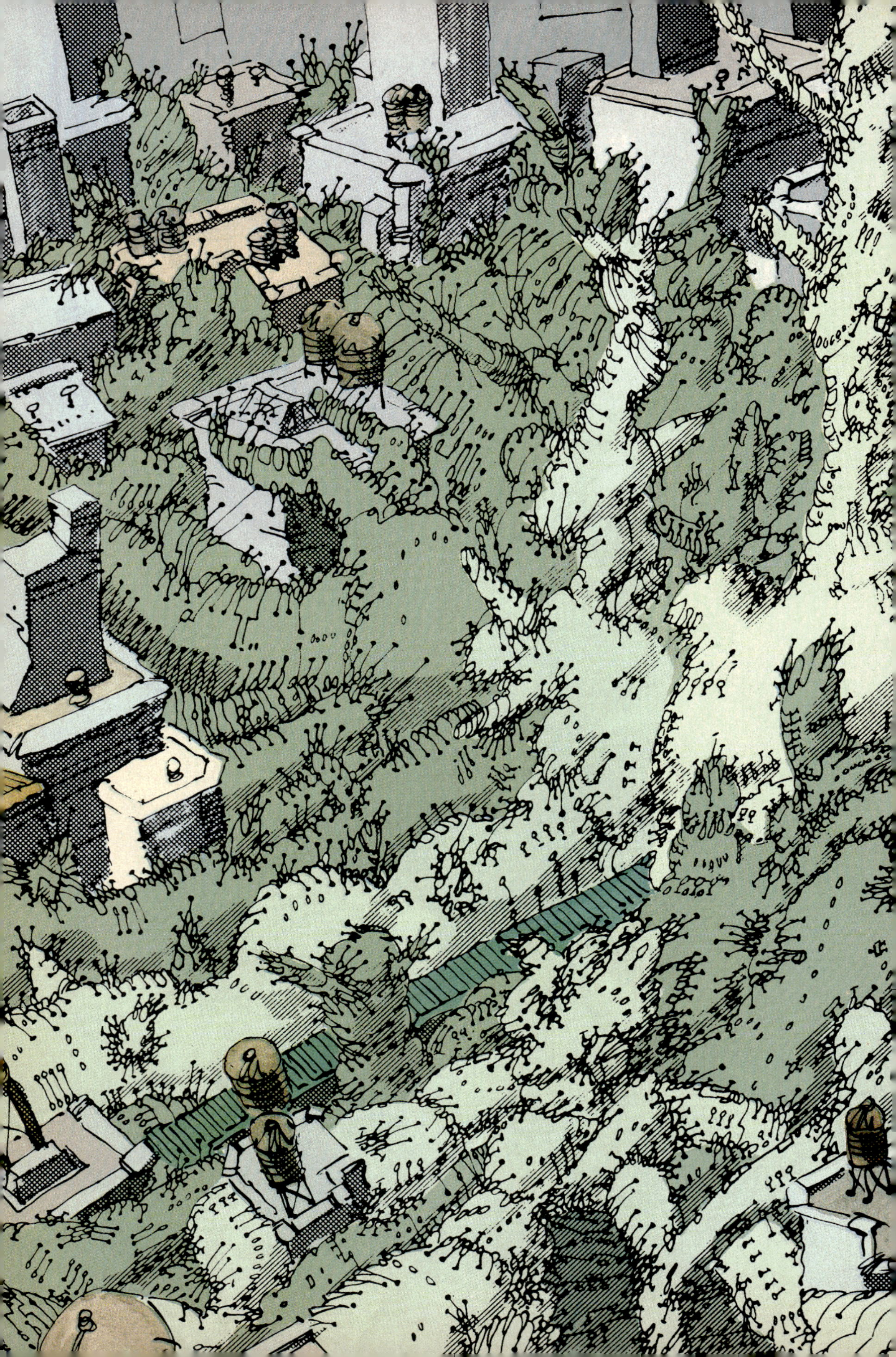

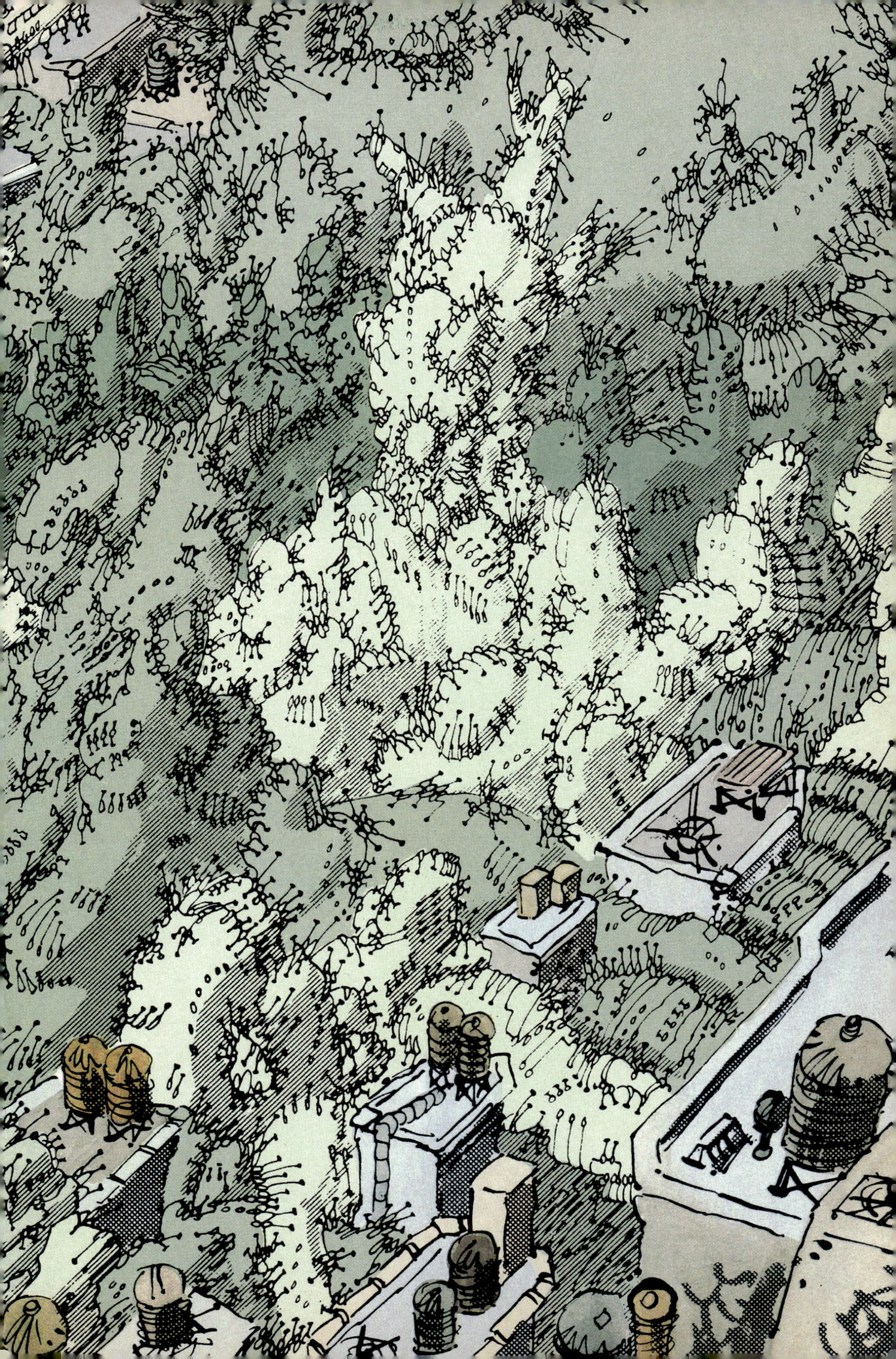

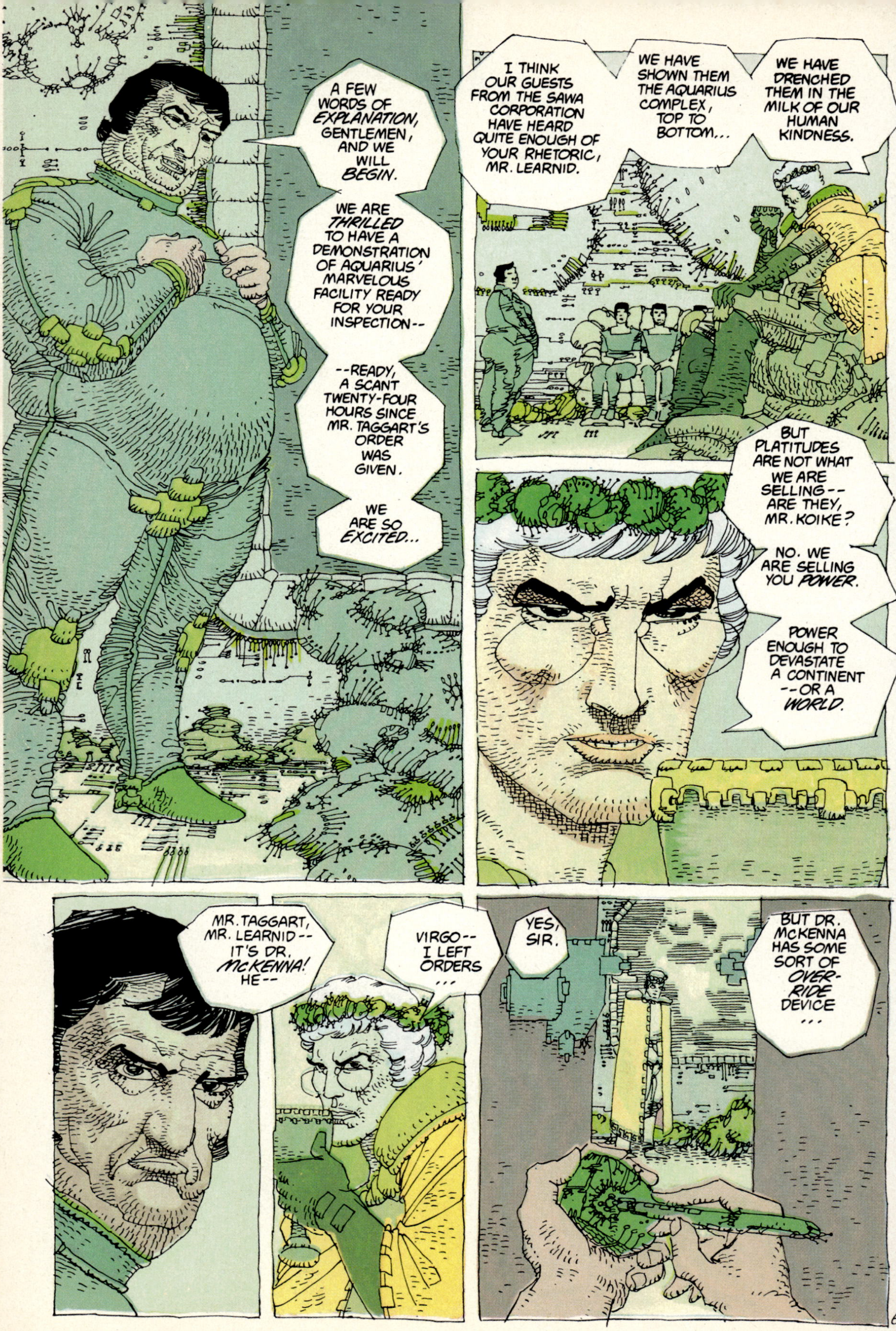
A FEW WORDS OF EXPLANATION, GENTLEMEN, AND WE WILL BEGIN.
WE ARE THRILLED TO HAVE A DEMONSTRATION OF AQUARIUS' MARVELOUS FACILITY READY FOR YOUR INSPECTION--
--READY, A SCANT TWENTY-FOUR HOURS SINCE MR. TAGGART'S ORDER WAS GIVEN.
WE ARE SO EXCITED...
I THINK OUR GUESTS FROM THE SAWA CORPORATION HAVE HEARD QUITE ENOUGH OF YOUR RHETORIC, MR. LEARNID.
WE HAVE SHOWN THEM THE AQUARIUS COMPLEX, TOP TO BOTTOM...
WE HAVE DRENCHED THEM IN THE MILK OF OUR HUMAN KINDNESS.
BUT PLATITUDES ARE NOT WHAT WE ARE SELLING-- ARE THEY, MR. KOIKE?
NO. WE ARE SELLING YOU POWER.
POWER ENOUGH TO DEVASTATE A CONTINENT --OR A WORLD.
MR. TAGGART, MR. LEARNID-- IT'S DR. McKENNA! HE--
VIRGO-- I LEFT ORDERS...
YES, SIR.
BUT DR. McKENNA HAS SOME SORT OF OVER-RIDE DEVICE...

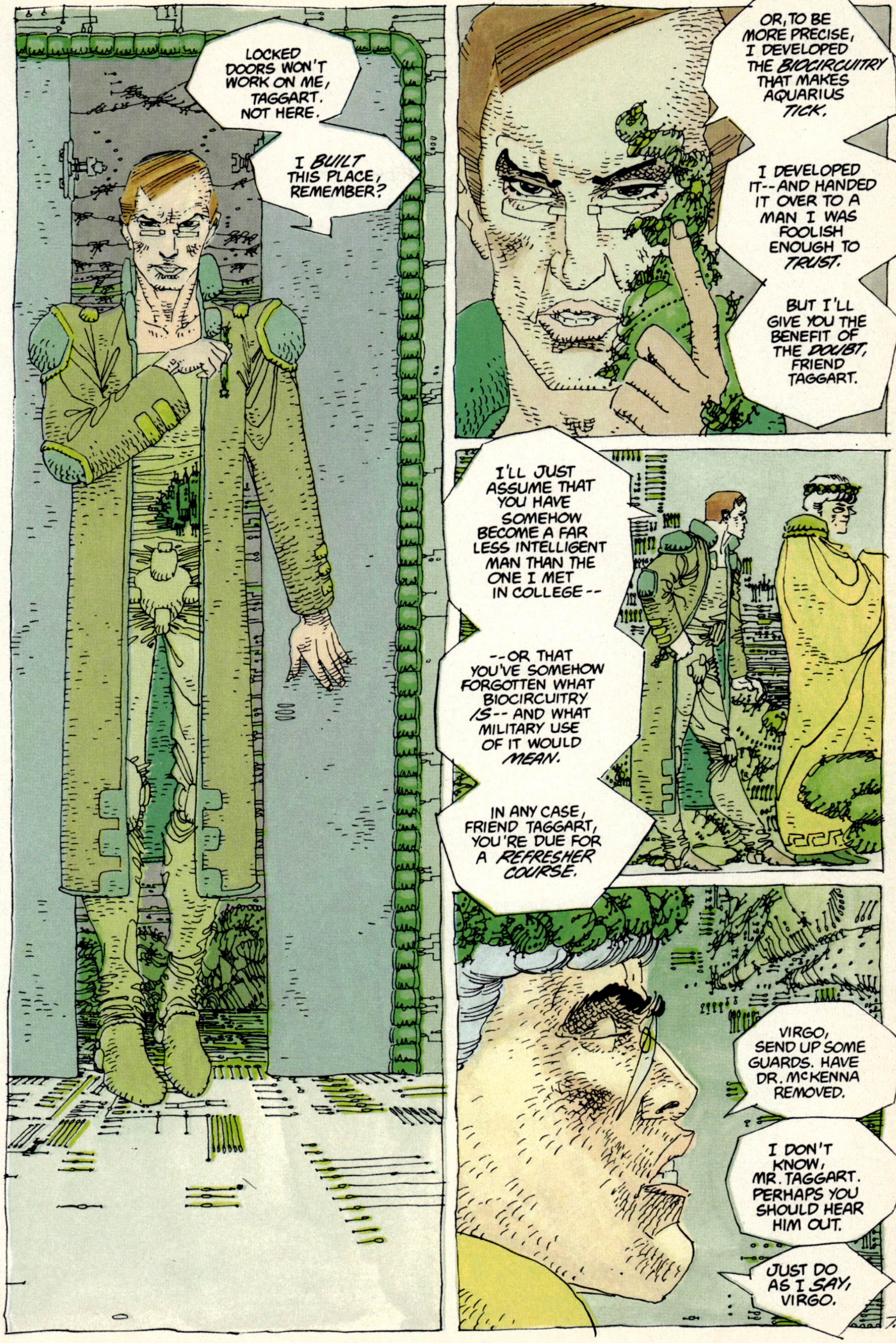

LOCKED DOORS WON'T WORK ON ME, TAGGART. NOT HERE.
I BUILT THIS PLACE, REMEMBER?
OR, TO BE MORE PRECISE, I DEVELOPED THE BIOCIRCUITRY THAT MAKES AQUARIUS TICK.
I DEVELOPED IT--AND HANDED IT OVER TO A MAN I WAS FOOLISH ENOUGH TO TRUST.
BUT I'LL GIVE YOU THE BENEFIT OF THE DOUBT, FRIEND TAGGART.
I'LL JUST ASSUME THAT YOU HAVE SOMEHOW BECOME A FAR LESS INTELLIGENT MAN THAN THE ONE I MET IN COLLEGE--
--OR THAT YOU'VE SOMEHOW FORGOTTEN WHAT BIOCIRCUITRY IS--AND WHAT MILITARY USE OF IT WOULD MEAN.
IN ANY CASE, FRIEND TAGGART, YOU'RE DUE FOR A REFRESHER COURSE.
VIRGO, SEND UP SOME GUARDS. HAVE DR. McKENNA REMOVED.
I DON'T KNOW, MR. TAGGART. PERHAPS YOU SHOULD HEAR HIM OUT.
JUST DO AS I SAY, VIRGO.
7.

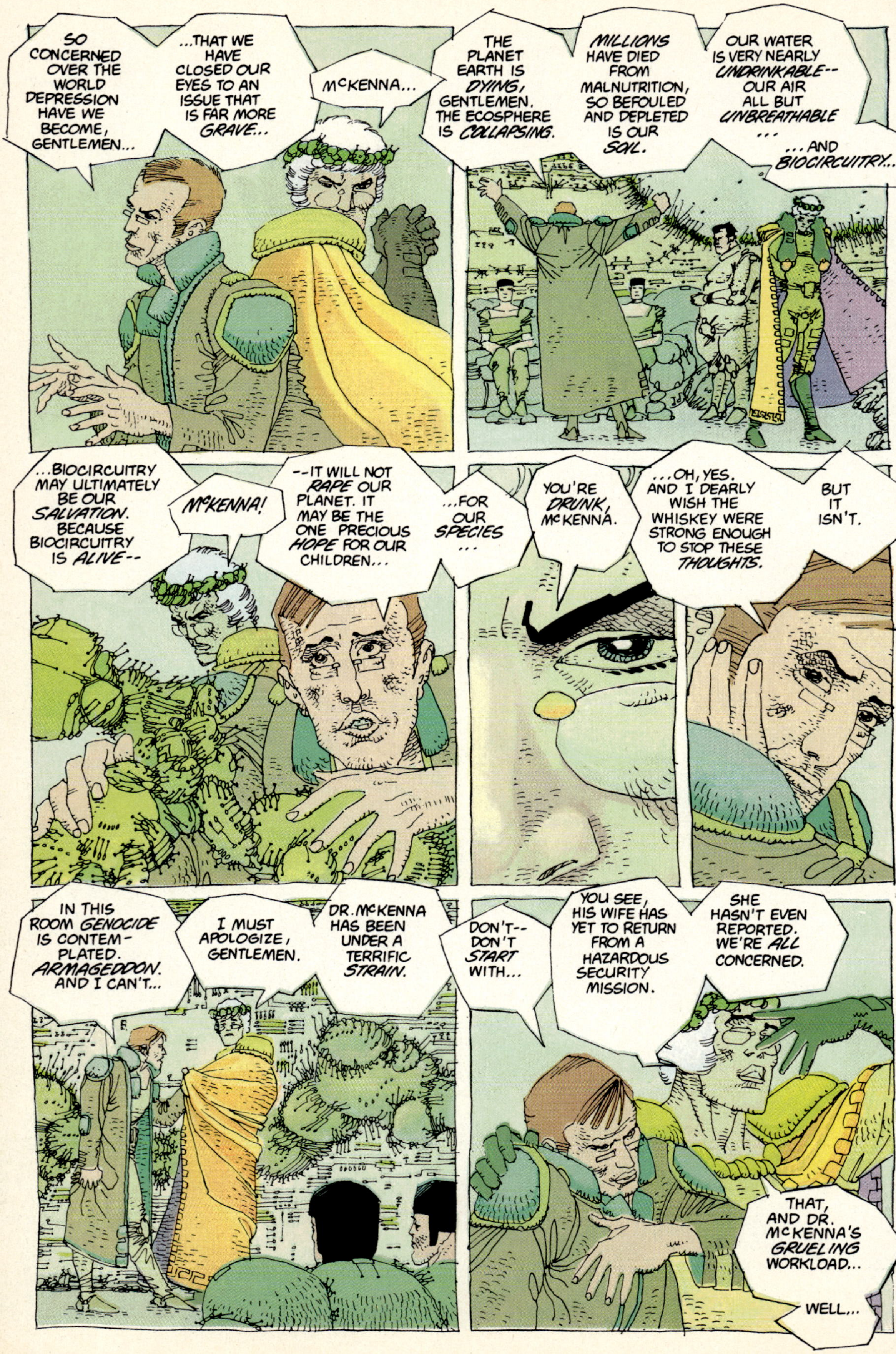
SO CONCERNED OVER THE WORLD DEPRESSION HAVE WE BECOME, GENTLEMEN...
...THAT WE HAVE CLOSED OUR EYES TO AN ISSUE THAT IS FAR MORE GRAVE...
McKENNA...
THE PLANET EARTH IS DYING, GENTLEMEN. THE ECOSPHERE IS COLLAPSING.
MILLIONS HAVE DIED FROM MALNUTRITION, SO BEFOULED AND DEPLETED IS OUR SOIL.
OUR WATER IS VERY NEARLY UNDRINKABLE-- OUR AIR ALL BUT UNBREATHABLE...
...AND BIOCIRCUITRY...
...BIOCIRCUITRY MAY ULTIMATELY BE OUR SALVATION. BECAUSE BIOCIRCUITRY IS ALIVE--
McKENNA!
--IT WILL NOT RAPE OUR PLANET. IT MAY BE THE ONE PRECIOUS HOPE FOR OUR CHILDREN...
...FOR OUR SPECIES...
YOU'RE DRUNK, McKENNA.
...OH, YES. AND I DEARLY WISH THE WHISKEY WERE STRONG ENOUGH TO STOP THESE THOUGHTS.
BUT IT ISN'T.
IN THIS ROOM GENOCIDE IS CONTEM-PLATED. ARMAGEDDON. AND I CAN'T...
I MUST APOLOGIZE, GENTLEMEN.
DR. McKENNA HAS BEEN UNDER A TERRIFIC STRAIN.
DON'T-- DON'T START WITH...
YOU SEE, HIS WIFE HAS YET TO RETURN FROM A HAZARDOUS SECURITY MISSION.
SHE HASN'T EVEN REPORTED. WE'RE ALL CONCERNED.
THAT, AND DR. McKENNA'S GRUELING WORKLOAD...
WELL...

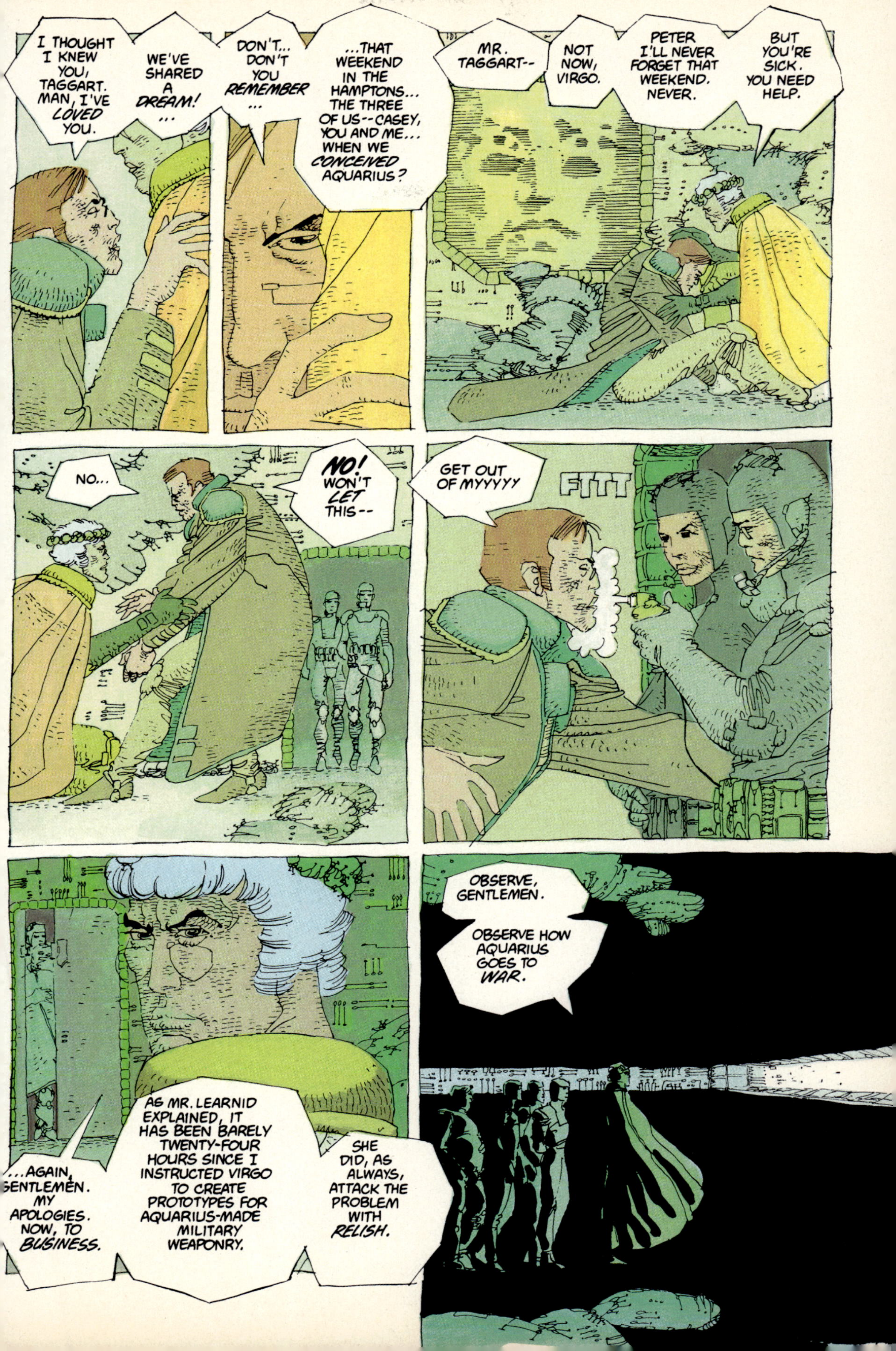
I THOUGHT I KNEW YOU, TAGGART. MAN, I'VE *LOVED* YOU.
WE'VE SHARED A *DREAM!* ...
DON'T... DON'T YOU *REMEMBER* ...
...THAT WEEKEND IN THE HAMPTONS... THE THREE OF US--CASEY, YOU AND ME... WHEN WE *CONCEIVED* AQUARIUS?
MR. TAGGART--
NOT NOW, VIRGO.
PETER I'LL NEVER FORGET THAT WEEKEND. NEVER.
BUT YOU'RE SICK. YOU NEED HELP.
NO...
NO! WON'T *LET* THIS--
GET OUT OF MYYYYY
FTTT
...AGAIN, GENTLEMEN. MY APOLOGIES. NOW, TO *BUSINESS*.
AS MR. LEARNID EXPLAINED, IT HAS BEEN BARELY TWENTY-FOUR HOURS SINCE I INSTRUCTED VIRGO TO CREATE PROTOTYPES FOR AQUARIUS-MADE MILITARY WEAPONRY.
SHE DID, AS ALWAYS, ATTACK THE PROBLEM WITH *RELISH*.
OBSERVE, GENTLEMEN.
OBSERVE HOW AQUARIUS GOES TO *WAR*.

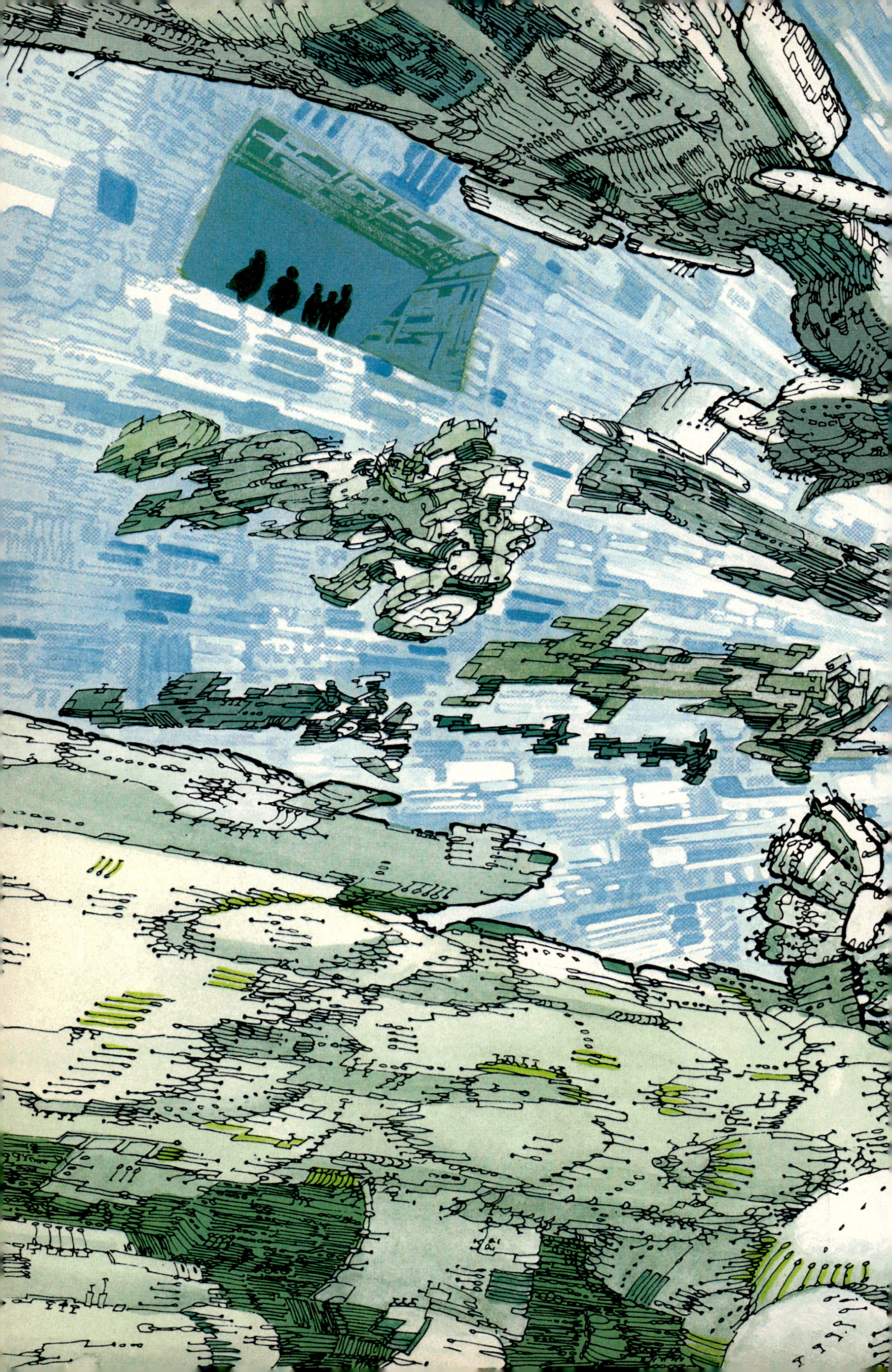

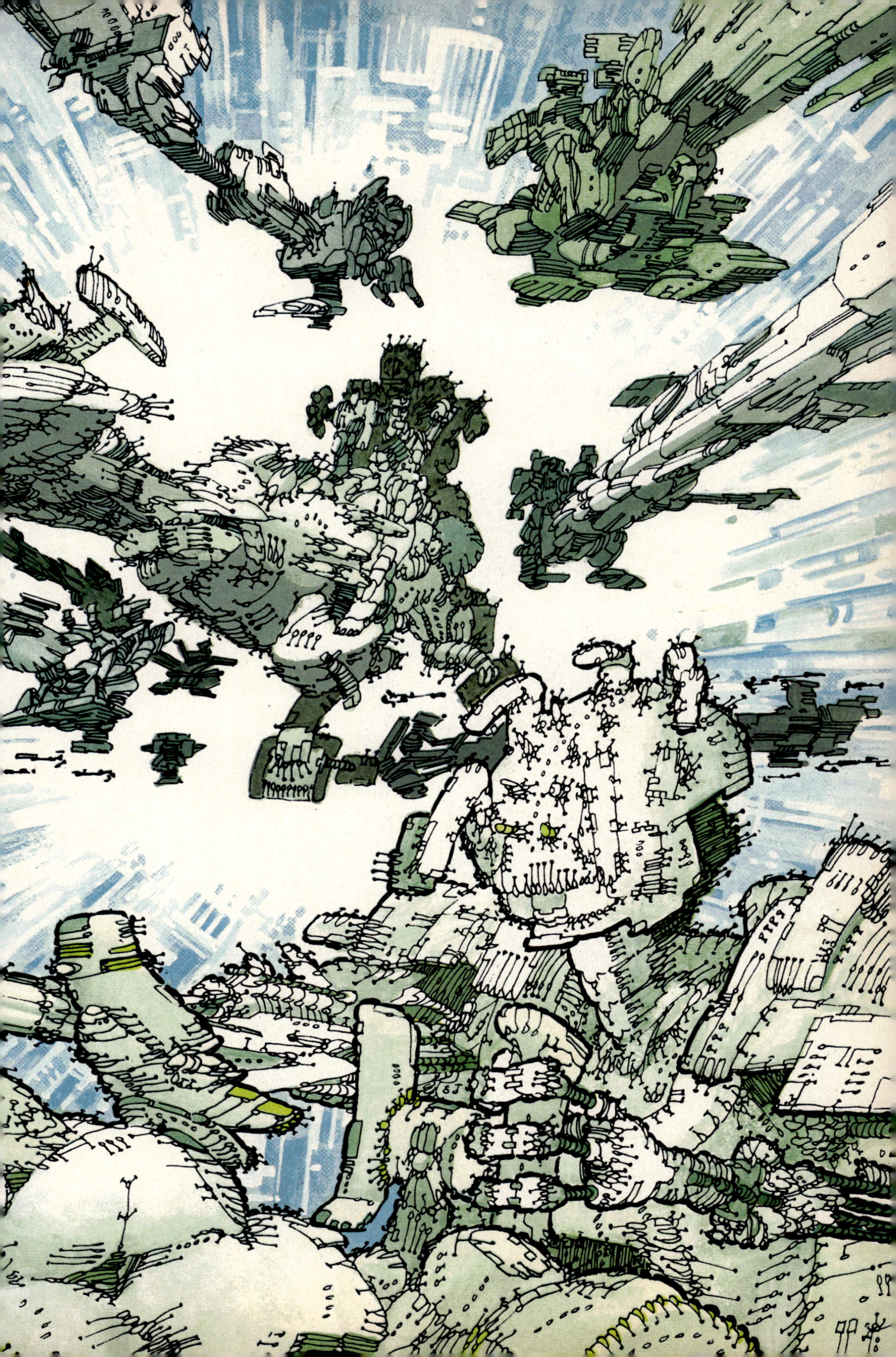

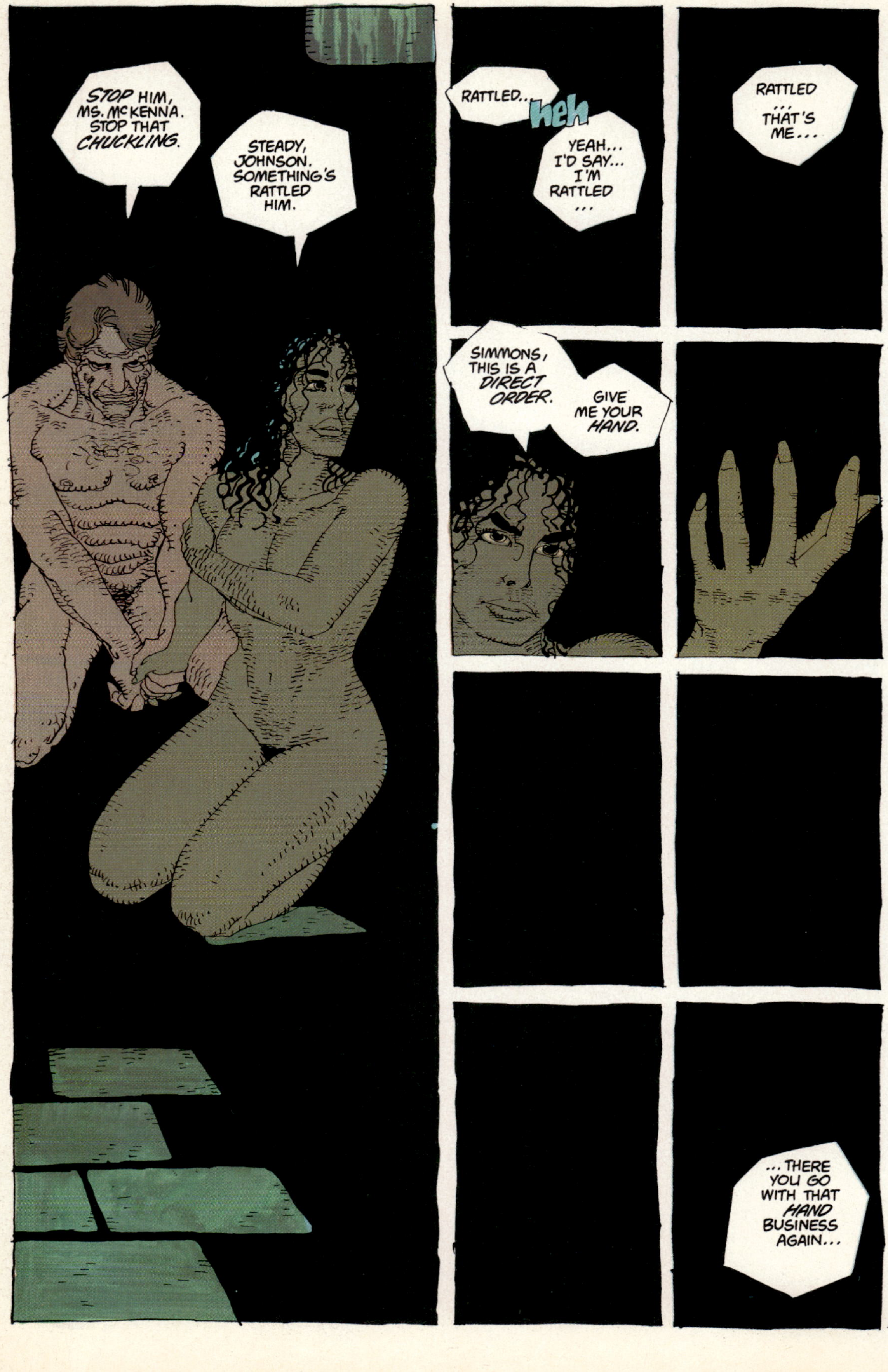
STOP HIM, MS. McKENNA. STOP THAT CHUCKLING.
STEADY, JOHNSON. SOMETHING'S RATTLED HIM.
RATTLED...
heh
YEAH... I'D SAY... I'M RATTLED ...
RATTLED ... THAT'S ME...
SIMMONS, THIS IS A DIRECT ORDER.
GIVE ME YOUR HAND.
...THERE YOU GO WITH THAT HAND BUSINESS AGAIN...

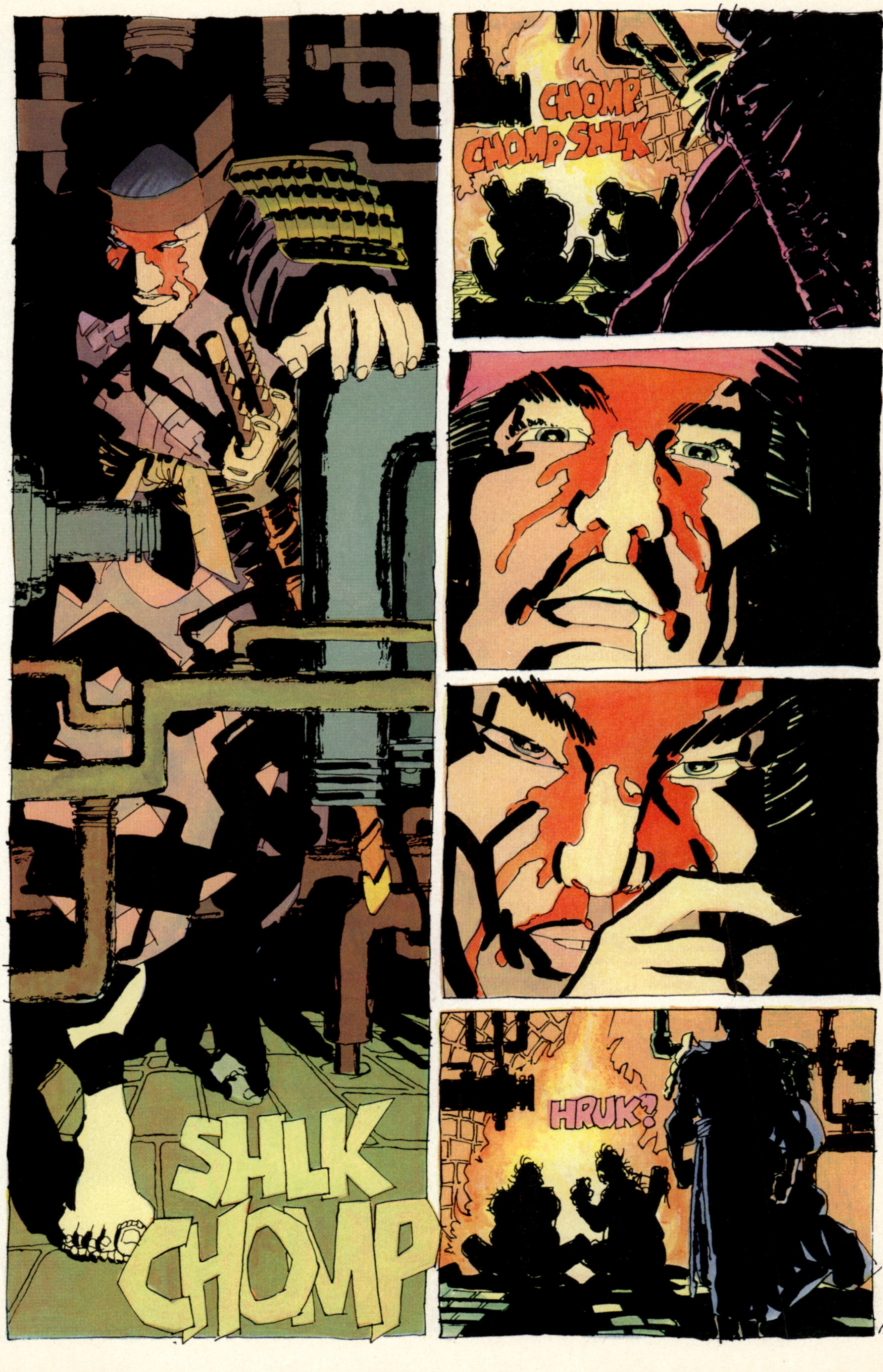
CHOMP
CHOMP SHLK
SHLK
CHOMP
HRUK?

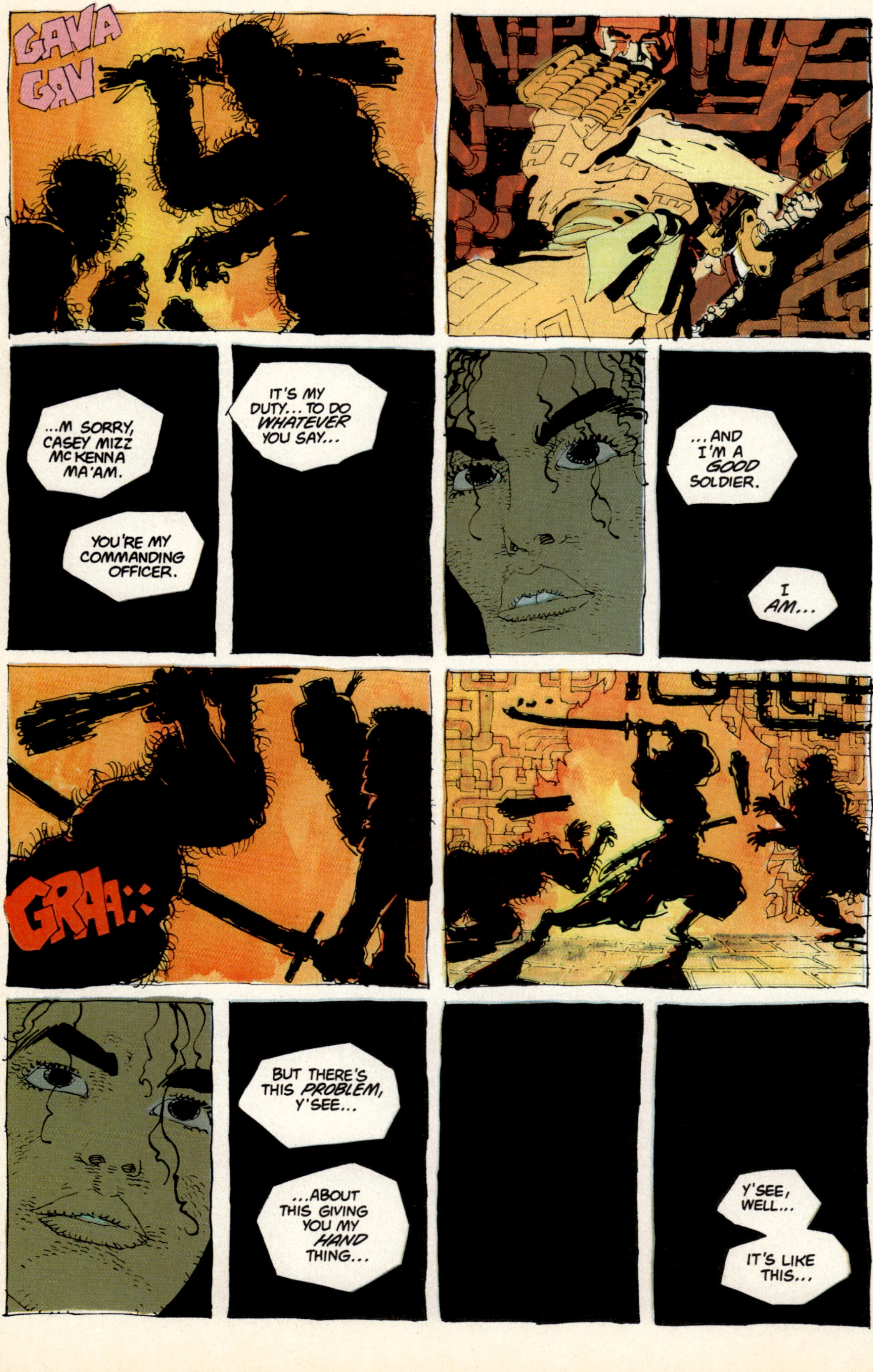
GAVA GAV
...M SORRY, CASEY MIZZ McKENNA MA'AM.
YOU'RE MY COMMANDING OFFICER.
IT'S MY DUTY... TO DO *WHATEVER* YOU SAY...
...AND I'M A *GOOD* SOLDIER.
I *AM*...
GRAA::
BUT THERE'S THIS *PROBLEM*, Y'SEE...
...ABOUT THIS GIVING YOU MY *HAND* THING...
Y'SEE, WELL...
IT'S LIKE THIS...

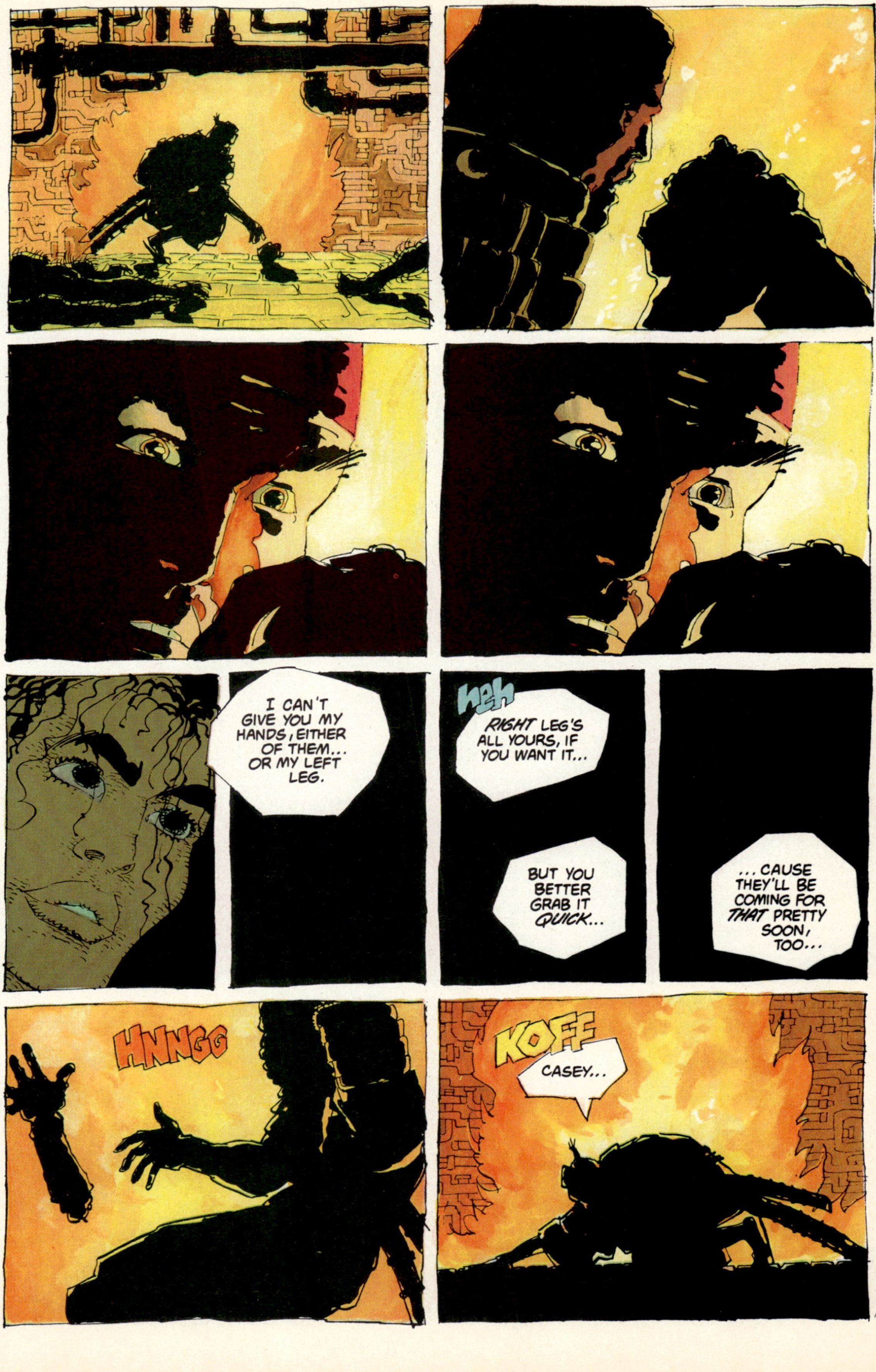
I CAN'T GIVE YOU MY HANDS, EITHER OF THEM... OR MY LEFT LEG.
heh
RIGHT LEG'S ALL YOURS, IF YOU WANT IT...
BUT YOU BETTER GRAB IT QUICK...
...CAUSE THEY'LL BE COMING FOR THAT PRETTY SOON, TOO...
HNNGG
KOFF
CASEY...

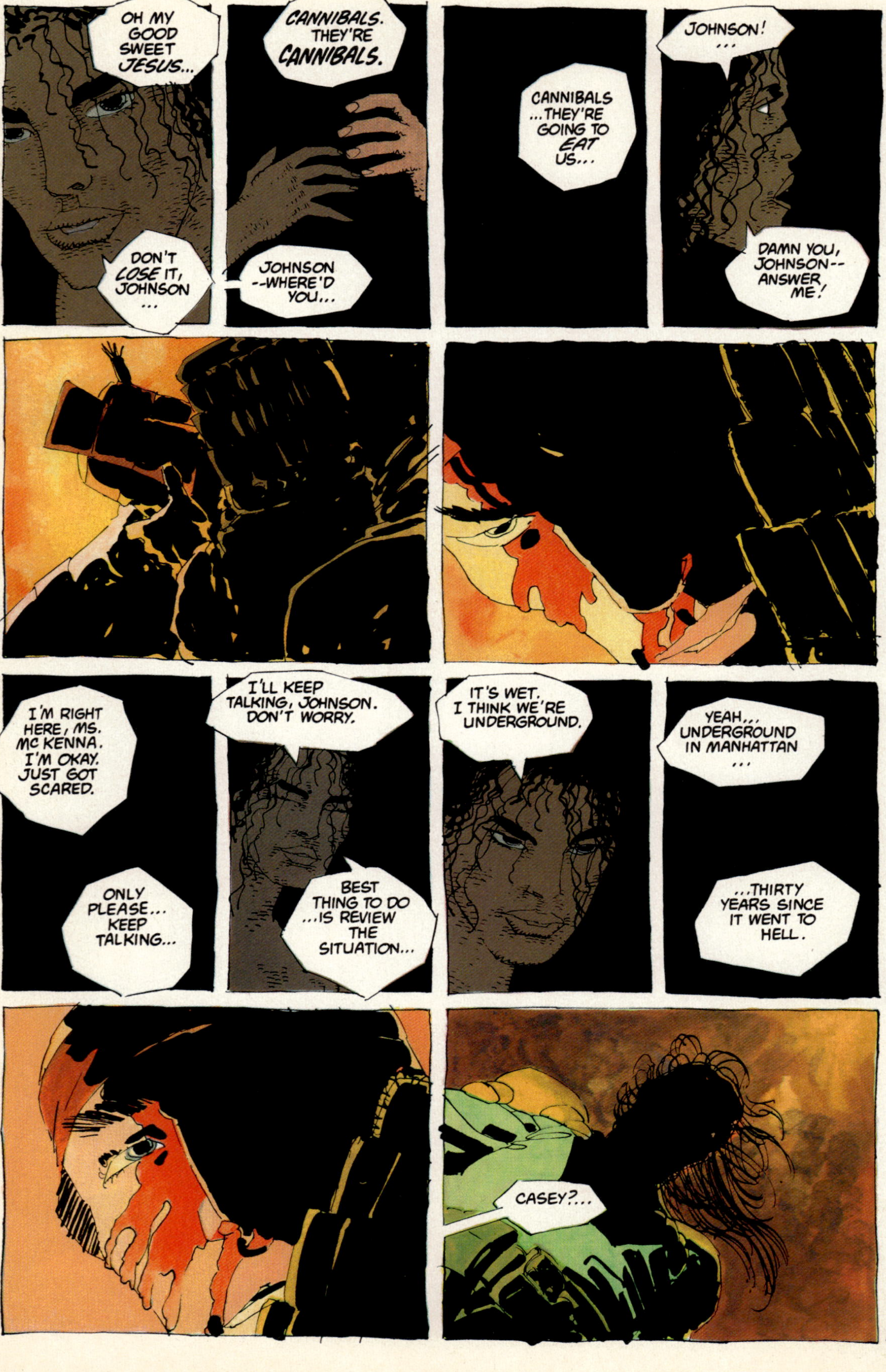
OH MY GOOD SWEET JESUS...
DON'T LOSE IT, JOHNSON ...
CANNIBALS. THEY'RE CANNIBALS.
JOHNSON --WHERE'D YOU...
CANNIBALS ...THEY'RE GOING TO EAT US...
JOHNSON! ...
DAMN YOU, JOHNSON-- ANSWER ME!
I'M RIGHT HERE, MS. MC KENNA. I'M OKAY. JUST GOT SCARED.
ONLY PLEASE... KEEP TALKING...
I'LL KEEP TALKING, JOHNSON. DON'T WORRY.
BEST THING TO DO ...IS REVIEW THE SITUATION...
IT'S WET. I THINK WE'RE UNDERGROUND.
YEAH... UNDERGROUND IN MANHATTAN ...
...THIRTY YEARS SINCE IT WENT TO HELL.
CASEY?...

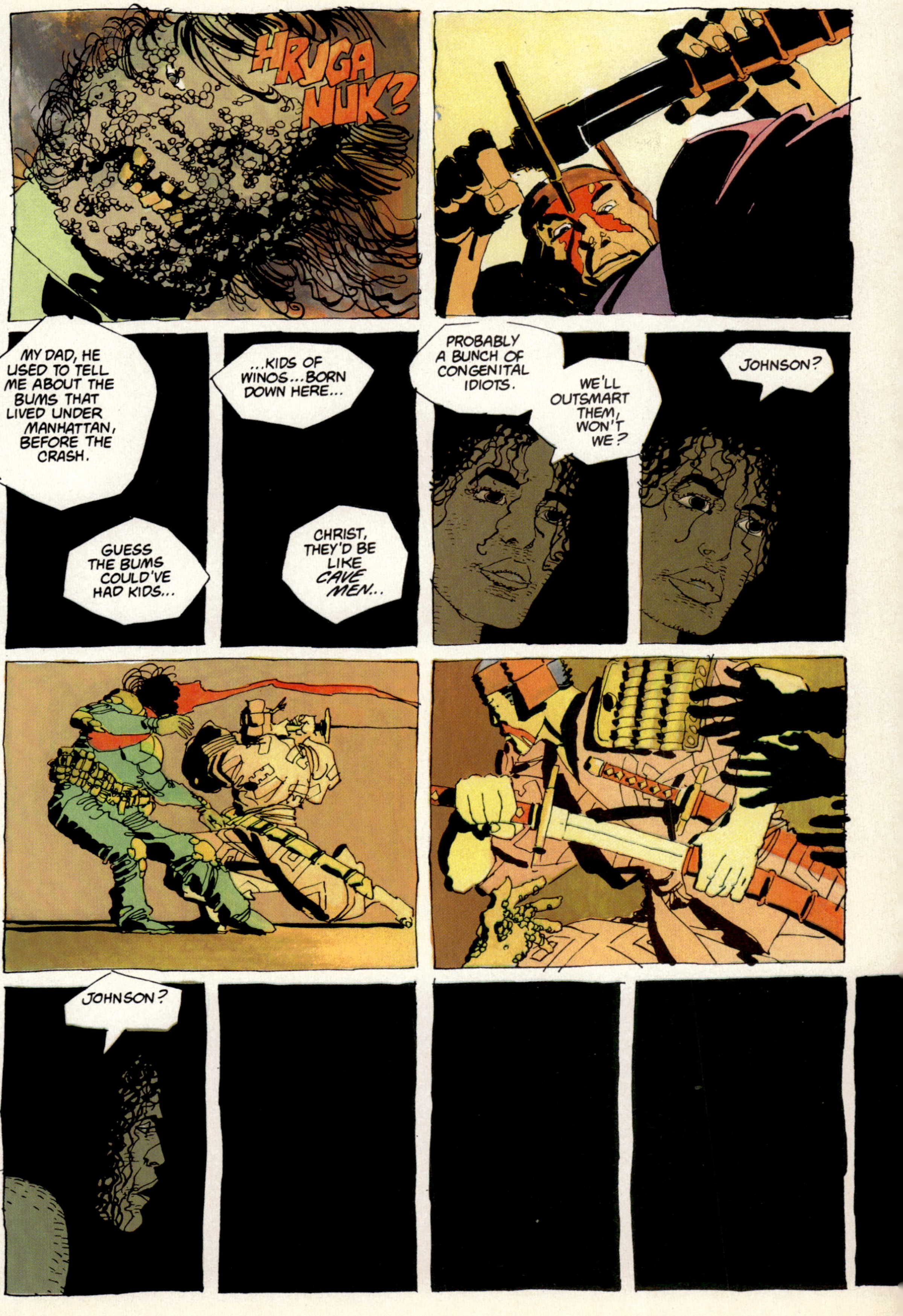
HRUGA NUK?
MY DAD, HE USED TO TELL ME ABOUT THE BUMS THAT LIVED UNDER MANHATTAN, BEFORE THE CRASH.
GUESS THE BUMS COULD'VE HAD KIDS...
...KIDS OF WINOS...BORN DOWN HERE...
CHRIST, THEY'D BE LIKE CAVE MEN...
PROBABLY A BUNCH OF CONGENITAL IDIOTS.
WE'LL OUTSMART THEM, WON'T WE?
JOHNSON?
JOHNSON?

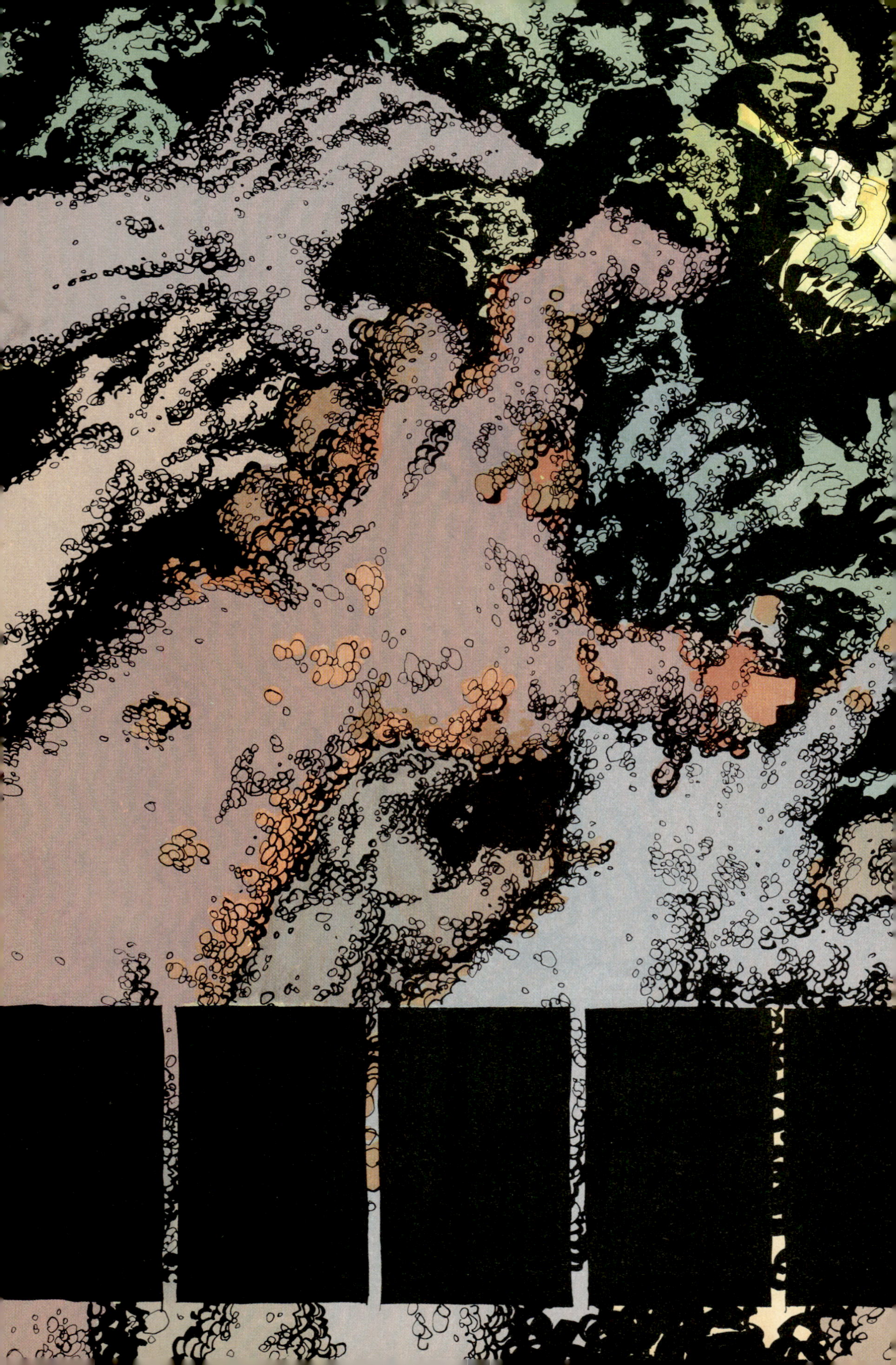

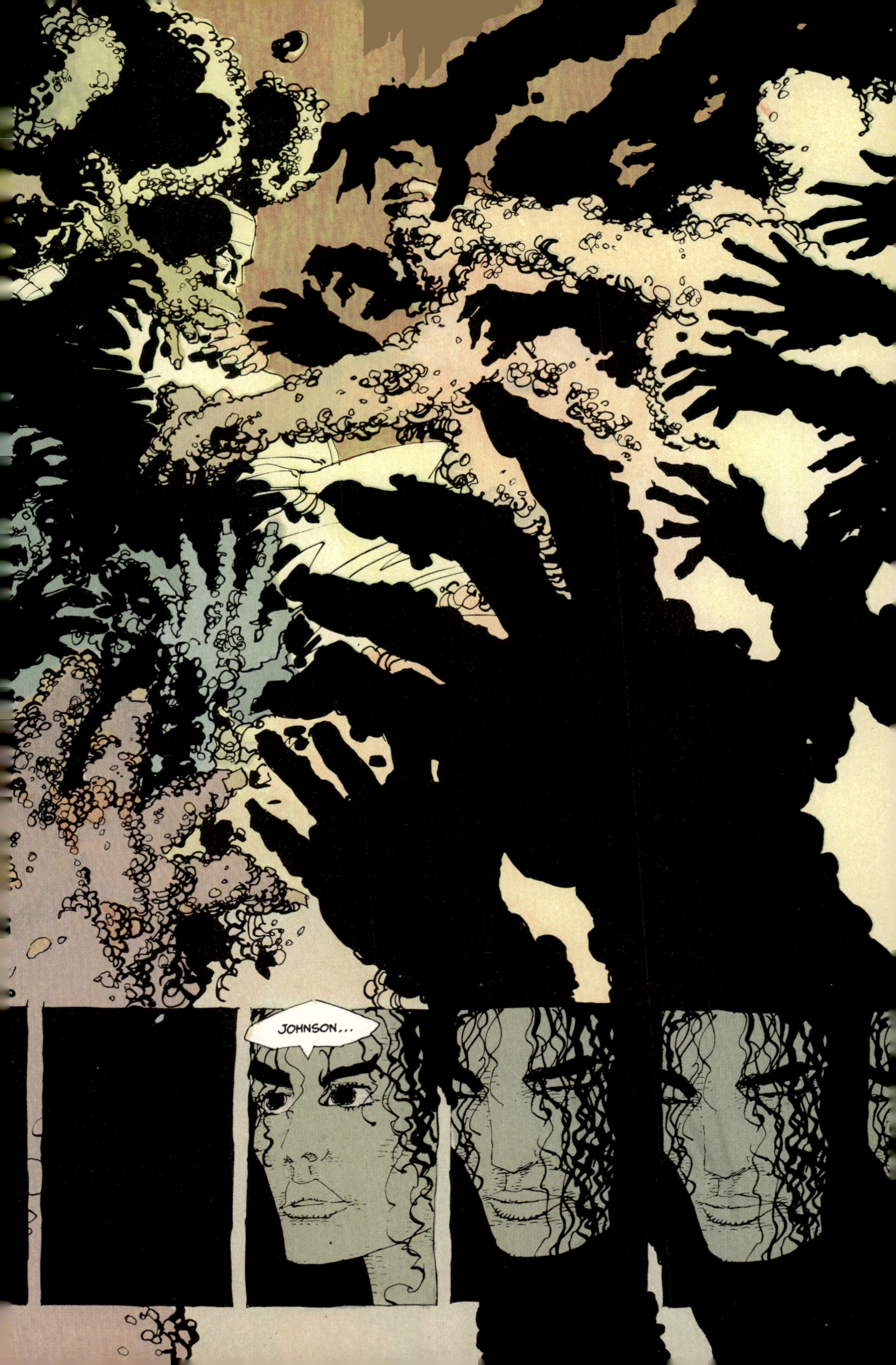
JOHNSON...

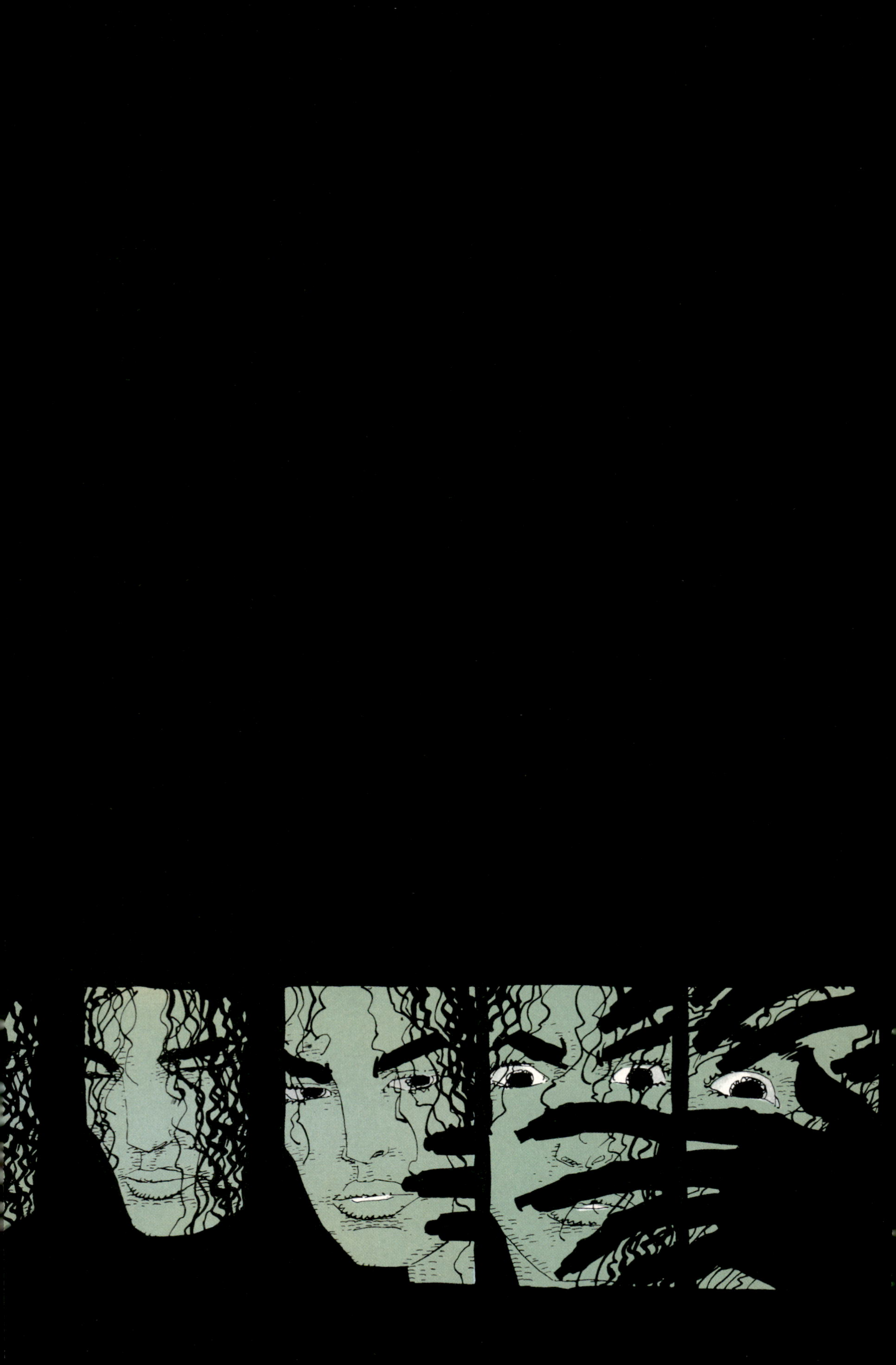

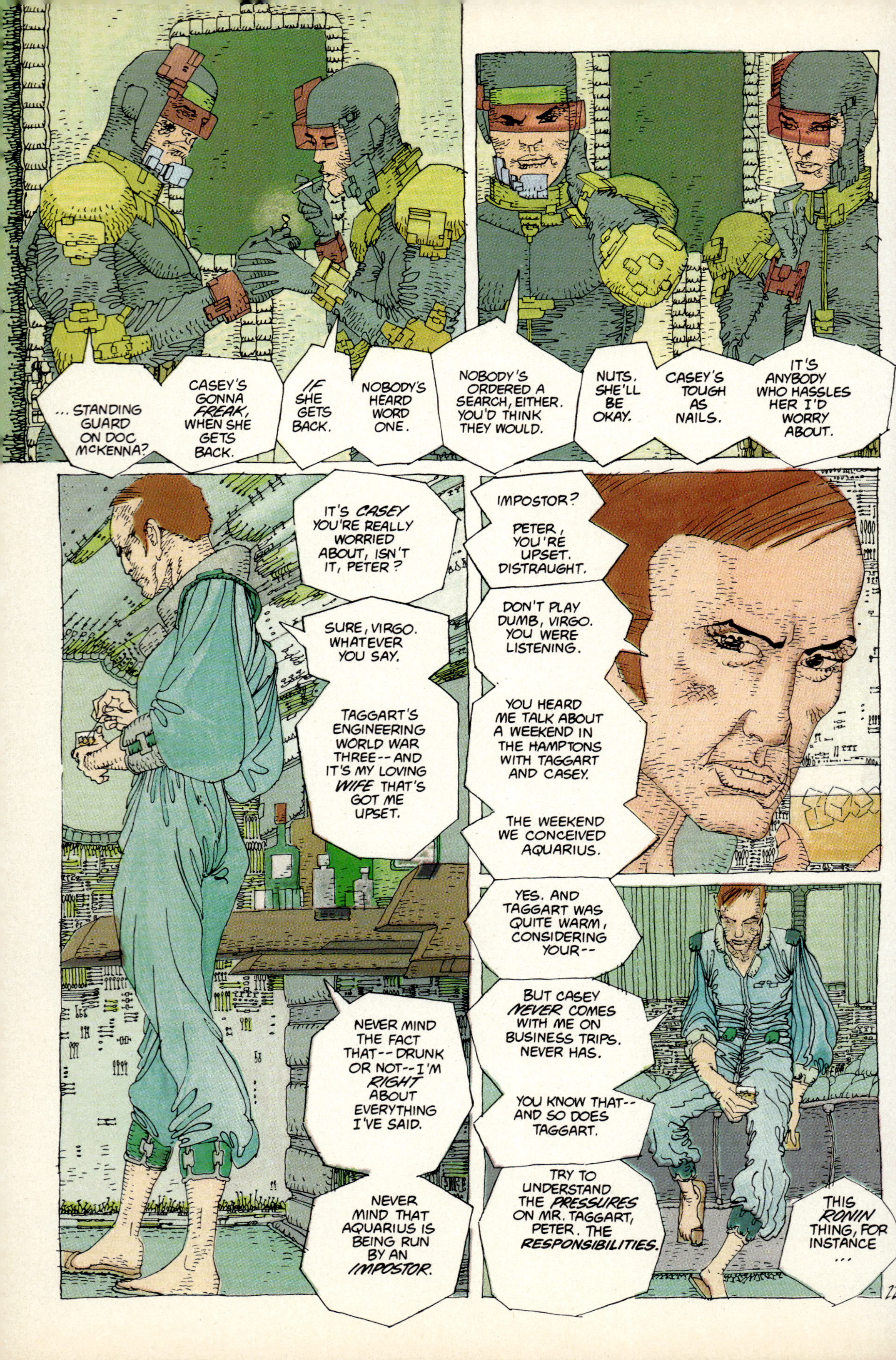
...STANDING GUARD ON DOC McKENNA?
CASEY'S GONNA FREAK, WHEN SHE GETS BACK.
IF SHE GETS BACK.
NOBODY'S HEARD WORD ONE.
NOBODY'S ORDERED A SEARCH, EITHER. YOU'D THINK THEY WOULD.
NUTS. SHE'LL BE OKAY.
CASEY'S TOUGH AS NAILS.
IT'S ANYBODY WHO HASSLES HER I'D WORRY ABOUT.
IT'S CASEY YOU'RE REALLY WORRIED ABOUT, ISN'T IT, PETER?
SURE, VIRGO. WHATEVER YOU SAY.
TAGGART'S ENGINEERING WORLD WAR THREE--AND IT'S MY LOVING WIFE THAT'S GOT ME UPSET.
NEVER MIND THE FACT THAT--DRUNK OR NOT--I'M RIGHT ABOUT EVERYTHING I'VE SAID.
NEVER MIND THAT AQUARIUS IS BEING RUN BY AN IMPOSTOR.
IMPOSTOR?
PETER, YOU'RE UPSET. DISTRAUGHT.
DON'T PLAY DUMB, VIRGO. YOU WERE LISTENING.
YOU HEARD ME TALK ABOUT A WEEKEND IN THE HAMPTONS WITH TAGGART AND CASEY.
THE WEEKEND WE CONCEIVED AQUARIUS.
YES. AND TAGGART WAS QUITE WARM, CONSIDERING YOUR--
BUT CASEY NEVER COMES WITH ME ON BUSINESS TRIPS. NEVER HAS.
YOU KNOW THAT--AND SO DOES TAGGART.
TRY TO UNDERSTAND THE PRESSURES ON MR. TAGGART, PETER. THE RESPONSIBILITIES.
THIS RONIN THING, FOR INSTANCE...

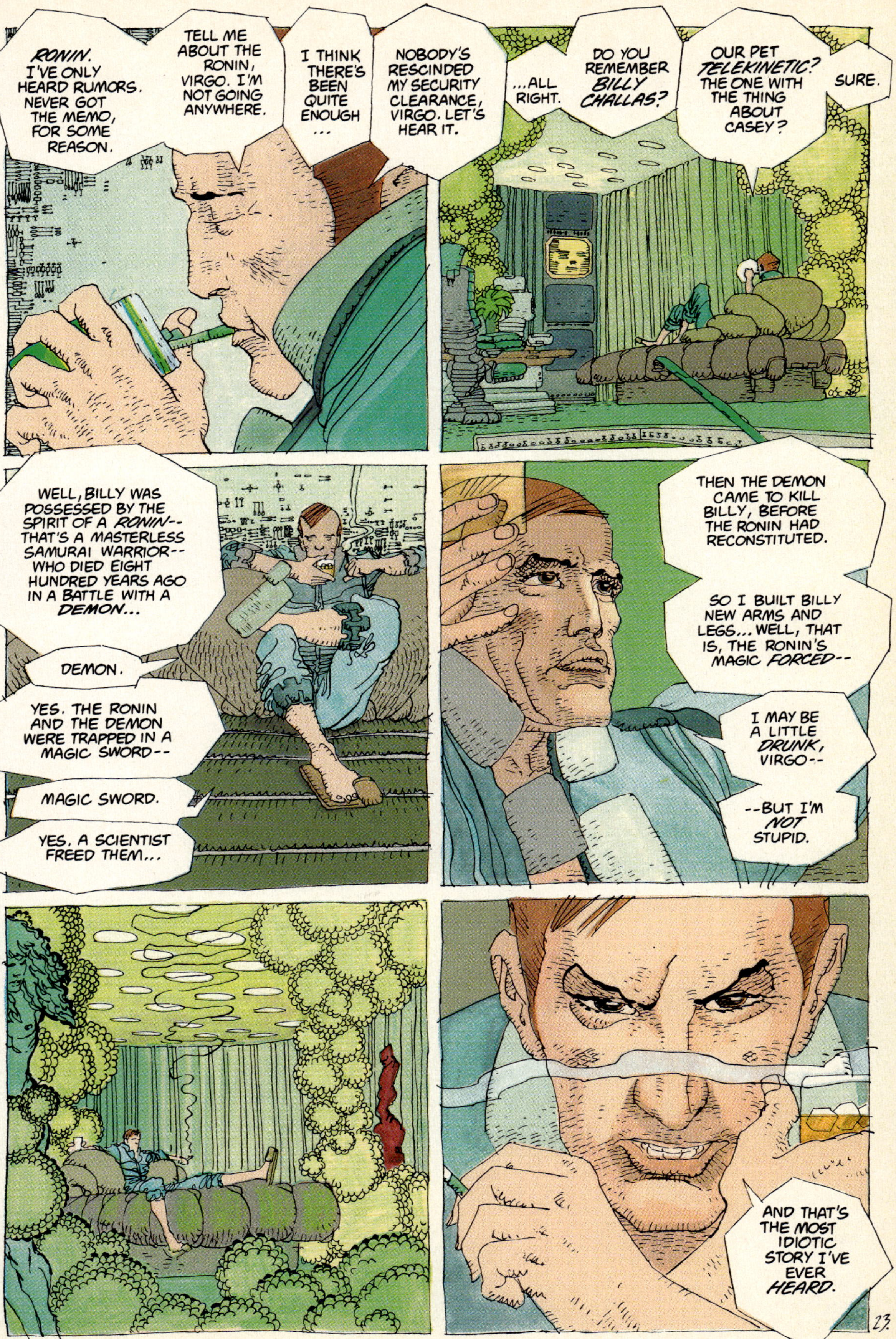
RONIN. I'VE ONLY HEARD RUMORS. NEVER GOT THE MEMO, FOR SOME REASON.
TELL ME ABOUT THE RONIN, VIRGO. I'M NOT GOING ANYWHERE.
I THINK THERE'S BEEN QUITE ENOUGH ...
NOBODY'S RESCINDED MY SECURITY CLEARANCE, VIRGO. LET'S HEAR IT.
...ALL RIGHT.
DO YOU REMEMBER BILLY CHALLAS?
OUR PET TELEKINETIC? THE ONE WITH THE THING ABOUT CASEY?
SURE.
WELL, BILLY WAS POSSESSED BY THE SPIRIT OF A RONIN-- THAT'S A MASTERLESS SAMURAI WARRIOR-- WHO DIED EIGHT HUNDRED YEARS AGO IN A BATTLE WITH A DEMON...
DEMON.
YES. THE RONIN AND THE DEMON WERE TRAPPED IN A MAGIC SWORD--
MAGIC SWORD.
YES. A SCIENTIST FREED THEM...
THEN THE DEMON CAME TO KILL BILLY, BEFORE THE RONIN HAD RECONSTITUTED.
SO I BUILT BILLY NEW ARMS AND LEGS... WELL, THAT IS, THE RONIN'S MAGIC FORCED--
I MAY BE A LITTLE DRUNK, VIRGO--
--BUT I'M NOT STUPID.
AND THAT'S THE MOST IDIOTIC STORY I'VE EVER HEARD.

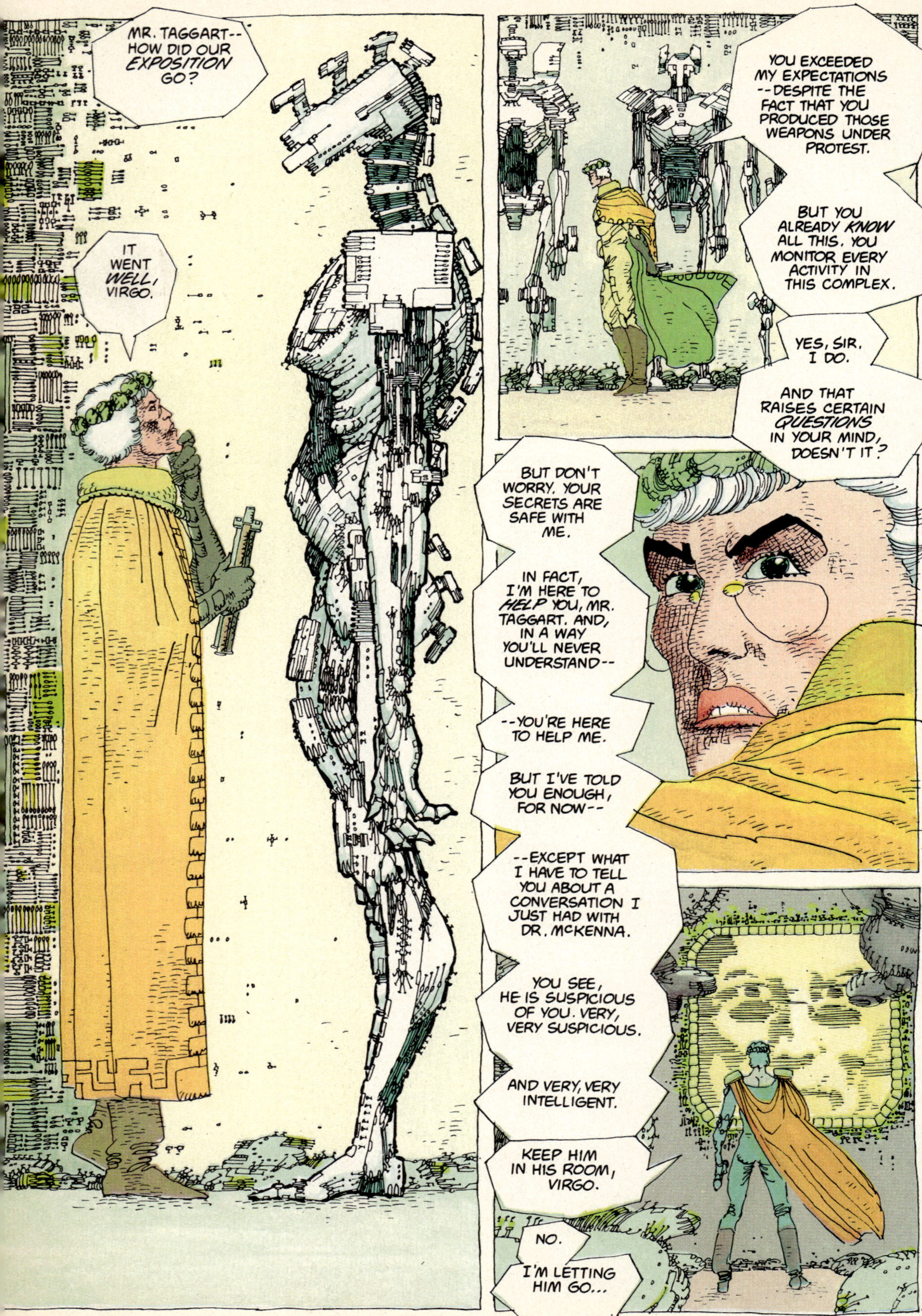

MR. TAGGART--
HOW DID OUR
EXPOSITION
GO?
IT WENT WELL, VIRGO.
YOU EXCEEDED MY EXPECTATIONS --DESPITE THE FACT THAT YOU PRODUCED THOSE WEAPONS UNDER PROTEST.
BUT YOU ALREADY KNOW ALL THIS. YOU MONITOR EVERY ACTIVITY IN THIS COMPLEX.
YES, SIR. I DO.
AND THAT RAISES CERTAIN QUESTIONS IN YOUR MIND, DOESN'T IT?
BUT DON'T WORRY. YOUR SECRETS ARE SAFE WITH ME.
IN FACT, I'M HERE TO HELP YOU, MR. TAGGART. AND, IN A WAY YOU'LL NEVER UNDERSTAND--
--YOU'RE HERE TO HELP ME.
BUT I'VE TOLD YOU ENOUGH, FOR NOW--
--EXCEPT WHAT I HAVE TO TELL YOU ABOUT A CONVERSATION I JUST HAD WITH DR. McKENNA.
YOU SEE, HE IS SUSPICIOUS OF YOU. VERY, VERY SUSPICIOUS.
AND VERY, VERY INTELLIGENT.
KEEP HIM IN HIS ROOM, VIRGO.
NO.
I'M LETTING HIM GO...

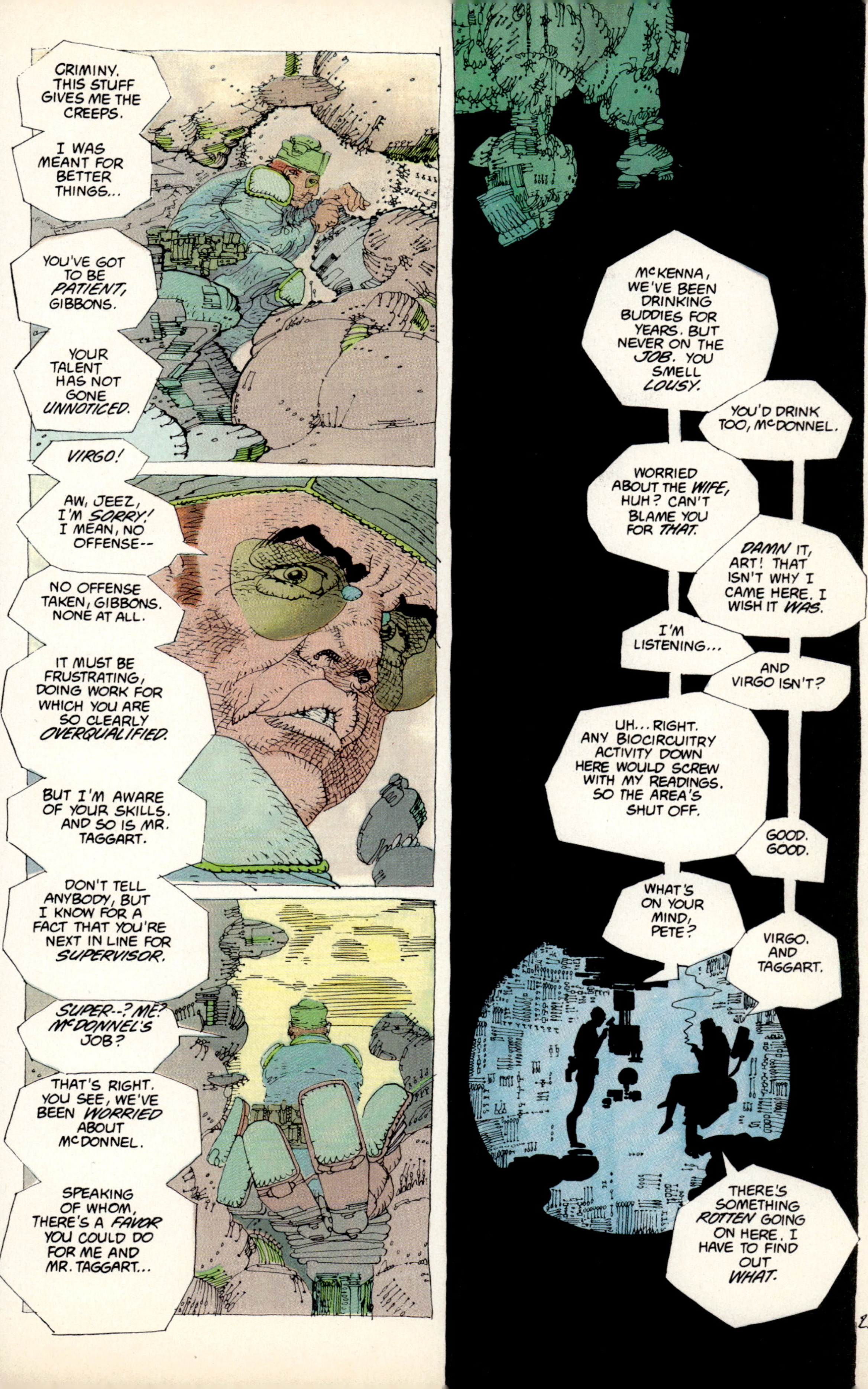
CRIMINY. THIS STUFF GIVES ME THE CREEPS.
I WAS MEANT FOR BETTER THINGS...
YOU'VE GOT TO BE PATIENT, GIBBONS.
YOUR TALENT HAS NOT GONE UNNOTICED.
VIRGO!
AW, JEEZ, I'M SORRY! I MEAN, NO OFFENSE--
NO OFFENSE TAKEN, GIBBONS. NONE AT ALL.
IT MUST BE FRUSTRATING, DOING WORK FOR WHICH YOU ARE SO CLEARLY OVERQUALIFIED.
BUT I'M AWARE OF YOUR SKILLS. AND SO IS MR. TAGGART.
DON'T TELL ANYBODY, BUT I KNOW FOR A FACT THAT YOU'RE NEXT IN LINE FOR SUPERVISOR.
SUPER--? ME? McDONNEL'S JOB?
THAT'S RIGHT. YOU SEE, WE'VE BEEN WORRIED ABOUT McDONNEL.
SPEAKING OF WHOM, THERE'S A FAVOR YOU COULD DO FOR ME AND MR. TAGGART...
McKENNA, WE'VE BEEN DRINKING BUDDIES FOR YEARS. BUT NEVER ON THE JOB. YOU SMELL LOUSY.
YOU'D DRINK TOO, McDONNEL.
WORRIED ABOUT THE WIFE, HUH? CAN'T BLAME YOU FOR THAT.
DAMN IT, ART! THAT ISN'T WHY I CAME HERE. I WISH IT WAS.
I'M LISTENING...
AND VIRGO ISN'T?
UH... RIGHT. ANY BIOCIRCUITRY ACTIVITY DOWN HERE WOULD SCREW WITH MY READINGS, SO THE AREA'S SHUT OFF.
GOOD. GOOD.
WHAT'S ON YOUR MIND, PETE?
VIRGO. AND TAGGART.
THERE'S SOMETHING ROTTEN GOING ON HERE. I HAVE TO FIND OUT WHAT.

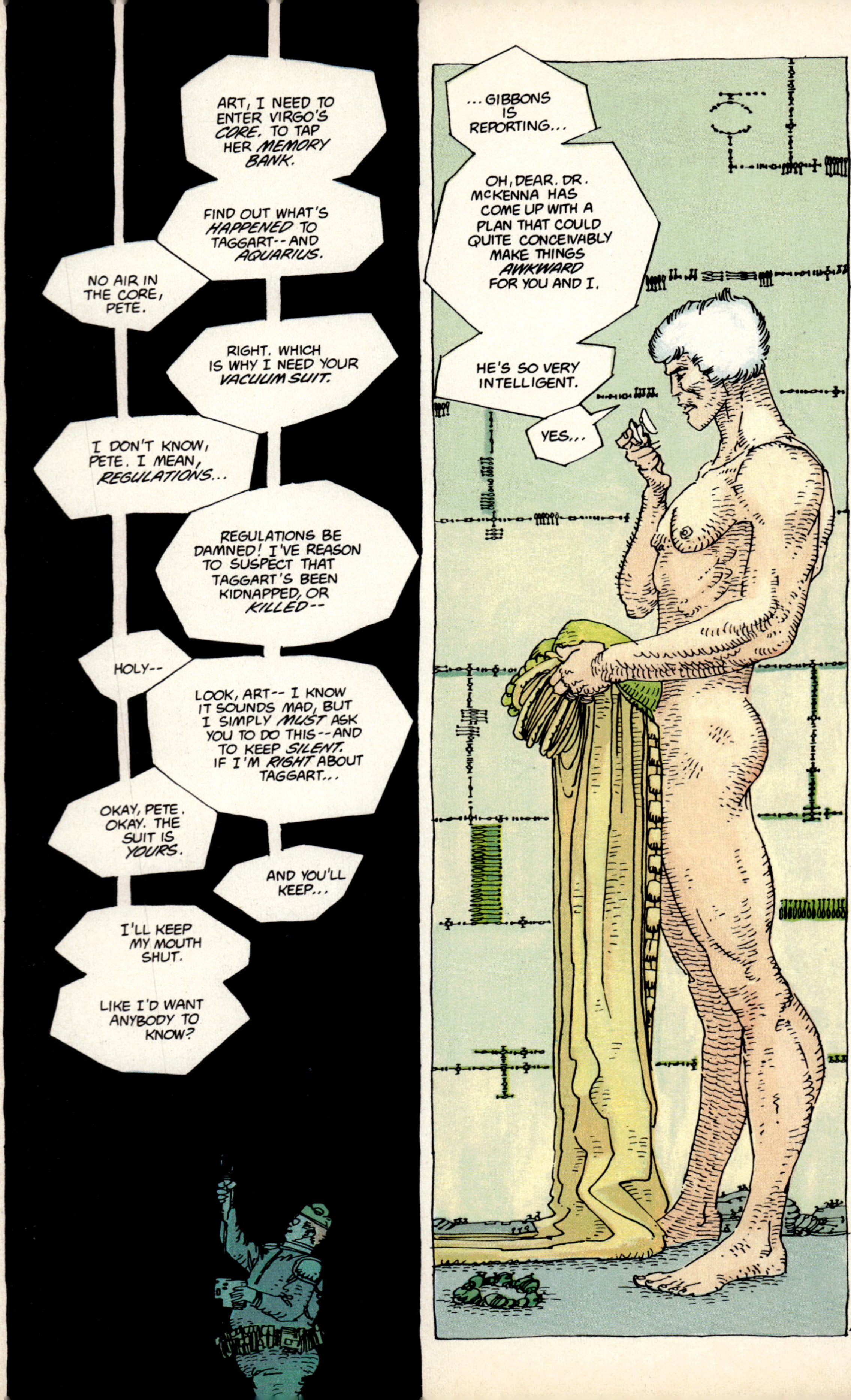

ART, I NEED TO ENTER VIRGO'S *CORE*, TO TAP HER *MEMORY BANK*.
FIND OUT WHAT'S *HAPPENED* TO TAGGART-- AND *AQUARIUS*.
NO AIR IN THE CORE, PETE.
RIGHT. WHICH IS WHY I NEED YOUR *VACUUM SUIT*.
I DON'T KNOW, PETE. I MEAN, *REGULATIONS*...
REGULATIONS BE DAMNED! I'VE REASON TO SUSPECT THAT TAGGART'S BEEN KIDNAPPED, OR *KILLED*--
HOLY--
LOOK, ART-- I KNOW IT SOUNDS MAD, BUT I SIMPLY *MUST* ASK YOU TO DO THIS--AND TO KEEP *SILENT*. IF I'M *RIGHT* ABOUT TAGGART...
OKAY, PETE. OKAY. THE SUIT IS *YOURS*.
AND YOU'LL KEEP...
I'LL KEEP MY MOUTH SHUT.
LIKE I'D WANT ANYBODY TO KNOW?
...GIBBONS IS REPORTING...
OH, DEAR. DR. McKENNA HAS COME UP WITH A PLAN THAT COULD QUITE CONCEIVABLY MAKE THINGS *AWKWARD* FOR YOU AND I.
HE'S SO VERY INTELLIGENT.
YES...

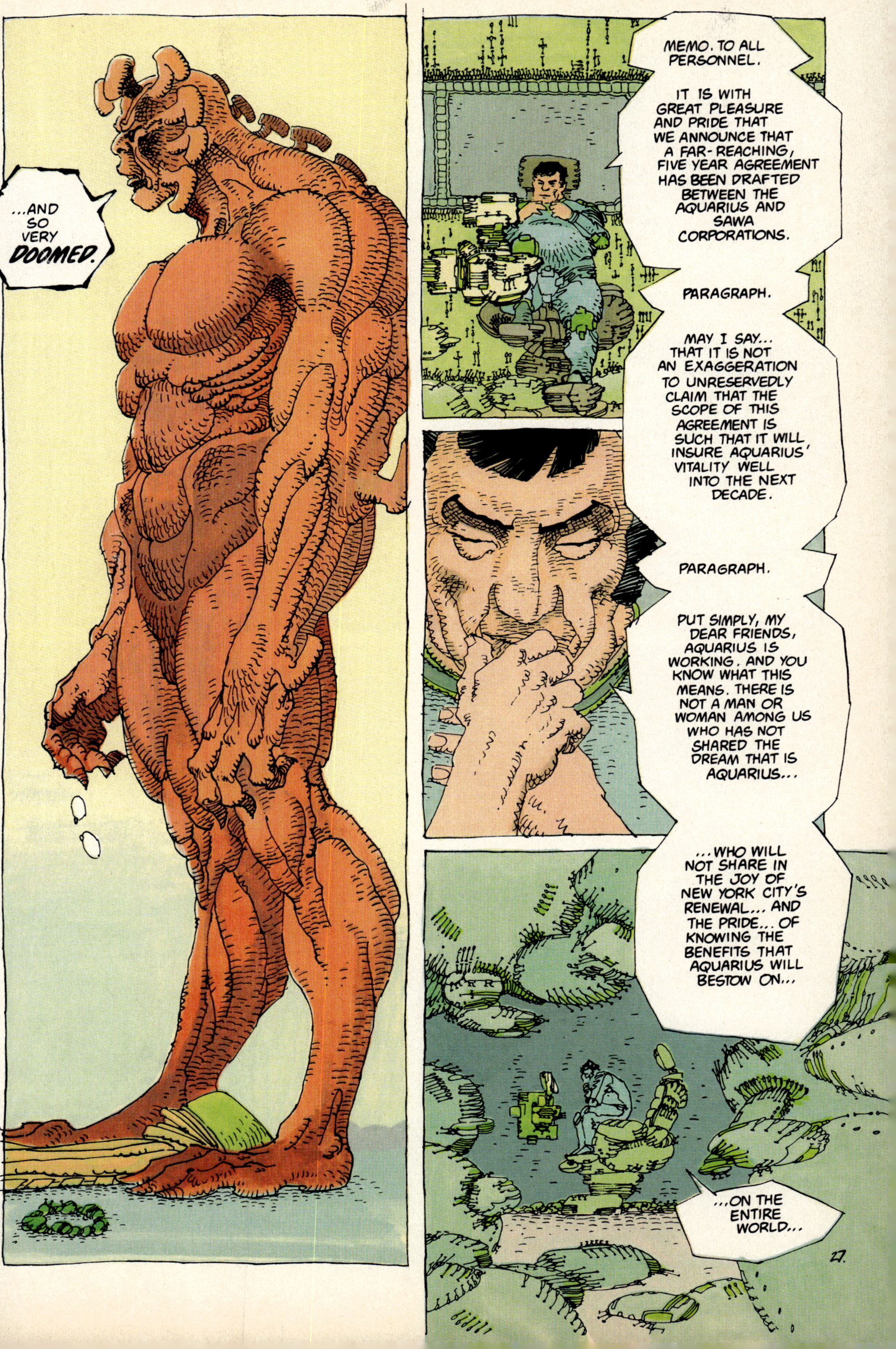

...AND SO VERY DOOMED.
MEMO. TO ALL PERSONNEL.
IT IS WITH GREAT PLEASURE AND PRIDE THAT WE ANNOUNCE THAT A FAR-REACHING, FIVE YEAR AGREEMENT HAS BEEN DRAFTED BETWEEN THE AQUARIUS AND SAWA CORPORATIONS.
PARAGRAPH.
MAY I SAY... THAT IT IS NOT AN EXAGGERATION TO UNRESERVEDLY CLAIM THAT THE SCOPE OF THIS AGREEMENT IS SUCH THAT IT WILL INSURE AQUARIUS' VITALITY WELL INTO THE NEXT DECADE.
PARAGRAPH.
PUT SIMPLY, MY DEAR FRIENDS, AQUARIUS IS WORKING. AND YOU KNOW WHAT THIS MEANS. THERE IS NOT A MAN OR WOMAN AMONG US WHO HAS NOT SHARED THE DREAM THAT IS AQUARIUS...
...WHO WILL NOT SHARE IN THE JOY OF NEW YORK CITY'S RENEWAL... AND THE PRIDE... OF KNOWING THE BENEFITS THAT AQUARIUS WILL BESTOW ON...
...ON THE ENTIRE WORLD...
27.

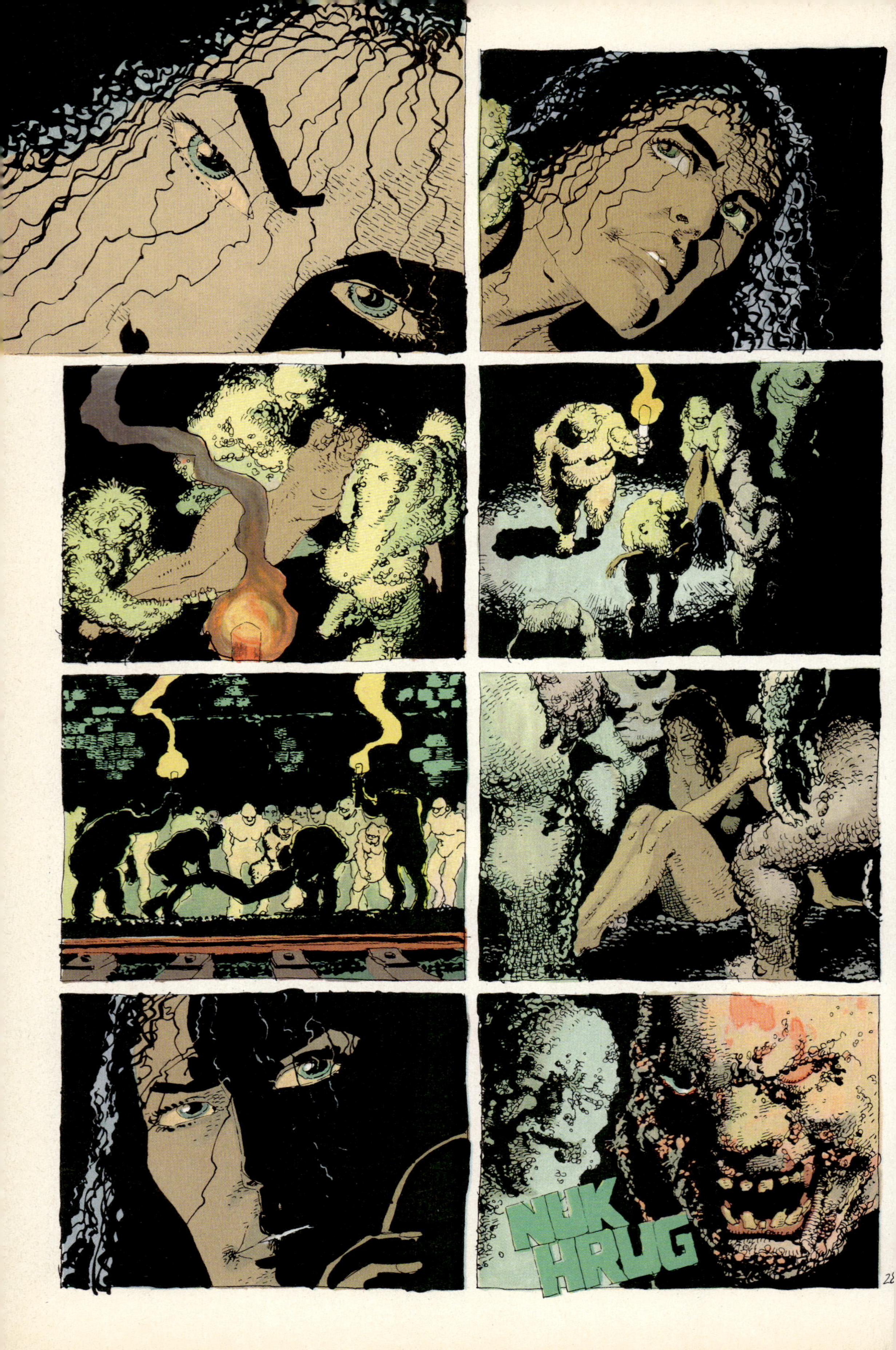
NUK
HRUG

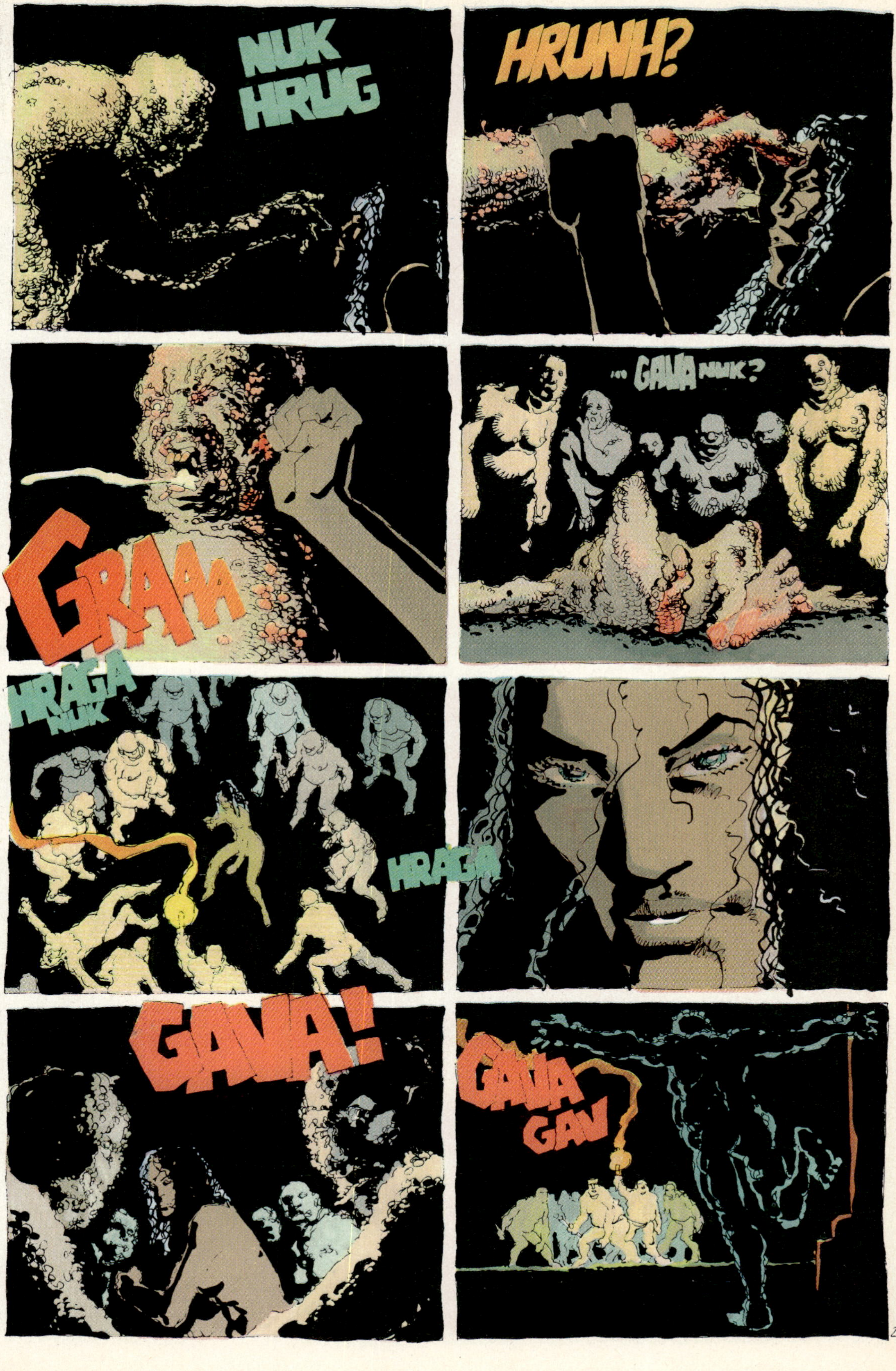
NUK HRUG
HRUNH?
GRAAA
... GANA NUK?
HRAGA NUK
HRAGA
GANA!
GANA GAN

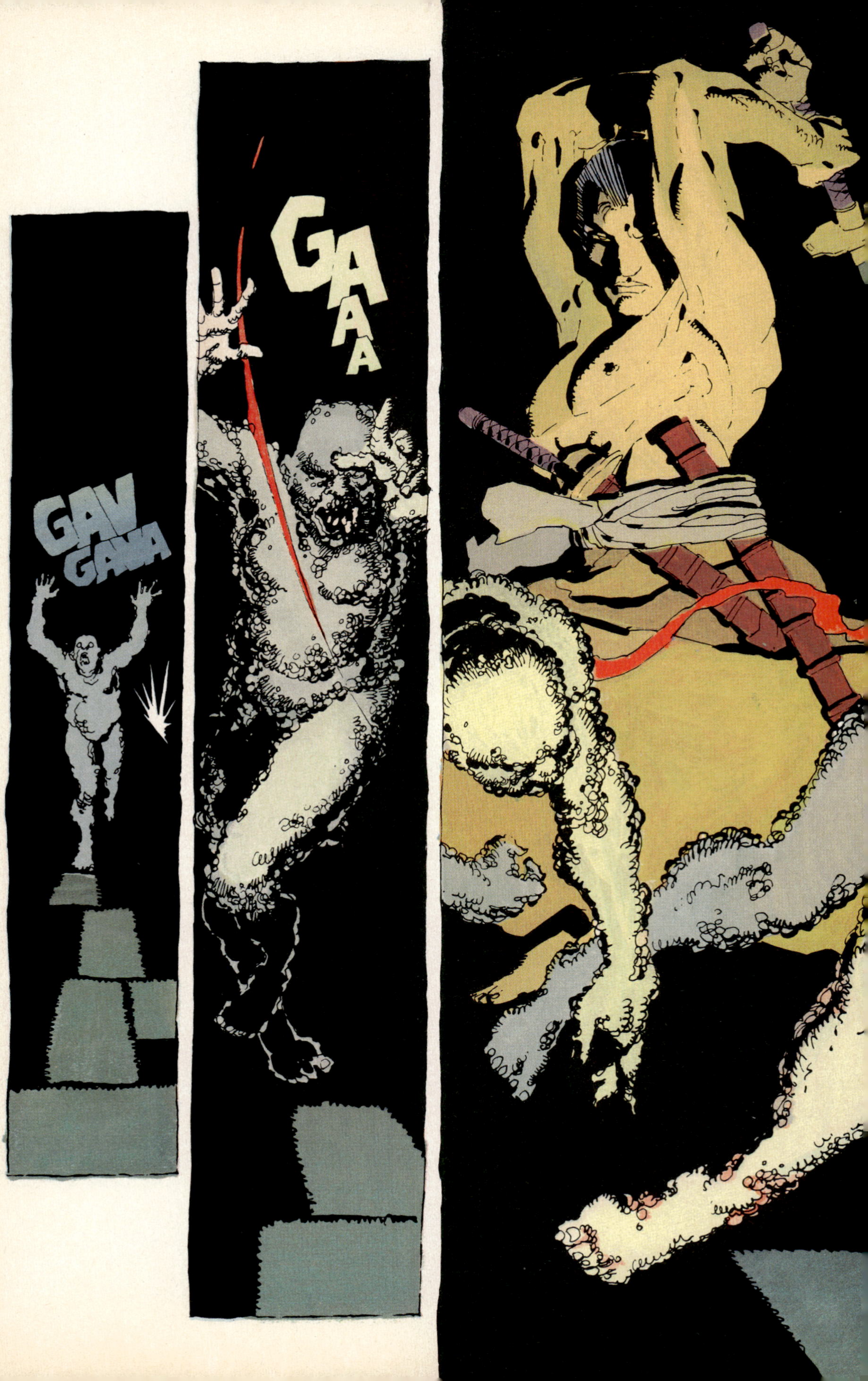
GAV
GAVA
GAAAA

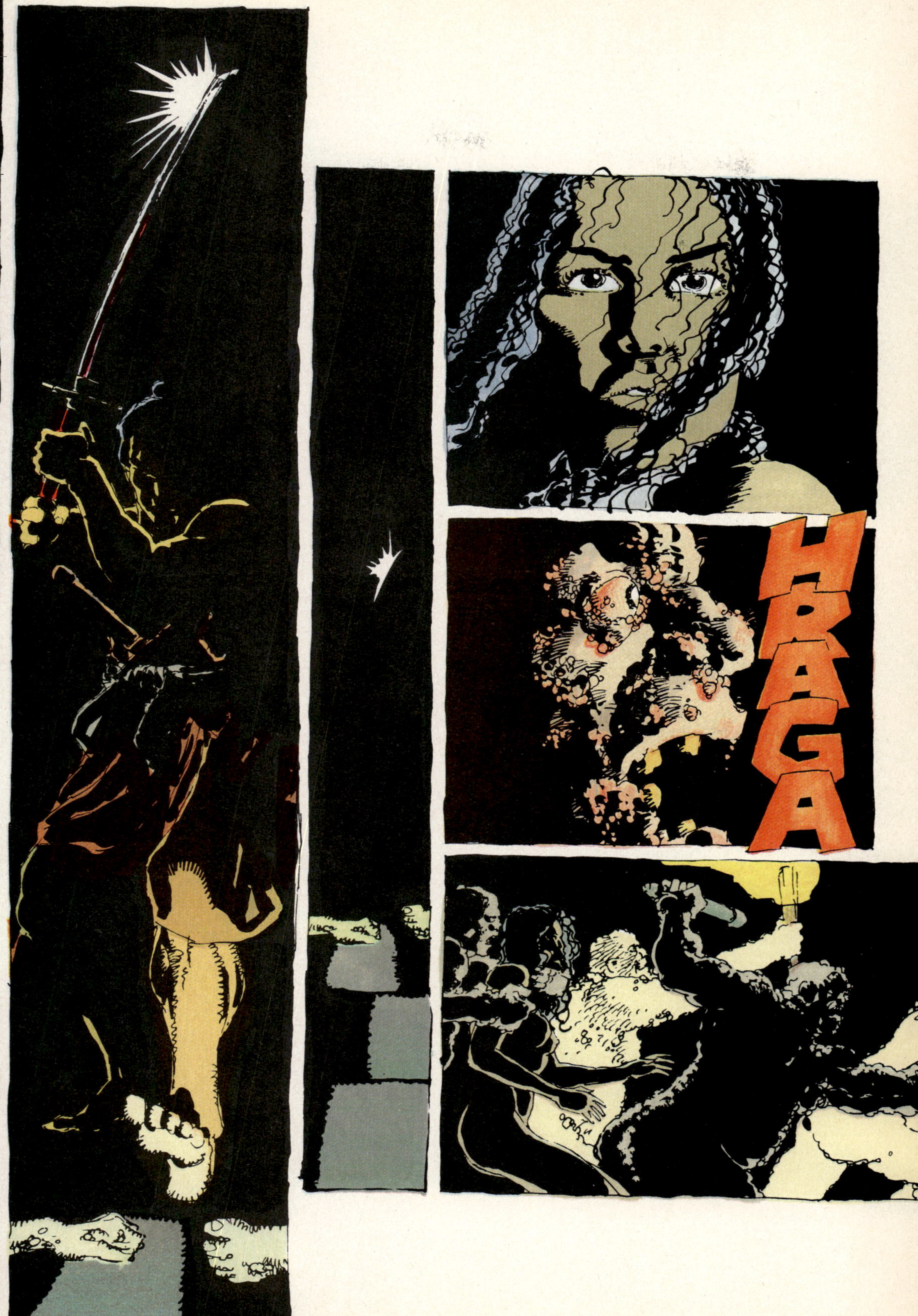
HRAGA

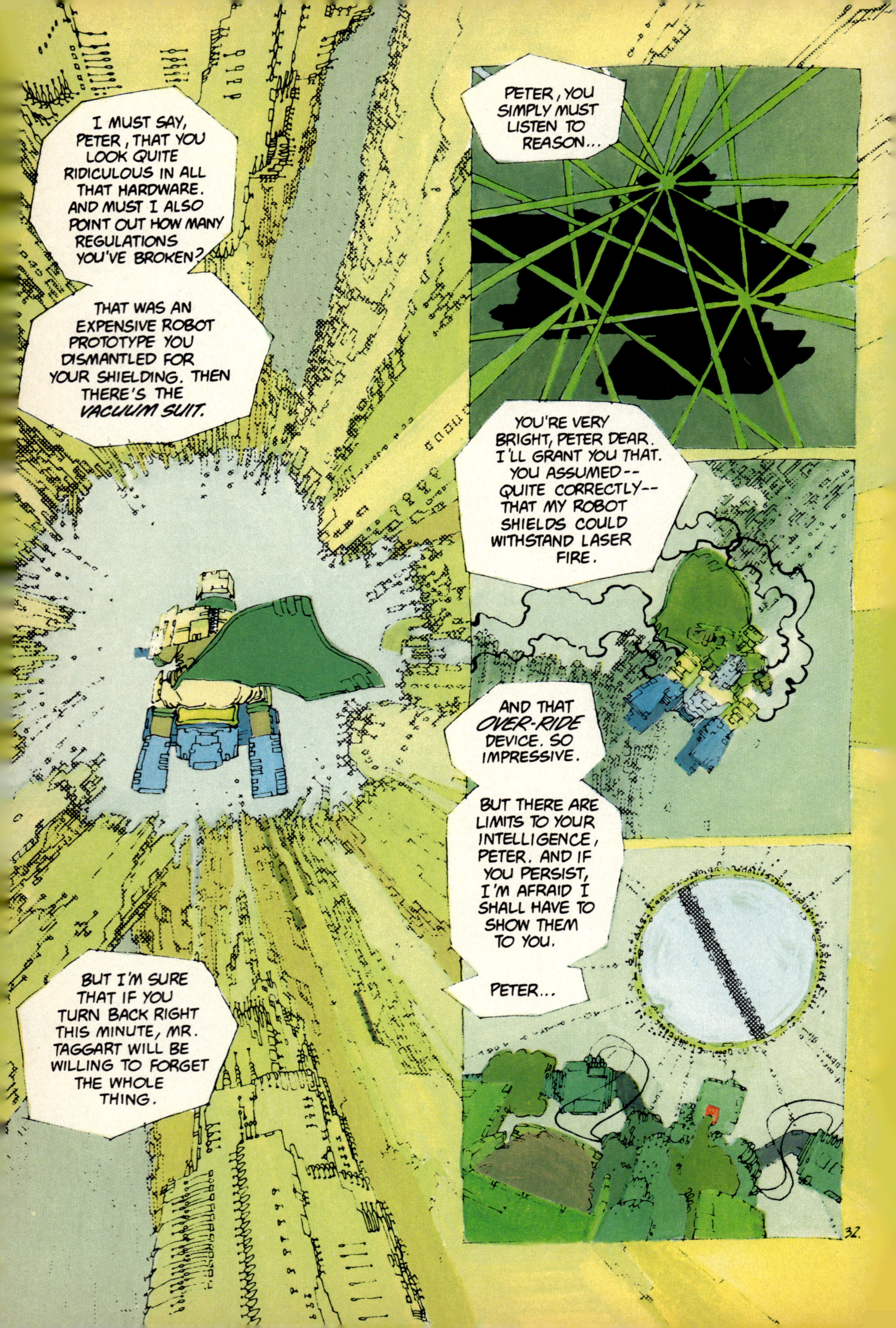
I MUST SAY, PETER, THAT YOU LOOK QUITE RIDICULOUS IN ALL THAT HARDWARE. AND MUST I ALSO POINT OUT HOW MANY REGULATIONS YOU'VE BROKEN?
THAT WAS AN EXPENSIVE ROBOT PROTOTYPE YOU DISMANTLED FOR YOUR SHIELDING. THEN THERE'S THE VACUUM SUIT.
BUT I'M SURE THAT IF YOU TURN BACK RIGHT THIS MINUTE, MR. TAGGART WILL BE WILLING TO FORGET THE WHOLE THING.
PETER, YOU SIMPLY MUST LISTEN TO REASON...
YOU'RE VERY BRIGHT, PETER DEAR. I'LL GRANT YOU THAT. YOU ASSUMED-- QUITE CORRECTLY-- THAT MY ROBOT SHIELDS COULD WITHSTAND LASER FIRE.
AND THAT OVER-RIDE DEVICE. SO IMPRESSIVE.
BUT THERE ARE LIMITS TO YOUR INTELLIGENCE, PETER. AND IF YOU PERSIST, I'M AFRAID I SHALL HAVE TO SHOW THEM TO YOU.
PETER...

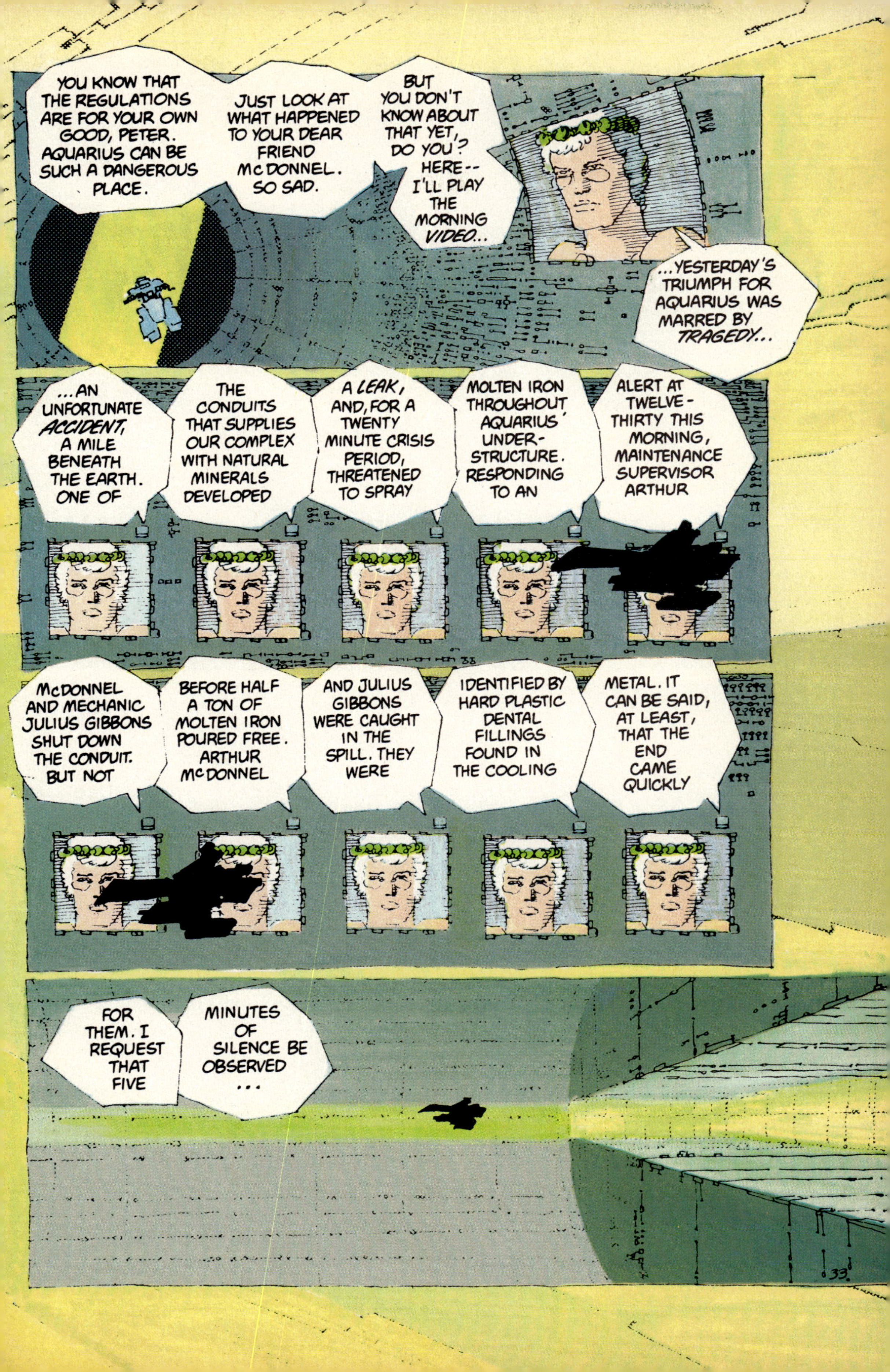
YOU KNOW THAT THE REGULATIONS ARE FOR YOUR OWN GOOD, PETER. AQUARIUS CAN BE SUCH A DANGEROUS PLACE.
JUST LOOK AT WHAT HAPPENED TO YOUR DEAR FRIEND McDONNEL. SO SAD.
BUT YOU DON'T KNOW ABOUT THAT YET, DO YOU? HERE-- I'LL PLAY THE MORNING *VIDEO*...
...YESTERDAY'S TRIUMPH FOR AQUARIUS WAS MARRED BY *TRAGEDY*...
...AN UNFORTUNATE *ACCIDENT*, A MILE BENEATH THE EARTH. ONE OF
THE CONDUITS THAT SUPPLIES OUR COMPLEX WITH NATURAL MINERALS DEVELOPED
A *LEAK*, AND, FOR A TWENTY MINUTE CRISIS PERIOD, THREATENED TO SPRAY
MOLTEN IRON THROUGHOUT AQUARIUS' UNDER-STRUCTURE. RESPONDING TO AN
ALERT AT TWELVE-THIRTY THIS MORNING, MAINTENANCE SUPERVISOR ARTHUR
McDONNEL AND MECHANIC JULIUS GIBBONS SHUT DOWN THE CONDUIT. BUT NOT
BEFORE HALF A TON OF MOLTEN IRON POURED FREE. ARTHUR McDONNEL
AND JULIUS GIBBONS WERE CAUGHT IN THE SPILL. THEY WERE
IDENTIFIED BY HARD PLASTIC DENTAL FILLINGS FOUND IN THE COOLING
METAL. IT CAN BE SAID, AT LEAST, THAT THE END CAME QUICKLY
FOR THEM. I REQUEST THAT FIVE
MINUTES OF SILENCE BE OBSERVED ...
33

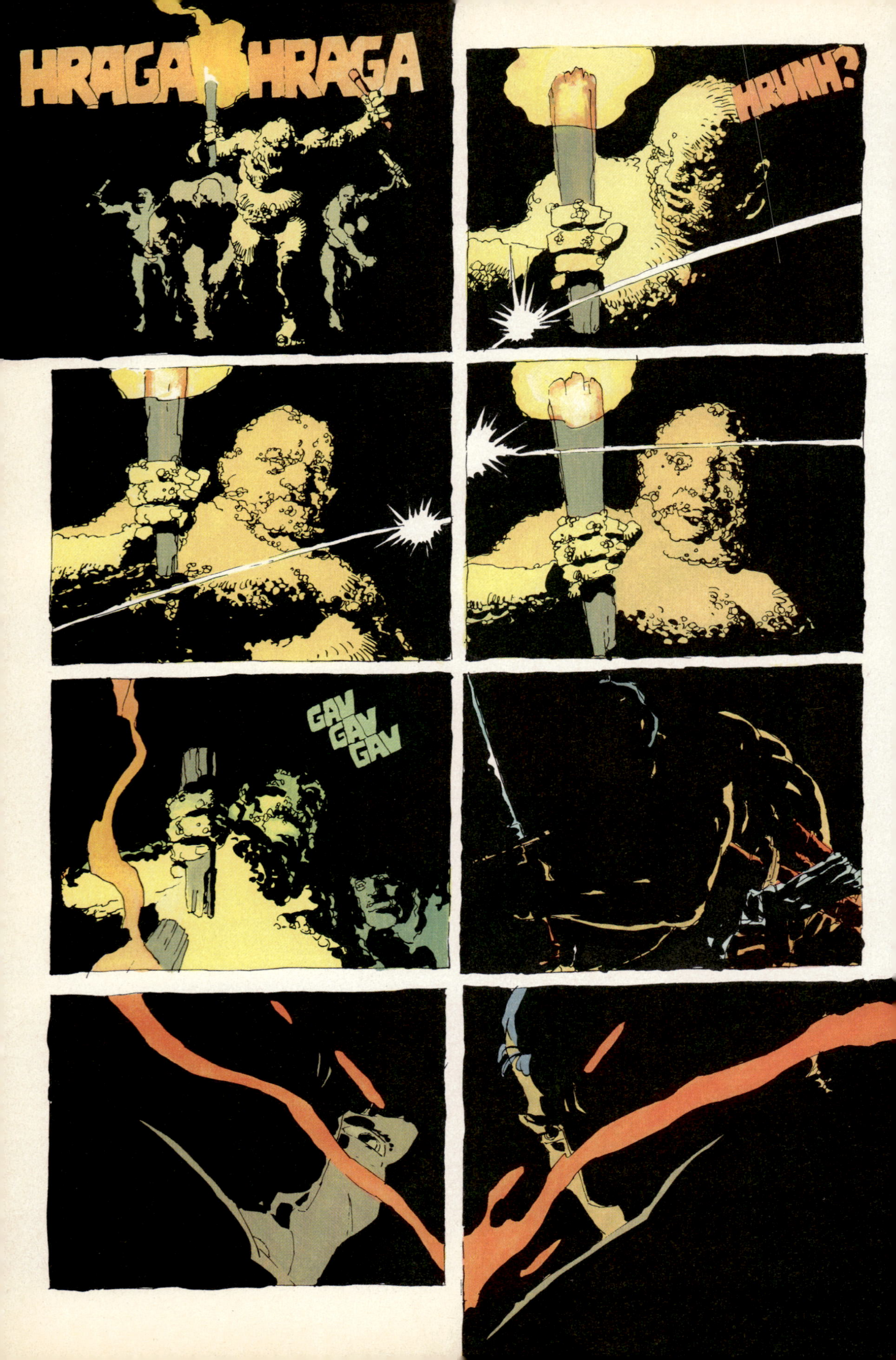
HRAGA HRAGA
HRUNH?
GAV GAV GAV

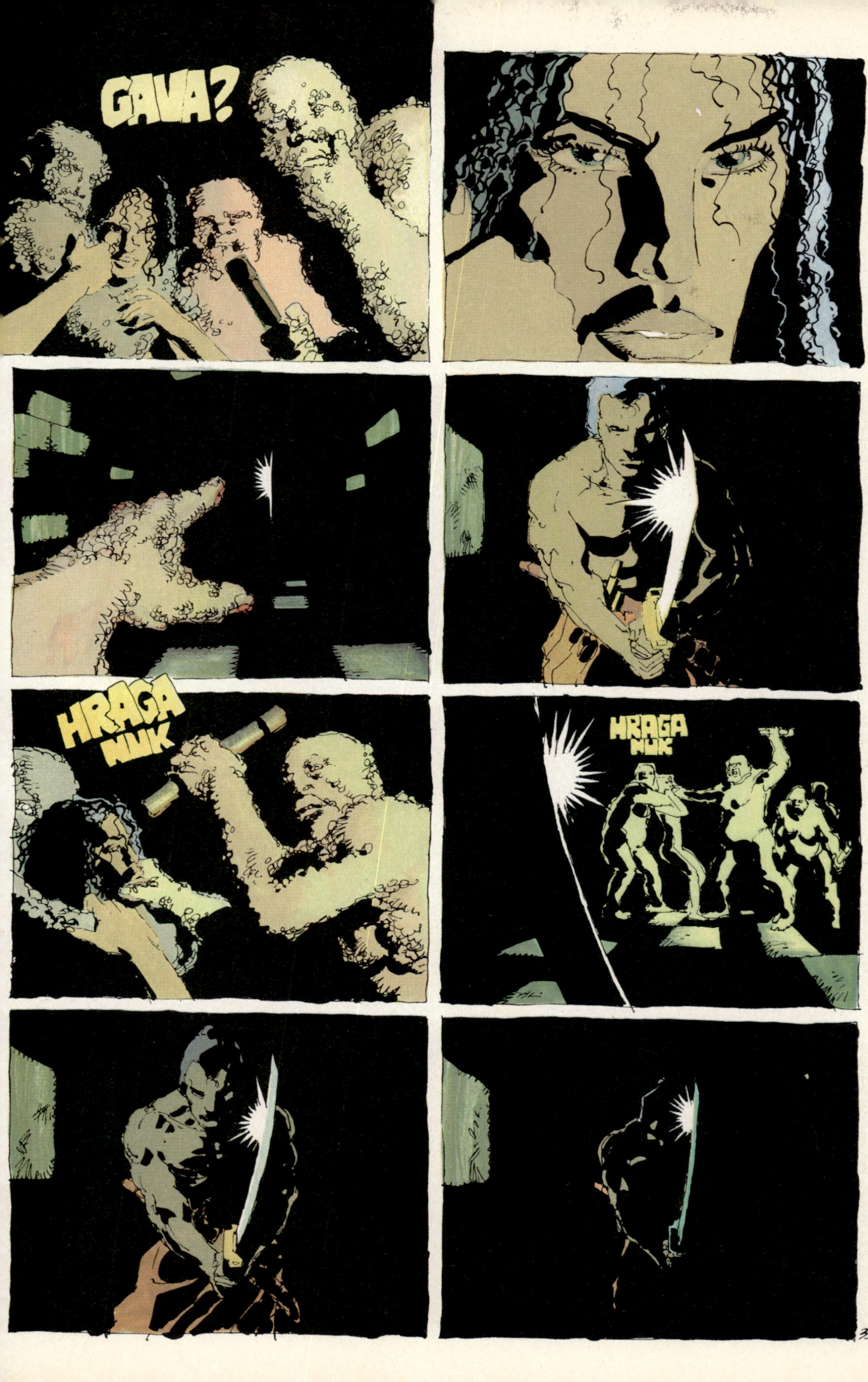
GAVA?
HRAGA NUK
HRAGA NUK

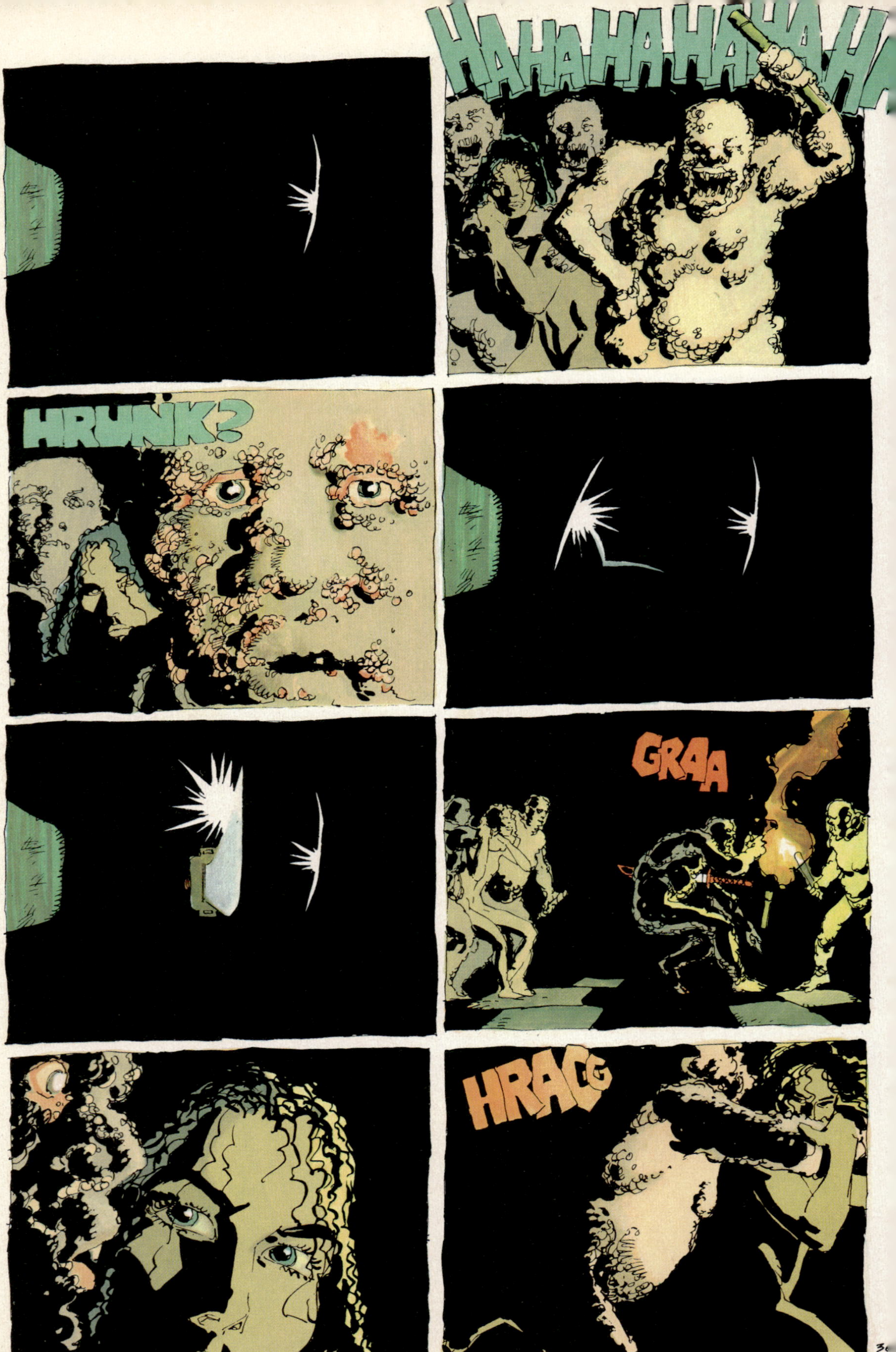

HAHAHAHAHAHA
HRUNK?
GRAA
HRACG

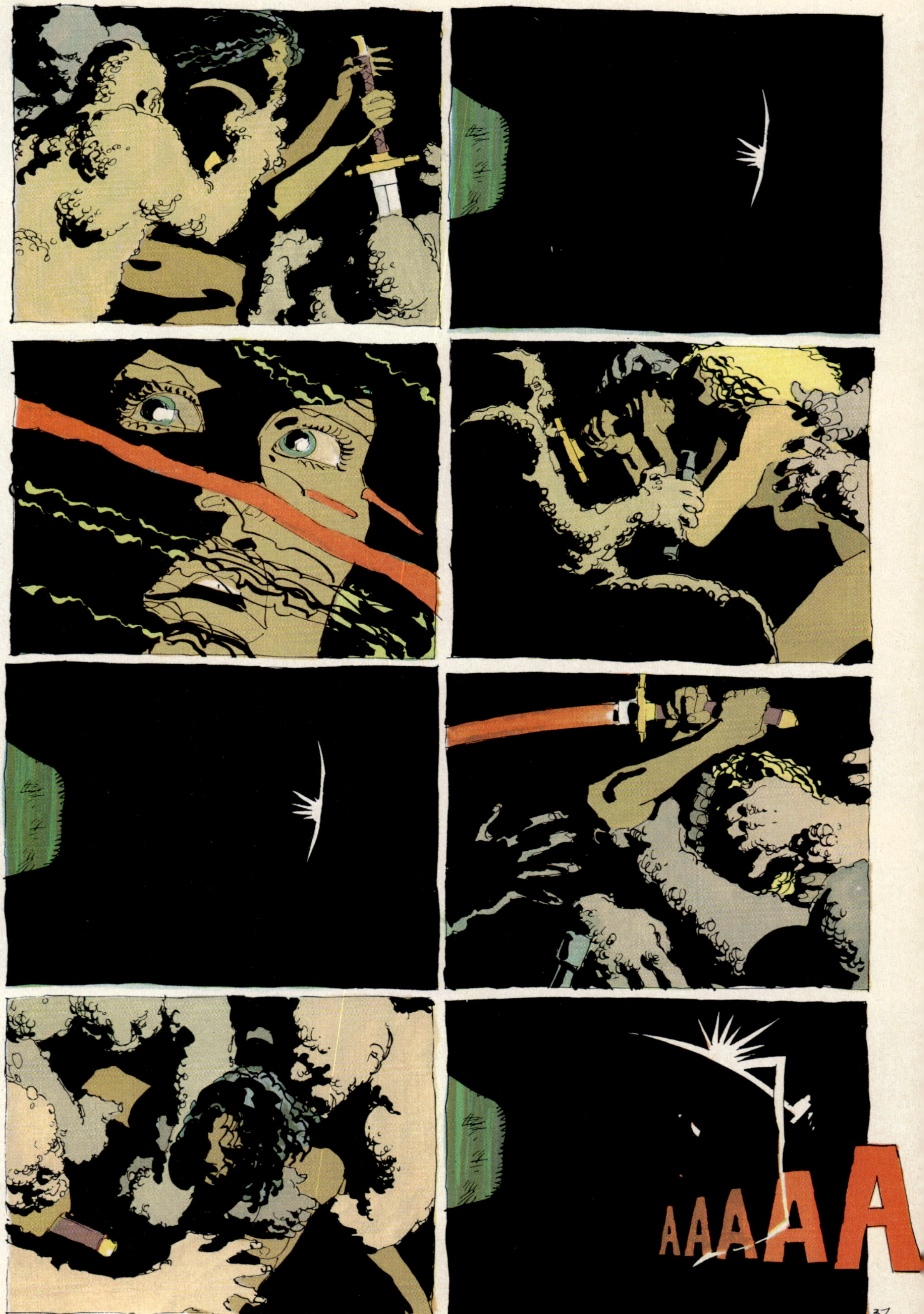
AAAAA

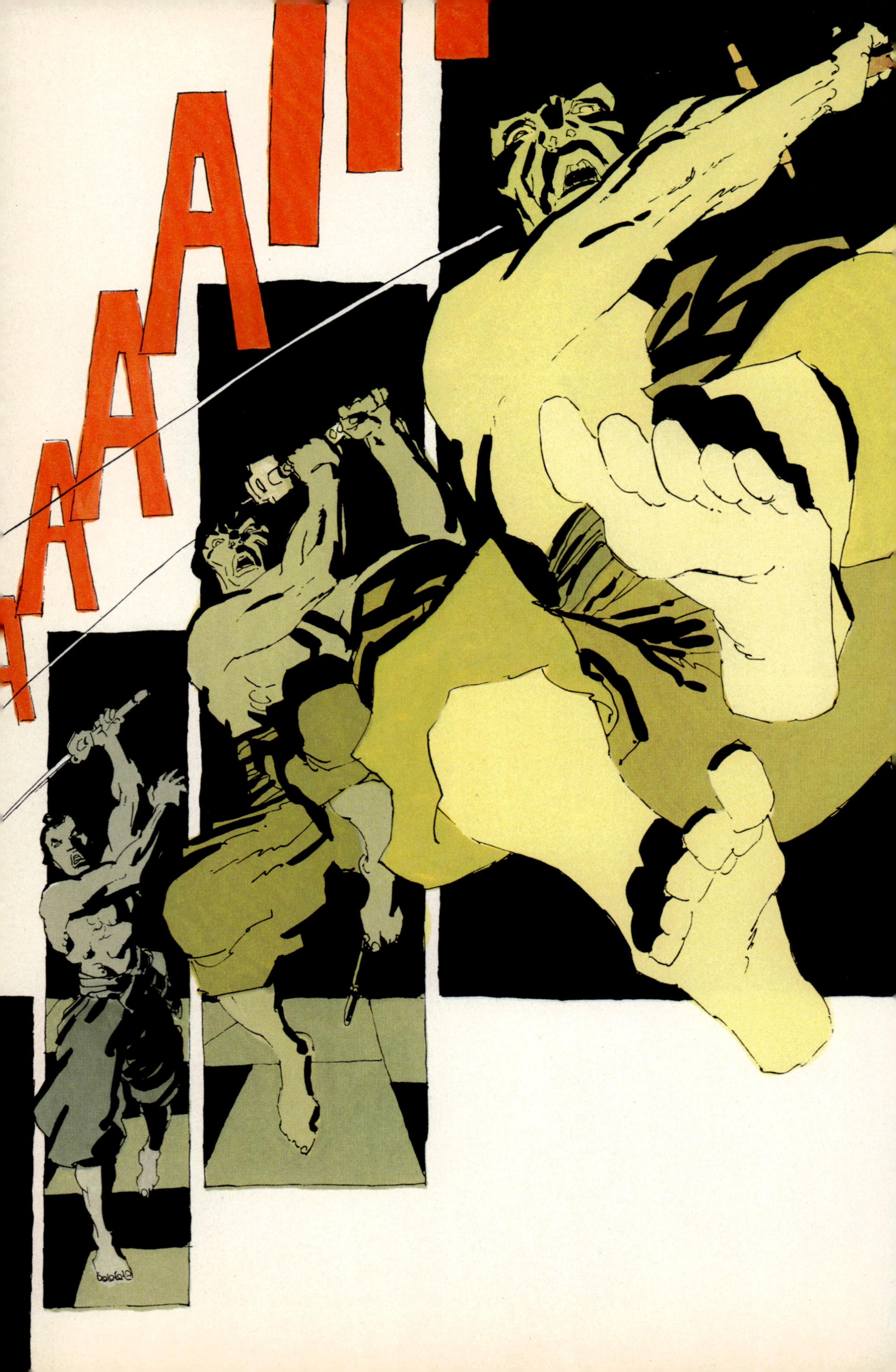
AAAAAIII

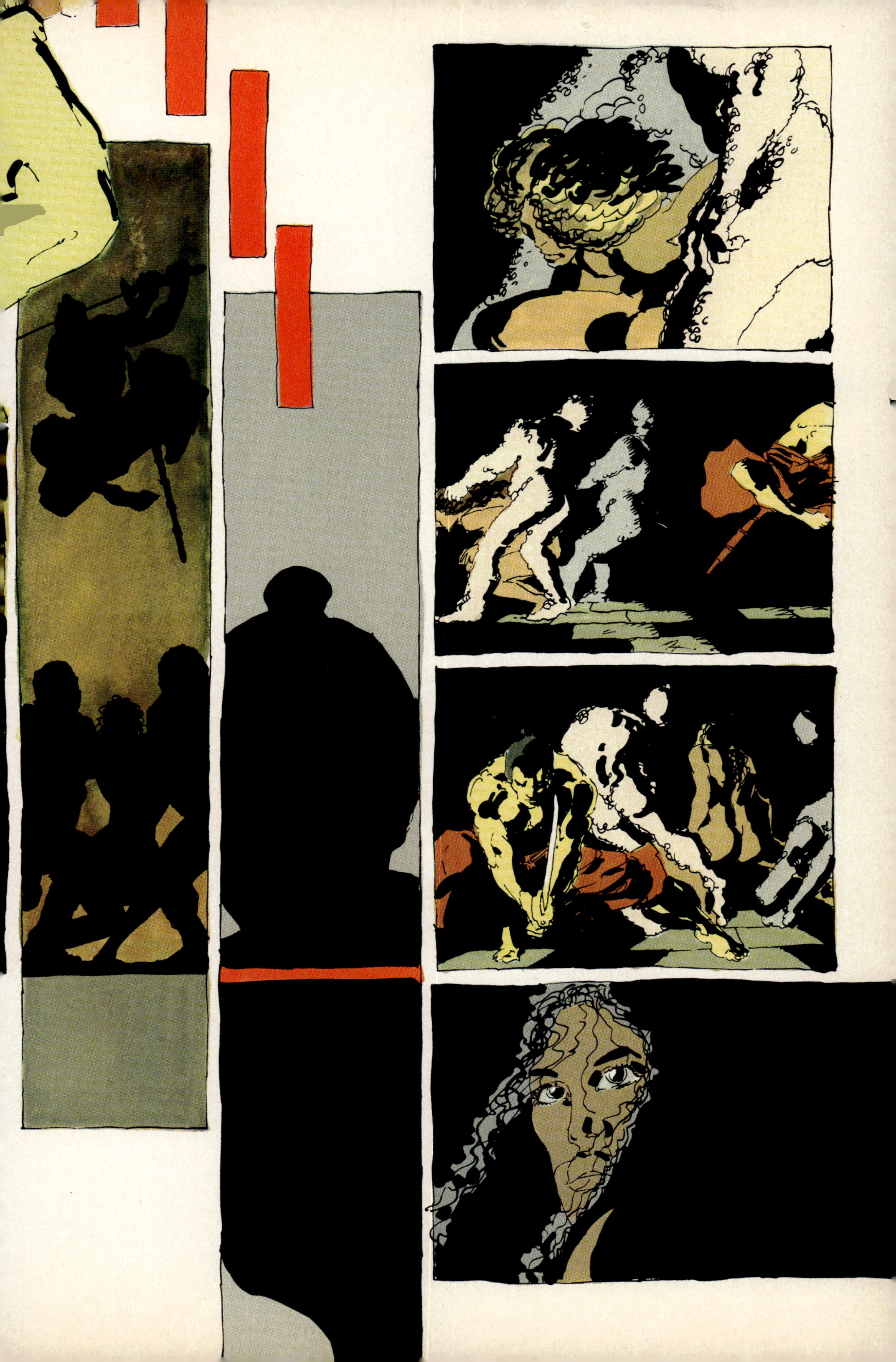

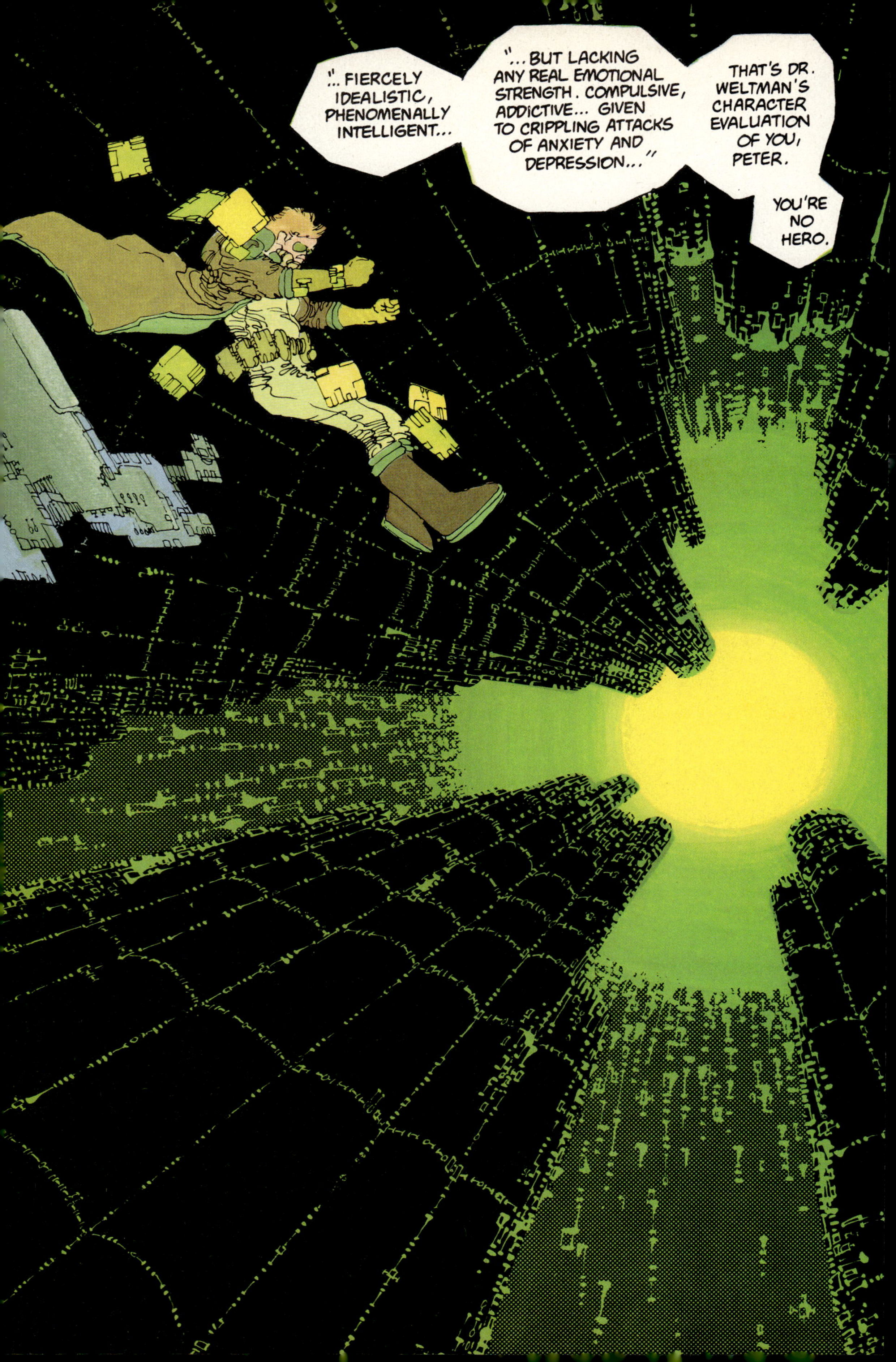
"... FIERCELY IDEALISTIC, PHENOMENALLY INTELLIGENT...
"... BUT LACKING ANY REAL EMOTIONAL STRENGTH. COMPULSIVE, ADDICTIVE... GIVEN TO CRIPPLING ATTACKS OF ANXIETY AND DEPRESSION..."
THAT'S DR. WELTMAN'S CHARACTER EVALUATION OF YOU, PETER.
YOU'RE NO HERO.

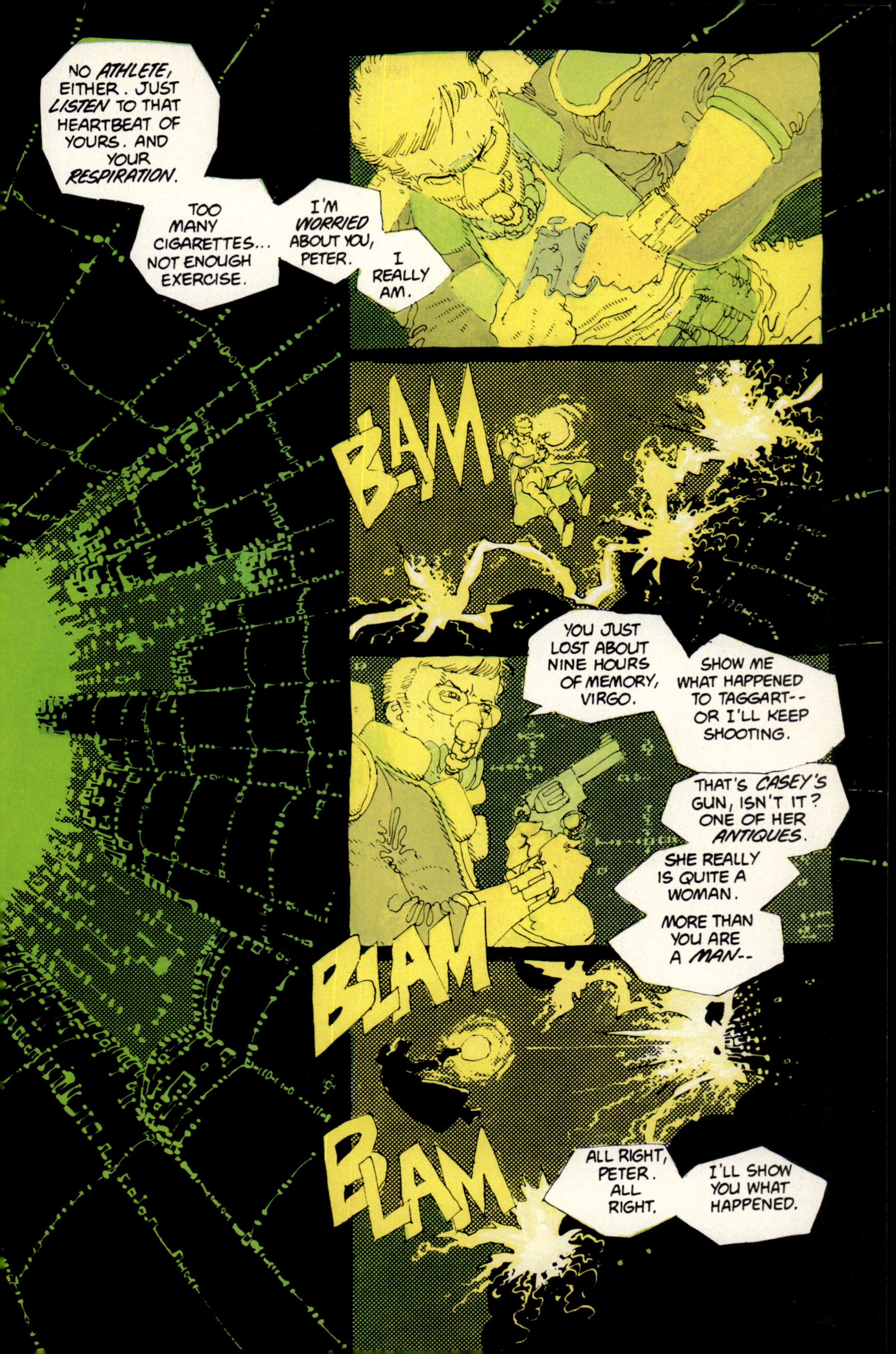
NO ATHLETE, EITHER. JUST LISTEN TO THAT HEARTBEAT OF YOURS. AND YOUR RESPIRATION.
TOO MANY CIGARETTES... NOT ENOUGH EXERCISE.
I'M WORRIED ABOUT YOU, PETER.
I REALLY AM.
BAM
YOU JUST LOST ABOUT NINE HOURS OF MEMORY, VIRGO.
SHOW ME WHAT HAPPENED TO TAGGART-- OR I'LL KEEP SHOOTING.
THAT'S CASEY'S GUN, ISN'T IT? ONE OF HER ANTIQUES.
SHE REALLY IS QUITE A WOMAN.
MORE THAN YOU ARE A MAN--
BLAM
BLAM
ALL RIGHT, PETER. ALL RIGHT.
I'LL SHOW YOU WHAT HAPPENED.

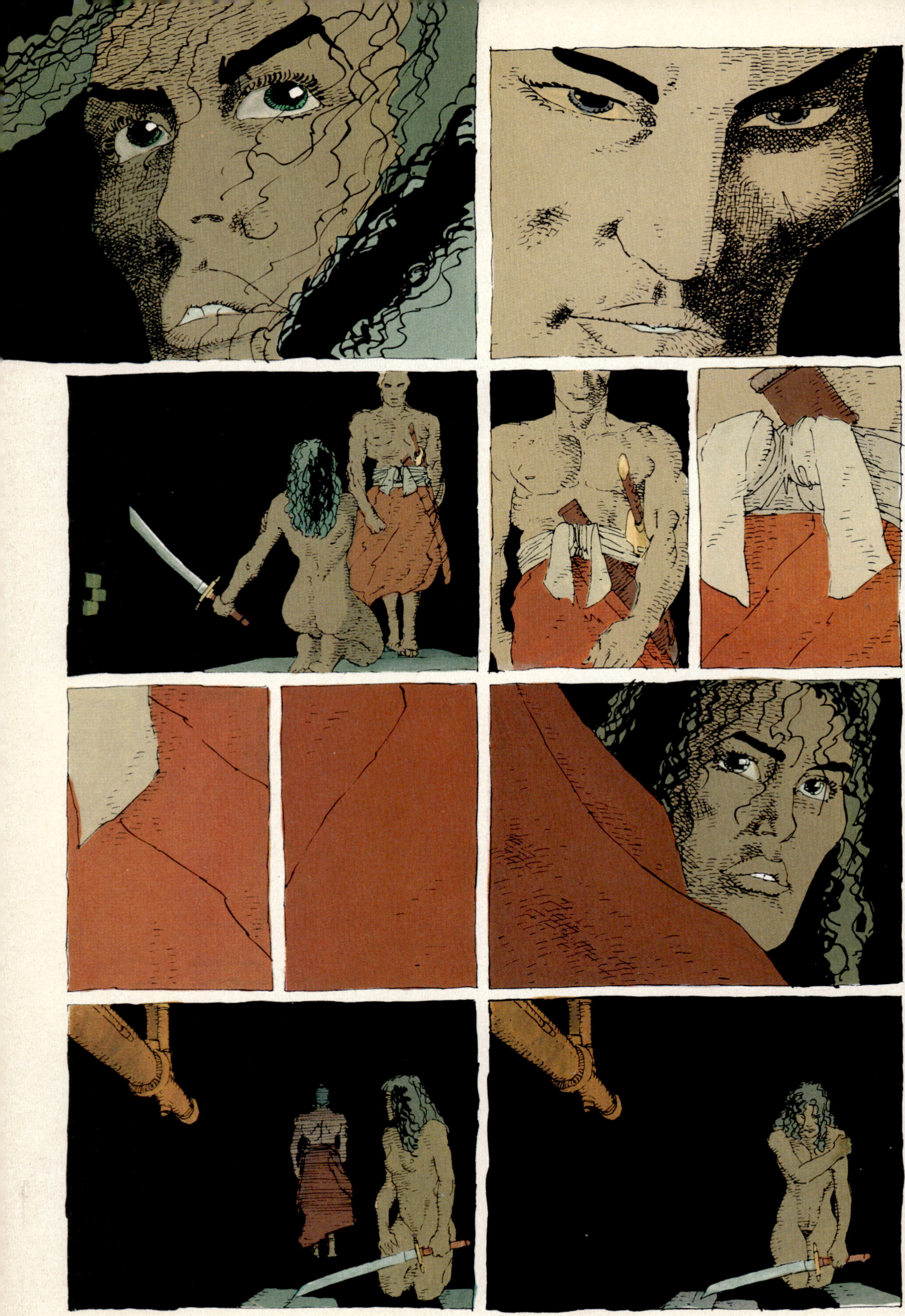

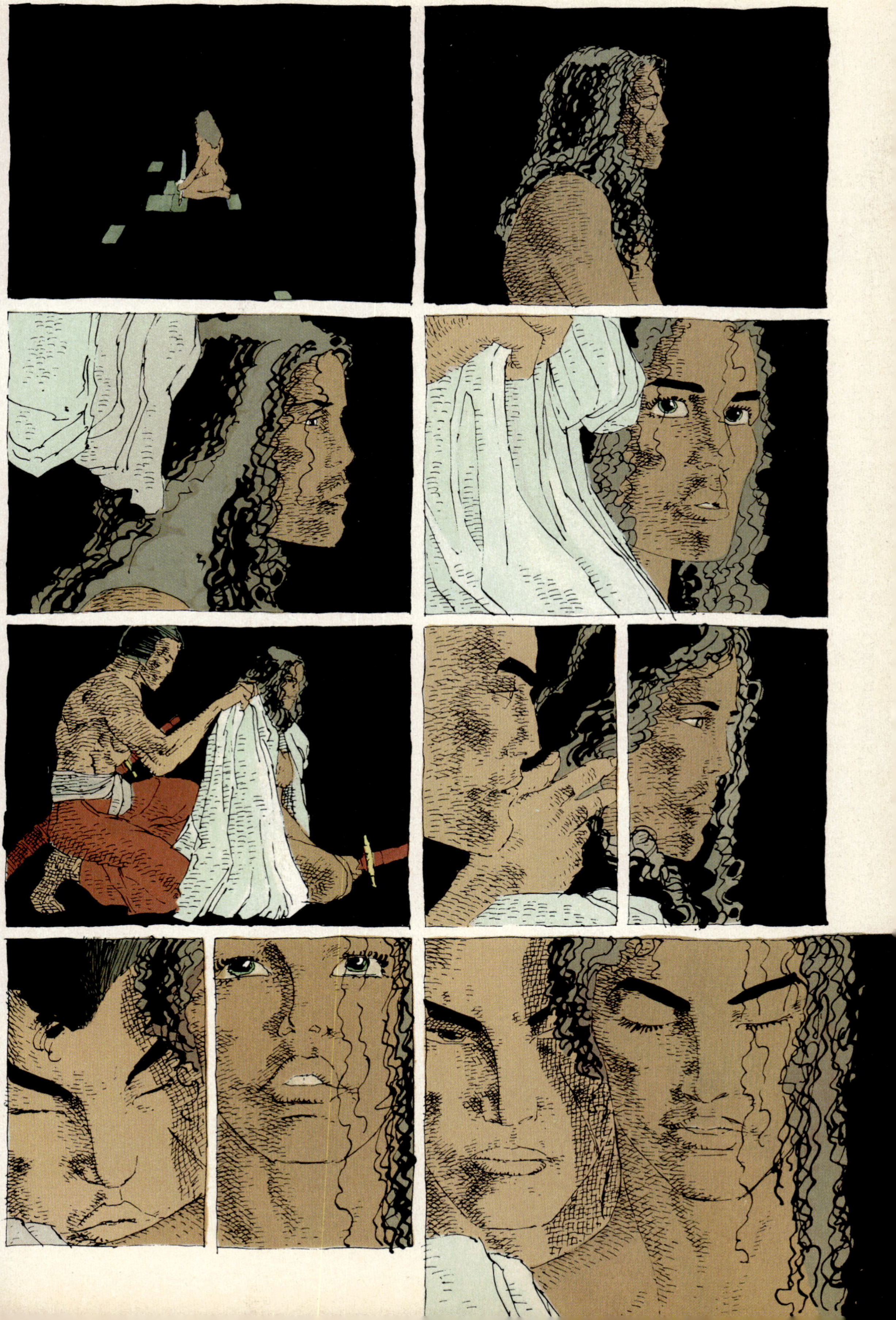

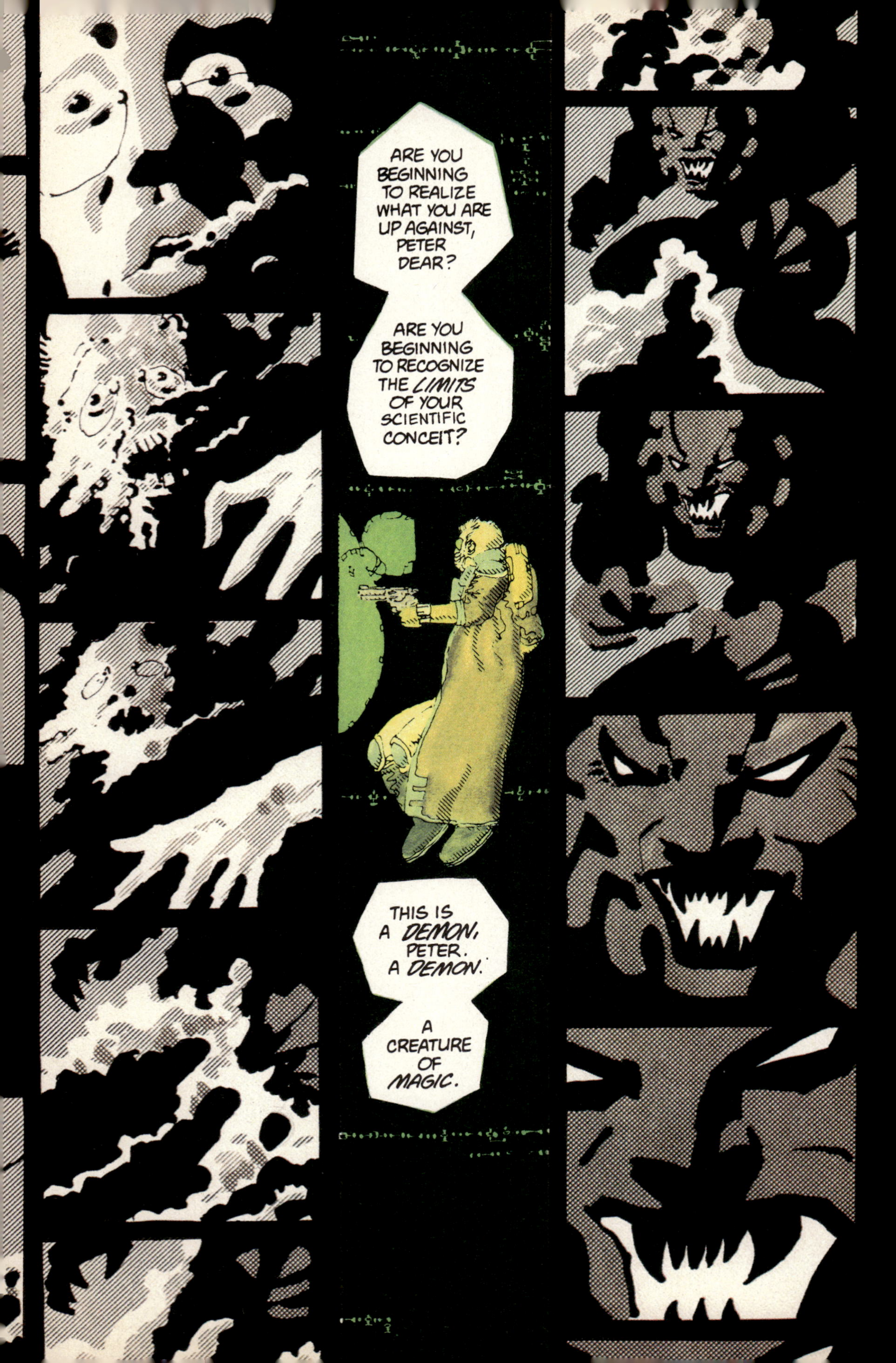
ARE YOU BEGINNING TO REALIZE WHAT YOU ARE UP AGAINST, PETER DEAR?
ARE YOU BEGINNING TO RECOGNIZE THE *LIMITS* OF YOUR SCIENTIFIC CONCEIT?
THIS IS A *DEMON*, PETER. A *DEMON*.
A CREATURE OF *MAGIC*.

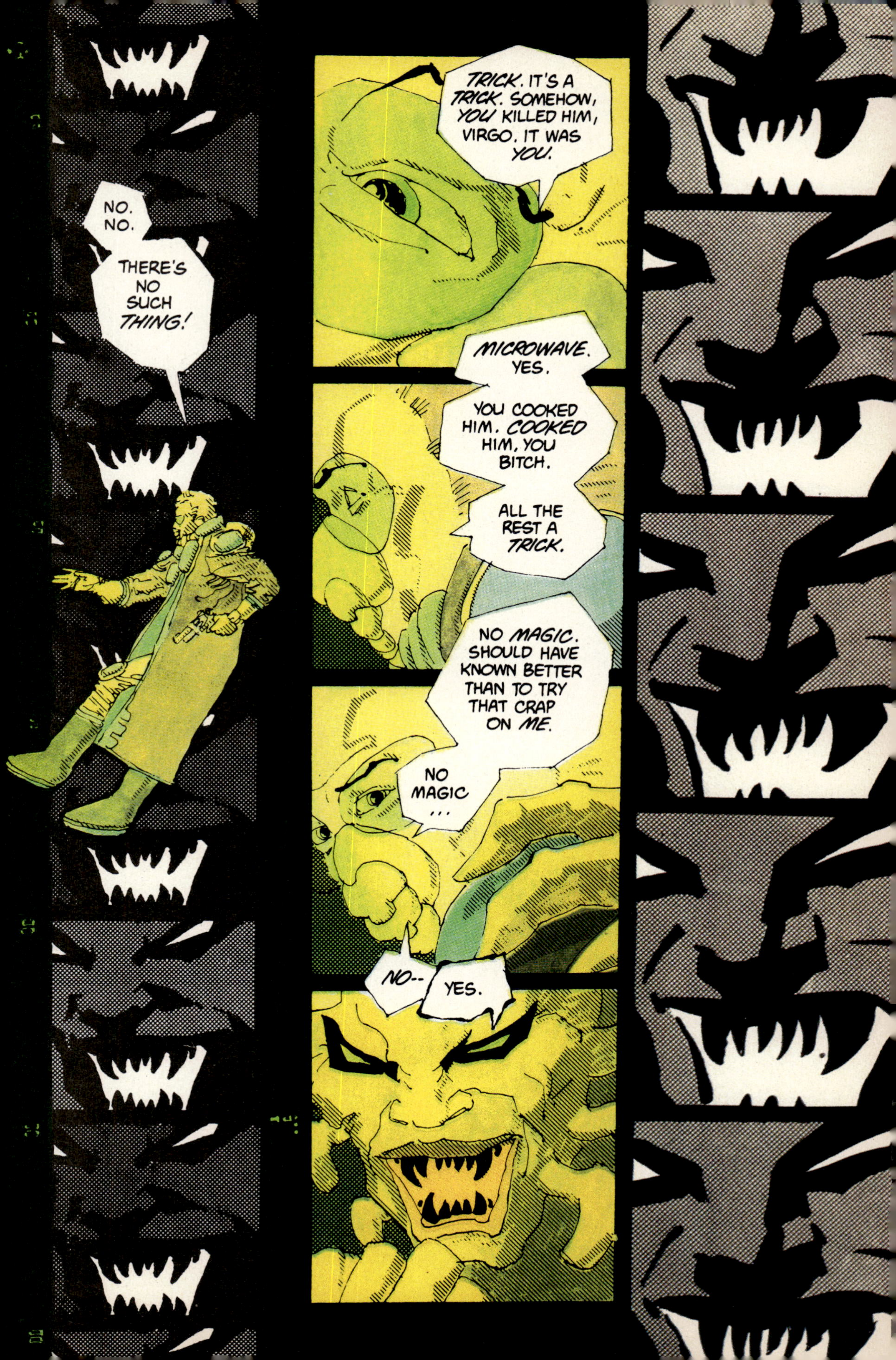
NO. NO.
THERE'S NO SUCH THING!
TRICK. IT'S A TRICK. SOMEHOW, YOU KILLED HIM, VIRGO. IT WAS YOU.
MICROWAVE. YES.
YOU COOKED HIM. COOKED HIM, YOU BITCH.
ALL THE REST A TRICK.
NO MAGIC. SHOULD HAVE KNOWN BETTER THAN TO TRY THAT CRAP ON ME.
NO MAGIC ...
NO--
YES.

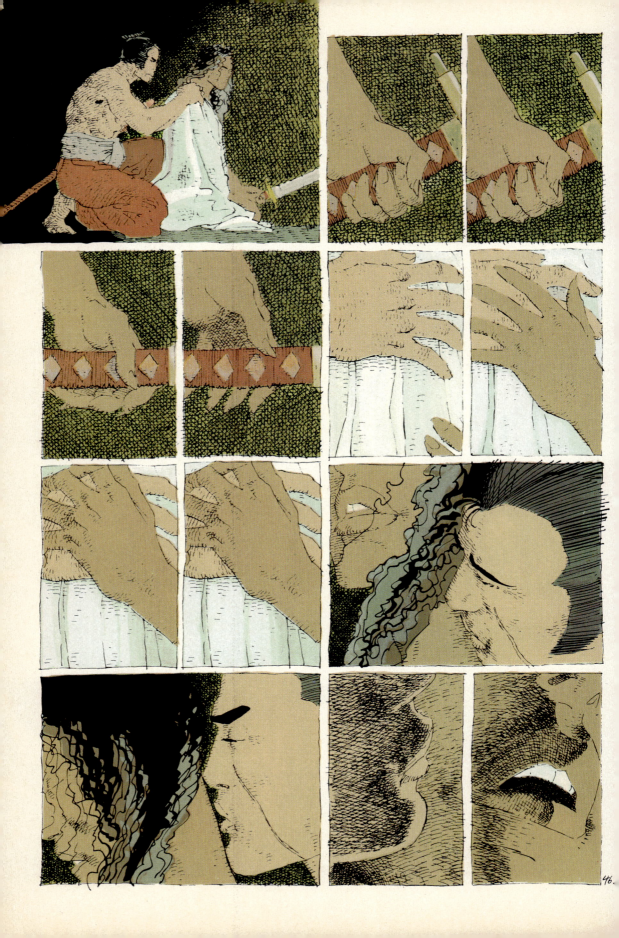

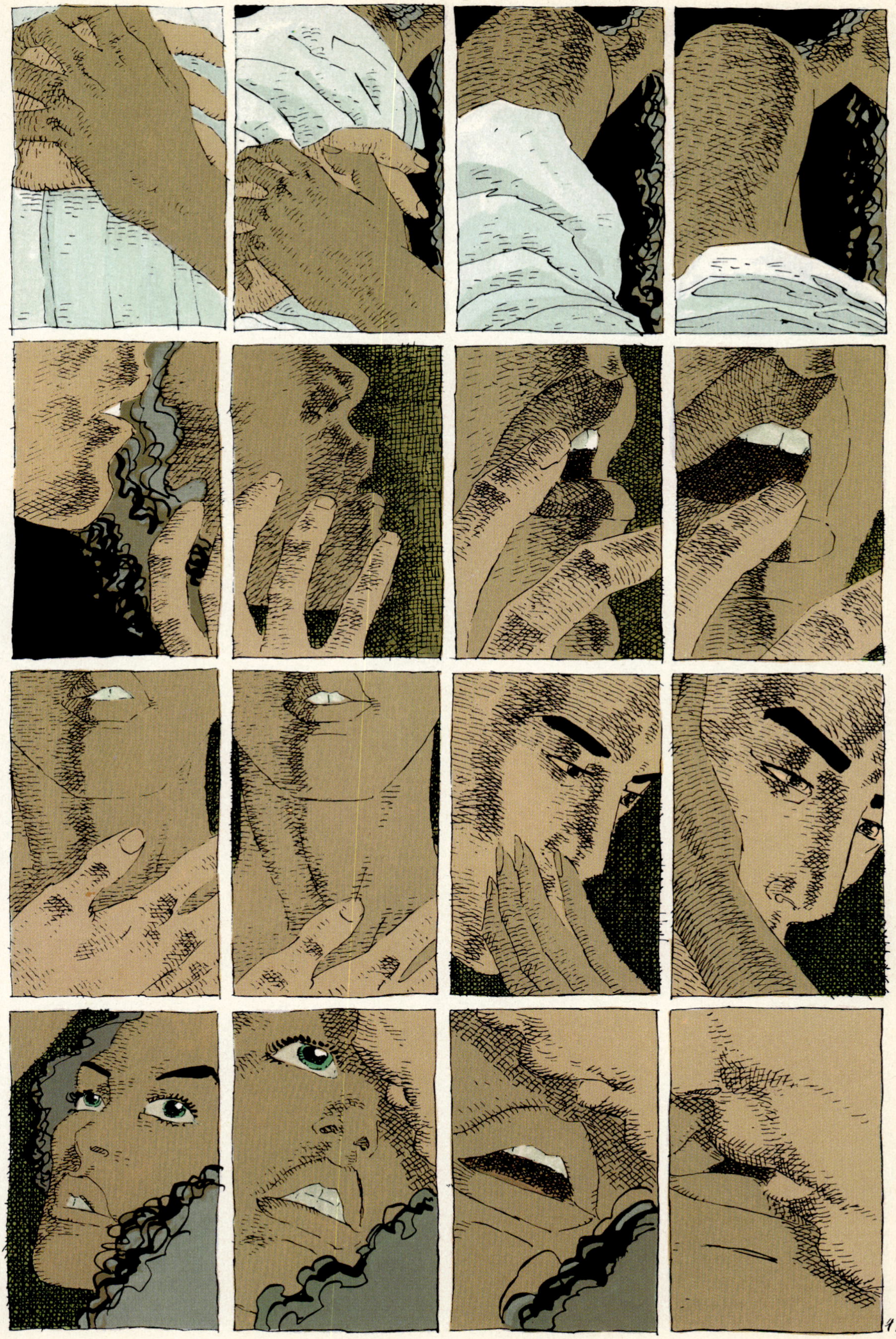

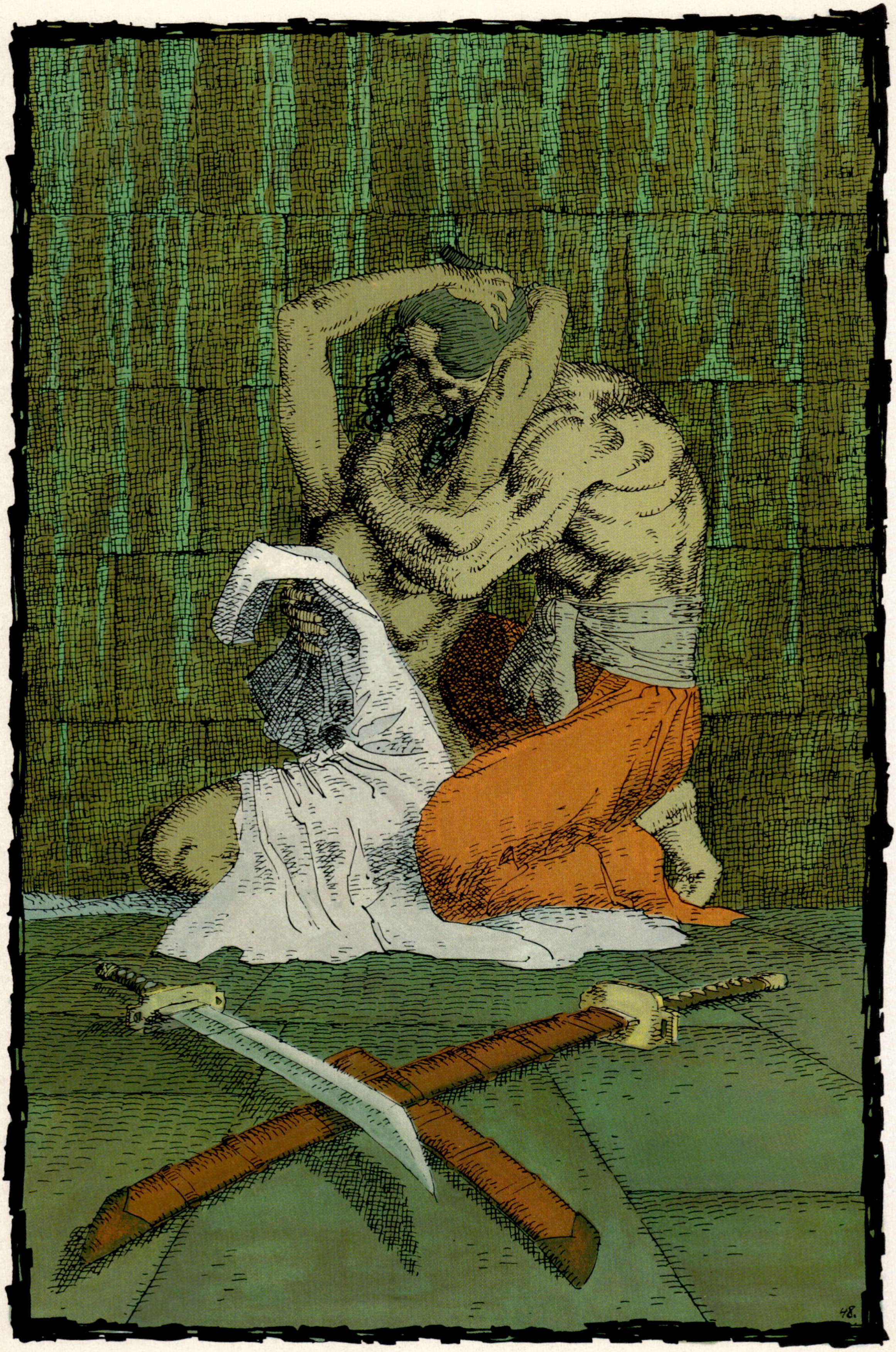

CHAPTER FIVE

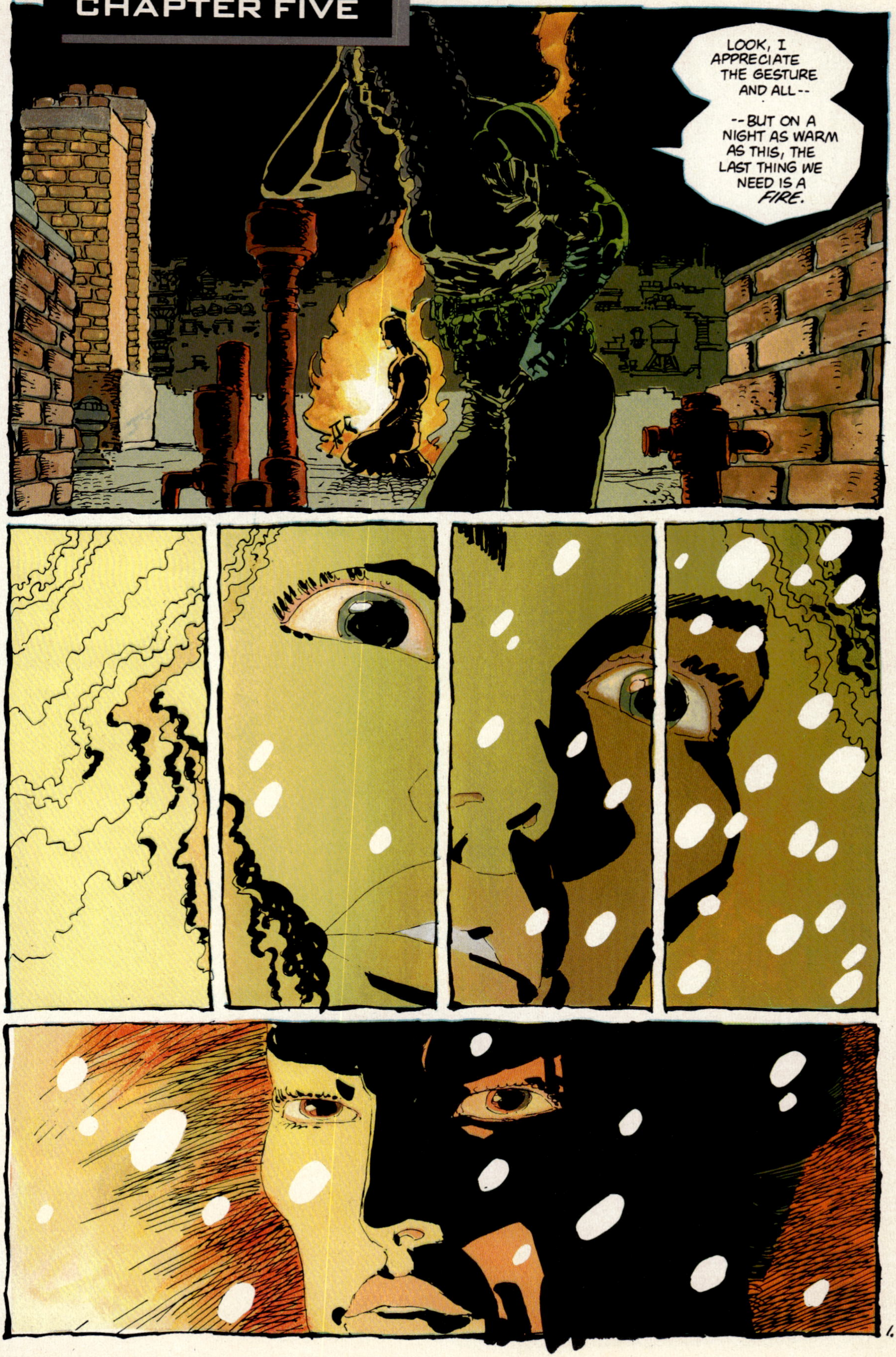

LOOK, I APPRECIATE THE GESTURE AND ALL--
--BUT ON A NIGHT AS WARM AS THIS, THE LAST THING WE NEED IS A *FIRE*.
1.

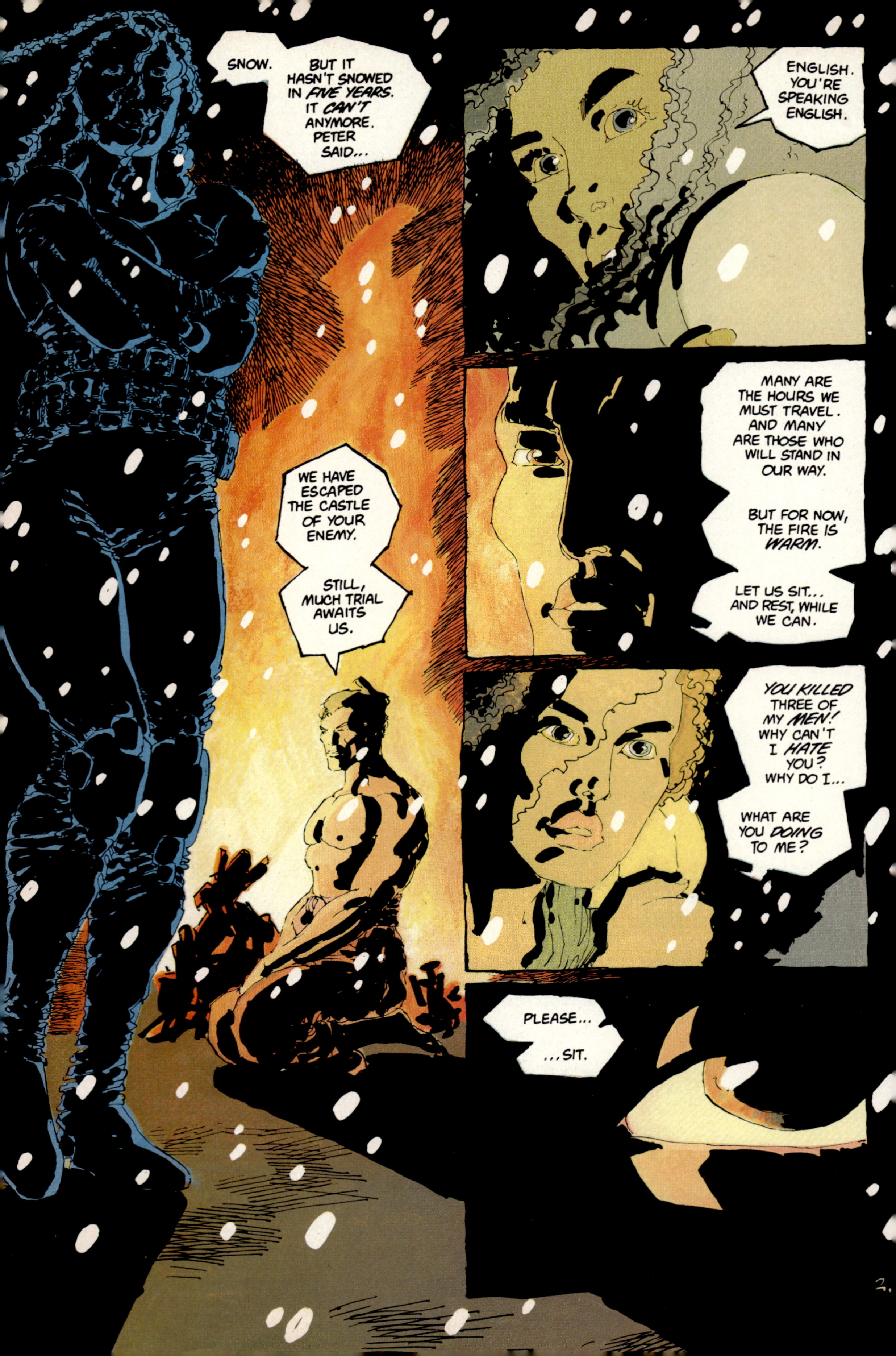

SNOW.
BUT IT HASN'T SNOWED IN FIVE YEARS. IT CAN'T ANYMORE. PETER SAID...
WE HAVE ESCAPED THE CASTLE OF YOUR ENEMY.
STILL, MUCH TRIAL AWAITS US.
ENGLISH. YOU'RE SPEAKING ENGLISH.
MANY ARE THE HOURS WE MUST TRAVEL. AND MANY ARE THOSE WHO WILL STAND IN OUR WAY.
BUT FOR NOW, THE FIRE IS WARM.
LET US SIT... AND REST, WHILE WE CAN.
YOU KILLED THREE OF MY MEN! WHY CAN'T I HATE YOU? WHY DO I...
WHAT ARE YOU DOING TO ME?
PLEASE...
...SIT.

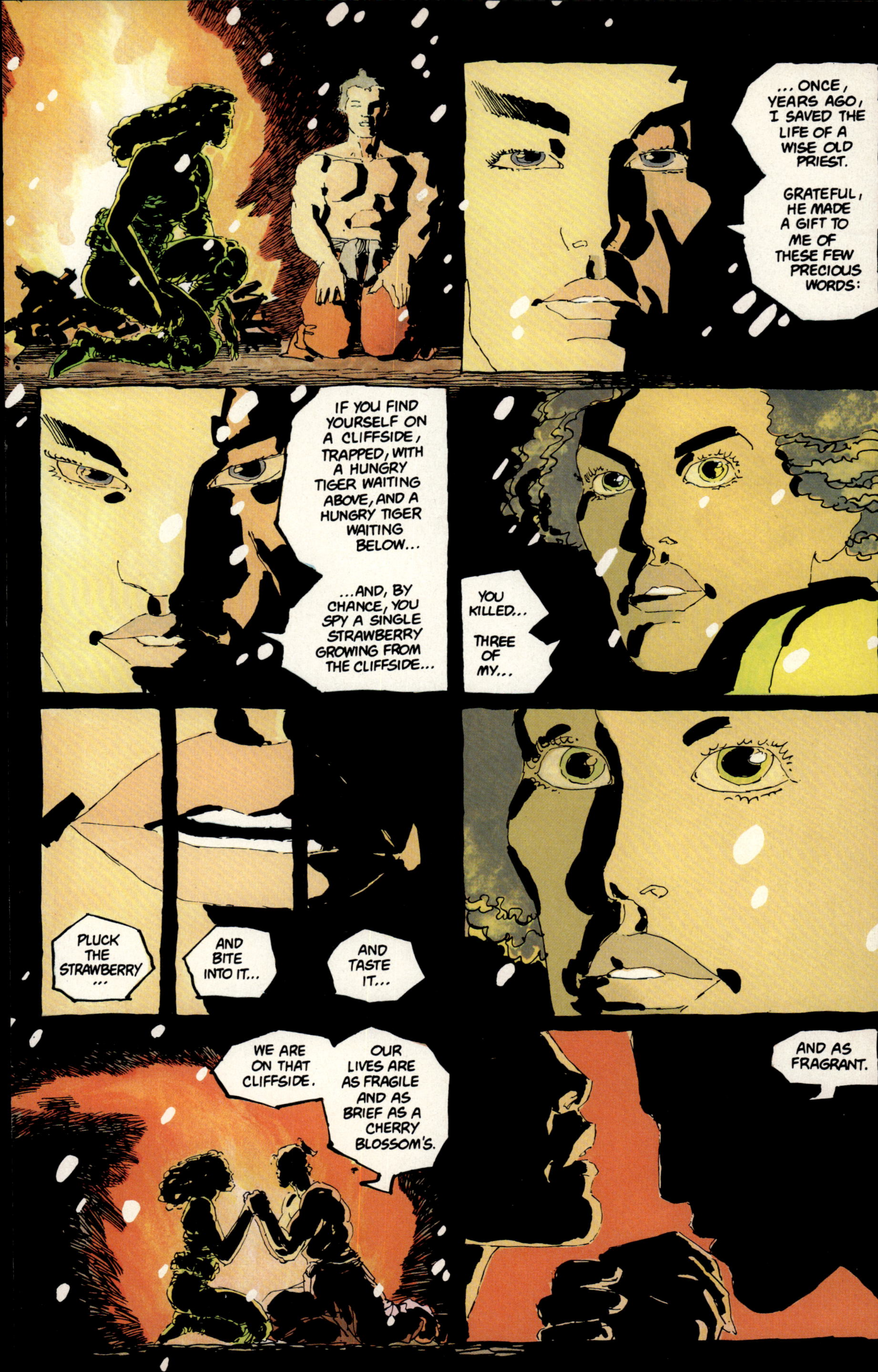

... ONCE, YEARS AGO, I SAVED THE LIFE OF A WISE OLD PRIEST.
GRATEFUL, HE MADE A GIFT TO ME OF THESE FEW PRECIOUS WORDS:
IF YOU FIND YOURSELF ON A CLIFFSIDE, TRAPPED, WITH A HUNGRY TIGER WAITING ABOVE, AND A HUNGRY TIGER WAITING BELOW...
...AND, BY CHANCE, YOU SPY A SINGLE STRAWBERRY GROWING FROM THE CLIFFSIDE...
YOU KILLED...
THREE OF MY...
PLUCK THE STRAWBERRY ...
AND BITE INTO IT...
AND TASTE IT...
WE ARE ON THAT CLIFFSIDE.
OUR LIVES ARE AS FRAGILE AND AS BRIEF AS A CHERRY BLOSSOM'S.
AND AS FRAGRANT.

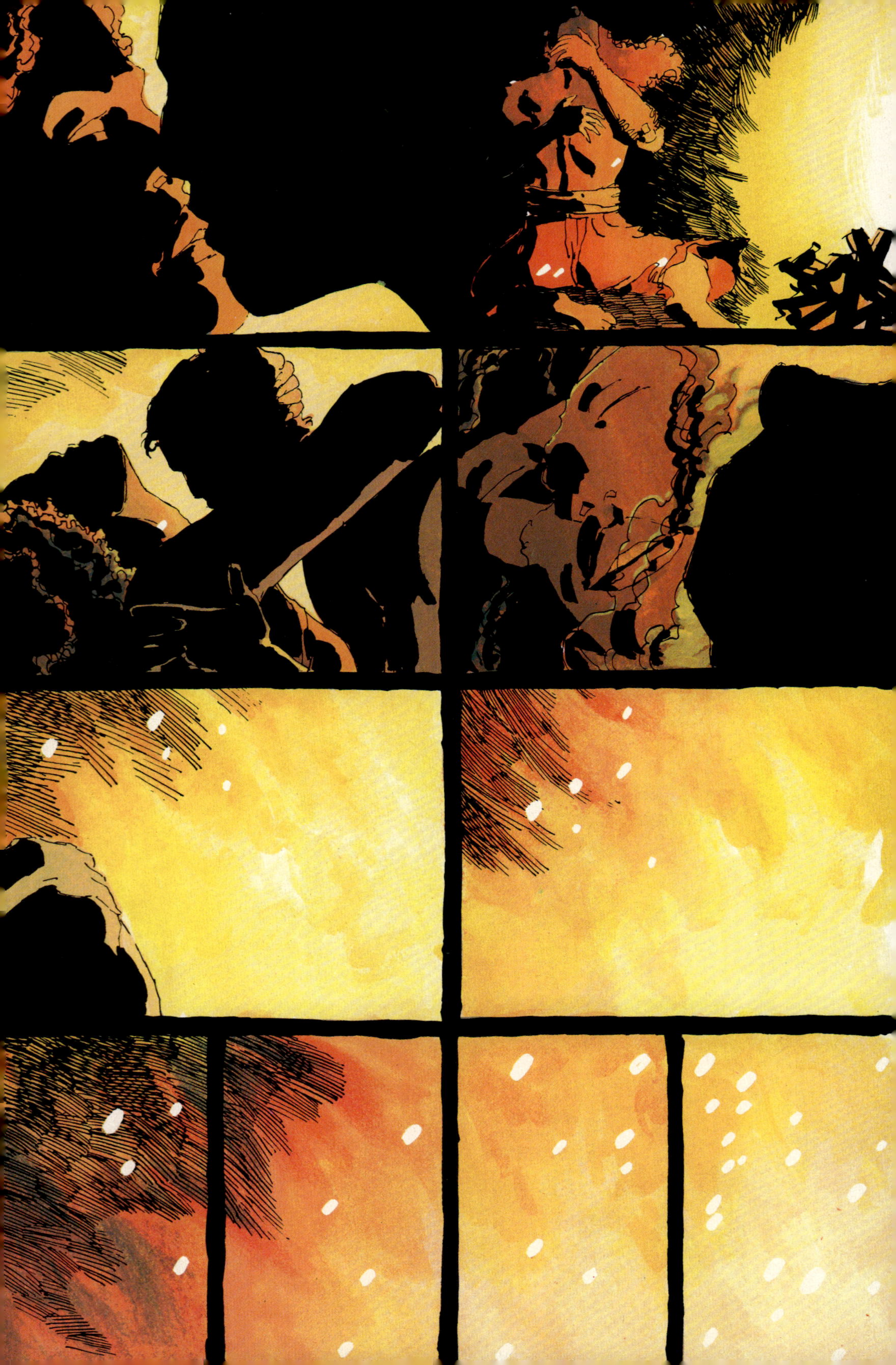

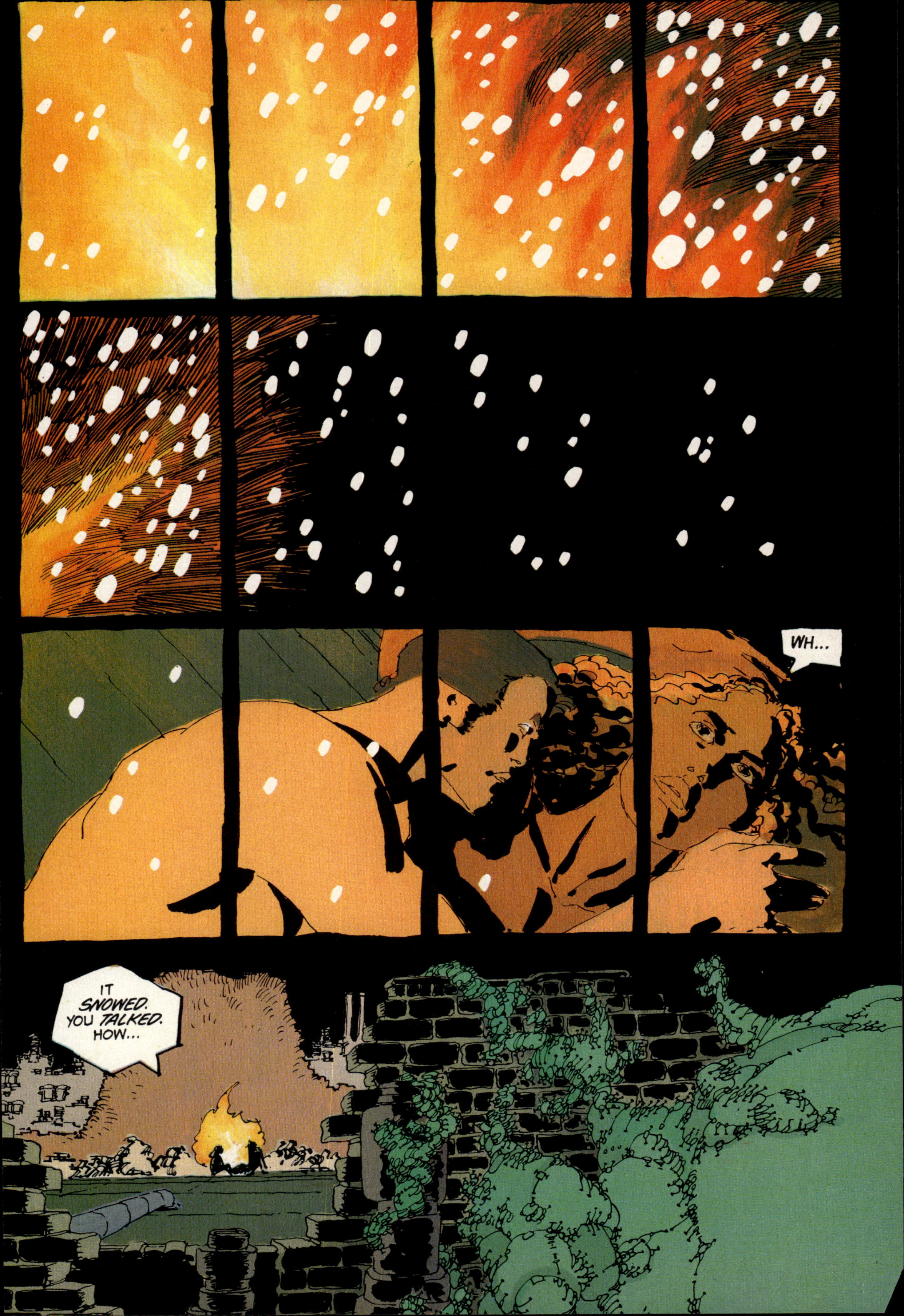
WH...
IT *SNOWED.* YOU *TALKED.* HOW...

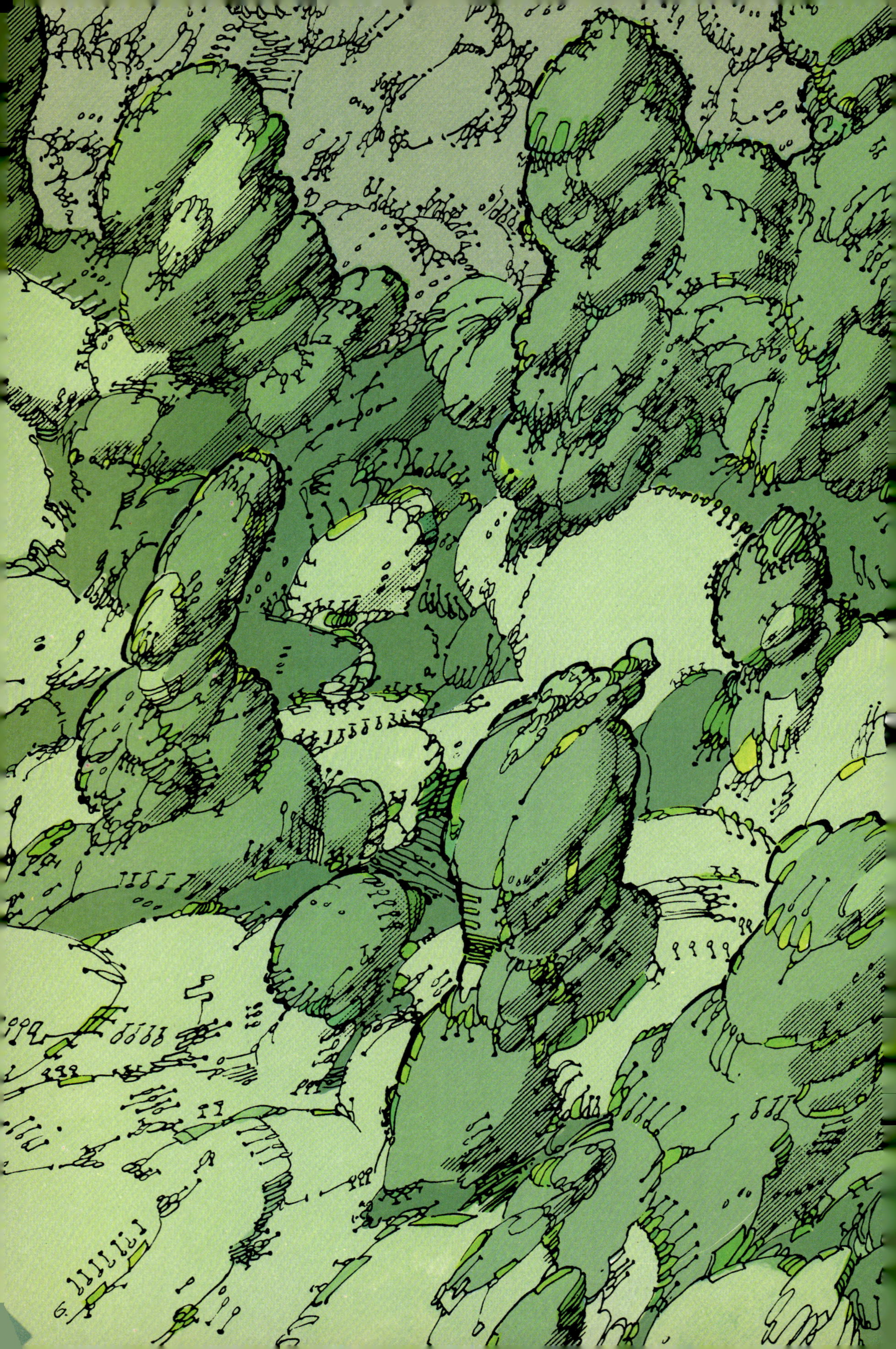

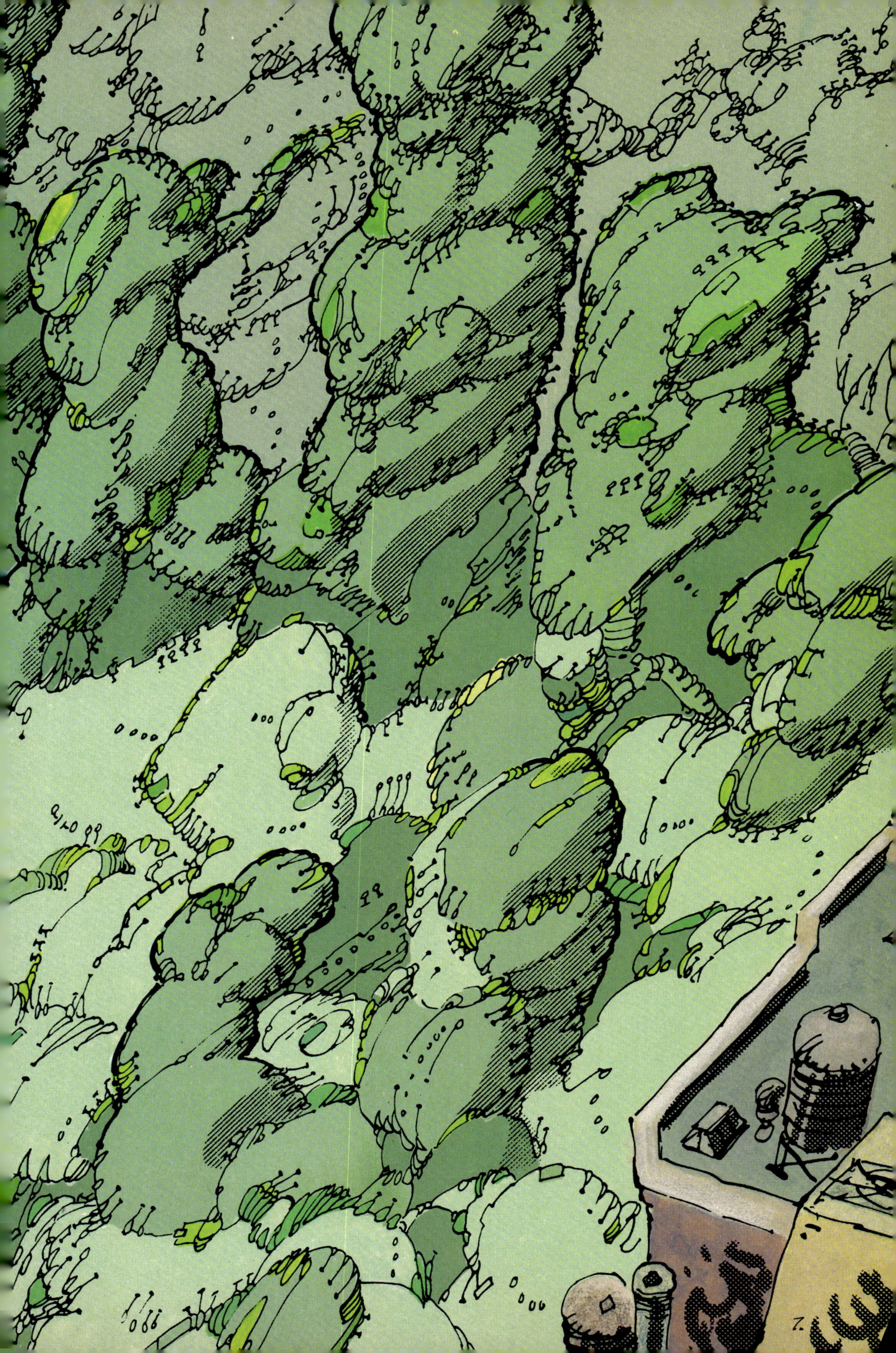

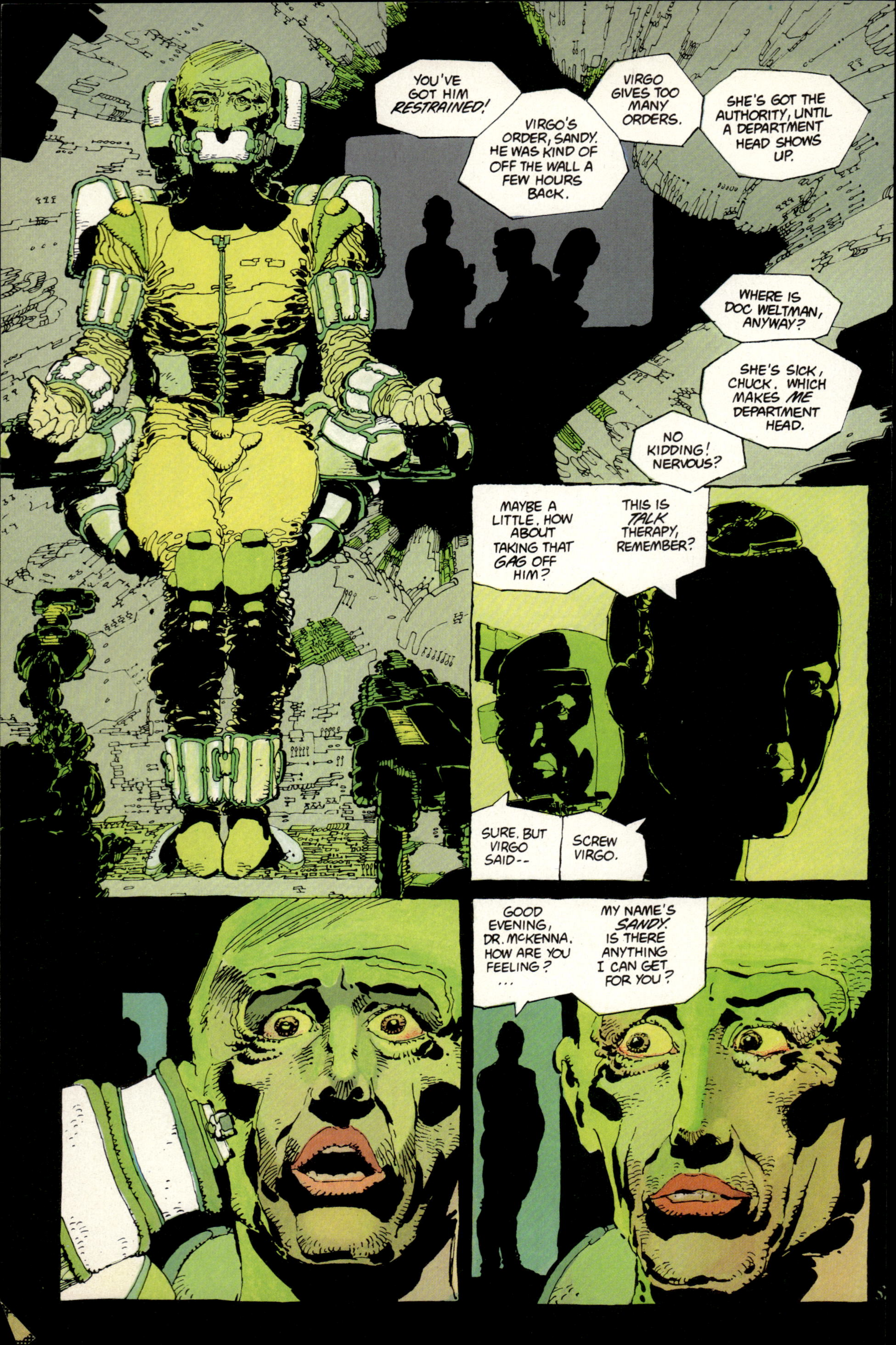
YOU'VE GOT HIM RESTRAINED!
VIRGO'S ORDER, SANDY. HE WAS KIND OF OFF THE WALL A FEW HOURS BACK.
VIRGO GIVES TOO MANY ORDERS.
SHE'S GOT THE AUTHORITY, UNTIL A DEPARTMENT HEAD SHOWS UP.
WHERE IS DOC WELTMAN, ANYWAY?
SHE'S SICK, CHUCK. WHICH MAKES ME DEPARTMENT HEAD.
NO KIDDING! NERVOUS?
MAYBE A LITTLE. HOW ABOUT TAKING THAT GAG OFF HIM?
THIS IS TALK THERAPY, REMEMBER?
SURE. BUT VIRGO SAID--
SCREW VIRGO.
GOOD EVENING, DR. McKENNA. HOW ARE YOU FEELING? ...
MY NAME'S SANDY. IS THERE ANYTHING I CAN GET FOR YOU?

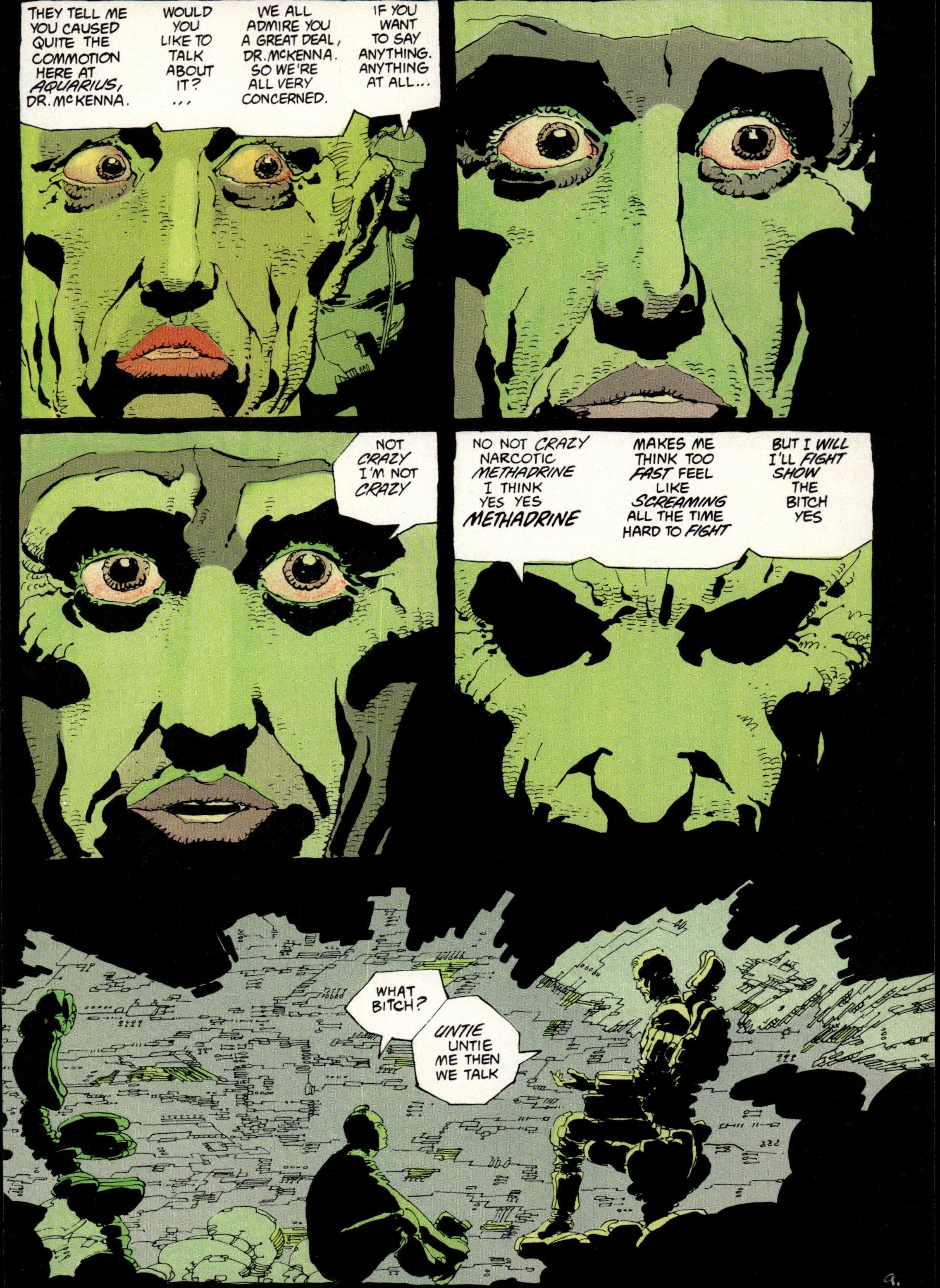

THEY TELL ME YOU CAUSED QUITE THE COMMOTION HERE AT AQUARIUS, DR. McKENNA.
WOULD YOU LIKE TO TALK ABOUT IT? ...
WE ALL ADMIRE YOU A GREAT DEAL, DR. McKENNA. SO WE'RE ALL VERY CONCERNED.
IF YOU WANT TO SAY ANYTHING. ANYTHING AT ALL...
NOT CRAZY I'M NOT CRAZY
NO NOT CRAZY NARCOTIC METHADRINE I THINK YES YES METHADRINE
MAKES ME THINK TOO FAST FEEL LIKE SCREAMING ALL THE TIME HARD TO FIGHT
BUT I WILL I'LL FIGHT SHOW THE BITCH YES
WHAT BITCH?
UNTIE UNTIE ME THEN WE TALK

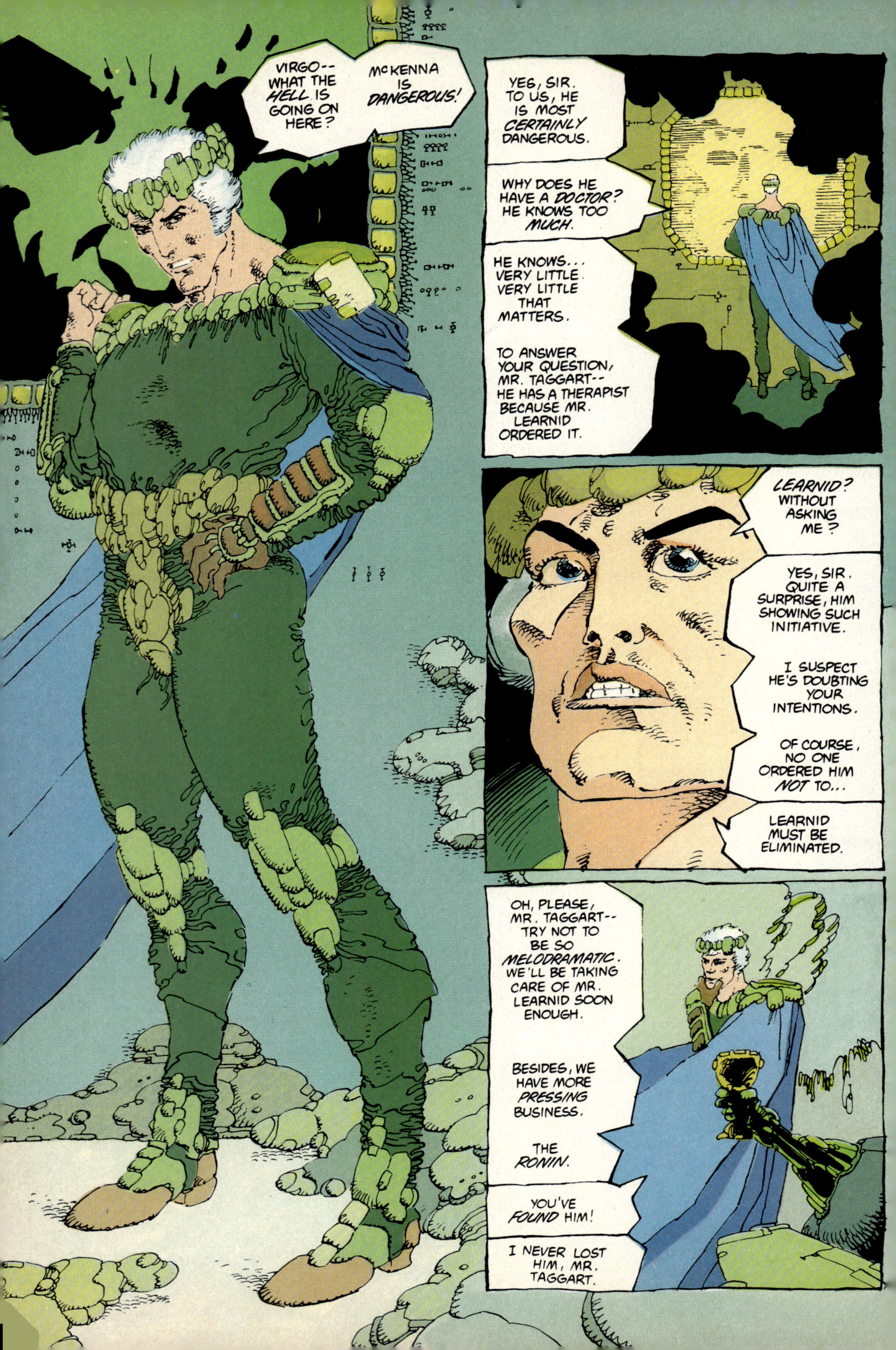

VIRGO-- WHAT THE HELL IS GOING ON HERE?
McKENNA IS DANGEROUS!
YES, SIR. TO US, HE IS MOST CERTAINLY DANGEROUS.
WHY DOES HE HAVE A DOCTOR? HE KNOWS TOO MUCH.
HE KNOWS... VERY LITTLE. VERY LITTLE THAT MATTERS.
TO ANSWER YOUR QUESTION, MR. TAGGART-- HE HAS A THERAPIST BECAUSE MR. LEARNID ORDERED IT.
LEARNID? WITHOUT ASKING ME?
YES, SIR. QUITE A SURPRISE, HIM SHOWING SUCH INITIATIVE.
I SUSPECT HE'S DOUBTING YOUR INTENTIONS.
OF COURSE, NO ONE ORDERED HIM NOT TO...
LEARNID MUST BE ELIMINATED.
OH, PLEASE, MR. TAGGART-- TRY NOT TO BE SO MELODRAMATIC. WE'LL BE TAKING CARE OF MR. LEARNID SOON ENOUGH.
BESIDES, WE HAVE MORE PRESSING BUSINESS.
THE RONIN.
YOU'VE FOUND HIM!
I NEVER LOST HIM, MR. TAGGART.

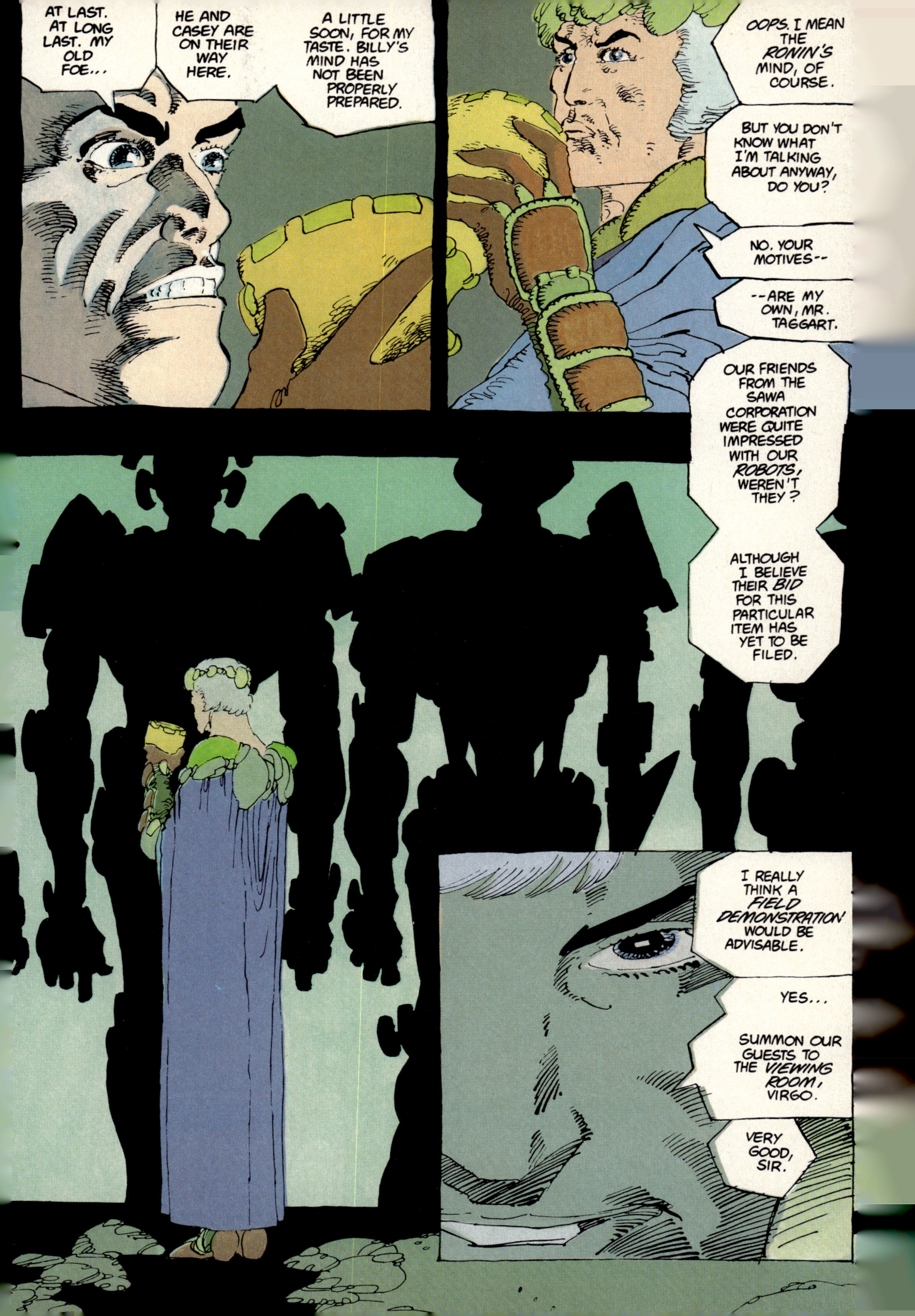

AT LAST. AT LONG LAST. MY OLD FOE...
HE AND CASEY ARE ON THEIR WAY HERE.
A LITTLE SOON, FOR MY TASTE. BILLY'S MIND HAS NOT BEEN PROPERLY PREPARED.
OOPS. I MEAN THE RONIN'S MIND, OF COURSE.
BUT YOU DON'T KNOW WHAT I'M TALKING ABOUT ANYWAY, DO YOU?
NO. YOUR MOTIVES--
--ARE MY OWN, MR. TAGGART.
OUR FRIENDS FROM THE SAWA CORPORATION WERE QUITE IMPRESSED WITH OUR ROBOTS, WEREN'T THEY?
ALTHOUGH I BELIEVE THEIR BID FOR THIS PARTICULAR ITEM HAS YET TO BE FILED.
I REALLY THINK A FIELD DEMONSTRATION WOULD BE ADVISABLE.
YES...
SUMMON OUR GUESTS TO THE VIEWING ROOM, VIRGO.
VERY GOOD, SIR.

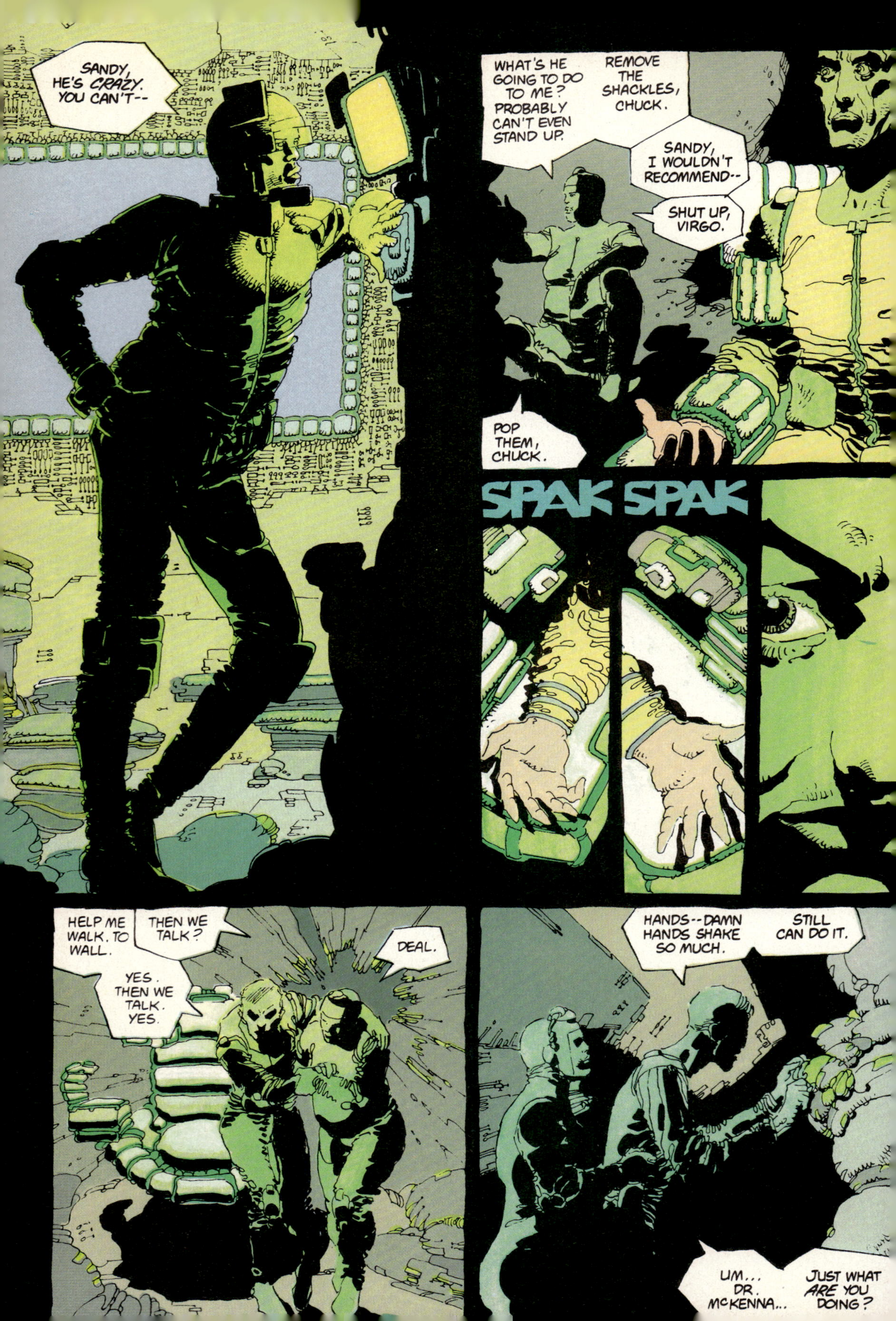
SANDY, HE'S CRAZY. YOU CAN'T--
WHAT'S HE GOING TO DO TO ME? PROBABLY CAN'T EVEN STAND UP.
REMOVE THE SHACKLES, CHUCK.
SANDY, I WOULDN'T RECOMMEND--
SHUT UP, VIRGO.
POP THEM, CHUCK.
SPAK SPAK
HELP ME WALK. TO WALL.
THEN WE TALK?
YES. THEN WE TALK. YES.
DEAL.
HANDS--DAMN HANDS SHAKE SO MUCH.
STILL CAN DO IT.
UM... DR. McKENNA...
JUST WHAT ARE YOU DOING?

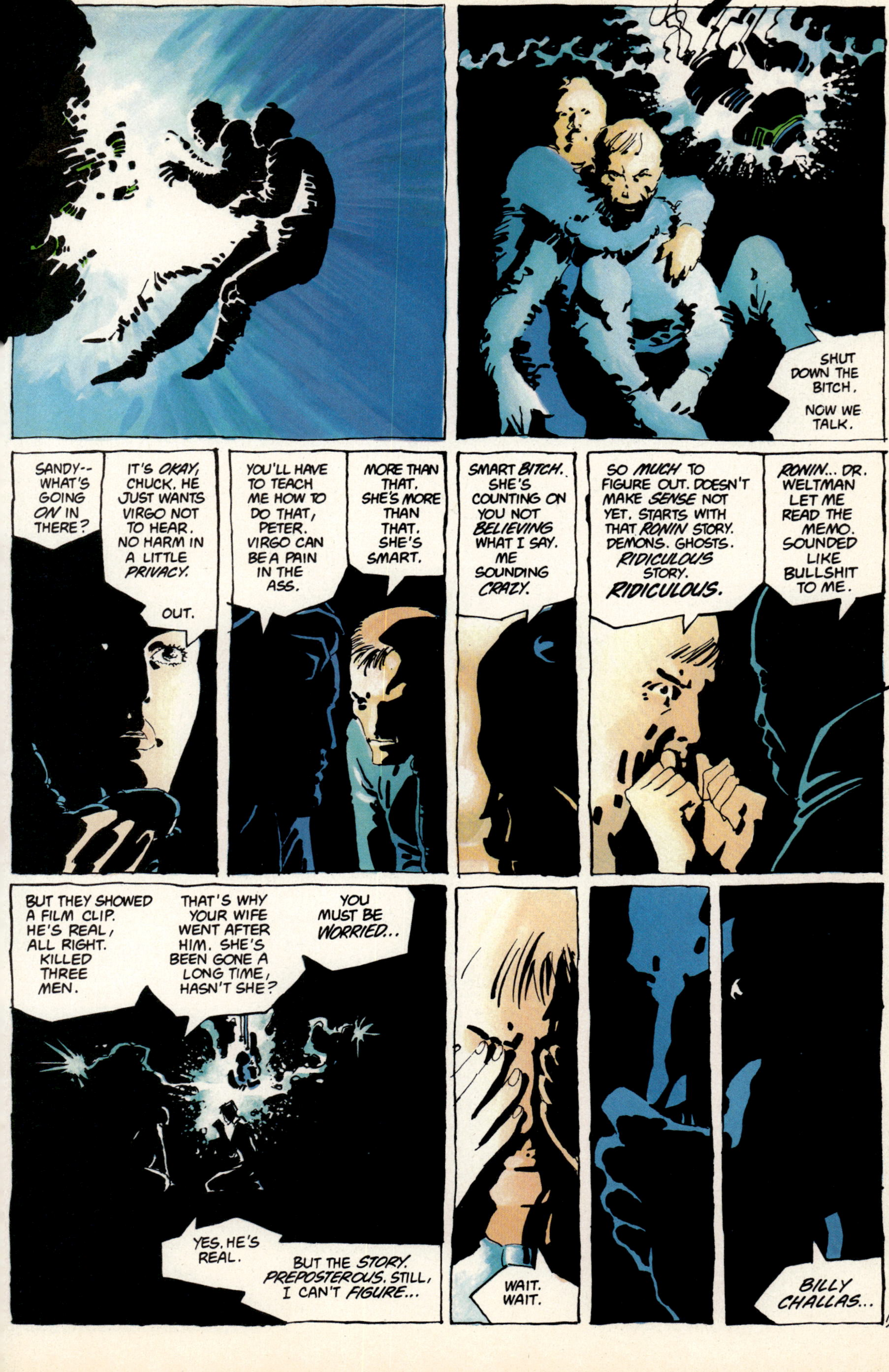
SHUT DOWN THE BITCH.
NOW WE TALK.
SANDY-- WHAT'S GOING ON IN THERE?
IT'S OKAY, CHUCK. HE JUST WANTS VIRGO NOT TO HEAR. NO HARM IN A LITTLE PRIVACY.
OUT.
YOU'LL HAVE TO TEACH ME HOW TO DO THAT, PETER. VIRGO CAN BE A PAIN IN THE ASS.
MORE THAN THAT. SHE'S MORE THAN THAT. SHE'S SMART.
SMART BITCH. SHE'S COUNTING ON YOU NOT BELIEVING WHAT I SAY. ME SOUNDING CRAZY.
SO MUCH TO FIGURE OUT. DOESN'T MAKE SENSE NOT YET. STARTS WITH THAT RONIN STORY. DEMONS. GHOSTS. RIDICULOUS STORY. RIDICULOUS.
RONIN... DR. WELTMAN LET ME READ THE MEMO. SOUNDED LIKE BULLSHIT TO ME.
BUT THEY SHOWED A FILM CLIP. HE'S REAL, ALL RIGHT. KILLED THREE MEN.
THAT'S WHY YOUR WIFE WENT AFTER HIM. SHE'S BEEN GONE A LONG TIME, HASN'T SHE?
YOU MUST BE WORRIED...
YES, HE'S REAL.
BUT THE STORY. PREPOSTEROUS. STILL, I CAN'T FIGURE...
WAIT. WAIT.
BILLY CHALLAS...

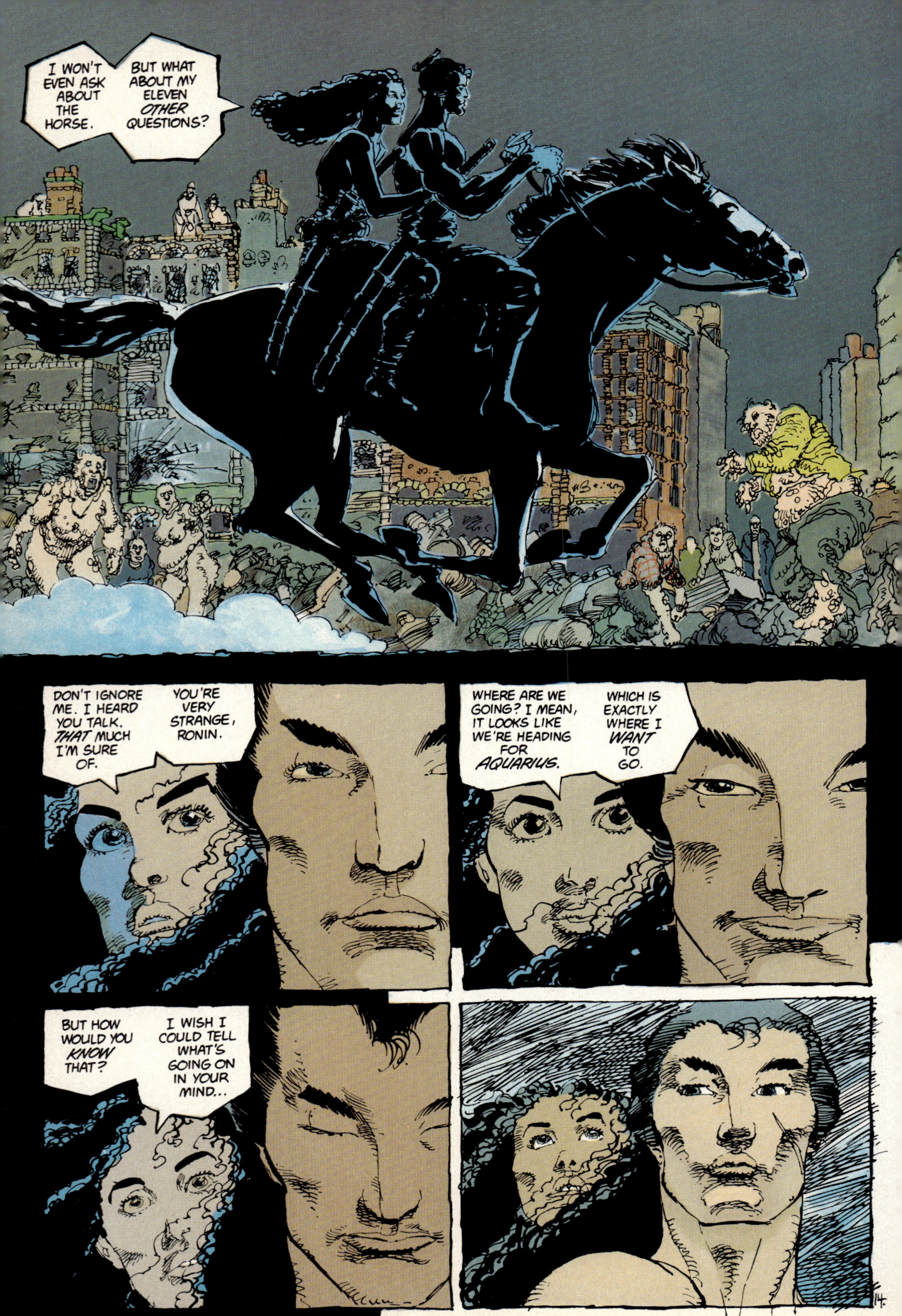
I WON'T EVEN ASK ABOUT THE HORSE.
BUT WHAT ABOUT MY ELEVEN *OTHER* QUESTIONS?
DON'T IGNORE ME. I HEARD YOU TALK. *THAT* MUCH I'M SURE OF.
YOU'RE VERY STRANGE, RONIN.
WHERE ARE WE GOING? I MEAN, IT LOOKS LIKE WE'RE HEADING FOR *AQUARIUS*.
WHICH IS EXACTLY WHERE I *WANT* TO GO.
BUT HOW WOULD YOU *KNOW* THAT?
I WISH I COULD TELL WHAT'S GOING ON IN YOUR MIND...
14.

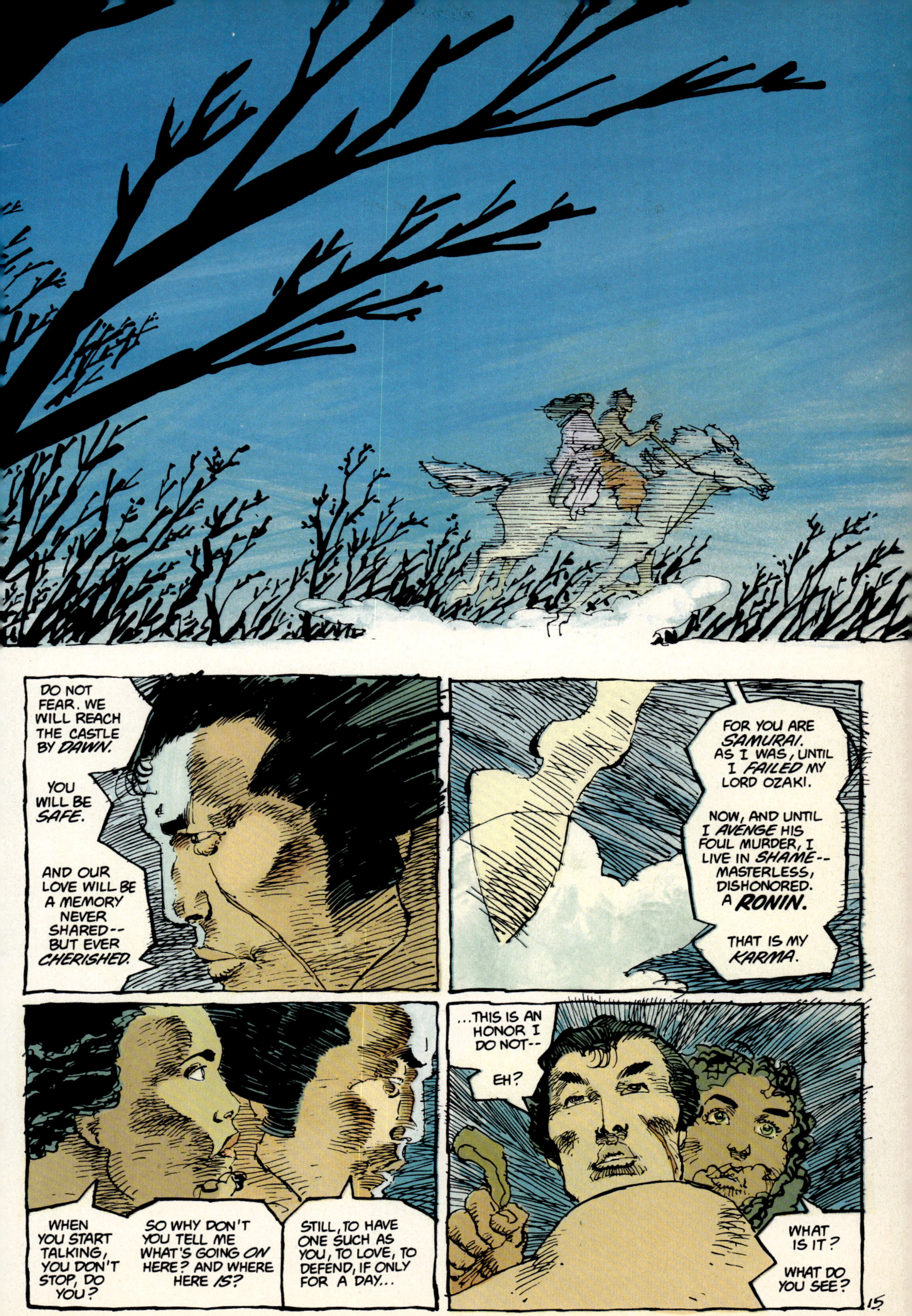
DO NOT FEAR. WE WILL REACH THE CASTLE BY DAWN.
YOU WILL BE SAFE.
AND OUR LOVE WILL BE A MEMORY NEVER SHARED-- BUT EVER CHERISHED.
FOR YOU ARE SAMURAI. AS I WAS, UNTIL I FAILED MY LORD OZAKI.
NOW, AND UNTIL I AVENGE HIS FOUL MURDER, I LIVE IN SHAME-- MASTERLESS, DISHONORED. A RONIN.
THAT IS MY KARMA.
WHEN YOU START TALKING, YOU DON'T STOP, DO YOU?
SO WHY DON'T YOU TELL ME WHAT'S GOING ON HERE? AND WHERE HERE IS?
STILL, TO HAVE ONE SUCH AS YOU, TO LOVE, TO DEFEND, IF ONLY FOR A DAY...
...THIS IS AN HONOR I DO NOT--
EH?
WHAT IS IT?
WHAT DO YOU SEE?

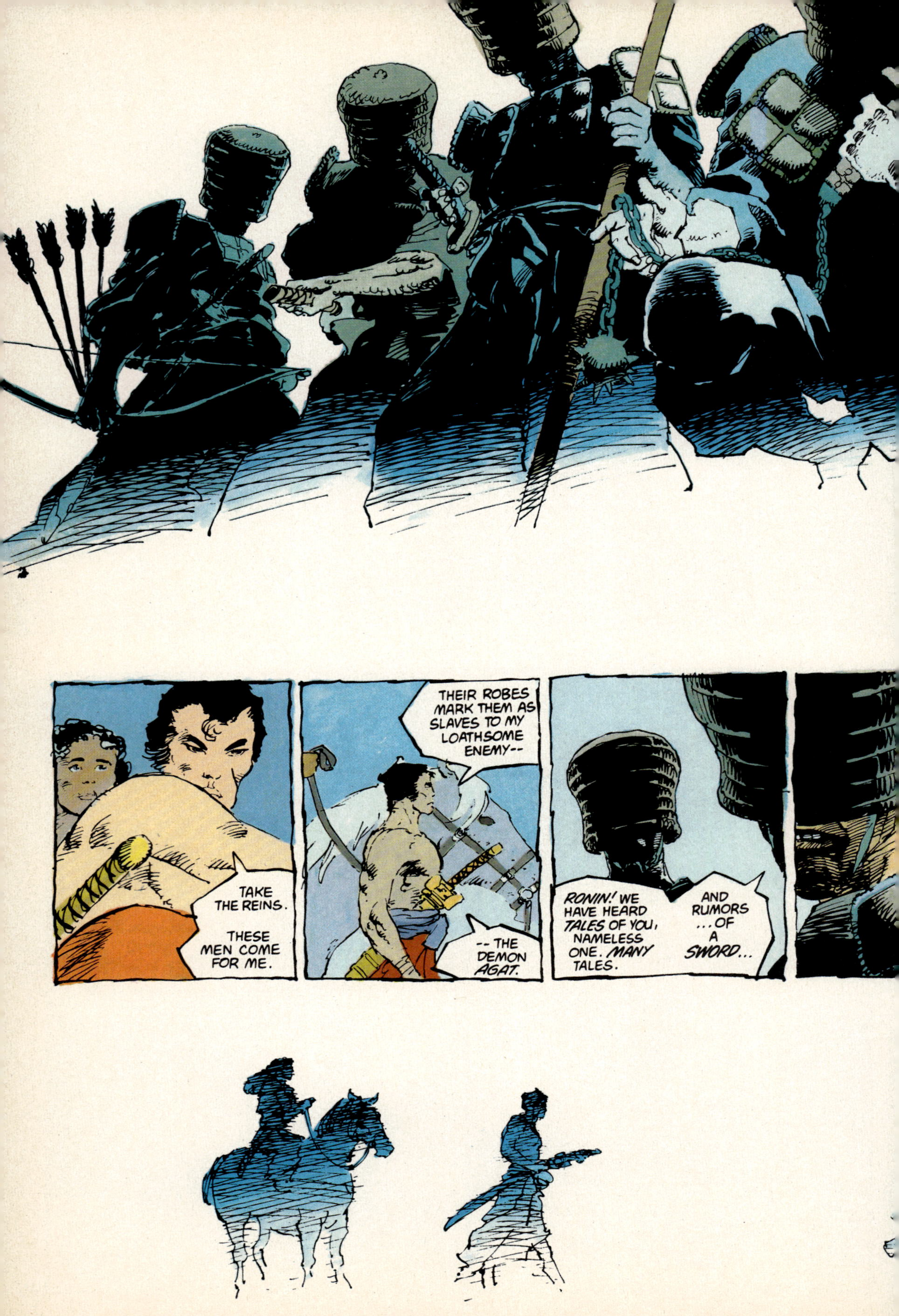
TAKE THE REINS.
THESE MEN COME FOR ME.
THEIR ROBES MARK THEM AS SLAVES TO MY LOATHSOME ENEMY--
-- THE DEMON *AGAT*.
RONIN! WE HAVE HEARD *TALES* OF YOU, NAMELESS ONE. *MANY* TALES.
AND RUMORS ...OF A *SWORD*...

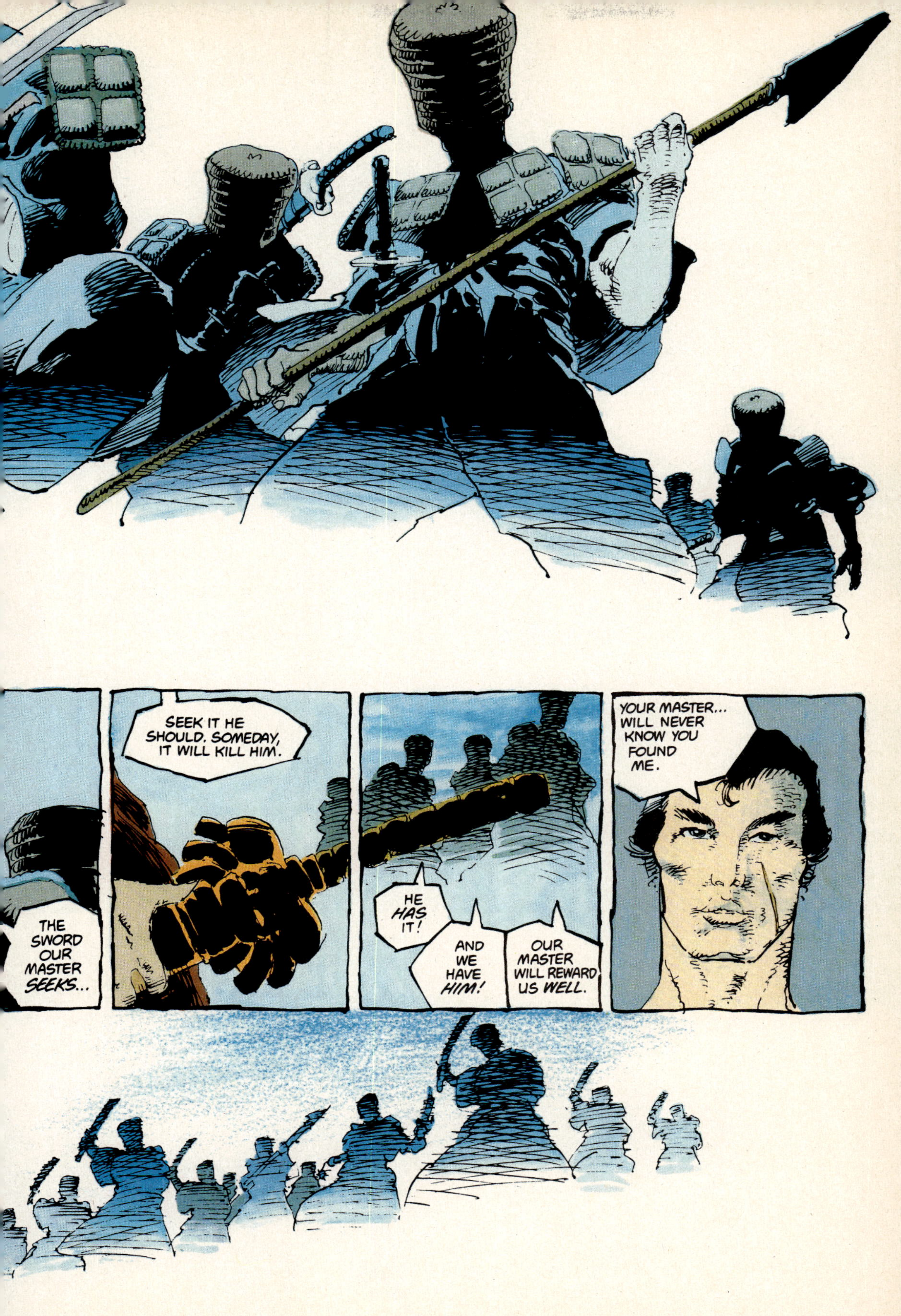
THE SWORD OUR MASTER SEEKS...
SEEK IT HE SHOULD. SOMEDAY, IT WILL KILL HIM.
HE HAS IT!
AND WE HAVE HIM!
OUR MASTER WILL REWARD US WELL.
YOUR MASTER... WILL NEVER KNOW YOU FOUND ME.

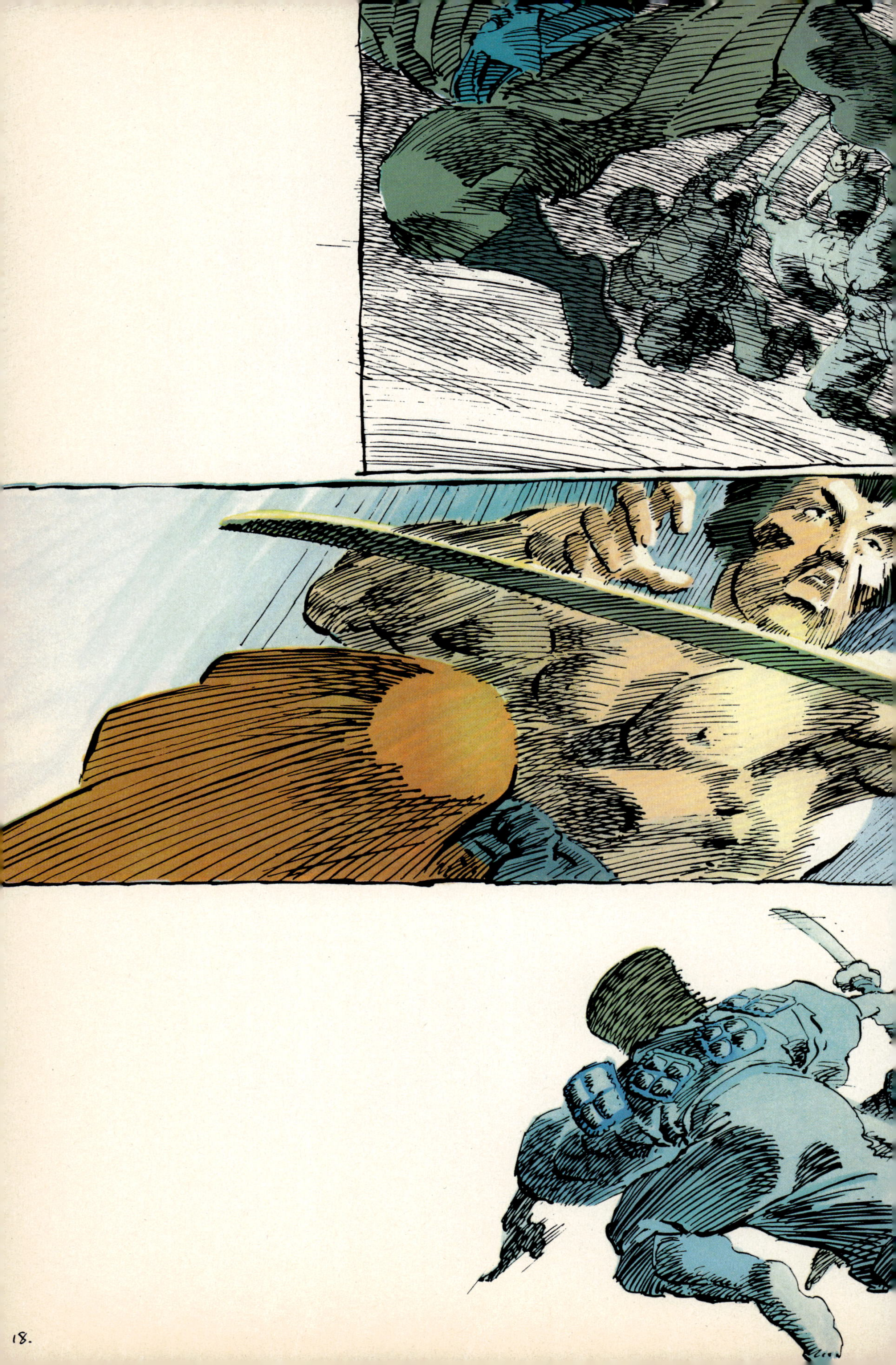

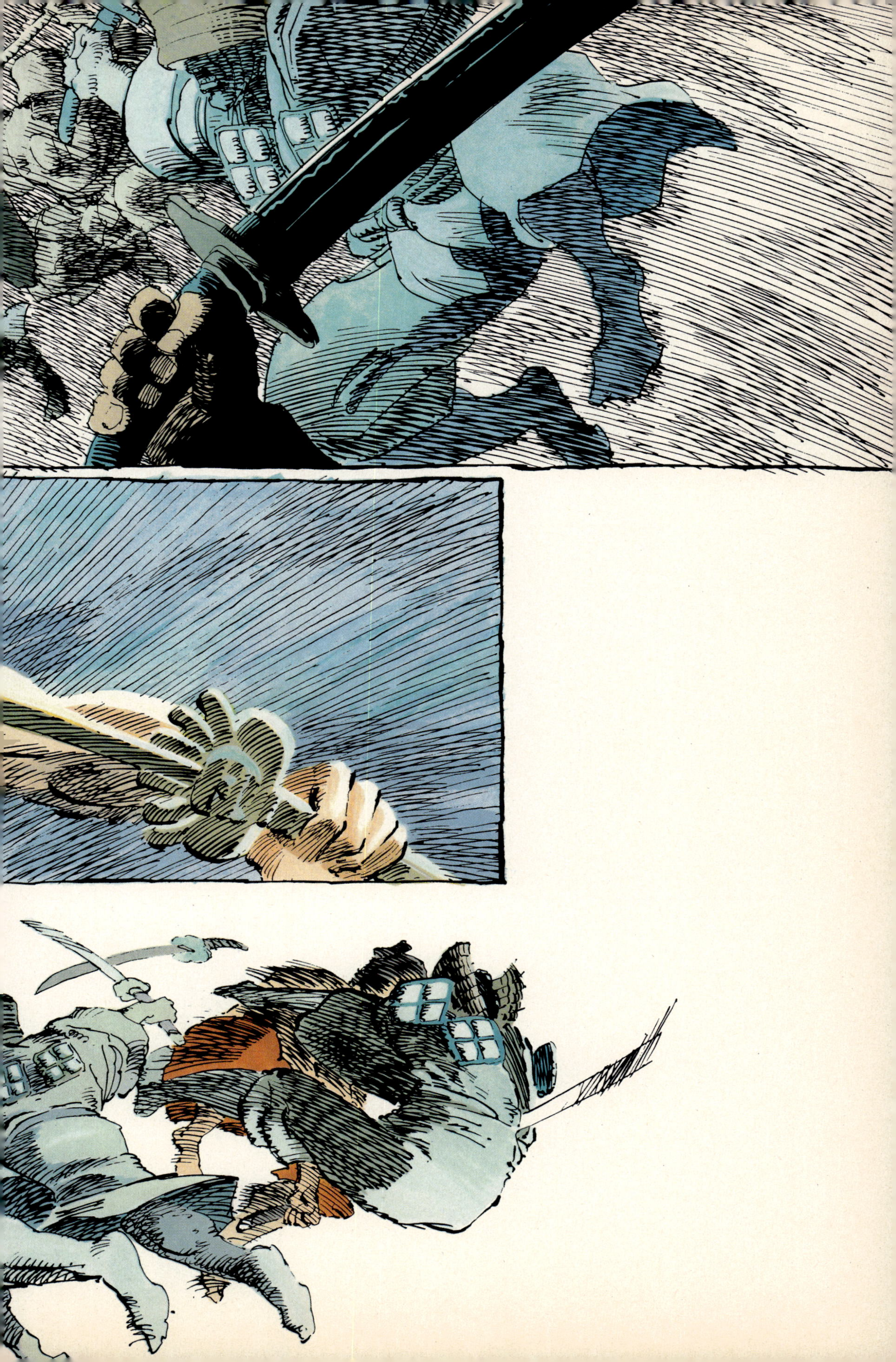

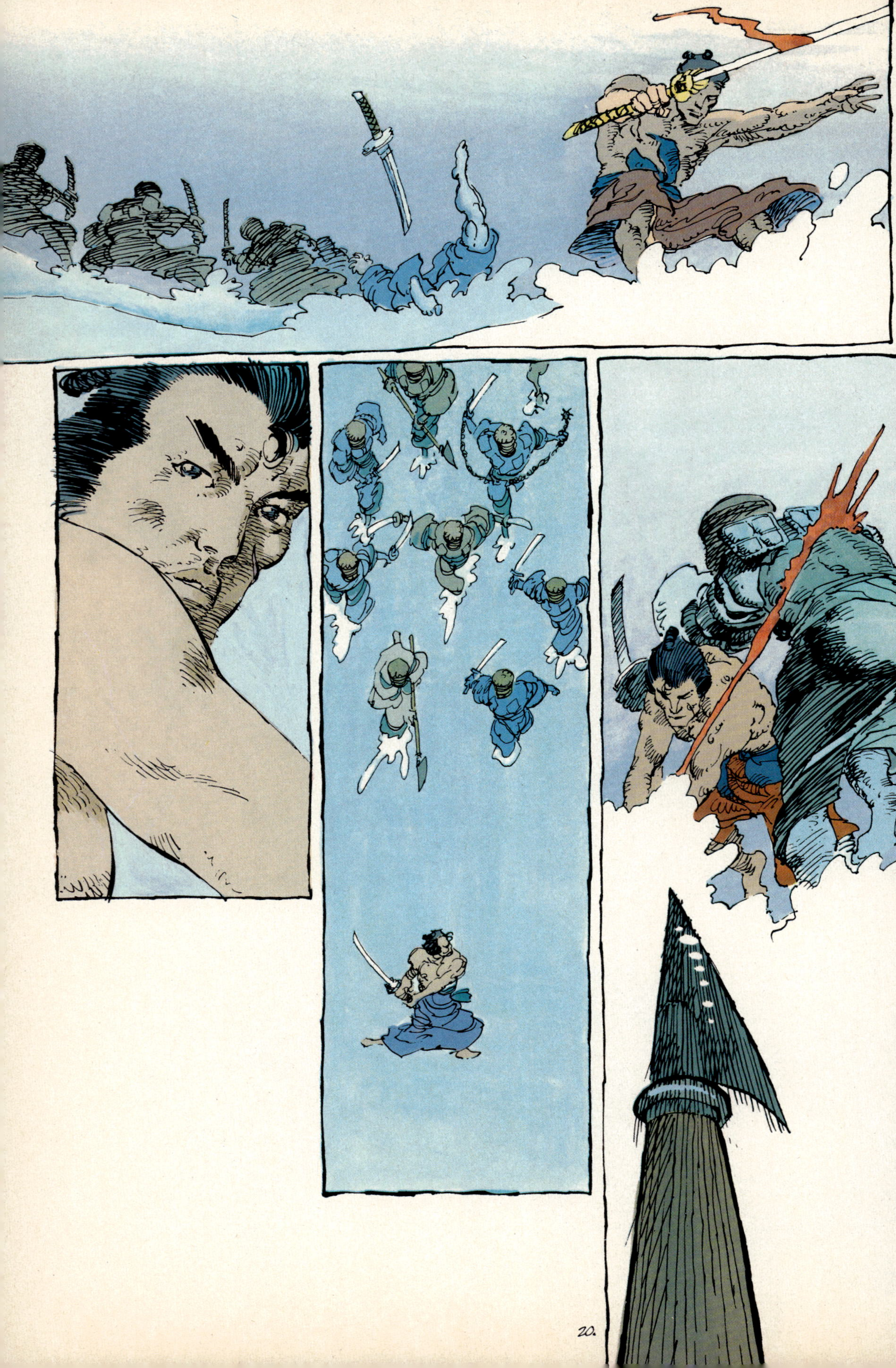

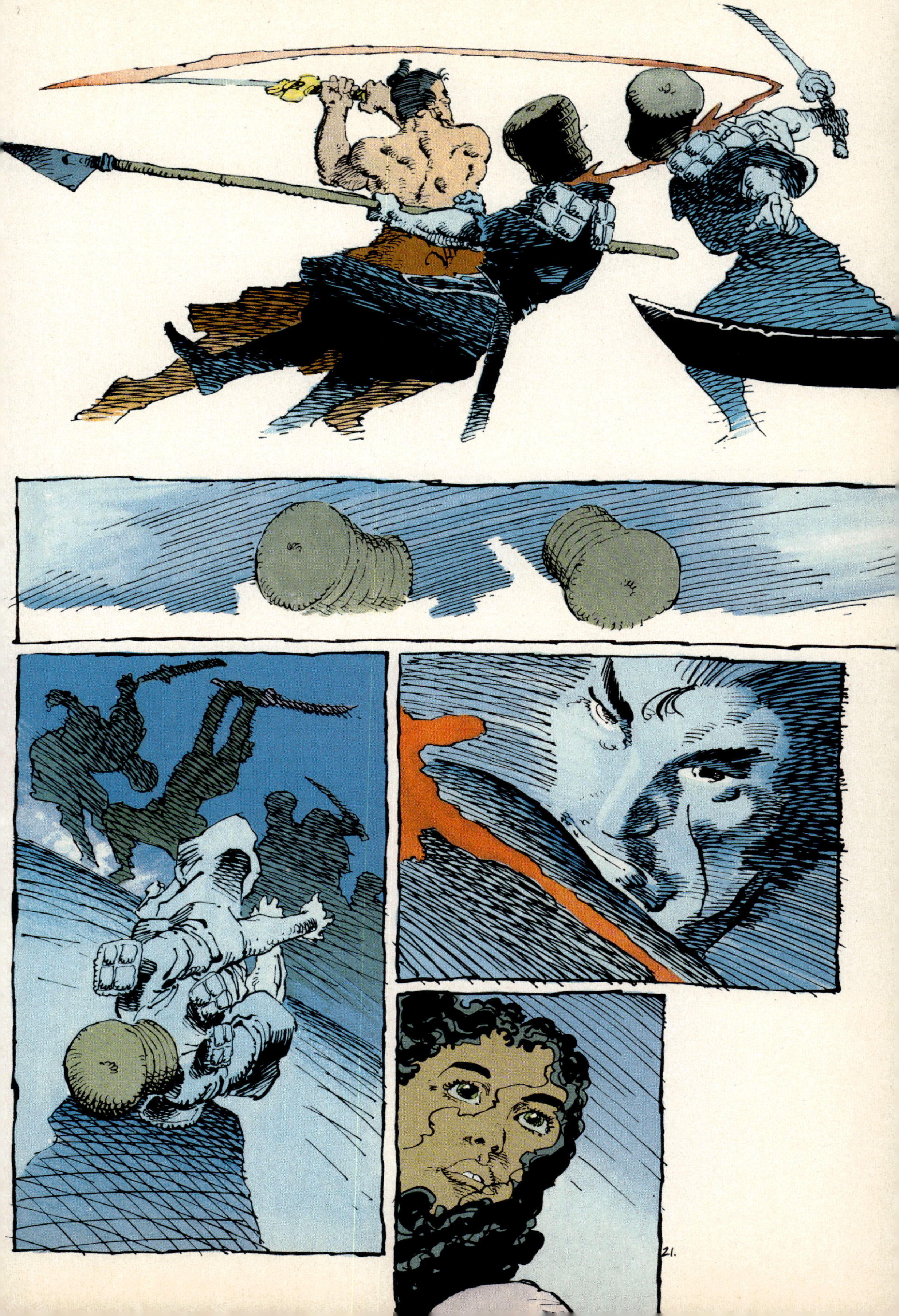

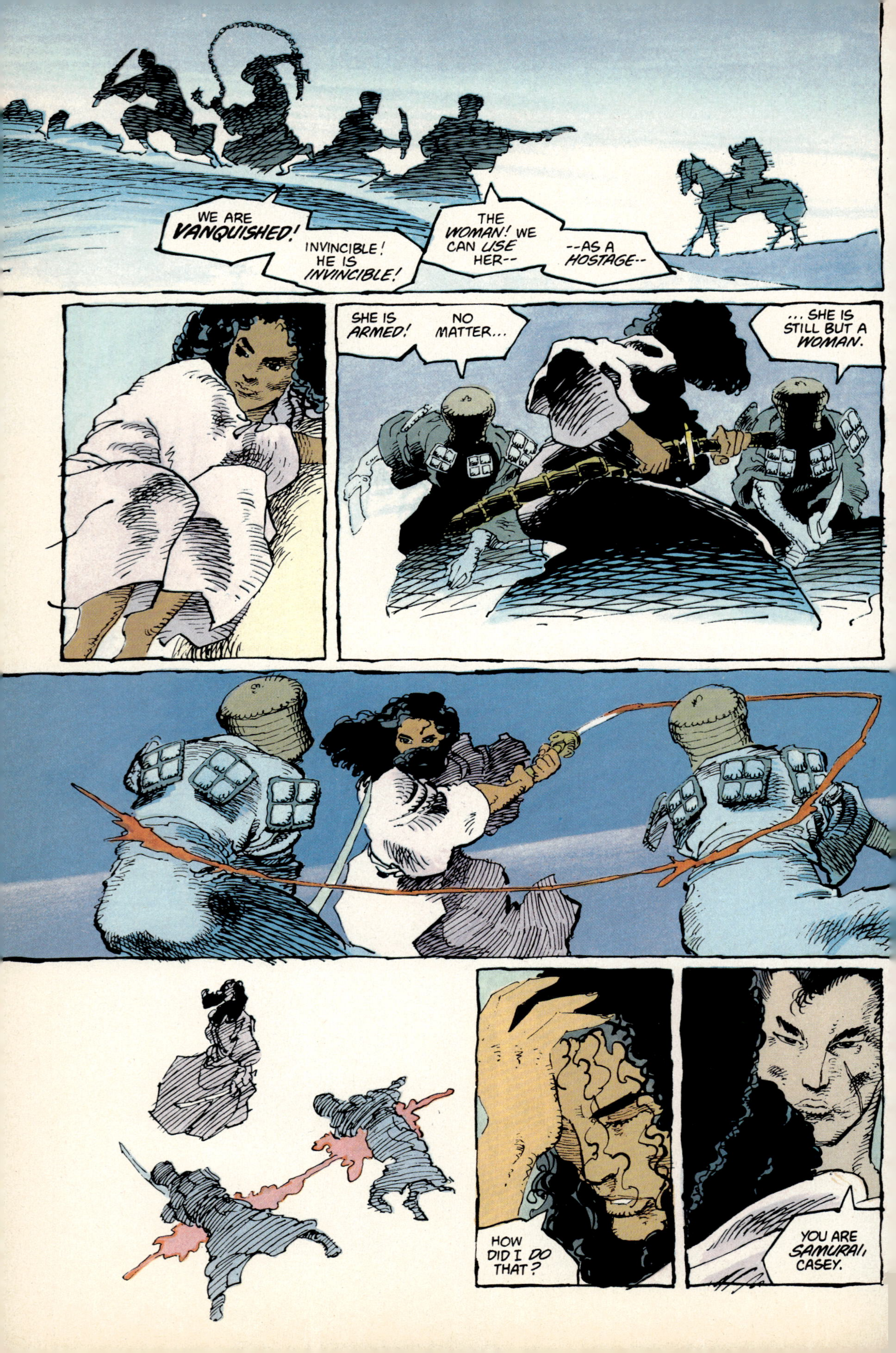
WE ARE VANQUISHED!
INVINCIBLE! HE IS INVINCIBLE!
THE WOMAN! WE CAN USE HER--
--AS A HOSTAGE--
SHE IS ARMED!
NO MATTER...
... SHE IS STILL BUT A WOMAN.
HOW DID I DO THAT?
YOU ARE SAMURAI, CASEY.

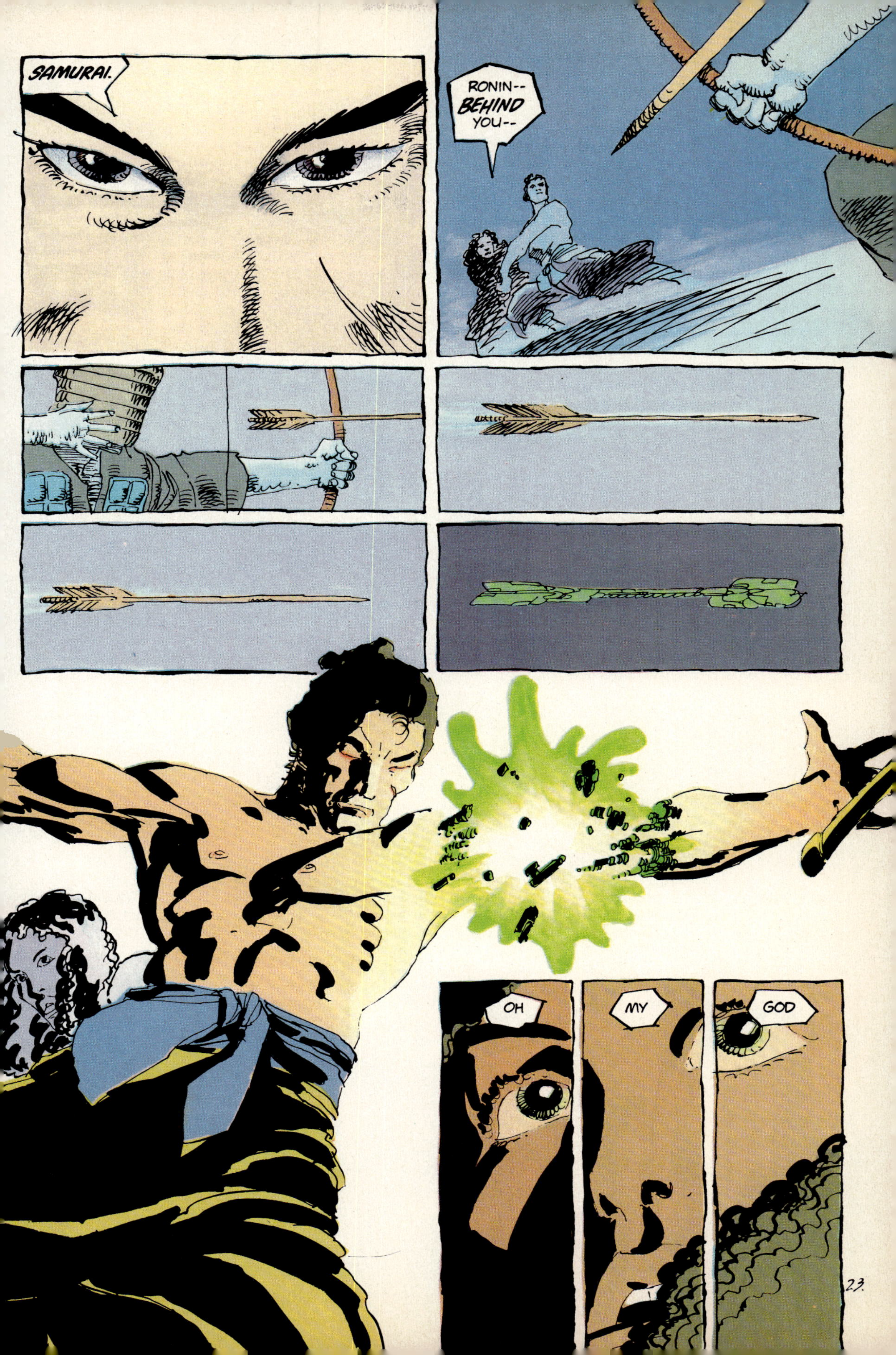
SAMURAI.
RONIN-- BEHIND YOU--
OH
MY
GOD

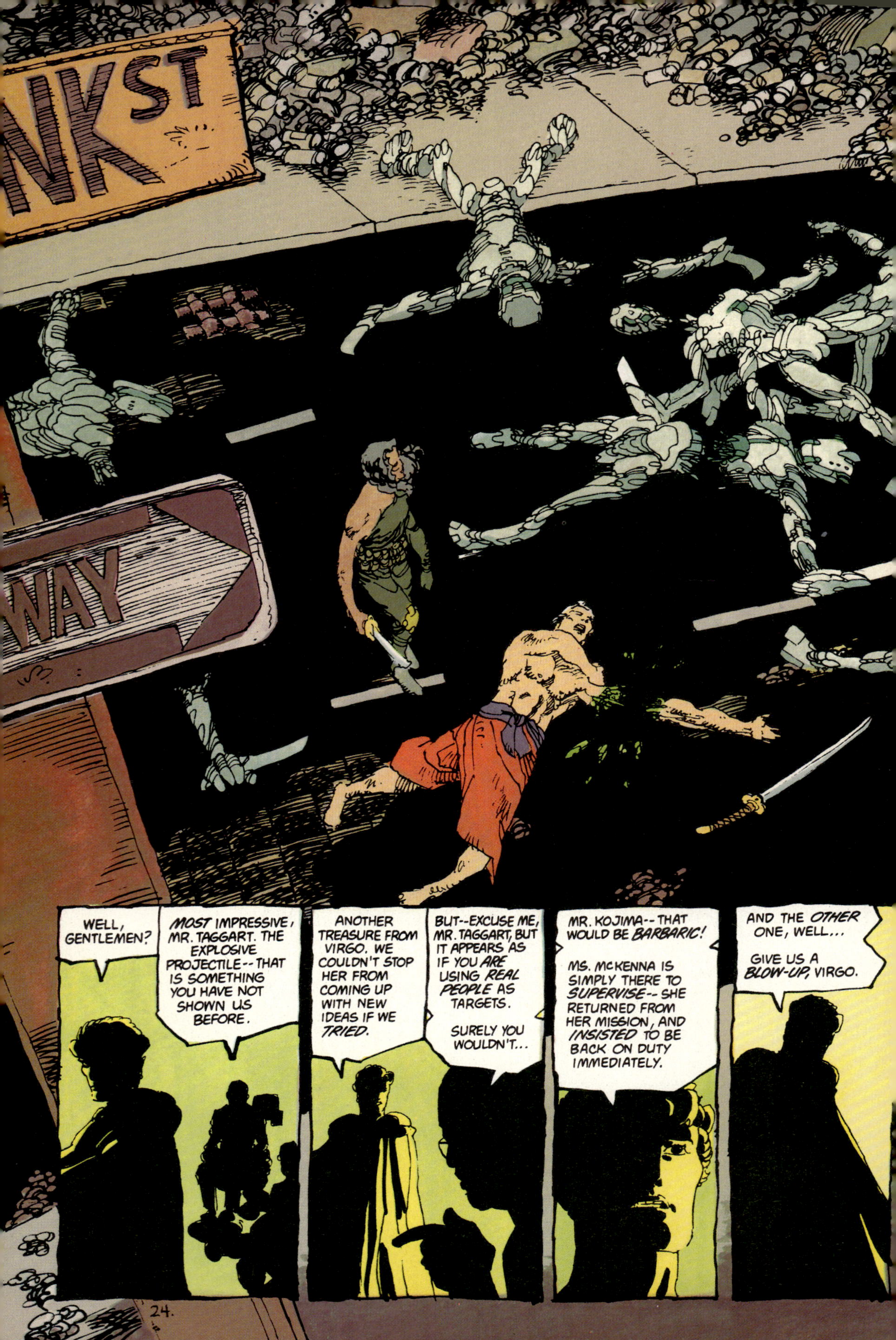
NK ST
WAY
WELL, GENTLEMEN?
MOST IMPRESSIVE, MR. TAGGART. THE EXPLOSIVE PROJECTILE--THAT IS SOMETHING YOU HAVE NOT SHOWN US BEFORE.
ANOTHER TREASURE FROM VIRGO. WE COULDN'T STOP HER FROM COMING UP WITH NEW IDEAS IF WE TRIED.
BUT--EXCUSE ME, MR. TAGGART, BUT IT APPEARS AS IF YOU ARE USING REAL PEOPLE AS TARGETS.
SURELY YOU WOULDN'T...
MR. KOJIMA--THAT WOULD BE BARBARIC!
MS. McKENNA IS SIMPLY THERE TO SUPERVISE--SHE RETURNED FROM HER MISSION, AND INSISTED TO BE BACK ON DUTY IMMEDIATELY.
AND THE OTHER ONE, WELL...
GIVE US A BLOW-UP, VIRGO.

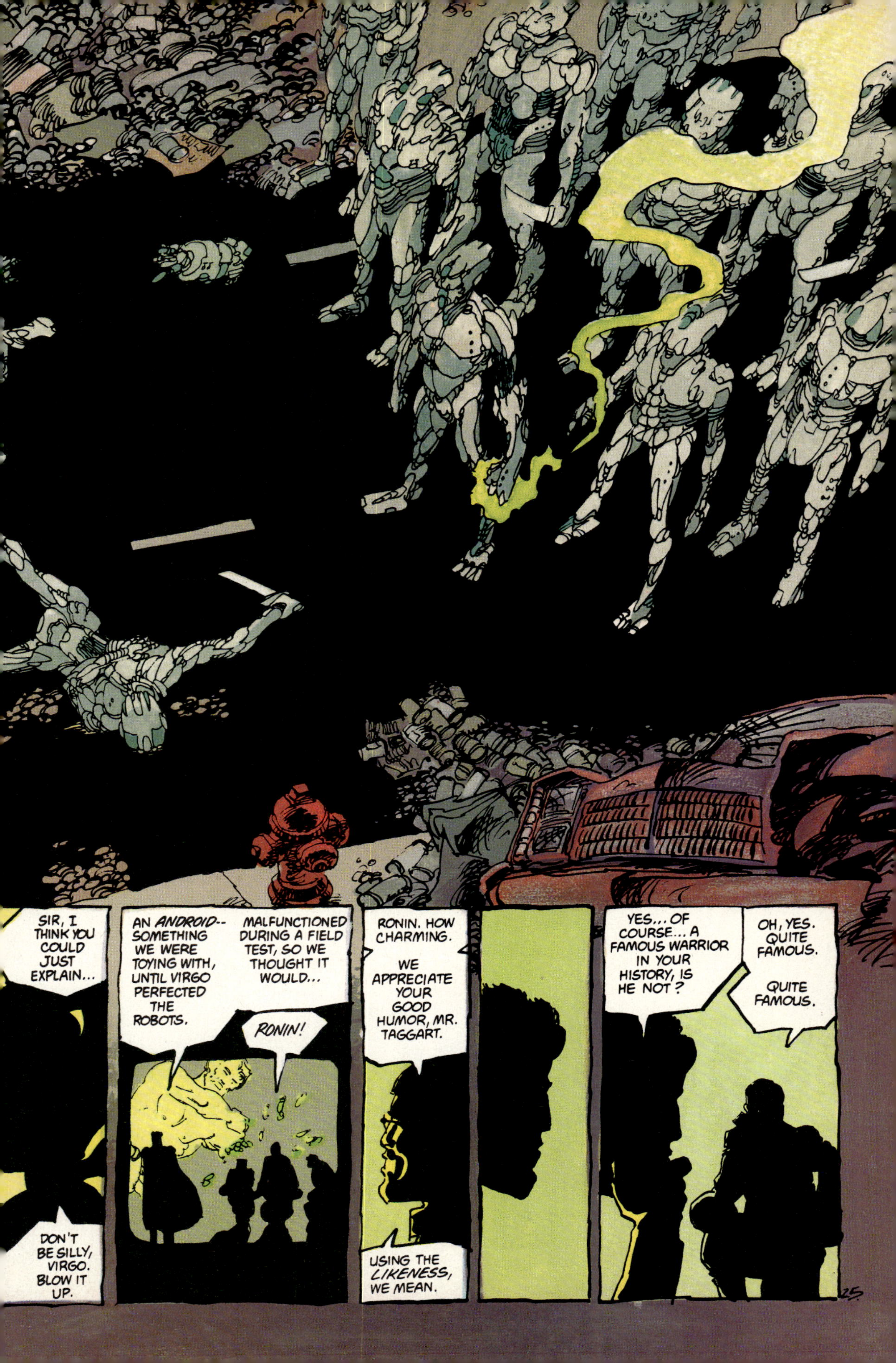
SIR, I THINK YOU COULD JUST EXPLAIN...
DON'T BE SILLY, VIRGO. BLOW IT UP.
AN *ANDROID*-- SOMETHING WE WERE TOYING WITH, UNTIL VIRGO PERFECTED THE ROBOTS.
MALFUNCTIONED DURING A FIELD TEST, SO WE THOUGHT IT WOULD...
RONIN!
RONIN. HOW CHARMING.
WE APPRECIATE YOUR GOOD HUMOR, MR. TAGGART.
USING THE *LIKENESS*, WE MEAN.
YES... OF COURSE... A FAMOUS WARRIOR IN YOUR HISTORY, IS HE NOT?
OH, YES. QUITE FAMOUS.
QUITE FAMOUS.
25

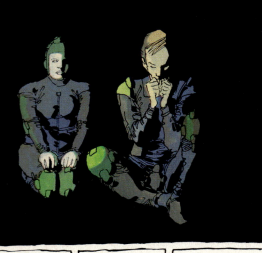

BILLY CHALLAS. *BILLY CHALLAS.* SOMETHING WITH BILLY CHALLAS.

HE TURNED INTO THE RONIN, SO *HE'S* GOT TO BE AT THE *ROOT* OF ALL THIS. BUT *HOW...*

HE WAS *TELEKINETIC.* THAT'S *MIND POWER.*

MIND... MIND...

MIND-- *PSYCHOLOGY.* MAYBE PSYCHOLOGY IS AT THE ROOT. YES--I'M NOT A *PSYCHOLOGIST.* THAT'S WHY I CAN'T *FIGURE--*

YOU. YOU COULD HELP ME WORK THIS OUT.

BUT I WANT TO KNOW WHAT *YOU'RE* FEELING, DR. McKENNA. THAT'S WHY I'M HERE.

FORGET FEELINGS. JUST FOR NOW. *HELP* ME THINK THIS OUT. TRY. *PLEASE. I BEG* YOU.

...ALL RIGHT, WHATEVER YOU LIKE.

BILLY CHALLAS. YOU EVER MEET HIM?

NO. NEITHER DID DR. WELTMAN. VIRGO INSISTED ON TAKING COMPLETE CARE OF HIM.

WELTMAN WAS *STEAMED...*

THAT WORKS. THAT WORKS. VIRGO KEEPING HIM ISOLATED... BEING THE ONLY ONE TO KNOW WHAT WENT ON IN HIS MIND. YES...

NOW...SUPPOSE-- SUPPOSE BILLY'S POWERS WERE GREATER THAN ANYONE KNEW...

WHY WOULD HE KEEP IT A SECRET?

YOU TELL ME.

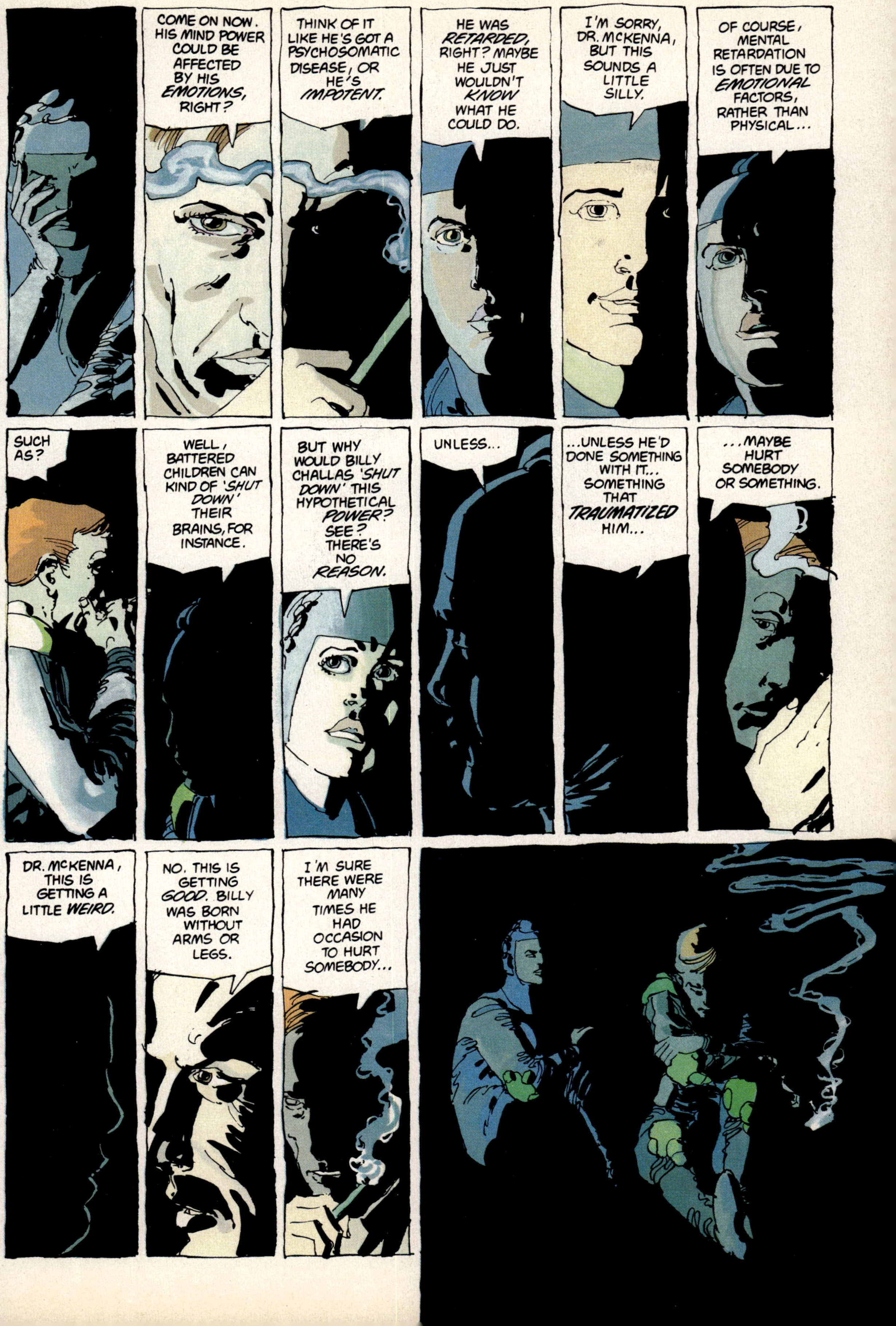
COME ON NOW. HIS MIND POWER COULD BE AFFECTED BY HIS EMOTIONS, RIGHT?
THINK OF IT LIKE HE'S GOT A PSYCHOSOMATIC DISEASE, OR HE'S IMPOTENT.
HE WAS RETARDED, RIGHT? MAYBE HE JUST WOULDN'T KNOW WHAT HE COULD DO.
I'M SORRY, DR. MCKENNA, BUT THIS SOUNDS A LITTLE SILLY.
OF COURSE, MENTAL RETARDATION IS OFTEN DUE TO EMOTIONAL FACTORS, RATHER THAN PHYSICAL...
SUCH AS?
WELL, BATTERED CHILDREN CAN KIND OF 'SHUT DOWN' THEIR BRAINS, FOR INSTANCE.
BUT WHY WOULD BILLY CHALLAS 'SHUT DOWN' THIS HYPOTHETICAL POWER? SEE? THERE'S NO REASON.
UNLESS...
...UNLESS HE'D DONE SOMETHING WITH IT... SOMETHING THAT TRAUMATIZED HIM...
...MAYBE HURT SOMEBODY OR SOMETHING.
DR. McKENNA, THIS IS GETTING A LITTLE WEIRD.
NO. THIS IS GETTING GOOD. BILLY WAS BORN WITHOUT ARMS OR LEGS.
I'M SURE THERE WERE MANY TIMES HE HAD OCCASION TO HURT SOMEBODY...

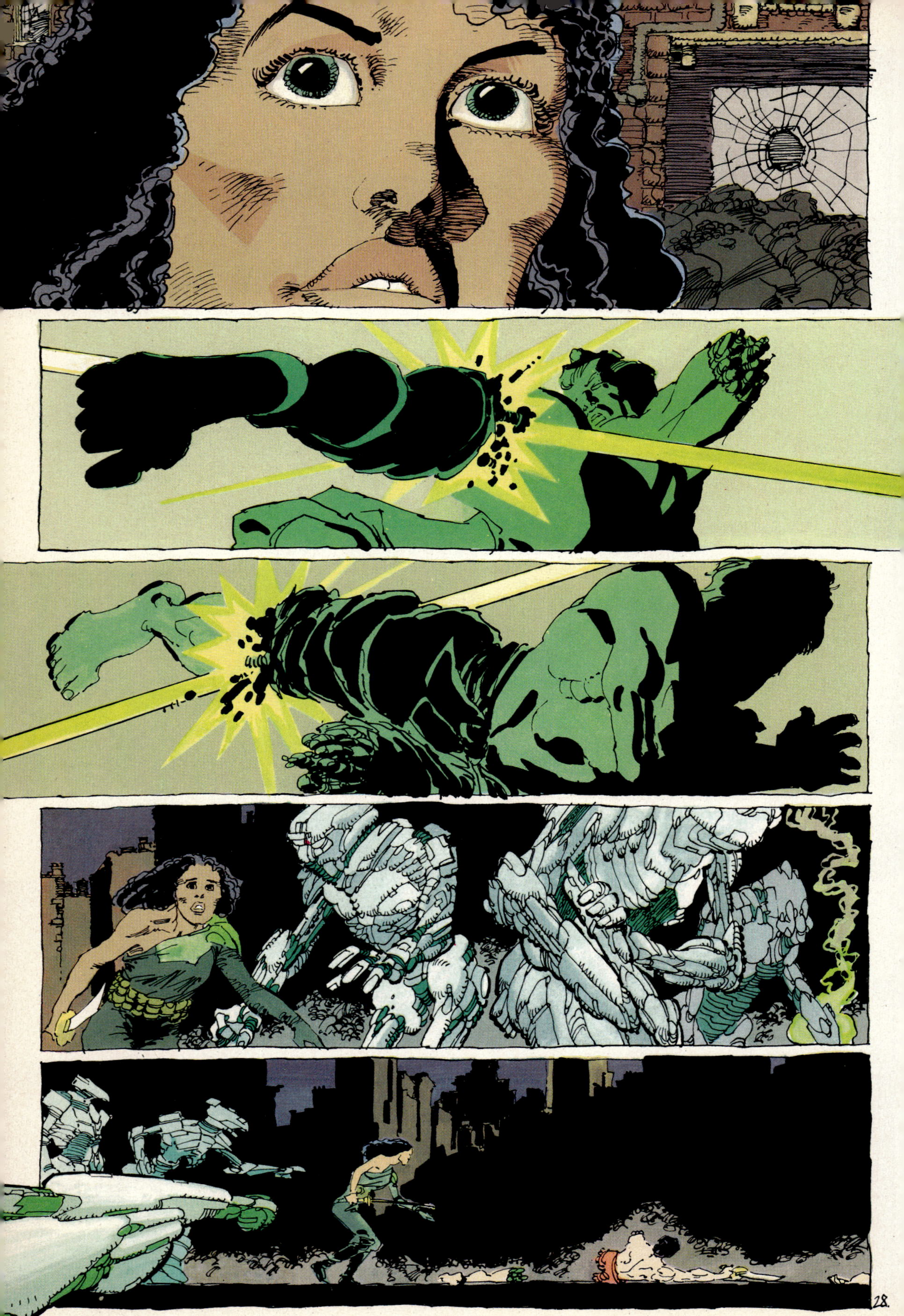

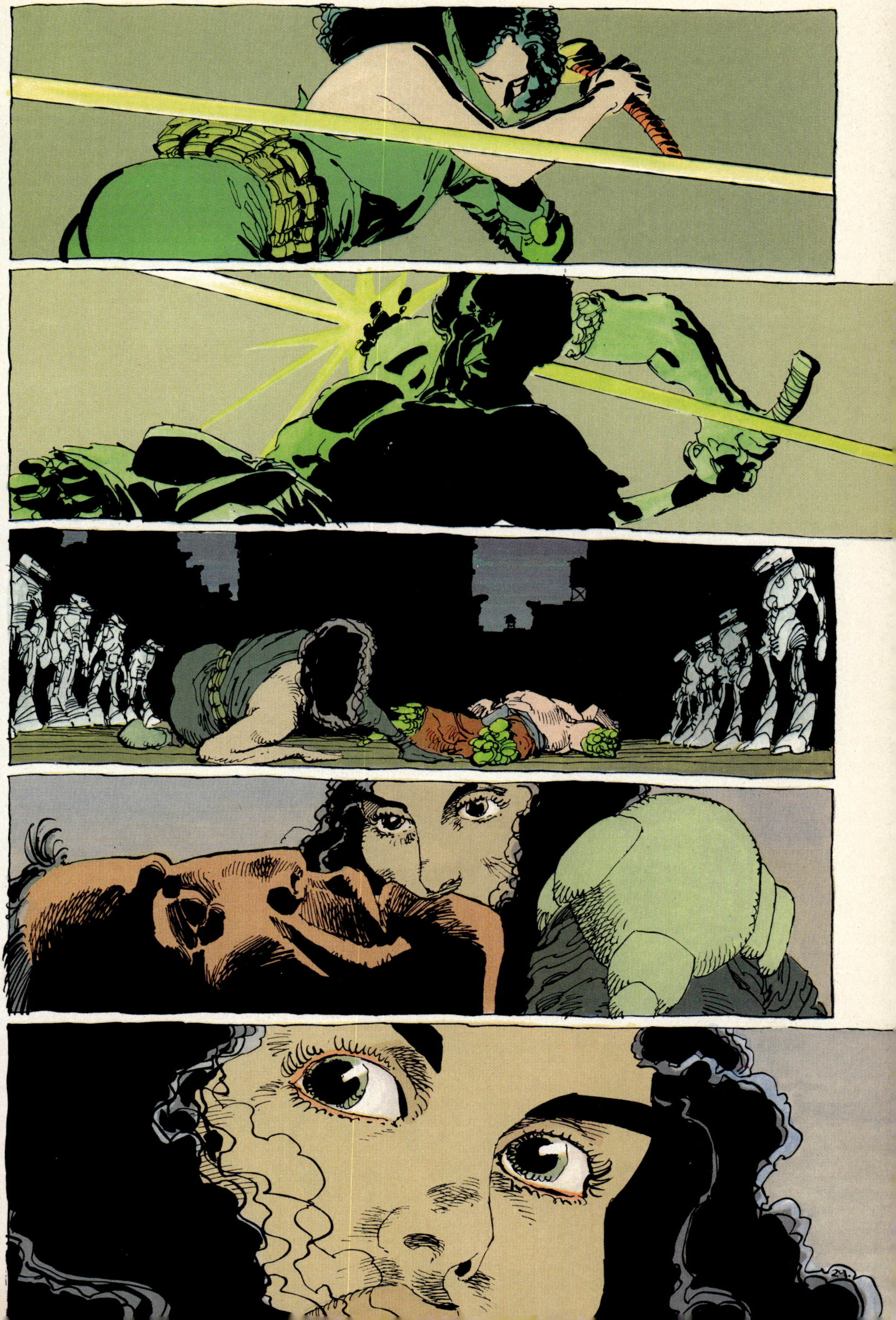

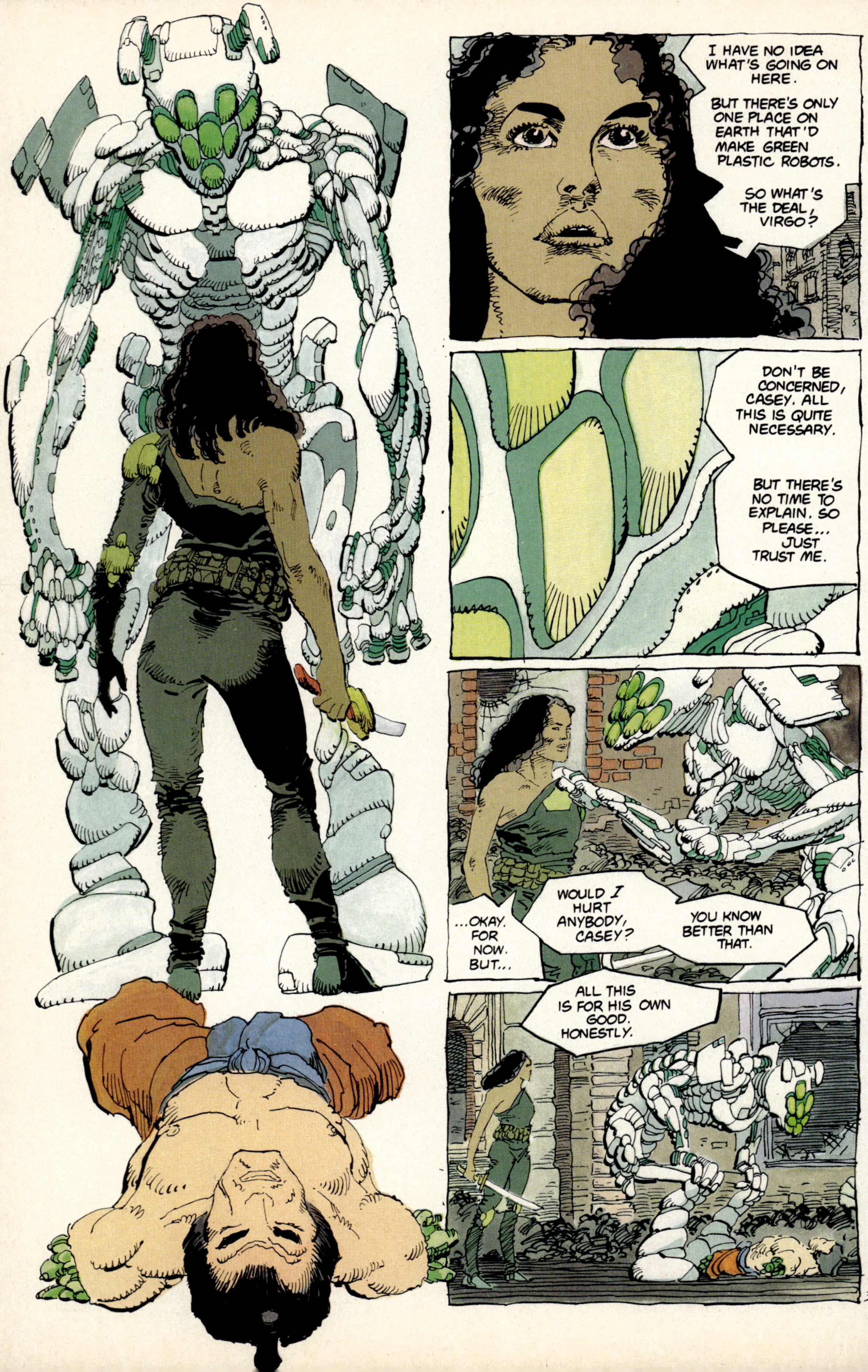
I HAVE NO IDEA WHAT'S GOING ON HERE.
BUT THERE'S ONLY ONE PLACE ON EARTH THAT'D MAKE GREEN PLASTIC ROBOTS.
SO WHAT'S THE DEAL, VIRGO?
DON'T BE CONCERNED, CASEY. ALL THIS IS QUITE NECESSARY.
BUT THERE'S NO TIME TO EXPLAIN. SO PLEASE... JUST TRUST ME.
...OKAY. FOR NOW. BUT...
WOULD I HURT ANYBODY, CASEY?
YOU KNOW BETTER THAN THAT.
ALL THIS IS FOR HIS OWN GOOD. HONESTLY.

HEY-- THIRD BASE! WATCHIN' TV AGAIN?
DON'T YOU WANT TO COME OUT AND PLAY WITH YOUR OLD PAL BART?
HEY-- THIRD BASE! WATCHIN' TV AGAIN?
DON'T YOU WANT TO COME OUT AND PLAY WITH YOUR OLD PAL BART?
MOMMA! MOMMA I'M SCARED!
YOUR MOMMA AIN'T HOME, BILLY. OUT BUYIN' GROCERIES.
LEFT YOU ALL ALONE...
YOU ALL ALONE...
BUT DON'T GET ASCARED, BASE. I AIN'T GONNA HURT YOU.
NAW. I WAS JUST WONDERIN...
...WONDERIN WHAT IT'S LIKE TO BE A TALKING PILLOW...
AND WONDERIN WHAT YOU DID--IF YOU GOT AN ITCH.
LIKE RIGHT HERE...
STOP IT...
OOH! HE'S TICKLISH!
REAL TICKLISH!
STOP-- STOP IT--
STOP IT--
STOP IT STOP IT--

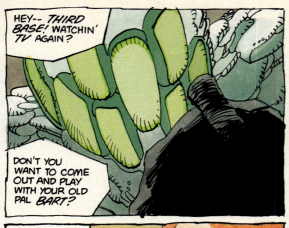

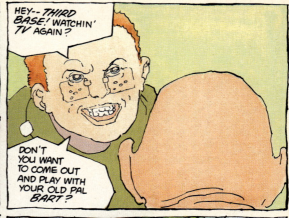

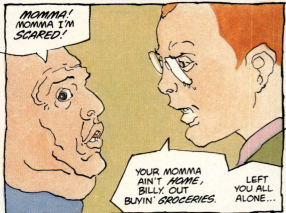

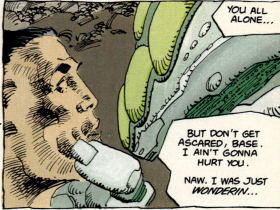

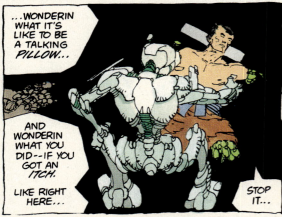

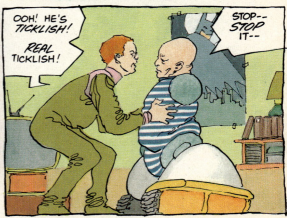

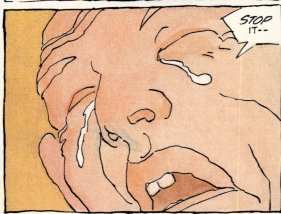

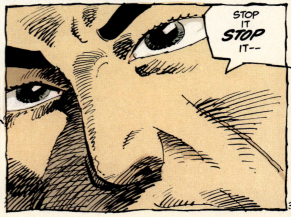

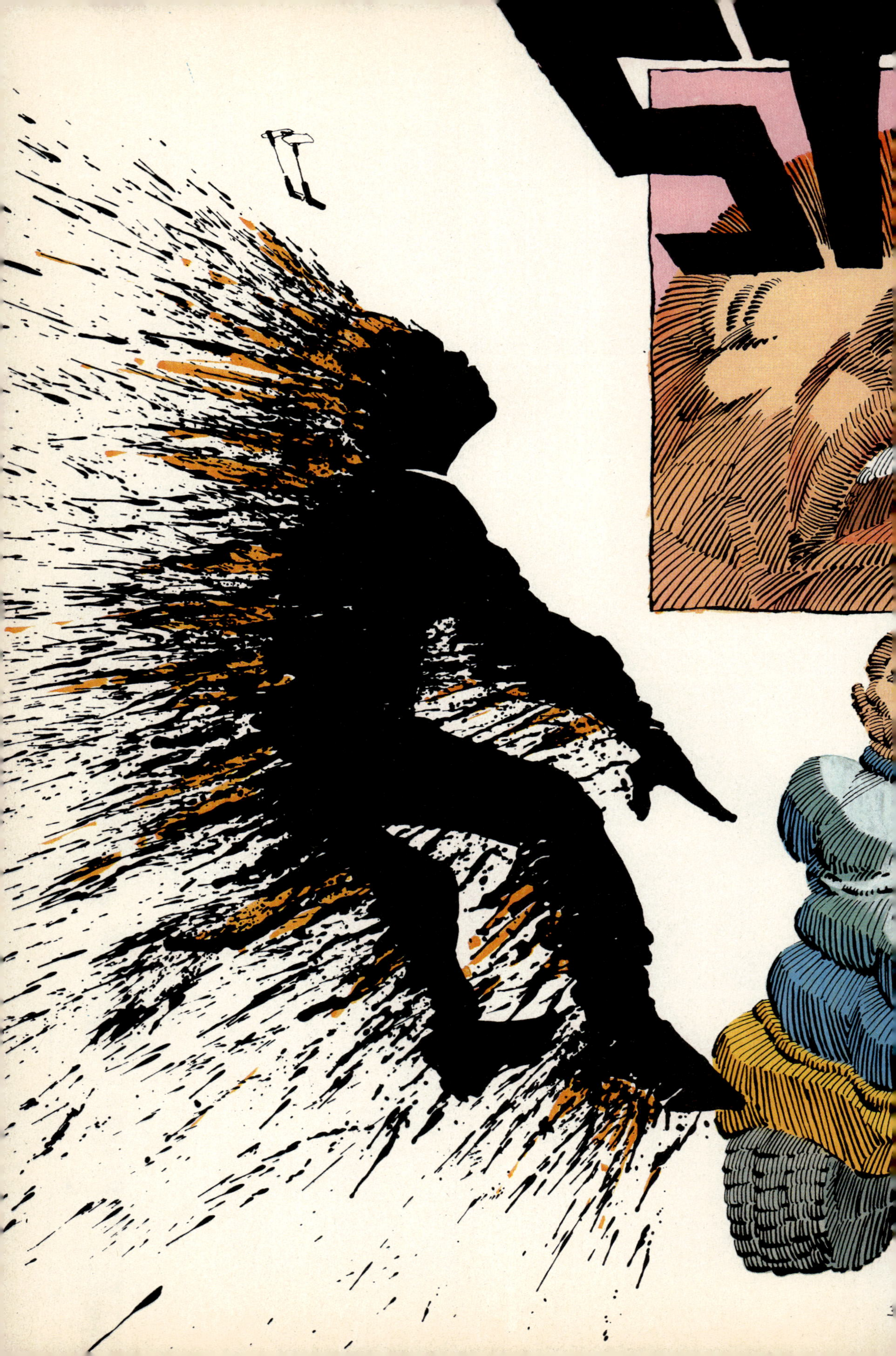

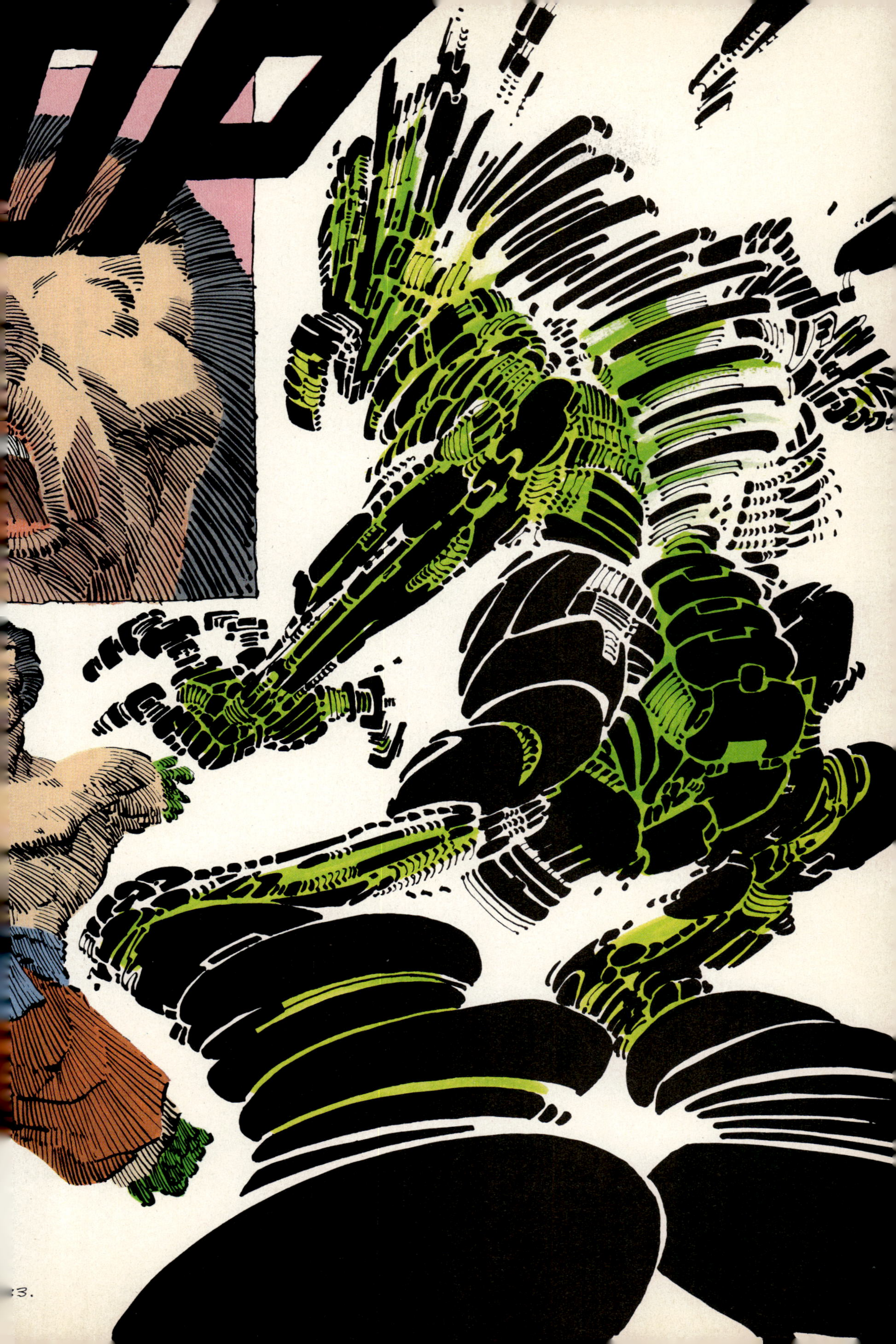

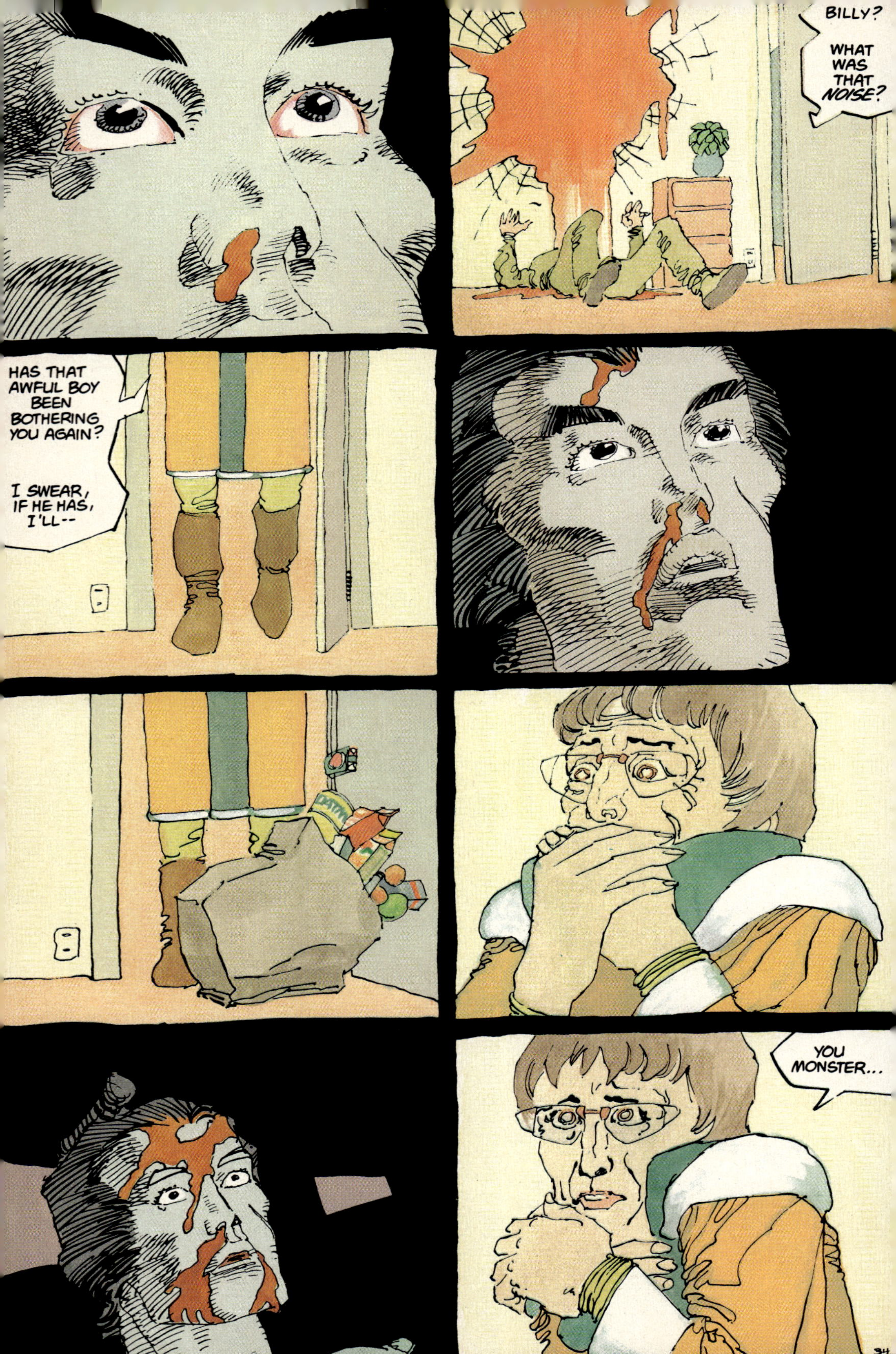
BILLY?
WHAT WAS THAT NOISE?
HAS THAT AWFUL BOY BEEN BOTHERING YOU AGAIN?
I SWEAR, IF HE HAS, I'LL--
YOU MONSTER...

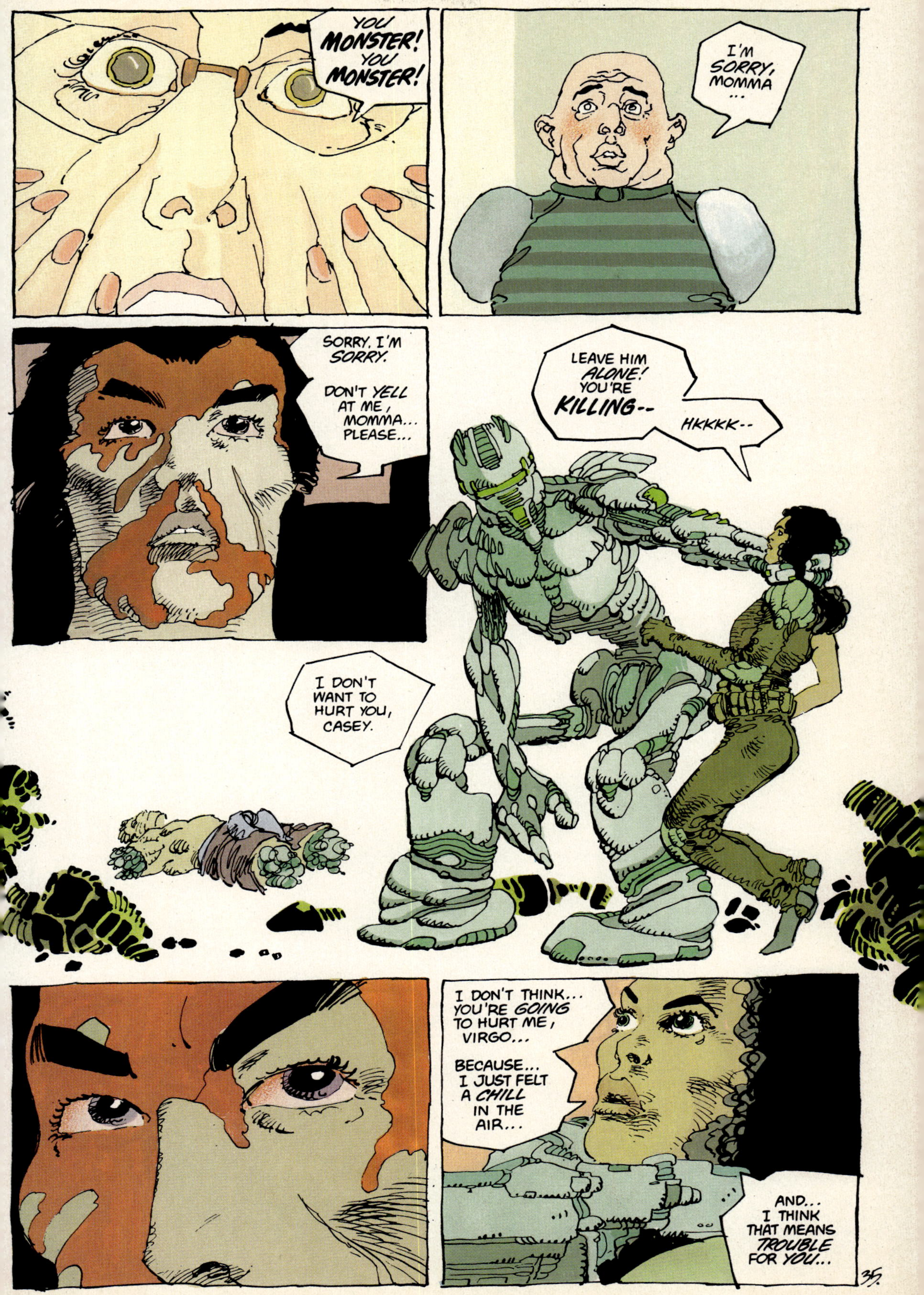
YOU MONSTER! YOU MONSTER!
I'M SORRY, MOMMA ...
SORRY, I'M SORRY.
DON'T YELL AT ME, MOMMA... PLEASE...
LEAVE HIM ALONE! YOU'RE KILLING--
HKKKK--
I DON'T WANT TO HURT YOU, CASEY.
I DON'T THINK... YOU'RE GOING TO HURT ME, VIRGO...
BECAUSE... I JUST FELT A CHILL IN THE AIR...
AND... I THINK THAT MEANS TROUBLE FOR YOU...

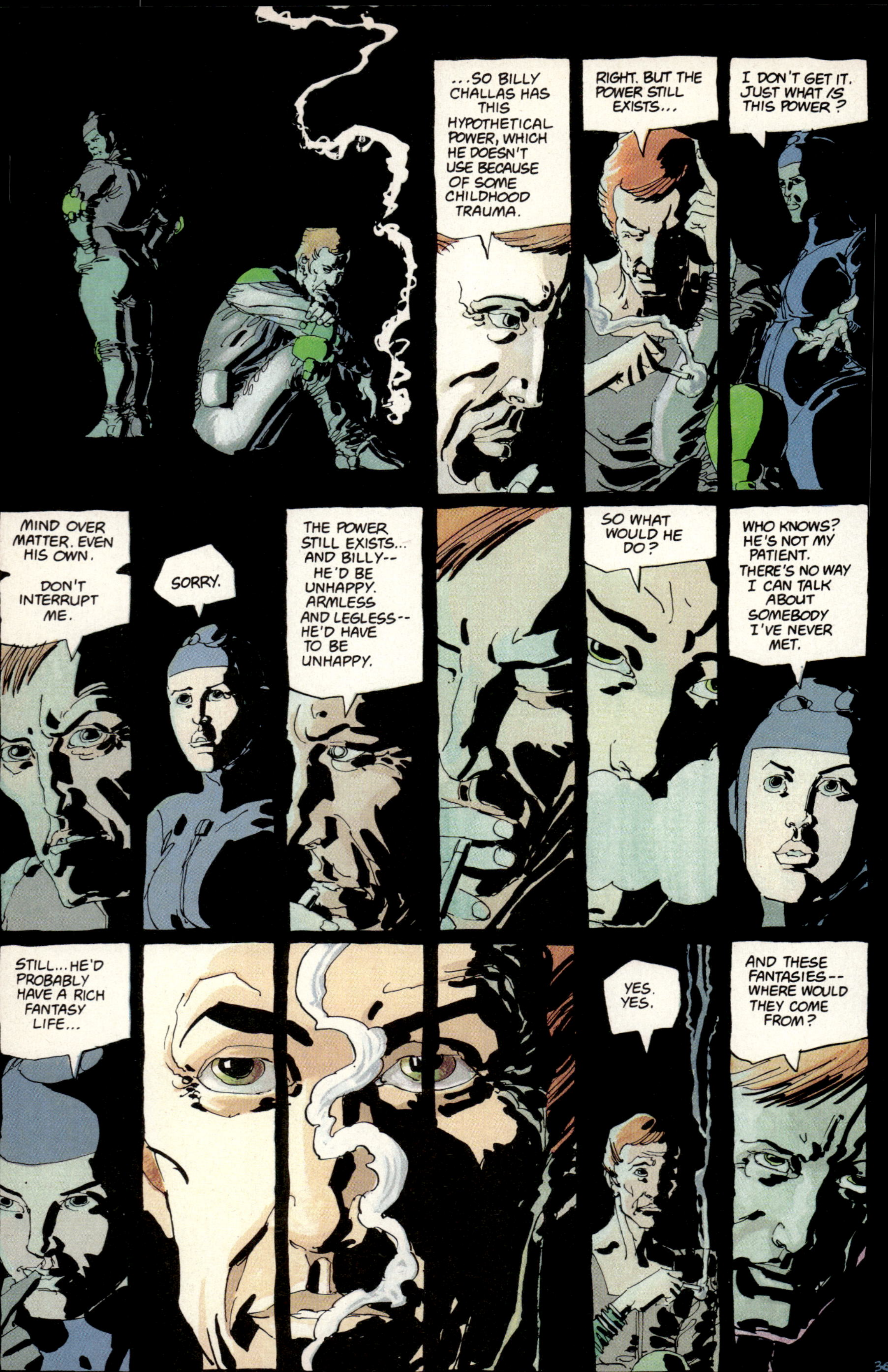
...SO BILLY CHALLAS HAS THIS HYPOTHETICAL POWER, WHICH HE DOESN'T USE BECAUSE OF SOME CHILDHOOD TRAUMA.
RIGHT. BUT THE POWER STILL EXISTS...
I DON'T GET IT. JUST WHAT *IS* THIS POWER?
MIND OVER MATTER. EVEN HIS OWN.
DON'T INTERRUPT ME.
SORRY.
THE POWER STILL EXISTS... AND BILLY-- HE'D BE UNHAPPY. ARMLESS AND LEGLESS-- HE'D HAVE TO BE UNHAPPY.
SO WHAT WOULD HE DO?
WHO KNOWS? HE'S NOT MY PATIENT. THERE'S NO WAY I CAN TALK ABOUT SOMEBODY I'VE NEVER MET.
STILL... HE'D PROBABLY HAVE A RICH FANTASY LIFE...
YES. YES.
AND THESE FANTASIES-- WHERE WOULD THEY COME FROM?

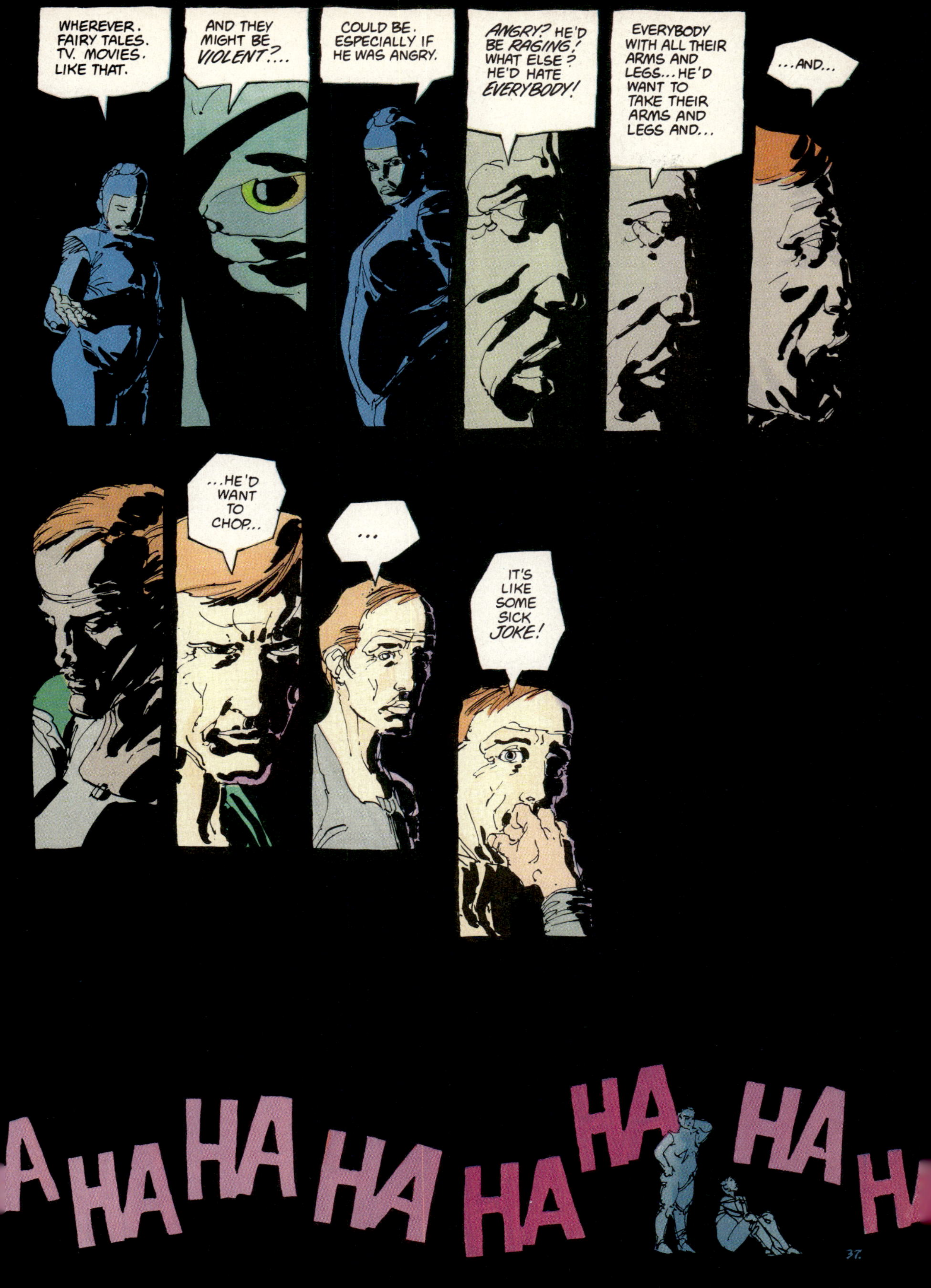
WHEREVER. FAIRY TALES. TV. MOVIES. LIKE THAT.
AND THEY MIGHT BE VIOLENT?....
COULD BE. ESPECIALLY IF HE WAS ANGRY.
ANGRY? HE'D BE RAGING! WHAT ELSE? HE'D HATE EVERYBODY!
EVERYBODY WITH ALL THEIR ARMS AND LEGS... HE'D WANT TO TAKE THEIR ARMS AND LEGS AND...
...AND...
...HE'D WANT TO CHOP...
...
IT'S LIKE SOME SICK JOKE!
HA HA HA HA HA HA HA HA HA
37.

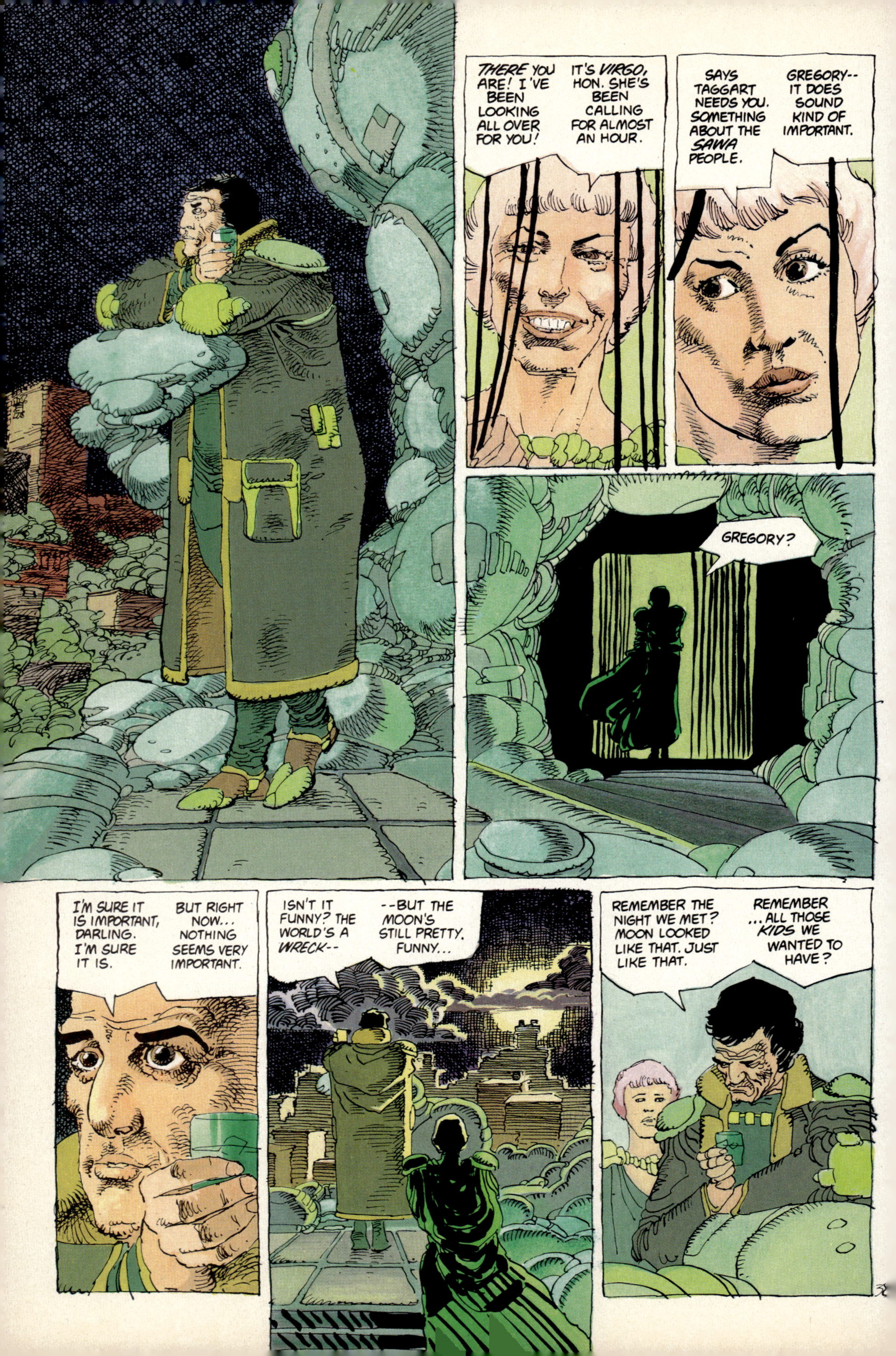
THERE YOU ARE! I'VE BEEN LOOKING ALL OVER FOR YOU!
IT'S VIRGO, HON. SHE'S BEEN CALLING FOR ALMOST AN HOUR.
SAYS TAGGART NEEDS YOU. SOMETHING ABOUT THE SAWA PEOPLE.
GREGORY-- IT DOES SOUND KIND OF IMPORTANT.
GREGORY?
I'M SURE IT IS IMPORTANT, DARLING. I'M SURE IT IS.
BUT RIGHT NOW... NOTHING SEEMS VERY IMPORTANT.
ISN'T IT FUNNY? THE WORLD'S A WRECK--
--BUT THE MOON'S STILL PRETTY. FUNNY...
REMEMBER THE NIGHT WE MET? MOON LOOKED LIKE THAT. JUST LIKE THAT.
REMEMBER ...ALL THOSE KIDS WE WANTED TO HAVE?

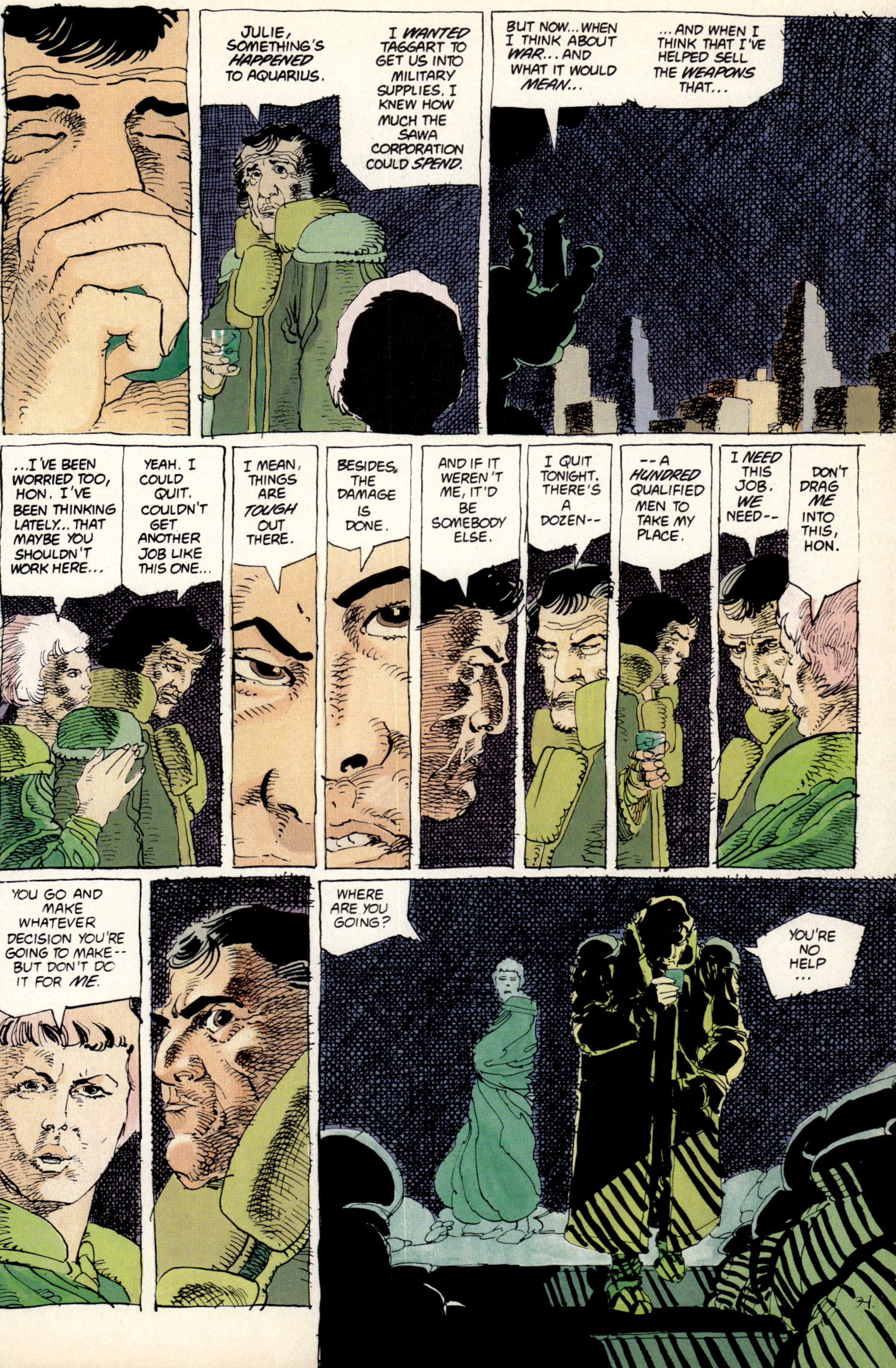

JULIE, SOMETHING'S *HAPPENED* TO AQUARIUS.
I *WANTED* TAGGART TO GET US INTO MILITARY SUPPLIES. I KNEW HOW MUCH THE SAWA CORPORATION COULD *SPEND*.
BUT NOW... WHEN I THINK ABOUT *WAR*... AND WHAT IT WOULD *MEAN*...
...AND WHEN I THINK THAT I'VE HELPED SELL THE *WEAPONS* THAT...
...I'VE BEEN WORRIED TOO, HON. I'VE BEEN THINKING LATELY... THAT MAYBE YOU SHOULDN'T WORK HERE...
YEAH. I COULD QUIT. COULDN'T GET ANOTHER JOB LIKE THIS ONE...
I MEAN, THINGS ARE *TOUGH* OUT THERE.
BESIDES, THE DAMAGE IS DONE.
AND IF IT WEREN'T ME, IT'D BE SOMEBODY ELSE.
I QUIT TONIGHT. THERE'S A DOZEN--
--A *HUNDRED* QUALIFIED MEN TO TAKE MY PLACE.
I *NEED* THIS JOB. *WE* NEED--
DON'T DRAG *ME* INTO THIS, HON.
YOU GO AND MAKE WHATEVER DECISION YOU'RE GOING TO MAKE-- BUT DON'T DO IT FOR *ME*.
WHERE ARE YOU GOING?
YOU'RE NO HELP ...

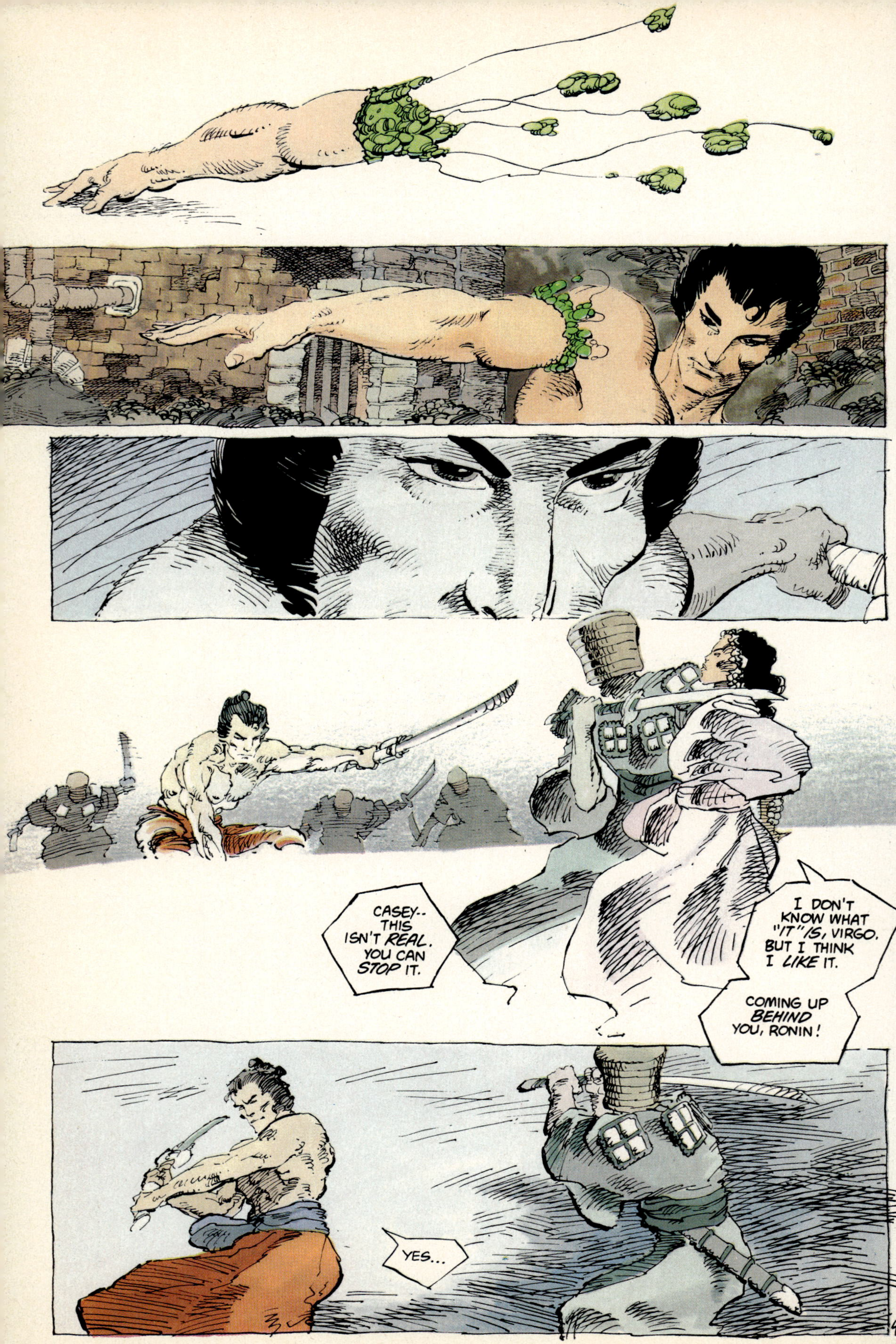
CASEY-- THIS ISN'T REAL. YOU CAN STOP IT.
I DON'T KNOW WHAT "IT" IS, VIRGO. BUT I THINK I LIKE IT.
COMING UP BEHIND YOU, RONIN!
YES...

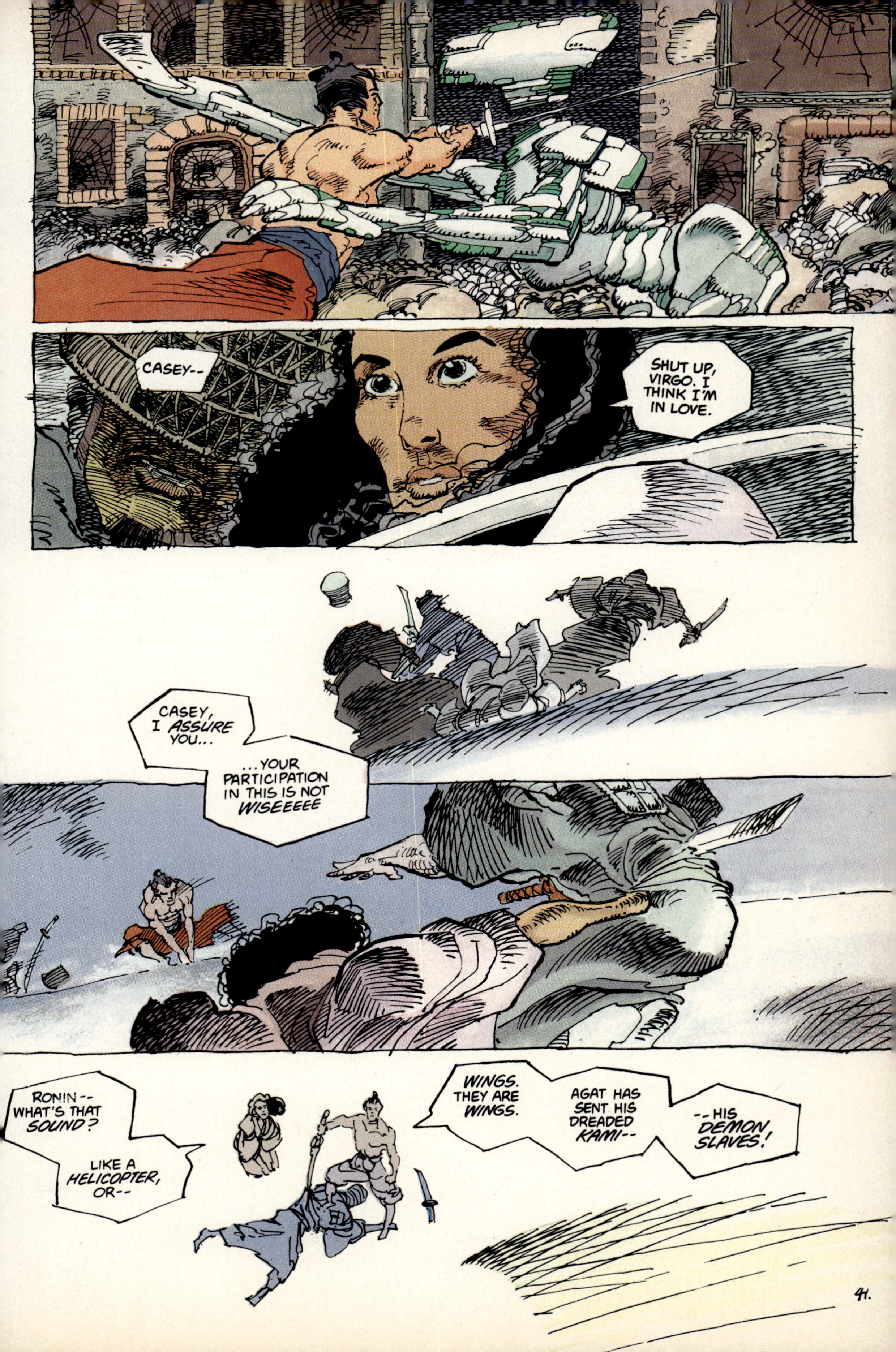
CASEY--
SHUT UP, VIRGO. I THINK I'M IN LOVE.
CASEY, I ASSURE YOU...
...YOUR PARTICIPATION IN THIS IS NOT WISEEEEE
RONIN-- WHAT'S THAT SOUND?
LIKE A HELICOPTER, OR--
WINGS. THEY ARE WINGS.
AGAT HAS SENT HIS DREADED KAMI--
--HIS DEMON SLAVES!

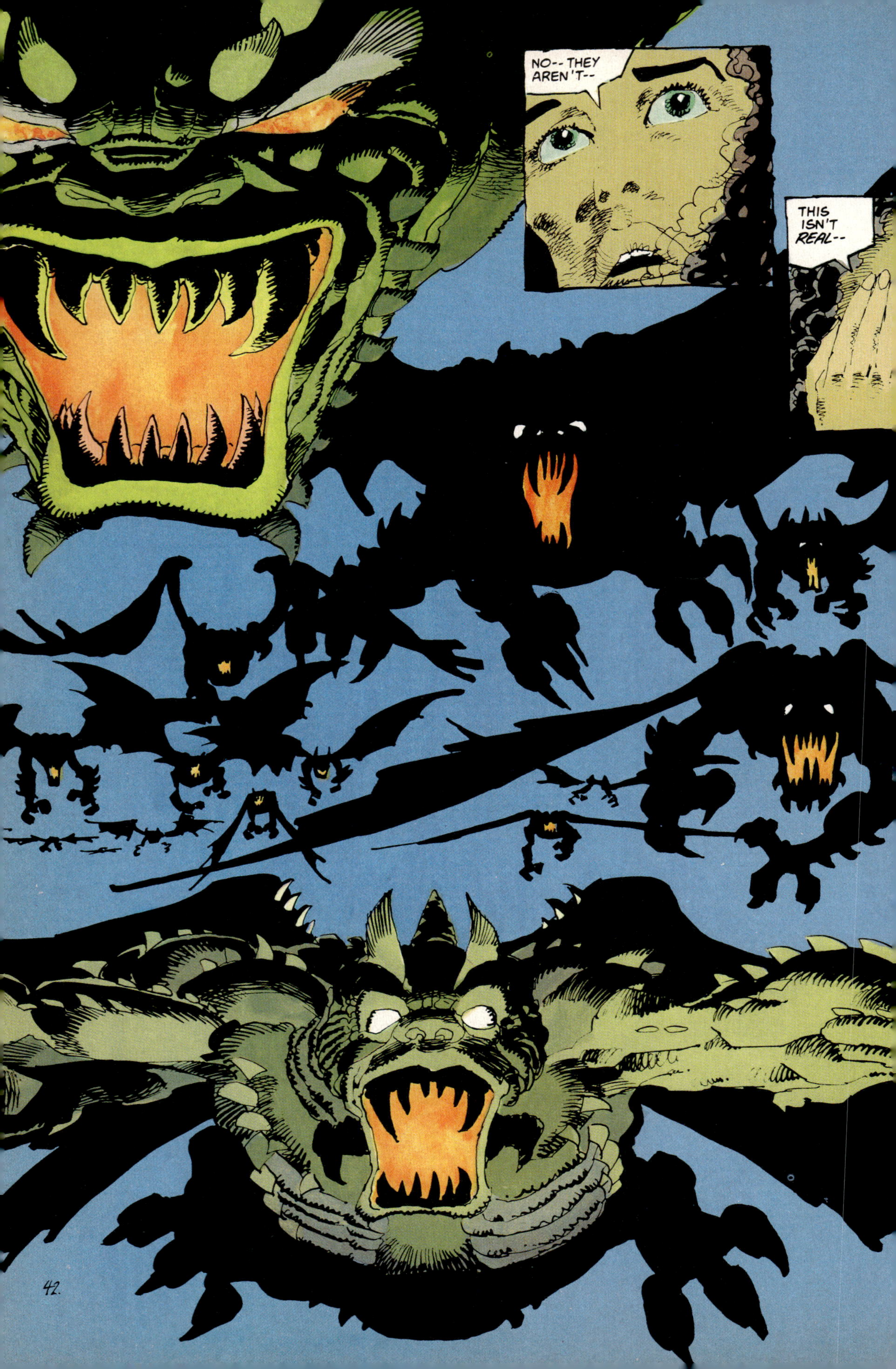
NO-- THEY AREN'T--
THIS ISN'T *REAL*--

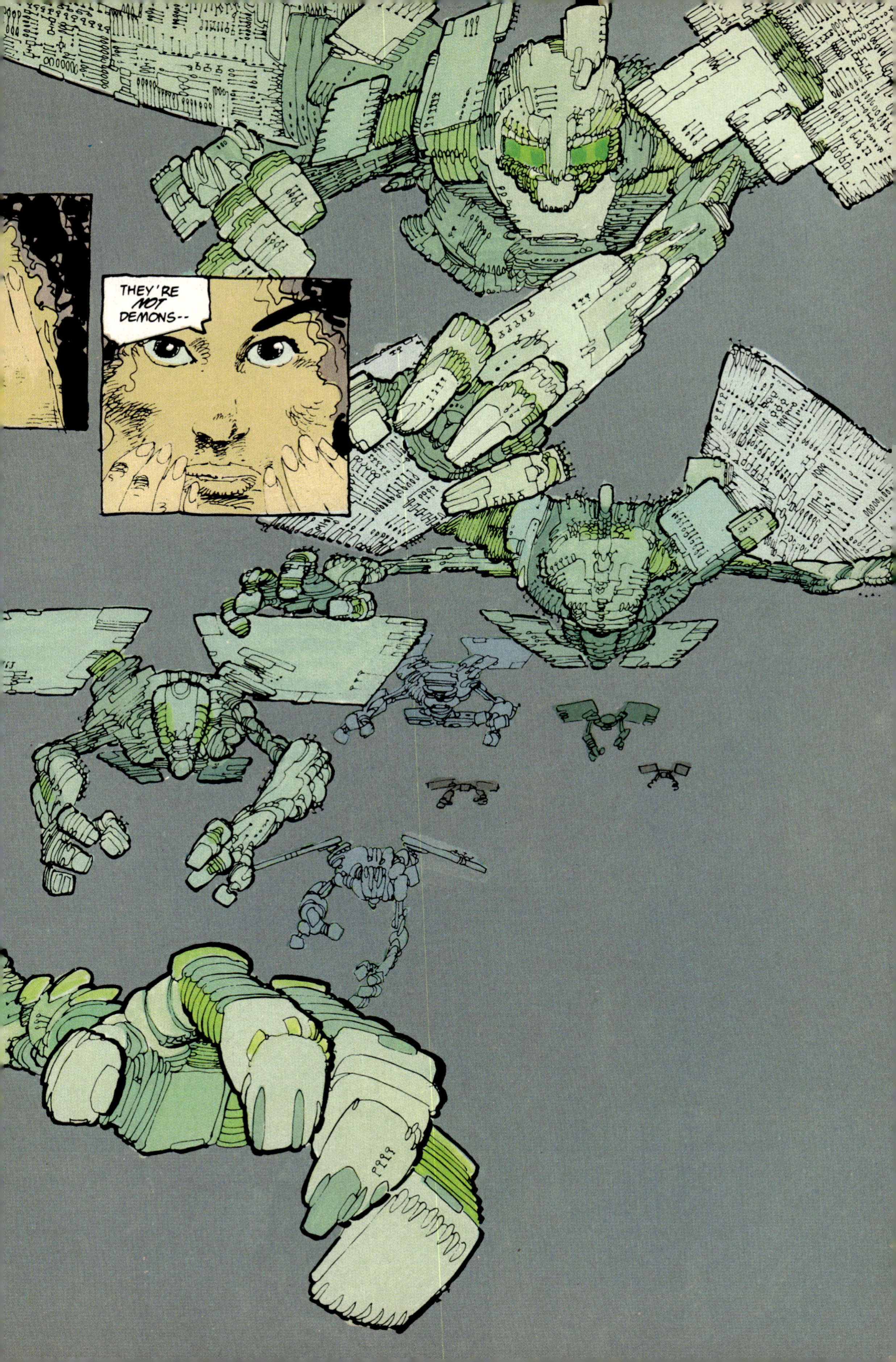
THEY'RE NOT DEMONS--

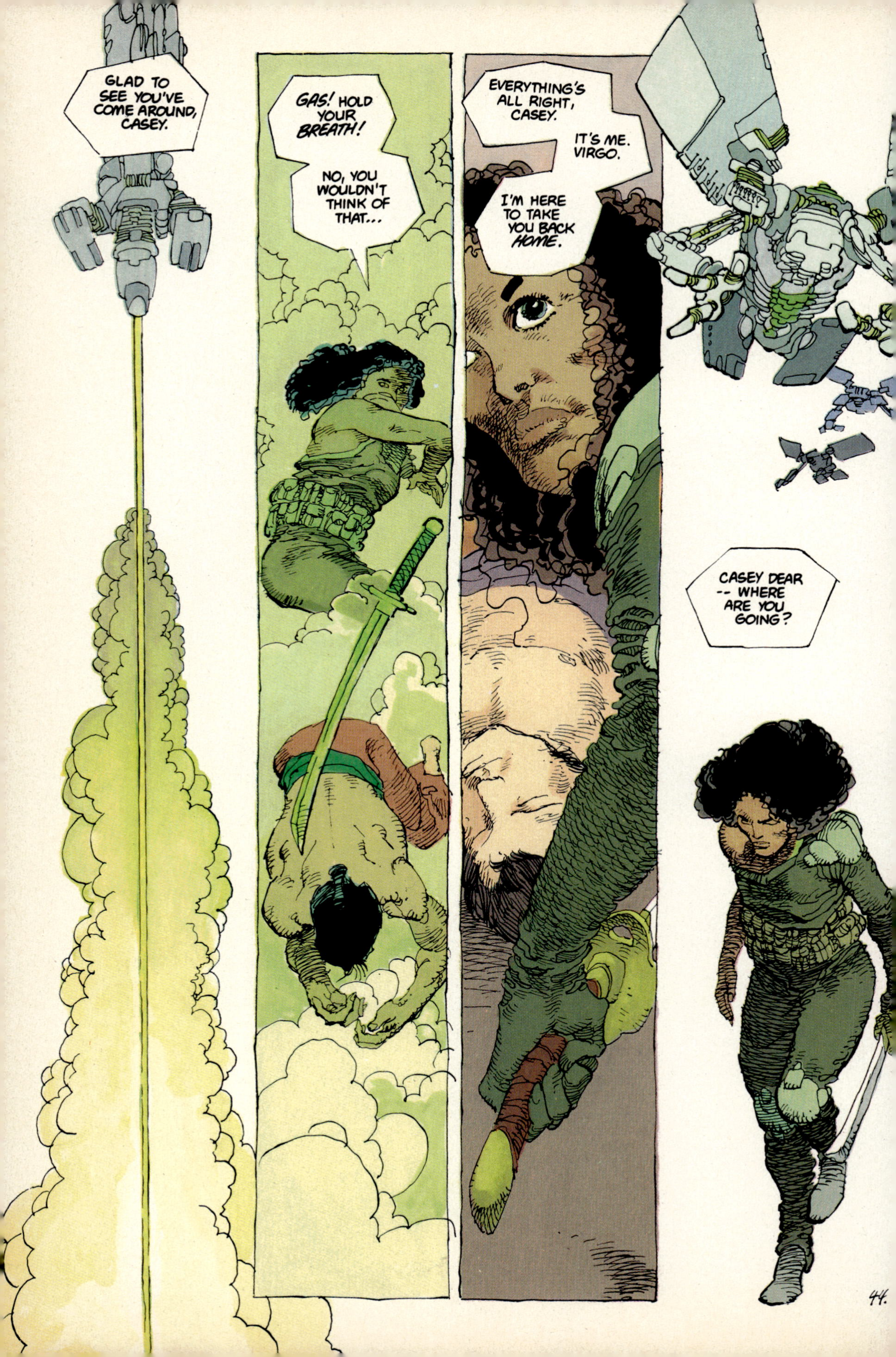
GLAD TO SEE YOU'VE COME AROUND, CASEY.
GAS! HOLD YOUR BREATH!
NO, YOU WOULDN'T THINK OF THAT...
EVERYTHING'S ALL RIGHT, CASEY.
IT'S ME. VIRGO.
I'M HERE TO TAKE YOU BACK HOME.
CASEY DEAR -- WHERE ARE YOU GOING?

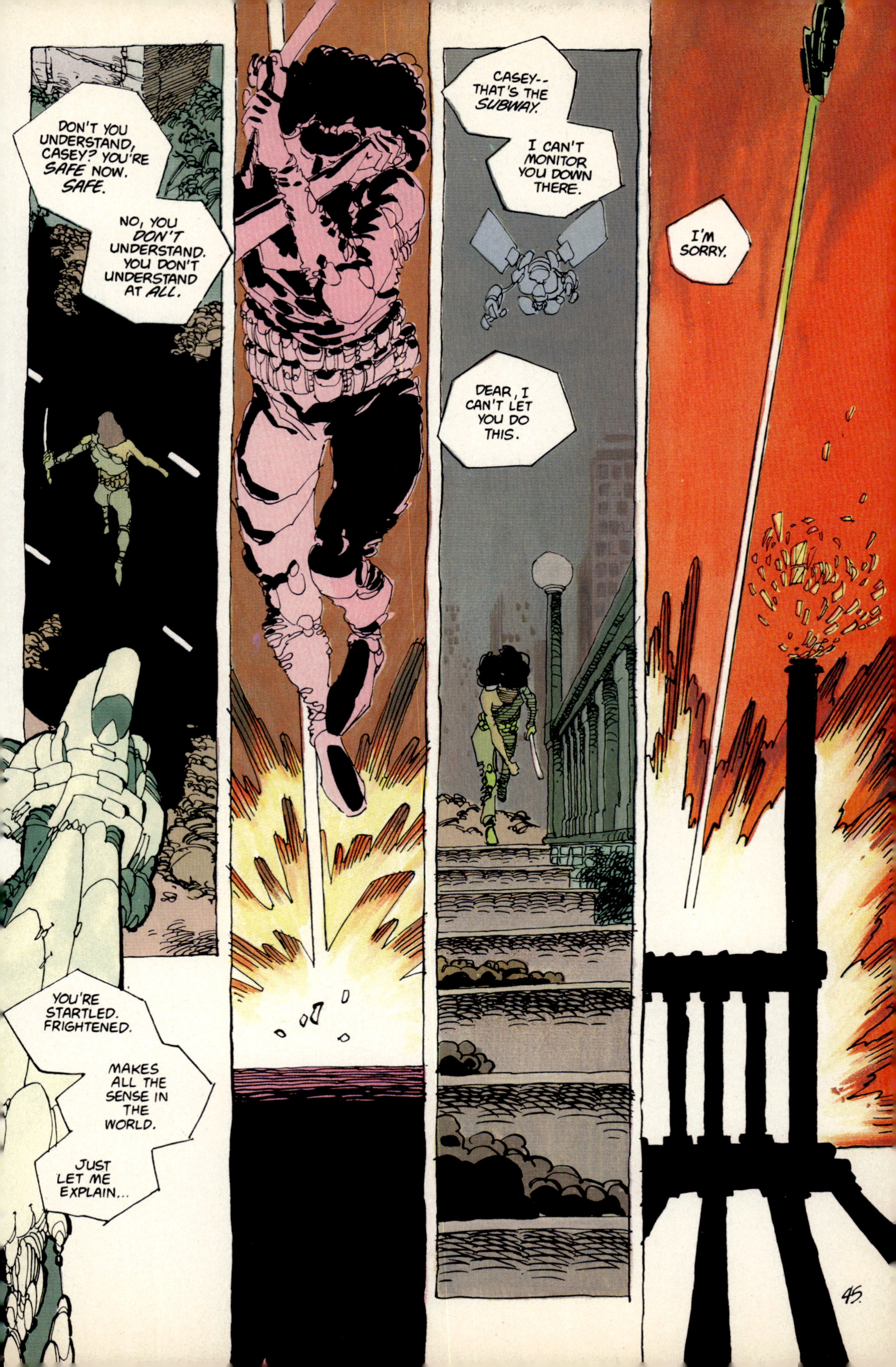
DON'T YOU UNDERSTAND, CASEY? YOU'RE *SAFE* NOW. *SAFE*.
NO, YOU *DON'T* UNDERSTAND. YOU DON'T UNDERSTAND AT *ALL*.
YOU'RE STARTLED. FRIGHTENED.
MAKES ALL THE SENSE IN THE WORLD.
JUST LET ME EXPLAIN...
CASEY-- THAT'S THE *SUBWAY*.
I CAN'T MONITOR YOU DOWN THERE.
DEAR, I CAN'T LET YOU DO THIS.
I'M SORRY.

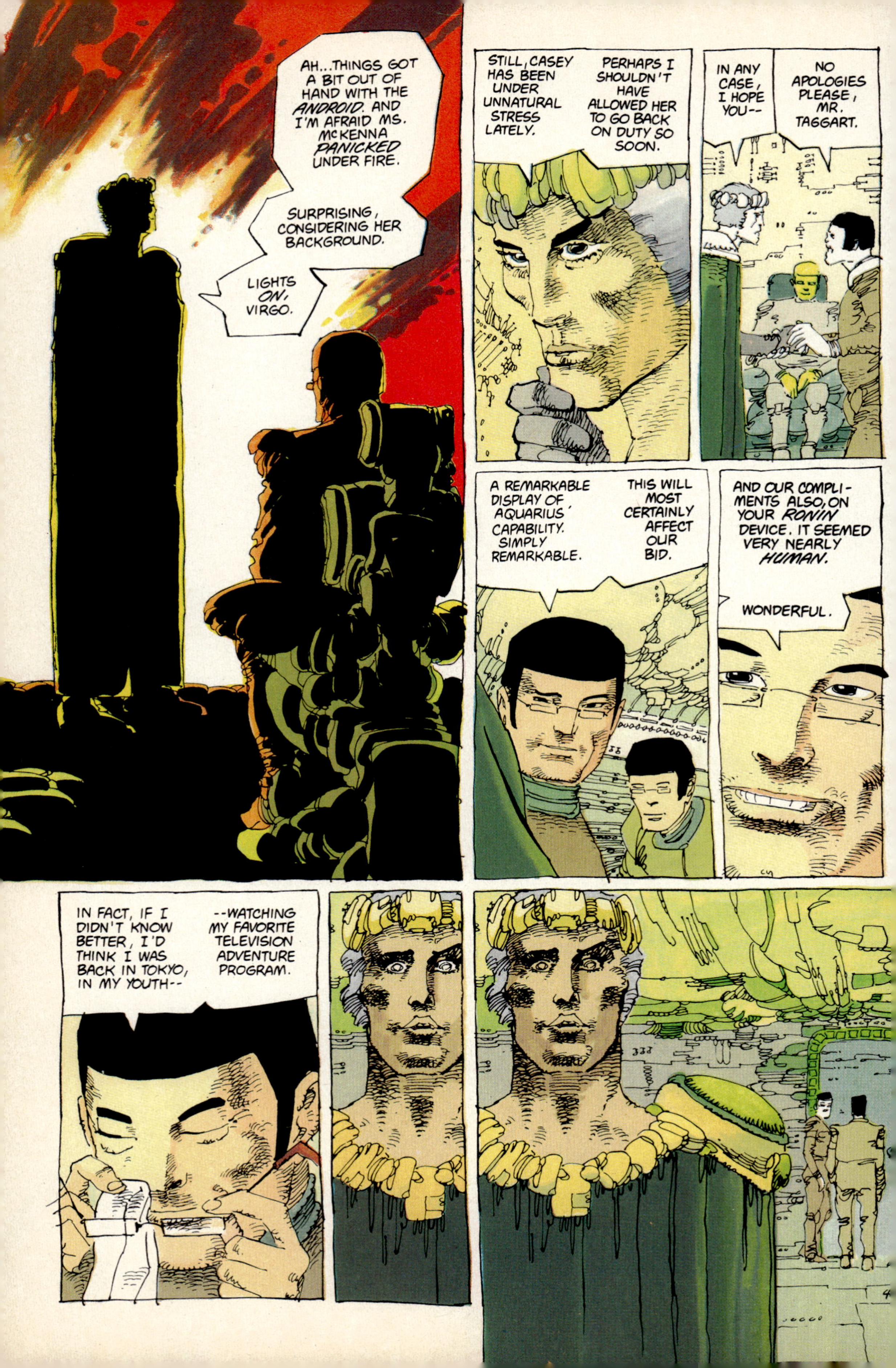

AH...THINGS GOT A BIT OUT OF HAND WITH THE ANDROID. AND I'M AFRAID MS. McKENNA PANICKED UNDER FIRE.
SURPRISING, CONSIDERING HER BACKGROUND.
LIGHTS ON, VIRGO.
STILL, CASEY HAS BEEN UNDER UNNATURAL STRESS LATELY.
PERHAPS I SHOULDN'T HAVE ALLOWED HER TO GO BACK ON DUTY SO SOON.
IN ANY CASE, I HOPE YOU--
NO APOLOGIES PLEASE, MR. TAGGART.
A REMARKABLE DISPLAY OF AQUARIUS' CAPABILITY. SIMPLY REMARKABLE.
THIS WILL MOST CERTAINLY AFFECT OUR BID.
AND OUR COMPLIMENTS ALSO, ON YOUR RONIN DEVICE. IT SEEMED VERY NEARLY HUMAN.
WONDERFUL.
IN FACT, IF I DIDN'T KNOW BETTER, I'D THINK I WAS BACK IN TOKYO, IN MY YOUTH--
--WATCHING MY FAVORITE TELEVISION ADVENTURE PROGRAM.

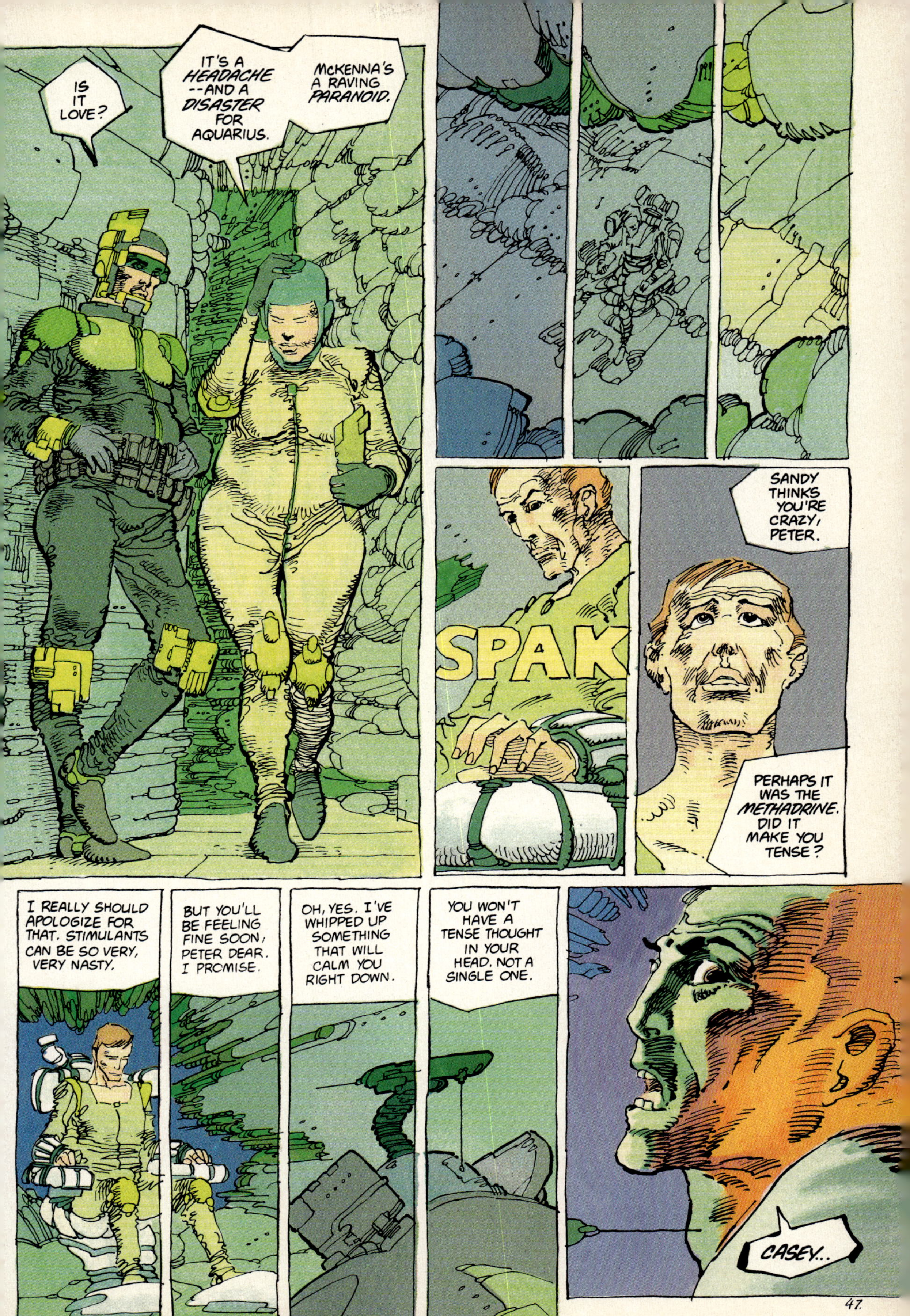
IS IT LOVE?
IT'S A HEADACHE --AND A DISASTER FOR AQUARIUS.
McKENNA'S A RAVING PARANOID.
SANDY THINKS YOU'RE CRAZY, PETER.
SPAK
PERHAPS IT WAS THE METHADRINE. DID IT MAKE YOU TENSE?
I REALLY SHOULD APOLOGIZE FOR THAT. STIMULANTS CAN BE SO VERY, VERY NASTY.
BUT YOU'LL BE FEELING FINE SOON, PETER DEAR. I PROMISE.
OH, YES. I'VE WHIPPED UP SOMETHING THAT WILL CALM YOU RIGHT DOWN.
YOU WON'T HAVE A TENSE THOUGHT IN YOUR HEAD. NOT A SINGLE ONE.
CASEY...

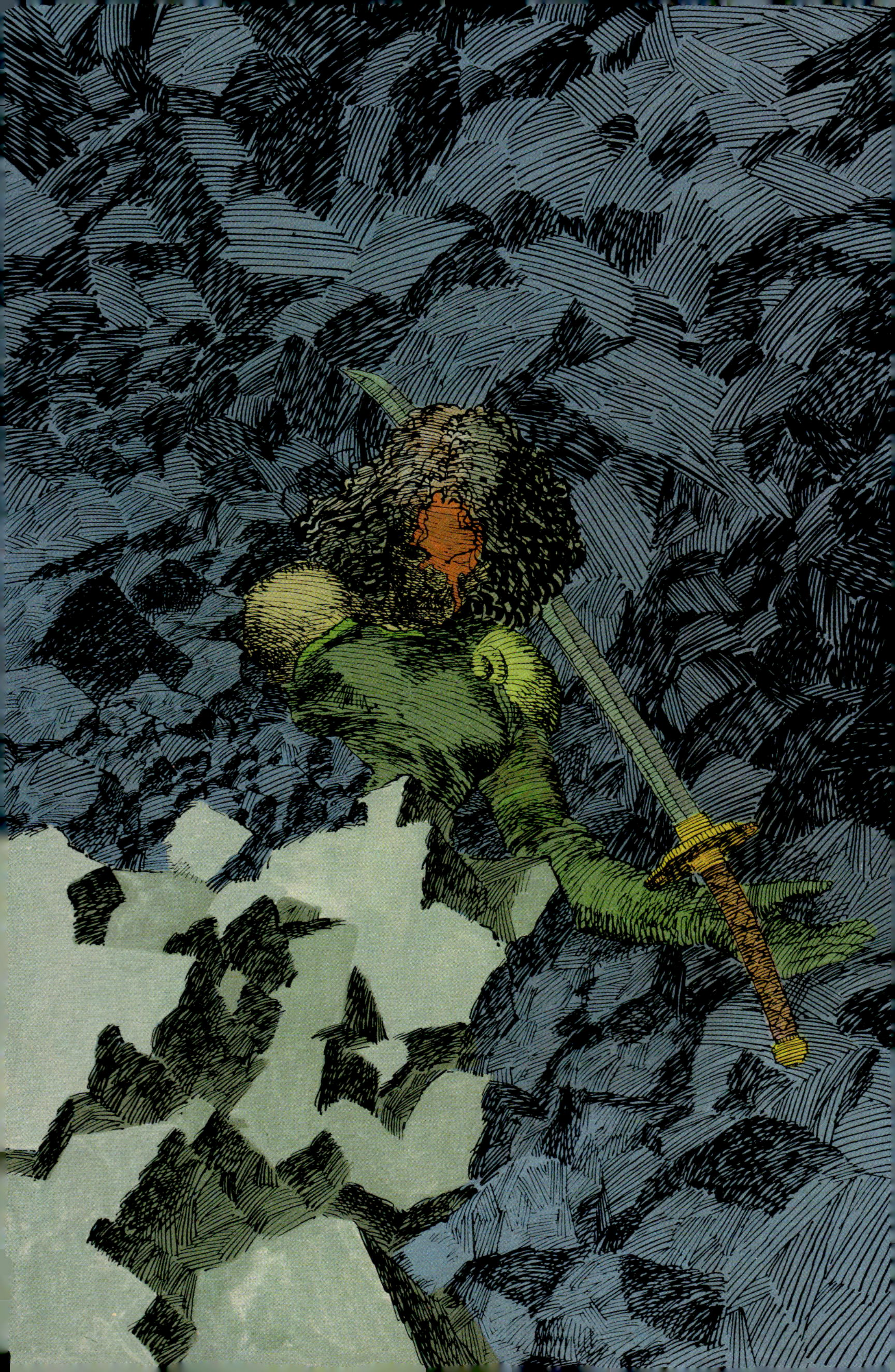

CHAPTER SIX

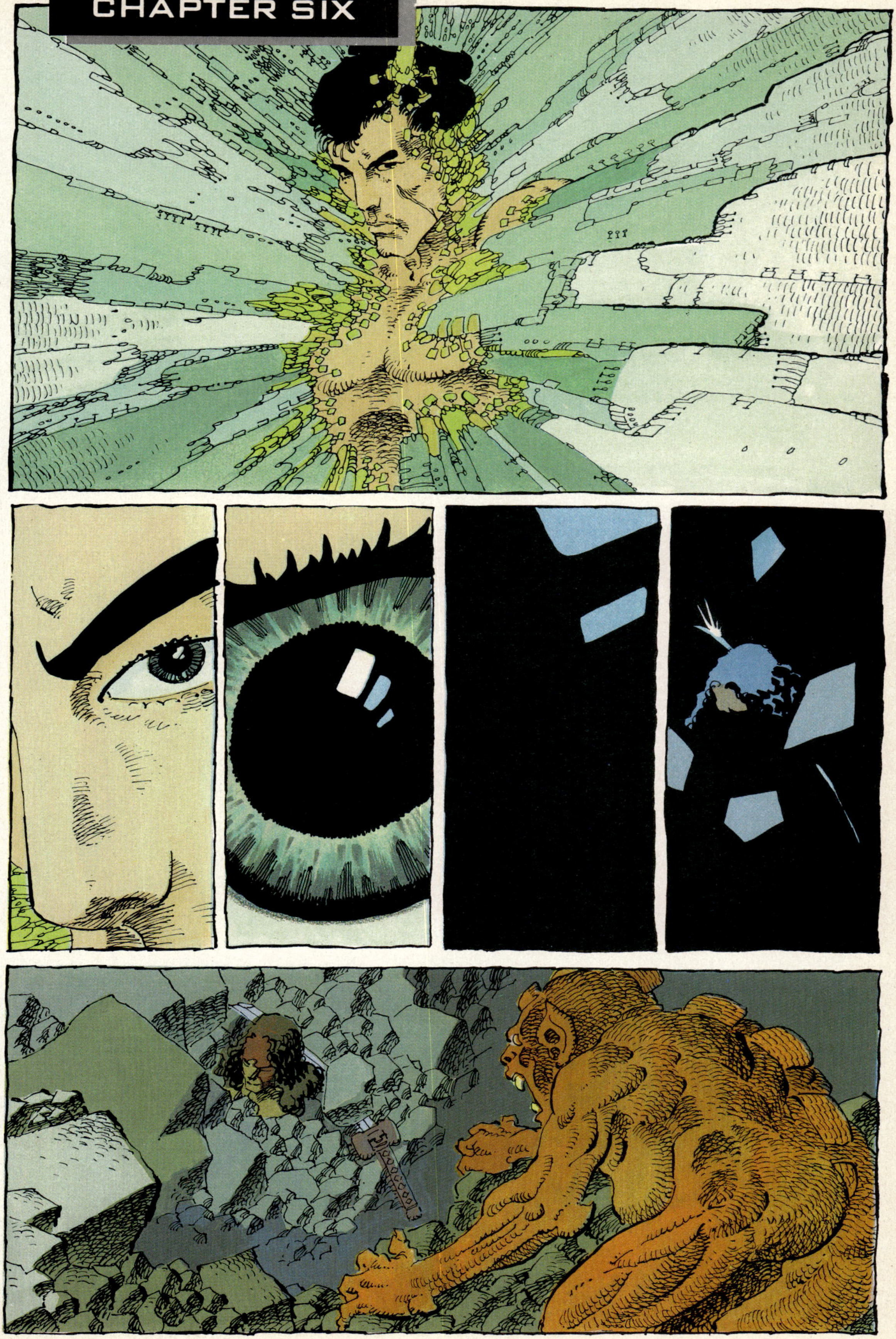

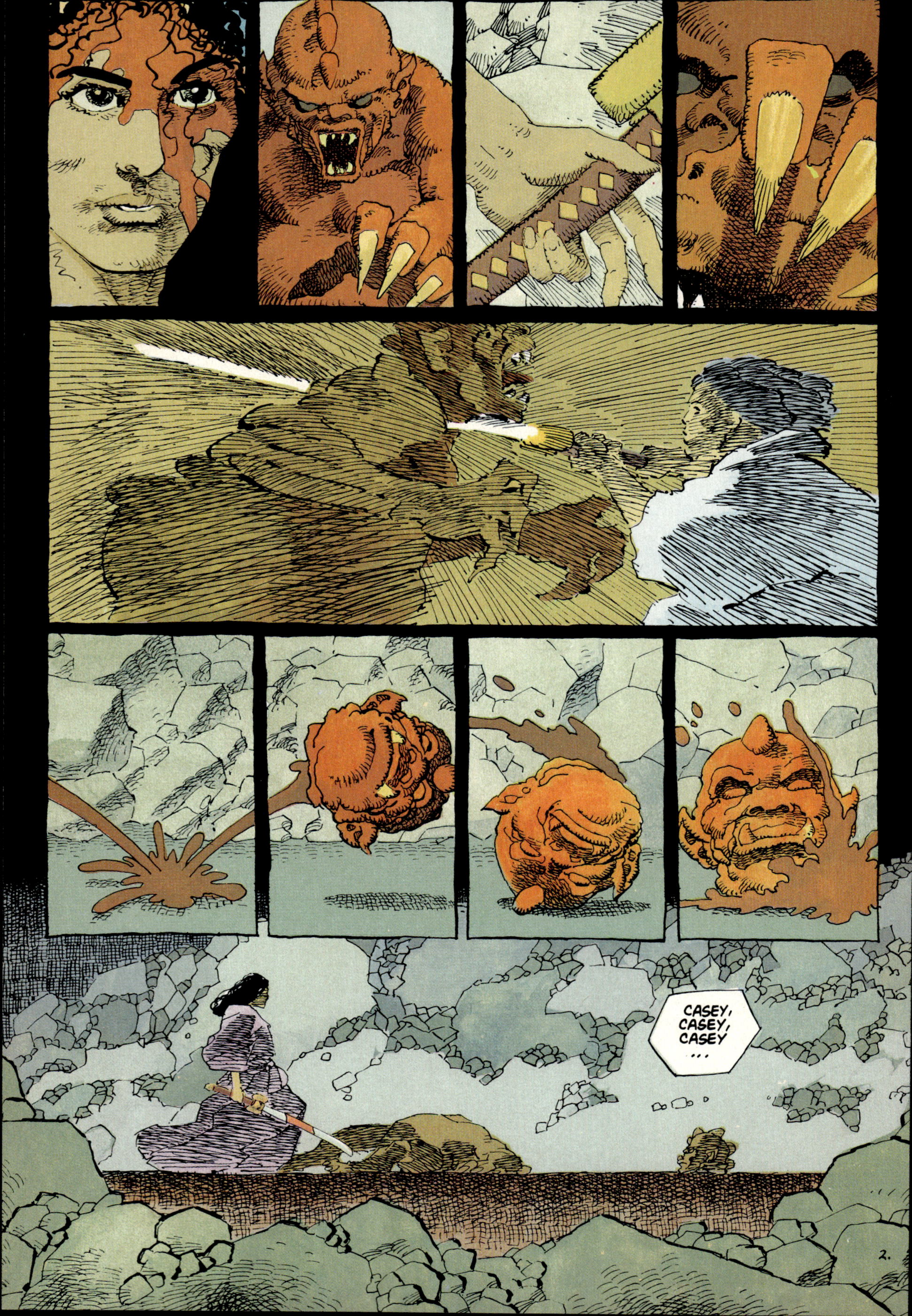
CASEY,
CASEY,
CASEY
...

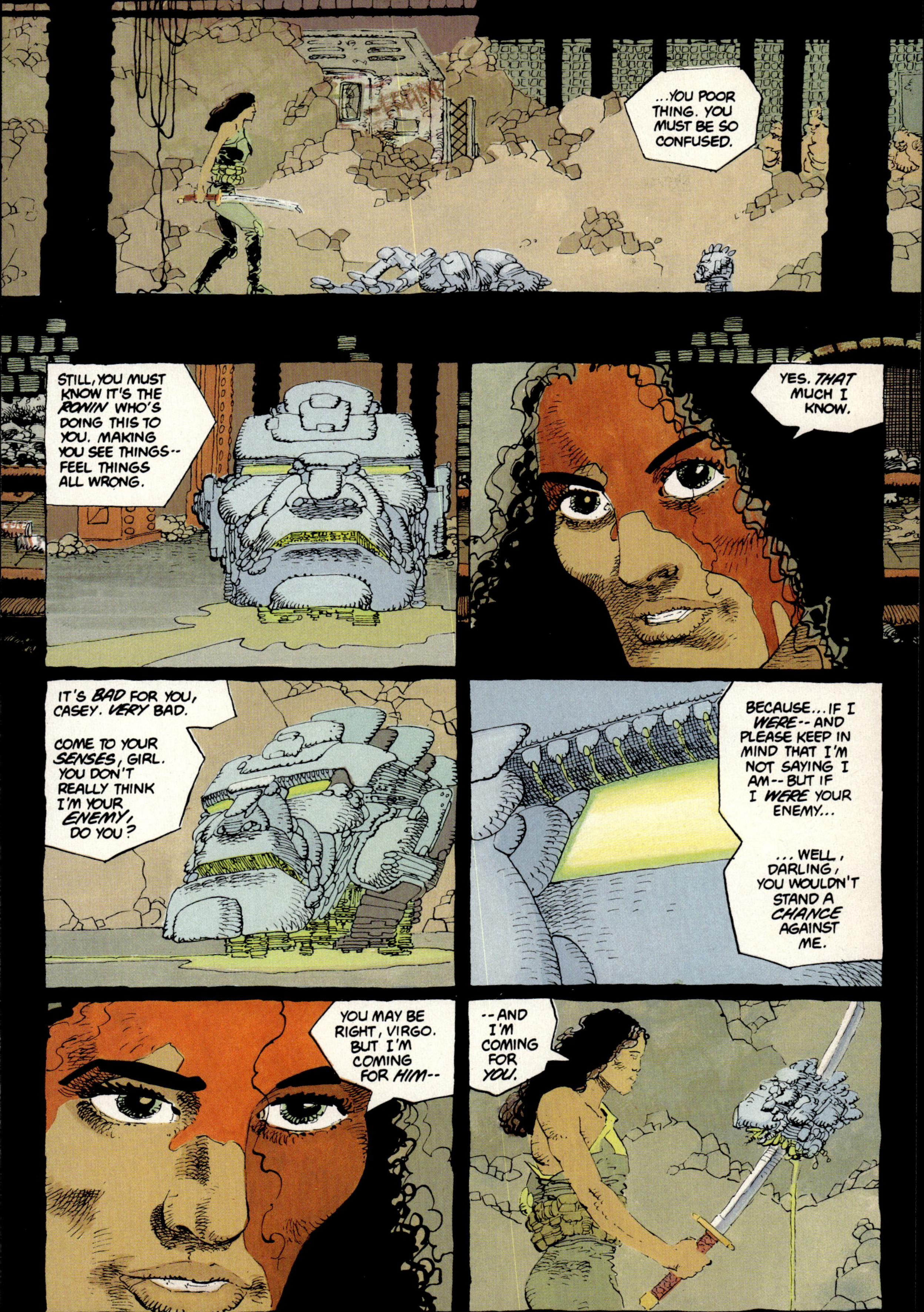
...YOU POOR THING. YOU MUST BE SO CONFUSED.
STILL, YOU MUST KNOW IT'S THE RONIN WHO'S DOING THIS TO YOU. MAKING YOU SEE THINGS-- FEEL THINGS ALL WRONG.
YES. THAT MUCH I KNOW.
IT'S BAD FOR YOU, CASEY. VERY BAD.
COME TO YOUR SENSES, GIRL. YOU DON'T REALLY THINK I'M YOUR ENEMY, DO YOU?
BECAUSE...IF I WERE-- AND PLEASE KEEP IN MIND THAT I'M NOT SAYING I AM-- BUT IF I WERE YOUR ENEMY...
...WELL, DARLING, YOU WOULDN'T STAND A CHANCE AGAINST ME.
YOU MAY BE RIGHT, VIRGO. BUT I'M COMING FOR HIM--
--AND I'M COMING FOR YOU.

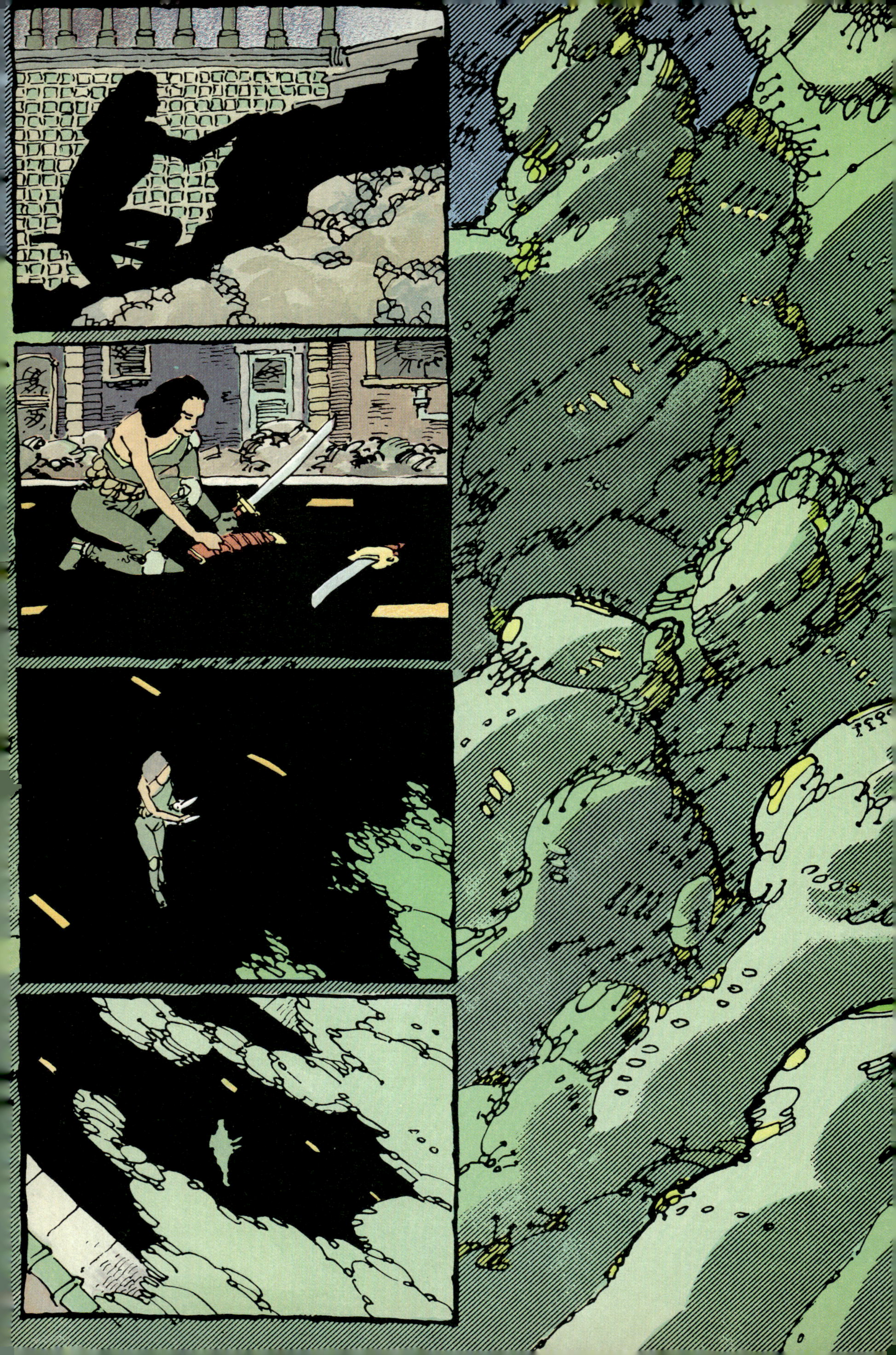

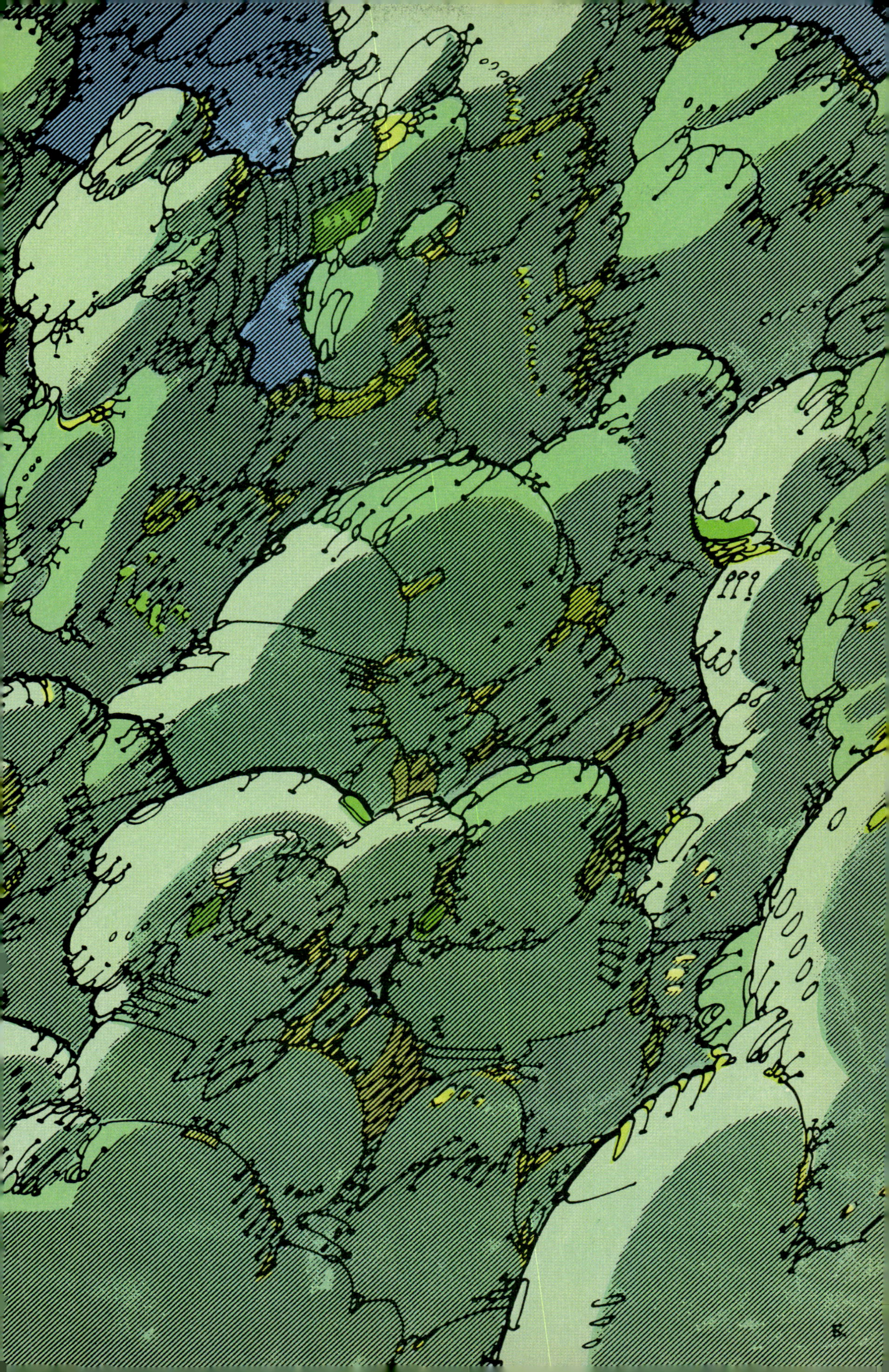

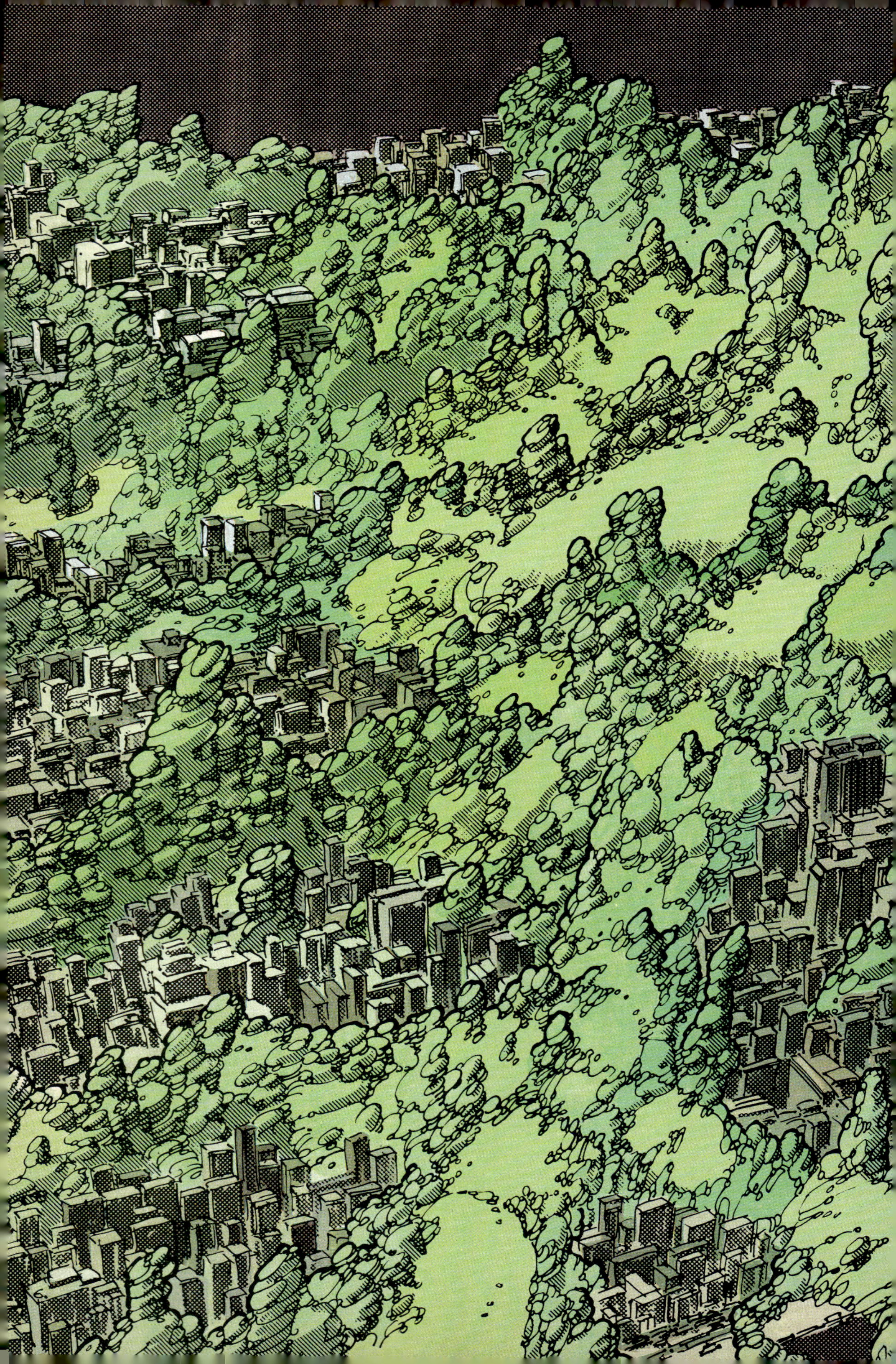

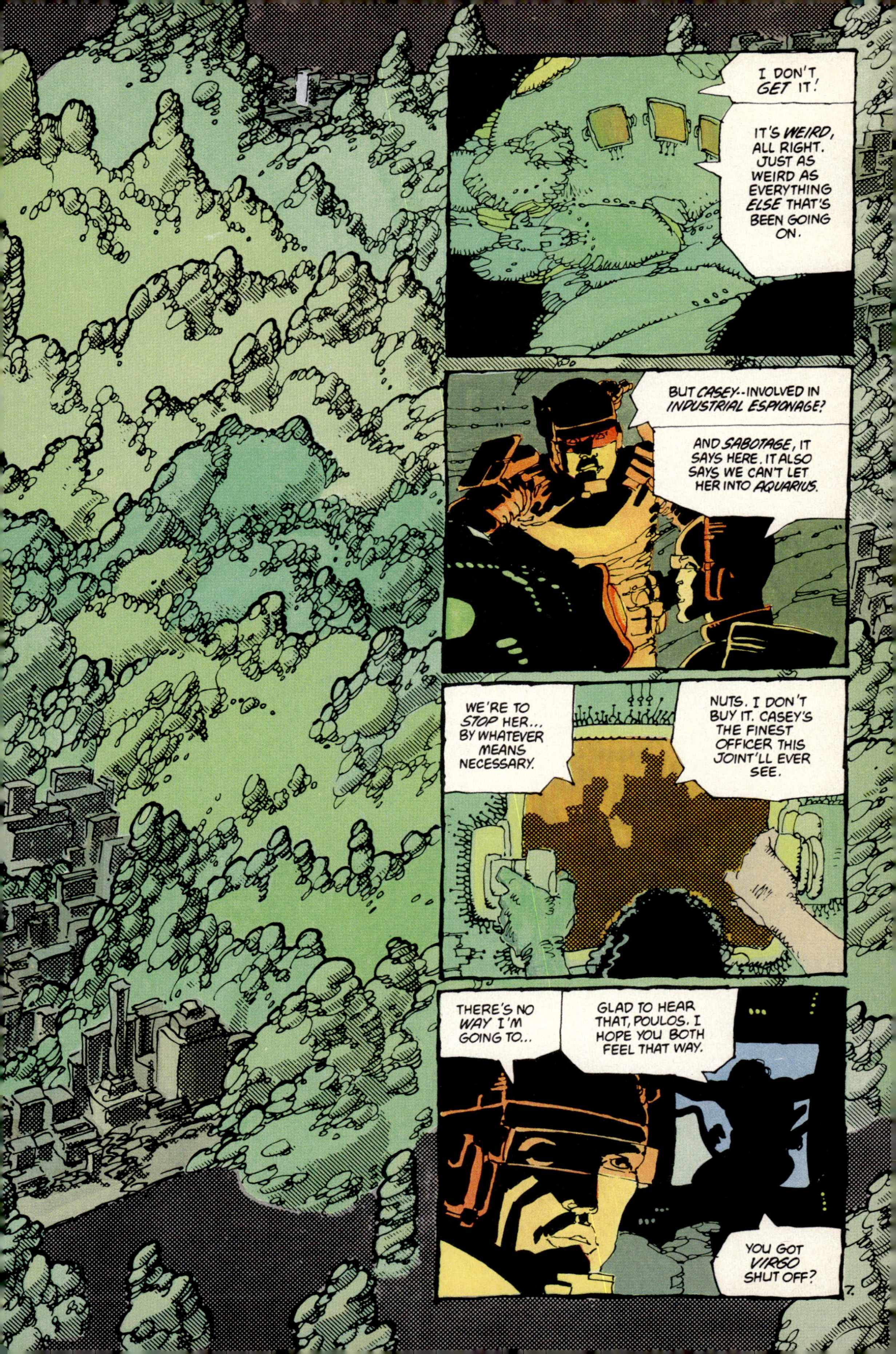
I DON'T GET IT!
IT'S WEIRD, ALL RIGHT. JUST AS WEIRD AS EVERYTHING ELSE THAT'S BEEN GOING ON.
BUT CASEY--INVOLVED IN INDUSTRIAL ESPIONAGE?
AND SABOTAGE, IT SAYS HERE. IT ALSO SAYS WE CAN'T LET HER INTO AQUARIUS.
WE'RE TO STOP HER... BY WHATEVER MEANS NECESSARY.
NUTS. I DON'T BUY IT. CASEY'S THE FINEST OFFICER THIS JOINT'LL EVER SEE.
THERE'S NO WAY I'M GOING TO...
GLAD TO HEAR THAT, POULOS. I HOPE YOU BOTH FEEL THAT WAY.
YOU GOT VIRGO SHUT OFF?
7.

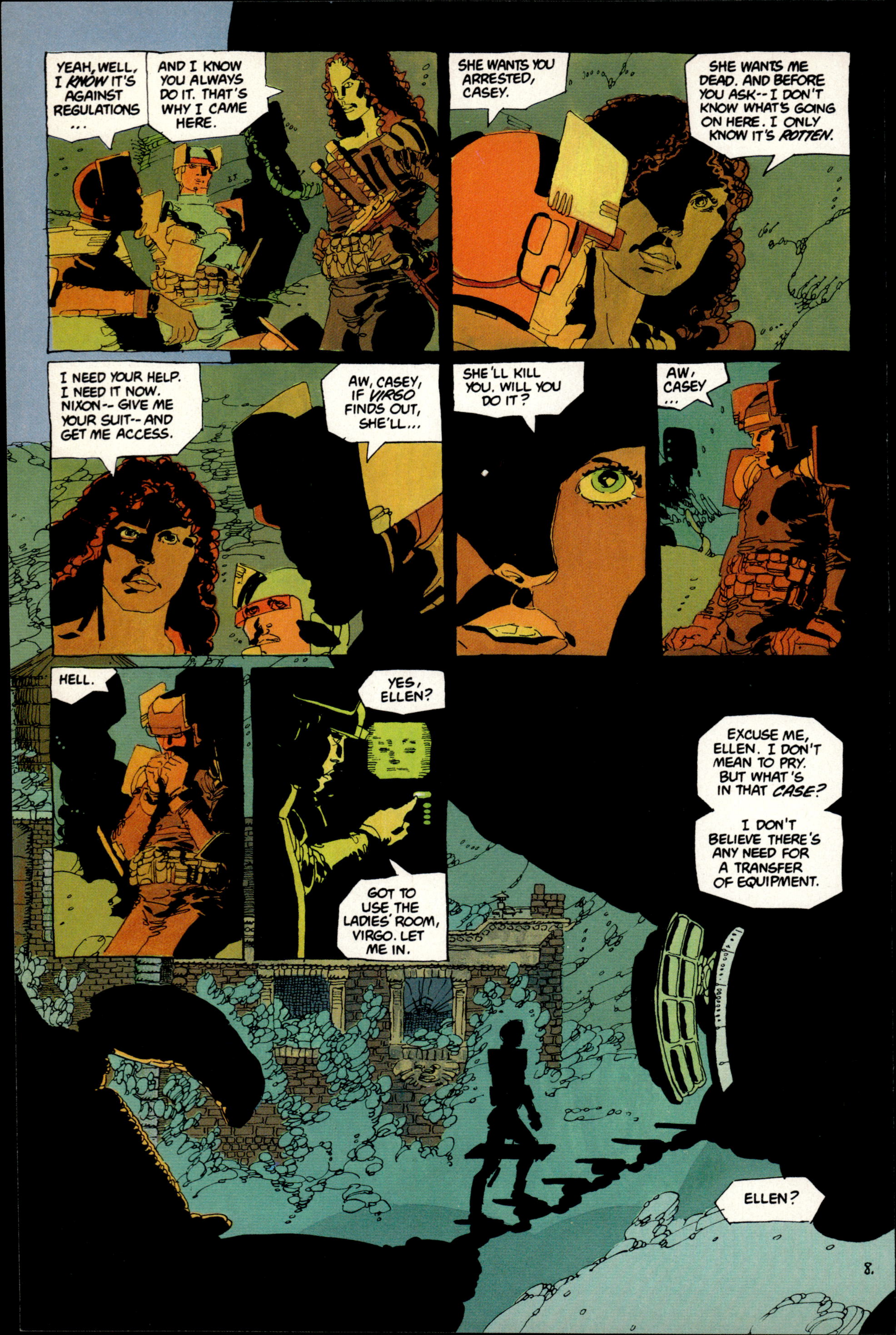
YEAH, WELL, I KNOW IT'S AGAINST REGULATIONS ...
AND I KNOW YOU ALWAYS DO IT. THAT'S WHY I CAME HERE.
SHE WANTS YOU ARRESTED, CASEY.
SHE WANTS ME DEAD. AND BEFORE YOU ASK-- I DON'T KNOW WHAT'S GOING ON HERE. I ONLY KNOW IT'S ROTTEN.
I NEED YOUR HELP. I NEED IT NOW. NIXON-- GIVE ME YOUR SUIT-- AND GET ME ACCESS.
AW, CASEY, IF VIRGO FINDS OUT, SHE'LL...
SHE'LL KILL YOU. WILL YOU DO IT?
AW, CASEY ...
HELL.
YES, ELLEN?
GOT TO USE THE LADIES' ROOM, VIRGO. LET ME IN.
EXCUSE ME, ELLEN. I DON'T MEAN TO PRY. BUT WHAT'S IN THAT CASE?
I DON'T BELIEVE THERE'S ANY NEED FOR A TRANSFER OF EQUIPMENT.
ELLEN?

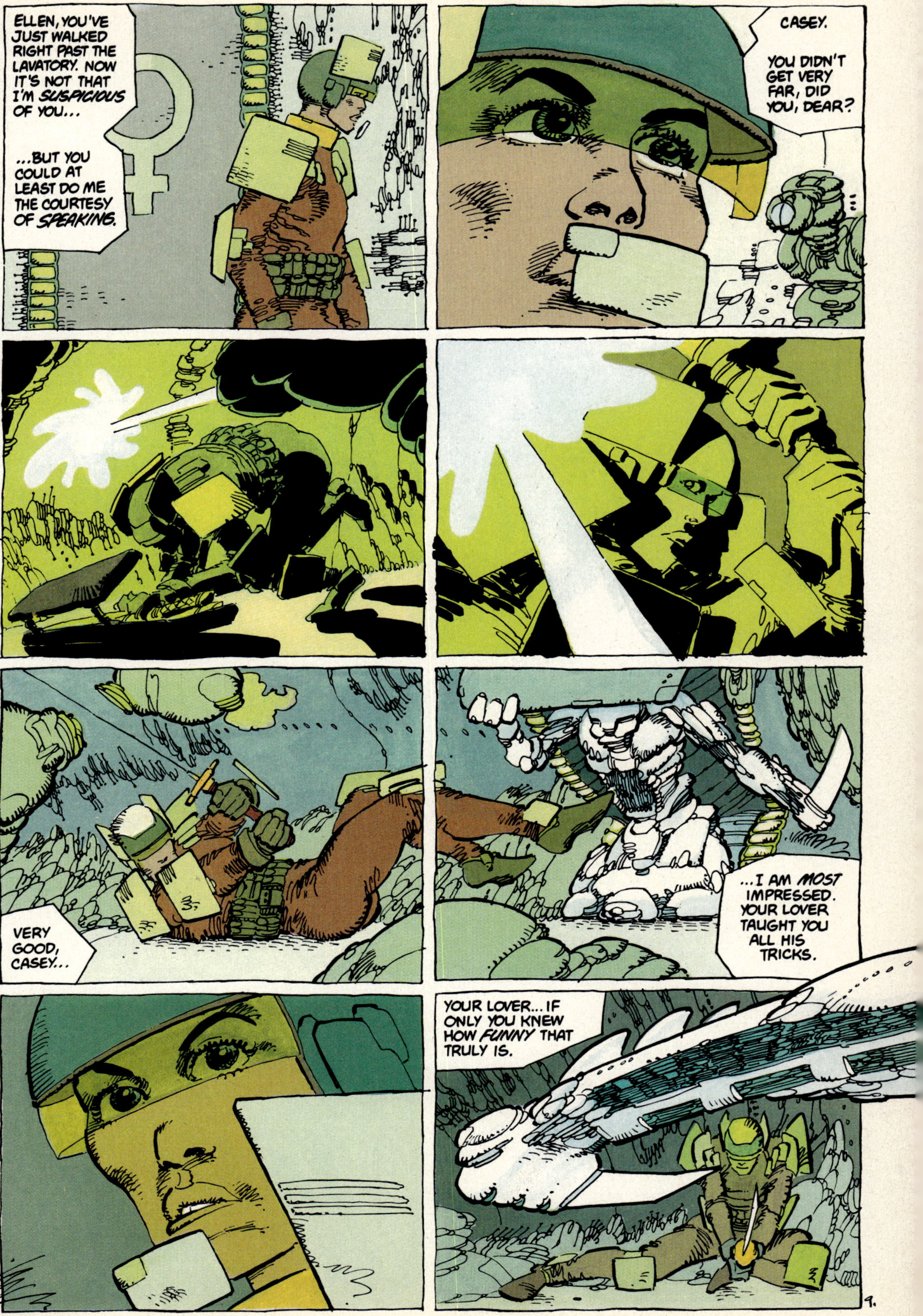
ELLEN, YOU'VE JUST WALKED RIGHT PAST THE LAVATORY. NOW IT'S NOT THAT I'M SUSPICIOUS OF YOU...
...BUT YOU COULD AT LEAST DO ME THE COURTESY OF SPEAKING.
CASEY.
YOU DIDN'T GET VERY FAR, DID YOU, DEAR?
VERY GOOD, CASEY...
...I AM MOST IMPRESSED. YOUR LOVER TAUGHT YOU ALL HIS TRICKS.
YOUR LOVER... IF ONLY YOU KNEW HOW FUNNY THAT TRULY IS.

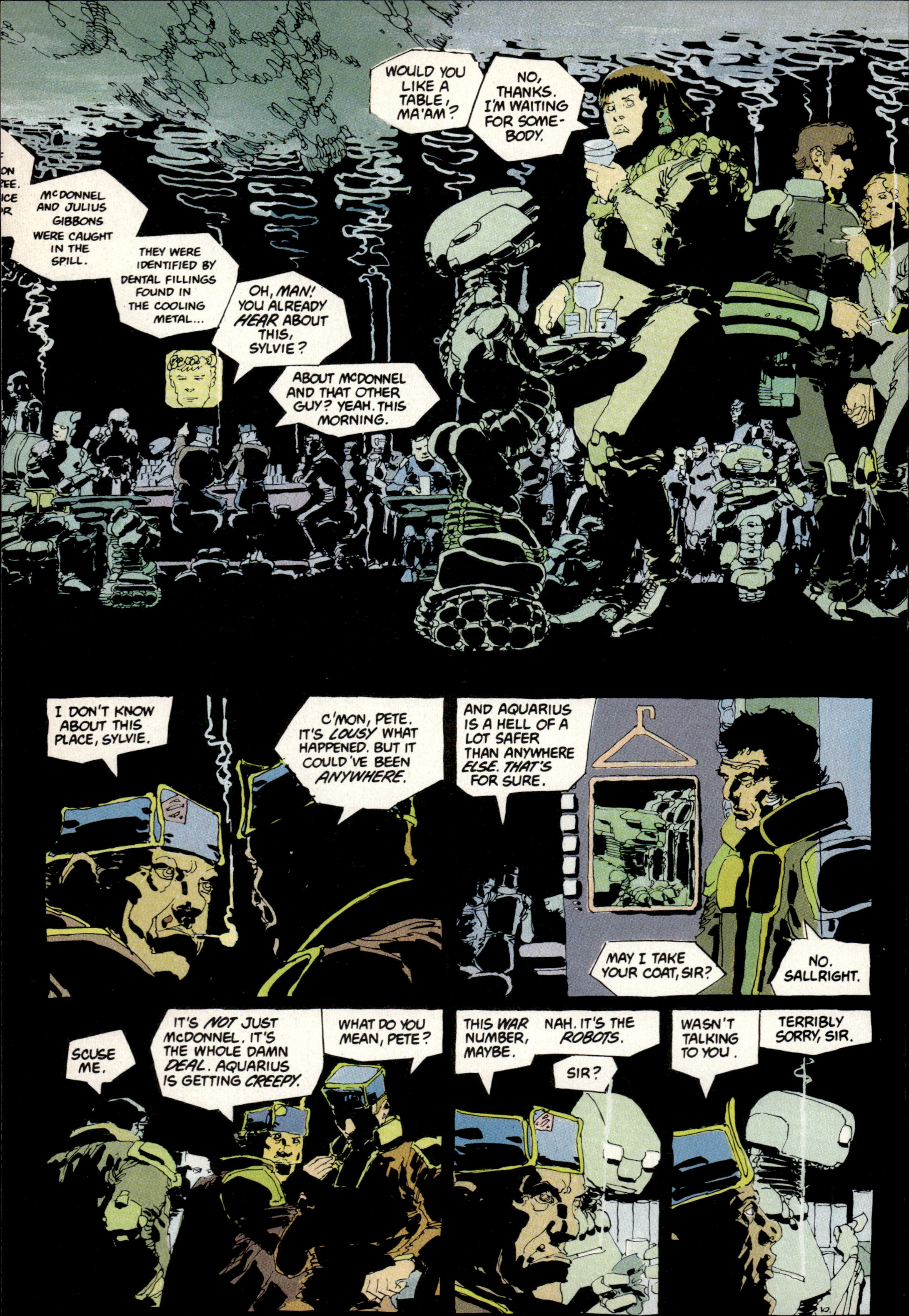

McDONNEL AND JULIUS GIBBONS WERE CAUGHT IN THE SPILL.
THEY WERE IDENTIFIED BY DENTAL FILLINGS FOUND IN THE COOLING METAL...
OH, MAN! YOU ALREADY HEAR ABOUT THIS, SYLVIE?
ABOUT McDONNEL AND THAT OTHER GUY? YEAH. THIS MORNING.
WOULD YOU LIKE A TABLE, MA'AM?
NO, THANKS. I'M WAITING FOR SOME-BODY.
I DON'T KNOW ABOUT THIS PLACE, SYLVIE.
C'MON, PETE. IT'S LOUSY WHAT HAPPENED. BUT IT COULD'VE BEEN ANYWHERE.
AND AQUARIUS IS A HELL OF A LOT SAFER THAN ANYWHERE ELSE. THAT'S FOR SURE.
MAY I TAKE YOUR COAT, SIR?
NO. SALLRIGHT.
SCUSE ME.
IT'S NOT JUST McDONNEL. IT'S THE WHOLE DAMN DEAL. AQUARIUS IS GETTING CREEPY.
WHAT DO YOU MEAN, PETE?
THIS WAR NUMBER, MAYBE.
NAH. IT'S THE ROBOTS.
SIR?
WASN'T TALKING TO YOU.
TERRIBLY SORRY, SIR.

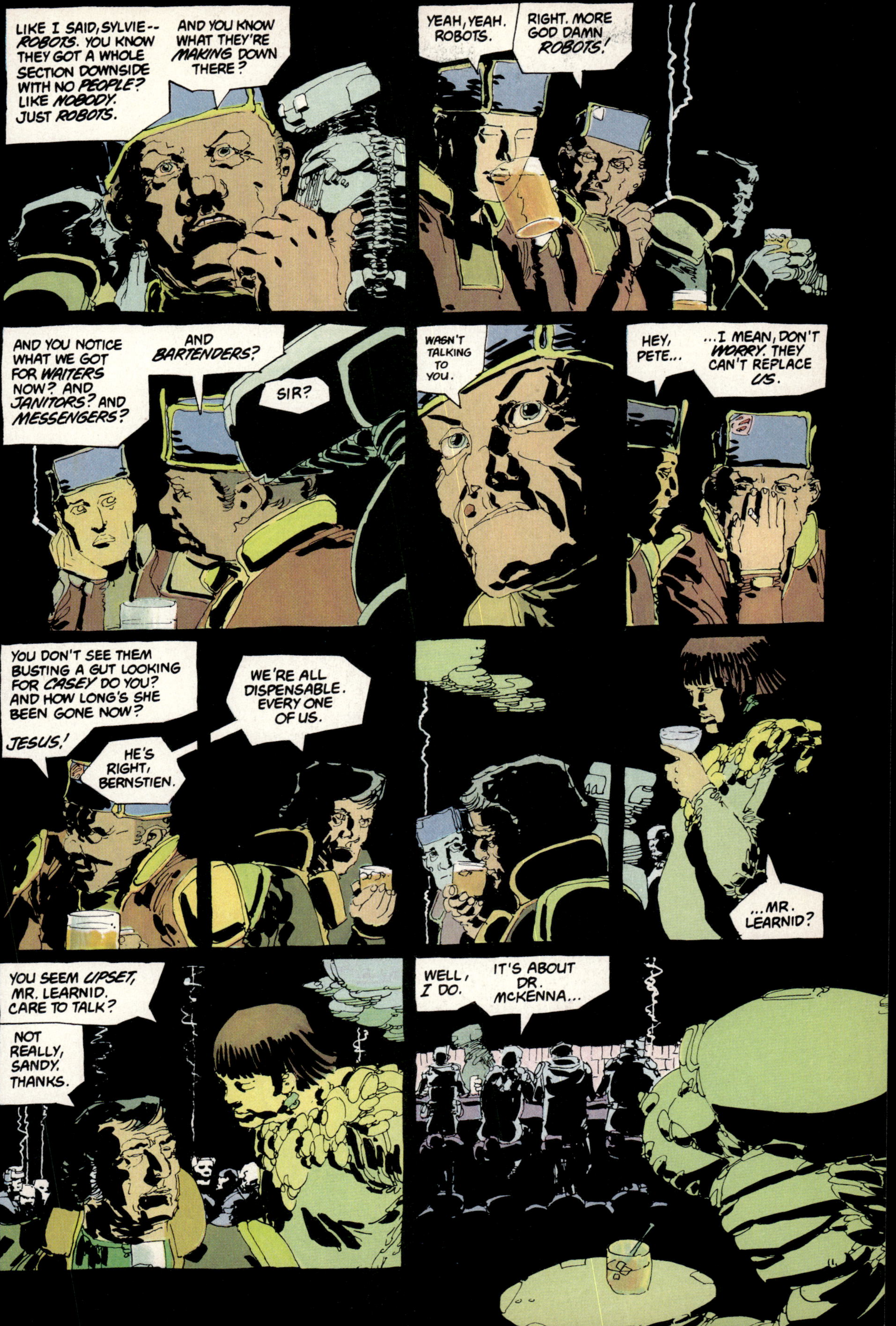

LIKE I SAID, SYLVIE-- ROBOTS. YOU KNOW THEY GOT A WHOLE SECTION DOWNSIDE WITH NO PEOPLE? LIKE NOBODY. JUST ROBOTS.
AND YOU KNOW WHAT THEY'RE MAKING DOWN THERE?
YEAH, YEAH. ROBOTS.
RIGHT. MORE GOD DAMN ROBOTS!
AND YOU NOTICE WHAT WE GOT FOR WAITERS NOW? AND JANITORS? AND MESSENGERS?
AND BARTENDERS?
SIR?
WASN'T TALKING TO YOU.
HEY, PETE...
...I MEAN, DON'T WORRY. THEY CAN'T REPLACE US.
YOU DON'T SEE THEM BUSTING A GUT LOOKING FOR CASEY DO YOU? AND HOW LONG'S SHE BEEN GONE NOW?
JESUS!
WE'RE ALL DISPENSABLE. EVERY ONE OF US.
HE'S RIGHT, BERNSTIEN.
...MR. LEARNID?
YOU SEEM UPSET, MR. LEARNID. CARE TO TALK?
NOT REALLY, SANDY. THANKS.
WELL, I DO.
IT'S ABOUT DR. McKENNA...

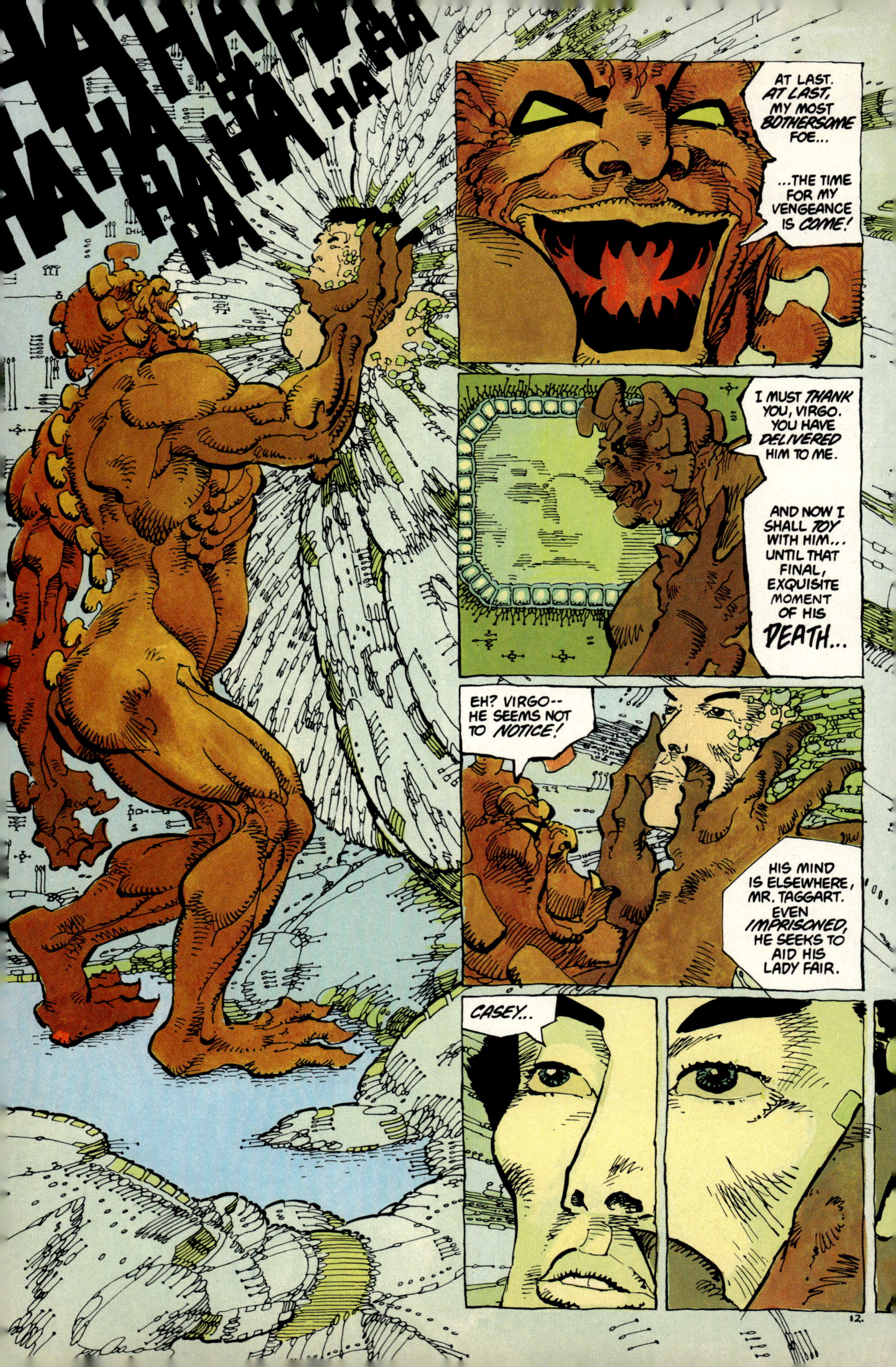
HAHAHAHAHAHA HA HA HA HA HA HA HA HA
AT LAST. AT LAST, MY MOST BOTHERSOME FOE...
...THE TIME FOR MY VENGEANCE IS COME!
I MUST THANK YOU, VIRGO. YOU HAVE DELIVERED HIM TO ME.
AND NOW I SHALL TOY WITH HIM... UNTIL THAT FINAL, EXQUISITE MOMENT OF HIS DEATH...
EH? VIRGO-- HE SEEMS NOT TO NOTICE!
HIS MIND IS ELSEWHERE, MR. TAGGART. EVEN IMPRISONED, HE SEEKS TO AID HIS LADY FAIR.
CASEY...
12.

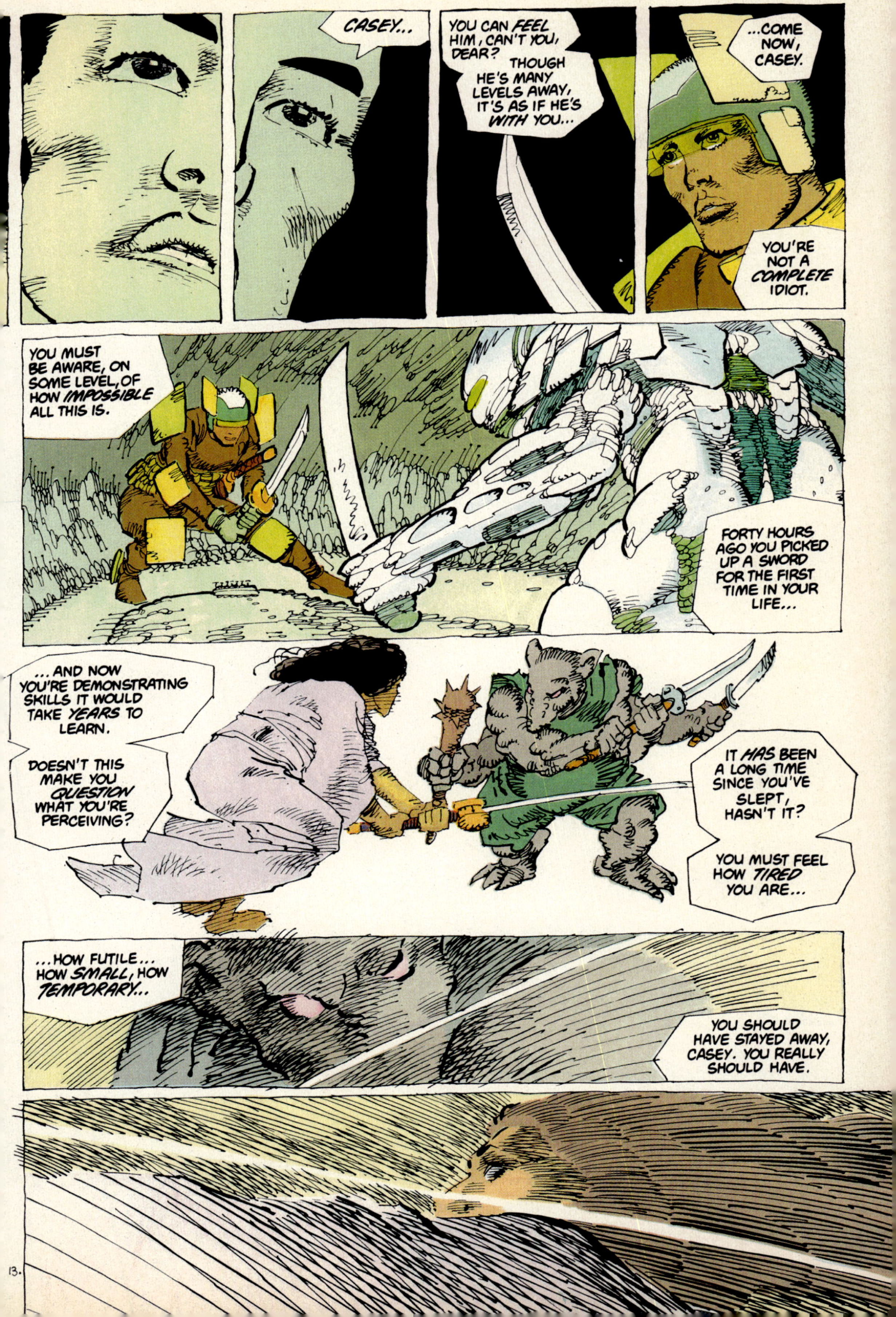
CASEY...
YOU CAN FEEL HIM, CAN'T YOU, DEAR?
THOUGH HE'S MANY LEVELS AWAY, IT'S AS IF HE'S WITH YOU...
...COME NOW, CASEY.
YOU'RE NOT A COMPLETE IDIOT.
YOU MUST BE AWARE, ON SOME LEVEL, OF HOW IMPOSSIBLE ALL THIS IS.
FORTY HOURS AGO YOU PICKED UP A SWORD FOR THE FIRST TIME IN YOUR LIFE...
...AND NOW YOU'RE DEMONSTRATING SKILLS IT WOULD TAKE YEARS TO LEARN.
DOESN'T THIS MAKE YOU QUESTION WHAT YOU'RE PERCEIVING?
IT HAS BEEN A LONG TIME SINCE YOU'VE SLEPT, HASN'T IT?
YOU MUST FEEL HOW TIRED YOU ARE...
...HOW FUTILE... HOW SMALL, HOW TEMPORARY...
YOU SHOULD HAVE STAYED AWAY, CASEY. YOU REALLY SHOULD HAVE.

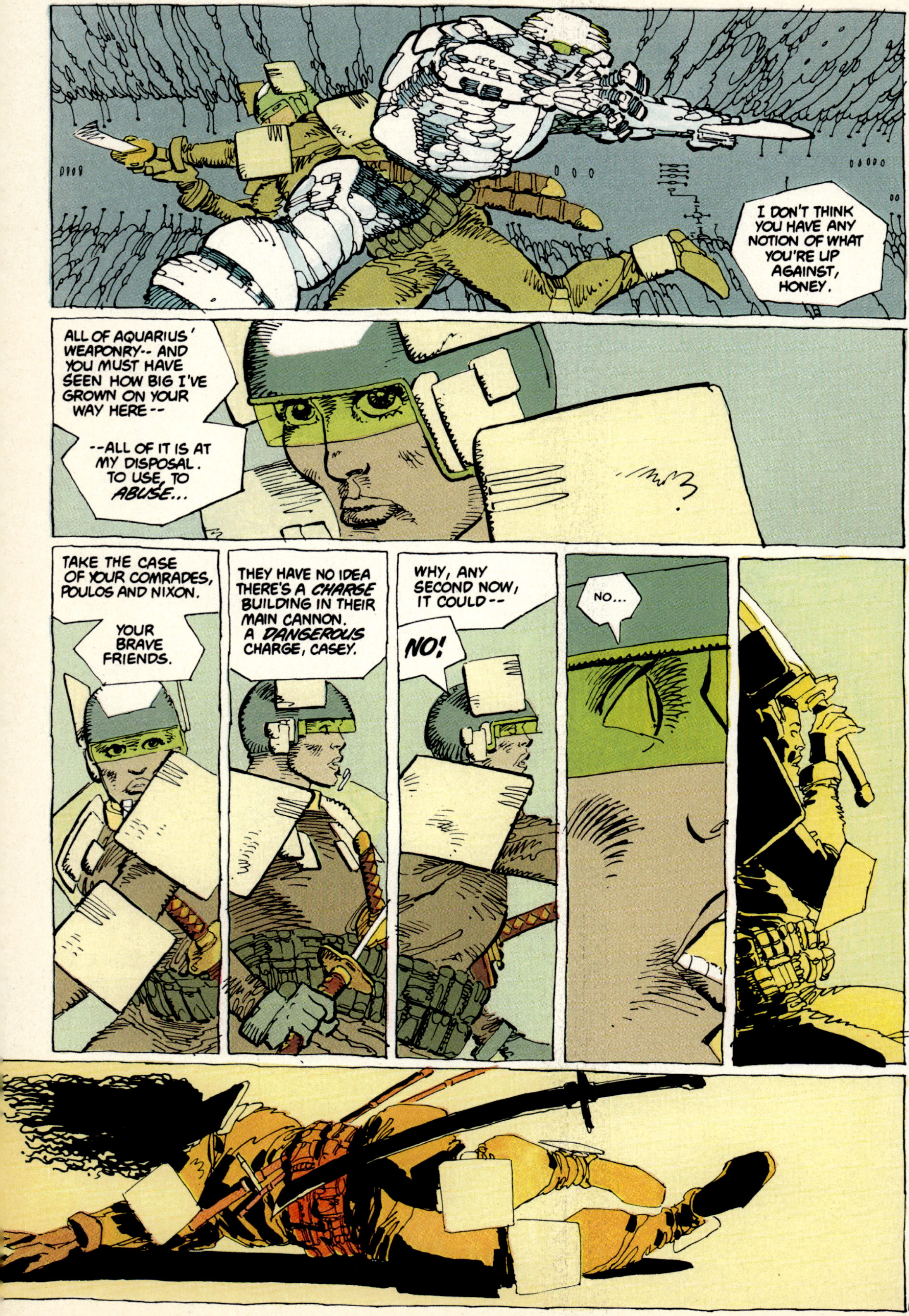
I DON'T THINK YOU HAVE ANY NOTION OF WHAT YOU'RE UP AGAINST, HONEY.
ALL OF AQUARIUS' WEAPONRY-- AND YOU MUST HAVE SEEN HOW BIG I'VE GROWN ON YOUR WAY HERE--
--ALL OF IT IS AT MY DISPOSAL. TO USE, TO ABUSE...
TAKE THE CASE OF YOUR COMRADES, POULOS AND NIXON.
YOUR BRAVE FRIENDS.
THEY HAVE NO IDEA THERE'S A CHARGE BUILDING IN THEIR MAIN CANNON. A DANGEROUS CHARGE, CASEY.
WHY, ANY SECOND NOW, IT COULD--
NO!
NO...

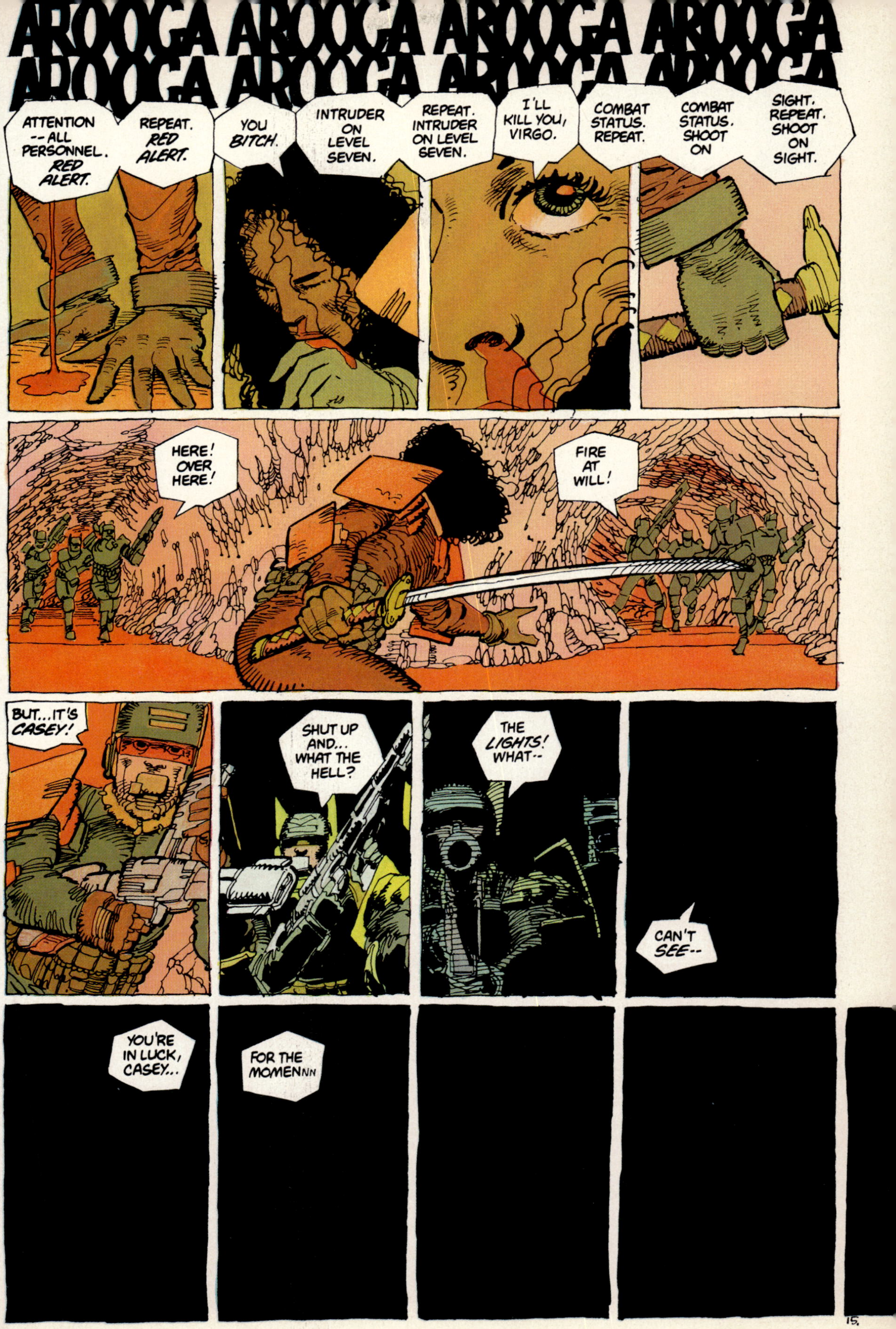
AROOGA AROOGA AROOGA AROOGA
AROOGA AROOGA AROOGA AROOGA
ATTENTION --ALL PERSONNEL. RED ALERT.
REPEAT. RED ALERT.
YOU BITCH.
INTRUDER ON LEVEL SEVEN.
REPEAT. INTRUDER ON LEVEL SEVEN.
I'LL KILL YOU, VIRGO.
COMBAT STATUS. REPEAT.
COMBAT STATUS. SHOOT ON
SIGHT. REPEAT. SHOOT ON SIGHT.
HERE! OVER HERE!
FIRE AT WILL!
BUT...IT'S CASEY!
SHUT UP AND... WHAT THE HELL?
THE LIGHTS! WHAT--
CAN'T SEE--
YOU'RE IN LUCK, CASEY...
FOR THE MOMENNN

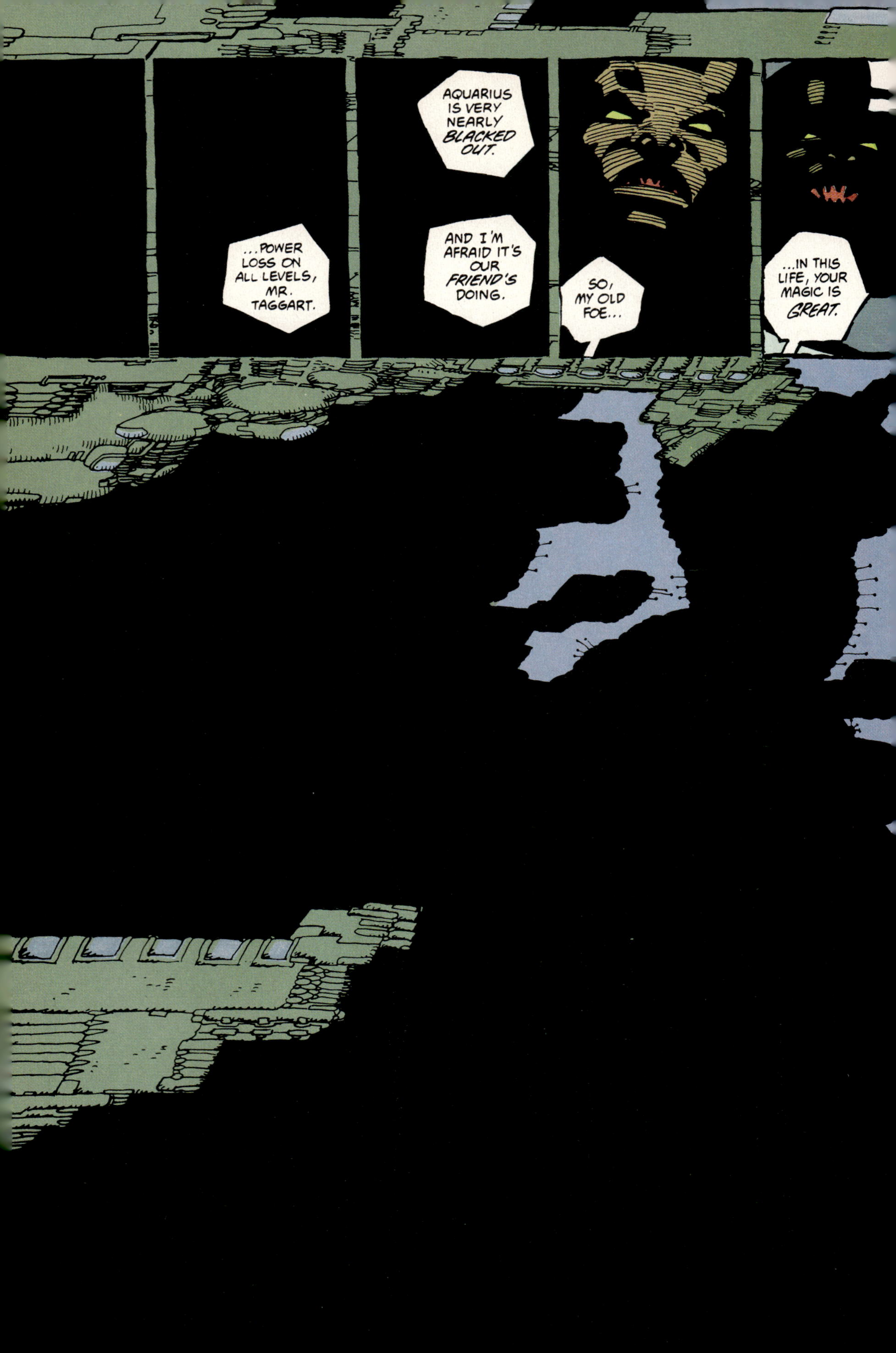
...POWER LOSS ON ALL LEVELS, MR. TAGGART.
AQUARIUS IS VERY NEARLY BLACKED OUT.
AND I'M AFRAID IT'S OUR FRIEND'S DOING.
SO, MY OLD FOE...
...IN THIS LIFE, YOUR MAGIC IS GREAT.

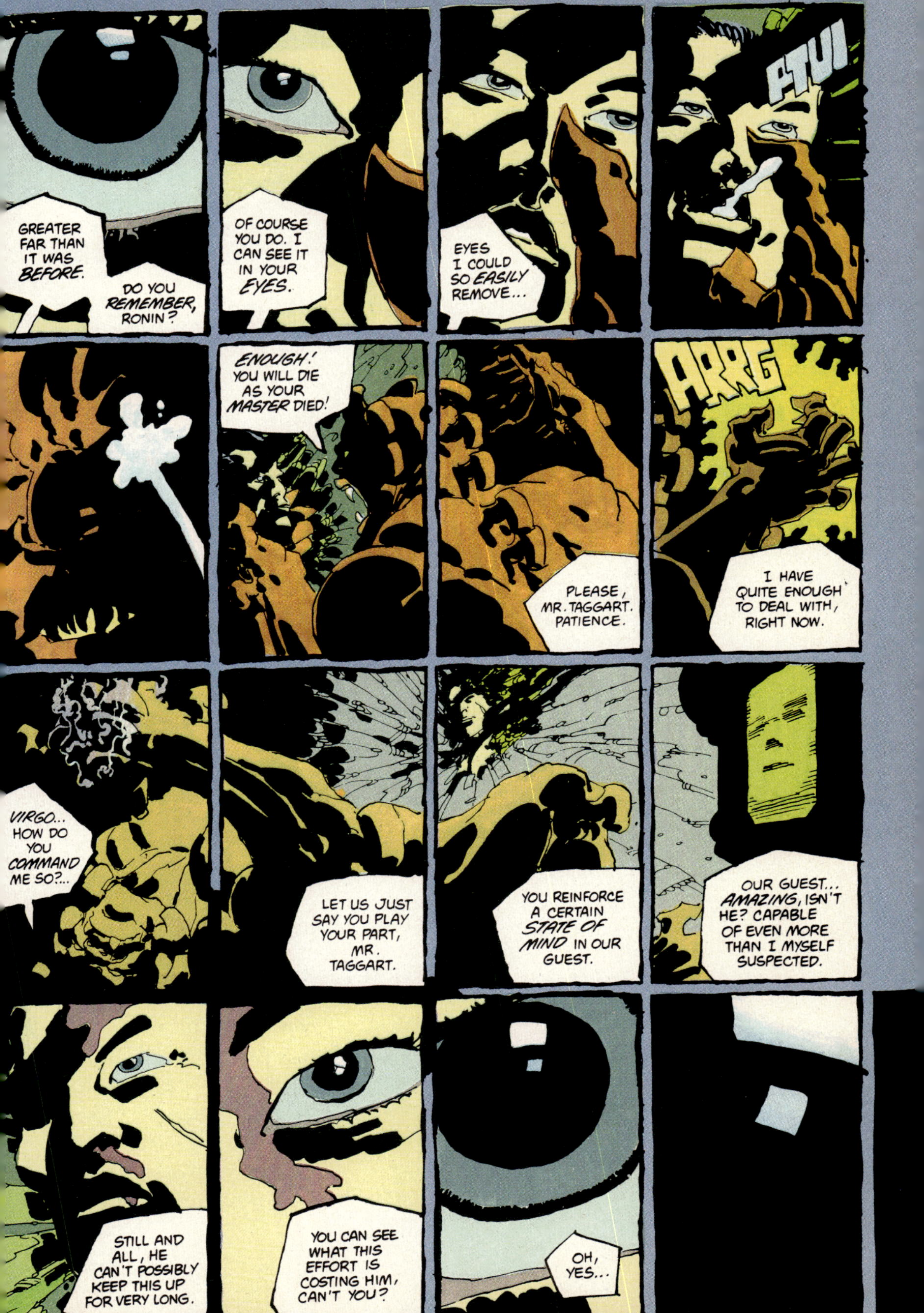
GREATER FAR THAN IT WAS BEFORE.
DO YOU REMEMBER, RONIN?
OF COURSE YOU DO. I CAN SEE IT IN YOUR EYES.
EYES I COULD SO EASILY REMOVE...
PTUI
ENOUGH! YOU WILL DIE AS YOUR MASTER DIED!
PLEASE, MR. TAGGART. PATIENCE.
ARRG
I HAVE QUITE ENOUGH TO DEAL WITH, RIGHT NOW.
VIRGO... HOW DO YOU COMMAND ME SO?...
LET US JUST SAY YOU PLAY YOUR PART, MR. TAGGART.
YOU REINFORCE A CERTAIN STATE OF MIND IN OUR GUEST.
OUR GUEST... AMAZING, ISN'T HE? CAPABLE OF EVEN MORE THAN I MYSELF SUSPECTED.
STILL AND ALL, HE CAN'T POSSIBLY KEEP THIS UP FOR VERY LONG.
YOU CAN SEE WHAT THIS EFFORT IS COSTING HIM, CAN'T YOU?
OH, YES...

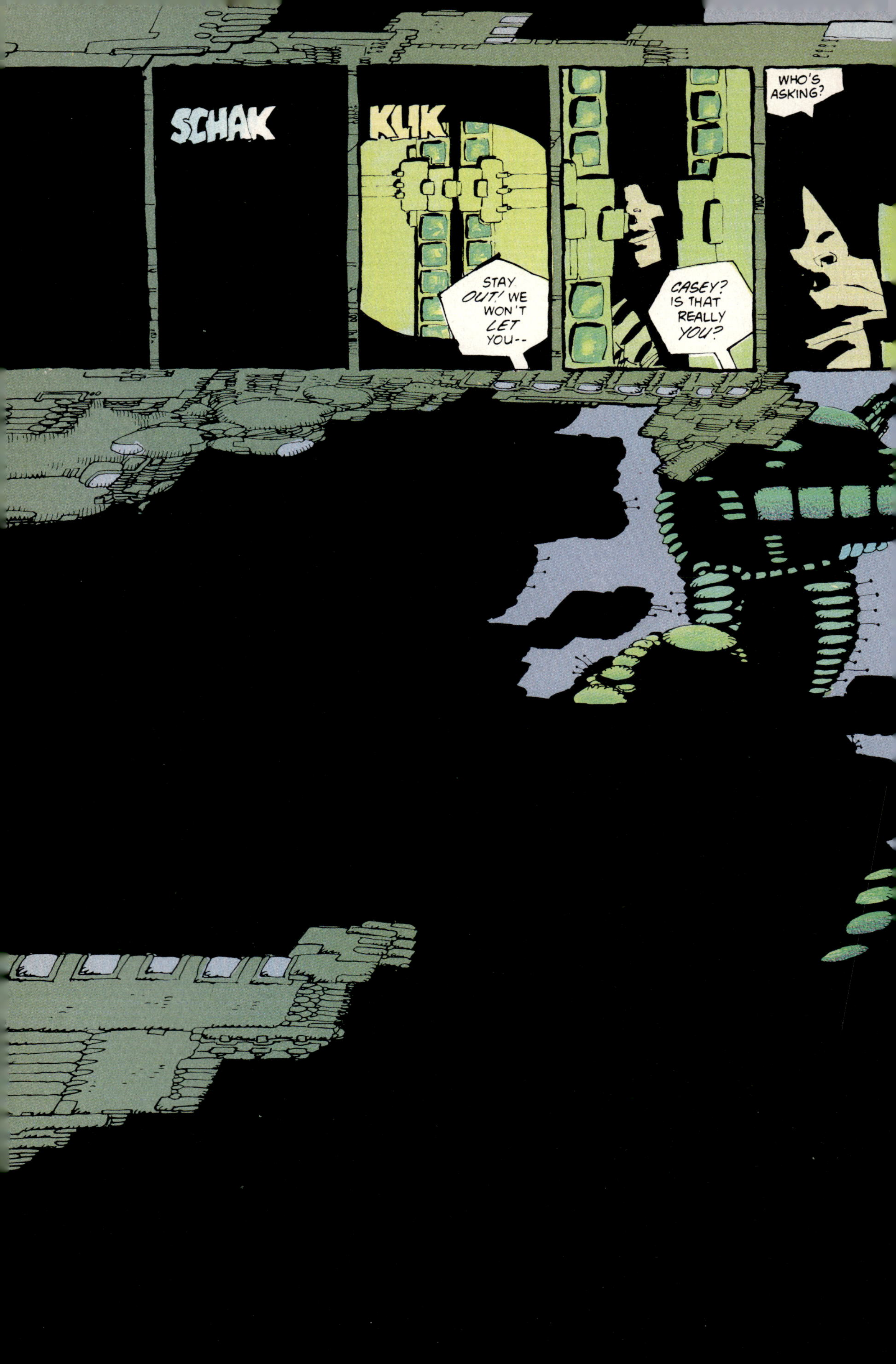
SCHAK
KLIK
STAY OUT! WE WON'T LET YOU--
CASEY? IS THAT REALLY YOU?
WHO'S ASKING?

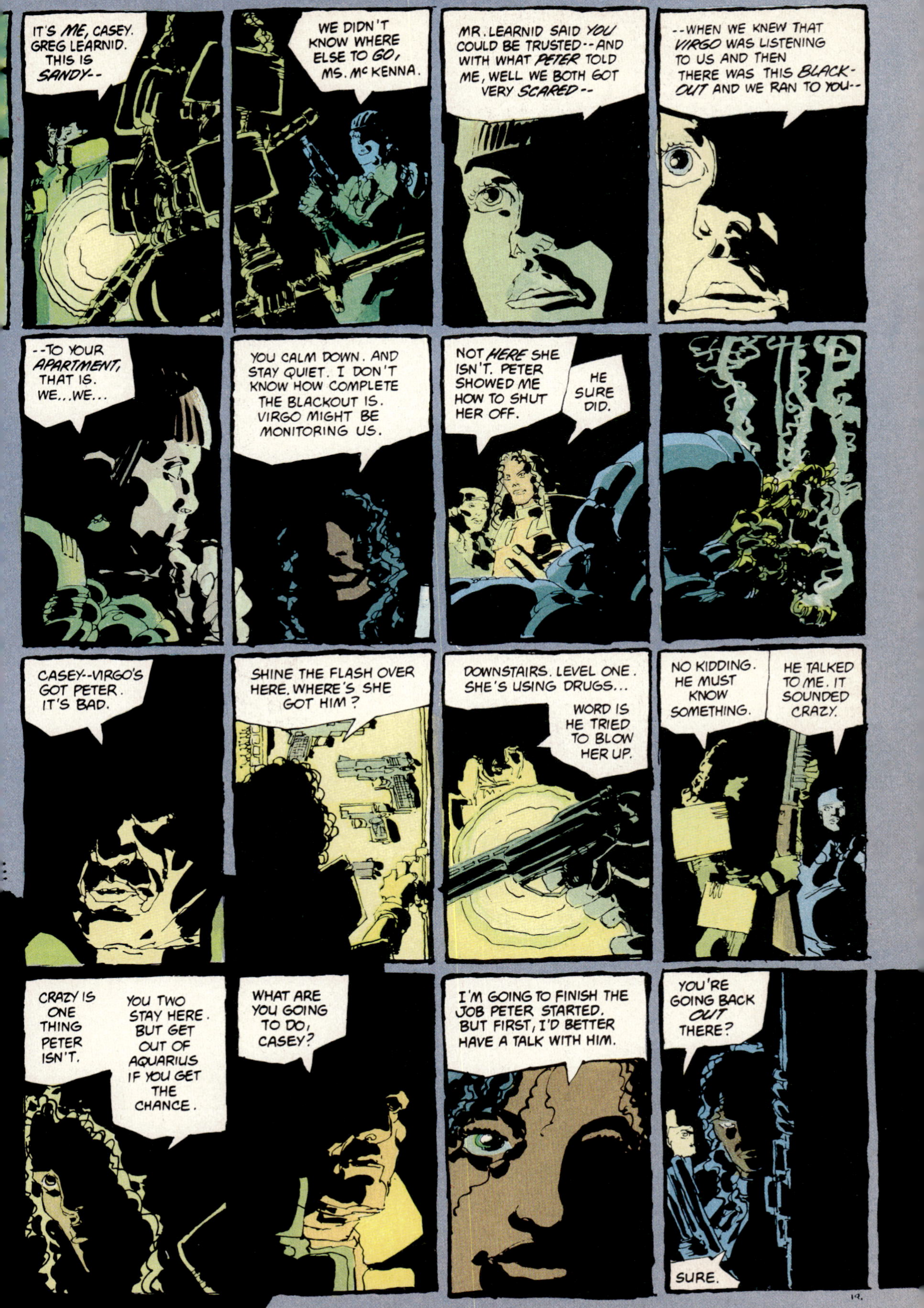

IT'S ME, CASEY. GREG LEARNID. THIS IS SANDY--
WE DIDN'T KNOW WHERE ELSE TO GO, MS. McKENNA.
MR. LEARNID SAID YOU COULD BE TRUSTED--AND WITH WHAT PETER TOLD ME, WELL WE BOTH GOT VERY SCARED--
--WHEN WE KNEW THAT VIRGO WAS LISTENING TO US AND THEN THERE WAS THIS BLACK-OUT AND WE RAN TO YOU--
--TO YOUR APARTMENT, THAT IS. WE...WE...
YOU CALM DOWN. AND STAY QUIET. I DON'T KNOW HOW COMPLETE THE BLACKOUT IS. VIRGO MIGHT BE MONITORING US.
NOT HERE SHE ISN'T. PETER SHOWED ME HOW TO SHUT HER OFF.
HE SURE DID.
CASEY--VIRGO'S GOT PETER. IT'S BAD.
SHINE THE FLASH OVER HERE. WHERE'S SHE GOT HIM?
DOWNSTAIRS. LEVEL ONE. SHE'S USING DRUGS...
WORD IS HE TRIED TO BLOW HER UP.
NO KIDDING. HE MUST KNOW SOMETHING.
HE TALKED TO ME. IT SOUNDED CRAZY.
CRAZY IS ONE THING PETER ISN'T.
YOU TWO STAY HERE. BUT GET OUT OF AQUARIUS IF YOU GET THE CHANCE.
WHAT ARE YOU GOING TO DO, CASEY?
I'M GOING TO FINISH THE JOB PETER STARTED. BUT FIRST, I'D BETTER HAVE A TALK WITH HIM.
YOU'RE GOING BACK OUT THERE?
SURE.

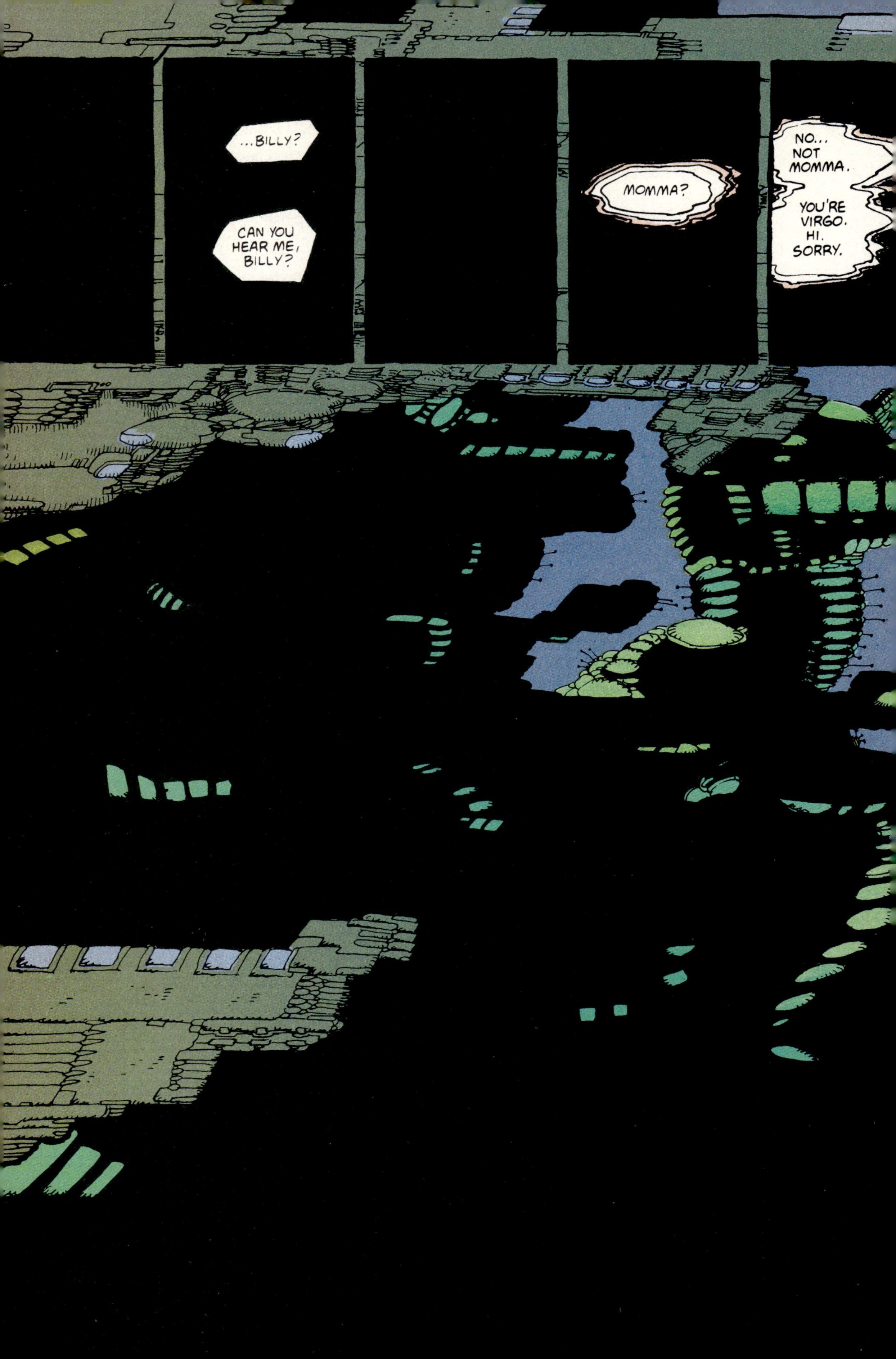

...BILLY?
CAN YOU HEAR ME, BILLY?
MOMMA?
NO... NOT MOMMA.
YOU'RE VIRGO. HI. SORRY.

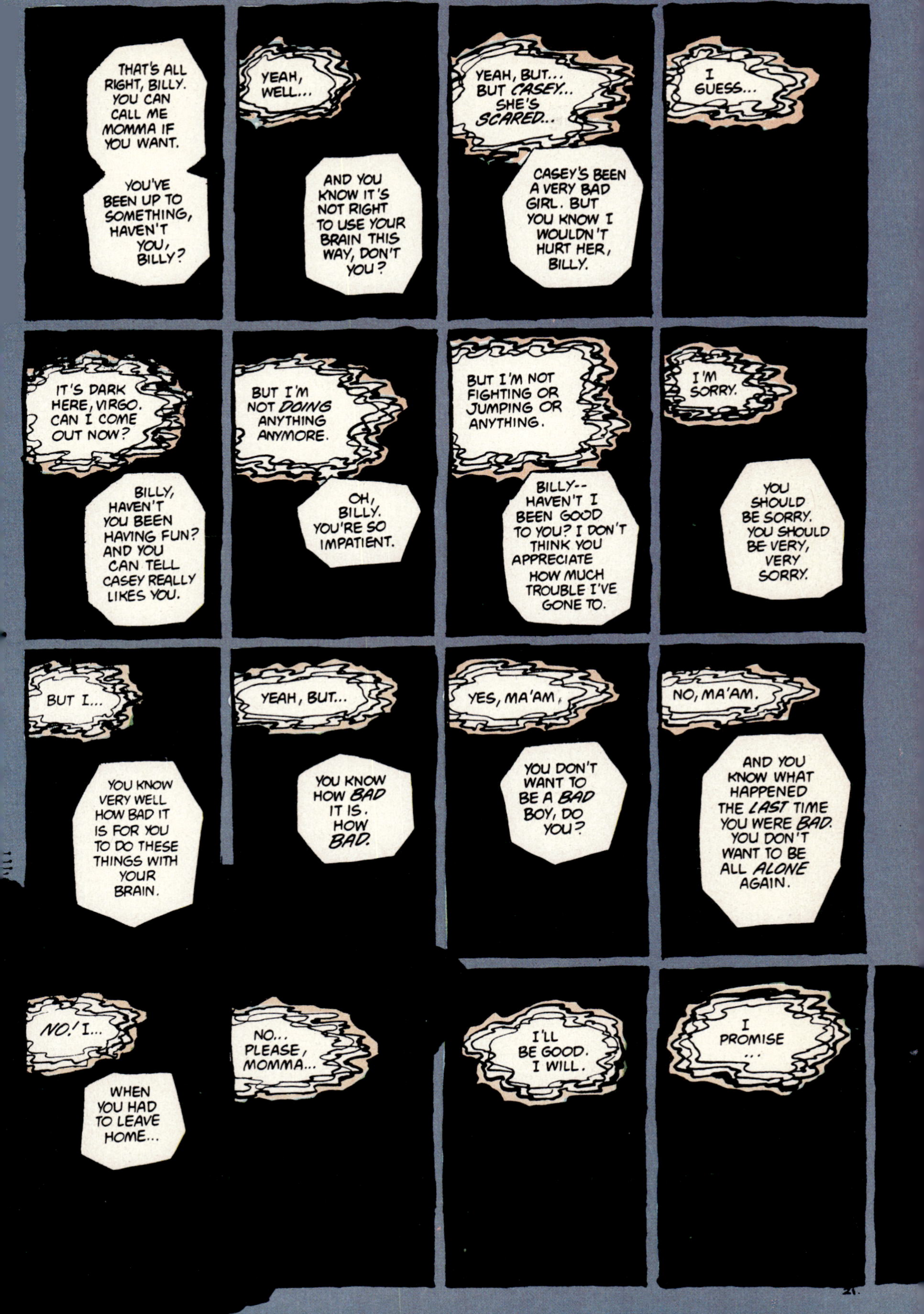
THAT'S ALL RIGHT, BILLY. YOU CAN CALL ME MOMMA IF YOU WANT.
YOU'VE BEEN UP TO SOMETHING, HAVEN'T YOU, BILLY?
YEAH, WELL...
AND YOU KNOW IT'S NOT RIGHT TO USE YOUR BRAIN THIS WAY, DON'T YOU?
YEAH, BUT... BUT CASEY... SHE'S SCARED...
CASEY'S BEEN A VERY BAD GIRL. BUT YOU KNOW I WOULDN'T HURT HER, BILLY.
I GUESS...
IT'S DARK HERE, VIRGO. CAN I COME OUT NOW?
BILLY, HAVEN'T YOU BEEN HAVING FUN? AND YOU CAN TELL CASEY REALLY LIKES YOU.
BUT I'M NOT DOING ANYTHING ANYMORE.
OH, BILLY. YOU'RE SO IMPATIENT.
BUT I'M NOT FIGHTING OR JUMPING OR ANYTHING.
BILLY-- HAVEN'T I BEEN GOOD TO YOU? I DON'T THINK YOU APPRECIATE HOW MUCH TROUBLE I'VE GONE TO.
I'M SORRY.
YOU SHOULD BE SORRY. YOU SHOULD BE VERY, VERY SORRY.
BUT I...
YOU KNOW VERY WELL HOW BAD IT IS FOR YOU TO DO THESE THINGS WITH YOUR BRAIN.
YEAH, BUT...
YOU KNOW HOW BAD IT IS. HOW BAD.
YES, MA'AM.
YOU DON'T WANT TO BE A BAD BOY, DO YOU?
NO, MA'AM.
AND YOU KNOW WHAT HAPPENED THE LAST TIME YOU WERE BAD. YOU DON'T WANT TO BE ALL ALONE AGAIN.
NO! I...
WHEN YOU HAD TO LEAVE HOME...
NO... PLEASE, MOMMA...
I'LL BE GOOD. I WILL.
I PROMISE ...

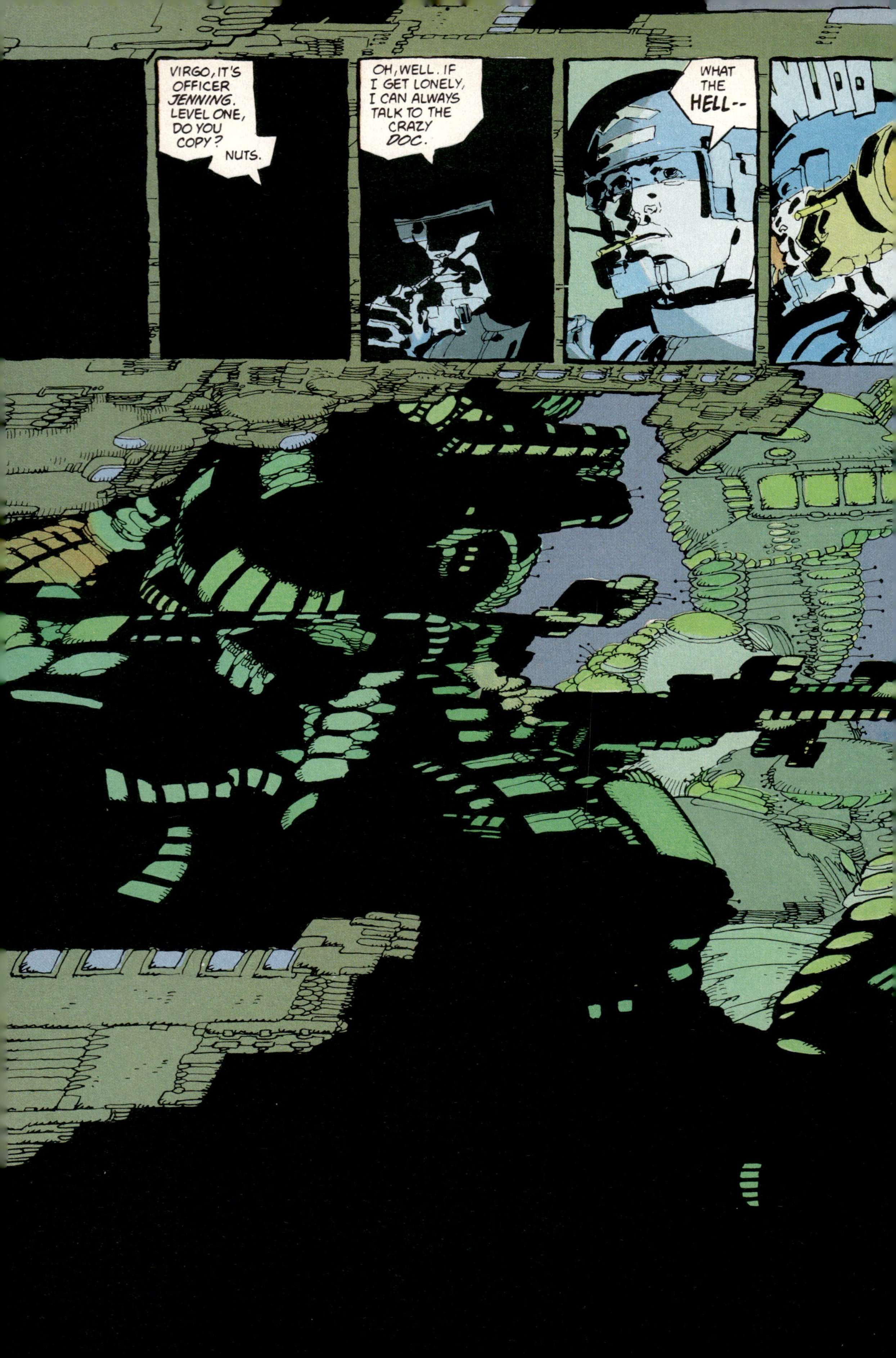
VIRGO, IT'S OFFICER JENNING. LEVEL ONE, DO YOU COPY?
NUTS.
OH, WELL. IF I GET LONELY, I CAN ALWAYS TALK TO THE CRAZY DOC.
WHAT THE HELL--

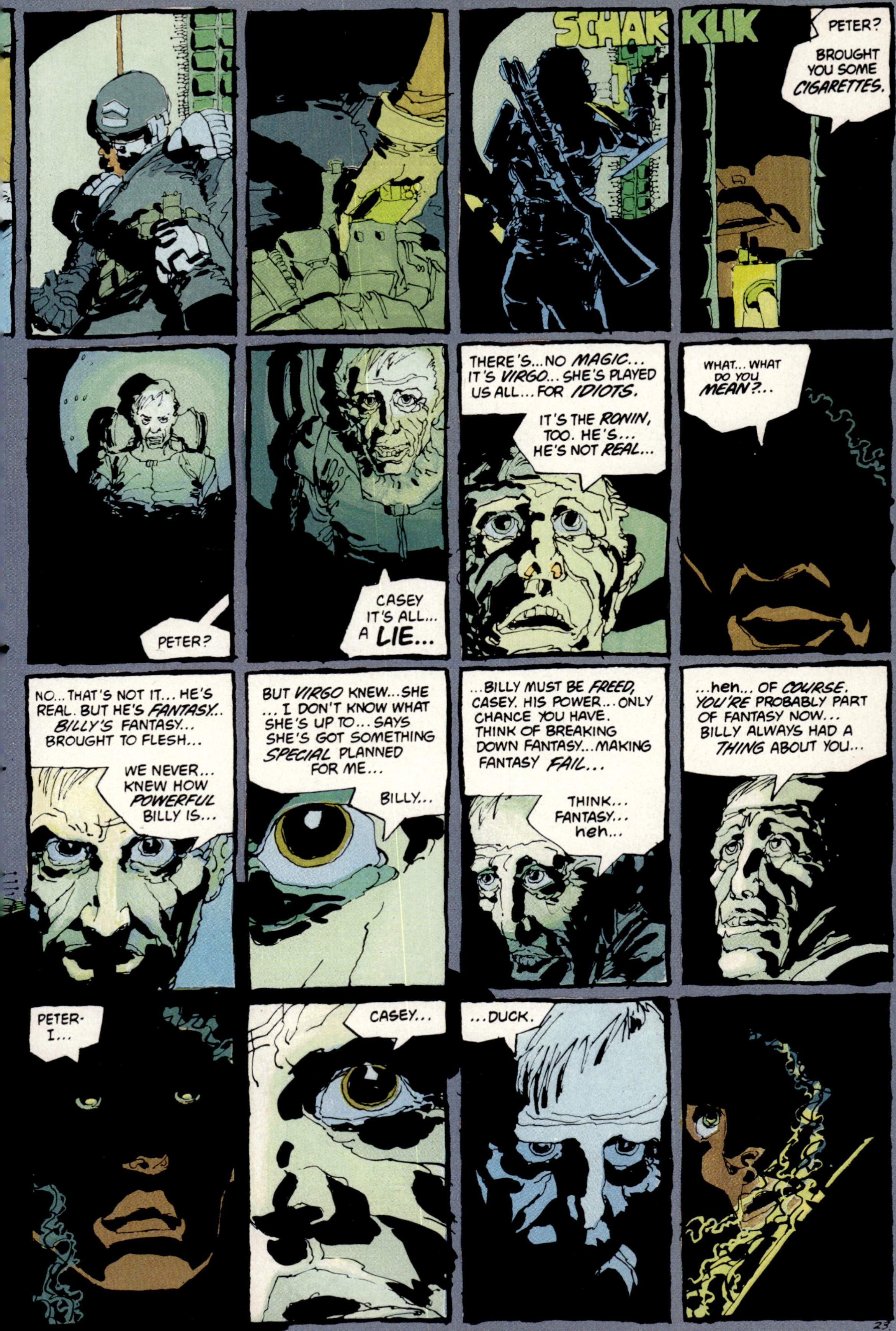
SCHAK KLIK
PETER?
BROUGHT YOU SOME CIGARETTES.
PETER?
CASEY IT'S ALL... A LIE...
THERE'S... NO MAGIC... IT'S VIRGO... SHE'S PLAYED US ALL... FOR IDIOTS.
IT'S THE RONIN, TOO. HE'S... HE'S NOT REAL...
WHAT... WHAT DO YOU MEAN?...
NO... THAT'S NOT IT... HE'S REAL. BUT HE'S FANTASY... BILLY'S FANTASY... BROUGHT TO FLESH...
WE NEVER... KNEW HOW POWERFUL BILLY IS...
BUT VIRGO KNEW... SHE ... I DON'T KNOW WHAT SHE'S UP TO... SAYS SHE'S GOT SOMETHING SPECIAL PLANNED FOR ME...
BILLY...
...BILLY MUST BE FREED, CASEY. HIS POWER... ONLY CHANCE YOU HAVE. THINK OF BREAKING DOWN FANTASY... MAKING FANTASY FAIL...
THINK... FANTASY... heh...
...heh... OF COURSE. YOU'RE PROBABLY PART OF FANTASY NOW... BILLY ALWAYS HAD A THING ABOUT YOU...
PETER- I...
CASEY...
...DUCK.

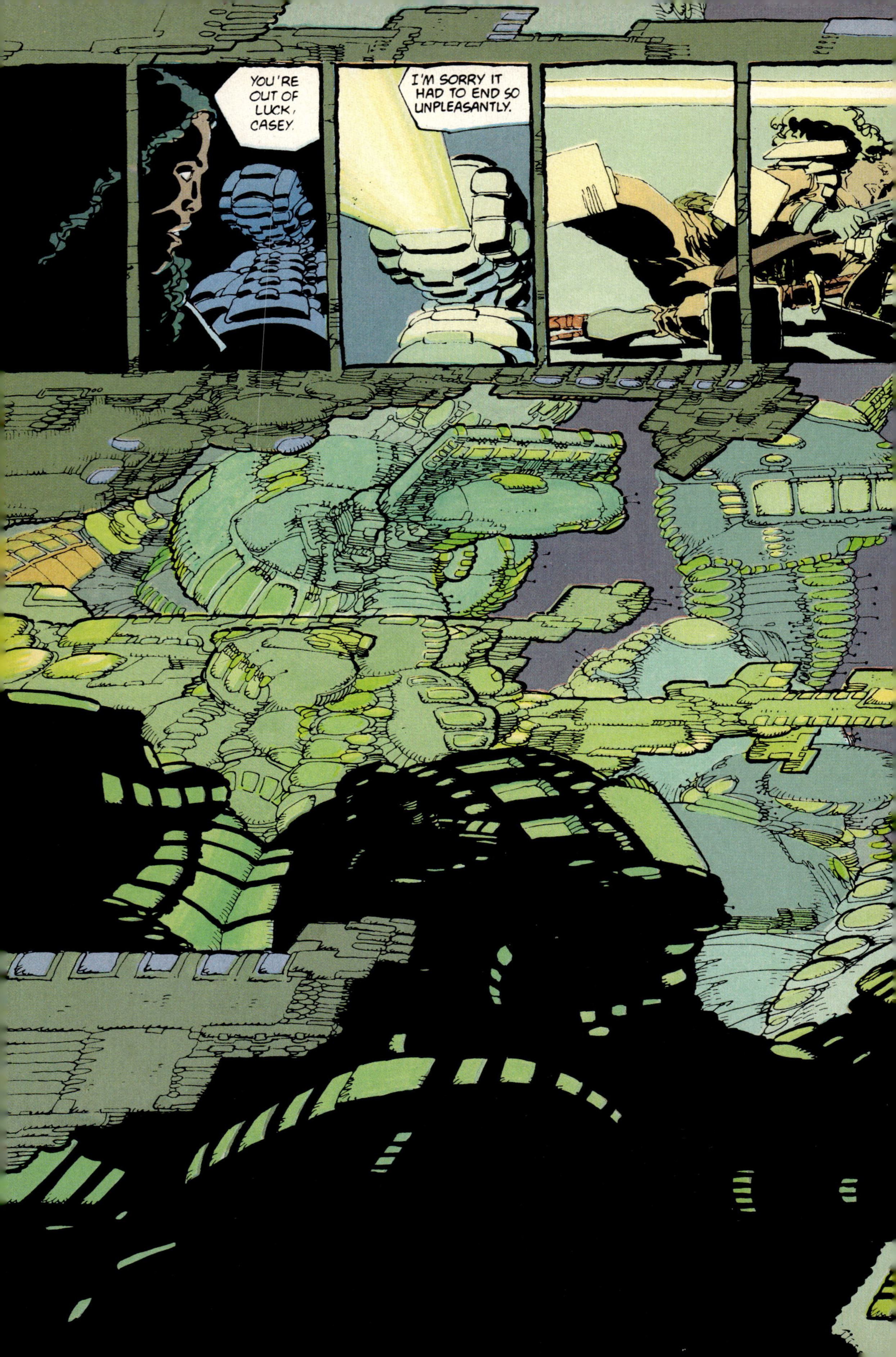
YOU'RE OUT OF LUCK, CASEY.
I'M SORRY IT HAD TO END SO UNPLEASANTLY.

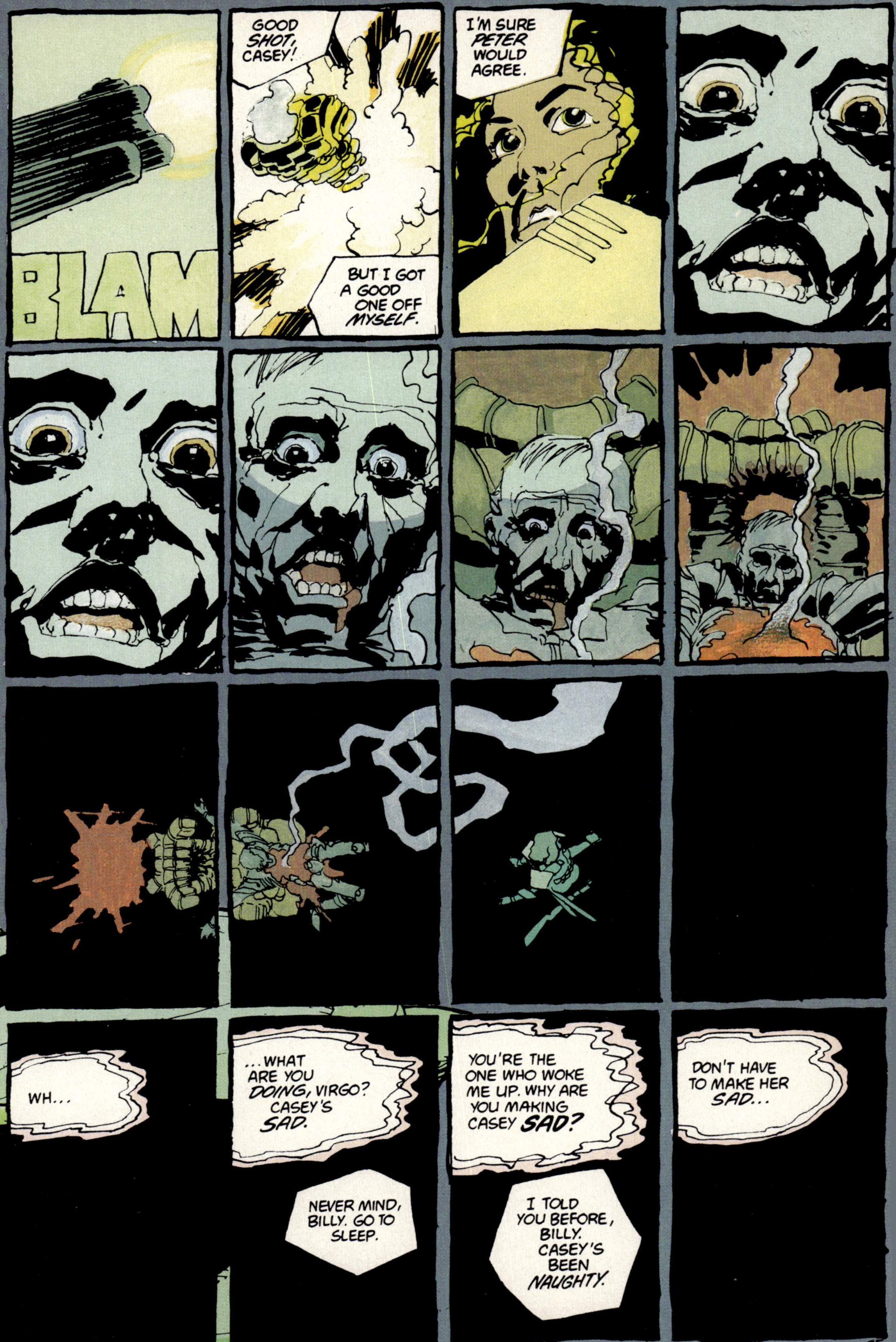
BLAM
GOOD SHOT, CASEY!
BUT I GOT A GOOD ONE OFF MYSELF.
I'M SURE PETER WOULD AGREE.
WH...
...WHAT ARE YOU DOING, VIRGO? CASEY'S SAD.
NEVER MIND, BILLY. GO TO SLEEP.
YOU'RE THE ONE WHO WOKE ME UP. WHY ARE YOU MAKING CASEY SAD?
I TOLD YOU BEFORE, BILLY. CASEY'S BEEN NAUGHTY.
DON'T HAVE TO MAKE HER SAD...

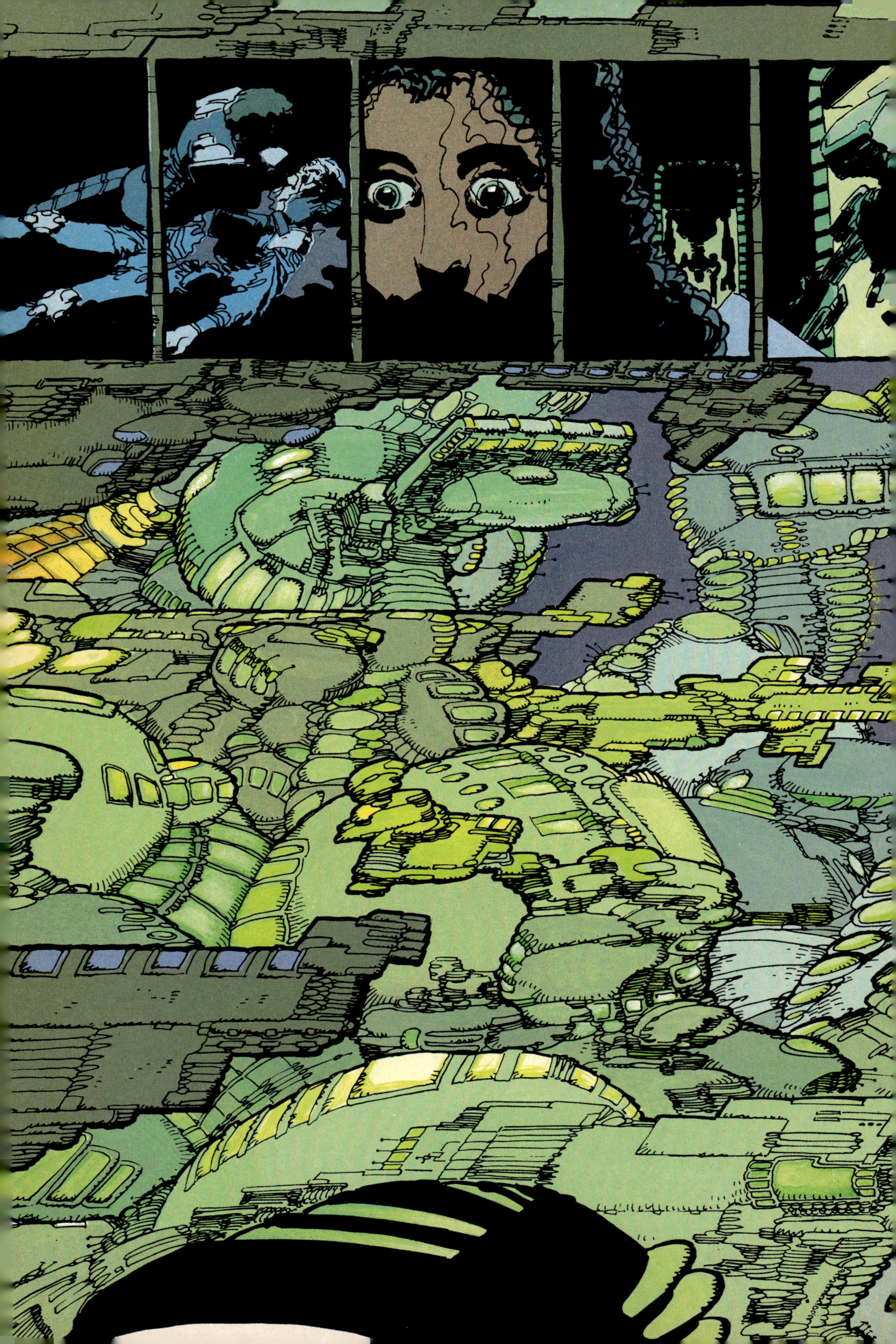

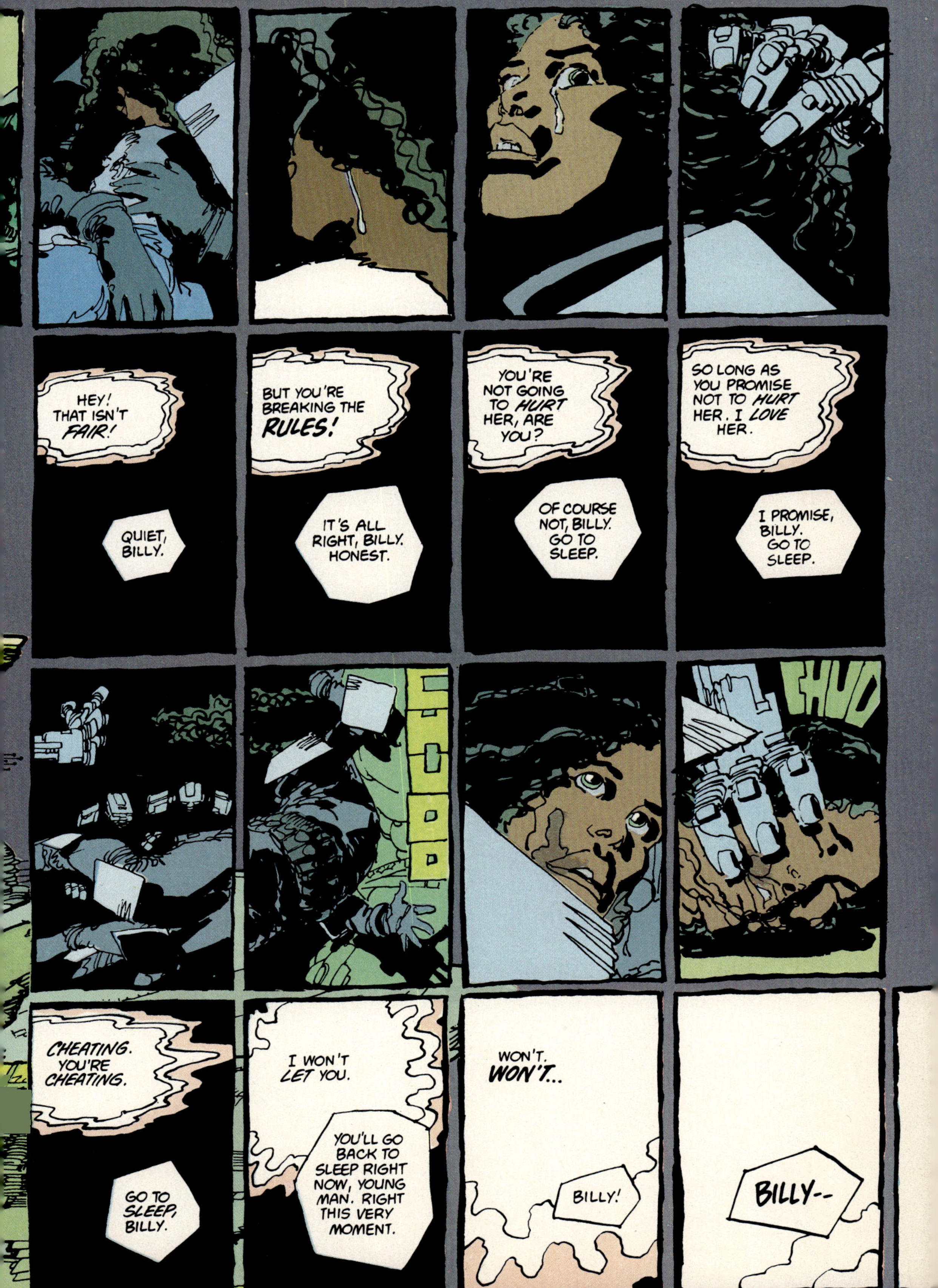
HEY! THAT ISN'T FAIR!
QUIET, BILLY.
BUT YOU'RE BREAKING THE RULES!
IT'S ALL RIGHT, BILLY. HONEST.
YOU'RE NOT GOING TO HURT HER, ARE YOU?
OF COURSE NOT, BILLY. GO TO SLEEP.
SO LONG AS YOU PROMISE NOT TO HURT HER. I LOVE HER.
I PROMISE, BILLY. GO TO SLEEP.
CHUD
CHEATING. YOU'RE CHEATING.
GO TO SLEEP, BILLY.
I WON'T LET YOU.
YOU'LL GO BACK TO SLEEP RIGHT NOW, YOUNG MAN. RIGHT THIS VERY MOMENT.
WON'T. WON'T...
BILLY!
BILLY--
22.

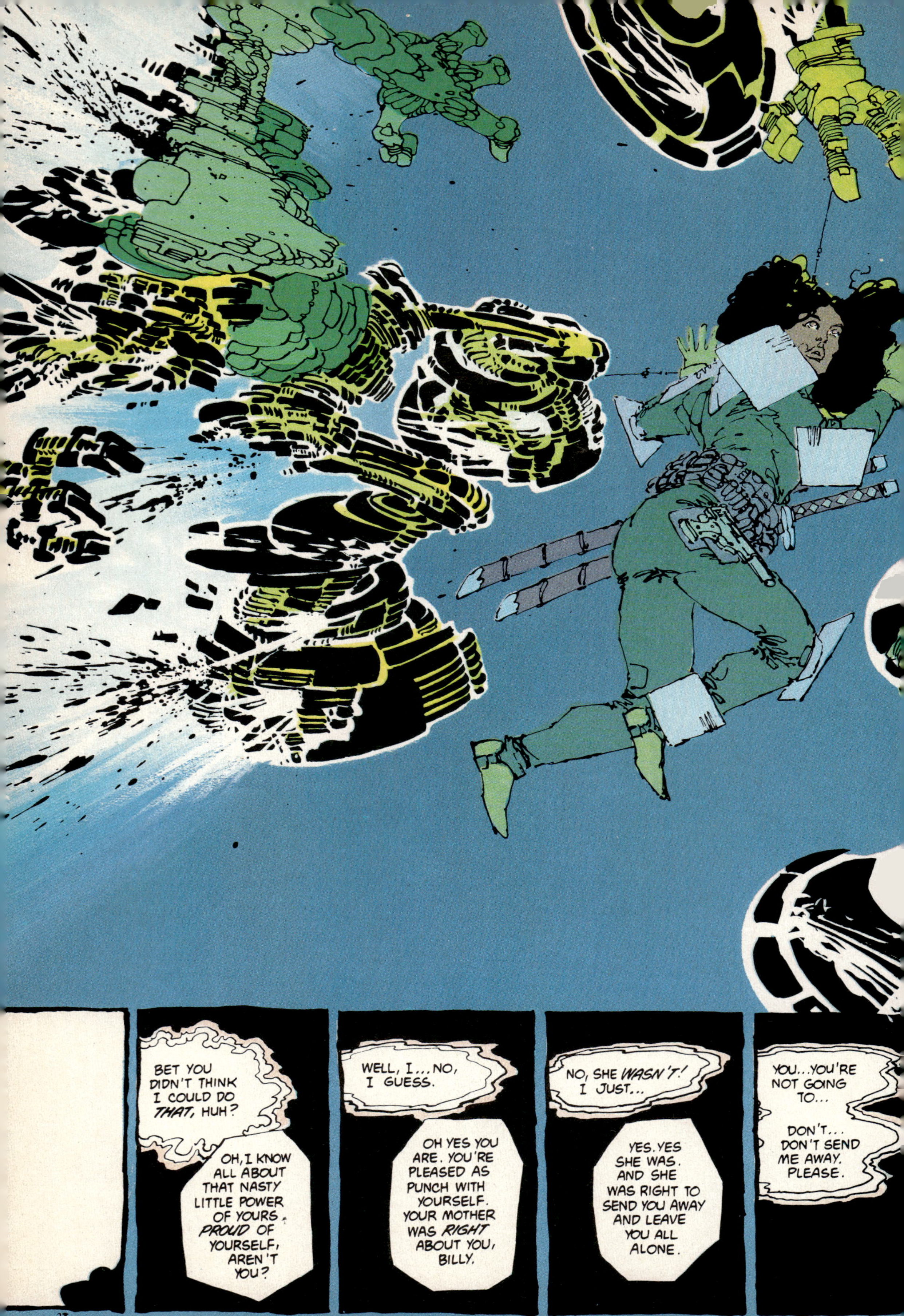
BET YOU DIDN'T THINK I COULD DO *THAT*, HUH?
OH, I KNOW ALL ABOUT THAT NASTY LITTLE POWER OF YOURS. *PROUD* OF YOURSELF, AREN'T YOU?
WELL, I... NO, I GUESS.
OH YES YOU ARE. YOU'RE PLEASED AS PUNCH WITH YOURSELF. YOUR MOTHER WAS *RIGHT* ABOUT YOU, BILLY.
NO, SHE *WASN'T!* I JUST...
YES. YES SHE WAS. AND SHE WAS RIGHT TO SEND YOU AWAY AND LEAVE YOU ALL ALONE.
YOU... YOU'RE NOT GOING TO...
DON'T... DON'T SEND ME AWAY. PLEASE.

I DON'T KNOW, BILLY. RIGHT NOW, I JUST DON'T KNOW WHAT TO DO WITH YOU. IF YOU WON'T *MIND* ME...

I *WILL!* I'M SORRY. I'LL MIND. I'LL GO TO SLEEP AND EVERYTHING.

THAT'S A GOOD BOY.

VIRGO?

YES, BILLY?

IS IT OKAY IF I JUST *WATCH?* I MEAN, I WON'T *DO* ANYTHING.

BILLY...

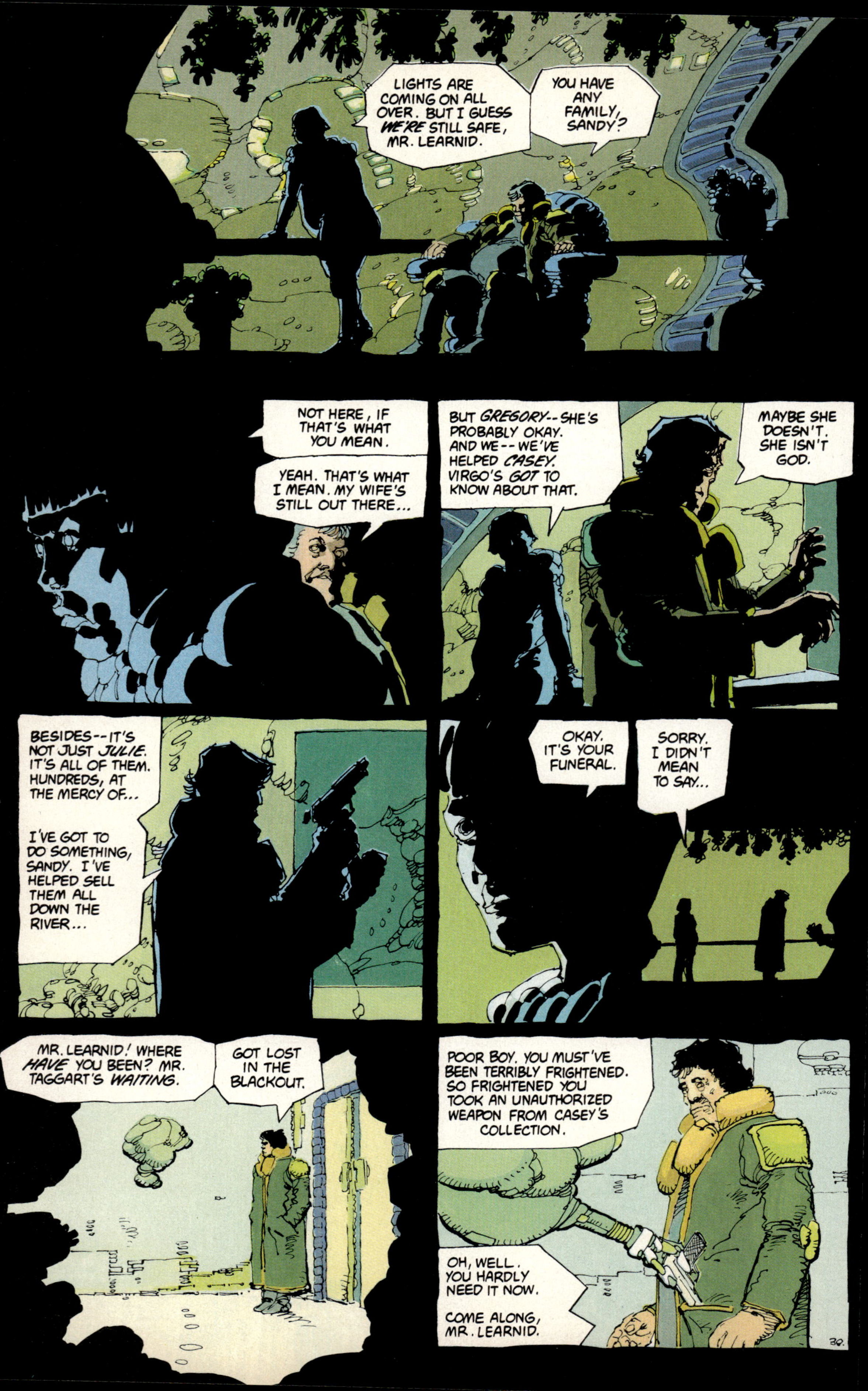
LIGHTS ARE COMING ON ALL OVER. BUT I GUESS WE'RE STILL SAFE, MR. LEARNID.
YOU HAVE ANY FAMILY, SANDY?
NOT HERE, IF THAT'S WHAT YOU MEAN.
YEAH. THAT'S WHAT I MEAN. MY WIFE'S STILL OUT THERE...
BUT GREGORY--SHE'S PROBABLY OKAY. AND WE--WE'VE HELPED CASEY. VIRGO'S GOT TO KNOW ABOUT THAT.
MAYBE SHE DOESN'T. SHE ISN'T GOD.
BESIDES--IT'S NOT JUST JULIE. IT'S ALL OF THEM. HUNDREDS, AT THE MERCY OF...
I'VE GOT TO DO SOMETHING, SANDY. I'VE HELPED SELL THEM ALL DOWN THE RIVER...
OKAY. IT'S YOUR FUNERAL.
SORRY. I DIDN'T MEAN TO SAY...
MR. LEARNID! WHERE HAVE YOU BEEN? MR. TAGGART'S WAITING.
GOT LOST IN THE BLACKOUT.
POOR BOY. YOU MUST'VE BEEN TERRIBLY FRIGHTENED. SO FRIGHTENED YOU TOOK AN UNAUTHORIZED WEAPON FROM CASEY'S COLLECTION.
OH, WELL. YOU HARDLY NEED IT NOW.
COME ALONG, MR. LEARNID.
38.

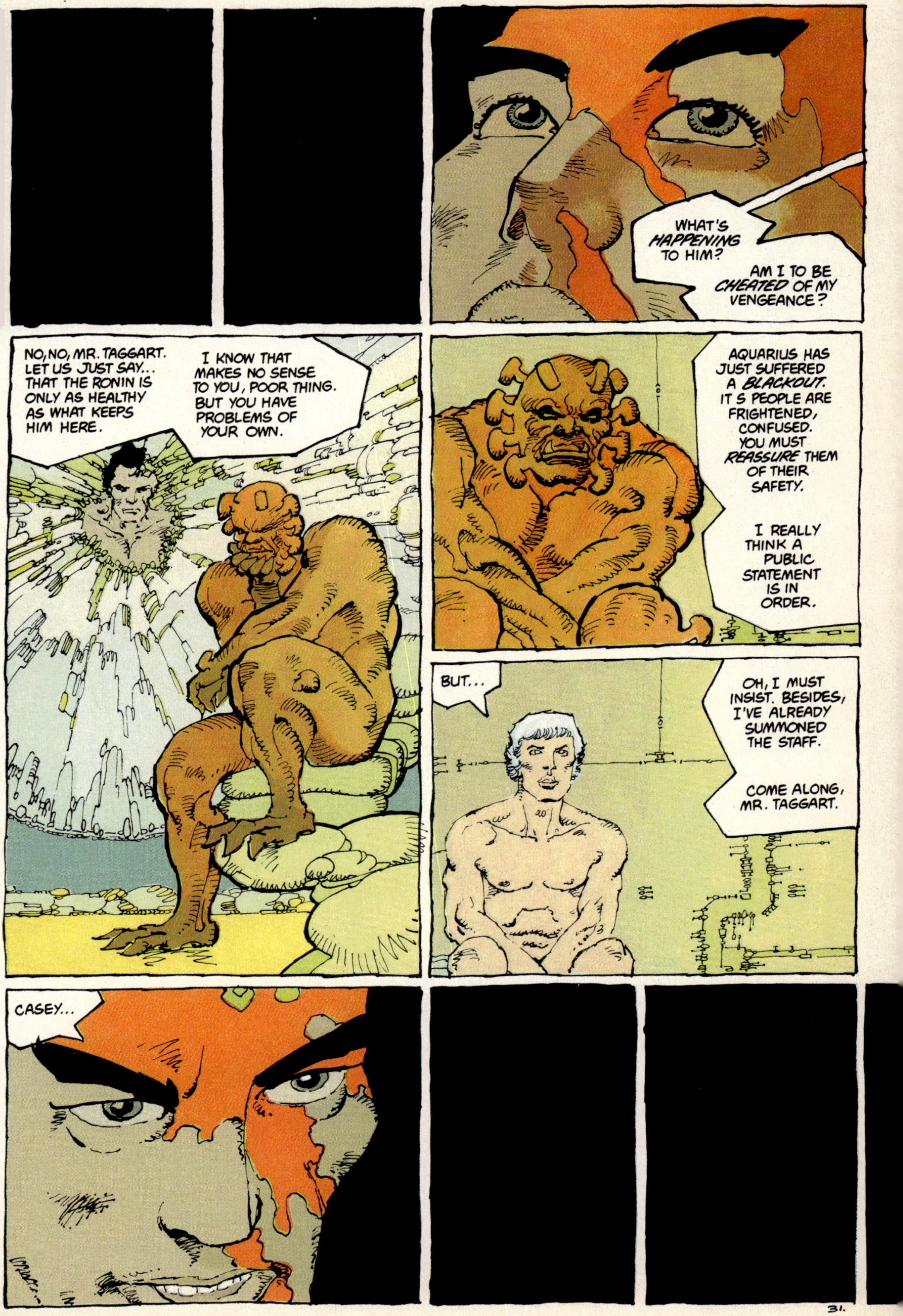
WHAT'S HAPPENING TO HIM?
AM I TO BE CHEATED OF MY VENGEANCE?
NO, NO, MR. TAGGART. LET US JUST SAY... THAT THE RONIN IS ONLY AS HEALTHY AS WHAT KEEPS HIM HERE.
I KNOW THAT MAKES NO SENSE TO YOU, POOR THING. BUT YOU HAVE PROBLEMS OF YOUR OWN.
AQUARIUS HAS JUST SUFFERED A BLACKOUT. IT S PEOPLE ARE FRIGHTENED, CONFUSED. YOU MUST REASSURE THEM OF THEIR SAFETY.
I REALLY THINK A PUBLIC STATEMENT IS IN ORDER.
BUT...
OH, I MUST INSIST. BESIDES, I'VE ALREADY SUMMONED THE STAFF.
COME ALONG, MR. TAGGART.
CASEY...

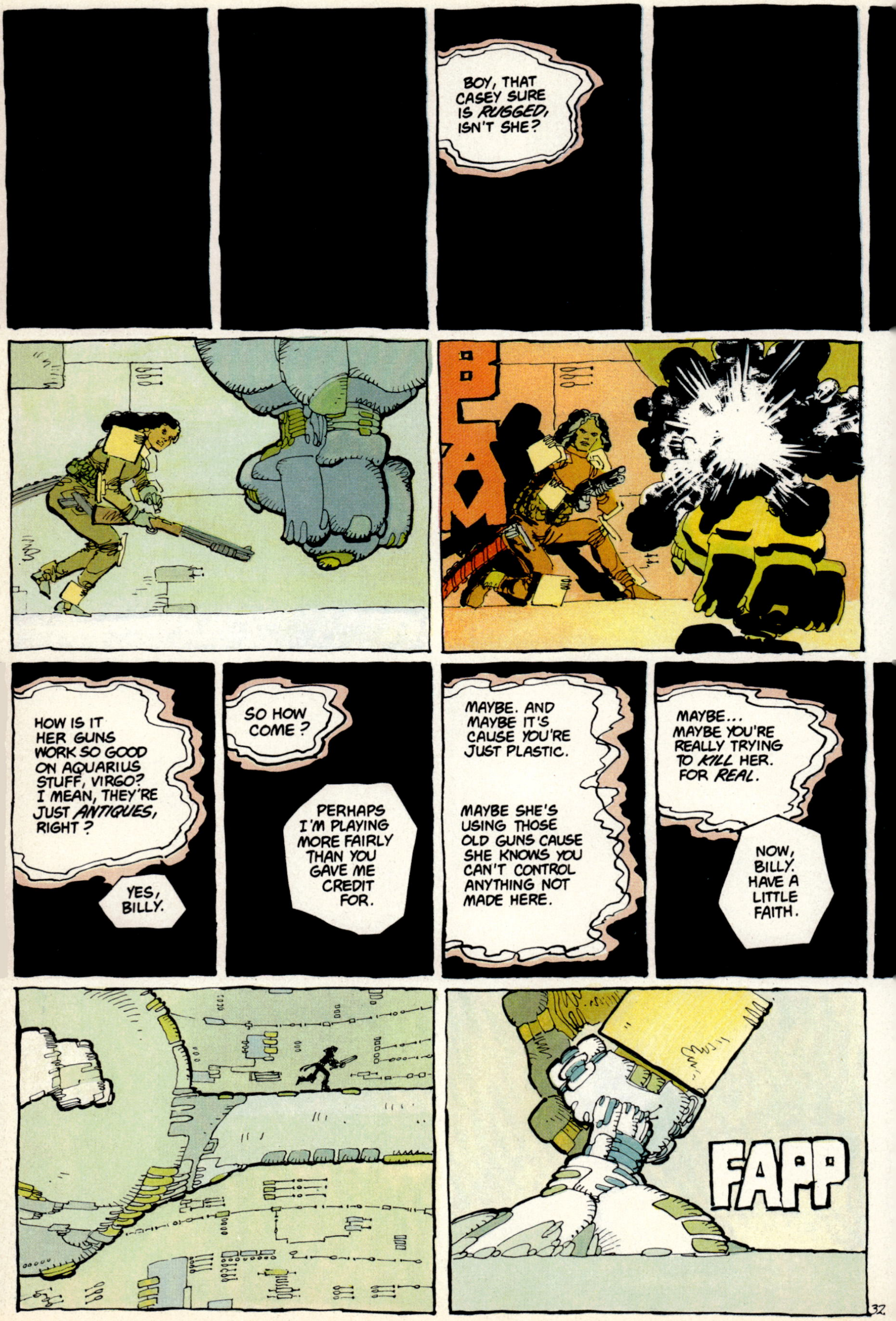
BOY, THAT CASEY SURE IS RUGGED, ISN'T SHE?
HOW IS IT HER GUNS WORK SO GOOD ON AQUARIUS STUFF, VIRGO? I MEAN, THEY'RE JUST ANTIQUES, RIGHT?
YES, BILLY.
SO HOW COME?
PERHAPS I'M PLAYING MORE FAIRLY THAN YOU GAVE ME CREDIT FOR.
MAYBE. AND MAYBE IT'S CAUSE YOU'RE JUST PLASTIC.
MAYBE SHE'S USING THOSE OLD GUNS CAUSE SHE KNOWS YOU CAN'T CONTROL ANYTHING NOT MADE HERE.
MAYBE... MAYBE YOU'RE REALLY TRYING TO KILL HER. FOR REAL.
NOW, BILLY. HAVE A LITTLE FAITH.
FAPP

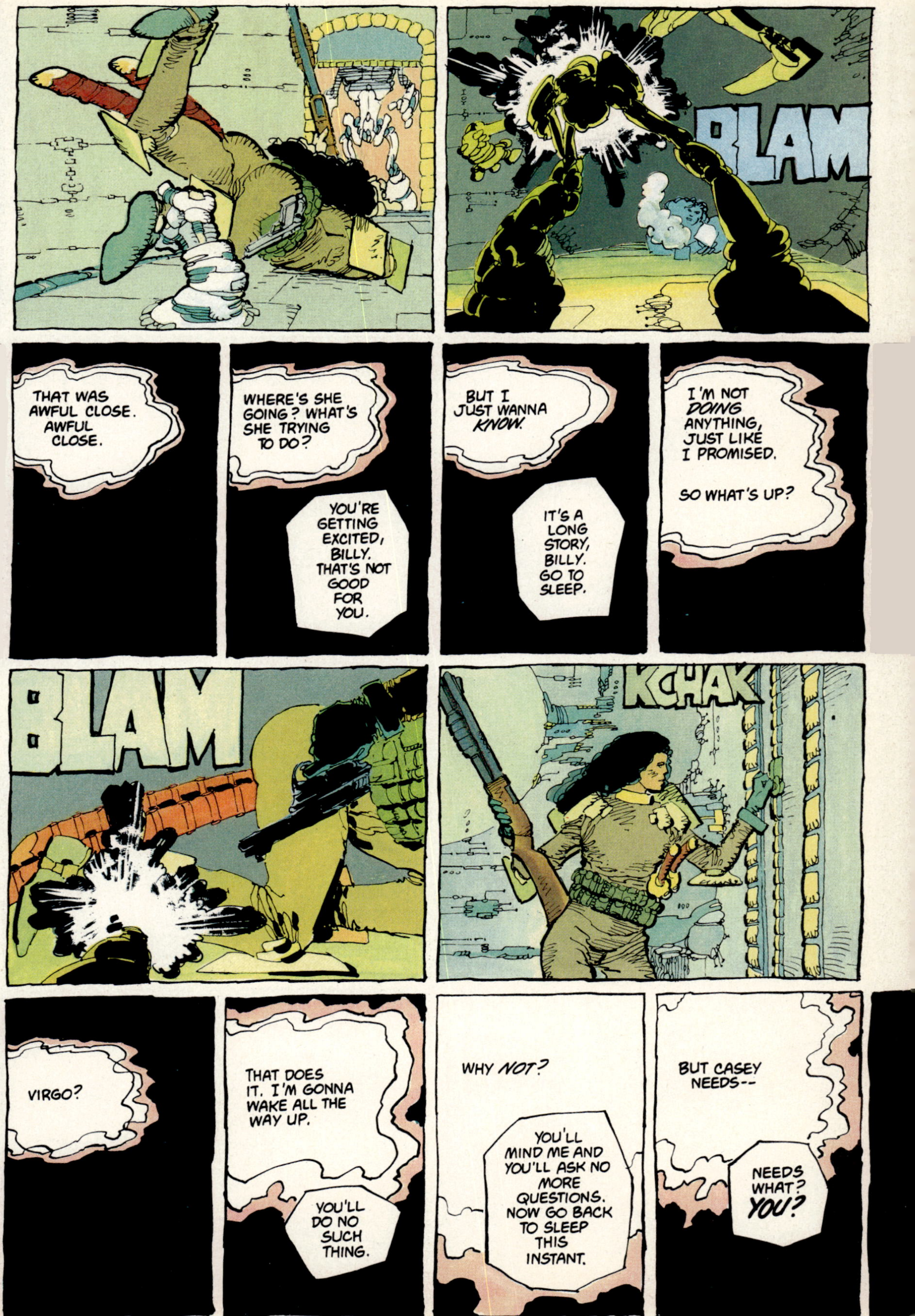
BLAM
THAT WAS AWFUL CLOSE. AWFUL CLOSE.
WHERE'S SHE GOING? WHAT'S SHE TRYING TO DO?
YOU'RE GETTING EXCITED, BILLY. THAT'S NOT GOOD FOR YOU.
BUT I JUST WANNA KNOW.
IT'S A LONG STORY, BILLY. GO TO SLEEP.
I'M NOT DOING ANYTHING, JUST LIKE I PROMISED.
SO WHAT'S UP?
BLAM
KCHAK
VIRGO?
THAT DOES IT. I'M GONNA WAKE ALL THE WAY UP.
YOU'LL DO NO SUCH THING.
WHY NOT?
YOU'LL MIND ME AND YOU'LL ASK NO MORE QUESTIONS. NOW GO BACK TO SLEEP THIS INSTANT.
BUT CASEY NEEDS--
NEEDS WHAT? YOU?

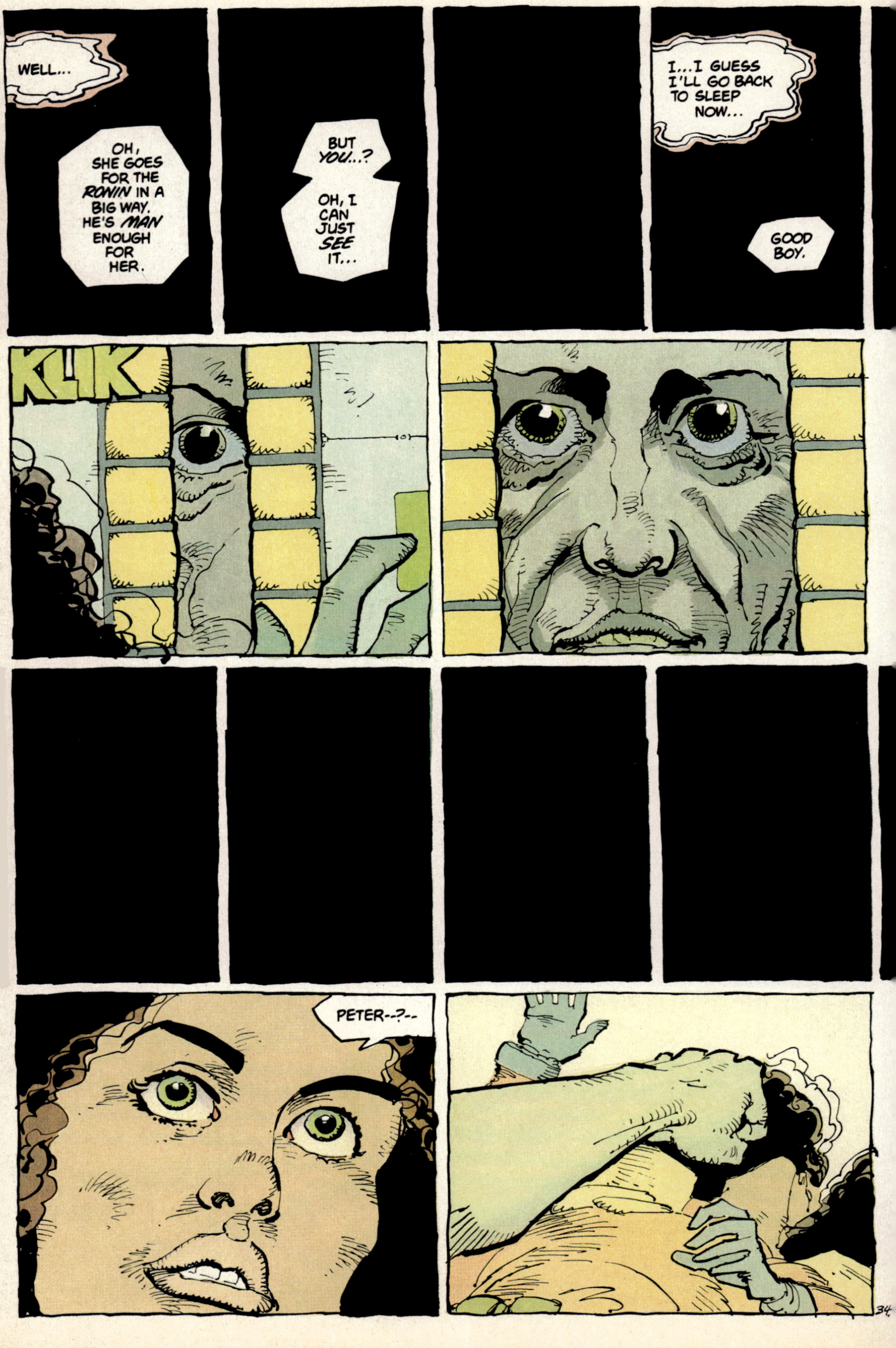
WELL...
OH, SHE GOES FOR THE *RONIN* IN A BIG WAY. HE'S *MAN* ENOUGH FOR HER.
BUT *YOU*...?
OH, I CAN JUST *SEE* IT...
I...I GUESS I'LL GO BACK TO SLEEP NOW...
GOOD BOY.
KLIK
PETER--?--

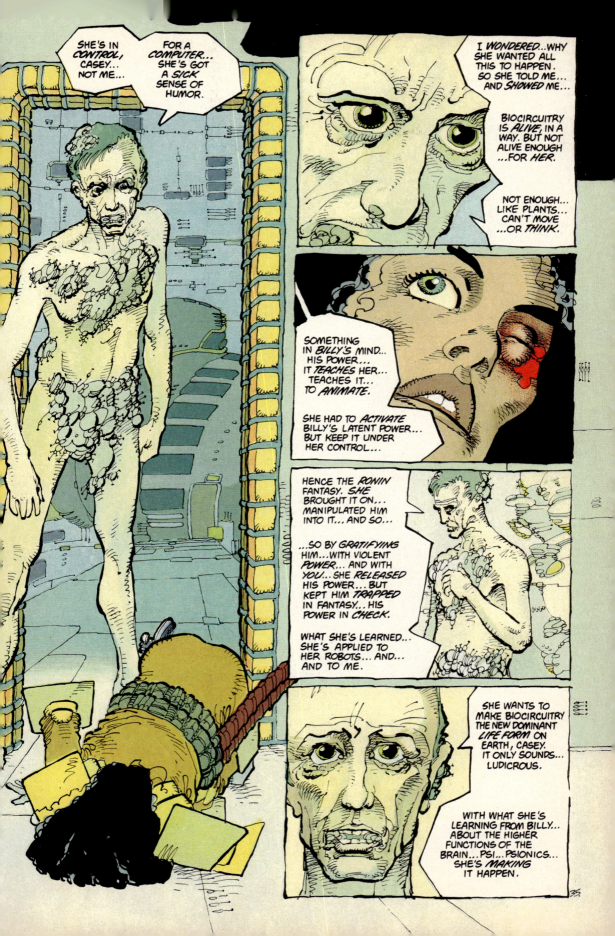

SHE'S IN *CONTROL,* CASEY... NOT ME...

FOR A *COMPUTER*... SHE'S GOT A *SICK* SENSE OF HUMOR.

I *WONDERED*... WHY SHE WANTED ALL THIS TO HAPPEN. SO SHE TOLD ME... AND *SHOWED* ME...

BIOCIRCUITRY IS *ALIVE,* IN A WAY. BUT NOT ALIVE ENOUGH ...FOR *HER.*

NOT ENOUGH... LIKE PLANTS... CAN'T *MOVE* ...OR *THINK.*

SOMETHING IN *BILLY'S* MIND... HIS POWER... IT *TEACHES* HER... TEACHES IT... TO *ANIMATE.*

SHE HAD TO *ACTIVATE* BILLY'S LATENT POWER... BUT KEEP IT UNDER HER CONTROL...

HENCE THE *RONIN* FANTASY. *SHE* BROUGHT IT ON... MANIPULATED HIM INTO IT... AND SO...

...SO BY *GRATIFYING* HIM...WITH VIOLENT *POWER*... AND WITH *YOU*... SHE *RELEASED* HIS POWER... BUT KEPT HIM *TRAPPED* IN FANTASY... HIS POWER IN *CHECK.*

WHAT SHE'S LEARNED... SHE'S APPLIED TO HER ROBOTS... AND... AND TO ME.

SHE WANTS TO MAKE BIOCIRCUITRY THE NEW DOMINANT *LIFE FORM* ON EARTH, CASEY. IT ONLY SOUNDS... LUDICROUS.

WITH WHAT SHE'S LEARNING FROM BILLY... ABOUT THE HIGHER FUNCTIONS OF THE BRAIN...PSI...PSIONICS... SHE'S *MAKING* IT HAPPEN.

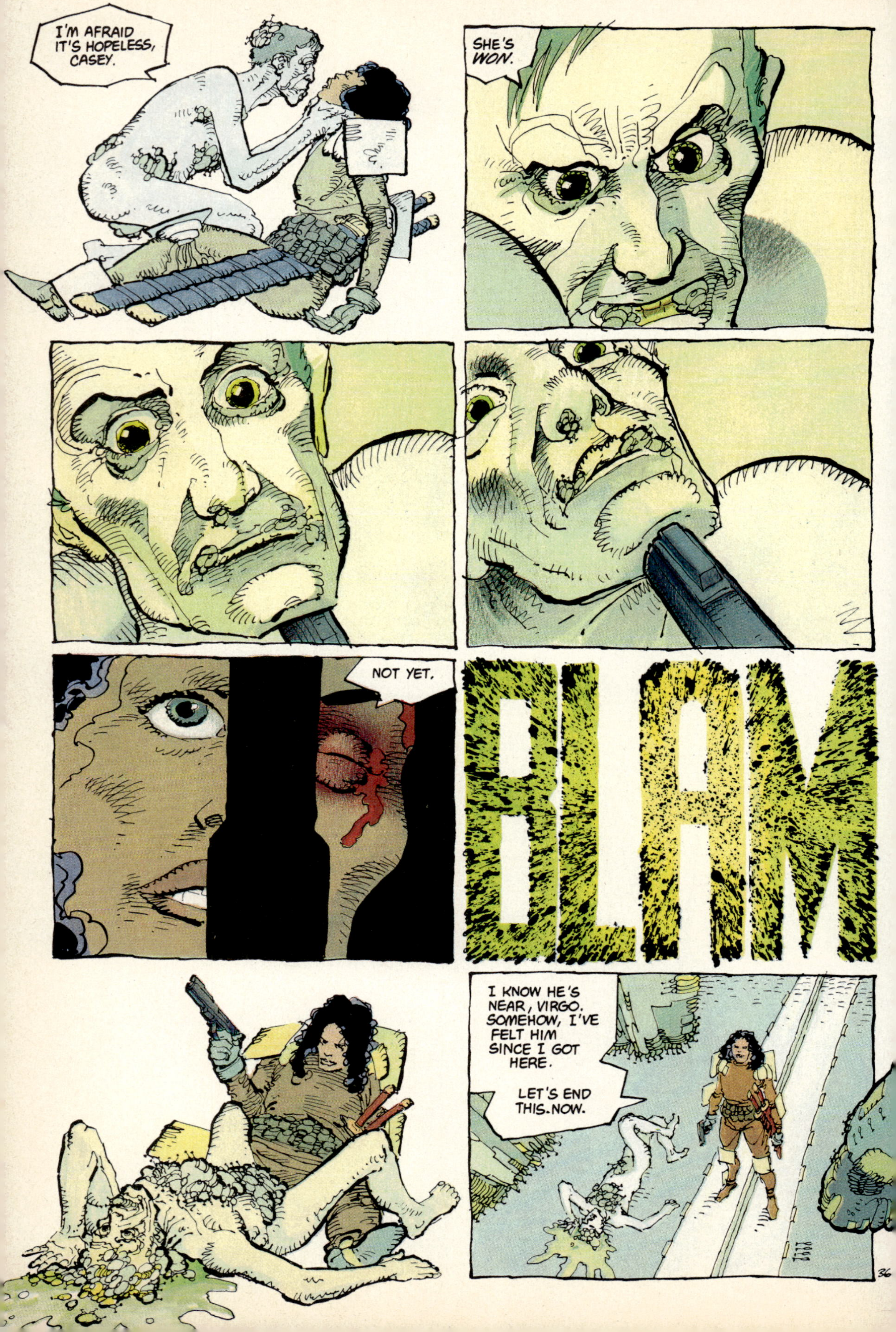
I'M AFRAID IT'S HOPELESS, CASEY.
SHE'S WON.
NOT YET.
BLAM
I KNOW HE'S NEAR, VIRGO. SOMEHOW, I'VE FELT HIM SINCE I GOT HERE.
LET'S END THIS. NOW.

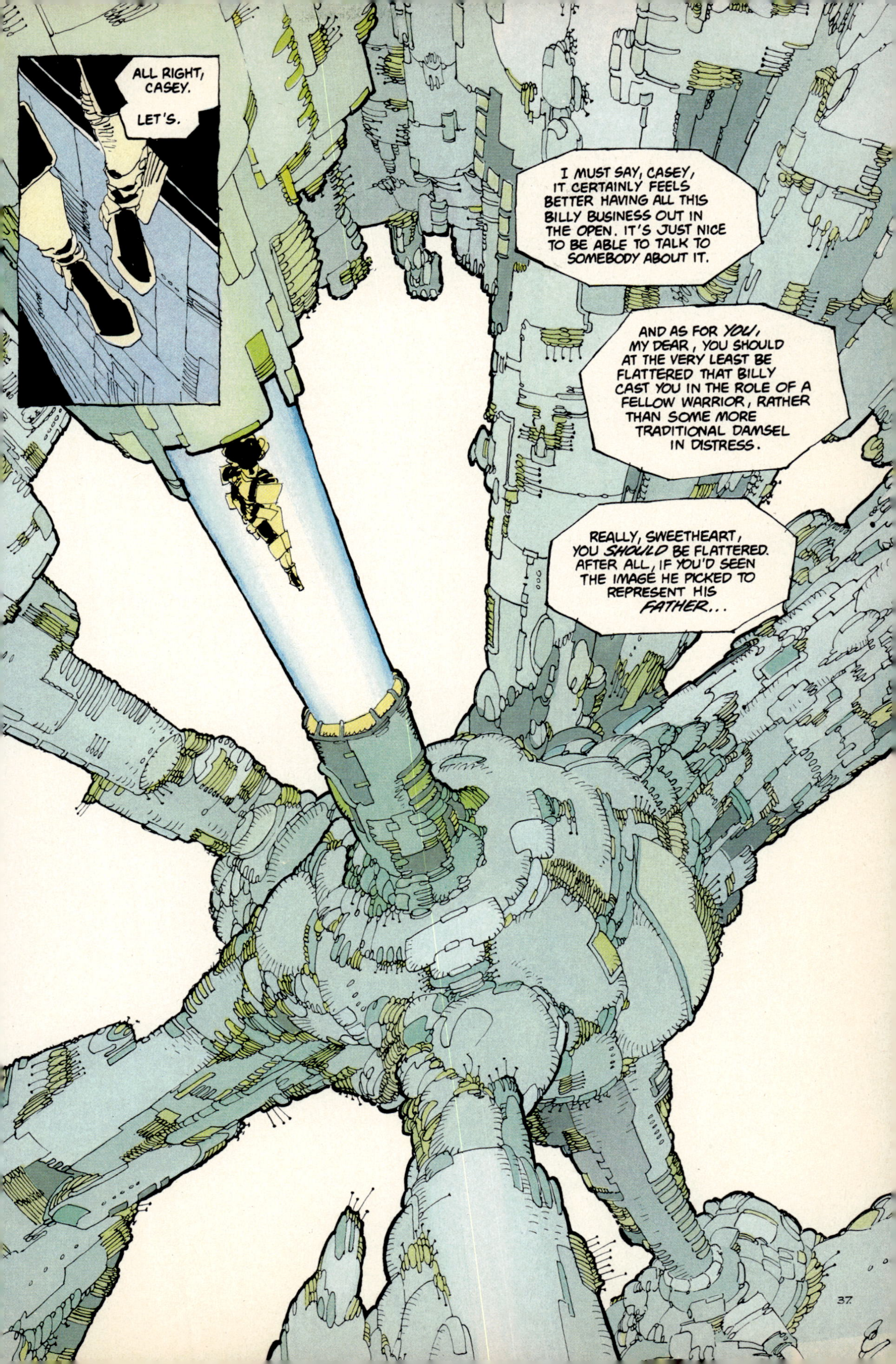
ALL RIGHT, CASEY.
LET'S.
I MUST SAY, CASEY, IT CERTAINLY FEELS BETTER HAVING ALL THIS BILLY BUSINESS OUT IN THE OPEN. IT'S JUST NICE TO BE ABLE TO TALK TO SOMEBODY ABOUT IT.
AND AS FOR YOU, MY DEAR, YOU SHOULD AT THE VERY LEAST BE FLATTERED THAT BILLY CAST YOU IN THE ROLE OF A FELLOW WARRIOR, RATHER THAN SOME MORE TRADITIONAL DAMSEL IN DISTRESS.
REALLY, SWEETHEART, YOU SHOULD BE FLATTERED. AFTER ALL, IF YOU'D SEEN THE IMAGE HE PICKED TO REPRESENT HIS FATHER...

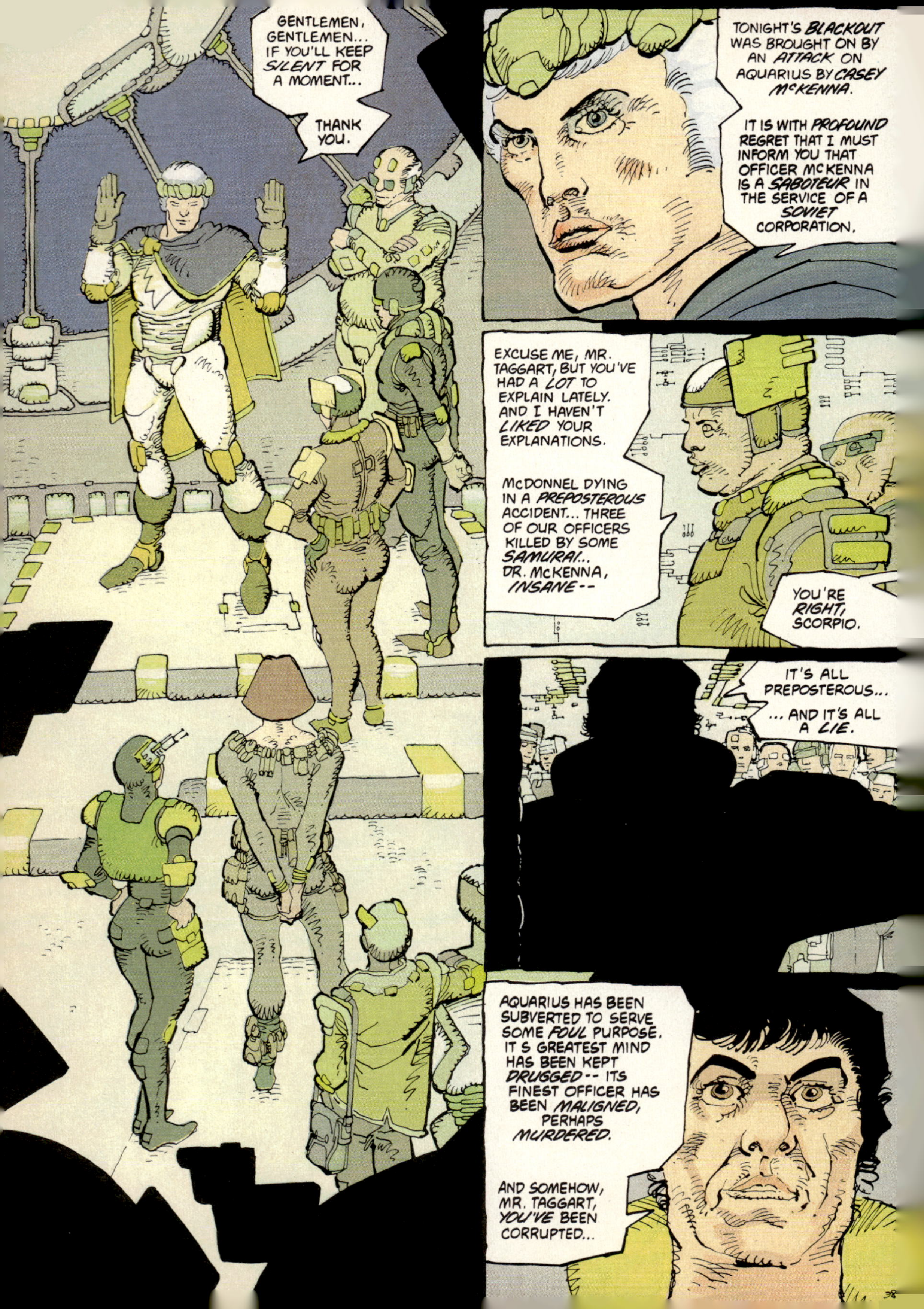
GENTLEMEN, GENTLEMEN... IF YOU'LL KEEP SILENT FOR A MOMENT...
THANK YOU.
TONIGHT'S BLACKOUT WAS BROUGHT ON BY AN ATTACK ON AQUARIUS BY CASEY McKENNA.
IT IS WITH PROFOUND REGRET THAT I MUST INFORM YOU THAT OFFICER McKENNA IS A SABOTEUR IN THE SERVICE OF A SOVIET CORPORATION.
EXCUSE ME, MR. TAGGART, BUT YOU'VE HAD A LOT TO EXPLAIN LATELY. AND I HAVEN'T LIKED YOUR EXPLANATIONS.
McDONNEL DYING IN A PREPOSTEROUS ACCIDENT... THREE OF OUR OFFICERS KILLED BY SOME SAMURAI... DR. McKENNA, INSANE--
YOU'RE RIGHT, SCORPIO.
IT'S ALL PREPOSTEROUS...
... AND IT'S ALL A LIE.
AQUARIUS HAS BEEN SUBVERTED TO SERVE SOME FOUL PURPOSE. IT S GREATEST MIND HAS BEEN KEPT DRUGGED-- ITS FINEST OFFICER HAS BEEN MALIGNED, PERHAPS MURDERED.
AND SOMEHOW, MR. TAGGART, YOU'VE BEEN CORRUPTED...
38

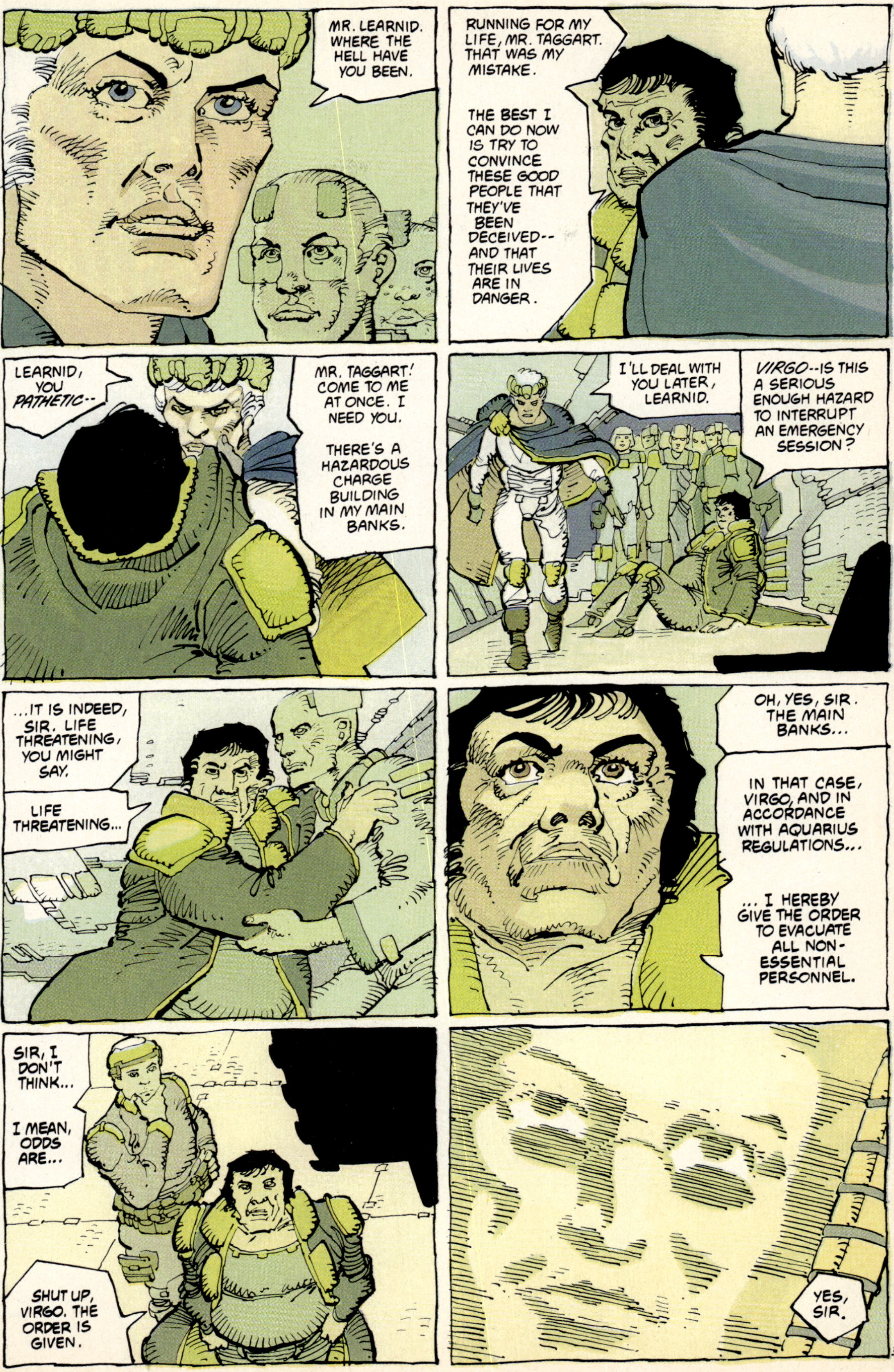
MR. LEARNID. WHERE THE HELL HAVE YOU BEEN.
RUNNING FOR MY LIFE, MR. TAGGART. THAT WAS MY MISTAKE.
THE BEST I CAN DO NOW IS TRY TO CONVINCE THESE GOOD PEOPLE THAT THEY'VE BEEN DECEIVED-- AND THAT THEIR LIVES ARE IN DANGER.
LEARNID, YOU *PATHETIC*--
MR. TAGGART! COME TO ME AT ONCE. I NEED YOU.
THERE'S A HAZARDOUS CHARGE BUILDING IN MY MAIN BANKS.
I'LL DEAL WITH YOU LATER, LEARNID.
VIRGO--IS THIS A SERIOUS ENOUGH HAZARD TO INTERRUPT AN EMERGENCY SESSION?
...IT IS INDEED, SIR. LIFE THREATENING, YOU MIGHT SAY.
LIFE THREATENING...
OH, YES, SIR. THE MAIN BANKS...
IN THAT CASE, VIRGO, AND IN ACCORDANCE WITH AQUARIUS REGULATIONS...
... I HEREBY GIVE THE ORDER TO EVACUATE ALL NON-ESSENTIAL PERSONNEL.
SIR, I DON'T THINK...
I MEAN, ODDS ARE...
SHUT UP, VIRGO. THE ORDER IS GIVEN.
YES, SIR.

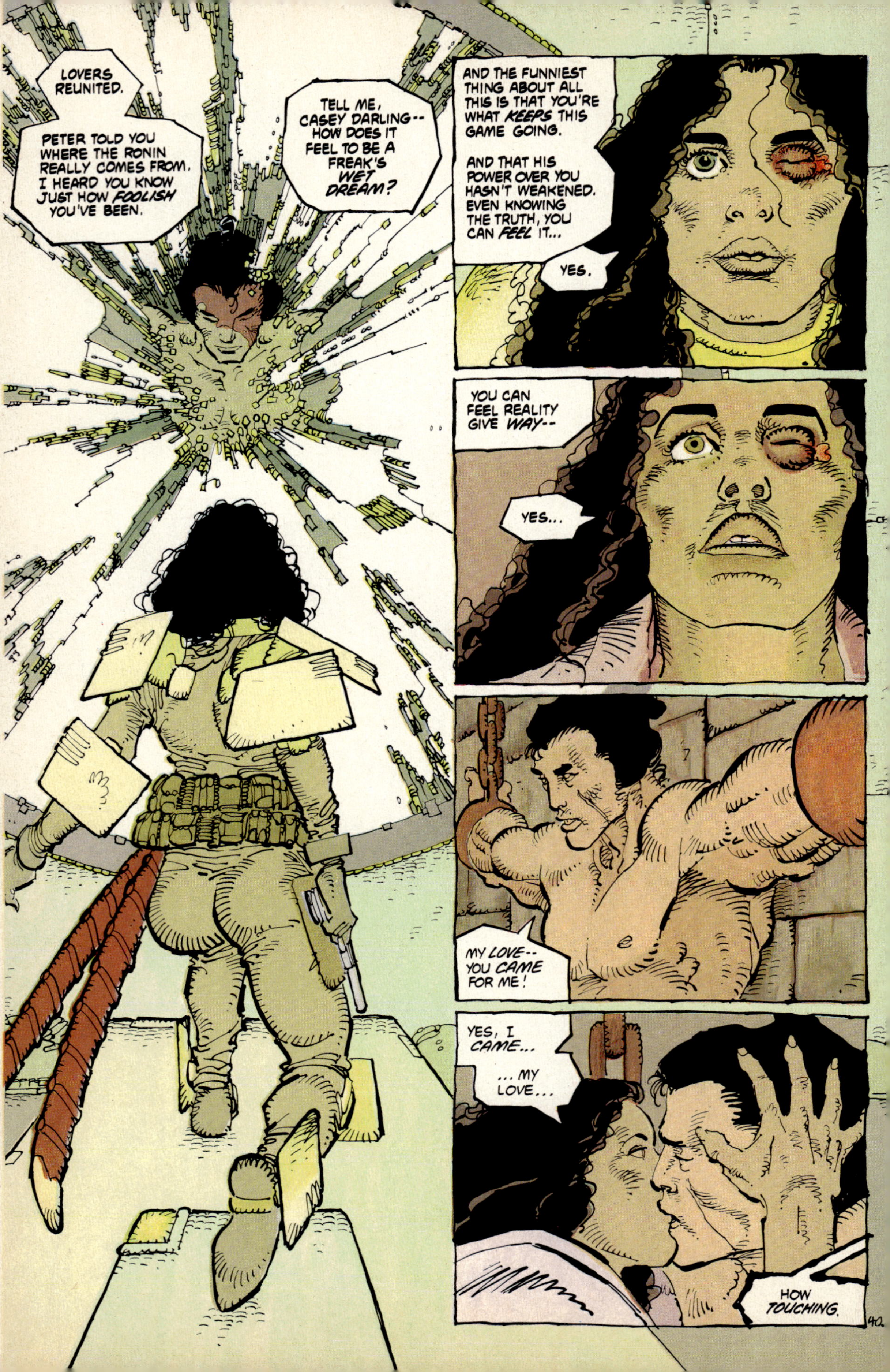
LOVERS REUNITED.
PETER TOLD YOU WHERE THE RONIN REALLY COMES FROM. I HEARD YOU KNOW JUST HOW FOOLISH YOU'VE BEEN.
TELL ME, CASEY DARLING-- HOW DOES IT FEEL TO BE A FREAK'S WET DREAM?
AND THE FUNNIEST THING ABOUT ALL THIS IS THAT YOU'RE WHAT KEEPS THIS GAME GOING.
AND THAT HIS POWER OVER YOU HASN'T WEAKENED. EVEN KNOWING THE TRUTH, YOU CAN FEEL IT...
YES.
YOU CAN FEEL REALITY GIVE WAY--
YES...
MY LOVE-- YOU CAME FOR ME!
YES, I CAME...
... MY LOVE...
HOW TOUCHING.

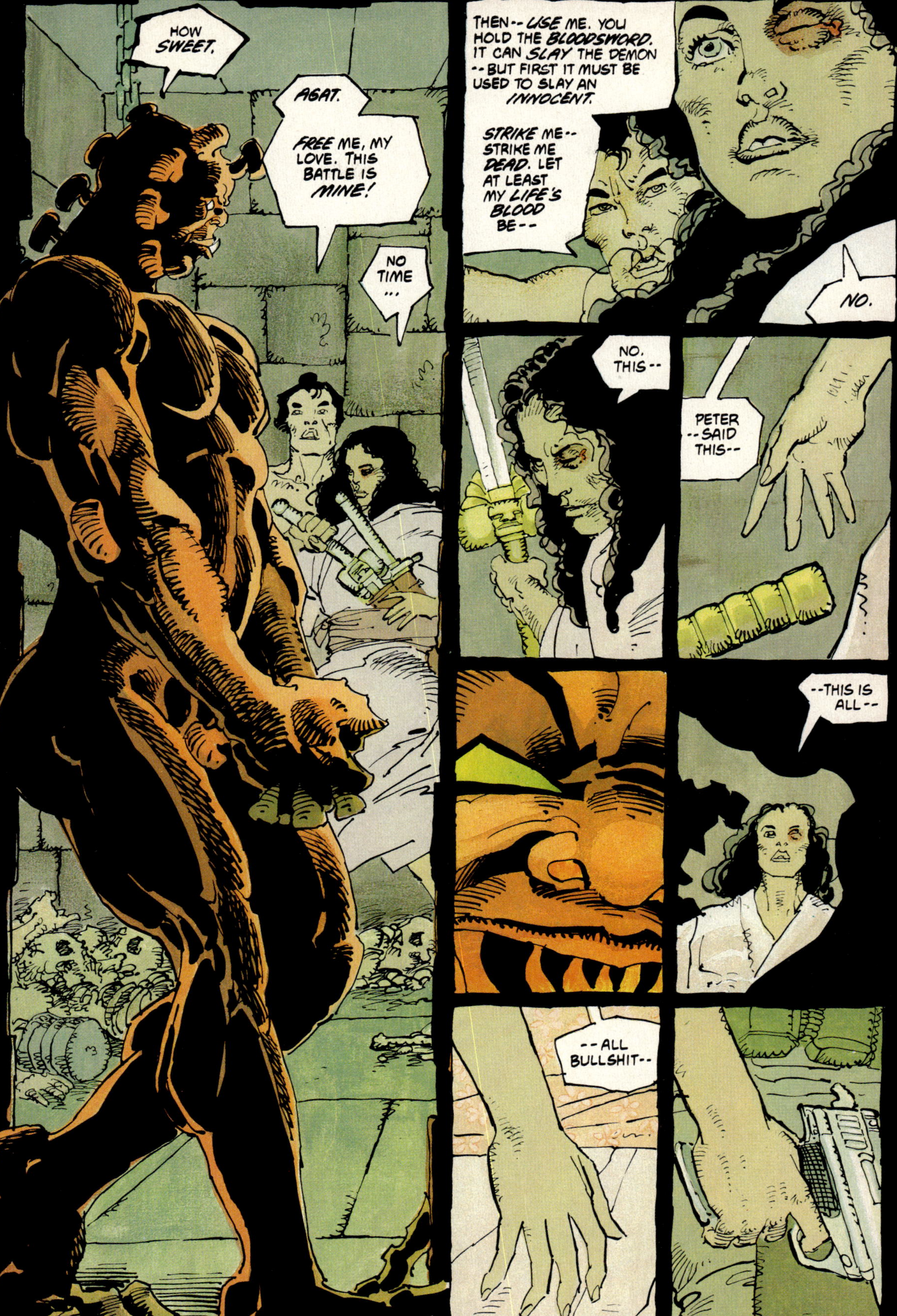

HOW SWEET.
AGAT.
FREE ME, MY LOVE. THIS BATTLE IS MINE!
NO TIME ...
THEN-- USE ME. YOU HOLD THE BLOODSWORD. IT CAN SLAY THE DEMON -- BUT FIRST IT MUST BE USED TO SLAY AN INNOCENT.
STRIKE ME-- STRIKE ME DEAD. LET AT LEAST MY LIFE'S BLOOD BE--
NO.
NO. THIS--
PETER --SAID THIS--
--THIS IS ALL--
--ALL BULLSHIT--

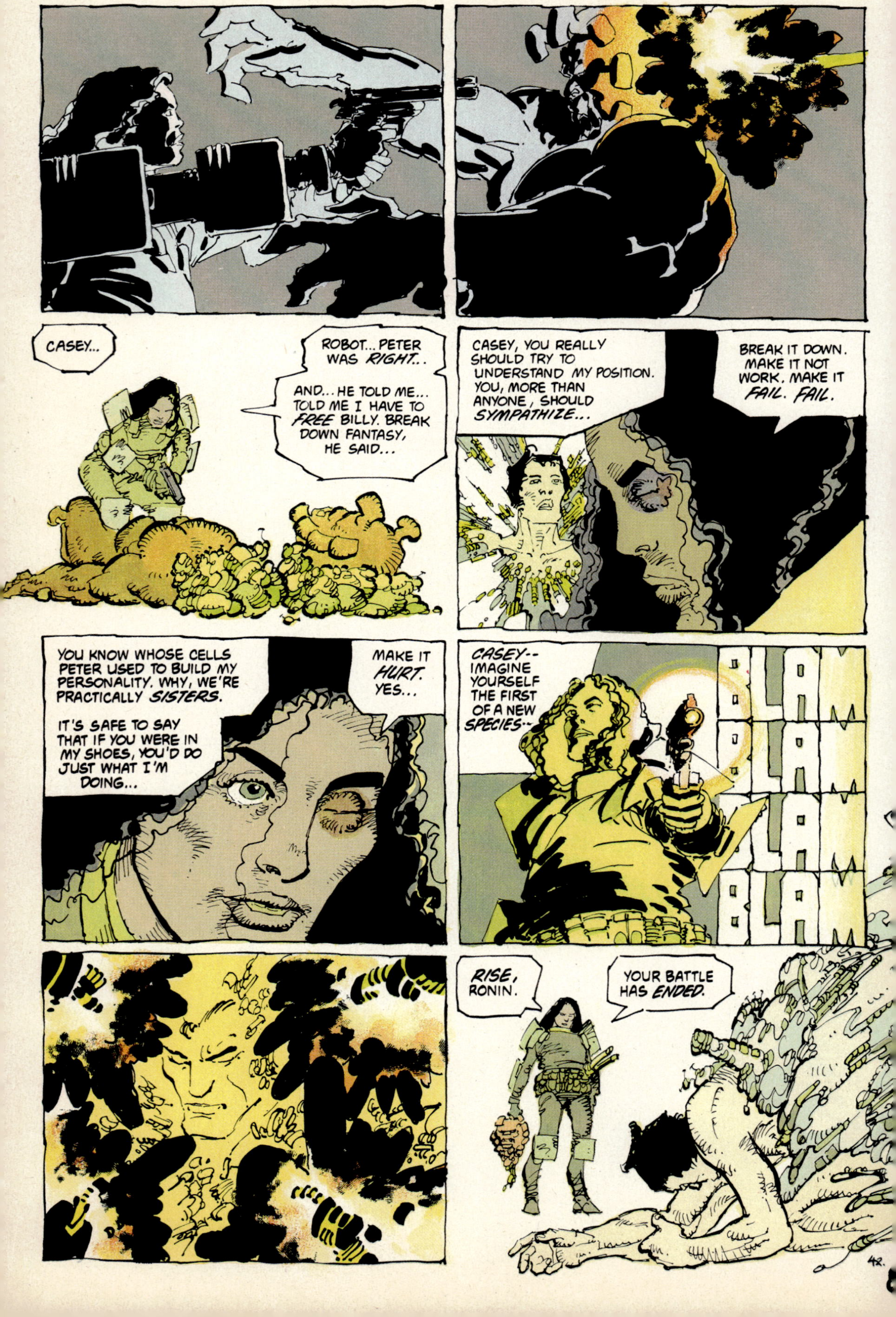
CASEY...
ROBOT... PETER WAS RIGHT...
AND... HE TOLD ME... TOLD ME I HAVE TO FREE BILLY. BREAK DOWN FANTASY, HE SAID...
CASEY, YOU REALLY SHOULD TRY TO UNDERSTAND MY POSITION. YOU, MORE THAN ANYONE, SHOULD SYMPATHIZE...
BREAK IT DOWN. MAKE IT NOT WORK. MAKE IT FAIL. FAIL.
YOU KNOW WHOSE CELLS PETER USED TO BUILD MY PERSONALITY. WHY, WE'RE PRACTICALLY SISTERS.
IT'S SAFE TO SAY THAT IF YOU WERE IN MY SHOES, YOU'D DO JUST WHAT I'M DOING...
MAKE IT HURT. YES...
CASEY-- IMAGINE YOURSELF THE FIRST OF A NEW SPECIES--
BLAM
BLAM
BLAM
BLAM
RISE, RONIN.
YOUR BATTLE HAS ENDED.
42.

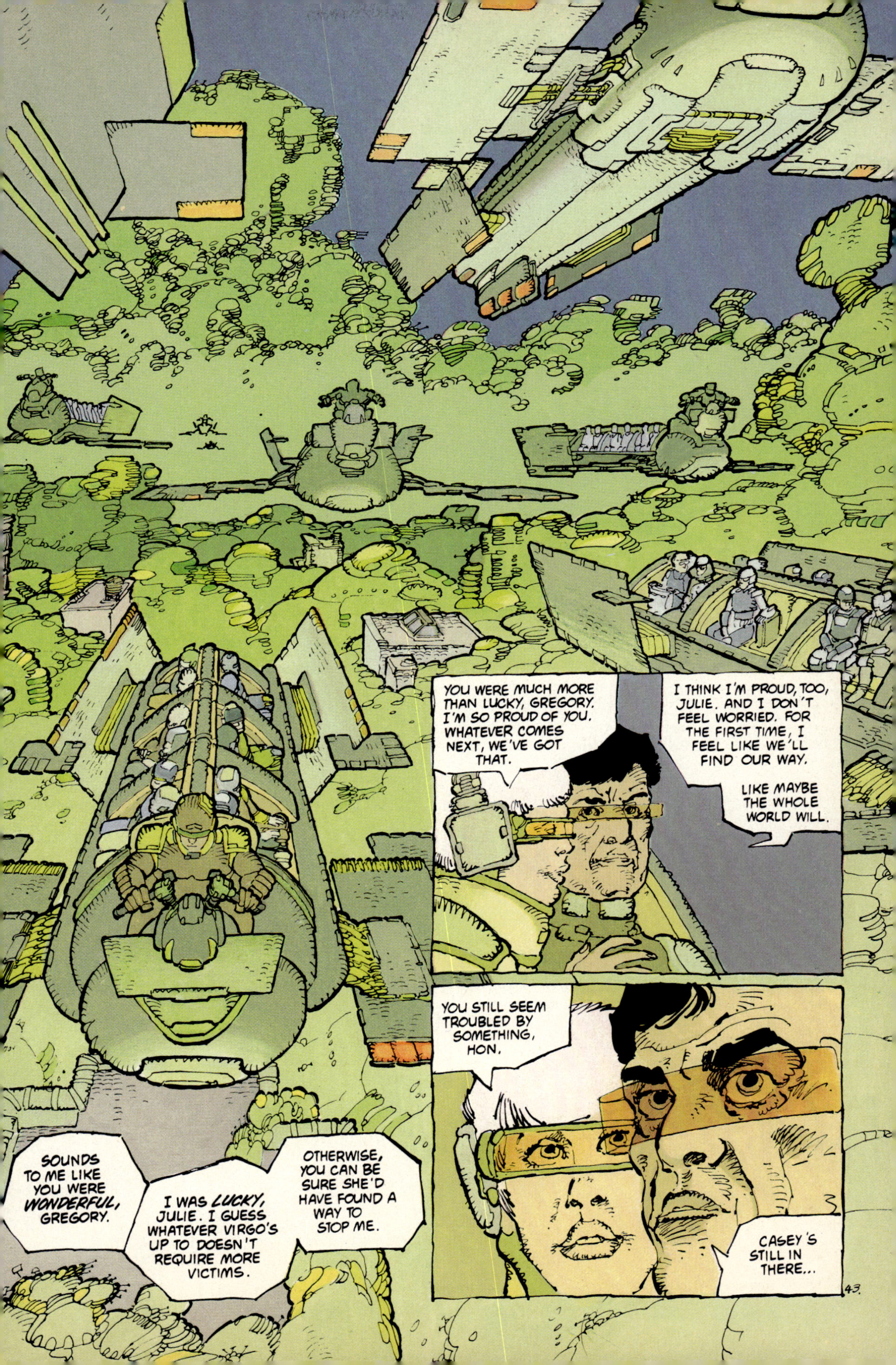
YOU WERE MUCH MORE THAN LUCKY, GREGORY. I'M SO PROUD OF YOU. WHATEVER COMES NEXT, WE'VE GOT THAT.
I THINK I'M PROUD, TOO, JULIE. AND I DON'T FEEL WORRIED. FOR THE FIRST TIME, I FEEL LIKE WE'LL FIND OUR WAY.
LIKE MAYBE THE WHOLE WORLD WILL.
YOU STILL SEEM TROUBLED BY SOMETHING, HON.
SOUNDS TO ME LIKE YOU WERE *WONDERFUL*, GREGORY.
I WAS *LUCKY*, JULIE. I GUESS WHATEVER VIRGO'S UP TO DOESN'T REQUIRE MORE VICTIMS.
OTHERWISE, YOU CAN BE SURE SHE'D HAVE FOUND A WAY TO STOP ME.
CASEY'S STILL IN THERE...

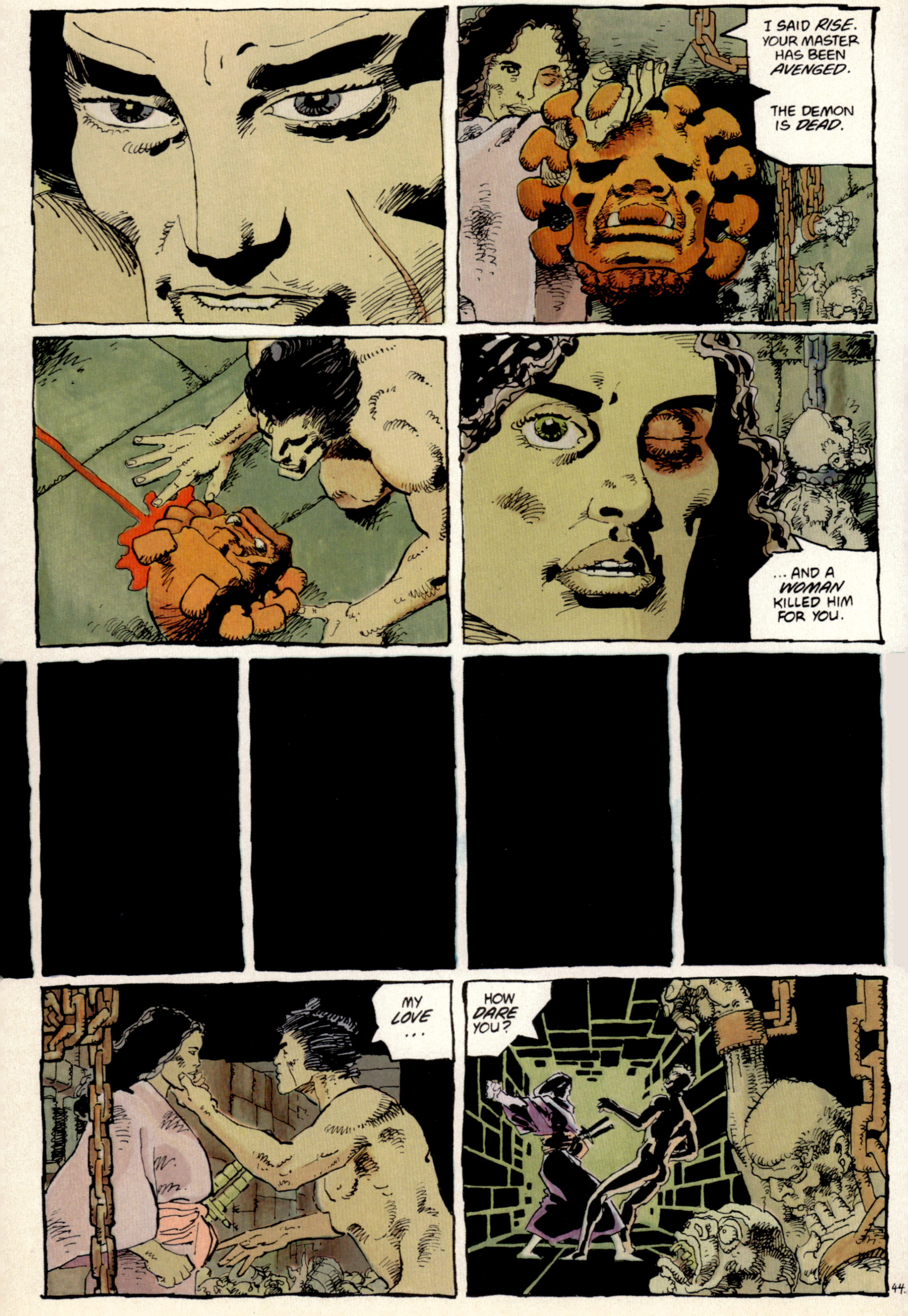
I SAID RISE. YOUR MASTER HAS BEEN AVENGED.
THE DEMON IS DEAD.
... AND A WOMAN KILLED HIM FOR YOU.
MY LOVE . . .
HOW DARE YOU?

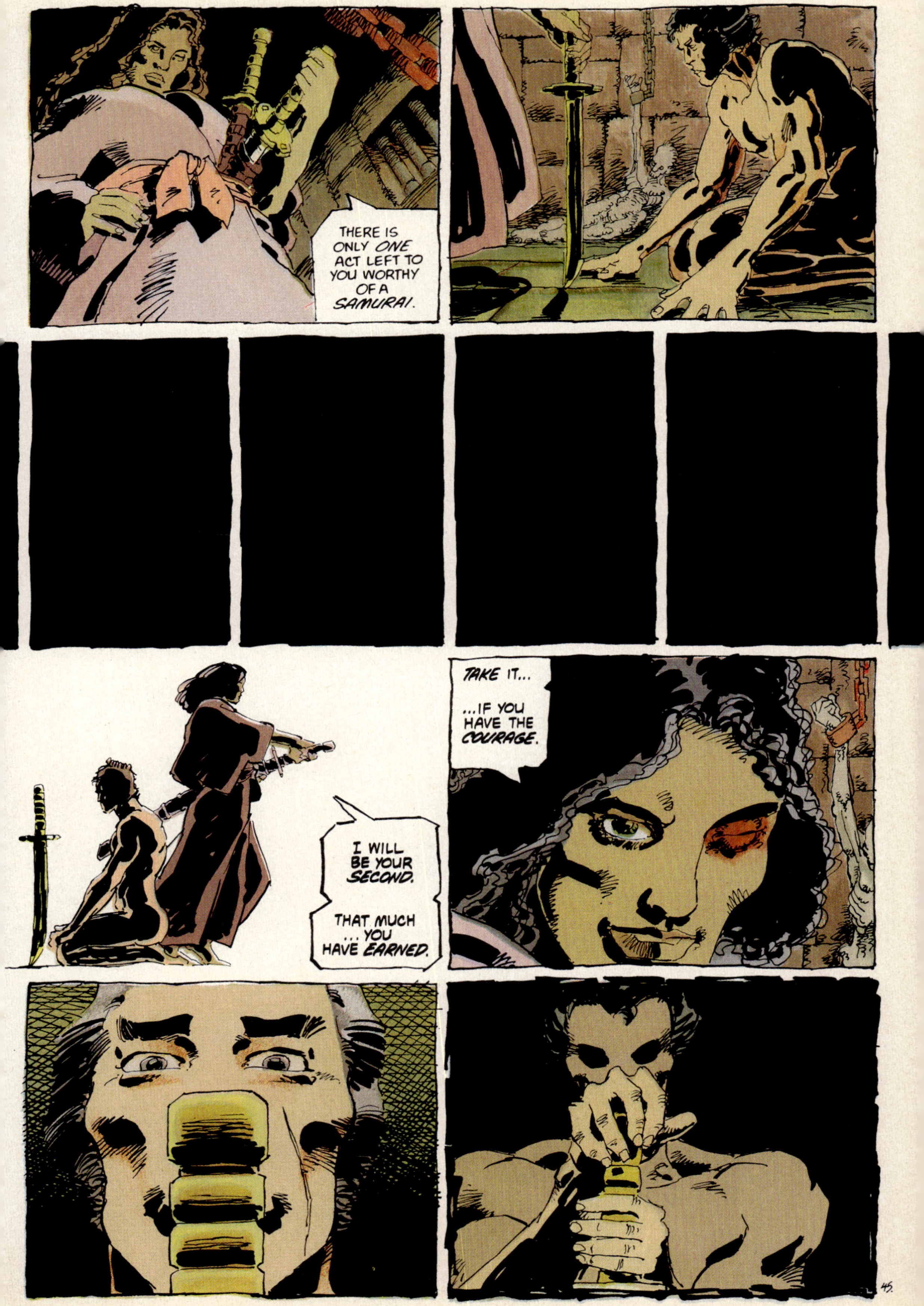
THERE IS ONLY *ONE* ACT LEFT TO YOU WORTHY OF A *SAMURAI*.
I WILL BE YOUR *SECOND*.
THAT MUCH ... YOU HAVE *EARNED*.
TAKE IT...
...IF YOU HAVE THE *COURAGE*.

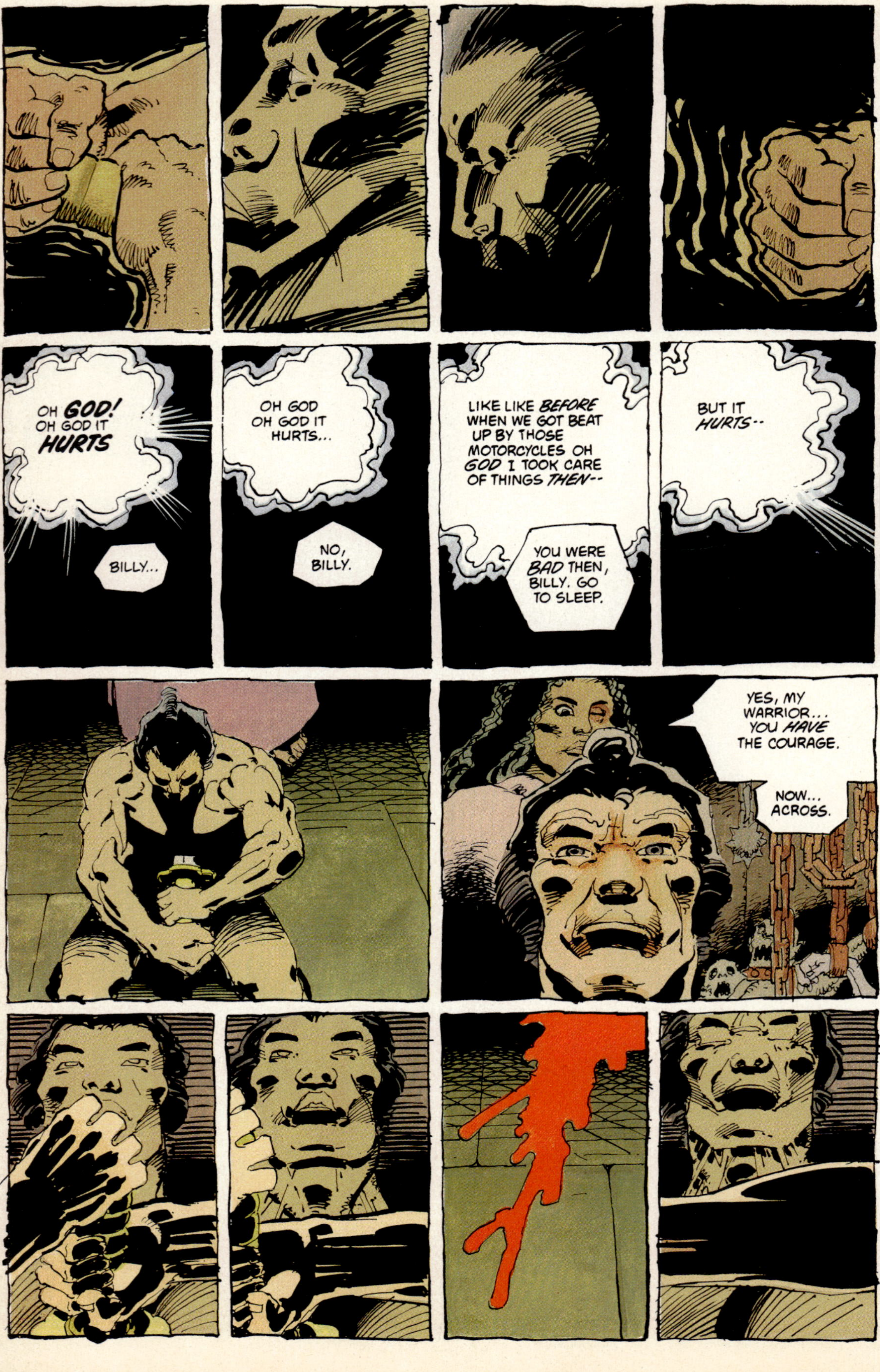

OH GOD! OH GOD IT HURTS
BILLY...
OH GOD OH GOD IT HURTS...
NO, BILLY.
LIKE LIKE BEFORE WHEN WE GOT BEAT UP BY THOSE MOTORCYCLES OH GOD I TOOK CARE OF THINGS THEN--
YOU WERE BAD THEN, BILLY. GO TO SLEEP.
BUT IT HURTS--
YES, MY WARRIOR... YOU HAVE THE COURAGE.
NOW... ACROSS.

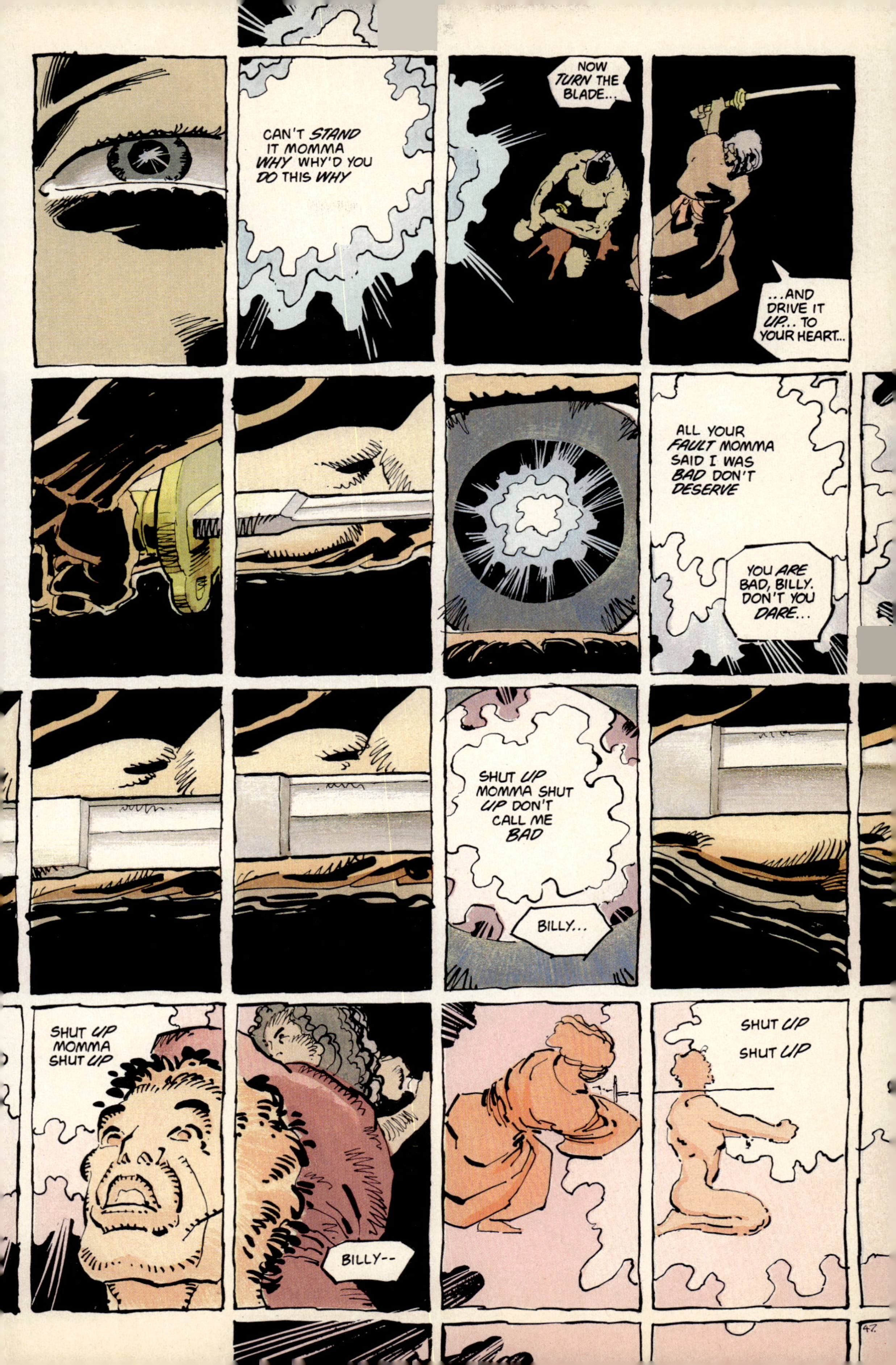
CAN'T STAND IT MOMMA WHY WHY'D YOU DO THIS WHY
NOW TURN THE BLADE...
...AND DRIVE IT UP... TO YOUR HEART...
ALL YOUR FAULT MOMMA SAID I WAS BAD DON'T DESERVE
YOU ARE BAD, BILLY. DON'T YOU DARE...
SHUT UP MOMMA SHUT UP DON'T CALL ME BAD
BILLY...
SHUT UP MOMMA SHUT UP
BILLY--
SHUT UP
SHUT UP

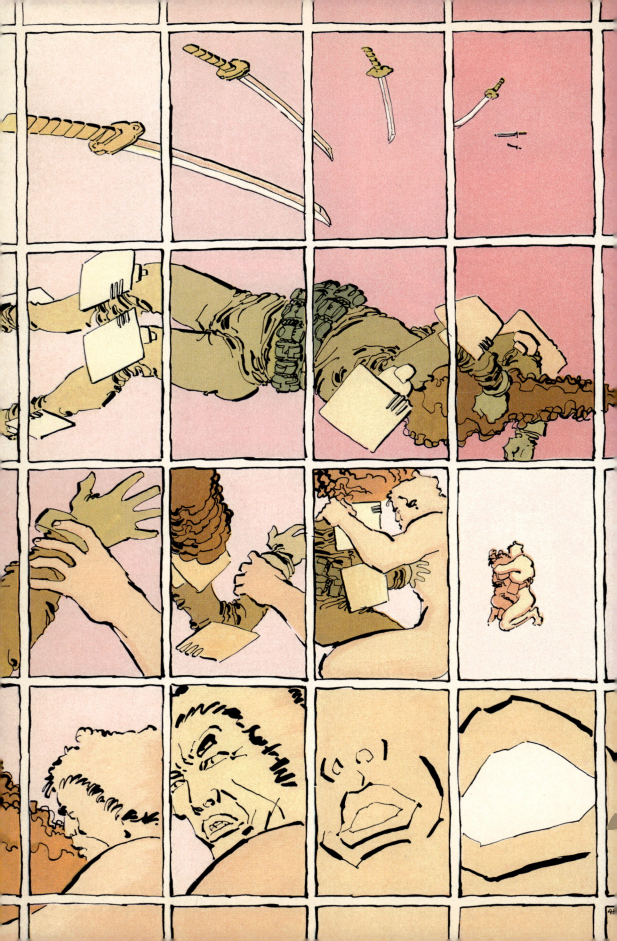

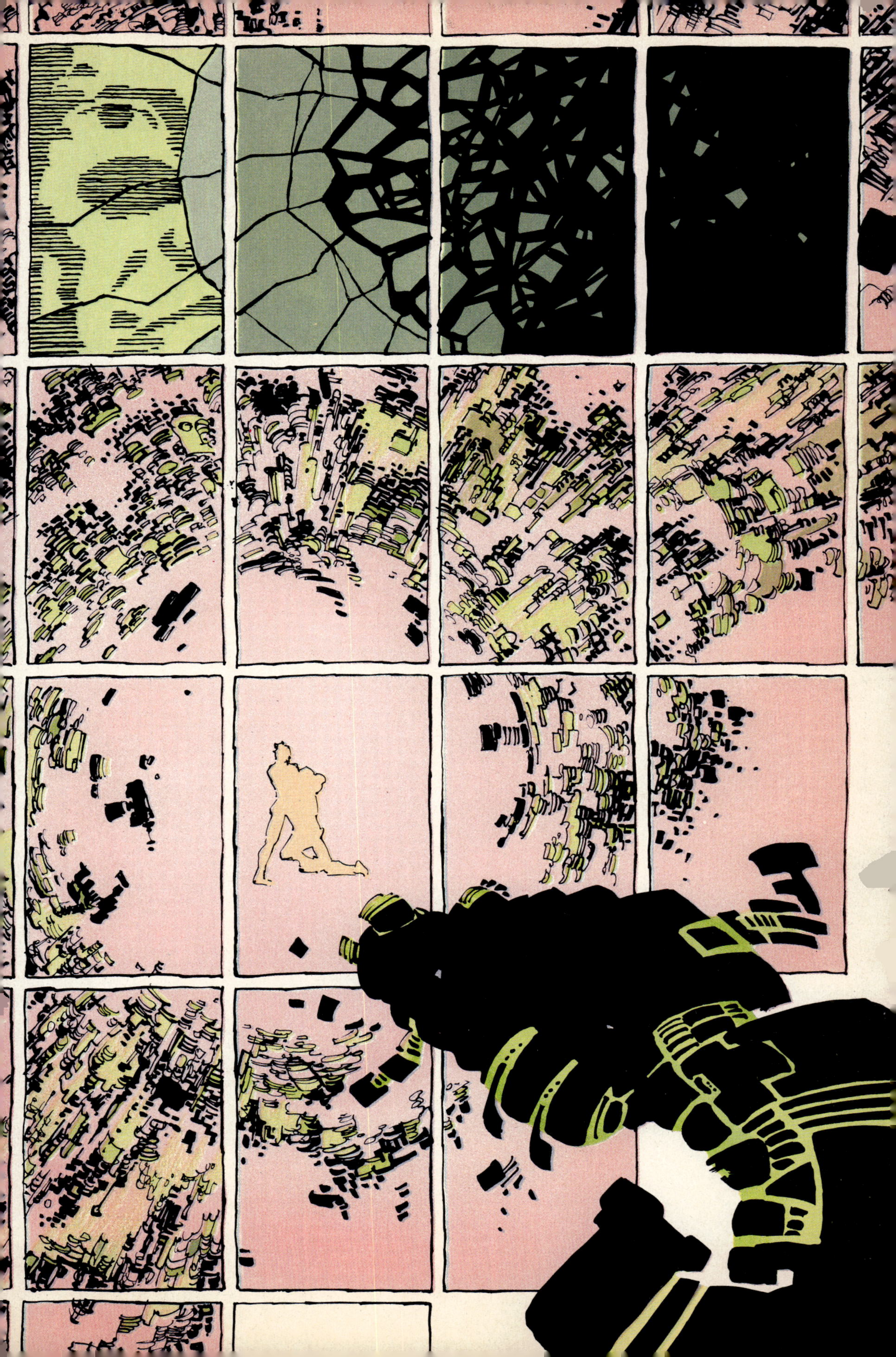

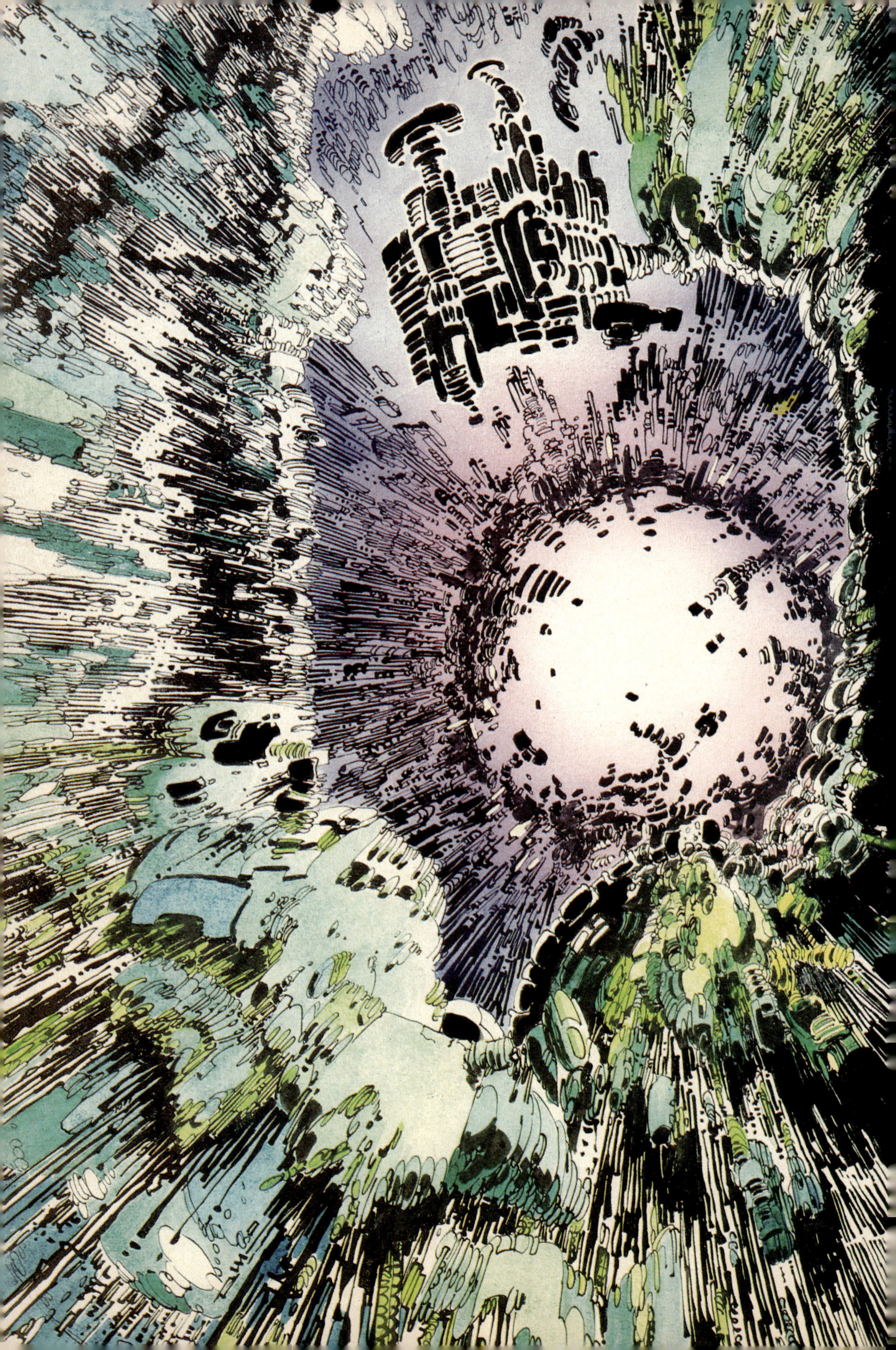